"With the precision of a surgeon's scalpel, Edwin Hui cuts through the layers of moral sentiment and ideological bias to the critical core of contemporary issues surrounding the question of the beginning and sustaining of human life. Holding that human personhood is actually present from the time of conception with varying potentials for development, Hui offers a compelling theological way of viewing human persons as embodied, social and moral beings.

"This book will provide scholars, pastors and laypersons alike with a scientifically sound, biblically based and morally measured approach to issues pertaining to reproductive technology, pre-natal screening, surrogate motherhood, abortion, human cloning and the most recent developments with regard to the human genome project.

"This is a stunning book in its breadth of knowledge and carefully nuanced argument for the recognition and preservation of human life from its precarious beginning endowed with actual personhood and its precipitous journey through the maze of human proclivities and scientific possibilities. I predict that it will become a standard reference for pastoral care as well as for public policy making."

RAY S. ANDERSON
Professor of Theology and Ministry, Fuller Theological Seminary

"Few Christian writers or indeed writers of any persuasion have the expertise in science, theology and philosophy that Edwin Hui displays in this work. It is a notable contribution to an ethic of personhood and the implications of that ethic for the beginnings of human life."

C. STEPHEN EVANS
University Professor of Philosophy and Humanities, Baylor University

"Over recent years, quite a body of literature has been produced by Christians on the contemporary ethical issues and dilemmas which bear on the beginnings of life. Frustratingly, this has all too often been written by specialists in one of the key fields of ethics, medical science and theology but whose knowledge of the other relevant fields is limited. In stark contrast this book is written by one who is not only a highly experienced and successful physician but a profound academic theologian and ethicist. The result is an incisive analysis which integrates supremely well a medically, philosophically and theologically informed perspective on one of the most significant ethical challenges of our time. This volume is nothing less than obligatory reading for thinking Christians and academics who wish to address these questions in depth. I could not recommend it more highly."

ALAN J. TORRANCE
Chair of Systematic Theology,
St Mary's College, University of St. Andrews, St. Andrews, Scotland

At the Beginning of Life

Dilemmas in
Theological
Bioethics

EDWIN C. HUI
(Xu Zhi-Wei)

InterVarsity Press
Downers Grove, Illinois

InterVarsity Press
P.O. Box 1400, Downers Grove, IL 60515-1426
World Wide Web: www.ivpress.com
E-mail: mail@ivpress.com

*InterVarsity Press® is the book-publishing division of InterVarsity Christian Fellowship/USA®, a student
movement active on campus at hundreds of universities, colleges and schools of nursing in the
United States of America, and a member movement of the International Fellowship of Evangelical Students.
For information about local and regional activities, write Public Relations Dept., InterVarsity Christian
Fellowship/USA, 6400 Schroeder Rd., P.O. Box 7895, Madison, WI 53707-7895, or visit the IVCF
website at <www.ivcf.org>.*

Scripture quotations, unless otherwise noted, are from the New Revised Standard Version of the Bible,
*copyright 1989 by the Division of Christian Education of the National Council of the Churches of
brist in the USA. Used by permission. All rights reserved.*

Cover photograph: K. Kjeldsen/Photo Researchers Inc.

ISBN 0-8308-2667-X

Printed in the United States of America ∞

Library of Congress Cataloging-in-Publication Data

Hui, Edwin C., 1946-
  At the beginning of life: dilemmas in theological bioethics/Edwin
C. Hui.
     p. cm.
Includes bibliographical references and index.
  ISBN 0-8308-2667-X (pbk.: alk. paper)
   *1. Human reproductive technology—Moral and ethical aspects. 2. Human
   reproductive technology—Religious aspects—Christianity. 3.
   Abortion—Moral and ethical aspects. 4. Abortion—Religious
   aspects—Christianity. 5. Bioethics. 6. Christian ethics. I. Title.*
     RG133.5 .H85 2002
176—dc21   2002005639

P	19	18	17	16	15	14	13	12	11	10	9	8	7	6	5	4	3	2	1
Y	17	16	15	14	13	12	11	10	09	08	07	06	05	04	03	02			

To Winnie

Contents

PART THREE

ABORTION AND PERSONHOOD

Acknowledgments

I'd like to express my gratitude to all the patients I treated in the early years of my career, and to all the students I have taught at Regent College and elsewhere, for their contributions to this work are invaluable though not easily recognizable.

The able research assistance of Amy Sharon, Gary Lepine, Jacob Vette and Randy Rauser is much appreciated. Randy also read through the entire manuscript and made many stylistic improvements.

My colleagues Jim Houston and Craig Gay read different parts of this work and made many valuable comments, and the general support and encouragement provided by Walt Wright, Jim Packer, Sven Soderlund, Gordon Fee, John Toews, Bill Reimer and Don Lewis are also much appreciated.

Terries and Chilly typed and retyped the manuscripts many times. Without their commitment, the completion of this work would have been even more difficult.

I am deeply indebted to my wife for her support, and in honor of her perseverence in tolerating my absence from family life in order to engage this work and others, I dedicate this book to her.

Introduction

This book is written with two objectives in mind—one theoretical and the other practical. The more theoretical objective is to elucidate the various dimensions of the nature of a human person within the context of a bioethical discourse; the second, more practical purpose is to employ this understanding of the human person to evaluate some of the particular moral dilemmas of our day as they relate to the beginning of human life. Hence, part one of this book will discuss the theoretical underpinnings of human personhood, while parts two and three will then apply an ethic derived from such a theological account of personhood to the contemporary debate of certain moral issues. Specifically, part two discusses the various issues arising from the recent remarkable scientific accomplishments in "creating" human lives technologically, and part three addresses the ongoing issue of abortion. As this study progresses, a particular irony—a paradoxical concatenation between artificial reproductive technologies and abortion—will become apparent: as life is created, it becomes aborted with increasing abandon.

I like to emphasize that I am not suggesting an ethic of personhood can be rigidly applied to all bioethical issues and used to resolve each and every moral dilemma at hand. In other words, I reject the tendency among modern philosophical ethicists to argue that personhood necessarily exercises such a normative force as to be decisive in every turn of the complex maze of our moral world. This ethic not only regards the concept of personhood as moral, but also accords it with such an exalted normative status as to determine the right to life. As we shall see, this entails the adoption of a narrow and exclusive definition of personhood, usually on some psychological or rationalistic basis. Rather, my view is that because personhood is first and foremost an ontological concept that describes our human nature, while an ethic of personhood may exercise normative and prescriptive functions, it should not be exhausted by them. The ethic of personhood I advocate here serves us best by providing a conceptual context that directs our moral orientation, nurtures our moral character, shapes our moral thoughts, determines our moral intention and inclines us to identify and act in a manner most appropriate for human persons.

My discussion of personhood is guided by a question posed in the original title of this manuscript: Who and what is a human person? This may prompt one to ask what category of questions "who" and "what" belong to. That is to say, are they scientific, philosophical, theological, moral or social questions? Or perhaps are they a combination of all the above? Much depends on which of the two pronouns is believed to be more appropriate when referring to a human person. Those who believe *what* is the correct word to use in asking the "person" question likely will believe these questions can be answered by empirically verifiable biological, sociological and anthropological facts; those who think that "person" questions are best raised with the pronoun *who* will tend to answer them from metaphysical or theological grounds. As readers will soon find out, since I believe that both who and what are important questions, I am of the opinion that these questions can only be answered by serious philosophical/theological reflections (who) on a wide range of scientific data (what).

In contrast, some authors feel that these questions are shaped largely by a more pragmatic question: for what purpose are these questions being asked? These authors are of the opinion that ethical concerns and social policies often find their way into the scientific interpretations of empirical biological facts and the resulting philosophical/theological reflection. For example, prominent American bioethicist Daniel Callahan says, "Scientific data as such are open to different readings and [are] compatible with different moral policies. . . . The biological facts may be evident enough, but the facts are open to a variety of interpretations none of which is undeniably entailed by the facts."[1] Specifically, because biological data do not carry self-evident philosophical interpretations, the data will have a different bearing depending on why a certain question is being asked in the first place. This allows Callahan and others to take a more pragmatic approach, which interprets scientific data in light of existing moral policy and social norms. In other words, the values embedded in the prevailing moral policy and social norms are allowed to influence the interpretation of scientific facts and philosophical/theological reflections. Writing in the context of the abortion debate, Callahan himself argues that the question, When does human life begin? should be replaced by, When does human life begin when an abortion is needed or necessary? On this view, the combination of a serious reason to have an abortion and a particular moral ethos in society will contribute significantly and decisively to the conclusion of whether there is a

---

[1]Daniel Callahan, *Abortion, Law, Choice and Morality* (New York: Macmillan, 1970), pp. 351-54.

human life present when abortion is being considered.[2] A sobering implication of such an approach is the net effect of allowing human desires and public consensus to determine human nature.

While we may not agree with Callahan's pragmatic approach to define the beginning of human personhood, we must at the same time frankly acknowledge that social and public-policy pressures have undeniably influenced many interpretations of and arguments about the determination of the beginning of human life and human personhood. For example, while there is general agreement within the so-called genetic school that genetic endowment confers humanness, consensus has not been reached as to when an individual human life begins. One of the main reasons for this lack of consensus is that there are many "social" advantages to defining the beginning of the individual human life two to three weeks after the biological fertilization of the ovum (conception). For instance, this would allow the use of abortive contraceptive devices (e.g., intrauterine devices) and abortifacient agents (e.g., RU 486), and it would justify many assisted reproductive technologies that involve embryo manipulation and experimentation. Social and policy factors play an even larger role within the so-called developmental school, which defines the beginning of human personhood on the basis of the emergence of certain chosen criteria such as self-consciousness, rationality and so on. In this case, the human desire to be autonomous and the social necessity of economic efficiency play a crucial role in deciding the various criteria of personhood. For this reason many interpret the explosive developments in bioethics over the last half century from a cultural perspective, and they see in moral issues such as abortion, assisted reproductive technologies, genetic engineering and euthanasia expressions of a much wider agenda aimed at "the reconstruction of human nature for the purpose of the post-Christian culture."[3]

Hence, it is important for us to realize that the question of personhood is not merely a moral one but that it should be taken as an expression of society's struggle with human nature and identity. It is "cultural shadow work . . . on a grand scale,"[4] through which human nature is being constantly redefined. Unfortunately the issue has been either given an ad hoc treatment or bracketed altogether in the course of discussing other, more practical bioethical issues. But the question of personhood cannot be easily avoided; indeed it would be irresponsible to do ignore it. I share the view that

---

[2]Ibid., pp. 377-78.

[3]Nigel M. de S. Cameron, "The Christian Stake in Bioethics: The State of the Question," in *Bioethics and the Future of Medicine*, ed. John F. Kilner, Nigel M. de S. Cameron and David L. Schiedermayer (Grand Rapids, Mich.: Eerdmans, 1995), p. 8.

[4]Bette-Jane Crigger, "At the Center," *Hastings Center Report* 22 (January/February 1992), inside front cover.

in talking about the nature of personhood, . . . we continually renegotiate the social order. In ways that we do not fully intend and could never control, our discourse is part of the even more complex shadow work that will bring (perhaps already has brought) a new culture into being.[5]

Precisely for this reason, I believe that the urgent and fundamental matter of personhood deserves and demands a clear and definitive treatment as a basis for the deliberation of other methodological and material issues in bioethics. As we will soon find out, this is the purpose and goal of part one of this book.

In recent years, several books with similar titles have been published on personhood: for example, *What Is a Person?* and *Who Is a Person?*[6] I do not intend to exaggerate the difference between the terms who and what, for both raise the same issue as to what kind of a person the human person is. One may even defend using the term *what* as a noun to refer to the substance or essence of an entity. For example, it is possible to say, "This is a book on the what and how of the human person." In this case, there is nothing wrong with employing the term *what* to refer to the human person. Yet, in the syntactic grammatical structure of the ordinary question, "What or who is a human person?" the terms *who* and *what* are being used as pronouns. As a pronoun, *who* is commonly used to refer to a living being—usually a human being, unless the context requires the inclusion of being or beings of a divine origin. The pronoun *who* anticipates other human (or divine) pronouns such as *I, she* or *he* and so on. By contrast, as a pronoun, *what* is used to refer to either an inanimate object (e.g., a stone, a piece of wood) or an animate object in the plant or animal kingdom. As such, questions addressed with *what* anticipate an answer with the nonhuman pronoun *it*. Even though a relationship may exist between an *I* and an *it,* according to Martin Buber that relation would not be one which promotes genuine personhood. (I will explore this further in chapter five.) By using a reified *it,* one either removes or significantly weakens the personal relational dimension, which I would advocate as a constitutive component of a person.[7]

Yet I believe that both *who* and *what* are equally important for raising questions about the human person. Without answering the "what" question, the nature of the human person remains incompletely described and inadequately defined. The biblical description of "I AM WHO I AM"[8] is, after all, reserved for Yahweh, who chooses to reveal himself in this way as a divine Person. Not sur-

---

[5]Ibid.

[6]For example, see Michael F. Goodman, ed., *What Is a Person?* (Clifton, N.J.: Humana, 1988), and James W. Walters, *What Is a Person?* (Urbana, Ill.: University of Illinois Press, 1997).

[7]See chapter five, "The Relational Dimension of Human Personhood."

[8]Ex 3:14 NRSV. The description is chosen by God to describe himself when Moses asked God to help him to identify God.

prisingly, Moses remains somewhat mystified by this description. Hence, to describe the human person with the who question alone, without finding recourse to the what question, renders the human "I" unacceptably and unnecessarily enigmatic. On the other hand, the what question considered alone reifies the human person into an object, and replaces the "I" with an "it." Furthermore, the replacement of an "I" with an "it" removes the specificity particular to the "I" since an "it" refers to descriptions that are shared by many. As we shall explore later, in response to the question, "What is a human person?" we may be able to come up with many legitimate descriptions: a human is a rational, conscious, self-conscious or communicative being and so on. However, these admirable qualities are shared by many other "its." Only the question, "Who is the human person?" leads to the unique and irreplaceable "I." So I believe that the human person must be apprehended as both an "I" and an "it," and thus both "who" and "what" are necessary questions in seeking the human person. Each complements rather than exhausts the other.[9]

Modernity's inclination to view human persons exclusively as things is not justified by the fact that each human person possesses many attributes shared by others; for while human persons share many attributes in common, there is no human person who is an individual and in-exchangeable human person like me (or you). As Orthodox theologian John Zizioulas puts it, "Many things 'are' but no one else is me. . . . This assertion is absolute: not simply because nothing else is 'me,' but also because nothing else [and, I may add, no one else] can ever be me."[10] In rejecting modernity's understanding of the human person as "it," I am not thereby ignoring or dismissing the "it" aspects of the person; rather I would argue that there is a dynamic interaction between the "I" and the "it" (things, qualities), one complementing and enabling the other, and both working hand in hand toward the fulfillment of the whole human person. This is what will be referred to as the "dyadic" or bipolar structure of the human person: the substantiality that primarily gives rise to the qualities of the "it" structure and the relationality that is mainly responsible for the unique

---

[9]In this regard, veteran evangelical theologian Professor Ray S. Anderson's works (Anderson, *On Being Human* [Grand Rapids, Mich.: Eerdmans, 1982], and Anderson and Dennis B. Guernsey, *On Being Family* [Grand Rapids, Mich.: Eerdmans, 1982]) were essentially in agreement with my point of view here. Also, J. P. Moreland and Scott Rae's *Body and Soul* (Downers Grove, Ill.: InterVarsity Press, 2000) and Gary Deddo's *Karl Barth's Theology of Relations: Trinitarian, Christological and Human: Towards an Ethic of the Family* (Washington, D.C.: P. Lang, 1999) are superb philosophical and theological (respectively) treatments on the subject of personhood that are also in sympathy with the stand I take here. Unfortunately, these works are too recent for me to engage them in this volume.

[10]John Zizioulas, "On Being a Person: Towards an Ontology of Personhood," in *Persons, Divine and Human*, ed. Christoph Schwöbel and Colin E. Gunton (Edinburgh: T & T Clark, 1991), p. 35.

"I" structure. Yet the two cannot be separated into distinct compartments,[11] for the personal ontology of the human being requires that both are given to us as an integrated whole. The Christian tradition has marvelously captured this dual aspect of the human person in the belief that a personal God creates humanity in his image (relation) and calls each human being into existence as an unique "I" from the dust of the ground with the breath of his life (substance). "And the man became a living being [person]" (Gen 2:7 NRSV).

Furthermore, part of orthodox Christian theology is the concept of personhood as archetypically found in God's triune self-revelation as the Persons of Father, Son and Holy Spirit. Since the Christian tradition holds that human beings are created as images of God, there is a strong connection between the divine personhood and human personhood. The existence of such a divine-human connection unavoidably raises a host of theological and anthropological questions that cannot be treated here, but it is important to stress that in most Christian traditions the connection between divine and human personhood is analogical rather than essential. As we shall see below, understood as an analogy, divine personhood is capable of enriching our understanding of human personhood in terms of human relationality. It provides an eschatological basis of human development and allows for the transformation of human personhood by the Holy Spirit, thus enabling the Christian person to live a moral life of imitation of and conformity to Jesus Christ, who alone submits perfectly to the moral demands and wishes of God the Father. In other words, the Christian trinitarian understanding of God does not permit us to "read off" from divine personhood the proper course of action when confronted with some of the specific dilemmas discussed in parts two and three of this book. Nonetheless, God's revelation to the world as a personal God and the human being's affirmation and experience of God as personal should shape human self-understanding as personal and should compel human morality to be personal. In this sense, Christians of all confessions affirm that the theology of divine personhood does have a bearing on the anthropology and the morality of human personhood. It is my hope that the moral arenas presented in parts two and three may provide the occasion and venue to explore the moral landscape in light of this understanding of personhood, both human and divine.

But to begin with, the six chapters in part one are devoted to a brief discussion of the philosophical and theological meanings of basic terms such as being, nature and substance and to a more detailed examination of the various dimensions that together constitute human personhood. In chapter one, I suggest that while human nature is a unity of the intellectual spirit and the material body, human being and human person are coterminous concepts and both are

---

[11]Hence my qualifiers *primarily* and *mainly*.

reducible to the same substance. As substance, the human being/person possesses an "it-selfness" property that endows her with unity, identity and wholeness; at the same time, the human being/person possesses a "toward otherness" property that imparts to her the self-expressive and self-communicative potential. This gives the human being/person her dyadic structure: as "presence-in-self" and as "self-in-communication." In short, a human person is a "being-in-communion," a living synthesis of substantiality and relationality.

In chapter two, "The Biologic Dimension of Human Personhood," I have two goals in mind: first, to use genetic information to argue in favor of conception as the beginning of human personhood and, second, to show the importance of embodiment in a balanced Christian theology of human personhood. In support of the first goal, I have cited the genetic uniqueness of the zygote, the genetic continuity of the zygote and adult, the zygote's capacity for self-development and the ontological identity of the zygote adult as my main support. I specifically argue against the significance of the fourteenth day of embryogenesis—when the so-called primitive streak of the embryo first appears and when the possibility of the embryo's twinning all but disappears—as the beginning of human personhood. I also believe that a genetic-ontological continuum from zygote to adulthood would refute a "no-subject" view embraced by David Hume, William James, Bertrand Russell and others of the same school of thought. The importance of embodiment is almost self-evident, given (as emphasized in chapter one) human personhood as a unity of body and spirit. I want to emphasize this because we have been accustomed to a Cartesian disembodied way of thinking, living and, indeed, being. In the second part of chapter two, I point out that the body is in fact the basis of our self-consciousness, presence, identity, particularity, sexuality, communication, relation and action. The Christian doctrines of creation, incarnation and resurrection are support for treating the body with the highest regard.

In chapter three, I trace the modern predominance of the use of psychological faculties—such as sentience, consciousness, self-awareness, self-interest, self-consciousness, desire and so on—in defining human personhood to early church fathers, who inherited their rationalistic bias from the Greek tradition. For example, Irenaeus believed that human beings are most like God because they are endowed with reason. Origen taught that only the human soul, but not the body, is the image of God. By the fifth century, Augustine proposed his famous psycho-theological analogy of the Holy Trinity in the human psyche as "memory, understanding and will," an analogy that has remained influential for more than fifteen hundred years. Boethius in turn defined a person as "an individual substance of a rational nature" about one hundred years after Augustine. Given this rich tradition, it should be of no major surprise for René Descartes to have made his error of "I think therefore I am," which was followed by John

Locke's understanding of a person as "a thinking intelligent being that has reason reflection." Other medieval and Enlightenment thinkers with a rationalistic bias briefly reviewed in this chapter include Thomas Aquinas, John Calvin, David Hume and Immanuel Kant. My main focus in the second half of this chapter is to critically review contemporary bioethicists who in one form or the other espouse a rationalistic definition of human personhood. For example, Michael Tooley, easily the most influential advocate of the "rationalist" position, confers personhood only on a human life capable of having an interest in its own continued existence. John Harris, on the other hand, emphasizes the importance of the ability to be conscious of oneself and one's own future. Mary Ann Warren relies entirely on cognitive functions for defining personhood, whereas Helga Kuhse and Peter Singer consider self-awareness and awareness of the future determinative of personhood. Interestingly enough, Joseph Fletcher, a pioneer Christian writer in bioethics, insists that neocortical function is "the cardinal indicator" of human personhood. The same bias is seen in Christian philosopher Robert Wennberg, who conceives of a person as one with the developed capacity of intellect, emotion and will. I conclude that such a rationalistic account of personhood not only is individualistic and hence incomplete, but is at the same time both reductionistic and exclusionistic.

In chapter four I want to introduce the important concept that the human person is multidimensional rather than a composite of several dimensions. I argue that the modern concept of psychosomatic medicine is useful in illustrating the interactions and interdependencies between the various dimensions of the person's proper functioning. Modern philosophical schools, especially existentialism and phenomenology, have also proposed holistic theories to emphasize a strong sense of the "mutually within-each-otherness" of the dimensions of the person in health or disease. I observe that this holistic personhood is entirely consistent with Christian theology and biblical tradition. The church fathers, Greek and Latin alike, in spite of the intellectual pressure of the time to despise the body, maintained a genuine effort to integrate and unify the body and soul as properly ordered members of the person. This is seen in the teachings of Athanasius, the Cappadocian fathers, Augustine, John Calvin and Karl Barth. I argue as well that the biblical data also support a holistic anthropology. The term *nephesh* is often translated as "soul," but in the original Hebrew it denotes both spiritual and physical organs and functions. The Hebrew people do not know that a person has a soul. A person is soul. Paul, in the New Testament, apparently retained this Judaic tradition when he used both corporeal and incorporeal terms that usually only designate one particular aspect of the person to refer to the whole person. In these instances, Paul was neither contradicting himself nor confusing others; rather he was either viewing the whole self from a particular standpoint or stressing the contribution of a particular aspect of the self to the functioning of the whole. I conclude that this inte-grated psychosomatic "whole"—the embodied soul or ensouled body—gives rise primarily to the being/person as "presence-in-self." This self or ego pro-vides each person with a center of direction, subjective inwardness and indi-viduality, with which each person first relates to oneself and then reaches out toward the other.

Chapter five is devoted to discussing the second pole of the dyadic structure of my understanding of human personhood: "relationality." I observe that human beings are born with sexual and linguistic faculties to be social beings and that culturally, as well, human family patterns and economic arrangements are adapted in interdependent fashions; yet human personhood is understood almost exclusively on the basis of an individual in the modern West since the Enlightenment movement, as maintained in chapter three. But in the last cen-tury or so, philosophers—notably Martin Buber, Gabriel Marcel and John Mac-murray and others—have adopted a more "antirationalistic" approach to their understanding of personhood. Specifically, they believed that the isolated Car-tesian self contradicts the real human nature as social being. As Buber puts it, "The fundamental fact of human existence is man with man. . . . It is a primal category of human reality."[12] I argue in favor of these writers that an exclusive psychological definition of human personhood yields a purely privatized self that can only be an unrealistic abstraction. The second part of chapter five unpacks the rich resources from both biblical and theological traditions that support a Christian anthropology fundamentally relational in nature. The Chris-tian concept of God as three Persons leads to an understanding of personhood in ontological terms and of the relations between the three divine Persons as "onto-relations." This theology has been worked out by the church fathers, particularly the Cappadocians; and I argue, following Barth and others, it is well supported by the biblical tradition of the imago Dei.

In chapter six, which concludes part one, I discuss the temporal dimension of human personhood in order to provide the proper context for understand-ing the significance of the potentiality, actuality and the teleology of the human person. I argue that the moral distinction between potentiality and actuality is often overstated: that is, the distinction between a potential person and a per-son with potential is confused, and the distinction between being a person and functioning as a person is conflated. I suggest that some of these conceptual difficulties arise from the faulty assumption that all teleologically organized biological systems are necessarily hierarchically arranged. For example, the biological, psychological and the social dimensions of humans are roughly

---

[12]Martin Buber, *Between Man and Man,* trans. Ronald Gregor Smith (Glasgow: William Col-lins's Sons, 1979), p. 203.

teleologically organized, but their respective structures are organized in such a way that they show their interdependency on and indebtedness to each other rather than their gradation of one over the other. Another common mistake is to overstate the difference between the capacity for and the potentiality of a certain function. For example, a "rationalist" would argue that a five-week-old neonate only has the potentiality to do arithmetic, whereas his five-year-old sister, who is having an afternoon sleep, has the actual capacity to do the arithmetic when she wakes up. The rationalist is ready to pronounce that the five-week-old is at best a potential person, whereas his sister is a person. I argue that the rationalist has made two errors, possibly three, in this judgment. The five-year-old wakes up, say, in a half hour and shows her capacity to do the arithmetic and thus justifies her personhood to the rationalist; the five-week-old neonate, who speeds up his brain development to catch up with his sister and to compensate for this discriminatory insult, is able to do the same arithmetic when he reaches the age of three and is then pronounced a person. I argue that the difference between potentiality and actual capacity is merely a matter of the immediacy of a particular function's "exercisability." It seems to me that to call someone a nonperson simply because he is not immediately exercising some arbitrarily chosen functions is no small mistake. I also argue that to call the five-week-old neonate a *potential person* is equally fallacious. I am alarmed by the popularity of the term even among Christian writers. I consider sperms and ova potential persons that may or may not come about, whereas embryos, fetuses and neonates are *persons with potentials* that will be actualized with time. Perhaps the fundamental error in this approach is the failure to distinguish between the "being" and "doing" of the person. To have and to actualize potentials is "to become." But we are created first "to be" and then "to become." The rationalists have turned it upside down by saying that we have first "to become" something in order "to be" someone. I conclude part one by presenting the true human Person, Jesus Christ, the perfect *imago Dei,* as the paradigmatic eschatological dimension that the human person will become by the grace of God.

The second part of the book consists of seven chapters, and all but one of these chapters are related to new advances in reproductive technologies in laboratories where human lives are being created. I review and evaluate the morality of each of these procedures in light of an ethic of personhood described in the first part of the book. I note in chapter seven that infertility, which affects about 8 percent of all couples, is a problem faced by an age group that has relatively little experience dealing with major life crises. Infertility can be emotionally disturbing, leading to various degrees of physical distresses, marital conflicts and even divorces. I also raise the sensitive but practical question of whether infertility should be treated as a disease for which treatment may be provided or whether having children is merely a desire that cannot always be fulfilled. Several responses to these questions are evaluated. In relation to treating infertility as a disease, I also discuss human procreation as a right. I point out the important difference between positive and negative rights in procreation, since no society can afford to grant all infertile couples the positive rights to use in vitro fertilization (IVF) technology. As well, I believe we should also distinguish the right to procreate a child and the right to create a family, for a natural capacity for the former provides a moral structure to gain the right for the latter. I conclude the chapter by showing how the ethic of personhood relieves the burden of the infertile to pursue technological assistance to become fertile.

In chapter eight, I discuss perhaps the oldest form of assisted reproductive technology: artificial insemination. When a donor sperm is used, this technology creates numerous moral issues with respect to the identity of the offspring, the confidentiality of the donor and the bonding of the married couple. In one way or another, I argue that the integrity of the persons involved may have been compromised. The Roman Catholic Church is particularly insistent in its objection to the use of donor gametes because it holds that the unitive and procreative aspects of the conjugal act are thereby disconnected. Most Protestant theologians argue that no intrinsic connection between these two aspects of the sexual act exists, since there are other nonprocreative meanings of the sexual act that are also unconnected with the act's procreative meaning. I show in this chapter the respective inadequacies of these two positions and the awkward moral implications they entail, and I demonstrate how the ethic of personhood may provide a more flexible moral framework to deal with a much more demanding and complex reproductive ethics today.

In chapter nine, I discuss the technology of in vitro fertilization and embryo transfer (IVF-ET), which opens up an arena of scientific and technological pursuit matched only by the invention of the steam engine of the eighteenth century. The rest of part two deals primarily with the various medical applications and extensions of this radical twentieth-century technological innovation. I argue that the data available suggest that children conceived through this technology sustain harm both physically and emotionally. Some argue that IVF may do some harm, but these children are better off harmed than nonexistent. I reject this because in the state of nonexistence there is no child waiting to be born, and because we are not aware of the harm of nonexistence. I also discuss the physical and emotional harm inflicted on the couple employing this technology as the last resort to have children, and I wonder whether in some cases the cure is not worse than the disease. I conclude the chapter by expressing my primary concern that the advent of IVF and other adventitious technologies represents a cultural shift of human values with regard to procreation from one of personal intimacy, sexuality and conjugal activity with unitive-procreative connectivity to one of impersonal medicalization and commercialization of human reproduction.

Surrogate motherhood, one of the most dramatic byproducts of IVF technology, is an excellent example of a shift in value of human procreation. In chapter ten, I introduce several classic cases to illustrate some of the many moral issues that are known to beset this particular reproductive arrangement. Since all commercial contracts involve monetary rewards, economic exploitation of the surrogate mother simply cannot be avoided, and I argue that this cannot be dismissed and legitimized just because the surrogate freely agrees to the arrangement. The surrogate is subject to further depersonalization by having to ignore her emotional attachment to the infant and by giving her up to the contracting couple after delivery. The harm to the child conceived through this arrangement can be considerable if custody is in dispute after her delivery, and at a later stage, her identity may be in jeopardy. I argue that when contracting couples are using donor gametes or when single parents or parents of same-sex orientation are legally allowed to have families through IVF and surrogate mothers, this will lead to a blurring of the notion of the conventional family as well as the notion of the self. I argue that the modern exercise of oneself's autonomy, whereby we decide to do whatever we technologically are empowered to do in order to have a child even at the expense of the welfare of another woman and the identity of the child, cannot be justified by the personhood ethic that I espouse.

Once an ovum is successfully fertilized, it is susceptible to manipulation by scientists before it is transferred to the womb to be gestated to term. This is this subject of chapter eleven, where I begin by evaluating the various positions on the embryo's right to life. I critically examine the biological basis for claiming the notion of a "pre-embryo," and for claiming distinctions between "genetic individuality" and "developmental individuality"—which the pre-embryo is said not to possess until it matures and becomes an embryo after fourteen days— and I find both claims to be insufficient and arbitrary. The availability of embryos in vitro also permits preimplantation embryo diagnosis and embryo screening. Before embryo genetic therapy can be done economically and on a large scale, the common practice will be to screen and subsequently discard embryos with abnormal genes. Hence, I believe that preimplantation genetic screening is only supported by the ethic of personhood I espouse in cases where the family knows of severe sex-linked genetic diseases, such as Duchenne's muscular dystrophy. In the latter half of the chapter, I discuss the particularly controversial subject of embryo experimentation. Many scientists believe that embryos should not be created specifically for the purpose of experimentation because that would be creating human lives as a means; but as long as the embryos are "surplus" or "redundant," never to be implanted and to be discarded sooner or later anyway, they believe that it would be a waste not to put them to use in order to yield scientific information for the benefit of humanity. I argue that I would have grave objection to both: in the first case, it amounts to a blatant violation of a nascent life's right to life; and in the second case, a self-deceptive evasion of the crucial question as to why there is a surplus of human life in the first place. I conclude the chapter by discussing the implications of the agnostic nature of embryo research as it affects the present and future generations and that humanity should not put its hope in a perfect human genome.

Chapter twelve is devoted to the subject of reproductive and therapeutic cloning at the genetic, cellular and human levels. As there is always a high level of uncertainty involved in embryo manipulation and experimentation, cloning is not exempted. That the cloned sheep Dolly was the one success after 277 failed attempts is a good testimony to this. I also argue in this chapter that if human cloning is being practiced in a significantly large scale, it may impact the individual, the society and the bioeconomy negatively: individually, it may threaten certain individuals' rights to identity and uniqueness; socially, it will destroy family structures within that region, which may in turn have far-reaching implications for human civilization; and bioecologically, reproductive cloning restricts biodiversity as a closed system. More significantly, reproductive cloning will more likely be practiced in a much smaller scale for eugenic reasons. I argue that this is motivated by modern people's desire to be some sort of a creator. In so doing, the foolish co-creators are replacing the wise Creator's open high-efficient sexual reproductive system with a closed low-efficient asexual replicative system. In the second half of chapter twelve, I also include the discussion of stem cells, since cloning is potentially one of the major sources of stem cells. I classify stem cells in terms of their origins because the latter has significant bearing on the ethical consideration of the former. Pluripotent stem cells are derived from "surplus" embryos donated by parents who have been treated in the IVF clinics, and similar stem cells are obtained from embryos created specifically for the purpose of harvesting stem cells for experimentation. These embryos may be created by the technique of "somatic cell nuclear transfer" (SCNT). Both sources of pluripotent stem cells involve the destruction of the embryos after the stem cells have been extracted, which seriously conflicts with the ethic of personhood presented in this book. I also discuss a second group of stem cells that bypass the embryo: they include fetal tissue, bone marrow of children and adults, the placenta and umbilical cord blood in live births and even adult nerve tissues. I agree that these sources of stem cells may be less "potent" than the embryonic stem cells. But there is also no question as to both the immense medical use and the moral risk of the use of the stem cells that originate from embryos. Hence, I recommend that more resources be devoted to maximize the utilization of fetal and adult stem cells.

In chapter thirteen, the final chapter of part two, I review the history of the ambitious Human Genome Project (HGP), which has been finished ahead of schedule and through which the total number of genes and the sequencing of the entire human genome are made known. I next discuss the potential moral issues arising from the information derived from the human genome, including privacy and the so-called diagnostic-therapeutic gap. Also, I express concern that the focus on genetic makeup may inadvertently promote a deterministic view of human life and that the HGP has become modern people's new hope for their utopia. Paradoxically, it is also a symbol of modern people's rebellion against their own finitude and embodiment. Through controlling the human genome, human beings try to transcend the limits imposed by the genome itself. Hence, I argue that technology has been encouraged by both the innovators as well as the consumers—the former by their vanity and the latter by desire. I end the second part of the book by suggesting ten questions one might ask to assess whether a technology should be adopted. I also caution that the scientific culture of the West has put our eyes on a false *eschaton* of a perfect genome, yet the eschatological dimension of our personhood clearly points to the promise of Jesus Christ as the hope on which we should be anchored, for only when we see him we will be perfectly like him.

In the context of the ethic of personhood developed in the first part of the book and in dialogue with a number of ethicists cum philosophers/theologians in this field of interest, I attempt in part three to evaluate the emotionally charged yet intellectually nuanced subject of abortion, which leaves very few people in modern society unaffected in one way or the other.

I begin chapter fourteen by presenting the extreme conservative and extreme liberal positions on abortion, the so-called pro-life and pro-choice positions, which I feel is better labeled as "extreme anti-abortion" and "extreme pro-abortion" respectively, if labels are really needed. I am critical of the philosophical basis offered by extreme pro-abortionist writers such as Michael Tooley and Mary Ann Warren, whose criteria of personhood are faulted for being arbitrary and exclusive but ultimately can be extended to justify infanticide, for which they offer no good philosophical defense. On the other hand, the extreme anti-abortion position awards human life with moral standing at the time of conception. I point out that this position is fundamentally based on the natural-law tradition, which is defended biologically on the basis that the conceptus possesses the full human genome, theologically on the basis of a primary creational relationship with God and philosophically by the species principle itself. I argue, on the basis of the ethic of personhood I have developed, that fetal lives including embryonic lives are human lives with moral status and the right to life and that this right to life, though not absolute, cannot taken away without the clearest and best justification.

In chapter fifteen, I trace, evaluate, comment on and summarize a body of literature that can be characterized, in retrospect, as an attempt by various authors to moderate the extreme pro-abortionist position. I am aware that at times it might not even be the exact intention of a particular author to do what I claim his or her work has achieved, but the effect has been produced nonetheless. The most liberal pro-abortionists designate the fetus as a property and the woman as a property owner who has property rights. But I suspect this analogy would have very limited application in maternal-fetal relationships not only because of its overly commercial connotation, but because recent tenant-landlord legislation seems to have granted more rights to tenants than are granted to fetuses. Others see the fetus as an aggressor against whom the woman uses her right of self-defense. I argue that the aggression of the fetus is not adequately established, and so fetal innocence is retained. Furthermore, even if aggression can be established, it is usually not proportional to the retaliation—death by abortion. Judith Thomson's famous "plugged-in violinist" is intended to illustrate a moderate form of bodily autonomy, not by necessarily killing the fetus but by having the right to relieve the woman of the burden of the pregnancy. At the same time, Thomson's analogy seeks to claim that the fetus's right to life is a negative right, limited by the mother's right of bodily autonomy. I reject Thomson's well-intentioned but impractical proposition for the simple reason that the vast majority of all abortions are fully intended for the death of the fetus and not for the removal of the pregnancy. I critically review the landmark 1973 *Roe* v. *Wade* case, in which the woman's right to privacy is guaranteed by the United States Constitution and that right is then extended to the case of abortion. In light of the personhood ethic I espouse, I support the general concept of privacy as related to one's independence and dignity. But ultimately, *privacy* is a relational term, and regarding the decision to abort, I argue that the woman's right to privacy can only be properly exercised in the normal but complex relational network that involves the spouse, other children, parents, other significant family members, physicians and important personal friends. I end the chapter by reflecting on some of the thoughtful critiques of maternal rights and responsibilities by feminist anti-abortionists.

Chapter sixteen is a kind of mirror image of the last chapter, reflecting the anti-abortionists' effort to moderate their more extremist colleagues' position based on the species principle, which many consider to be arbitrary and superficial. As a result, a number of "decisive moments" have been postulated to replace the acquisition of the human genome as the beginning of human life with the right to life. One point nominated as a decisive moment is the emergence of the brain or brain-life between the sixth and tenth weeks, assuming that the beginning and the end of life can be naturally correlated to the emergence and cessation of brain function. I reject this on the basis that in the first trimester, the fetus has not reached the stage of maturity for functioning independently as a whole, and so the brain does not have to serve any integrative function yet, whereas at the other end of the life spectrum, when the brain ceases to function, the whole human organism ceases to function. There is no symmetry between the beginning and the end of life as far as the function of the brain is concerned. Other decisive moments including sentience, viability, birth, rationality and potentiality have been discussed and critiqued. I have discussed in some length the popularity of the "gradualist theory," which may justify terminating some very early pregnancies and make it increasingly more difficult to abort as the fetus becomes more mature. The proponents of this theory win much popular support by associating this theory to the principle of potentiality, but I argue that it is actually connected with the principle of proportionality that is not relevant in the assessment of personhood. In the ethic of personhood, the right to life is an all-or-none matter rather than a matter of degrees.

In chapter seventeen, I discuss the importance of pragmatic factors that ought to be seriously considered whenever a pregnant woman requests an abortion. I strongly believe that the pragmatic factors are to be found largely in the pregnant woman's immediate contexts: physical, mental, spiritual, social, personal, familial, marital, medical, professional, financial, historical—indeed all the various dimensions that constitute her personhood. I do not mean to argue that pragmatic factors can always override the fetal right to life; but I argue that even when the pragmatic factors are to be overridden and the fetal life ends up being protected, they have to be assessed carefully and seriously and explained with clarity to the pregnant woman, and in most if not all cases accepted by the woman. For example, I evaluate the case of a rape-induced pregnancy and argue that even though the four theoretical reasons traditionally given to justify an abortion can be easily countered by other theoretical considerations, the woman's choice must be respected in view of the traumatic context, which no one else can claim to have shared. The socioeconomic condition of the pregnant woman is another contextual factor often overlooked when a pregnant woman requests an abortion. I argue it is not a coincidence that both the most liberal abortion law and the weakest social support system for women, mothers and children are be found in the same nation, the United States. I also discuss the general psychological effect of abortion on women and find that even though the literature documenting this is, as a whole, poorly standardized and does not readily lend itself to easy and absolutely valid comparison, I believe one may safely draw the conclusion that abortion affects some but not all women, some of whom are affected with emotional scars that can never be erased. I argue that it is morally irresponsible to either overstate or understate the importance of the psychological effects of an abortion. I conclude the chapter by discussing the importance of the special relationship between the pregnant woman and her family and her physician. I argue that when the physician acquiesces to "a request on demand," the physician is reduced from a moral professional to an amoral technician. I also discuss the moral significance of the father's role in an abortion decision, which so far has been largely ignored. I am critical of Western society's preoccupation with individualism and autonomy, societal values that are incompatible with the ethic of personhood this book endorses.

In chapter eighteen, I discuss the specific cases of prenatal diagnosis of fetal abnormalities and genetic screening, in the case of a strong family history of certain inheritable diseases, followed by abortion. I examine the notion of "wrongful life"—a notion based on the premise that there is a fetal right not to be born—as a justification for aborting these defective fetuses for their own good. I conclude that such an argument carries a high moral premium and is rarely applicable, if at all. I also argue that aborting nonfatal defective fetuses for the good of the society is hardly justifiable, and one of the several reasons I give is that we are never sure whether the defective gene that we eliminate regularly does not also carry with it one or more very essential genes valuable for human survival. Further, many so-called nonlethal defective fetal conditions are considered to be below a certain "decent minimum" in quality of life, and therefore fetuses with them should not be born. Likewise, pregnancies in women over a particular age are labeled as "high risk" and must be monitored with screening. I argue that this in fact decreases rather than increases the woman's reproductive choice and control. In turn, the routine use of screening followed by abortion exerts an enormous pressure on the existing community of the disabled, who are impaired more by the obstacles set up by an insensitive and uncaring society rather than by their own physical or mental handicap. Based on the account of personhood I have developed, the defective fetus—whether she is nonfatal or as fatal as an anencephalic—will be valued as a human person who deserves to be respected and treated with dignity and more so with love and compassion, given her more needy disposition.

The last chapter presents two modern innovations in medicine that have produced two diametrically opposite moral attitudes toward the moral nature and status of the fetus. I speculate that in turn this may alter the public viewpoint on abortion. The first development is a type of birth-control agent called abortifacients that are "oral contraceptives" which in fact act either by destroying the developing embryo or preventing the implantation of the embryo. I review the physiology of these agents in this chapter, and I believe that in some cases regular oral contraceptives may actually operate as abortifacient agents rather than truly preventing the fertilization of an egg. I am also concerned by the persistent confusion and conflation between contraceptives and abortifacients, which, from the woman's point of view, is a serious compromise of the ethic of personhood because it robs her of the right to make the right choice. But from the fetus's point of view, this lack of clarity robs her of the right to life. On the balance, the advantages gained from an abortifacient agent such as RU 486—including safety, expediency and economy—are more than offset by the destruction of and insensitivity toward the nascent human life. At the same time, even as nascent lives are being aborted, incredible effort and ingenuity are being used to save fetal lives in an area of surgical subspecialty: fetal surgery. In the second part of this chapter, I introduce briefly this cutting-edge innovation of modern medicine because I believe it is destined to radically change our view of the pregnant woman as a maternal-fetal dyad that is one complex patient to a maternal-fetal dyad that is a duality. As a duality, the fetus will then be recognized as a distinct human being with his own identity and personhood. Next I review different scholars' positions on this matter, which may be outright rejection, conditional duality or full acceptance; I believe that those who reject the duality model are largely biased by their original extreme anti-abortionist position. I conclude the chapter by discussing the difficult issue of resolving conflicts between the duality in the event that certain surgical treatments benefiting only the fetus are required, involving some harm to the pregnant woman. I review some legal cases in the United States and Canada to show that because of the ambiguity of the moral standing the fetus, both the rights of the fetus and the pregnant woman can be abused. I believe that the ethic of personhood I espouse, which emphasizes relationship over autonomy-based rights, offers the best chance for conflict resolution. By extending herself to protect the fetus, who wholly depends on her for surviving as a human person, the mother thereby becomes even more a person.

Part One

Foundations of Human Personhood

1

Being, Person and Human Nature

*B*eing, Person and the Structure of Human Nature

In our attempts to describe humanity, we encounter several potentially confusing terms that convey distinct, yet overlapping ideas: *human being, human person* and *human nature*. For a long time, the terms *human being* and *human person* have been considered interchangeable, a practice continued by many modern thinkers working in the field of biomedical ethics, including John Noonan, Germain Grisez and others. This view has been variously labeled the "genetic," "speciest" or "substantialist" school because it purports that once the existence of the "substance" of a human life, or a human being possessing a genome, is ascertained, a human person is then said to be present. As Noonan puts it, "The criterion for humanity, thus, was simple and all embracing: if you are conceived by human parents, you are human."[1] This view tends to see the human being as an entity or substance, and it understands human personhood in metaphysical terms independent of any human potentialities or activities. It resists any suggestion that human personhood requires the human being to complete further phases of development or to develop certain relationships. Rather, human beings are persons simply by virtue of what they are. Despite its appeal among conservative thinkers, such a view runs the risk of treating human beings merely as static objects or passive products of the blind impersonal forces of nature, thus undermining human

---

[1]John T. Noonan Jr., "An Almost Absolute Value in History," in *The Morality of Abortion*, ed. John T. Noonan Jr. (Cambridge: Harvard University Press, 1970), p. 51.

beings as free and autonomous beings with a mind to know and a will to act. Above all, this narrow and static substantialist view overlooks the more dynamic relational aspect of the human being, which, as I shall demonstrate below, is an essential ontological aspect of the human being as a person. Hence, I believe that while this understanding of personhood has many merits which should be preserved, the concept of "substance" must be expanded and revitalized before it can truly and more completely elucidate the dynamic nature of human personhood. I will return to this issue in due course.

In contrast with the substantialists, another perspective of humanity, the "developmentalist" school, views *human being* and *human person* as anything but synonyms. This tendency to disconnect the two terms is particularly pronounced in the debate on the status of fetuses, infants and human persons who have become irreversibly comatose. On this view, these human entities may be considered only as "qualified human beings" whose "human" status is either granted or preserved on the basis of certain biological criteria that are also possessed by other members of the species *Homo sapiens:* for example, the human genome. But their status as human persons is denied or removed because they have not yet gained or they forever have lost the higher integrative functions that have arbitrarily been deemed essential for personhood. Philosophers who espouse this view include Michael Tooley, Mary Ann Warren, Peter Singer, John Harris, H. Tristram Engelhardt Jr. and others. Not only do they insist that human beings and human persons are not necessarily coterminous and thus may be separate entities, but they also make the normative claim that only human persons possess the right to life. Specifically, they believe that *human being* is a purely descriptive term of biological life, possessing no moral significance, and that a morally neutral human being has to go through further development, which includes the addition of some mature qualities and characteristics, especially those related to cognitive functions. Only at this point of human development does the human being become a human person, and the evaluative or normative term *person* refers to a moral agent with the right to life. In other words, only when a human being fulfills both the biological criteria and certain arbitrarily chosen "personal" criteria will she become a human person.

This high valuation of personhood has quite obviously been influenced by the Enlightenment philosophy of John Locke and Immanuel Kant as well as by the long-held Christian belief that persons possess souls. It is ironic that this secular exaltation of personhood—which excludes a large number of human beings from personhood, including fetuses, infants, the severely retarded and the irreversibly comatose—is claimed to be supported by the Christian doctrine of humanity's being created in the image of God. As we will see below, this approach underestimates the moral significance of human biological embodiment and overlooks the normative and evaluative features of the term *human being*. Such a bifurcated understanding of human beings/persons misses what our basic intuition tells us, that "most single human beings just are unproblematically, single persons . . . [with] the obvious and trivial point that the normal human being is our sole paradigm of personhood."[2] The so-called higher and morally more significant qualities that developmentalist philosophers require all human persons to possess are found everywhere in human beings anyway. Hence, the criteria that supposedly separate the human being from the human person give a distinct impression that they are in fact superfluous and unjustified.

Within this development/achievement school some have found the category of relations to be an attractive criterion for personhood. On this view, human personhood is grounded on the basis of the relationships people participate in and the social roles they assume. This view is especially favored by those with an existentialist or personalist bent, who advocate that we become persons as we relate to other persons. This rather heterogeneous group includes thinkers such as Martin Buber, Miguel de Unamuno, Gabriel Marcel, John Macmurray and others. Many Christian theologians also find this relational approach very attractive, for it seems to provide a firm ground for securing personhood in one's relationship to God. There is much merit to the idea that human personhood is constituted by a divine-human relationship, but as we will see later, this relation cannot be understood in abstract or spiritual terms. Rather, it is the exact *sort* of relation or the concrete nature of the divine-human relation that ultimately determines whether relations will constitute personhood. In any case, regardless of whether cognitive functions or relations are chosen as endpoints of development or as indicators of achievement, developmentalists share one belief in common: namely, that human persons are not what they *are*, but what they *become*. While this view is praiseworthy for its refusal to see the human being as a reified Cartesian object passively produced by nature, it overlooks the rather obvious point that the human has to be a "being" in order to be a "becoming." One must in some sense be "something" that endures over time before one becomes anything else. That is to say, there needs to be a substantial entity present to serve as the enduring human structure that develops, functions, achieves and enters into relations.

Thus substantialist and developmentalist views are both reductionistic: the former reduces the person to an inert, self-enclosed and unresponsive object; the latter treats the person purely as a set of possibilities. I take the position that both substance and relations, both being and becoming, are essential categories for a complete understanding and definition of human personhood. In

---

[2]Kathleen V. Wilkes, *Real People* (Oxford: Clarendon, 1987), p. 22.

other words, there is a bipolar or dyadic structure to human personhood comprised in a substantial pole and a relational pole. These poles need to be resynthesized or reintegrated as the substantiality and the relationality of the human being in order for us to see the person in proper focus. Catholic philosopher W. Norris Clarke argues that only when the dyadic structure of the human being is actualized does the human person becomes manifest.[3] In a similar vein, Protestant philosopher C. Stephen Evans affirms this view when he says that "a person is someone whose being involves becoming," and yet a person only becomes what one already is.[4] I will explore in more detail Clarke's notion of the person as substance-in-relation and Evans's person as a substantial achiever.[5] But before I do that, I must first explain the meaning of being, the relationship between being and person and the role human nature plays in being a human person.

The Nature of Being the Human Person

What then is the nature of the human being or person? To begin with, I take the view that the notions of being and person are essentially coterminous concepts, and, as suggested above, I believe that the contemporary trend to bifurcate humanity into a human being as a biological entity and a human person as a moral agent is ill-conceived, unnecessary and unjustified. I wish to emphasize that person is not some special mode of being added on from the outside; rather, person is "the fullness of being itself"[6] such that to be *personal* is *being* in its fullest expression. It is existence coming into its own, "being" allowed to be fully what it is and what it can be. The implication is that being and person differ not in kind but only in the degree of expression, and in general, a human being will fully manifest itself as a human person under optimal conditions. (In the Christian tradition God is understood to be the ultimate Being and hence is experienced only as a personal God—in fact, a person par excellence.) These statements are true for all beings, human or divine, although the expression of being as person will be conditioned by the being's respective nature. In the case of a human being, the fullness of being is conditioned by the limitations imposed by and proper to its material mode of being. Therefore

---

[3]W. Norris Clarke, S.J., "To Be Is to Be Substance-in-Relation," in *Metaphysics as Foundation,* ed. Paul A. Boggaard and Gordon Treash (New York: State University of New York Press, 1993), pp. 164-81.

[4]C. Stephen Evans, "Human Persons as Substantial Achievers," *Philosophia Reformata* 58, no. 1 (1993): 108.

[5]In shaping my understanding of the dyadic structure of personhood, I am indebted to Clarke and Evans for their articles cited above.

[6]W. Norris Clarke, S.J., *Person and Being* (Milwaukee: Marquette University Press, 1993), p. 25.

it is important to recognize that to speak of a person is not to refer to the nature of the being; *nature* refers to properties and conditions that qualify the expression of the being as person, but *person* always refers to the concrete reality of a being as unique, undivided, autonomous and noninterchangeable. The unique reality of a person is the actual reality of a being that belongs to itself, in itself.[7]

What then is the relationship between human nature and human being (and, in the latter's fullest expression, a human person)? A human being/person is a being possessing a soul of an intellectual nature united with a body of a material nature. When Aristotle calls the human being a "rational animal," he is recognizing that the human in her deepest level of being is a spirit, but a spirit that needs the cooperation and complementation of the body as the mediating instrument to fulfill her destiny in the material world. For Thomas Aquinas, who improves on Aristotle's somewhat crude formulation, the human being is better known as an "embodied spirit" whose body enables her to journey through the material cosmos to God—*homo viator*, the human traveler. In this unity of physical body and intellectual spirit or soul, the soul is often seen by those from the traditions of Roman Catholicism and conservative Protestantism to be capable of purely spiritual acts that transcend bodily functions. In this way the soul may therefore be considered to possess its own act of existence. Specifically, the soul retains its existence when separated from the body at death. Furthermore, according to Christian orthodoxy, the soul is thought to have an intrinsic orientation toward or affinity with the body such that the two will be rejoined in the final resurrection of the body. Thus, in contrast to Aristotle, the Christian human soul is not limited as the form of the body but also transcends the body in that it is capable of an independent spiritual existence. The soul thus is both a form and a spirit. However, not all Christian theologians think that the soul is capable of existing independent of the body. Karl Barth, for example, says in his *Church Dogmatics* that "the soul is not a being for itself, and it cannot exist for itself. Soul can awake and be only as soul of a body."[8] But all strands of Christian thought agree that the soul—as the unifying center of all vital activities of the human being/person—"needs" the body as the necessary "partner" for the journey of self-realization in and through the material cosmos. As such, the soul and body form a single, unified existing nature.[9]

---

[7]See also Max Müller and Alois Halder, "Person: I Concept," in *Sacramentum Mundi: An Encyclopedia of Theology,* ed. Karl Rahner et al. (New York: Herder & Herder, 1968-1970), 4:404.

[8]Karl Barth, *Church Dogmatics* 3/2, ed. G. W. Bromiley and T. F. Torrance (Edinburgh: T & T Clark, 1960), §46.3.

[9]For another discussion of the interconnection between soul and body from a different perspective, please refer to chapter four, "Person as a Psychosomatic Unity," below.

Christian orthodoxy also holds the view that as ensouled body or embodied soul, the human person *has* spirit, in the sense that the spirit is not essentially part of the human nature but is given to and received by the human being. Barth describes the relation between man and his spirit[10] well when he says, "Man has spirit, as one who is possessed by it."[11] Unlike the soul and body, the spirit is neither a third constitutive "component" of the human person, nor a capacity or an ability of the human's own nature; rather it is "foreign to his nature which has come to it from God."[12] The Spirit—given to the human being as a principle of his creaturely reality—grounds, constitutes and maintains him as soul of his body. Without the Spirit "man cannot in any sense be man, nor in any sense soul of his body. As he has the Spirit from God, he lives, he becomes and is soul, his material body becomes and is a physical body, and he is soul of this body."[13] The Spirit unifies and holds the human being as soul and body. Barth calls the Spirit given to the human being the creative action of God that, as a "transcendental determination of the human constitution"[14] and as a life-giving event, has to be continually repeated by God in order for the human to live. The human being "owes its being and existence to the Spirit."[15] To say that the human being has the Spirit, however, is not to say that the human being has divine essence. While the Spirit is in the human being, the Spirit is not identical with the human being. The Spirit may have created the human soul and taken up residence in it, but the Spirit is not thereby transformed to become the human soul. When the human being dies, the Spirit who is immortal returns to God who first sent him forth. On this view, "whether or not death is the last word concerning man depends upon whether He [the Spirit] is given again."[16]

She, as a human being, with her nature as ensouled body or embodied soul, discovers herself as both historical and social. She is historical because with her almost unrestricted intellectual power and interests corresponding with the freedom of her will, she is endowed with a creativity that enables her to make her own history as she journeys toward her destiny through time and space; she is also social because the journey through the material cosmos cannot be done alone. As *homo viator,* human beings are not only mutually dependent on and

---

[10]Throughout this book, the feminine pronouns *she* and *her* are used randomly and interchangeably with masculine pronouns except where the discussion is in dialogue with a particular author whose writings employ the masculine pronouns.

[11]Barth, *Church Dogmatics* 3/2, §46.2.

[12]Ibid.

[13]Ibid.

[14]Ibid.

[15]Ibid., §46.3.

[16]Ibid., §46.2.

complementary to each other, but by their sexual nature are attracted to and enjoy the company of each other. Human nature as embodied soul or ensouled body therefore does not imply a static and rigidly determined structure; rather, as we shall see in more detail below, it provides the condition for the human being to be a dynamic center of free and creative actions, constantly opening toward others even as she writes the history of her own unique life.

Finally, one may wonder why a human being, with his primary nature as body and soul, and derivatively as historical and social, should necessarily journey *toward* a destiny—and one may also wonder what that destiny is. To answer this question, we should consider a long tradition in Western (Christian) thought that envisions the human being with his dual nature of body and soul, matter and spirit, constituted and maintained by the Spirit, as a microcosm—a miniaturized synthesis of the whole universe. Barth says, "As soul of his body, man is obviously heavenly as he is earthly."[17] As a body-soul microcosm, the human being is sharing in the "twofold mystery" of the macrocosm of heaven and earth. By his body, the human being sinks his roots deep into the material cosmos, which is the source of his inspiration (thought), aspiration (desire) and indeed perspiration (action) as well as the theater of life where he realizes his being as human. But by his spiritual soul, he is also capable of rising above the limitations of time and space to participate in the spiritual worlds of supramaterial meanings and values. For this reason, Barth sees that

> the benefit of creation consists in the fact that man may be the soul of his body, that as a living material body he is not restricted to space and the world of bodies, but may also be and exist temporally and belong to the invisible upper cosmos.[18]

Clarke calls this human dynamism "the dynamic a priori of the human spirit," which drives the person constantly to new levels of growth and development.[19] Thus as "soul of his body" and as "body of his soul," the human being is like an "amphibian," as the Greek fathers used to say, living on the frontier of matter and spirit, journeying through matter in his destiny toward a fulfillment beyond the material realm. Specifically, the human will, by virtue of the soul's intellectual capacity and as its faculty of action, is necessarily oriented toward the ultimate Infinite Good as the infinite source and fullness of all meaning, value and being—namely, God. Barth explicitly states that "man's soul *per se* has an affinity to the Spirit by whom it is made. And thus it is created *a priori* in this affinity, i.e. for the realization of a connection between man and his creator."[20] It is perhaps for this reason that human beings are fun-

---

[17]Ibid.
[18]Ibid.
[19]Clarke, *Person and Being*, p. 37.
[20]Barth, *Church Dogmatics* 3/2, §46.4.

damentally religious, endowed with an innate, unrestricted drive toward God. As Augustine proclaimed so long ago, "Our hearts are restless, O Lord, till they find rest in you."[21]

In light of what has been said so far, we may summarize a Christian perspective of the human nature as follows: a human being is by nature an embodied soul or an ensouled body, possessed by the Spirit who constitutes and maintains the finite (and fallen) human being, living in social solidarity with her fellow human beings, and journeying historically through this material cosmos toward her final supranatural destiny, in search for the infinite God who creates her.[22]

Being and Person as Substance

Having considered the nature of the human being/person, I now turn to the meaning of the terms *being* and *person*. In the West, there is a venerable tradition that considers both *being* and *person* in terms of "substance." The concept of substance as the primary instance of real being, and hence the person, can be traced back to the thought of Aristotle, if not Plato or even to the ancient pre-Socratics.[23] The concept of substance as developed by Aristotle and many philosophers after him is understood

☐ to possess the aptitude to exist in itself as a concrete individual thing and not as a part of any other being

☐ to be the unifying center of the various characteristics, attributes and properties that it possesses at any one moment (the Latin *substance* means to "stand under" all its attributes as their ultimate subject)

☐ in the case of change, to persist as the same individual "numerically one and the same" throughout the change

As such, the substance is the abiding center of the being over time, a fact that Aristotle calls "the most distinctive mark of substance."[24] As a primary instance of real being, this power to exist *in itself* as an ultimate subject of action and attribution and not as a part of any other being is perhaps the most important mark of substance.[25] This emphasis on the "in itselfness" of the substance is necessary because wherever there is real being, there must be sub-

---

[21]St. Augustine, *The Confessions of St. Augustine* (Westwood, N.J.: Christian Library, 1984), p. 5.

[22]Compare Clarke, who provides a very similar Christian definition of human nature (*Person and Being,* p. 41).

[23]For a brief summary of this complex concept in Western philosophy, see D. J. O'Connor, "Substance and Attributes," in *The Encyclopedia of Philosophy,* ed. Paul Edwards (New York: Macmillan, 1967), 8:36-40.

[24]Ibid., 8:37.

[25]Compare Clarke, "To Be," p. 166.

stance to ground whatever else is there as the being's ultimate subject of inherence. Consequently, without the "in itselfness" of the substance, every instance of real being would be a part of, or inhering in, some other being, and the necessary conditions for any being to exist would be deferred indefinitely. Substance with its "in itself" characteristic is necessary in making a being what Bernard Lonergan has called a "unity, identity, whole."[26]

But it must be stressed that to be "in itself" does not mean that being is thereby unrelated to others; one of the most overlooked aspects of the notion of substance is its intrinsic dynamic orientation toward the self-expressive and self-communicative action that generates relations. Clarke, as a Catholic philosopher, seeks to retrieve the pre-Cartesian notion of substance as a dynamic center of self-communication and relations, involving both acting and being acted upon.[27] Similarly, Evans, a Protestant philosopher, holds the view that human persons are substances which must be thought of and treated in a dynamic fashion.[28] To overlook the active and self-communicative aspects of substance/real being is costly because simultaneously and consequently one ignores the relational dimension of substance/real being. In fact, the main distortion of the modern notion of substance is the loss of this "toward-others" relational dimension of substance. The classical notion of substance as active nature imbedded in a network of relations of acting and being acted upon has been stripped away by the Cartesian substance as "that which exists by itself, that which needs nothing else but itself to exist,"[29] and as substance in itself, it is the unchanging substratum and the primary ground of all attributes. On this view, relations are ontologically subordinate to substance and thus of secondary importance.

Clarke lays the blame for the ongoing misconstruction of substance not only on René Descartes's self-enclosed substance, but also on John Locke's inert substance as unknowable substratum and on the separable substance of David Hume.[30] As a result of this distortion, the two notions of substance and relation have not simply been separated but have become increasingly antithetical to each other in the modern philosophy of ontology and personhood. Drawing support from Aquinas's teaching on the personhood of the triune God,[31] Clarke argues that in real being, there are two fundamental poles: the "in itself" and

---

[26]Bernard Lonergan, quoted in Clarke, "To Be," p. 167.

[27]Clarke's writings on this subject are collected in W. Norris Clarke, S.J., *Explorations in Metaphysics: Being-God-Person* (Notre Dame: University of Notre Dame Press, 1994).

[28]Evans, "Human Persons," p. 106.

[29]Quoted in Clarke, "To Be," p. 171.

[30]Clarke, "To Be," pp. 171-74; for further discussion on Locke and Hume, see chapter three, "The Psychological Dimension of Human Personhood," below.

[31]For example, in *Summa Theologica* 1.Q29.A4 (trans. Fathers of the English Dominican Province [Westminster, Md.: Christian Classics, 1981]), Aquinas discusses the claim that "in God the individual—i.e., distinct and incommunicable substance—includes the idea of relation."

the "toward other," the "self-possessing" and the "self-communicative." These two poles are distinct but inseparable—indissoluble and complementary aspects of real being. As I will discuss below, the "in itself" is the necessary point from which "it" launches toward the "other." It is therefore necessary for us to realize that these two aspects of real being: substantiality (the in-itself dimension of being) and relationality (the toward-others dimension of being) are equally important in the order of being. They both constitute being and, hence, person as the supreme instance of being. To favor one at the expense of the other is to "upset the dyadic balance of being." As Clarke summarizes it, "to be real is to be a *dyadic synthesis* of substance and relation; it is to be *substance-in-relation*."[32]

Being and Person as Presence-in-Itself

Before I explore the concept of "being as substance-in-relation" and its implications for the human person, we should first consider the significance of the in-itself aspect of substance for the human being/person.[33] If, as we have seen, every real being exists first as present in itself, on its own as a "unity-identity-whole," in the company of but not as a part of any other existents, then it is true with the person and specifically the human person. This "presence-in-itself," at the level of personal being, manifests and expresses itself consciously in two ways: in the order of knowledge as self-consciousness and in the order of action as self-determination.

Self-presence as self-consciousness enables a personal being to be aware of itself as subject "immediately present to itself from within"[34] and conscious of itself as the source of its own actions such that the person can meaningfully say, "I." This ability to be "self-present" or self-conscious is considered primarily the function of the spiritual soul and not the physical body.[35] In the higher form of spiritual being, as in God and the angels, this self-presence is immediate and complete; but the self-presence of the human being, as an embodied soul, is less than immediate. Instead, it remains incomplete and must be activated from without, relying on the stimulation of the senses by the outside world of objects and existents. The explicit awakening to self-awareness as an

---

[32]Clarke, "To Be," p. 166, emphasis added.

[33]In this section and the next ("Being and Person as Self-Communicative Act and Relation"), I draw on and further develop the thoughts in Clarke's *Person and Being*.

[34]Clarke, *Person and Being*, p. 44.

[35]This is because physical material occupies space and is governed by physical laws, and as such it is not possible for one part of a physical substance to coincide or be identical with another part. In the act of self-awareness, the subject and the object of the same act are identical, with both the knower and the known coinciding fully. Such an event is possible only if the subject of such an activity is able to transcend the material, necessitating that it belong to the spiritual mode of being.

"I," therefore, is dependent on an "other" encountering us, to provide us with the "wake-up call," so to speak, by reaching out to us and calling us into an "I-Thou" relation.[36] So it seems that in order for the human self-presence to emerge, human beings cannot exist on their own; we need the outside world and particularly other persons before we even become self-conscious. There is something misleading about the "self" in the "self-conscious," for we become conscious of others before we become conscious of ourselves.[37]

This process of "self-consciousness" in a human person continues on through one's whole life. This implies that there is a progressive and incremental character to one's self-awareness as one journeys through life. As *homo viators* we increasingly discover not only the world outside of us, but also the world of the self within us, the "who I am" as a unique person among other persons in the world. As I have already shown, this seemingly infinite or inexhaustible depth of the self is interpreted by Christian orthodoxy as due to the fact that as spirit, even as embodied spirit, we are naturally open to the Infinite Spirit, God. As German mystic Angelus Silesius puts it, "The abyss in man cries out to the abyss in God. Tell me, which is deeper?"[38] John Scotus Eriugena thinks that "God and man are paradigms of each other"—both are ineffable because of their subjectivity and their inexhaustible depth. Hence, our self-awareness is like "a partial zone of light within us, ever in fluid expansion or recession, surrounded by a penumbra of shadow shading off into an (at present) impenetrable darkness,"[39] only to be gradually and increasingly illuminated as we approach the true light. In the same way that we as limited embodied spirits will never be able to fathom the spirit of God, so we will never be completely conscious of "our selves" as God is conscious of us. Put differently, short of a direct vision of God himself or a step into the visual horizon of God-self where we shall see ourselves totally as God sees us, we shall never see ourselves as we really are. As embodied spirit, we discover ourselves more as we grow to know the Spirit. This dual knowledge of God and self has been expressed well by Augustine when he says, "Let me know thee O God, let me know myself"; and the knowledge of God and self advance together, reciprocally illuminating each other in an alternating spiral of enlightenment and vision. For much the same reason, John Calvin opens book one of his *Institutes of the Christian Religion* by stating that "the knowledge of God and that of ourselves are connected. . . . Without knowledge of the self there is no

---

[36]A brief discussion of Martin Buber's "I-Thou" relation will be found in chapter five, "The Relational Dimension of Human Personhood," below.

[37]Compare John MacMurray, *Persons in Relation* (London: Humanities Press, 1991), esp. chaps. 1-4.

[38]Angelus Silesius, quoted in Clarke, *Person and Being*, p. 47.

[39]Ibid.

knowledge of God."[40]

The self-presence of the personal being also manifests itself in the order of action as self-determination: that is, self-presence as the self exercises mastery or control of one's own actions by freedom of the will. Through this second mode of self-presence, the "I" becomes responsible for its own actions. Moral responsibility arises from this self-determination through freedom, and a personal being is a self-governing—autonomous—being. But in exercising one's freedom to choose, one is not merely freely determining certain particular actions but also is determining one's own self as a person, "who I am." My action displays my personhood. Every consciously, freely and responsibly chosen action shapes, builds and determines my identity and the kind of person I am. In this sense, the self-determination of our freely chosen actions is in fact determining the self. In every free action, there is "the outward-oriented intentionality of the act towards its object . . . [as well as an] inward-oriented effect of *self*-determination or *self*-making that goes hand in hand with the former."[41] In other words, while the intentionality of an act is object-oriented, there is a concomitant intentionality of self-determination that is subject-oriented. Admittedly, one's self-determination, like one's self-consciousness, is never complete and perfect. Our intellect and will are conditioned and limited by many influences external to our self-possessive consciousness, including our culture, family, childhood experience, emotions and unconscious drives as well as our various bodily needs. We only gradually learn to exercise self-mastery over our "freely chosen" choices. Like self-consciousness, self-determination is a journey, an ongoing life project.

In sum, the self-presence of the person, as expressed by self-consciousness and self-determination, is the manifestation of one of the two complementary poles of the ontological structure of any real being and person, namely, the "in-itselfness" or substantiality of the person. It is here that the unique interiority and individuality of the personal self reside. It is also this in-itselfness which protects the self from fusing with the other selves.

Being and Person as Self-Communicative Act and Relation

I now turn to the "toward-other," or "self-communicative," aspect of being: the notion of "being" as substance-in-relation. In the following discussion, substance is assumed to be the primary instance of being, but as I have said, there remains a need to reestablish the notion of substance as substance-in-relation. In this regard, I appeal to Aquinas who said the following:

---

[40]John Calvin, *Institutes of the Christian Religion,* ed. John T. McNeill, trans. Ford Lewis Battles (Philadelphia: Westminster Press, 1960), p. 35.

[41]Clarke, *Person and Being,* p. 56.

☐ Real being—that is, actually existing being—is intrinsically active and self-communicating.

☐ "Every substance exists for the sake of its operation,"[42] which he sees as "the ultimate perfection of each thing."[43]

☐ All operations or actions of a being are ways of self-communication of that being, and hence "it is the nature of every actuality to communicate itself insofar as it is possible."[44]

☐ It is the very nature of rational being to communicate: "communication follows upon the very intelligibility *(ratio)* of actuality."[45]

Contrary to many modern conceptions of substance as an inert, static, isolated, enclosed and unknowable substratum of being, this conception of substance argues that action is precisely the way an existing substance manifests its existence and essence. "Not: to be, then to act, but: to be is to act,"[46] and "action is the manifestation or epiphany of the silence of being."[47]

The dynamic act in every being to be self-communicative may be due to both the being's own poverty (i.e., his lacking the fullness of existence) and so striving to enrich himself from the richness of his surroundings as well as the being's own richness of existence and so the tendency to communicate and share it with others.[48] On this view, if there is any being at all, it can only be understood as intrinsically active, self-manifesting and self-communicating. This notion of substance or real being as dynamic self-communication in action provides the core of the notion that every real being is constituted by its *esse* or act of existence, "conceived not as form or whatness or essence but as active presence—power-filled presence."[49] Because of this dynamic inner core, there is a tendency for every being to flow into action, by its very nature as existing being. As one philosopher puts it, "The act of existence *(esse)* is not a state, it is an act, the act of all acts. . . . *Esse* is dynamic impulse, energy, act."[50]

If self-communication is a fundamental aspect of real being, then so is receptivity since communication cannot be truly consummated without recep-

---

[42]Thomas Aquinas *Summa contra Gentiles* 3.26, quoted in Clarke, "To Be," p. 167.

[43]Aquinas *Summa contra Gentiles* 1.45, quoted in Clarke, "To Be," p. 167.

[44]Aquinas *Summa contra Gentiles* 3.113, quoted in Clarke, "To Be," p. 168.

[45]Thomas Aquinas *Exposition in Libros Sententiarum* 1.4.1.1, quoted in Clarke, "To Be," p. 168.

[46]Etienne Gilson, *Being and Some Philosophers* (Toronto: Pontifical Institute of Mediaeval Studies, 1952), p. 184, quoted in Clarke, *Person and Being,* p. 8.

[47]James Sommerville, "Maurice Blondel and the Philosophy of Action," *Spiritual Life* 7, no. 2 (1961): 114.

[48]Clarke, *Person and Being,* p. 10.

[49]Clarke, "To Be," p. 169.

[50]Gerald Phelan, "The Existentialism of St. Thomas" in *Selected Papers* (Toronto: Pontifical Institute of Mediaeval Studies, 1967), p. 90, quoted in Clarke, *Person and Being,* p. 9.

tivity as the complementary pole of self-communication. They are two complementary and inseparable sides of the dynamic process of being itself, and as such real being or substance is a center of both activity and receptivity.[51] The most important corollary of this understanding of being as dynamic substance of activity and receptivity is that every substance cannot help but generate a network of relations to become the center of a web of relations to other beings around it. Just as a real being is inseparable from its action, so the substantiality of every real being is inseparable from its relationality. This means that all self-communicative beings are oriented through action to the community of other beings. Real being, "as intrinsically self-communication and relational through action, tends naturally toward modes of being-together that we can justifiably call the mode of community."[52] To be is to-be-together. Being and community are inseparable. On this view, then, being as substance, as existing *in itself,* naturally flows over into being as relational, as turned *toward others* by its self-communicating action. *"To be fully is to be substance-in-relation."*[53]

While this line of reasoning may be said to reflect Aquinas's integration of the Aristotelian and Neo-Platonic traditions of the self-diffusiveness of the Good into his metaphysics of being, in reality he locates the ultimate reason of the dynamism of self-communicative action of all beings in the infinite goodness of the Source, the Supreme Being itself—the triune God whose inner nature is an ecstatic process of self-communicative love. In this context, the Father is the self-giving mode of the being of God, and the Son and Spirit are the receiving mode. As perfect Love, both self-communication and receptivity are present as the fundamental dimensions of real being and are generative of relations. This self-communicative love subsequently flows over freely in the finite self-communication that is creation. It is for this reason that "self-communication is written into the very heart of all beings, as finite but positive images of their Source."[54] Philosophy and theology agree, then, that to be and to be active are distinguishable but inseparable.

If real being is an act of existence *(esse)* with its dynamic, self-communicating, relational aspect—and because person is the highest and most intense expression of being—we may expect this self-communicative aspect of being to have developed fully in the realm of persons. Everything that has been said about the dyadic ontological structure of all being, with both of its poles of "in-itselfness" and "toward-otherness" applies to the person. To be a person, then, is intrinsically expansive and ecstatic, ordered toward self-manifes-

---

[51]Clarke, *Person and Being,* p. 85.
[52]Ibid., p. 14.
[53]Ibid.
[54]Ibid., p. 12.

tation and self-communication of one's own richness to others, while providing the person with an innate drive toward other beings to form relations. This Thomistic substance is considerably more advanced than the Aristotelian substance, which, though possessing an intrinsic dynamism, is nevertheless ordered toward self-realization and self-fulfillment rather than self-communication.

Just as a human person's consciousness of the self needs to be actualized from the outside, so the relational dimension of the human person also begins from its passive side as receptivity. The human person starts out as a fetus, infant and child—poor and needy, on the receiving end. As the mother actively relates to the child, the child becomes progressively an "I," responding to her mother as a "Thou." In this process of personalization, the child's potentiality for self-consciousness and responsiveness is being actualized; and as the child matures, with both the self-presence and the self-communication aspects of the person growing more established, the child becomes the source of both giving and receiving, consciously expressing the dyadic rhythm of all existential being in its most intense form as a personal being. While the consideration of receptivity as poverty or deficiency may be more pronounced in the case of infants and children, it does not imply that receptivity is eliminated once personhood becomes more progressively expressed; receptivity is retained by a maturing person because there is a positive side to receptivity that is an essential component of mutuality. This is best seen in the highest mode of love, the love of friendship, which requires mutuality and reciprocity to be initiated and maintained; in the absence of receptivity, this mode of relation can never be exercised. Hence, as part of the essence of the highest love, receptivity acquires its ontological value as a positive perfection of being. Christian orthodoxy may readily trace this refutation of receptivity as passivity or inferiority from the fact that in the triune life of God, the Son and the Spirit are both subsistent Receptivity, while they are ontologically equally perfect and worthy as the Father, who is subsistent Self-Communicative.

If there is an acquisitive side to the self-communication of the human person's reaching out to others seeking self-fulfillment due to one's own incompleteness, there is also a drive to communicate in order to share one's richness. In other words, self-communication turns into a form of love. This primal mystery of self-openness to the other as love, as an intrinsic property of all beings, and even more so of persons, can rightly be traced back to its ultimate source in the divine being—the personal triune God who reveals himself as self-communicative and interpersonal love. This relational pole of the human person naturally leads to the formation of all kinds of human bonds, including filial, fraternal and that of friendship, which in turn interconnect into community. This is consistent with the observation that every viable human community involves some kind of communion of love of friendship. Ultimately to be means to-be-in-communion. Clarke summarizes the relation between being, person and communion as follows:

> To be, in the full deployment of its actuality, is to *commune* with one's fellow existents, and the most intense and luminous manifestation of this shines forth in the life of the person, as self-conscious, free, communion with other persons. . . . There is no viable substitute for communion; this is the law of being itself.[55]

So in the final analysis, to be—and, more intensely, to be persons—is to be caught up in this dynamic process of receptivity and self-communication, giving and receiving, mutuality and reciprocity, and ultimately moving toward communion. The reason why all beings and particularly all persons are this way is precisely because that is the way of the Supreme Being. As the apostle John tells us, "God is love," and the doctrine of the Trinity makes it clear that God's nature is to be self-communicative love. Made in the image of God, human beings will mirror, however dimly, in some character-istic way the divine mode of being as love. "To be an actualized human per-son, then, is to be a lover, to live a life of inter-personal self-giving and receiving."[56]

Conclusion: Person as "Substance-in-Relation" or "Substantial Achiever"
This analysis leads to the conclusion that a human being, like all being, is caught up in an unending dialectic between the "in-itself" and "toward-others" dimensions. Hence, a human person, like all real being, is a living synthesis of substantiality and relationality. The substantial pole, the in-itself dimension of the person, provides the basis for one's abiding presence in the world as pres-ence in oneself and to oneself, as self-presence through self-consciousness and self-determination; the relational pole, the toward-others dimension, provides through its self-communication and receptivity the basis for one's entry into a web of relationships. The two poles are mutually dependent on each other; for without "the inward-facing act of existential presence in itself," no "outward-facing act of self-expression and self-manifestation to others" is possible.[57] Yet it is through the relational dimension of the person that the self as substance is actualized from its latent state as potentiality and fulfilled in its maturity. As we have seen, only through the mediation of the other can one return to discover oneself as the self-conscious "I," unique and individuated. I only positively become fully aware of who and what I am when other human persons with

---

[55]Ibid., p. 82; also see the writings of John Zizioulas.
[56]Ibid., p. 76.
[57]W. Norris Clarke, *Person and Being* (Milwaukee: Marquette University Press, 1993), p. 64.

the same actualized capacity of self-consciousness decide to treat me as a "Thou" in an interpersonal matrix and invite me into an "I-Thou" relation. As I will discuss later in more detail, Buber believes that the "I" only arises out of the "I-Thou." The importance of the relational dimension lies in the fact that unless another "I" appeals to me to respond as another self, as a "Thou," I can never wake up to myself as an "I," as a person. Personhood only emerges gradually through dialogue and encounter in a growing matrix of persons to other persons and the world.

One can readily envision that the entire growth, development and maturation of one's personal life can be seen to unfold through this dialectic of substantiality and relationality. In the maturing process of a person, it is never a one-sided immersion in relation to others but an alternating rhythm between self and other. In response to the other's call, we go out of our selves toward others in relation, but in turn we also return to our own center to evaluate what that act of going out means for the self and how that act may build up and enrich the self in the process. The self, thus enriched, is encouraged to reach out to establish more relations with greater self-confidence and a deeper sense of self-possession. Clarke puts it this way:

> Paradoxically the more intensely I am present to myself at one pole, the more intensely I am present and open to others at the other. And reciprocally, the more I make myself truly present to the others as an "I" or self, the more I must also be present to myself, in order that it may be truly *I* that is present to them, not a mask.[58]

This progression of "person building" goes on, alternating harmoniously between the two poles of substantiality and relationality, mutually facilitating and enriching each other.

One of the problems with some contemporary trends of thought, especially those from the school of phenomenology, is the tendency to reject substance as a mode of being in favor of relations. On this view, being is reduced to nothing but a relation or a set of relations, and the person is treated as purely relational and interpersonal. Phenomenologist viewpoints come in two varieties: moderate and radical. Those who hold a moderate phenomenologist view acknowledge that while the person may possess a substantial pole, the "in-itselfness" or self-presence is constituted by one's relations to others, such as a child's being called to personhood by her mother. But such a view, as Evans points out, is "self-deificatory," because if human persons constitute themselves socially by relating to each other, we are claiming in essence that humans are "autonomous, self-creating beings."[59] Clarke also argues that we simply cannot

[58]Ibid., pp. 69-70.
[59]Evans, "Human Persons," p. 106.

bring anything into being by simply relating to it, any more than we can make a tree into a person by relating to it. In metaphysical terms, "the being to which we relate must already be of the type that *can* respond to such an invitation by intrinsic powers already within it."[60] For example, a child's gradual acquisition of personal consciousness in response to her mother's loving relation is best viewed as the awakening or actualizing of the potential personal nature latent but inherent in the child's own being. What the mother does is to apply the appropriate stimulus to facilitate the conversion of this potentiality to actuality. Self-awareness, indeed, only appears subsequent to the "I-Thou" encounter, but the role played by these relations is best seen as facilitative rather than constitutive. "The person is awakened to actual exercise of its personhood by the initiatives of others, but is not constituted in being as person by them."[61]

The second and more radical phenomenological interpretation only magnifies these problems. It sees the whole category of substance as inappropriate to the description of human being, and thereby it reduces the human person to a set of relations to others, with no substantial subject to ground them. Real being thus becomes pure relatedness to others. Such a move to replace substance with relation as the exclusive ground of being is as serious an error as that which it seeks to correct. For a relation to be real, it must relate to something. "If all beings are relations, such that A is nothing but a relation to B, and B is nothing but a relation to A, then neither one has its 'own being' and both disappear into 'emptiness.' "[62] Eliminating the substantial pole from the ontological structure amounts to evacuating any "own-being" from all persons so that they disappear into a Buddhist type of emptiness. Further, it removes from the person all dimensions of privacy, interiority, uniqueness and *self*-possession so that the person "becomes a totally extroverted presence *to* others without a genuine self-presence."[63] This reduction appears to be particularly favored by postmodern deconstructionist thinkers who deprive the person of his inner self and leaves him with nothing to share or receive from others, resulting in the loss of a necessary component in the formation of relation. To dispense with substance in favor of relations is therefore itself self-destructive of relations and ultimately of personhood; by contrast, to conceive substance as a center of activity and receptivity, and hence generative of relationality and community, makes this either/or dichotomy between substance and relation unnecessary and ultimately renders genuine personhood possible.

---

[60]Clarke, *Person and Being,* p. 59.
[61]Ibid.
[62]Clarke, "To Be," p. 166.
[63]Clarke, *Person and Being,* p. 60.

Substantiality as a mode of being is therefore both indispensable and necessary as a grounding for relationality itself, for relation implies a connection between two "relateds." A related is neither identical with nor reducible to the relation of which it is a part in its constitution; for "no relation can be self-supporting by itself . . . [and] there must be an *in-itself* somewhere along the line to ground the betweenness."[64] The ontological role of substance in a being, then, is to provide the abiding unifying center for all the being's relations and other attributes. As Joseph Pieper puts it, "Only in reference to an inside can there be an outside. Without a self-contained 'subject' there can be no 'object.' Relating-to, conforming-with, being-oriented-toward—all these notions presuppose an inside starting point."[65] But emphasizing the necessity of substance does not make relations any less primordial than substance since being as substance, as existing in itself, flows naturally into being as relation. Relationality as proceeding from substantiality would not be secondary in its ontological importance if relation is in fact the self-expression of the substance itself: that is, the goal and fulfillment of substance, indeed, the ultimate raison d'être of substance.[66] Christian orthodoxy readily finds a theological basis for this in the doctrine of the Trinity, which is expressive of the same truth in that the relations between the Father, Son and Spirit are manifesting and fulfilling of the divine substance. If relationality and substantiality are equally primordial and necessary in the being of God, then all created beings must similarly assume this dyadic structure of being, an "in-itself" dimension as substance, and a "toward-others" dimension as relations. These two dimensions are inseparable, complementary to each other and equally important. The intrinsic structure of all beings and persons—divine and human—is irreducibly dyadic, "a polarity of active substance and relation, of in-self interiority and self-transcending outreach toward others."[67]

This approach to reintegrate or synthesize substance and relation is also advocated by Evans, who, though appreciative of the aims and concerns of what he calls a "relational anthropology," nevertheless insists that a "substance anthropology" should not thereby be replaced. He believes that relational anthropology has rightly emphasized the importance of relations for the existence of human persons, especially the view that everything about

---

[64]Ibid., p. 16.

[65]Joseph Pieper, *The Truth of All Things* (San Francisco: Ignatius Press, 1989), pp. 82-83, quoted in Clarke, *Person and Being,* p. 18.

[66]In the same manner, a book exists to be read. Recognizing that purpose as its reason for being allows the substance of the book (paper and ink) to be actualized in the relation of the book being read, thus maintaining both poles.

[67]Clarke, "To Be," p. 176.

human beings is fundamentally dependent on God and derived from a relationship to God. This is consistent with the Reformation view that the image
of God is to be found not in any intrinsic human qualities, such as rationality
or morality, but in the righteousness of people who have been redeemed and
reconciled to be in proper relation to God. But Evans is also keen to point
out that to say that human "natures" (qualities) can only come out of God's
redemptive purpose does not mean that human nature is reduced to the
redemptive relation between the human person and God.[68] In terms of the
imago, there is no question that the human being as the image of God can
only be derived from a relationship with God, but it will be wrong to thereby
equate the image with the relationship. As far as Evans is concerned, all
human beings possess a definite human nature and with this nature, definite
powers; as well, all human beings exist as individual persons and essentially
relate to God and other persons in various ways, particularly through such
institutions as the family. But Evans insists that all of these categories are
terms for substances that enter into various relations.[69] Hence, he insists that
both relational and substantial categories are needed to do justice to the
Christian view of the person. In sum, Evans holds the view that a human person is both an entity and an achievement, a substance and a relation; persons
are what we are and what we must become.

Evans also argues that the notion of substance as applied to human beings
is qualitatively different from other natural objects, because the substance of a
person has the "nature" of "personal substance" with unique capacities. Hence,
"a person can be an *object* without being a *mere* object."[70] He then treats the
various unique human activities such as self-consciousness and relationality as
capacities that are essential to this personal substance. In particular, he stresses
the importance of free choice or autonomy as one of the most essential capacities for personhood because it underlines the unfinished and open-ended
character of the personal being. But he is also insistent that genuine freedom is
possessed only by a substantial agent because for an action to be genuine, it
has to be produced by a personal agent and not by any event or set of events
occurring in the agent. This means that a truly free agent has to be "a substantial agent, who is not reducible to a set of events."[71] Hence, as essential as freedom is to human personhood, personhood still cannot be equated with pure
freedom. To be a person is to be faced with the possibilities as to what one can

---

[68]C. Stephen Evans, "Healing Old Wounds and Recovering Old Insights: Toward a Christian
   View of the Person for Today," in *Christian Faith in the Modern World,* ed. Mark Noll and
   David Wells (Grand Rapids, Mich.: Eerdmans, 1988), pp. 68-86.
[69]Ibid., p. 71.
[70]Evans, "Human Persons," p. 107.
[71]Ibid., pp. 107-8.

and should become, but nonetheless one must in some sense already *be* a person. One has *to be* before one can choose *to become*. Evans concludes that

> a person who develops the capacity to choose, to reflect, and to relate is therefore becoming what he or she already is, essentially. A person is a being who has these capacities and characteristically actualizes them, though a person who fails to realize such capacities remains a person.[72]

In arriving at this conclusion, Evans is dependent on what Søren Kierkegaard noted more than a century ago: that the basic human task is "to strive to become what one already is."[73] Kierkegaard was emphasizing not only the becoming of the self, but also the self humans already are. Hence, Evans finds support from Kierkegaard in his claim that personhood is a category of both being and becoming, substance and relation.

Another reason why it is important to recapture the category of substance in our understanding of human personhood is because it is a reality grounded in God's creation. In linking human personal substance to God's creative activity, we can thereby provide "substantive" contents to the divine-human relationship, which in Protestant theology is often understood exclusively on soteriological grounds. But God's redemptive activity can only be fully apprehended against the backdrop of his creative activity, just as the doctrine of soteriology cannot be understood independently of the doctrine of creation. Protestant theology tends to overemphasize the doctrine of soteriology at the expense of the doctrine of creation, an imbalance that is also reflected in the preference of relation to substance in Protestant anthropology. But the two need not be, and indeed cannot be, mutually exclusive; for in fact substance and relation are interdependent and dynamically related in God's act of creation. As Evans correctly sees it, "The most fundamental relation humans possess to God is that of creation, and God's creation is reality, not illusion."[74] Plainly put, creation leads to the reality of substance, including substantial human beings. With the help of Kierkegaard's analysis of personal being, Evans attempts an account of the person as substance-in-relation in the context of such a creational theistic metaphysics. In *Philosophical Fragments,* Kierkegaard reminds us that for us as human beings, our historical existence involves possibility; however, it is not pure possibility but a set of possibilities rooted in an actuality. In other words, human possibilities occur within a context of a reality or actuality that is already in existence. This is what Kierkegaard means when he says that human historical existence involves a "coming into existence within a coming into

---

[72]Ibid., p. 108.

[73]Søren Kierkegaard, *Concluding Unscientific Postscript* (Princeton, N.J.: Princeton University Press, 1941), p. 116, quoted in Evans, "Human Persons," p. 109.

[74]Evans, "Human Persons," p. 102.

existence."[75] It is the actuality of human persons that makes possible this second "coming into existence," and such an actuality points back "ultimately to a freely effecting cause."[76] This leads to the conclusion that

> the power of human persons to be "relatively freely effecting causes" is grounded in the power of an "absolutely freely effecting cause." The substantiality of the historical self is thus tied to its ontological status as a created object.[77]

This notion of the self as a created object is confirmed by another passage where Kierkegaard defines a "self" as a "relation that relates itself to itself."[78] While this statement may suggest that Kierkegaard is in favor of a relational anthropology, Kierkegaard is quick to add that a relation that relates itself to itself must "either have established itself or have been established by another."[79] In fact, he believes that the human self "as a relation that relates itself to itself and in relating itself to itself relates itself to another" is "a derived, established relation."[80] Furthermore, even if it is God who establishes this relationship, the nature of that relation is one which specifically involves creation and not "merely that of the self knowing God, or even being known and loved by God."[81] Such a creational relation means that some substantial realities are being established, for as Kierkegaard argues, creation is the relation where God creates an authentic something, rather than a something which is nothing.[82]

Hence, the doctrines of creation and the *imago Dei* make it possible for us to see human persons as substantial beings with capacities to become and also as substantial realities that are opened rather than closed to possibilities. Rooted in God's creational activities, the self is both a substantial entity and a relational possibility. I concur with Evans's conclusion that "God has made us to be becomers; hence that is what we *are,* even if, paradoxically, we fail to become. . . . The status of persons as persons does not depend on their achievements, however, but on their status as God's *creatures.*"[83]

From the above discussion it is obvious that I bring to the philosophical/

---

[75]Søren Kierkegaard, *Philosophical Fragments,* quoted in Evans, "Human Persons," p. 109.
[76]Evans, "Human Persons," p. 110.
[77]Ibid.
[78]Søren Kierkegaard, *The Sickness unto Death,* trans. Howard V. Hong and Edna H. Hong (Princeton, N.J.: Princeton University Press, 1980), p. 13, quoted in Evans, "Human Persons," p. 110.
[79]Ibid.
[80]Ibid.
[81]Kierkegaard, *Concluding Unscientific Postscript,* p. 116, quoted in Evans, "Human Persons," p. 110.
[82]Ibid.
[83]Ibid., p. 111.

metaphysical reflection on human personhood my own Christian backgrounds and heritage. Specifically, as I shall demonstrate below in more detail, I have been informed by a Christian trinitarian faith, which holds the belief that the one substance of God is "founded" on the relations between the three Persons. As a consequence, I also hold the belief that human beings, created in God's image as embodied spirits, are also created in the likeness of this dyadic structure. On the basis of this understanding of the human person as substance and relation, actuality and possibility, or being and becoming, I shall explore in what follows the various dimensions of the dyadic structure of the human person in more detail: how each dimension may relate to the other and how as a multi-dimensional whole the human person is constituted. Specifically, I will discuss the human biological and psychological dimensions and see how they together as a psychosomatic unity constitute the "substantial" core of the human being who is endowed with the various potentialities and capacities to become, relate and transcend. We shall see that all human dimensions—including biological, psychological, relational, temporal and eschatological—are necessarily part and parcel of the human person as an integrated dyadic whole. Each functions as a part of the whole, but none on its own is capable of defining the whole.

2

The Biological Dimension of Human Personhood

*T*he Significance of the Genetic Endowment

In general, people find it easier to reach a consensus as to what constitutes a biological human. John Noonan suggests that a biological human is a living organism with a genetic endowment which is genetically identical with that of the species *Homo sapiens.*[1] When the male and female germ cells (a sperm and an ovum) form a zygote, in a process that takes from twenty-four to thirty-six hours, a genetically unique biologically human entity is brought into existence. Given the proper nurturing, a zygote will grow into an individual member of the species *Homo sapiens.* No one will deny that the entity so formed is indeed "human" (e.g., human embryo, human fetus, and so on), distinguishable from other nonhuman entities. The acknowledgment of the biological humanness of these entities can best be seen in the overwhelming preference for human organs when organ transplant is being considered; this is because these organs are fully biologically human, and the genetic material they contain is sufficiently generically similar that maximal tissue compatibility can be expected. Much of these commonsense practices are consistent with Noonan's view that "the criterion for humanity, thus, was simple and all embracing: if you are con-

---

[1]John T. Noonan Jr., "An Almost Absolute Value in History," in *The Morality of Abortion,* ed. John T. Noonan Jr. (Cambridge: Harvard University Press, 1970), pp. 1-59.

ceived by human parents, you are human."[2]

But the crucial question we must ask is whether these biologically living human entities are entitled to the right to life. Many people, while acknowledging these biologically human entities as humans, are reluctant to grant them the moral rights to life possessed by human persons. On the other hand, many feel that the significance of the biological entity's genetic endowment is sufficient to regard the human embryo as the beginning of a human individual, or a human person with the right to life. Noonan is one of the best known proponents of this position. He regards conception as the decisive moment of humanization because it is at this point when the new being receives the genetic code. "A being with a human genetic code is man."[3] This genetic argument is supported by Germain Grisez, who argues that a new individual begins when the sperm and ovum have completed the process of uniting with each other to form a whole.[4] Thus this author views genetic uniqueness to be sufficient to grant the zygote (and later the embryo) the status of a living, human individual. Even though Grisez admits that establishing personhood is a question of metaphysics, he sees "no compelling reason to deny that the embryo is a human person . . . [or] at the very least, that the embryo can as well be considered a person as not."[5]

Four genetic arguments have been cited in support of conception as the beginning of human personhood. First, there is the genetic uniqueness of the human diploid single-cell zygote (except when monozygotic twinning occurs). The mixing of the paternal and maternal chromosomes leading to a genetically unique unicellular zygote remains the most biologically significant event in the whole process of the transmission of human life. There is no other reproductive process with a comparably radical discontinuity to mark the beginning of an individual human life. "On this notion, most human people begin when a human sperm and ovum fuse."[6]

Second, there is the genetic continuity of the human zygote with the future adult. The mitotic cleavages and multiplication of cells from fertilization onward do not compromise the genetic continuity of the zygote as the same ontological individual; this same genetic uniqueness continues in the multicellular embryo, in the fetus, in the infant, in the child and eventually in the adult person. This genetic identity provides strong support for the ontological and

---

[2]Ibid., p. 51.

[3]Ibid., p. 57.

[4]Germain Grisez, *Abortion: The Myths, the Realities, and the Arguments* (New York: Corpus, 1970), p. 14.

[5]Ibid., p. 307.

[6]Germain Grisez, "When Do People Begin? The Ethics of Having Children," *Proceedings of the American Catholic Philosophical Association* 63 (1989): 28.

personal identity of the zygote and the adult human that develops from it. But in most cases where only one individual human life results from that unicellular zygote, the zygote is a distinct living being with a unique, independent and autonomous genetic endowment that programs its own orderly development into an adult. In these cases, the zygote and the adult that develops from it have the same genetic, ontological and personal identity. Norman Ford argues against this viewpoint on the basis that ontological identity cannot be established as long as twinning is possible before the primitive-streak stage.[7] I will discuss his arguments and the twinning process that occurs in approximately one out of two hundred pregnancies in greater detail below. Suffice it to say here that his argument is based on the mistaken assumption that all zygotes have an active potential to become twins and, excepting unforeseen interference, would do so. Scientific facts seem to indicate otherwise: that all zygotes usually actively develop continuously into single individuals. At most, the facts indicate that early embryos could, under some yet unexplained circumstances, passively undergo division or combination to become twins or chimeras. Nonetheless, the existence of such exceptions does not nullify the general conclusion that the zygote is genetically and ontologically identical with the adult it eventually becomes.

The third genetic argument is the zygote's capacity for self-development: by virtue of its unique genetic endowment, the zygote possesses an inherent and naturally active capacity, encoded in its genome, to control and coordinate all its systematic development and differentiation throughout the entire life process from fertilization onward. Even though the unicellular zygote depends on the mother for survival, it shows all the signs of an autonomous organism with an intrinsic life principle within it, directing all its activities to maintain and develop itself. This principle is the genetic code contained in the primordial nucleus. One writer calls this genetic capacity for organic self-development the human soul.[8] Because the zygote is endowed with this inherently vital capacity to direct and organize its own self-development into what is phenotypically a human person, it is justifiable to claim the zygote as the beginning of individuation (i.e., the beginning of a living individual human being), genetically and ontologically, which will endure throughout subsequent development.

Finally, the fourth genetic argument exploits the concept of continuum to show that the zygote's individuality or ontological identity is shared with the adult. If one takes a newborn infant and moves her back in time from birth to conception, one will observe that even though the physical appearance of

---

[7]Norman M. Ford, *When Did I Begin?* (Cambridge: Cambridge University Press, 1988), p. 117.
[8]B. M. Ashley, O.P., "Pro-Life Evangelization," in *New Technologies of Birth and Death* (St. Louis: Pope John XXIII Medical-Moral Research and Education Center, 1980), p. 85.

the developing fetus may have changed due to the addition of new organs or to an increase in tissue mass, there is no change in the nature of the developing human being radical or abrupt enough to suggest that a new human individual emerges in any one particular developmental stage. In other words, if one traces an adult's development back to the moment of fertilization, one will find no demonstrable difference in identity between the adult, the infant, the fetus and the originating zygote. No evidence shows that stages and degrees of development and growth are in any way disruptive to the continuing presence of the same human individual, provided an ontological human individual exists in the first place. And this ontological human individual is found in the zygote, who, as an individual human life, will exist as a progressive, ongoing, continuum until death. A similar conclusion is reached by the Australian Senate Select Committee on Human Embryo Experimentation, which states that "the embryo [zygote] may be properly described as genetically new human life organized as a distinct entity oriented towards further development . . . of a biologically individuated member of the human species."[9] In sum, these arguments support the contention that the genetic endowment of the zygote is sufficiently significant to be considered as the beginning of human personhood.

As expected, not everyone finds the biological/genetic arguments of human personhood quite so convincing. Two main arguments have been advanced to refute the case that a human person begins at the formation of the zygote. The first argument contends that although the genetic endowment found in a human zygote is unique, it is not sufficient to establish the ontological individuality of the adult. This case is built around certain biological evidences which arguably suggest that the genetic identity of the zygote can be proven to be different from the ontological identity of the adult it later becomes. I shall call this "the non-identity of genetic and ontological continuity argument." The second approach seeks to refute the genetic argument of human personhood by arguing that no demonstrable continuity exists between the physical organism of the zygote and the mental experiences of the adult it eventually becomes. I shall call this "the non-identity of genetic and psychological continuity argument."

The Non-identity of Genetic and Ontological Continuity Argument
Thomas Shannon and Allan Wolter observe that it takes about twenty-four to thirty-six hours from the time the sperm begins to penetrate the various lay-

---

[9]Human Embryo Experimentation in Australia, Senate Select Committee on the Human Embryo Experimentation, Bill 1985 (Carbetta: Australia Government Publishing Service, 1986), p. 25, quoted in Ford, *When Did I Begin?* p. 179.

ers of the ovum to the fusion of the nuclear contents of the sperm and ovum (a process called *syngamy*), at which point a new entity (the zygote) is created with a diploid set of chromosomes.[10] Three to four cellular divisions ensue in the following sixty hours, yielding the eight-cell stage as it migrates down the fallopian tube to the uterus. Around the sixth or seventh day after fertilization, the early embryo (or "pre-embryo," a term which I believe is misleading but which some writers prefer for embryos up to fourteen days of development), now called the *blastocyst,* reaches the uterine wall and begins the process of implantation; implantation is completed by the end of the second week, at which time primitive utero-placental circulation is established. Within the primitive embryo, the process of cellular differentiation occurs simultaneously with implantation. In this process, two types of cells appear: the trophectoderm, which occupies the outer wall of the blastocyst and later becomes the placental tissue, and the inner cell mass, which becomes the precursor of the embryo proper. At the end of the second week, the primitive streak appears, providing the earliest evidence of the embryonic axis and the formation of the embryo proper. The inner cell mass continues to differentiate into three distinct layers (gastrulation)—the ectoderm, endoderm and mesoderm—which ultimately give rise to the fetal tissues and organs. Gastrulation is completed at the end of the third week. At this time, each cell is genetically committed to developing along a particular pathway. All other genetic expressions are switched off, and all cells cease to be totipotent.

Based on these embryological observations, Shannon and Wolter raise three objections to the view that the zygote or the early embryo up to two to three weeks of its development is a human individual warranting the status of a person:

☐ the possibility of twinning and recombination resulting in something other than a human (hydatidiform mole)[11]

☐ the totipotentiality of the cells in the early embryo

☐ the early embryo's reliance on "supplementary genetic information" in its own development so that the zygote is "neither self-contained nor self-sufficient"[12]

I will review these objections, beginning with the claim that the zygote lacks sufficient genetic information for its own development and hence presumably lacks the completeness and autonomy of being—that is, the capacity to exist in

---

[10]Thomas A. Shannon and Allan B. Wolter, "Reflections on the Moral Status of the Pre-embryo," *Theological Studies* 51 (December 1990): 603-26.

[11]This is a group of fluid-filled sacs that develop after the abnormal fusion of egg and sperm when the membrane which surrounds the embryo degenerates early in pregnancy.

[12]Shannon and Wolter, "Reflections," p. 608.

and by itself, which is traditionally assumed to exist in an individual human being.[13]

Zygotic Dependence on Maternal Genetic Material

It is an undisputed fact of biology that up to the second or third cellular divisions of the zygote, the fertilized mammalian ovum is largely dependent on the messenger ribonucleic acid (mRNA) found originally in the mother's ovum for its vital activity. This means that in most animals, including human beings, the earliest stages of embryonic development are regulated by maternally inherited information.[14] These maternal mRNAs support all or most of the biosynthetic activities carried out in the early embryo,[15] persisting until they are replaced by zygotic transcripts emanating from the blastomeres of the early embryo.[16] For the human, it has been shown that it is only at the four- to eight-cell stage of embryonic development that the embryonic genes begin to be expressed.[17] This four- to eight-cell stage of embryonic development is achieved around seventy-two hours after fertilization (i.e., on the third day of life). It is only at this stage of the "switching on" of the embryonic genes that the embryo begins to assume genetic control and, in one sense, begins to function autonomously as a genetically distinct individual. Prior to this switching on of the embryonic genome, the embryo expresses a set of genetic sequences that are largely the same as that of the mother.

André Hellegers even suggests that not until after the appearance of the primitive streak (end of the second week) or even the completion of gastrulation (end of the third week) can all the internal activities of the conceptus be specifically and completely attributed to the fetal messenger RNA, because only then will the genetic apparatus in the embryo become crucially acti-

---

[13]The notion of autonomy of being as a characteristic of personhood is traditionally developed in Thomas Aquinas's theology. See, e.g., Gabriel Pastrana, "Personhood and the Beginning of Human Life," *The Thomist* 41, no. 1 (1977): 286-90.

[14]Mark B. Devorkin and Eva Devorkin-Rastl, "Functions of Maternal mRNA in Early Development," *Molecular Reproduction and Development* 26 (July 1990). 261-97.

[15]Eric H. Davidson, *Gene Activity in Early Development* (London: Harcourt Brace Jovanovich, 1986), pp. 4-7.

[16]The period of total embryonic dependence on the maternal mRNAs varies from species to species. In the mouse, the new embryonic genes take over at the two-cell stage (see V. N. Bolton, P. J. Oades and M. H. Johnson, "The Relationship Between Cleavage, DNA Replication and Gene Expression in the Mouse 2-Cell Embryo," *Embryology and Experimental Morphology* 79 [1984]: 139-63), whereas this does not occur until the four-cell stage in the pig and the eight-cell stage in sheep (see I. M. Crosby, F. Gandolfi and R. M. Moor, "Control of Protein Synthesis During Early Cleavage of Sheep Embryos," *Journal of Reproduction and Fertility* 82, no. 2 [1988]: 769-75).

[17]Peter Braude, V. Bolton and S. Moore, "Human Gene Expression First Occurs Between the Four- and Eight-Cell Stages of Preimplantation Development," *Nature* 332 (March 1988): 459-61.

vated.[18] Based on similar observations, C. A. Bedate and R. C. Cefalo argue that it is wrong to say that the zygote possesses all the informing molecules for embryo development; rather, the zygote has the potential to acquire informing capacity through some necessary interactions between "molecules of the zygote and extra-zygote molecules." At that point the zygote forms certain new molecules with a particular informing capacity that is not originally coded in the genome of the zygote. Hence, they conclude that the zygote only makes possible the existence of a human embryo but that it does not in and of itself possess enough information to form an embryo. The formation of the embryo depends on certain ontogenetic events that are outside the control of the zygote's genetic program.[19] Shannon and Wolter conclude that

> the development of the zygote depends at each moment on several factors: the progressive actualization of its own genetically coded information, the actualiza- tion of pieces of information that originate de novo during the embryonic process, and exogenous information independent of the control of the zygote.[20]

However, Antoine Suarez disagrees with Bedate's and Cefalo's conclusion that the early embryo is physiologically dependent on the mother. Based on studies of abnormal embryos, such as hydatidiform moles (which are the result of certain abnormal fusions of eggs and sperm) and teratomas (which arise from the abnormal parthenogenic division of germ cells), Suarez argues that since these abnormal embryonic developments can be shown to have devel- oped independently of any maternal information, they provide strong indirect evidence that maternal molecules do not have any informational influence on the embryo, which is itself the sole source of all the organizing information, including abnormal ones.[21] Furthermore, even if during the course of normal embryogenesis certain maternal RNA molecules are found to contain organiz- ing information, it does not automatically follow that the zygote or early embryo is thus "genetically silent" and passively controlled by maternal infor- mational molecules. In this regard Shannon and Wolter concede that develop- mental information of the human embryo probably originates from three sources—the zygote, the mother and the "embryonic process" itself—with highly complex interactions among these various sources of genetic informa- tion.[22] These maternal-fetal interactions, which begin on the first day of the

---

[18]André E. Hellegers, "Fetal Development," *Theological Studies* 31 (March 1970): 3-5.
[19]C. A. Bedate and R. C. Cefalo, "The Zygote: To Be or Not to Be a Person," *Journal of Medi- cine and Philosophy* 14, no. 6 (1989): 642-44.
[20]Shannon and Wolter, "Reflections," p. 608.
[21]Antoine Suarez, "Hydatidiform Moles and Teratomas Confirm the Human Identity of the Pre- implantation Embryo," *Journal of Medicine and Philosophy* 15, no. 6 (1990): 627-35.
[22]Shannon and Wolter, "Reflections," p. 608.

embryo's existence, are to continue throughout the entire gestational period.

I believe that embryogenesis and fetal development are better seen as the result of an interplay between the new human life and its environment. Environmental conditions, including maternal molecules, can influence the formation of many characteristics of the developing organism, but that does not mean that the maternal influences are to be taken as determinative and decisive. Instead, they are reminders that maternal-fetal relationships are established at the very early stage of the formation of the new life. There is no question that maternal sources of information are made available to and are used by the zygote/embryo, but the role and integration of this information into the organism's development are determined by the organism itself. In short, even if maternal molecules are being used, the zygote/embryo controls this use. The zygote/embryo remains the primary organizer of its own growth process, and so the observation that the embryo is partially dependent on exogenous genetic information does not compromise its integrity as a complete, autonomous human individual.[23]

Totipotentiality of Early Embryonic Cells

A second objection to the claim that the zygote or the early embryo has attained ontological individuality is based on the fact that prior to the blastocyst stage (four to six days after fertilization), the embryonic cells are still so undifferentiated that they remain totipotential: that is, each of the cells is still able to develop into a whole, mature organism when isolated from other cells. On this basis, some consider that the cellular divisions of the zygote and the early embryo merely produce a collection of cells and that each one of these cells has the potential equivalent to a zygote to become all or part of an embryo and its extra-embryonic structure.[24] As development progresses, the cells become increasingly "committed" or "restricted" in their potency, and the process of restriction is completed about three weeks into embryonic development, when all the cells are finally committed to their respective "developmental fate." On the basis of this observation, Shannon and Wolter argue that the loss of totipotency of the cells is reliable proof of human singleness and individuality; hence not until all the cells have lost their totipotency, about three weeks after fertilization, would the embryo be granted the status of a single individual organism.[25]

Ford also argues that not only is the loss of totipotency significant for deter-

---

[23]See also Patrick Lee, *Abortion and Unborn Human Life* (Washington, D.C.: Catholic University of America Press, 1996), p. 101.

[24]Clifford Grobstein, *Science and the Unborn: Choosing Human Futures* (New York: Basic, 1988), p. 235, cited in Shannon and Wolter, "Reflections," p. 612.

[25]Shannon and Wolter, "Reflections," p. 613.

mining the time when an actual individual human being has been formed, it is also an indication that species-specific individuation had taken place, with the formation of a distinct multicellular individual endowed with differentiated parts for structures, organs and tissues.[26] Ford argues that if the embryo with its cluster of totipotential cells were an actual person, then one would have to admit that the embryo was both one person and more than one person. Since he finds this unacceptable, he believes that "it would be reasonable to deny that the zygote and cluster of cells are persons."[27] On a similar basis, Shannon and Wolter conclude that

> given the biological evidence, there is no reasonable way in which the fertilized egg can be considered a physical individual minimally until after implantation. Maximally, one could argue that full individuality is not achieved until the restriction process is completed and cells have lost their totipotency.[28]

Others reject the philosophical interpretations of the totipotentiality of blastomeres provided by Ford, Shannon and Wolter. For example, Teresa Iglesias argues that despite the presence of totipotential cells, other molecular, cellular and morphological evidences do not support the view that the early embryo is an undifferentiated being; rather, both intracellular and intercellular differentiating activities are present from the beginning, leading to the embryo's full differentiation and formation. For example, at the eight-cell stage on the third day after fertilization, the differences in position between the cells are readily observable, suggesting different cellular functions within the early embryo.[29] Later in the eight-cell stage the cells of the early embryo are seen to develop differential adhesion and inside-outside polarity to maximize cellular contact.[30] This internal differentiation and organization of cellular activities takes place much earlier than the formation of the primitive streak and is determined from within the zygote, and hence it justifies the conclusion that the early embryo exhibits all the unity of an individual organism with an intrinsic goal-directness.[31]

Diane Nutwell-Irving also contends that it is wrong to view the early embryonic cells as undifferentiated because the original single-cell human zygote is simply the *most determined* and specialized cell in the entire pro-

---

[26]Ford, *When Did I Begin?* p. 163.

[27]Ibid., pp. 135-36.

[28]Shannon and Wolter, "Reflections," pp. 619-20.

[29]C. R. Austin, *Human Embryos: The Debate on Assisted Reproduction* (Oxford: Oxford University Press, 1989), pp. 10-11.

[30]William J. Larsen, *Human Embryology* (New York: Churchill Livingstone, 1993), p. 19.

[31]Teresa Iglesias, "What Kind of Being Is the Human Embryo?" in *Embryos and Ethics: The Warnock Report in Debate,* ed. Nigel M. de S. Cameron (Edinburgh: Rutherford House, 1987), p. 70.

cess of human development.[32] She points out that the differentiated cells which develop later on in fact continue to possess *all* of the information that was in the original zygote. Cellular differentiation is merely the "loss of ability" to *use* all the information available due to methylation and other chemical processes that activate or deactivate genes to aid in the specialization of certain cells. She concludes:

> There is nothing vague, undirected or undecided about [the zygote]. It is the *human zygote* which represents the greatest fullness of human content and useable information, of directedness and decisive action—more than that found in any of the later cells.[33]

Patrick Lee responds to the totipotentiality argument by citing the case of a dividing flatworm. He argues that if we cut a flatworm into two and the two halves each become flatworms, we do not conclude that the original flatworm was not a single organism prior to the division. The totipotency of a part does not entail that prior to the division of the whole (early embryo), the parts (the cells of the early embryo) are not functioning as specialized parts within an integrated ontological whole.[34] Cellular totipotency and differentiation are thus not necessarily incompatible and to deny the zygote/early embryo the individuality it possesses on this ground is therefore faulty. I believe this and other similar conclusions can be further supported by recent success in animal cloning using the nucleus of the fully differentiated cell from an adult animal (somatic cell nuclear transfer, or SCNT), which illustrates that the process of differentiation is reversible under certain circumstances.[35] It will be difficult to accept an argument that claims the somatic cell nucleus animal donor is originally not an individual animal.

Disunity of Early Embryonic Cells

Another reason for denying the early embryo the status of an individual organism is the contention that it only exists as a cluster of cells with very little evidence of the intrinsic unity required of a single individual organism. Ford claims that up to the eight-cell stage, there are no "tight junctions" holding cells together, as are characteristically found later at the thirty-two-cell morula stage. He also notes that prior to implantation, each of the eight cells takes in its own nutrients, thereby demonstrating its own autonomy.[36] On the basis of these

---

[32]Diane Nutwell-Irving, "Scientific and Philosophical Expertise: An Evaluation of the Arguments on Personhood," *Linacre Quarterly* 60 (February 1993): 18-46.

[33]Ibid., p. 28.

[34]Lee, *Abortion,* pp. 94-95.

[35]Ian Wilmut et al., "Viable Offspring Derived from Fetal and Adult Mammalian Cells," *Nature* 385 (February 27, 1997): 810-13.

[36]Ford, *When Did I Begin?* p. 137.

observations, Ford determines that

> the early human embryo is really a cluster of distinct individual cells, each one of
> which is a centrally organized living individual or ontological entity in simple con-
> tact with the others enclosed in the protective zona pellucida. It would be difficult
> to justify attributing the natural unity proper to a single ontological individual to
> the cluster of cells as a whole.[37]

But this is a peculiar way to understand the function of the zona; for most embryologists, the most important sign that the developing embryo is deter-mined to exist as a single organism of unity and organization is the very fact that prior to implantation, the early embryonic cells are contained within the zona pellucida.

Anthony Fisher also disagrees with Ford's claim that the cells of an early embryo are merely touching and are loosely held together by the zona pellucida, on the basis of high-resolution photographic images that show the cells pressing against each other and restricting each other's shape and position. Furthermore, the fact that embryonic tissues such as the zona and placenta originate from the embryo rather than from maternal tissue is evidence that the embryo is capable of goal-oriented activities to preserve its own integrity and survival as an individual organism.[38] This intrinsic embryonic goal-directedness is also evidenced by the genetic restriction and cellular differentiation of the early embryonic cells alluded to earlier. There is no evidence that this process is initiated or imposed by mater-nal influences. Rather, biological evidence indicates that the time when restriction and differentiation begin is determined by a precise intrinsic "clock mechanism" within the developing embryo, providing strong support that the zygote/embryo is a substantial unity with an intrinsic goal-directedness that ensures and maintains its growth as a whole individual organism.[39] This is in sharp contrast to Ford's vision that early embryonic divisions give rise to a small army of distinct individu-als which are somehow subsequently grouped together to form the true human individual. If Ford's view of the early embryo is right, then all the totipotent cells should become individual organisms. The fact that they do not—unless they are artificially separated—suggests that within the zona pellucida some interaction is taking place that prevents them from developing into whole organisms individu-ally and that directs them collectively to continue as parts of the zygotic whole.[40]

---

[37]Ibid., p. 139.

[38]Anthony Fisher, " 'When Did I Begin?' Revisited," *Linacre Quarterly* 58 (August 1991): 60.

[39]Anne McLaren, "The Embryo," cited in Lee, *Abortion,* p. 86.

[40]Benedict Ashley and Albert Moraczewski, "Is the Biological Subject of Human Rights Present from Conception?" in *The Fetal Tissue Issue: Medical and Ethical Aspects,* ed. Peter Cataldo and Albert Moraczewski (Braintree, Mass.: Pope John Center, 1994), p. 49, cited in Lee, *Abortion,* p. 98.

The Possibility of Twinning

One of the strongest arguments used by Ford, Shannon and Wolter to deny individuality to the zygote/early embryo is the possibility of twinning (up to but not beyond gastrulation) and, in rare situations, the recombining (untwinning) of two early embryos to form one living embryo. On this basis, it is contended that before the development of the primitive streak, around the fourteenth day after fertilization when twinning can still occur, "the philosophical definition of individual . . . as 'undivided in itself' *(indivisium in se)* is not yet realized, at least not as strictly as the individuality of the human person demands."[41] On the same basis, Shannon and Wolter reject the unicellular zygote as the beginning of a specific, genetically unique individual human being, contending that "while the zygote is the beginning of genetically distinct life, it is neither an ontological individual nor necessarily the immediate precursor of one."[42] For Ford, the possibility of twinning is also the main reason for denying ontological individuality and identity to the early embryo. He invites us to suppose that a certain cluster of cells really is a multicellular individual embryo—a person, say, "Susan." When twinning occurs, Susan, as one whole living individual, would asexually give origin to her identical twin sister. Ford asks, Of the two sisters, who is the original Susan? He goes on to answer the question by suggesting that Susan would actually cease to exist when she "splits" and gives "birth" to her offspring, Margaret and Sally. In Ford's view, if we grant the early embryo the status of an ontological individual, its ontological individuality will be lost in the process of twinning: "There could not be the same human individual present before and after the twinning process, notwithstanding the continuing genetic identity present in each twin."[43] But Ford apparently realizes the difficulty of his thesis that a human individual simply ceases to exist in the twinning process, and so he decides that it would be more plausible to argue that an ontological human individual had not yet begun to exist. In other words, if an entity is capable of being divided into two or more entities, then that "divisible" entity cannot be an individual entity prior to division.

Several comments need to be made regarding the twinning argument. For one thing, Ford apparently assumes that the potentiality for twinning is always present in the normal conditions of embryogenesis, under which an embryo matures into one adult person. But in reality, monozygotic twinning is essentially rare, occurring in only three or four out of a thousand births. Scientists

---

[41]Pete Schoonenberg, *God's World in the Making,* quoted in Joseph Donceel, "Immediate Animation and Delayed Hominization," *Theological Studies* 31, no. 1 (1970): 98-99.

[42]Shannon and Wolter, "Reflections," p. 612.

[43]Ford, *When Did I Begin?* p. 136.

are still uncertain as to why it actually takes place. However, we do know that some unknown agents seem to be needed to break down the intercellular bonds that normally hold the cells of the embryo together as an individual organism. There are some indications that twins are genetically determined and hence the two beings that emerge as twins are in actuality two from conception, although in a "latent" form.[44] Furthermore, as a rare event, monozygotic twinning can take place after the fourteen-day period and the formation of the primitive streak, at which point even Ford does not deny the embryo ontological individuality.

It would seem that these scientific observations do not support Ford's claim. Further, the analogy of the divisible tapeworm can again be used to refute his thesis. The subsequent emergence of two tapeworms in no way compromises the initial organism's integrity as an individual before it is cut into half. Ford acknowledges the available evidence for a genetic cause for twinning, but he essentially disregards it as unimportant. Ford also acknowledges the possibility of twinning after the formation of the primitive streak, but he dismisses it as an exception that does not affect his position, giving the impression that he is somewhat arbitrary about what he chooses to accept as being important. Nonetheless, his main problem remains in his faulty assumption that all embryos possess the ability to actively twin.

As for the concern with embryonic recombination, Grisez has pointed out that zygotes/embryos do not have the active tendency to fuse and form a chimera any more than they have the active tendency to split and form twins. Rather, at most the facts may indicate that for unknown reasons early embryos may passively divide and become twins or combine and become chimeras.[45] It is important to distinguish what an embryo can do actively from what can passively happen to it. Iglesias has also pointed out that the recombination of embryos to form a single chimera has been seen only in laboratory conditions. This fact suggests that early embryos possess a certain regulatory capacity and ability to repair themselves in the event that a substantial part of the organism has been removed or damaged. In other words, the possibility to form chimeras under laboratory conditions probably suggests that the powers of "grafting," "transplant," "healing," "regeneration" and so on are present in the early embryos[46] but never naturally mobilized to form chimeras. Hence, I concur with the conclusion that most babies develop with their accessory tissues from a single zygote, as an individual organism, despite the possibility of twinning or chimerization.[47]

---

[44]Iglesias, "What Kind of Being," p. 69.

[45]Grisez, *Abortion,* p. 38.

[46]Iglesias, "What Kind of Being," p. 70.

[47]Grisez, *Abortion,* p. 37.

The Non-identity of Genetic and Psychological Continuity Argument

The argument that the genetic and psychological individual is discontinuous or non-identical claims support from two views: the dualistic view and the no-subject view.

The dualistic view. In Michael Tooley's definition of the human person,[48] the physical aspect of the organism is specifically excluded from consideration. The first reason he provides for maintaining that the embryo/fetus/infant[49] cannot be considered a person and thus lacks a right to life is its lack of capacity for self-consciousness or other mental states. This is an important argument but one that even he himself cannot consistently hold. His second reason, which he considers to be more decisive, is the lack of identity between the fetus and any later subject of consciousness.[50] Comparing a temporarily comatose individual to a fetus, he argues that the former remains a person because the subject of the consciousness of the comatose patient is the same subject if she survives the coma and recovers, and such an identity of subjects of consciousness is established mainly by psychological connections such as memory. But according to Tooley the same cannot be said about the fetus, since memory links between a fetus and the subsequent adult have not been demonstrated to exist. Hence, Tooley maintains that one cannot claim the fetus and adult are one and the same subject of consciousness and, on this basis, the personhood of the fetus cannot be established; to destroy a fetus cannot be considered a frustration of the desires of the adult whom it would have otherwise become. What Tooley has done is to claim that only psychological continuity—not genetic/physical continuity—should be given ontological significance, and in so doing he has dissociated the subject of the physical organism (of the fetus) from the subject of consciousness of this same entity. In other words, Tooley holds a dualistic view whereby the physical organism (of the fetus) may exist without the subject of consciousness existing at the same time; they are two different things distinct from each other, and the existence of one does not necessarily entail the existence of the other.

But such a dualism contradicts the ordinary human experience that as subjects of experience, our sense/experience is dependent on our bodies. In a sense, it is the body that sees, touches and so on, although these sensations are dependent on a conscious subject for their comprehension (i.e., organizing these sensual stimulations so that they can be understood as meaningful).

---

[48]Tooley's position will be discussed in more detail in the section on abortion below.

[49]From this point on in the present discussion on Tooley, I will use the term *fetus* in a metanymic sense to include embryo/fetus/infant. However, after my critique of Tooley, I will no longer use this shorthand.

[50]Michael Tooley, *Abortion and Infanticide* (New York: Oxford University Press, 1983), pp. 118-21.

Since my sensations and consciousness together constitute my subjectivity and enable me to be an "I" as a subject of experience, my body as a necessary component and condition of subjectivity must also be considered as subject.[51] Once we accept the body as subject, either we accept it as the same subject as the "I" that I am conscious of, or we hold that there are two subjects involved. This is in fact Tooley's dualistic claim: the person as a subject of consciousness is somehow associated with the human organism but at the same time is or can be other than it. Clearly such an essentially Cartesian position is untenable since it entails an "unreal situation of having one subject (the conscious disembodied self), with no means of experience, and the other subject (the body), with all the experience but no consciousness."[52] I am obliged to conclude that my body, which is a necessary condition of my subjectivity, is an indispensable part of the person "I." This means that the human body is part of the human person. And if the human person essentially includes the physical organism, one would be obliged to agree that "one cannot hold that the human organism comes to be at one time while the person comes to be at a later time."[53] Therefore, the human person is identical with the human physical organism, which begins with the zygote.

The no-subject view. A second approach used to argue against the zygote's ontological identity is to see the person as a continuity of experiences. There is a strong tradition in modern Western philosophy—articulated first by David Hume and maintained by William James to Bertrand Russell—which holds that the person is a series of experiences, or "a train of consciousness," that has certain psychological relations or continuities within it rather than a subject or substance underlying experiences or consciousness.[54] Such a series of experiences may be linked together by memory to constitute a human person, and since these psychological relations cannot be shown to occur in embryonic or early fetal life or even in the early infant, these latter human entities cannot be said to be persons.

Such an approach, which bases personal identity on psychological continuity, in effect denies that a human person is a physical organism, or a physical subject or a subject at all (hence it is called the "no-subject view").[55] It overlooks the fact that actual experiences involve actions and that actions involve agents. For example, the "I" that desires, decides, understands and writes this

---

[51]Kevin Doran and Patrick Lee both hold a similar view; for their respective arguments see Doran, *What Is a Person: The Concept and the Implications for Ethics* (Lewiston, N.Y.: Edwin Mellen Press, 1989), pp. 64-66; and Lee, *Abortion,* pp. 34-43.

[52]Doran, *What Is a Person,* p. 65.

[53]Lee, *Abortion,* p. 37.

[54]See also chapter three, "The Psychological Dimension of Human Personhood," below.

[55]Lee, *Abortion,* p. 37.

essay is the same "I" that persists throughout the afternoon (time) in front of the desk (place). In other words, the direct awareness of the experiences of desiring, deciding and writing requires the entity "I" to persist through time and space as an agent, and not as an inert "container" of the series of experiences or events. Human persons both are physical organisms as well as *persisting* substances as *agents* performing actions in time and space that result in experiences, and to abstract experience from an underlying substance ignores the role of the agent in human actions and experiences.[56] One is most conscious of "the unity of oneself when one is conscious of oneself as an agent."[57] This means that a human person is a persistent substance/subject of various actions and events; and if a person is a substance/subject that persists through time and space, then a human person is essentially a human physical organism. The person comes to be when the human physical organism comes to be.

I conclude that both the genetic-ontological discontinuity argument and the physical-psychological discontinuity argument fail to refute the genetic/physical basis of human personhood. I think that the notion of continuum in a developing human being is not only philosophically more sustainable but also more consistent with ordinary experience. Most people recognize that newborn babies are human persons, even though the babies have not yet acquired cognition or other mental states. The basis for recognizing the personal status of the infant is found not in the fact that it will someday grow and develop into a human individual, but in the fact that now it *is* the same individual being that gradually grows and develops into the adult human individual. Most of us do not doubt that we are the same person today that was born many years ago, and no philosophical definition of a person can discount this fact of experience. The growth and development of a zygote, a fetus or an infant are the growth and development of a human being/person to maturity, not merely the growth and development of "something" into a human being. The developing zygote, fetus or infant gradually realizes its natural potential to express more fully what it already is. It does not develop and mature into something else. The same ontological individual reality, the same identical being, continues in existence through the various stages of growth and development. The zygote,

---

[56]Ibid., pp. 41-42. Applying such an "agential" approach to action/experience, Lee shows that an action and its structure are often explained only by the kind of agent that produces it and sustains it. For example, a dog will chase a rabbit whereas a horse will not. The no-subject view, which supposes that there are only experiences strung together in various ways, somehow loses sight of the simple fact that the dog is a certain particular type of agent (i.e., "a persistent source of predictable actions and reactions: [and] given certain circumstances, this type of agent will act or react in certain ways," pp. 41-42) and that a human being is a certain type of agent: given certain circumstances, it will act or react in certain ways.

[57]Ibid.

fetus and infant are the same one person, genetically and ontologically.[58] Based on the human zygote's genetic uniqueness, its ontological identity and continuity and its innate capacity for self-development, I see not a *potential* human person but a human person with a potential to develop. Life, including biological life, is a dynamic rather than static reality. It goes on to develop, change and grow certainly for a long time after an infant is born.

The Meaning of Human Embodiment

Both the dualistic and the no-subject views express the tendency in the West to reject the biological dimension of the human being as offering a serious indicator of personhood; this Western anthropology, which has been found from antiquity to modern times, has consistently treated the body as something from which the person should be freed or, failing that, upon which disciplines should be imposed.[59] At the beginning of the Christian era, the West was pervaded by Plato's preoccupation with liberating the soul from the "tomb" of the body; in medieval Europe the body was subjected to the regulation and determination of the Aristotelian soul; and in modern times, the body, the Cartesian *res extensa*, continues to be dominated by its more superior *res cogitan*. In this long tradition, the more the person can detach himself from the body, the more the person is said to be free. As German theologian Jürgen Moltmann observes, this has apparently been "an essential element in the history of freedom in the Western world."[60]

In modern times, the human body has been further devalued by so-called empiricist materialism, advanced by a group of Enlightenment philosophers including Francis Bacon, John Locke, René Descartes and others. Bacon is chiefly responsible for "demythologizing" nature, stripping away its veil of mystery and leaving it naked for the human mind to investigate, understand, master and manipulate. Since the human body behaves as a part of nature in following natural laws, it belongs to the realm of nature and hence is amenable to being treated in the same manner. This empirical conceptualization of the body as raw matter is further advanced by Descartes's interpretation of the body as a machine, which can be understood mechanically and controlled by the human soul. If the human body is basically the raw material of nature, it is conveniently treated under the paradigm of property rights, which Locke develops primarily for other inanimate objects and which is applied by modern day pro-abortionists to fetuses (see below). All these contribute toward a view

---

[58]See also Ford, *When Did I Begin?* pp. 75-79, but note that Ford believes the notion of "continuum" only applies after the appearance of the "primitive streak."

[59]John Y. Fenton, ed., *Theology and Body* (Philadelphia: Westminster Press, 1974).

[60]Jürgen Moltmann, *God in Creation* (San Francisco: HarperSanFrancisco, 1991), p. 244.

of the body as morally neutral, thus rendering any further ethical reflection unnecessary and superfluous.

However, alternative approaches to the body have been advanced by phenomenologists and feminist thinkers, particularly in the twentieth century. The phenomenological approach notes that the human body always exists in a unique relationship with the self. Far from experiencing the body as inert material, the self experiences the body both as familiar and strange, mine and other, intimate yet alien—a dialectical phenomenon that Richard Zaner considers as "the core of human body-as-experienced."[61] As ambiguous as our experience of embodiment may be, phenomenologists argue that it provides the fundamental sense of being human. The body declares the presence of the human being and expresses different and even conflicting feelings, desires, intentions and actions in the ongoing life of the person. Hence, morally the body is far from being neutral.

This emphasis on the moral worth of the body has been further endorsed and enthusiastically articulated by feminist writers since the 1980s. Writing primarily in the context of protest against gender discrimination, they specifically reject both the sexual dualism that views man as superior to woman and the correlative spiritual dualism that sees the mind as man's strength controlling the woman's body. Feminists regard Cartesian and other such dualisms of modern culture as anomalies in Western thought that overlook the importance of embodiment and undervalue the many bodily functions traditionally associated with women (including bearing, rearing and nurturing children) in favor of the mind and cognitive functions traditionally considered more as men's domain.[62] Instead, feminists argue that the human person and human body are essentially coextensive and coterminous and that embodiment is sine qua non for any definition of personhood. This means respect for a person entails respect for the embodied person, a perspective that necessitates a reevaluation of many feminine roles, such as caring and nurturing, and calls for a revision of traditional moral theories that assign superior status to timeless, universal truths of reason at the expense of the contextual and contingent factors of bodily experience.[63]

---

[61]Richard Zaner, "Body—I. Embodiment: The Phenomenological Tradition," in *Encyclopedia of Bioethics,* ed. Warren T. Reich (New York: Macmillan, 1995), 1:292. For detail see Richard Zaner, *The Context of Self: A Phenomenological Inquiry Using Medicine as a Clue* (Athens: Ohio University Press, 1980).

[62]See, e.g., Carol Gilligan, *In a Different Voice* (Cambridge, Mass.: Harvard University Press, 1982).

[63]A feminist perspective of the body also renders some medical procedures morally problematic, especially certain cosmetic surgical procedures that alter the appearance of the female body to narrowly set social stereotypes of beauty. Even in the more legitimate areas of women's health care (such as childbirth, infertility and assisted reproductive technologies),

This feminist viewpoint confirms our common sense that one's body serves as more than an instrumental function in one's life as a person, and it may be credited for having forcefully confronted our society with the importance of embodiment. One hardly feels that one is a full person if part of one's body is in anyway compromised, violated or injured; and with the rapid advance in our knowledge of the human body, especially in the field of human genetics, it is "more obvious than ever that there is no human self that stands outside the processes of biology, unaffected by them."[64] Furthermore, across different cultures since time immemorial, people have treated dead human bodies with an inexplicable reverence. This suggests that people perceive a special meaning in the human body, even when the person is deceased. If a dead body deserves that much respect, how much more seriously must the living body be viewed not just as an object, but as part of our life insofar as that life is organized by the body. Arthur Vogel reminds us that the body organizes our time in deciding when we do something with our self; the body also organizes our space in determining where its activities are to take place. By organizing our time and space, the body becomes the center of our actions and experiences. In what is to follow I will briefly review the various "personal" meanings of the body as that by means of which the person is worlded.[65]

The body as the basis of one's presence and action. Human beings exist in space through their bodies. To the extent that we are placed in the world through our bodies, we are spatial beings, and our bodily location is always made in reference to other objects. The use of prepositions illustrates the fact that our bodies are the center around which the field of physical objects external to us is spatially organized. This means that our body is the primary location of our presence by which we are located in, presented to and rendered as part of the world. Furthermore, we are present in the world as a personal agent so that fundamentally the body is an actional center from which one's

---

feminists are sensitive to the fact that the male-dominated medical world will ensure the good of women is still largely determined by men. This situation, which may be argued to be only partially true, prompts feminists to maintain that as an embodied self, the person should assume responsibility for her own body. The physician's role, regardless of whether the medical profession is in fact dominated by men, is to provide advice and support for the "diseased" person and to restore and maintain her body. The physician's complete control over a patient's body is thus ethically suspicious. See, e.g., Christine E. Gudorf, "A Feminist Critique of Biomedical Principlism" in *A Matter of Principles? Ferment in U. S. Bioethics,* ed. Edwin R. DuBose, Ron Hamel and Laurence J. O'Connell (Valley Forge, Penn.: Trinity Press International, 1994), pp. 164-81.

[64]Roger Lincoln Shinn, *The New Genetics: Challenges for Science, Faith and Politics* (London: Moyer Bell, 1996), p. 51.

[65]Arthur A. Vogel, *God's Presence in Man's World* (London: Geoffrey Chapman, 1973), p. 88. I am indebted to Vogel's insights, presented in this thoughtful book, for much of the discussion in the balance of this chapter.

action is originated and around which all external physical objects are spatially organized. Earlier, I used this important fact to refute the no-subject view, which sees the person as a mere collection of experiences. This personal presence as an agent means that our body has an intrinsic meaning of its own: it is human presence and action located. Hence, the body contributes significantly to the in-itself aspect of the human substance and provides the basis for the self-presence of the human being and person. Of course, personal presence, especially for humans, also includes a nonmaterial transcendent aspect and so is not identical to embodiment; but without the body, the transcendent property of one's personal presence will not be easily known or appreciated. Even God's presence in the world is mediated through a human body in the incarnation of his Son. As Vogel puts it, "Human presence needs the body in order to be itself, for body meaning anchors us in the world."[66]

The body as the basis of one's identity, particularity and self-consciousness. As the person's experiential center, the body is the means by which other objects of the world are known; it is also differentiated from other objects by being experienced as "mine." In other words, there are certain experiences that we are able to have only in relation to our own body (e.g., hunger or pain) because they can only be mediated by our own particular body. The body and its organs are experienced through their needs and powers, and the person is one with herself only when these needs are satisfied and the powers harmonized. In this bodily unity and harmony, the person then forms an identity with herself and finds herself dependable. This means a person relates first and foremost to her own body. It is true that in some chronically disabled states, bodily functions are so compromised that the person loses identity with her own body and thus with herself. Also in the conditions collectively labeled as gender dysphoria (the most extreme form being transsexualism), the person in fact feels alienated from her own body, regarding it as untrustworthy or even as an enemy.[67] But in general, regardless of its condition, a person's body is experienced as particularly "mine." When someone hits me in my face, I don't respond by saying, "Why did you hit my body?" Instead, I say, "Why did you hit me?" The body has the ability to impart such uniqueness to the person because it is solely through that particular body that everything else is experienced by the person. While we may share common ideas, thoughts, beliefs and values, we do not and cannot share our bodies. Although the process whereby we become conscious of ourselves as independent and self-determining is largely a function of the soul, it is necessarily mediated through the body

---

[66]Ibid.

[67]Eric J. Casell, *The Nature of Suffering and the Goals of Medicine* (Oxford: Oxford University Press, 1991), chaps. 3 and 4.

so that any act we perform includes our material bodies and immaterial souls. Without the material body, we cannot be aware of objects different from ourselves; neither can we distinguish ourselves from others as the object or therefore recognize ourselves as the subject.[68] This understanding of self-consciousness and particularity highlights the importance of physical embodiment as the source of one's personal identity. The physical body, despite developmental or degenerative changes, remains the strongest mark of personal identity.

The body as the basis of relations. The body not only locates us in the time/space world, but also allows us to relate to others and express ourselves to them. In other words, as spatial and temporal beings mediated through our bodies, we constantly seek to organize a self-presence that extends and relates to other people and objects. As we have seen, all beings possess a "toward-other" aspect (an openness to other beings and objects), and this openness makes us live through our bodies as personal projects: a projection of embodied self in relating to other people and other things. Our openness to extending ourselves as personal projects is because as bodies we are also beings of need; the body is not able to be itself by itself, and it needs to always refer beyond itself.

A significant part of our personal project also involves activities that reflect the feelings of our bodies, and they in turn affect how we respond to the world external to us. For example, to hate or love one's body may be translated as a hatred or love of the world respectively. In a way, the external world is an extension of the desires, needs and feelings of one's body. These bodily elements significantly contribute to the communal/relational aspect of our being, and hence any kind of personal relation in this world cannot be actualized without some bodily dimension. As Alistair McFadyen points out, "The possibilities of community and of communication are rooted first in the physical organization of the human organism,"[69] although the human person is not thereby reducible to a physical object. Just as the physical and psychological are distinct but inseparable components of the human life (as I will discuss in more detail later), so too the physical and social are distinct but interdependent dimensions of human personhood. The body is the indispensable substantial pole of the dyadic structure of the human being; it is the base-line "substance" through which one's individual existence and personal relationships are mediated.

---

[68]For an interesting discussion of the roles of the body and soul in one's subjectivity, see Karl Barth, *Church Dogmatics* 3/2, ed. G. W. Bromiley and T. F. Torrance (Edinburgh: T & T Clark, 1960), §46.3.

[69]Alistair I. McFadyen, *The Call to Personhood: A Christian Theory of the Individual in Social Relationships* (Cambridge: Cambridge University Press, 1990), p. 77.

The body as the basis of sexuality. Human beings are fundamentally relational also because we are sexual beings, and we are sexual because we are embodied—a glorious truth which is expressed in our being either female or male. As a distinctive human capacity, and in contrast to the mere sexual drive in other subhuman species, human sexuality enables us to engage in love-giving and life-giving activities mediated in and through the human body. Christian doctrine refers to these as the unitive and procreative meanings of human sexuality. Human sexuality profoundly actualizes the relationality pole of the human person; it is "the personal power to *share* (physically, psychically, and spiritually) *the gift of self* with self and with others."[70] This mode of sharing, giving and receiving of the self is supremely mediated through our sexuality, made possible by the human body.

Although sexuality permeates all human relationship, it is uniquely expressed in the procreation of offspring, which enables two human beings to join in an equal share of partnership toward the "begetting" of a new human being. It allows the expression of two persons' capacity "to be forever-gift—the genesis of every individual child meant to be a creative 'third,' the expression of selves offered totally, and received unreservedly."[71] This procreative expression of human sexuality enables each one of us to have the privilege of living bodily within another human being, to share flesh and blood with the uttermost degree of intimacy and immediacy. In addition, it confers the gestating woman with the unique experience of providing abode to the developing human person. It is this human sexuality, mediated through the human body, that allows us to be in touch with "those incommunicable depths where each person is called into union with God as well as with other human persons."[72]

The body as the basis of communication. As relational beings, we communicate through language, but the body itself is a form of language. To the extent that every *body* is situated in the world and shares a common orientation to life, our bodies speak a universal language (e.g., a smile or grimace). It is our nature to be body-meaning. Our lived-bodies are words through which we communicate even before we acquire verbal skills. Infants communicate their needs for security through "body words," and mothers communicate their trustworthy provision through the same; adults may communicate equally effectively through body or language. Vogel suggests that "man is able to use words only because his being has the nature of a word."[73] Hence, a human person does not just use words; he or she *is* a word. We can "be" our words

---

[70]Mary Timothy Prokes, F.S.E., *Toward a Theology of the Body* (Grand Rapids, Mich.: Eerdmans, 1996), p. 95.
[71]Ibid., p. 97.
[72]Ibid., p. 98.
[73]Vogel, *God's Presence,* p. 92.

because we are first our bodies and can stand behind our words. Words, then, are the extension of the body, constituting our selves and announcing our presence in the world. When our bodies and our words contradict each other, the person is falsified.

The body as the basis of personal history. One's bodily life, in its totality, constitutes a personal history. Our lives are a constant synthesis of our past, present and future, and our ordinary experiences confirm that everything truly personal is temporal and everything most significantly temporal is personal. But the dimensions of time are constitutive of our beings only because of our material and bodily nature. Paul Ramsey proclaims that as ensouled bodies, our lives have the body's shape and trajectory.[74] Such a natural trajectory provides the person with both history and destiny. The growth and development of one's bodily life through youth and adulthood and its subsequent decline toward old age and death together are the personal history and destiny of the embodied self. Likewise, our personal history is first marked by our bodily ties with our parents, through whom we acquire our family history and identity. With time, we establish more bodily ties with significant others, including our spouses and children, colleagues at work and neighbors in the community we live—relationships that allow us to have a history, a biography. As such, there is a deep and indissoluble connection between a person and the natural trajectory of her bodily life. At times we may desire a different trajectory and want to change its course, but we can only transcend the body's history and destiny to some degree, for the person cannot be divorced from the body and its natural trajectory. As embodied soul or ensouled body, we both make and are made by history.

Gilbert Meilaender notes Augustine's description of the human being as *"terraes animata"* (animated earth),[75] which suggests that the preeminent church father grasped the personal and historical significance of the body. To have a life is to be *terra animata,* a living body whose natural history has a trajectory. To be *terra animata* is to be a someone with a history, not merely a someone with certain capacities or characteristics. To truly know ourselves entails a willingness to embrace our own histories, and to truly know other persons requires our willingness to enter into their histories. A complete personal history encompasses one's whole life with its high points and lows, "from potentiality to zenith to residuality."[76] The zenith may be the best part of the history, but it is only one part of the history, and the zenith is not the person. As John Kleing says:

---

[74]Paul Ramsey, *The Patient as Person* (New Haven, Conn.: Yale University Press, 1970), p. xiii.

[75]Augustine, *The City of God* 20.20, trans. Henry Bettenson (New York: Penguin, 1972), quoted in Gilbert C. Meilaender, *Body, Soul and Bioethics* (Notre Dame: University of Notre Dame Press, 1995), p. 38.

[76]John Kleinig, *Valuing Life* (Princeton: Princeton University Press, 1991), p. 201.

> Human beings are continuants, organisms with a history that extends beyond their immediate present, usually forward and backward. What has come to be seen as "personhood," a selected segment of that organismic trajectory, is connected to its earlier and later phases by a complex of factors—physical, social, psychological—that constitute part of a single history.[77]

To point to some specific moment in this history at which point we have personhood is to assume the ability to extricate ourselves from the bodily nature of history and "to suppose that in such a moment we are rather like God, no longer having our personal presence in the body."[78] Or in our arrogance we may even want to exceed God, who after all assumed a human body as the incarnate Word to be present in this world. Every human life is the unfolding of a story; and as a living body, that story begins before we are conscious of it, and some of us believe that it continues after we are no longer conscious of it. Yet each story is about someone who, as a *terra animata,* has a single history of how his being makes other becoming possible.

The embodiment of human nature is not only ontologically but also morally significant because it imparts to the person a strong sense of worth. Our embodiment "lies at the root of the moral sense of inviolability of personhood."[79] Our moral knowledge too seems to be more bodily dependent than we admit. We know cruelty, mercilessness or injustice because we somehow feel them in our guts.[80] James W. Walters observes that the American public readily accepts early abortion of fetuses with relative ease but rejects killing the most disabled newborn even though both do not attain the threshold of personhood by the criterion of self-consciousness. This is the case because in society's mind, as well as in the eyes of the law, the difference between killing a fetus and killing a newborn is a highly significant one: it is a distinction based primarily on the great difference in their physical developments.[81]

It is important to realize that the physical development of the human person from the embryo stage to the toddler has moral relevance not merely because the embryo-fetus has grown in physical size but because this growth is the progressive physical growth of the human person. This is an increasingly powerful symbol of the personal history it embodies and of the full personal life it will eventually embrace. As I will discuss later, with the development of ultrasonography, through which the features and movements of the fetus can be visualized, the fetus increasingly appears to look like a lit-

---

[77]Ibid.

[78]Meilaender, *Body, Soul and Bioethics,* p. 49.

[79]Zaner, "Body," 1:297.

[80]James B. Nelson, *Body Theology* (Louisville, Ky.: John Knox Press, 1992), p. 43.

[81]James W. Walters, *What Is a Person? An Ethical Exploration* (Urbana: University of Illinois Press, 1997), p. 68.

tle baby. It may be argued that this level of physical growth is emotionally powerful not only because it appeals to human sentiment but because it anticipates the variety of emotions that encompass a full personal life in which the fetus will soon be involved. "Quickening" may be said to have similar effects and implications; at all times of human history and across all cultures, quickening, as experienced by the pregnant woman, has always assumed particular significance because at this point the pregnant woman does not merely think and imagine her child, but actually feels the child's physical movement. "The fetus becomes a tactile reality."[82] The talk of the fetus's reacting to a variety of maternal emotions and even "playing" with the mother may often be exaggerated, but it does not remove the actual significance, both emotional and moral, of this milestone of fetal physical development and especially of the personal life it both mediates and symbolizes. Similarly, the attainment of viability as a milestone of physical development may have many other philosophical implications, but its symbolic value of relational life and emotional power is not morally irrelevant.[83] This is evidenced in the United States Supreme Court's judgment in *Roe* v. *Wade* (1973) that fetal viability is the point of development at which the state has an obligation to legally protect the interest of the fetus.

In sum, the significance of the body explains the profound moral feelings that accompany all interventions and intrusions in the embodied person. Whatever is done to my body is, after all, done to me; therefore the nature of human embodiment renders medicine an inherently personal and moral enterprise. Bioethics in the West has employed a philosophical framework that reduces persons to their psychological faculties, effectively excluding the body from ethical and moral reflection. Yet medical technologies such as genetic screening and therapy exert enormous normative power in determining which lives are most valuable and which human characteristics are unacceptable; in this way medical technology gradually redefines human nature primarily through the alterations of the body.

The Christian doctrine of incarnation—the belief that the second person of the Trinity took on a human body and was born in the world—has provided support for treating the body with high regard. Such an incarnational faith prompts numerous questions with respect to the meaning of human embodiment, especially human sexuality, aging, physical suffering, death and the future resurrected body. But more pertinent to the subject at hand—when life begins—the Christian incarnational faith serves to highlight the essential physicality of humanness. The

---

[82]Ibid., p. 71.
[83]See the separate discussion on the fetus as a patient in chapter nineteen, "Medical Technological Innovations and the Status of the Unborn," below.

tendency in the Christian West has always been to spiritualize human beings as if the "spiritual" is more worthy in God's sight. But a proper theology informed by an incarnational faith will insist that the physical is the authentic and necessary basis for humanity's covenantal relation with God. A person must not strive to transcend his physical body in order to be a fuller human being or a more perfect bearer of God's image; rather, we only come before God as "full humanity" when we are embodied through the physical. Stanley Hauerwas aptly points out that in our failure to treat and regard the physical life of the fetus as full human life, we deny the most significant aspect of our own being.[84]

Contemporary Christians need to be reminded that the Christian church has, in fact, a long tradition which teaches that the flesh is not the hindrance to, but the hinge of, salvation. As Tertullian writes in his *De resurrectione carne:*

> To such a degree is the flesh the hinge of salvation, by which, with the soul, it is bound to God. It is the very flesh which makes it possible that the soul is able to be chosen by God. But also: the flesh is washed in order that the soul may be cleansed; the flesh is anointed in order that the soul may be consecrated; the flesh is signed in order that the soul may be fortified; the flesh is overshadowed by the imposition of the hand in order that the soul may be illumined by the Spirit. The body feeds on the flesh and blood of Christ so that the soul might feast upon God.[85]

The body, then, is the hinge not only for the relationship between God and humanity, but also for the relationship between the human being and his self, neighbors, and the world. It is true that science and philosophy in the modern West have made it rather difficult to see the bodily significance of an incarnational faith. But the Christian faith requires us to apprehend God bodily—not simply so we can make religious pronouncements about the bodily life, but so one's life may be redefined as "body words" of love, mediating God's love for the world and his divine presence in the world.[86]

---

[84]Stanley Hauerwas, *Vision and Virtue* (Notre Dame: University of Notre Dame Press, 1981), pp. 150-51.

[85]Tertullian *De resurrectione carnis,* trans. Sr. M. Timothy Prokes, quoted in Prokes, *Toward a Theology of the Body,* p. 44.

[86]Nelson, *Body Theology,* pp. 52-53.

3

The Psychological Dimension of Human Personhood

*T*raditional Philosophical Viewpoints

"Neocortical function is the key to humanness, the essential trait, the human *sine qua non.*"[1] These words, uttered by Joseph Fletcher, one of the earliest pioneers of modern bioethics in America, reflect the tradition in modern Western thought to define human personhood in terms of the human psychological, especially cognitive, faculty. Paul Ramsey, another pioneer in bioethics, employs the notion of person to safeguard the patient's right to autonomy and self-determination. In practical terms, this safeguarding is translated into a right to be *informed* of everything that is to be done to the patient either therapeutically or experimentally. In other words, the notion of the person exercises a protective role against patient abuse and provides a Kantian check on the utilitarian bias of modern technological medicine. But in order to be informed, the person must be capable of cognitive activities; hence, cognitive functions become the sine qua non for defining personhood.[2] But why does human rationality so preoccupy contemporary bioethicists that it is considered almost the sole criterion of personhood? To identify the origin of this contemporary

---

[1]Joseph Fletcher, "Four Indicators of Humanhood: The Enquiry Matures," *Hastings Center Report* 4 (December 1974): 5.
[2]Paul Ramsey, *The Patient as Person* (New Haven, Conn.: Yale University Press, 1970).

preoccupation, we have to go back to at least the beginning of the Enlightenment movement in the seventeenth century.

René Descartes. The tradition of regarding the self as a thinking substance has a long heritage, dating back originally to ancient Greek philosophy. However, it did not reach its apogee until René Descartes (1596-1650), the "father of modern thinking," who based the self in the act of cerebration: *"Cogito ergo sum,"* "I think, therefore I am." However, before arriving at this triumphant dictum of the modern mind, Descartes finds it necessary to initiate his search for an indubitable grounding of the self, knowledge and truth in the principle of universal doubt. One by one, by means of his "methodical doubt," he eliminates sense experience, geometric reasoning, demonstration and judgments. In a serendipitous moment, while doubting (thinking) everything, he realizes that one piece of indubitable knowledge remains: the doubting (thinking) "I." If I am thinking, I undoubtedly exist.[3] On this basis, Descartes concludes what he judges to be a human being: a thing that thinks—that is, a mind, a mental substance (which he calls "soul" in order to make it intelligible to the audience of his time). He considers this a truth beyond reproach and the first principle of philosophy.

By presupposing the "I" as a substance in which thinking is realized—that is, thinking itself presupposes the existence of the substance "self" or the self-conscious "I"—Descartes's formulation "I think, therefore I am" affirms his own existence as a thinking self, but it proves little beyond that. For instance, it still leaves one ignorant as to the *nature* of the person: if I am a thing that thinks, what is a thing that thinks? While he is right in retaining the concept of the "self" as substance, the grounding for that self, *"cogito ergo sum,"* conceives of it as a thinking substance that has no need of the world for its existence, that subsists in its own consciousness, with all the eternal truths innate. He declares that "I can have no knowledge of what is outside me except by means of the ideas I have within me." In this tradition, person is defined as an ego subject subsisting in itself, endowed with reason in his

---

[3]As Descartes remarks, "I noticed that, whilst I thus wished to think all things false, it was absolutely essential that the I who thought this should be something." Furthermore, in Descartes's view, this mental substance, the mind, is not only distinguishable from, but ultimately independent of, the body. As such, it continues to exist even when the body no longer exists; for Descartes, this immateriality provides the basis for personal immortality. In his own words: "I knew that I was a substance the whole essence or nature of which is to think, and that for its existence there is no need of any place, nor does it depend on any material thing; so that this 'me,' that is to say, the soul by which I am what I am, is entirely distinct from its body, and is even more easy to know than is the latter; and even if the body were not, the soul would not cease to be what it is." René Descartes, "Discourse on Method," quoted in *Images of the Human*, ed. Hunter Brown, Dennis L. Hudecki, Lenard A. Kennedy and John J. Snyder (Chicago: Loyola Press, 1995), p. 156.

inner being; in short, a person is a rational individual.

John Locke. If Descartes places absolute confidence in the rational nature of the human person, his optimism is not shared by empiricists such as John Locke (1632-1704), George Berkeley (1685-1753) and David Hume (1711-1776), who insist that experience is a more reliable indicator of truth than is reason. Locke, for example, attacks the then-fashionable theory of innate ideas,[4] arguing instead that such ideas do not exist and that all knowledge comes from the human senses which allow "an impression or motion made in some part of the body to produce some perception in the understanding,"[5] which is a function of the soul. Although Locke is ambivalent about the nature and exact role of this human soul which "understands," he affirms that it is a "substance that thinks" which stands (stance) beneath (sub) the various mental experiences. Thus, Locke defines a person as "a thinking intelligent being that has reason and reflection, and can consider itself as itself, the same thinking thing, in different times and places."[6] Locke basically relies on intuition to justify his claim of the existence of the "thinking thing," "something-I-know-not what," since he cannot identify an impression that corresponds with the idea of the mental substance or self. The self as a real entity that underlies the various mental phenomena experienced day to day can only be assumed but not empirically proven.

David Hume. Both Locke and Berkeley are willing to assume the self, but for Hume, such a substantive notion of selfhood, however intuitively attractive, fails to live up to the rigorous test of the canons of empiricism. Hume defines experience through two kinds of "perceptions": "impressions" and "ideas." In Hume's system, sensory experiences of realities in the world create impressions, and ideas are but copies of these impressions. There is no fundamental difference between impressions and ideas; they differ only in terms of degree, not in kind. In contrast to Descartes's certainty that the self is a thinking substance, Hume insists that the origin of the idea of self must be found in some impressions derived from concrete experiences in reality, even mental reality, in order to justify the idea of self. In other words, Hume assumes that if such a self does exist, there has to be a continuous and identical reality that forms the idea of the self and, in turn, one corresponding impression that is invariably associated with the idea of self. Such an impression of the self must be shown to exist as an enduring presence throughout life, if personal identity is to be

---

[4]John Locke, *An Essay Concerning Human Understanding,* abr. ed., ed. A. D. Woozley (New York: Meridian Printing, 1974), pp. 66-68.

[5]Ibid., p. 97. Locke regards the human mind more like a *tabula rasa,* a blank slate or "white sheet," so that nothing can be said to be innate.

[6]John Locke, *An Essay Concerning Human Understanding in Four Books* (London: Tho. Basset, 1690), 2.9.29.

considered a constant feature of an individual's life. Hume undertakes an introspective reflection in his search for the self, or an impression of the self, concentrating exclusively on what is disclosed by experience. The result of Hume's search for such a self is ultimately negative. His introspection yields a number of impressions, including pain, pleasure, grief, joy and so on, but they do not provide the basis to establish an underlying self.[7]

As a result, even though Hume concedes that there is a powerful "propensity" to posit a self as the enduring seat of human experiences, he nevertheless insists that human beings "are nothing but a bundle or collection of different perceptions."[8] Hume declares that

> for my part, when I enter most intimately into what I call *myself*, I always stumble on some particular perception or other, of heat or cold, light or shade, love or hatred, pain or pleasure. I never can catch *myself* at any time without a perception, and never can observe anything but the perception. When my perceptions are removed for any time, as by sound sleep, so long am I insensible of myself, and may truly be said not to exist. . . . If anyone . . . thinks he has a different notion of *himself*, . . . he may, perhaps, perceive something simple and continued, which he calls *himself*, though I am certain there is no such principle in me.[9]

Hume concludes that it is only our memory which gives the (illusory) impression of our continuous identity.[10]

Ultimately the most important premise leading to Hume's denial of the continuous self that retains its identity through time is his rejection of any form of substance, a notion which Locke retains as "something-we-know-not what" and which Berkeley is willing to preserve as the idea of spiritual substances. If the self exists in some form of substance, then no such substance, Hume argues, can be derived from our impressions of sensation. A person, to Hume,

---

[7]For Hume, "if any impression gives rise to the idea of self, that impression must continue invariably the same, through the whole course of our lives, since self is supposed to exist after that manner." Instead, all the perceptions he can experience "are different, and distinguishable, and separable from each other, and may be separately considered, and may exist separately, and have no need of anything to support their existence." This incessant dynamic fluctuation, in Hume's estimation, cannot give rise to the idea of self. Hume also notes that perceptions come with such "an inconceivable rapidity, and are in a perpetual flux and movement," that for him it is impossible to conceive of "any single power of the soul which remains unalterably the same, perhaps for one moment." David Hume, *A Treatise of Human Nature*, 1.4.6, quoted in *Images of the Human*, ed. Hunter Brown, Dennis L. Hudecki, Lenard A. Kennedy and John J. Snyder (Chicago: Loyola Press, 1995), pp. 192-93.

[8]Ibid., p. 192.

[9]Ibid.

[10]This Humean notion may be important for understanding the source of some contemporary bioethical discussions about whether an advance directive is ever valid, since the person who executes such a document when he is mentally competent may no longer be the same person when he becomes incompetent.

is no more than "just a train of consciousness," and even the unity of that consciousness is at best circumstantial. However, he fails to recognize that in order for changes to take place, even changes in perceptions, there must be an underlying substance—the Lockean "something"—in which the changes occur and which endures through time. As I initially noted, one must have "being" in order for "becoming" to take place.

Immanuel Kant. Another philosopher who has left an indelible impression on the modern understanding of human personhood is Immanuel Kant (1724-1804). Kant has not directly written on the concept of person per se; rather it is in the explication of his metaphysics of morality that his understanding of personhood is revealed. Kant is convinced that the grounding of a metaphysics of morals is to be found in pure reason.[11] He further claims that it is a moral categorical imperative to only treat human beings as ends in themselves and never merely as a means because as persons they are rational.[12] Kant is essentially arguing that the human being is the actual embodiment of rationality; and as a rational being, he possesses freedom and autonomy, which constitute the foundation of all moral actions of *rational* beings.[13] Because the human being can freely determine his will by reason, he possesses "dignity," which Kant defines as "absolute inner worth." On this view, Kant's rational, autonomous person is a superman with the attributes of a godlike agent. It is clear that one of Kant's main problems is the inordinate amount of credit allotted to rationality in his understanding of persons. Rationality is the only thing that is the essence of moral agency and that is valued as an end in itself. When Kant speaks of respect for the human person, the respect can not be extended to a human being who is not capable of rational thinking. In short, rationality is the only qualification both for being a moral agent and for being an object of moral concern. With that, Kant crystallizes for modern Western thought what the West has long held—that rationality is constitutive of personhood.

---

[11]For Kant, "the basis of obligation must not be sought in human nature or in the circumstances of the world in which he (man) is placed, but *a priori* simply in the concepts of pure reason." See Immanuel Kant, "Preface," in *Groundwork of the Metaphysics of Morals,* trans. H. J. Paton (London: n.p., 1950), p. 389, quoted in Frederick Copleston, S.J., *A History of Philosophy,* vol. 6, bk. 2 (Garden City, N.Y.: Image, 1964), p. 105.

[12]Kant argues that, "assuming that there is something *the existence of which* has *in itself* absolute value, something which, *as an end in itself* could be the ground of determine laws, then in it and in it alone would lie the ground of a possible categorical imperative." So Kant goes on to postulate that the human being is an end in itself. From this, a practical moral principle follows: "So act as to treat humanity, whether in your own person or in that of any other, always at the same time as an end, and never merely as a means." Kant, *Groundwork,* p. 429, quoted in Copleston, *History of Philosophy,* p. 120.

[13]Immanuel Kant, *Fundamental Principles of the Metaphysic of Morals* (Indianapolis: Bobbs-Merrill, 1949), p. 282.

Contemporary Bioethical Viewpoints

Joseph Fletcher. This highly individualistic, introspective and intellectualistic account of a person as one who possesses some psychological faculties, such as consciousness or rationality, continues to dominate the modern bioethical discourse, especially within the secular academic circle. It has been argued that these psychological faculties are prerequisites for "the possibility of the moral community"[14] and, hence, for personhood. On this view, to qualify as a human person, mere biological/genetic humanness or membership in the species *Homo sapiens* is not sufficient. Fletcher, whom I cited in the introduction of this chapter, initially proposed fifteen positive and five negative necessary and sufficient criteria for human personhood! The positive indicators include minimal intelligence, self-awareness, self-control, a sense of time (both of the past and the future), the capability to relate to others, the capacity to show concern for others, communication, control of existence, curiosity, change and changeability, idiosyncrasy, balance of rationality and feeling, and neocortical function; negative indicators include that humans are not anti-artificial, not essentially parental, not essentially sexual, not a bundle of rights and not worshipers.[15]

Despite its thoroughness, the list is theoretically too vague and empirically too ill-specified to be of any practical use as a set of operational criteria. For instance, how does one demonstrate a balance of rationality and feeling? What are the signs and manifestations that one has control of existence? Later, Fletcher reduced the list of traits of personhood to essentially four: neocortical function, self-awareness, relational ability and happiness.[16] Since the first two are directly related to one's rational faculty, there is a clear bias for this human function to be an indicator for humanhood or personhood. His assumption is simply that to be human is to be rational: "*Homo* is indeed *sapiens,* in order to be *homo.* The *ratio,* in another term of speech, is what makes a person of the *vita.*"[17] For Fletcher, minimal intelligence as provided by the neocortical function is the necessary criterion, "the cardinal indicator," for humanhood. Any individual who scores below forty on the IQ test is questionably a person, and those who score twenty or below are definitely not persons. He concludes that "mere biological life, before minimal intelligence is achieved or after it is lost irretrievably, is without personal status."[18]

---

[14]H. Tristram Engelhardt Jr., *The Foundations of Bioethics* (Oxford: Oxford University Press, 1986), pp. 105-7.

[15]Joseph Fletcher, "Indicators of Humanhood: A Tentative Profile of Man," *Hastings Center Report* 2, no. 5 (1972): 1-3.

[16]Fletcher, "Four Indicators," pp. 4-7.

[17]Fletcher, "Indicators of Humanhood," p. 1.

[18]Ibid.

Michael Tooley. Michael Tooley is another influential advocate of the "rationalist" position. He first defines human personhood in a normative sense as a human entity that possesses a right to life. Next, he argues that a human entity cannot have a right to life unless it is capable of having an interest in its own continued existence.[19] To have an interest involves the capacity for having desires; and a human entity, however, cannot have such a desire for its continued existence unless it possesses, at some time, the concept of a continuing self, or subject of experiences.[20] A continuing self in turn depends on the existence of a simple, continuing subject of consciousness and experience, which is only made possible by psychological connections (i.e., memory). Since the fetus or infant does not possess these psychological faculties, it lacks a concept of a continuing self and thus a right to life. In Tooley's view, fetuses and infants may well be biologic human beings as members of the species *Homo sapiens,* but they are not human persons with a right to life—not until they become a continuing subject of consciousness.

It is important to understand that Tooley is not denying the fetus's "interest" in life, since many nonconscious beings, such as plants, may be said to have such an interest. Rather, he is arguing that these interests are not morally relevant to the endowment of the right to life, on account of the fact that these interests do not belong to a continuing subject of consciousness.[21]

> What is needed, apparently, is that the continued existence of the individual will make possible the satisfaction of some desires existing at other times. But not just any desires existing at other times will do. . . . It is not even sufficient that they be desires associated with the same physical organism. It is crucial that they be desires that belong to one and the same subject of consciousness.[22]

This ultimately exposes the overall weakness of Tooley's argument, which entails a sort of value judgment for the determination of the kind of interests that should be considered for the purpose of assigning the right to life. Specifically, it is not clear why a fetus has to be able to conceptualize her interest in life as a continuing subject of consciousness before her interest wins her the right to life. Since rights are transactions exchanged in a social context, can and should not the fetus's interest in and right to life be located in her immediate network of relationships rather than in her self-consciousness? Presumably,

---

[19]"It is a conceptual truth that an entity cannot have a particular right *R* unless it is at least capable of having some interest *I* which is furthered by its having right *R.*" Michael Tooley, *Abortion and Infanticide* (New York: Oxford University Press, 1983), p. 99.

[20]"To have a desire for one's own continued existence presupposes that one possesses the concept of a continuing subject of experiences, and that one is aware of oneself as a subject of experiences." Ibid., p. 105.

[21]Ibid., p. 117.

[22]Ibid., p. 120.

Tooley has already assumed the latter to be of higher value.

John Harris. Consciousness as the basis of assigning personhood is also advocated by British philosopher John Harris. Specifically, he emphasizes the importance of an entity's ability to be conscious of itself and its own future. Such a consciousness endows the human entity with a capacity to value its own life. Linking interests to the right to life in a manner somewhat similar to Tooley's, Harris argues that the most important justification for regarding human life as more worthy of special care and protection than other living beings has to do with the fact that human beings are capable of valuing their own lives and the lives of others:

> A person will thus be any individual capable of valuing its own life. . . . Such a being will, at the very least, be able to conceive of itself as an independent center of consciousness, existing over time, with a future that it is capable of envisaging and wishing to experience.[23]

Evidently, Harris appeals to the distinction between fact and value to distinguish between the human being and human person. On this basis, embryos, fetuses and infants will not possess the necessary degree of self-consciousness required to value their own lives, and so they remain indistinguishable from many animals.[24] In this regard, Harris is explicit in his rejection of the notion that membership in the species *Homo sapiens* is an adequate ground for personhood with an entitlement of special care and protection. He labels this as "a form of species prejudice."[25]

The problem in Harris's reasoning lies not only in the fact that "person" becomes an embodiment of value, but also in his transferring the dichotomy of fact/value to human being/person, which should at most be seen as a continuity and not a dichotomy. As Mary Ann Warren points out in an explicit reference to Harris's position, this creates an extraordinarily confusing concept because, on one hand, it is not possible to demonstrate that neonates, whom Harris explicitly excludes, do not value their lives and want to live; on the other hand, people with suicidal tendencies do not value their lives and should then be excluded, although Harris does not exclude them.[26] Harris's account, therefore, does not adequately justify the distinction between person and human being on the basis of values and facts, and it is arbitrarily prejudiced against those who are on the edges of human life.

---

[23]John Harris, "In Vitro Fertilization: The Ethical Issues," *Philosophical Quarterly* 33 (July 1983): 225.

[24]Ibid., p. 226.

[25]Ibid., p. 224.

[26]Mary Ann Warren, "In Vitro Fertilization: The Ethical Issues," *Philosophical Quarterly* 33 (July 1983): 241-42.

Mary Ann Warren. Unlike Tooley or Harris, Warren does not see an inherent problem with "speciesism," and in fact she argues that it is virtually impossible to fully purge such tendencies from one's judgments. To the contrary, she regards it as a desirable and important moral principle: "To live in a universe in which we were genuinely species indifferent would be impossible, or . . . undesirable."[27] At times Warren appears to want to do away with the term *person* altogether; instead she prefers the term *human*. Warren distinguishes between two distinct senses of the term *human:* human as genetically part of a certain species and human as part of a moral community. Embryos and fetuses are humans only in the first sense, and to be a "person" requires that one to be human in the second sense. Warren maintains that we have no right to assume a priori that genetic humanity necessitates membership of a moral community, and she suggests that personhood or "humanity in the moral sense" should exhibit five characteristics:

☐ consciousness, and particularly the capacity to feel pain

☐ reasoning, with the developed capacity to solve new and relatively complex problems

☐ self-motivated activity that is relatively independent of either genetic or direct external control

☐ the capacity to communicate

☐ the presence of self-concepts and self-awareness, either individual or racial, or both.[28]

If these categories are central to membership in a moral community, they should also be central to the concept of personhood. As with Fletcher's original criteria, Warren's position is not arguing that an entity must possess all of these traits to be considered a person; but she is claiming that any being that satisfies none of these criteria is certainly not a person. Thus, despite her acceptance of speciesism, at the end, Warren's reliance on cognitive functions for personhood is hardly different from that of Tooley and Harris.

Helga Kuhse and Peter Singer. The loudest voices denouncing any form of speciesism come from Helga Kuhse and Peter Singer, who reject membership of the species *Homo sapiens* as a morally relevant criterion for personhood. In fact, they consider speciesism to be as indefensible as racism and sexism.[29] Taking their position to its logical end would mean that feeding your two-month-old infant before you attend to your two-year-old dog, simply because the infant is a human, is a crime as serious as having unjustly discriminated

---

[27]Ibid., p. 242.

[28]Ibid., pp. 241-42.

[29]Helga Kuhse and Peter Singer, *Should the Baby Live?* (Oxford: Oxford University Press, 1985), p. 123.

against a person of the opposite sex or of a different race. In Kuhse's and Singer's view, the notion of species is indirectly relevant only when it is demonstrated to function as a reliable indicator of other morally relevant capacities such as self-awareness and rationality. For these authors, it is precisely the sense of self-awareness and the awareness of the future that count as crucial in the determination of personhood. "When I think of myself as the person I now am, I realize that I did not come into existence until some time after my birth. At birth I had no sense of the future, and no experience which I can now remember as 'mine.' "[30] In Singer's more recent book *Rethinking Life and Death,* he makes the same point more clearly when he defines a person as "a being with awareness of her or his own existence over time, and the capacity to have wants and plans for the future."[31] If self-awareness and rationality are the criteria for personhood, then it follows that "not all members of the species *Homo sapiens* are persons, and not all persons are members of the species *Homo sapiens.*"[32]

On this view, the newborn infant is clearly not a person.[33] By contrast, Singer, who is well-known for his concern for animal rights, is particularly keen to point out that there is conclusive evidence that the great apes are persons; in fact, "whales, dolphins, elephants, monkeys, dogs, pigs and other animals may eventually also be shown to be aware of their own existence over time and capable of reasoning. Then they too will have to be considered as persons."[34] Kuhse and Singer emphasize that the term *person* is no mere descriptive label but that it carries with it a moral standing which confers the basic right to life. "It is the beginning of the life of the person, rather than of the physical organism, that is crucial so far as the right to life is concerned."[35] Since fetuses and infants are not persons, these authors do not believe that they possess the right to life. Ultimately, Kuhse and Singer appeal to an utilitarian justification for their positions on abortion, infanticide and animal rights. Many are skeptical that this position can be consistently sustained by utilitarianism; indeed, even if these utilitarian arguments can be sustained, it would only expose the very weakness of such an ethical theory that consistently pushes human beings to the fringes of the right to life.

Harry G. Frankfurt. Perhaps the most innovative psychologically based cri-

---

[30]Ibid., p. 133.
[31]Peter Singer, *Rethinking Life and Death: The Collapse of Our Traditional Ethics* (New York: St. Martin's Griffin, 1994), p. 218.
[32]Ibid., p. 206.
[33]Ibid., p. 217.
[34]Ibid., p. 182.
[35]Kuhse and Singer, *Should the Baby Live?* p. 133.

terion for personhood is Harry G. Frankfurt's "second-order volitions."[36] To qualify as a human person, Frankfurt contends, not only must one be capable of having desires (itself an ability that presupposes some forms of rationality), consciousness and perhaps some degree of self-consciousness, but also one must have the ability to counter such primary, or "first-order," desires. In other words, one must be able to desire not to desire—hence have a "second-order" desire. Further, one must possess the freedom of the will to act on the second-order desire. When a human individual demonstrates this type of second-order volition, then he is truly a person. In other words, to be a person one must possess the freedom of will to control one's own inclinations. Although this is an intriguing proposition, if we honestly reflect on the frequency with which we fail to exercise the faculty of second-order volitions, we may be less prepared to accept this criterion for personhood. Frankfurt offers scant argument to persuade me to accept such a demanding criterion.

Traditional Theological Viewpoints

Some may be surprised to discover that the psychological approach to the understanding of human personhood has enjoyed a vintage dating back almost two millennia within the Christian Church. Hence, the Christian theological tradition is an important resource for gaining further insights into the concept of personhood. After all, the term *person* was first used widely in the third and fourth centuries in an attempt to understand and enunciate certain mysteries of the Christian faith, especially that of the Trinity (the being of one God who is nevertheless three Persons) and the incarnation (the being of one person, Jesus Christ, who has two natures, the human and the divine). Tertullian is the first to refer to Christ as a "person," but it is in the Councils of Nicea (A.D. 325) and Chalcedon (A.D. 451) that the concepts became entrenched in Christian doctrine. Surprisingly, in maintaining that God is three Persons with one substance and that Christ is one Person with two natures (divine and human), the early councils neglected to define the word *person,* leaving the task for the later theologians and philosophers who tried to understand the concept of personhood mainly through the explication of the biblical concept of the *imago Dei* (the image of God).

Influenced by a Hellenistic dualism, many early church fathers hold a psychological or intellectualistic understanding of the *imago Dei*, and they argue that since God does not have a body, likewise, the divine image in human beings can have nothing to do with our bodies; they then conclude that human beings reflect the image of God by having an immaterial and rational

---

[36]Harry G. Frankfurt, "Freedom of the Will and the Concept of a Person," *Journal of Philosophy* 68 (January 1971): 15-20.

soul. This tradition has enjoyed a long history within the church, beginning with the church father Irenaeus, who has the honor of being the first expositor of this interpretation of the imago.[37] Despite the fact that he is concerned with maintaining the unity of the nature of humankind as body and soul, he nevertheless makes humankind's natural reason the decisive element in the concept of *imago Dei*. In *Against Heresies* 4.4.3, he says, "But man, being endowed with reason, and in this respect like to God . . ."[38] For Irenaeus, God is Reason proper and the rational nature of humanity is a kind of participation in God. He further distinguishes "image" from "likeness," understanding the former to consist in the freedom and rationality of human nature, which may not be lost, while the latter is humanity's gift of supernatural communion with God, which certainly has been lost since Adam's Fall. Some believe that this distinction may have started the process of making reason a chief ontological characteristic of humanity for the following fifteen hundred years in the history of the church.[39]

Origen, another church father, understands the first two chapters of Genesis to represent two distinct creations: the first one relates to the immaterial eternal realm wherein the soul, which alone is created in the image, resides; the second one is the inferior, changing, material realm. To him, the human soul is "the incorporeal and invisible image of the incorporeal and invisible Word."[40] And more specifically, the image is in the soul's higher element, the intellect or the logos (reason), which is in humankind. Another Greek church father, Athanasius, though more inclined toward seeing the unity of the human being as body and soul, nevertheless connects the idea of the *imago Dei* with the human soul. To Athanasius, the image or likeness refers to rationality, which is seen as God's continuous gift to enable the human person "to understand oneself and one's world rationally, . . . to appreciate the world as created, good and valuable, [and] to recognize creation's harmony and the Harmonizer of all creation."[41] Even though Athanasius insists that the rationality includes a "desire" for God, the intellectual and cognitive nature of the image is not mistaken.[42] Gregory of Nyssa, one of the Cappadocian fathers, affirms the impor-

---

[37]Emil Brunner, *Man in Revolt,* trans. Olive Wyon (Philadelphia: Westminster Press, 1939), p. 504.

[38]Irenaeus, *Against Heresies,* vol. 1 of Ante-Nicene Fathers (Grand Rapids, Mich.: Eerdmans, 1975).

[39]Ibid., p. 505.

[40]Henri Crouzel, *Origen: The Life and Thought of the First Great Theologian,* trans. A. S. Worrall (San Francisco: Harper and Row, 1989), p. 94.

[41]Alvyn Pettersen, *Athanasius* (Ridgefield, Conn.: Morehouse, 1995), p. 28.

[42]"He did not barely create man, as He did all the irrational creatures on the earth, but made them after His own image, giving them a portion even of the power of His own Word; so that having as it were a kind of reflexion of the Word, and being made rational, they might

tance of human embodiment. But man's excellence and greatness rest "not upon his likeness to the created universe, but upon the fact that he has been made in the image of the nature of the Creator."[43] And humankind is the faithful image of his Creator because its soul possesses reason, freedom of the will and supernatural grace.

When we turn to the Latin fathers, we note that Augustine, although rejecting much of Plato's teaching on the soul, nevertheless belies a Platonic influence by identifying the essential self with the soul, which directs the function of the body: "The true man is the soul, and the body is its instrument."[44] The soul acts on the body, but the body does not act on the soul, because the soul resembles and corresponds to the divine nature whereas the body is similar to other earthly creatures. Even though Augustine in his later teaching emphasizes a soul-body unity (see below), he persists in believing that the soul is superior to the body because the soul is where the image of the Trinity is located. For Augustine, the image of Trinity is not found in the exterior human but in the interior human[45]—in the mind as memory, understanding and love. In his treatment of the Trinity, Augustine is much more concerned with the oneness of the Trinity, hence the image of God is also essentially in the one soul. Augustine differentiates the unity of the soul in a trinitarian sense by saying that "man was made to God's image, inasmuch as we exist and know that we exist, and love this existence and knowledge."[46] In this inwardly subjective threefold differentiation into being, knowing and loving, the human soul corresponds to the three divine Persons—Father, Son and Holy Spirit, respectively. Augustine interprets the soul not so much as substance, but as subject with the inner threefold character of self-awareness, self-knowledge and self-love together composing the perfect image of the Trinity.[47] This implies that the image and our authentic humanness cannot be found in our embodiment. Thus we find Augustine declaring

---

be able to abide ever in blessedness, living the true life which belongs to the saints in paradise." Athanasius, *On the Incarnation of the Word* §3.3, in *The Nicene and Post-Nicene Fathers,* 2nd series, ed. Philip Schaff (1819-1893; repr. Grand Rapids, Mich.: Eerdmans, 1973), 4:37.

[43]Gregory of Nyssa, *De opticio hominis* C.16, MG 44, 180A, quoted in Johannes Quasten, *Patrology,* vol. 3 (Westminster, Md.: Christian Classics, 1994), p. 292.

[44]Augustine, *The Greatness of the Soul, The Teacher,* vol. 9 of Ancient Christian Writers, ed. Johannes Quasten and Joseph C. Plumpe (New York: Newman, 1978), p. 13.

[45]Augustine, *The Trinity,* trans. Edmund Hill, O.P. (New York: New York City Press, 1991), pp. 303-21.

[46]Augustine *De civitate Dei* 6.26, quoted in Thomas Aquinas *Summa Theologiae* 1.Q93.A7, trans. Fathers of the English Dominican Province (Westminster, Md.: Christian Classics, 1981), p. 474.

[47]See Mary T. Clark, "Christ and Trinity," in *Augustine* (Washington, D.C.: Georgetown University Press, 1994).

that "for not in the body but in the mind was man made in the image of God. In his own similitude let us seek God, in his own image recognize the creator."[48] Augustinian anthropology is therefore a two-substance dualism: soul and body with the image of God located exclusively in the former. These considerations all contribute to the Augustinian tradition of personhood as a matter mainly concerned with individual consciousness and its internal differentiations, making the social and communal dimensions relatively unimportant.

Augustine's influence can be seen particularly in the famous definition of the "person" tendered by Boethius one hundred years later (A.D. 480-524): he defined a person as "an individual substance of a rational nature." With this memorable definition, the individualistic and intellectualistic connotations of person as a center of consciousness are thus solidified. One should not have much difficulty in seeing how this Latin/Augustinian theological tradition may have influenced the Cartesian definition of humanity as a thinking individual thing, as we have previously seen. Christopher Kaiser correctly observes that in Augustine we have "a rather static concept of deity on the one hand, and an individualistic concept of humanity on the other."[49] I may add that in Augustine we have a highly rationalistic concept of human personhood as well. It is fair to say that the Augustinian tradition has contributed enormously to the church's understanding of the concept of a person, although Augustine's rationalistic emphasis has been exploited by later philosophers and theologians who have often constructed exclusively rationalistic accounts of human personhood.

In contrast to Augustine's Platonized two-substance dualism, Thomas Aquinas's approach is to adopt Aristotle's metaphysics to hold that substances are constituted by two metaphysical principles: form and matter. On this model, human beings are single substances/entities constituted by soul (form) and body (matter). In emphasizing the substantial unity of human nature, Aquinas is able to provide a more holistic or integrated account of human functioning. But despite this advance, his understanding of the *imago Dei* remains cognitive in nature:

> Since man is said to be the image of God by reason of his intellectual nature, he is the most perfectly like God according to that in which he can best imitate God in his intellectual nature. Now the intellectual nature imitates God chiefly in this, that God understands and loves Himself.[50]

---

[48]Augustine *In Joannis Evangelium Tractatus* 24.23.5, quoted in David J. A. Clines, "The Image of God in Man," *Tyndale Bulletin* 19 (1968): 86.

[49]Christopher B. Kaiser, *The Doctrine of God: A Historical Survey* (Westchester, Ill.: Crossway, 1982), p. 81.

[50]Aquinas *Summa Theologiae* 1.Q93.A.4.

In this latter affirmation, Aquinas expresses an anthropology that is more Augustinian than Aristotelian.

In the teaching of the great Reformer John Calvin on the *imago,* the Augustinian rather than the Thomist tradition is preserved. Calvin believes that the soul is the proper seat of God's image and that it animates all parts of the body and renders them useful for their actions.[51] More specifically, the image is expressed in humankind's understanding and reason; and, as far as Calvin is concerned, these intellectual qualities are retained by humankind even after the Fall as remnants of the image of God in fallen humanity. [52]

Contemporary Christian Viewpoints

This rationalistic definition of the *imago Dei* and, derivatively, human personhood persists in the writings of contemporary Christian philosophers. Protestant philosopher Robert Wennberg, writing on human personhood in a theological context, holds the view that personhood can be equated with the *imago Dei.*[53] Since Wennberg conceives of a person as a being in possession of the developed capacity to engage in acts of intellect, emotion and will, he believes that the way a human person images the divine Person, God, is also through such acts. In my opinion, this author has committed a methodological error of allowing a definition of human personhood to interpret the *imago Dei.* Although he grants that the biblical understanding of the *imago Dei* may include more than just a rational capacity (e.g., exercising headship over creation in general), he nevertheless states that "it would seem clear that humanity's rational capacity remains fundamental."[54] Wennberg concludes that infants and fetuses lack the image of God, for they do not possess the necessary rational faculties. On the other hand,[55] since Wennberg also subscribes to the concept of a potential person, he suggests that if we adopt a more "elastic understanding" of the *imago Dei,* which would include even those entities who possess these psychological faculties (to think, love and will) only in a latent form, "then we will be in a position to claim that not only infants but fetuses and newly fertilized ova are in the image of God because they will in due course be imaging God in full actuality."[56] As I will argue below, the concept of a potential person is itself fraught with problems.

---

[51]John Calvin *Institutes of the Christian Religion* 1.15.6 ed. John T. McNeill, trans. Ford Lewis Battles (Philadelphia: Westminster Press, 1960).

[52]Ibid., 1.15.3., 2.2.12.

[53]Robert N. Wennberg, *Life in the Balance: Exploring the Abortion Controversy* (Grand Rapids, Mich.: Eerdmans, 1985), chap. 3.

[54]Ibid., p. 37.

[55]For further discussion, please refer to part three, "Abortion and Personhood," below.

[56]Wennberg, *Life in the Balance,* p. 38.

Another approach that ultimately leads to a rationalistic understanding of the soul is the medieval hylomorphic theory advocated by some contemporary writers in the Christian tradition. Hylomorphic theory is an argument for the position that the embryo/fetus is not a human person until sometime after conception. According to this medieval scholastic theory, all living beings are composed of matter and a principle that determines what that matter is to be and to become. This principle is the substantial form or soul; as an organizing principle of the living being, the soul is related to matter in such a way that it comes into existence only when the matter is sufficiently organized. In other words, the soul is proportioned to its matter, and it can only exist in matter capable of receiving it. On the basis of this theory, Joseph Donceel argues that in order for a human soul to exist, there must first exist an organized body capable of engaging in spiritual activities, which require the brain and especially the cerebral cortex. Donceel concludes that the human soul does not exist in a fetus until the fetal brain/cortex is developed; it follows that a human person comes to be only when the cerebral cortex is present.[57]

Donceel's interpretation of the hylomorphic theory is supported by Thomas Shannon and Allan Wolter, who argue that the biological structures necessary to perform rational actions must be present before a being can be said to be of a rational nature; for the human fetus this happens around the twentieth week, when the integration of the cerebral cortex with the brain stem is achieved.[58] In sum, these writers assume that the human rational faculty is the defining characteristic/function distinctive of the human species and that it requires the presence of an organized brain. Until this crucial bodily organization is present, the soul is not present, and the conceptus without a soul is not a human person.

In response to this, we may agree with the general point of the hylomorphic theory that the human soul only comes into existence in the presence of some sort of an organized body. But this does not necessarily entail that the organized body has to include a brain capable of performing certain distinctive functions of the human species. As a counterexample, Patrick Lee argues that although the most distinctive operation for animals is reproduction, in most animals this ability is not functional for many years; yet prior to the emergence of this distinctive animal function, animals are never considered as anything other than animals, and it is not clear why such a requirement should be applied to human beings.[59] Furthermore, if one holds that the brain must be

---

[57]Joseph Donceel, "Immediate Animation and Delayed Hominization," *Theological Studies* 31, no. 1 (1970): 79-83.

[58]Thomas A. Shannon and Allan B. Wolter, "Reflections on the Moral Status of the Pre-Embryo," *Theological Studies* 51 (1990): 620.

[59]Patrick Lee, *Abortion and Unborn Human Life* (Washington, D.C.: Catholic University of America Press, 1996), pp. 79-90.

present before there is a human being with a rational soul, to the extent that the human brain is only capable of mental activities about three months after birth (during which time the number of neuronal synapses increases from 56 trillion to 1,000 trillion), one may arguably question whether a full-term infant is a human being with a soul. Yet few people are even willing to consider such a possibility.[60]

One of the main difficulties with this interpretation of the hylomorphic theory is again due to a rationalistic bias in the understanding of the function of the soul; in response Lee suggests that the soul's function should be seen more broadly as "the immanent design for the series of temporal events which, possessing a certain intelligible relation among them, are recognized as events belonging to a single organism."[61] On this understanding of the soul's "diachronic" function (i.e., the sequential effect of the soul spread out in time), one may be able to identify the presence of the soul even at the beginning and not just at the culmination of the series of intelligible events that begin to unfold the immanent design. As I have discussed earlier, a zygote/embryo indisputably acquires an intrinsic, self-directed design for its own eventual development and maturation at the time of conception, and hence the human soul is evidently present at conception. Surprisingly, Shannon and Wolter, who espouse the delayed hominization version of the hylomorphic theory, admit that "we have every reason to believe that the dynamic properties of the organic matter—the elements of the fully formed zygote—owe their existence to their organizational form or the system."[62] This being the case, I believe that it is more reasonable to conclude that for an organism with the actual unity a zygote/embryo clearly possesses, it is the soul that is providing the organizational form and that this ensouled organism begins to exist (at the time of conception) long before it develops the more mature psychological functions such as consciousness and rational and volitional activities that are characteristic of the human species. Hence, the contemporary use of the hylomorphic argument with a rationalistic bias overlooks the real function of the soul and the intimate union it has with the body (discussed in the next chapter) and deprives the early conceptus the personhood it possesses.

Evaluation of an Exclusively Psychological Definition of Personhood

The above review of an exclusively psychological definition of personhood—which emphasizes the achievement of rationality, consciousness, self-con-

---

[60]See Germain Grisez, "When Do People Begin? The Ethics of Having Children," *Proceedings of the American Catholic Philosophical Association* 63 (1990): 27-41.

[61]Lee, *Abortion*, p. 83.

[62]Shannon and Wolter, "Reflections," p. 620.

sciousness and so on—is susceptible to a host of criticisms. First and foremost, it is reductionistic in that it ignores the fact that a being, and person as a supreme instance of being, is both substance and achievement, being and becoming. To define personhood in terms of psychological functions at the expense of the underlying substance ignores the fact that the exercise and performance of desiring, rational reasoning, consciousness and self-awareness presuppose the being, the substance, that already exists as a prerequisite of the manifestation of these otherwise admirable functions. Hence, an exclusively psychological definition of personhood renders the person "more like the concept of a state than the concept of a thing."[63] In this regard, P. F. Strawson's definition of a person may be helpful:

> By the concept of a person is [meant] the concept of a type of entity, such that both predicates ascribing states of consciousness, and predicates ascribing corporeal characteristics, a physical situation, etc., are equally applicable to a single individual of that single type.[64]

What Strawson wants to emphasize here is that there has to be an entity—and in the case of a living human person, a physical entity—of some sort. An exclusively psychological definition of personhood insistently ignores the embodied nature of a human being and favors a disembodied person who remains an impoverished Cartesian "ghost in the machine."

Second, such a psychological account of personhood with its emphasis on the person's subjectivity also confuses what D. Connell distinguishes as "the interiority of consciousness" with "the interiority of being."[65] The interiority of being pertains to the unity of the existing self, whereas the interiority of consciousness pertains to the unity of the knowing self, and the two are clearly not identical. An exclusively psychological definition of personhood falsifies the meanings of both interiority and personhood by replacing the interiority of being with the interiority of consciousness. To be is an act of existing rather than knowing. Existing is prior to knowing; the former is a precondition for the latter. To confuse or to reverse the order of the two leads to either an unreal or an empty self.

Third, this account of personhood is highly introspective, individualistic and, hence, atomistic. It isolates the "in-itself" aspect of being from the "toward-others" aspect, leaving the relational dimension ontologically and morally irrelevant. What results is an independent, isolated and individualistic "self" disconnected

---

[63]J. Teichman, "The Definition of Person," *Philosophy* 60, no. 232 (1985): 180.

[64]P. F. Strawson, *Individuals* (London: University Paperbacks, 1964), p. 102.

[65]D. Connell, "Substance and the Interiority of Being," in *Neue Zeitschrift für Systematische Theologie und Religionsphilosophie* (Berlin: Walter de Gruyter, 1983), quoted in Kevin Doran, *What Is a Person: The Concept and the Implications for Ethics* (Lewiston, N.Y.: Edwin Mellen, 1989), p. 44.

from the rest of the world in which it lives and from which it derives its meaning and being. This alienation of the self from others is made worse because this exclusively psychological definition of personhood also overlooks other dimensions of the human psyche, including the integral aspects of human subconscious and emotion, which play a crucial role in the human nature of self-transcendence. By not taking into consideration one's emotional life and subconscious mental world, a person's inner emotional unity is jeopardized, resulting in inner conflicts or imbalances that manifest in the person's inability or reluctance to be open to others. Such a person tends to be rigidly enclosed in narcissistic self-absorption, and this has the net effect of undermining the person's freedom, which is grounded not only in the exercise of self-determination in choice but also in the response of self-transcendence—that is, in reaching out to others toward mutuality and community. The truly authentic free self is one that is neither imprisoned by nor burdened with itself, but that freely, creatively and responsively makes itself available to others. An exclusively psychological account of human personhood is thus incomplete and compromises the wholeness of the person by undermining the relational pole of our being.

This reductionistic and individualistic psychological account reveals itself to be severely inadequate when applied to concrete situations, for it excludes many members of *Homo sapiens*—including fetuses, neonates, the irreversibly comatose and the hopelessly senile—who otherwise are recognized as human persons. Its proponents often try to conceal this inadequacy by creating separate provisions to include those human beings whom they exclude. For example, infants cannot be killed and those in the permanent vegetative state cannot have their organs removed for transplant because the dominant social ethos does not permit them to be "defined out of existence," even though both categories of human beings are not persons. Charles Hartshorne, for example, is adamant that only human beings with the capacity to speak, reason and make decisions qualify to be called "actual persons," whereas fetuses and the hopelessly senile are only "possible persons." These "possible persons" may have to be treated as persons but only for "symbolic reasons,"[66] yet I am at a loss as to what they are meant to symbolize.

James W. Walters argues in his recent book that higher brain function is the fundamental requirement for the designation of the person.[67] Yet he admits that this position is inadequate in dealing with questions of marginal life, and he devotes a whole chapter of his book to providing a much more nuanced

---

[66]Charles Hartshorne, "Concerning Abortion: An Attempt at a Rational View," *Christian Century* 98 (January 1981): 42-45.

[67]James W. Walters, *What Is a Person? An Ethical Exploration* (Urbana: University of Illinois Press, 1997), p. 26.

account of what he calls "proximate personhood," which acknowledges the importance of human potentiality, physical development and social bonding in human existence.[68] H. Tristram Engelhardt Jr. basically adopts the same criterion of higher-brain capacity for human personhood, but he also recognizes that people respect human beings who do not yet possess or have lost their rational capacities. So he allows for a category of "social personhood," which is applied to biological human beings who are to be treated as "social persons" even when they do not meet the conditions for "strict personhood."[69] The net result of these well-intentioned adjustments on personhood is to put society's moral commitments to human individuals on a sliding scale based on what Loren Lomasky has called the "meritocracy of mind"[70] and to reduce personhood to a quantifiable quality that changes as a function of one's performance. As Singer boldly pronounces, "Hardly anyone really believes that all human life is of equal worth. . . . [We] should treat human beings in accordance with their ethically relevant characteristics."[71]

In conclusion, I should emphasize that while I oppose any definition of human personhood that is exclusively based on the person's psychological capabilities, I am not thereby dismissing the human psyche as an important dimension of the human person. I believe that the human psyche contributes to both the substantial and relational poles of the human person and that it establishes the human person as a unity and a center of the self with its own consciousness and self-consciousness. These capacities serve to underlie the one's coherence, consistency and identity as well as one's ability for self-reflection, highlighting a person's singularity and particularity. Furthermore, the possession of human freedom and willpower impart to each person her own unique autonomy, individuality and integrity, and together with the person's ability to appreciate worthiness of praise or blame, the person is able to construe herself as a moral being—to be a moral agent. And as a moral agent, she is ready to transcend herself to reach toward others as a relational being. These are all important functional capacities of the person that are enabled by her psychological faculties and are generally possessed and valued by persons; but on their own, they are neither necessary nor sufficient criteria of the human person. True personhood only emerges when the human being is considered as a complete psychosomatic unity with all its physical, psychological and social dimensions. And to this unity I will now turn.

---

[68]Ibid., pp. 62-77.
[69]Engelhardt, *Foundations of Bioethics*, p. 117.
[70]Loren E. Lomasky, *Persons, Rights and the Moral Community* (Oxford: Oxford University Press, 1987), p. 194.
[71]Singer, *Rethinking Life and Death*, pp. 190-91.

4

Person as a
Psychosomatic
Unity

*M*ultidimensional Humanness

One of the major problems with an exclusively psychological definition of personhood is the implication that the person is found only in a unique moment in life, usually the acquisition of neocortical function. As Joseph Fletcher says, "Neocortical function is the key to humanness, the essential trait, the human *sine qua non.* . . . [It] is the first-order requirement . . . of a human being."[1] Applying the same line of reasoning to the other end of the spectrum of life, L. J. Schneiderman and his associates declare that medical treatment which only preserves "continued biologic life without consciousness or autonomy" is futile because the body is being sustained without benefiting the person;[2] loss of neocortical function marks the loss of personhood, and consequently these "bodies" might best be abandoned to a nursing home, allowed to die or treated as already dead. Again, Fletcher says that "to be dead 'humanly' speaking is to be ex-cerebral, no matter how long the body remains."[3] As I have discussed, such an exclusively psychological understanding of personhood—which abstracts the person from his context

---

[1]Joseph Fletcher, "Four Indicators of Humanhood: The Enquiry Matures," *Hastings Center Report* 4 (December 1974): 5.

[2]L. J. Schneiderman, N. S. Jecker and A. R. Jonsen, "Medical Futility: Its Meaning and Ethical Implications," *Annals of Internal Medicine* 112, no. 12 (1990): 950.

[3]Fletcher, "Four Indicators," p. 5.

(bodily or otherwise) and divorces the person from the life of the body and its destiny—is ultimately unrealistic. On the other hand, an exclusively biological understanding of personhood is equally unrealistic, for there is obviously something incomplete about the person when the body is no longer animated by its spirit. Hence, the very nature of the human person militates against any "essentialist" reduction.

If one reflects on the various dimensions of humanness (biological, psychological, relational and historical), it becomes apparent that all these dimensions are essential in defining a human person. Each may play a different role with varying degrees of importance through one's life, but it is difficult, if not outright impossible (and certainly unwise), to single out any one dimension as normative and decisive in defining human personhood. The insights of modern psychosomatic medicine have emphasized the interdependencies and interactions between the body and the psyche for the proper functioning of the human being. Interhuman relations, in turn, are dependent on the attainment of a minimal level of biological and psychological functions. Any attempt to define human personhood in a single dimension necessarily overlooks the multidimensional (biological, psychological, relational and historical) interrelationships present in every human being. This mistake is often made by "essentialists," who assume that a common overriding characteristic of humankind's essence (such as genetics, rationality, sociality and so on) can be found. However, as I noted above, each dimension is vital; a person only emerges through a multidimensional matrix, including the total bio-psycho-socio-cultural-historical context. As Paul Tillich writes, "Man should not be considered as a composite of several levels, such as body, soul, spirit, but as a multidimensional unity."[4] In addition, one may incorporate the Christian tradition, which emphasizes that the transcendental dimension, that is, the human being's personal relationship with God, is the ultimate ground for this unity and thus human personhood.

Philosophical Traditions

As I have shown, René Descartes is more commonly remembered as the premiere advocate for a dualistic understanding of the human as comprising two mutually exclusive, self-subsistent and ontologically distinct entities: mind and body. But according to Richard Zaner, Descartes understands the body in two ways: first, in a mathematical or metaphysical way, and second, in a daily, ordinary-experience way. The body/soul dichotomy is applicable

---

[4]Paul Tillich, "Meaning of Health," in *On Moral Medicine: Theological Perspectives in Medical Ethics,* ed. Stephen E. Lammers and Allen Verhey (Grand Rapids, Mich.: Eerdmans, 1987), p. 162.

only in the first sense; in the second sense, the body exhibits the composite union of body and soul, which cannot be understood by mathematics or metaphysics. The body in clinical medicine belongs to the second sense, in which the mind is believed to be not only connected to the body, but "intimately" so.[5] "I am not lodged in my body merely as a pilot in a ship," Descartes says, "but so intimately conjoined, and as it were intermingled with it, that with it I form a unitary whole."[6] This analysis suggests that at least from the practical point of view, Descartes is more holistic than most critics give him credit for.

Descartes's contemporaries struggle with this same difficult task of trying to understand the "intimate union" of body and soul. Benedict de Spinoza argues that for the union to be comprehensible, mind and body need to be essential to one another: the body as a mirror of the soul and the mind the idea of the body.[7] Later on, Edmund Husserl attempts to characterize this intimate union as the "body-as-mine," a dictum echoed by Gabriel Marcel's "my body qua mine" and ultimately Jean-Paul Sartre's "I *am* my body." These existentialist and phenomenological inquires are consistent with scientific findings in modern psychosomatic medicine that the human "psyche and soma are inextricably bound together as constituents of an integral, contextual whole."[8] This psychosomatic unity endows the embodied person with a "valuative" character, which explains why every medical intervention that intrudes into the human person falls within the realm of the moral order.

Psychosomatic Medicine and a Holistic Model of Personhood

In the past half century, social scientists as well as clinical practitioners have become increasingly aware of the inadequacy of medicine that is strictly based on a biomedical model in which every living process, normal or pathological, is supposed to be traceable to an anatomical, physiological, biochemical or molecular basis, with no reference to the psychological, social, cultural or spiritual dimensions of the person. Social scientists, working in the fields of psychology, sociology, anthropology and religion, have observed that there are often complex "bio-psycho-socio-cultural-historical" antecedents contributing to the causation and influencing the outcome of the dynamic states of health

---

[5]Richard Zaner, *Ethics and the Clinical Encounter* (Englewood Cliffs, N.J.: Prentice-Hall, 1988), pp. 115-18.

[6]René Descartes, "Meditations on First Philosophy," in *The European Philosophers from Descartes to Nietzsche,* ed. Monroe Beardsley (New York: Modern Library, 1960), p. 71.

[7]Benedict de Spinoza, *Ethics,* vol. 2 of *Chief Works* (New York: Dover, 1951), quoted in Richard Zaner, "Body—I. Embodiment: The Phenomenological Tradition," in *Encyclopedia of Bioethics,* ed. Warren T. Reich (New York: Simon & Schuster Macmillan, 1995), 1:295.

[8]Zaner, "Body," 1:298.

and illness. They have rightly questioned the validity of the dichotomization of the human person into mind/body compartments and have begun to see the human person as essentially a multidimensional unity, consisting of mechanical, chemical, biological, psychological, spiritual, cultural and historical dimensions.

On this view, we need to assume a more "holistic" perspective from which each person is seen as "one," uniting within herself all dimensions of life so that in health as well as in sickness there is a "mutual within-each-otherness" of the dimensions.[9] This implies that whenever one dimension of the person is affected, all the other dimensions are involved as well, and the health of the person is ultimately sought in a return to wholeness. The World Health Organization has captured part of this ethos in its definition of health as "a state of complete physical, mental and social well-being and not merely the absence of disease or infirmity."[10] But the strongest impetus for encouraging the evolution of a bio-psycho-socio-cultural-historical (holistic) conceptualization of health and disease (and indirectly the person) has been provided in the last half of a century by the development of "psychosomatic" medicine.[11] This development has been stimulated, in turn, by the concept of the psychogenesis of disease and the notion of holism.[12]

The Psychogenic Concept

Psychogenesis simply states that bodily disease may be caused by psychological factors.[13] Since Galen proposes that passions (emotions) such as grief, anger, lust and fear represent definitive causes of diseases as early as the second century A.D., the role of emotions as putative pathogenic factors has rarely been disputed. But psychogenic etiology had not been substantiated by any empirical proof until 1833, when American physician William Beaumont reports that emotions such as anger and fear influence the appearance and function of a patient's exposed gastric mucosa (stomach lining). This landmark report demonstrates the first empirical psychophysiological correlation, which is corroborated by subsequent experimental studies of I. P. Pavlov and W. B. Cannon on the physiological correlates of emotions. On the basis of these observations, psychosomatic medicine has since evolved through three con-

---

[9]Paul Tillich, "Meaning of Health," p. 164.

[10]Tom L. Beauchamp and LeRoy Walters, eds., *Contemporary Issues in Bioethics,* 3rd ed. (Belmont, Calif.: Wadsworth, 1989), p. 80.

[11]A useful short review may be found in Erwin H. Ackerknecht, "The History of Psychosomatic Medicine," *Psychological Medicine* 12 (February 1982): 17-24.

[12]Z. J. Lipowski, "Psychosomatic Medicine: Past and Present, Part I: Historical Background," *Canadian Journal of Psychiatry* 31 (February 1986): 2.

[13]For a brief but useful review, see Z. J. Lipowski, "Psychosomatic Medicine, Part I."

ceptual and methodological stages: the psychoanalytic, the biopsychosocial and the psychophysiological.

The psychoanalytic stage is established by Sigmund Freud's psychoanalytic theories. While Freud himself remains uninterested in the correlation between psychogenic factors and the etiology of physical disease, his concept of conversion has been used by his followers to explain illnesses (physical) as symbolic representations of repressed inner conflicts within one's consciousness.[14] A more creative revision of Freud's theory, proposed by Franz Alexander, is to hypothesize psychological causation as *nonsymbolic,* suggesting that unresolved unconscious conflicts engender chronic emotional tensions, whose specific physiological correlates (e.g., gastric secretion) would result in dys-function of and eventually damage to the target organ. This nonsymbolic psychogenetic theory maintains that psychogenesis involves a simple linear causal chain: the first link consists of a cerebral process of that unconscious conflict of opposing and often repressed emotional forces acting in concert with other biological and constitutional factors to produce the harmful effect in the target organ.[15]

The psychoanalytic approach is improved further by the biopsychosocial understanding of health and disease of the person. In this second phase of development, psychosomatic medicine recognizes that personality and psychosocial factors may, through the activities of the brain, either disturb or maintain homeostasis and thereby affect health either negatively or positively. In general, epidemiological studies have confirmed that a stressful life situation either uncovers one's vulnerability to a particular illness, resulting in its manifest onset, or exacerbates a preexisting illness, whereas the availability of social supports may enhance the ability to cope with existing diseases. Furthermore, recent studies on the relationship between personality and health suggest that the connection between stress and disease is influenced by the meaning that a person assigns to a given stressful event. Specifically, this ascribed meaning modifies the emotional arousal and the physiological changes that disrupt homeostasis. Whether a given event will elicit an effect depends largely on the individual's personality, current emotional state, access to social support and other coping resources. Thus whether an event or situation will result in stress or health changes depends in part on the individual person and not solely on the environmental condition or event.[16]

---

[14]Ibid., p. 3.

[15]Ibid., pp. 3-4.

[16]Z. J. Lipowski, "Psychosomatic Medicine: Past and Present, Part II: Current State," *Canadian Journal of Psychiatry* 31 (February 1986): 10. While many studies in the past have concentrated on human responses to psychosocial factors as the cause of physical illness, some recent "somatopsychic" studies have investigated the effect of physical illness on the patient's

But both psychoanalytical and biopsychosocial models too simplistically attempt to linearly equate "psychogenic" with "psychosomatic" in the sense of something "psychic" causing something "somatic." What is ultimately required is the identification of physiological pathways and processes that allow mental states and events—derived either intrapsychically (i.e., within the psyche of the person) or indirectly through stressful life situations—to bring about changes in various body functions. In the past two to three decades, three mediating pathways or mechanisms have been identified: psychoendocrinology, psychoimmunology and psychoneurophysiology. The psychoendocrinal pathway refers to the effects of psychosocial stimuli on physiological functions through the secretion of hormones. For example, constantly working under the stress of deadlines has been found to lead to the increased secretion of "stress" hormones (e.g., adrenaline and cortisol); this in turn initiates changes in a wide range of specific physiological functions and metabolic processes. The psychoimmunologic pathway refers to the effects of the psychosocial stimulation of one's immune system. Animal studies have shown that subjecting rats to the stress of shock to the tail results in suppression of lymphocytic stimulation (LSS), a necessary defense mechanism of the body. This finding has been corroborated in human clinical studies showing the suppression of LSS following conjugal bereavement. In other animal studies, crowding, noise or exposure to a predator can increase susceptibility to diseases known to be influenced by the immune system. The psychoneurophysiological pathway is through direct activation of specific cerebral structures and mechanisms, such as the limbic system, by internal and external emotional events. Once activated, it will be released in the brain to influence motor and visceral target organs.[17] In a sense these psychoneurological pathways are not directly "psychosomatic," but they do serve "to delineate the highly com-

---

psychosocial functioning and behavior. For example, after studying over seven hundred chronically ill patients, B. R. Cassileth et al. found that those who suffered from a variety of physical illnesses remained psychologically intact despite their illnesses, indicating that in general, the chronically physically ill adapt well (Lipowski, "Psychosomatic Medicine," pp. 9-10). Their emotional state is dependent more on the *severity* of their illness rather than on the *kind* of illness with which they are afflicted. It seems that a patient's style of coping is significant for determining whether or not the illness will lead to psychological and social behavioral changes. The effects of physical illness on psychosocial and behavioral function serve to emphasize further the interplay of psychological and biological variables in a human person.

[17]Specifically, once stimulated, the limbic system, which includes the hypothalamus, will produce secretions to act on the pituitary-adrenal axis and the autonomic nervous system as well through hypothalamic-releasing hormones. Z. J. Lipowski, "Psychosomatic Medicine: Past and Present, Part III: Current Research," *Canadian Journal of Psychiatry* 31 (February 1986): 15-16.

plex neuro-physiological and neuro-endocrine pathways and processes whereby personally meaningful information and the consequent emotional arousal can exert effects on all physiological processes in the periphery."[18] Recent neuroscientific research suggests that the brain plays a major role in the maintenance of health and the pathogenesis of disease; it integrates all inputs, processes them in a variety of pathways and ultimately mediates responses to all psychosocial stimuli by either maintaining, disturbing or restoring homeostasis.[19]

The Concept of Holism

Holism, another basic concept in psychosomatic medicine, is derived from the Greek word *holos* (a whole) and entails certain notions about human nature, health and illness. Ancient Greek thinkers, including Plato, Aristotle and Hippocrates all view the *mind* and *body* as an *indivisible unity*. Plato, in *Charmides,* advises people "not to attempt to cure . . . the body without the soul . . . for the part will never be well unless the whole is well." In 1859, French physician Claude Bernard proposes that there is a *"milieu interieur"* (internal environment) within the body that mediates between living tissue and the external environment, and whose stability is essential for maintaining health.[20] In 1930, Cannon formulates the concept of *homeostasis,* which suggests that the internal milieu is a steady state that is normally maintained by the body's autonomic nervous system but that can be affected by physical and psychosocial factors, thereby affecting the function of the organism as a whole.[21] In this century, Adolf Meyer conceived, under the label of "psychobiology," of mind and body as distinct yet integral aspects of the whole psychobiological human organism. The holistic implication of psychobiology has greatly facilitated the course of psychosomatic medicine and enabled holism to become the second major connotation of the term *psychosomatic.*

Recently some writing from a phenomenological perspective have made further advancement in the consideration of the person as a "psychosomatic" whole. While crediting the psychosomatic approach for considering all the biopsychosocial determinants of health and illness, they propose that it is not enough to conceive of psyche, soma and the external world as separate entities that exert influence on each other, because the "whole" is more than the sum of the parts. Viewed this way, the psychosomatic whole remains a mere summation

---

[18]Ibid., p. 16.

[19]H. Weiner, "The Prospects for Psychosomatic Medicine: Selected Topics," *Psychosomatic Medicine* 44, no. 6 (1982): 491-517.

[20]Edward J. Kollar and Michael Alcalay, "The Physiological Basis for Psychosomatic Medicine: A Historical View," *Annals of Internal Medicine* 67, no. 4 (1967): 885-86.

[21]Ibid., pp. 886-87.

of separate fragments, and the addition of fragments and separate entities, no matter how comprehensive or exhaustive, can never reconstruct the whole living patient, in all her distinctly human aspects, inhabiting her individual world. Instead, these writers claim that psyche and soma arise as distinct aspects from a corporeal field, the lived body, which is in turn embedded in the world. They are not externally connected entities standing side by side; instead, they overlap and coexist and are intertwined and inseparably interconnected.[22]

Clearly, such a unified view of the multiple facets of human existence does not begin with an assumption of the separation of mind, body and world. Rather, the notion of the "lived body" as a corporeal field understands the body as consisting of networks of distinct aspects, with multiple intertwinings, so that it is impossible to say which alteration is "caused" by which network system. At most, we can only determine that in certain areas, particular influences are more concentrated.[23] Furthermore, phenomenological "holists" insist that the lived body is always embedded within the life world. On this view, body and world are distinguishable in that one cannot be reduced to or absorbed by the other; yet they should not be considered as two separate entities that stand side by side. Rather like body networks, body and world are interconnected and intertwined in multiple ways. Changes of the world and body are interdependent rather than independent occurrences. The body takes on a form or a figure such as a working figure, a fighting figure or a loving figure only in accordance with the world in which its task lies. Understanding the lived body as dynamically interconnected within itself and with the external world permits mutually simultaneous interaction and distinction between body and world. The meanings of the life-world get "mapped" onto the lived body (i.e., translated in and through the lived body), and the lived body with its meanings gets translated into the structures of the life-world. So closely are the body and world intertwined that these authors claim it is not certain "whether changes are primarily 'located' in the body or in the world: illness is always already 'located' in the world as well as in the body."[24]

Such a holistic view of human existence immediately calls into question the type of simplistic treatment of psychosomatic medicine in which psychological

---

[22]G. Northoff, M. A. Schwartz and O. P. Wiggins, "Psychosomatics, the Lived Body and Anthropological Medicine: Concerning a Case of Atopic Dermatitis," in *The Body in Medical Thought and Practice,* ed. Drew Leder (Dordrecht, Netherlands: Kluwer Academic, 1992), p. 141.

[23]The hypothalamic-pituitary is a good example of such an intertwining between the neural and endocrine networks, both of which are distributed through and compose the whole lived body, wherein they are influencing, regulating and mediating. But other network systems, e.g., the immunologic, also exert their influences.

[24]Northoff, Schwartz and Wiggins, "Psychosomatics," p. 141.

disturbances are seen to be primary and physiological secondary. By contrast, this view argues that psychic and physiological aspects are inextricably intertwined so that neither is primary or secondary. We can only say that certain physiological or psychological aspects arise and emerge as the lived body interacts with the life-world. On such a view, even the psychosomatic or bio-psychosocial model has to be viewed as a methodological reduction representing an abstraction from reality, although for the purpose of investigation it may be a necessary one. But the holistic view emphasizes the blurring of the boundaries and the "mutual within-each-otherness" of the various bio-psycho-socio-cultural-historical dimensions of human existence. It interprets the human reality as bio-psycho-socio-cultural-historical interpenetration and interdependency, existing in a psychosomatic understanding of health, disease and personhood. As such, it provides a rich insight not only into the multidimensional nature of human persons, but particularly into the inseparability and interconnectedness of the human person as a psychosomatic unity.

Theological Understanding of the Person as an Integrated Whole

As I have already noted, even though the church fathers are not always successful in resisting the Greek two-substance dualism of the body and soul, they manage to grasp the significance of the human being as an ensouled body or embodied soul—that is, as a psychosomatic unity. Irenaeus teaches a trichotomistic view of humans as consisting of body, soul and spirit;[25] and in his *Against Heresies,* he emphasizes the "commingling" and "blending" of the body and soul in order to attain perfection in the human person.[26] Similarly, Athanasius rejects the common Platonic antithesis of soul and body even though he acknowledges the immortality of the soul. To Athanasius, the human soul is not exterior to the body but is bound to it by God's will.[27] His respect for the human body is seen in his understanding of the incarnation of Christ, who, as far as he is concerned, cannot be worshiped apart from the body:

> And we neither divide the body, being such, from the Word, and worship it by itself, nor when we wish to worship the Word do we set Him far apart from the

---

[25]Johannes Quasten, *Patrology* (Alten, Tex.: Christian Classics, 1994), 1:308-10.

[26]Irenaeus *Adversus haereses* 5.6.1: "For the perfect man consists in the commingling and the union of the soul receiving the Spirit of the Father, and the mixture of that fleshly nature which was also moulded after the image of God. . . . For if anyone take away the substance of flesh, that is, of the handiwork of God, and consider the spirit only, such then would not be a spiritual man but would be the spirit of man, or the Spirit of God. But when the spirit here blended with the soul is united to the body, the man becomes spiritual and perfect" (*Ante-Nicene Fathers,* vol. 1, ed. James Donaldson [Grand Rapids, Mich.: Eerdmans, 1975]).

[27]Alvyn Pettersen, *Athanasius* (Ridgefield, Conn.: Morehouse, 1995), p. 28.

flesh. . . . Who is so senseless as to say to the Lord: "Leave the Body that I may worship Thee."[28]

Similarly the Cappadocians, especially Gregory of Nyssa, hold the view that humankind is from the beginning a mixture of body and soul. In writing a refutation to the doctrine of the preexistent human soul, Gregory of Nyssa says, "But as man is one, the being consisting of soul and body, we are to suppose that the beginning of his existence is one, common to both parts," and this is because when God breathes his own breath of life into a man or woman, "the divine nature produces in man a blending, *migma,* of the intelligible and the sensible."[29]

When we turn to the Latin fathers, we also observe that in spite of the pressure from the Greek dualism, they make a genuine effort to integrate and unify the body and soul as properly ordered members. Tertullian (A.D. 155-220) insists that the whole person is made of both body and soul.[30] Although the body is the servant of the soul, the body as God has created it is indispensable for the proper functioning of the soul:

> For what enjoyment of nature is there, what produce of the world, what relish of the elements, which is not imparted to the soul by means of the body? How can it be otherwise? . . . The sight, the hearing, the taste, the smell, the touch? . . . The acts come through the flesh [the body]; through the flesh also effect is given to the mind's pursuits and powers; all work, too, and business and offices of life, are accomplished by the flesh; so that the flesh, which is accounted the minister and servant of the soul, turns out to be also its associate and co-heir.[31]

The human person as a unity of the body and soul is so commingled that Tertullian says, "So intimate is the union, that it may be deemed to be uncertain whether the flesh bears about the soul, or the soul the flesh; or whether the flesh acts as *apparitor* to soul, or the soul to the flesh."[32]

Another Latin father, Augustine (A.D. 354-430), who is well known for his struggles against lust to live a life of chastity and for his famous lament that "the body weighs down the soul," nonetheless believes that ultimately "it is not the body, but the corruptibility of the body, which is a burden to the soul."[33]

---

[28]Athanasius *Epistula ad Adelphium* 3, quoted in Quasten, *Patrology,* 3:75.

[29]Gregory of Nyssa *On the Making of Man* 29.1, *The Nicene and Post-Nicene Fathers,* 2nd series, ed. Philip Schaff Grand Rapids, Mich.: Eerdmans, 1973), 5:420.

[30]Tertullian *Against Marcion* 1.24, *The Ante-Nicene Fathers,* ed. Alexander Roberts and James Donaldson Peabody, Mass.: Hendrickson, 1994), 3:290.

[31]Tertullian *The Resurrection of the Flesh* 7, *The Ante-Nicene Fathers,* ed. Alexander Roberts and James Donaldson Peabody, Mass.: Hendrickson, 1994), 3:550-51.

[32]Ibid.

[33]Augustine *The City of God* 13.16, *The Nicene and Post-Nicene Fathers,* 1st series, ed. Philip Schaff Grand Rapids, Mich.: Eerdmans, 1973), 2:252.

Augustine believes that despite the Fall, the human body continues to bear the marks of glory with which the Creator originally endows it.[34] Furthermore, the body serves a crucial function for the salvation of the sinful person:

> It is said, "the flesh profiteth nothing," . . . but this means of itself. Let the spirit be added to the flesh, as charity is added to knowledge, and it profiteth more. . . . But it is through the flesh that the spirit acted for our salvation. . . . For how should the sound of the Word reach us except through the voice of the flesh?[35]

In some of his later works, Augustine is more explicit in stating that the human being is not just the soul but a unity of body-soul. In *The City of God* he asks the rhetorical question, "Is it neither the soul by itself nor the body by itself that constitutes the man, but the two combined, the soul and the body being each a part of him, but the whole man consisting of both?"[36]

As I have previously discussed, in adopting the Aristotelian metaphysical principles of form and matter, Thomas Aquinas is able to formulate a more holistic account of human nature as soul and body in intimate unity. He says, "It is clear that man is not a soul only, but something composed of soul and body. . . . Hence a hand, or a foot is not called a hypostasis, or a person; nor, likewise, is the soul alone so-called, since it is a part of the human species."[37] But in the end, Aquinas has to part with the Aristotelian view that the soul is only the form of the body and is thus not capable of existence independent of the body. At this point Aquinas remains an Augustinian in claiming that the soul is both the form of the body and an intellectual substance on its own. But as long as the body still exists, the soul is united with it, for it has "an aptitude and a natural inclination to be united to the body."[38] And since the soul is united to the body as its substantial form, it is united to the body in such a way that it is not only in the whole body, but also in each part of the body.

Much of Augustine's teaching on this subject has been retained by the Protestant Reformers. Like Augustine, John Calvin subscribes to the doctrine of the immortality of the soul, which is seen to be united with the body just as someone dwells in a house. According to Calvin, the soul's function is divided into

---

[34]"Even in the body, though it dies like that of the beasts . . . what goodness of God, what providence of the Great Creator, is apparent! . . . And even apart from its adaptation to the work required of it, there is such a symmetry in its various parts, and so beautiful a proportion maintained, that one is at a loss to decide whether in creating the body, greater regard was paid to utility or to beauty" (Augustine *City of God* 22.24).

[35]Augustine *In Evangelium Johannis tractatus* 27.5, quoted in Margaret Ruth Miles, *Augustine on the Body* (Missoula, Mont.: Scholars Press, 1979), pp. 7-8.

[36]Augustine *The City of God*, trans. Henry Bettenson (London: Penguin, 1984), pp. 849-50.

[37]Thomas Aquinas *Summa Theologiae* 1.Q75.A4, trans. Fathers of the English Dominican Province (Westminster, Md.: Christian Classics, 1981), p. 366.

[38]Ibid., 1.Q76.A1 (p. 372).

mundane and more lofty activities. For the smooth operation of the body in one's earthly life, the soul has the function to "animate all its parts and render its organs fit and useful for their actions," but the chief activity of the soul is "to arouse him to honor God. . . . Just as man was made for meditation upon the heavenly life, so it is certain that the knowledge of it was engraved upon his soul."[39]

In the twentieth century, Swiss theologian Karl Barth is generally critical of the traditional Christian anthropology sketched above, saying it borrows too much from Hellenistic dualism. He does not deny that early church fathers and medieval theologians both in the Roman and Reformed traditions have tried to understand the human soul and body as "essentially and necessarily united," but he is critical that, despite these efforts, the soul and body have been treated "only as two 'parts' of human nature. . . . Each is to be understood as a special substance, self-contained and qualitatively different in relation to the other."[40] He is concerned that this unbiblical and unchristian view will lead ultimately to conflict and finally to separation between the two substances since they have no essential interrelation.[41] As far as Barth is concerned, it is not enough to speak of the interconnection, commingling, blending or mixture of the body and soul. Nothing less than the total unity of soul and body will suffice: "He is soul as he is a body and this is his body. Hence he is not only soul that has' a body, . . . but he is bodily soul, as he is also besouled body."[42] In other words, the soul would not be soul if it were not bodily, and the body would not be body if it were not besouled.

Barth is explicit in stating that the way the soul and body unite is not merely a "combination," "union" or "association"; rather, the person is "wholly and simultaneously both soul and body, always and in every relation soulful, and always and in every relation bodily . . . for the concrete reality of man consists in his being both, and only in both one."[43] Barth goes so far as to say that the soul cannot exist for itself. "Soul can awake and be only as soul of a body. Soul presupposes a body. . . . Thus in being soul, it is not without body. It is, only as it is soul of a body."[44] Likewise, the body is not merely an object of

---

[39]John Calvin, *Institutes of the Christian Religion,* ed. John T. McNeill, trans. Ford Lewis Battles (Philadelphia: Westminster Press, 1960), 1.15.6.

[40]Karl Barth *Church Dogmatics* 3/2, ed. G. W. Bromiley and T. F. Torrance (Edinburgh: T & T Clark, 1960).

[41]"In general, the character and result of this anthropology are marked by a separation of soul and body, an exaltation of the soul over the body, a humiliation of the body under the soul, in which both really become not merely abstractions but in fact two 'co-existing' figments" (Ibid., §46.3).

[42]Ibid., §46.2.

[43]Ibid., §46.3.

[44]Ibid.

self-movement or self-activity "but is for the soul as the soul is for it."[45] Barth sees that the human soul and body are united because a human being has spirit that is given by the Spirit, and to have spirit "means that he is grounded, constituted and maintained by God as the soul of his body."[46] For one to be soul of one's body entails the immediate action of Spirit. Without the Spirit, the human being cannot help but appear as a "puzzling duality" of body and soul, two conflicting substances alongside each other, "inadequately glued together. . . . Our statement that man is wholly and at the same time both soul and body presupposes the first statement that man is as he has Spirit."[47] It is therefore on the premise that the Spirit unifies the human being together as soul and body that a true Christian anthropology can be advocated: soul and body—a duality in unity.

Biblical Tradition of the Human Being as a Substantial Psychosomatic Unity

While the church fathers have to struggle between classical dualism, which tends to reduce the essence of human personhood to the soul, and the Christian doctrines of incarnation and resurrection, which favor the human person as a unity of body and soul, biblical writers do not experience this tension in their description of the relationship of body and soul (mind). Biblical anthropology maintains a consistently holistic view of a human being as a psychosomatic unity. Its point of departure is based on the text of Genesis 2:7: "The Lord formed the man from the dust of the ground and breathed into his nostrils the breath of life, and the man became a living soul [*nephesh*]." While *nephesh* is often translated as "soul," in other places it is correctly translated as "throat," "neck" or "stomach." The term thus denotes both spiritual and physical organs and functions, referring not so much to specific parts but to the life of the whole person.[48] As Bruce Waltke indicates, in the Hebrew mind, "man does not have a soul but . . . man is soul."[49] He is *nephesh,* a living soul. To that we may add that one does not merely have a body but is embodied—one is a living body. There is no hint in biblical anthropology of any systematic distinction between physical and spiritual organs;[50] a human being is made as a whole.

---

[45]Ibid.

[46]Ibid., §46.2.

[47]Ibid., §46.3.

[48]John W. Cooper, *Body, Soul and Life Everlasting* (Grand Rapids, Mich.: Eerdmans, 1989), p. 48.

[49]Bruce Waltke, "Reflections from the Old Testament on Abortion," *Journal of the Christian Medical Society* 19, no. 1 (1988): 26.

[50]For a comprehensive review of Old Testament anthropology, see Hans Walter Wolf, *Anthropology of the Old Testament,* trans. Margaret Kohl (Philadelphia: Fortress, 1974).

This Old Testament holistic understanding of human beings is also reflected in the variety and interchangeability of other anthropological terms such as *neshama, ruach, basar, qereb, leb* and so on. Their usage does not support the notion of an immortal, imperishable, immaterial soul that functions independently of the mortal, perishable, material body. On the contrary, Old Testament writers habitually localize different mental and emotional functions of the soul in different parts of the body. The "inner parts" of the human person are represented by the "kidneys" (*kilyoth,* Ps 7:10 Heb; "heart," Ps 7:9 NIV); grief is represented by the "liver" (*kabed,* Lam 2:11 Heb; "heart," NIV), so that the liver bile renders a person bitter; a person's will and desires originate from her heart. This correspondence between mental/emotional functions and bodily organs suggests that in biblical anthropology, body and soul—the outer and inner life—exist only in a relation of mutuality, complementarity, reciprocity, interdependence and interpenetration. This essential holism is best summarized in the Israelite Shema: "Love the LORD your God with all your heart and with all your soul and with all your strength" (Deut 6:5 NIV). To the ancient Israelites, a human being is created by and appears before God as a whole person.

If we turn to the New Testament and particularly the Pauline corpus, we find that Paul's anthropology is entirely consistent with his Jewish background, which views the self as an integrated whole. Paul acknowledges that this integrated whole has both corporeal and incorporeal dimensions, with the former represented by mainly two words: *soma* (body) and *sarx* (flesh), which are used synonymously in many occasions (see, e.g., 1 Cor 5:3; 2 Cor 4:10-11; Col 1:22; 2:5). The terms Paul uses to describe the incorporeal dimension include *pneuma* (spirit), *nous* (mind), *psyche* (soul) and *kardia* (heart). Again, these words do not differ significantly in meaning or usage (see, e.g., Rom 6:17; 1 Cor 2:11; 5:3; 14:14-16; 2 Cor 4:6; Eph 6:6; Phil 1:27; Col 3:23; 1 Tim 1:5). While Paul at times distinguishes the incorporeal from the corporeal—as when he exalts the believers of the Corinthian church "to be devoted in both body *[soma]* and spirit *[pneuma]*" (1 Cor 7:34)—he also describes certain incorporeal functions with conventional corporeal terms, such as when *kardia* (heart) and *splanchna* (liver) are used to denote human emotions. Indeed *kardia* stands for "the whole of the inner being of man"[51] in both its corporeal and incorporeal dimensions. The overlapping of these terms suggests that Paul apparently sees the corporeal and the incorporeal as a unity.

Paul often speaks of the whole self using both corporeal and incorporeal terms that in different contexts designate only one particular aspect of the per-

---

[51]Johannes Behm, "Kardia," in *Theological Dictionary of the New Testament,* ed. Gerhard Kittel and Gerhard Friedrich, trans. G. W. Bromiley (Grand Rapids, Mich.: Eerdmans, 1964-1976), 3:612.

son. In these instances, Paul is neither contradicting the various usages of these terms nor confusing the parts with the whole. Rather, "he is viewing the whole self from a particular standpoint, or stressing the contribution of a particular aspect of the self to the functioning of the whole."[52] For example, in Romans 12:1, to offer one's body *(soma)* is to offer one's entire self, corporeally and incorporeally as the whole person. Similarly, in Philippians 2:30, Paul writes that Epaphroditus nearly died, having risked his *psyche* (soul) for the work of Christ, in which case *psyche* obviously refers to the whole person, including his bodily existence. Likewise, while *soma* (body) and *pneuma* (spirit) are distinguishable, they are united in devotion to Christ (1 Cor 7:34); and both *sarx* (flash) and *pneuma* must be purified if the person is to become holy (2 Cor 7:1). The best yet most misunderstood verse highlighting Paul's view of the self as unity in diversity is found in 1 Thessalonians 5:23. This verse—which contains the triad spirit, soul and body *(pneuma, psyche* and *soma)*—has been used by many as a basis for arguing that Paul holds a trichotomistic anthropology; in reality Paul's intention is just the opposite. Paul blesses the believers, praying, "May God himself . . . sanctify you through and through *[holoteleis]*. May your whole *[holokleros]* spirit, soul and body be kept blameless" (NIV); he is trying to emphasize that they are preserved as integrated and whole human beings at Christ's return.

This biblical understanding of the human person as an integrated whole, body and soul, also finds support in the biblical concept of the *imago Dei*. David Clines says that "according to Genesis 1 man does not have the image of God, nor is he made *in* the image of God, but is himself the image of God."[53] This implies that the image of God is a matter pertaining to our entire authentic humanness and that it is not to be related to certain particular qualities, capacities or characteristics. By making reference to ancient Near Eastern understandings of the notion of image, Clines suggests that the image of God can only be understood as "a three-dimensional object,"[54] thus stressing the importance of the body as part of the image. The human flesh is just as much the image of God as is human psychology. "Man is the flesh-and-blood image of the invisible God,"[55] because God wills his image to be corporeal animated man.[56] This biblical teaching of the image of God as an indivisible unity of a psychosomatic whole is reaffirmed by the New Testament eschatology, in

---

[52]J. Knox Chamblin, *Paul and the Self: Apostolic Teaching for Personal Wholeness* (Grand Rapids, Mich.: Baker, 1993), p. 44.

[53]David J. A. Clines, "The Image of God in Man," *Tyndale Bulletin* 19 (1968): 80. This is based on Clines's conclusion that Genesis 1:26 should be translated "Let us make man as our image" or "to be our image."

[54]Ibid., p. 85.

[55]Ibid., p. 86.

[56]W. Eichrodt, *Theology of the Old Testament II* (London: SCM Press, 1967), p. 149.

which the resurrection of the body is emphasized. "The doctrine of the image is thus the protological counterpart of the eschatological doctrine of the resurrection." Man is incomplete without the body, and even in the new heaven and the new earth, humans will yet be given a new body.[57]

Another important theme in the New Testament anthropology is that, as a true human, Jesus Christ is the perfect image of God, body and soul. As Barth puts it, "Jesus is true man in the sense that He is whole man, a meaningfully ordered unity of soul and body."[58] And according to Paul's teaching, the Holy Spirit conforms every human being to be more like Christ, to be the *imago Christi,* the first-born among many. When the Holy Spirit brings life to the children of God (Rom 8:1-4), he renews their whole life, body and soul. All spheres of our life—our mindsets, worldviews, actions and relations—bear the fruits of the Holy Spirit and witness to his presence in our lives. In suffering the persecutions as Christ's apostle, Paul is mindful that "we [are] always carrying in the body the death of Jesus, so that the life of Jesus may also be made visible in our bodies" (2 Cor 4:10 NRSV). All this pertains to the experience of the whole person, so much so that the resurrection of the body may be like the glorious body of the risen Christ (Phil 3:21). Created *imago Dei,* we become *imago Christi* in the Spirit and arrive at the fulfillment of *Gloria Dei est homo.*[59]

If we follow the Augustinian tradition that the *imago Dei* is meant to be understood as the *imago Trinitatis,* and if the Trinity is understood to exist perichoretically in a relationship of mutual dependency, reciprocity and interpenetration (see the next chapter's section "Trinitarian Understanding of Being as Relation"), and if divine relationships are archetypal of created relationships, then the human being may also be viewed as composed of a fundamental differentiation of body and soul that is mutually complementary, interdependent and interpenetrating, with no one dimension assuming primacy or domination. The Holy Spirit who enables the perichoretic flow of life in God is the same Holy Spirit who constitutes, preserves and quickens the human life as body and soul. The modern conception of the human spirit is reductionistic in seeing the spirit as the cognitive mind capable of self-reflection, through which the person is abstracted from the body and isolated from others. But the true Spirit who can truly give human beings a true human spirit integrates the body and the soul. He creates, preserves and quickens the human soul with all of its consciousness, reflections, ideas, intentions, desires and feelings so that the human being is spirit-soul. He also forms, pervades and animates the human

---

[57]Ibid., p. 87.
[58]Barth *Church Dogmatics* 3/2.
[59]Compare Jürgen Moltmann, *God in Creation* (San Francisco: HarperSanFrancisco, 1991), pp. 228-30.

body with all its locutions, actions and relations so that the human being is also spirit-body. The person is a unity, and the Holy Spirit is the one who enables the perichoretic unity of the body and soul (the psychosomatic unity) to give a spirited human life worthy of being the true image of the triune God. In this way, the human being becomes an integrated lived life with its differentiated unity, in which there is constant conversation, input and presence, between the body and soul. As Jürgen Moltmann puts it, "In the lived Gestalt [total pattern of life], body and soul arrive intermittently at a tenable consensus. . . . [They] have made a covenant. They have arrived at a certain equilibrium."[60] It is in this equilibrium that the person as a psychosomatic unity is to be found; and it is as differentiated yet equilibrated unity that a person is enabled to engage "perichoretically" with the other dimensions (social, transcendental) of her life.[61]

Conclusion: Psychosomatic Unity as the Center of the Self

Many people define human personhood in terms of mental activities or social processes in favor of physical embodiment for fear of reducing a human to a physical object, a "thing" or a static substance in the world. But this fear is groundless because "a person can be an object without being a mere object."[62] As the person is seen as a being that involves becoming, as well as an actuality that involves possibility,[63] to the extent that this human actuality entails the mutual interdependence of the physical and personal dimensions of the human nature, it can only be understood in natural terms as a psychosomatic being. The category of natural being or "substance" is particularly important when we appreciate that human beings are not only physical but also profoundly historical beings, and there can be no historical being without physical entity or substance that occupies a physical space and endures over time as a particular life. Here I disagree with Moltmann that "the human being has really no substance in himself; he is a history,"[64] for it is both as an actuality with possibilities in the future, and as a physical and historical being with a past time and space, that the human person finds her ontological root as a created substance in the form of a psychosomatic being.

As an embodied soul or ensouled body, this psychosomatic unity provides a basic structure in every human being, which gives rise to the conscious, need-

---

[60]Ibid., p. 260.

[61]For a more detailed discussion on the concept of perichoresis, see chapter five, "The Relational Dimension of Human Personhood," below.

[62]C. Stephen Evans, "Human Persons as Substantial Achievers," *Philosophia Reformata* 58, no. 1 (1993): 107.

[63]Ibid., p. 109.

[64]Moltmann, *God in Creation,* p. 257.

ful, rational, intentional, purposeful, sensing, thinking, desiring, willing, unifying and acting self or ego—a self that can answer the question, "What is a person?" It is this self or ego that provides each person with a center of direction, a private and subjective inwardness that will never be entirely accessible by others. This self constitutes the core of one's individuality; each one has a self-identity with a life story that is unique and irreplaceable. As an individual ego-self, each also develops internal relations with oneself— we each relate to our self, with our own unique givens: physical, psychological and historical. In self's relation to self, there is both unity and conflict, or, as John Macquarrie puts it, there is "the conjunction of identity and otherness with the self."[65] Some of the statements we commonly use, such as "I am at peace with myself" or "I am angry with myself," are examples of unity or conflict within the individual. As we have seen, with the development of psychosomatic medicine, modern science testifies to the importance of the inner harmony for the well-being of an individual. Further, Christianity has always taught, in the tradition of Pauline anthropology, that a person's indwelling sin will split the self into two, one "true" and one "false," each at war with the other,[66] yet nevertheless both being part of the self.

It is possible to see that the conflict between the "true self" and "false self" is in fact related to some opposing forces deeply embedded in human nature; and one of the manifestations of these inherent forces is the tendency for an individual ego/self to be inclined either toward egoism or toward its opposite: transcendence. In leaning toward egoism, the self narcissistically makes itself an absolute center toward which everything and everyone is pulled and whose interest everyone is expected to serve. A self so inclined is "*incurvatus in se,* curved in upon himself"[67] as the "false self" because the self is finally stifled, choked and suffocated. Such a tendency toward egoism is understood by Martin Luther as the very nature of sin. But setting oneself up as the absolute center to enhance the self is self-defeating; and in the process, one's personhood is diminished because one ignores the relational pole of the being and upsets the dyadic structure of the person.

As we have seen, every being has another pole, relationality, which is the inclination (however weak that may be) for an individual ego/self to open toward that which is beyond the self—transcendence. It is possible for the self, however complete as a unique psychosomatic unity, to see the limitation and the finitude and hence the neediness of the self, constrained in time and space,

---

[65]John Macquarrie, *In Search of Humanity: A Theological and Philosophical Approach* (New York: Crossroad, 1989), p. 44.

[66]See, e.g., Romans 7.

[67]A phrase used by Macquarrie, *In Search of Humanity,* p. 46.

and thus to become aware of the possibility of transcending these limitations and becoming a richer and fuller self by breaking out of the self to the other. It seems, therefore, that each human self is inevitably involved with others in social relations. It is the "toward-other" pole of the human being that is manifested as the human characteristic of transcendence—especially a transcendence toward the other person(s). An individual self affirms and fulfills itself when it actualizes its own potential of freedom and transcendence, not to draw on the other to inflate itself but to enhance the other; and in so doing, the self answers the question, who is a person? This latter aspect of human nature is the social and relational dimension of human personhood, to which I shall now turn.

5

The Relational Dimension of Human Personhood

*T*he Individualistic Bias of the West

As I have demonstrated, both philosophical and theological traditions in the West have favored an individualistic and rationalistic understanding of the self and personhood. This emphasis can be traced back to ancient Greek philosophy, which is the primal fount of Western thought. Pre-Socratic philosophers postulate a rational order to the universe (i.e., a "cosmos" as opposed to "chaos"), and this order, or "physis," is completed in itself, self-subsistent and self-motivating. Because of this order, the totality of things in the universe are all on their own, existing in and through themselves without recourse to anything other than themselves. This objectivist concept of being as being-in-itself is further developed in Plato's notion of ideas. In his world of ideas, each idea is purely what it is in itself, so it is unnecessary for it to have any relation with other ideas. Likewise, a thing is an individual thing purely in itself, defined by its pure identity. Hence, relations with other things are not part of its defining characteristics. Plato's concept of reality is also a form of objectivism: ontologically that which is really real exists-in-itself and by-itself.

This idea of reality-in-itself is further developed in Aristotle's notion of substance. As I have discussed earlier, this notion allows him to give ontological priority to each concrete, determinate individual thing as the ultimate identifiable reality and also to explain and justify the inner content and structure of this reality. Aristotle thus arrives at a conclusion similar to his predecessors': the basic identifiable ontological units are individual substances, having particularity of their own and possessing within themselves the inherent principle governing all the changes and motions that are natural to them. Even though Aristotle's concept of substance allows for a certain degree of dynamism and transcendence, ultimately it continues to foster an inward-looking orientation, since the identity of a thing is defined in virtue of its inner structure and mechanism, and since these characteristics are primarily for the purpose of fulfilling the inherent goals of the substance itself and not of projecting outside of the substance toward the other. The world is thus composed of discrete substances with mechanism and *telos* within themselves.[1]

Any approach to define personhood exclusively from either a biological or psychological dimension may be said to have inherited this individualistic, Hellenistic bias. An exclusively biological definition depends on the appearance of a unique complement of genetic information in a new human being as the primary basis for determining the origin of the individual human person who is worthy of full moral standing; and, according to James W. Walters, this approach betrays an "insensitivity to larger social dimensions of the issue."[2] On the other hand, an exclusively psychological definition holds that only the actual possession of a certain higher-brain function by a particular individual warrants the title of a person. In this regard, I have already shown that the Cartesian "self" is particularly problematic in that the self is not only cognitive in nature but also understands itself to be isolated from the world about which it reflects. Such a Cartesian thinking self reduces the self to objects of its own thinking processes; it is determined to be freed from ties to anyone that it has not freely chosen to relate to; and it promotes a brand of individualism that "disposes each citizen to isolate himself from the mass of his fellows."[3]

Such an encapsulated self not only contradicts the real nature of humans as social beings, but also ignores the basic connections between the human dimensions of rationality and relationality. We have seen that both Joseph Fletcher and Michael Tooley claim self-consciousness as the sine qua non for personhood; but how can the embodied self be conscious of itself, a mental

---

[1] For a useful historical review of the idea of reality-in-itself, see Carver T. Yu, *Being and Relation: A Theological Critique of Western Dualism and Individualism* (Edinburgh: Scottish Academic Press, 1987), chap. 4.

[2] James W. Walters, *What Is a Person? An Ethical Exploration* (Urbana: University of Illinois Press, 1997), p. 51. This complaint would be true if that were the only defense of the fetal life.

[3] Alexis de Tocqueville, *Democracy in America*, ed. J. P. Mayer, trans. George Lawrence (New York: Doubleday/Anchor, 1969), p. 506.

activity, without the presence of someone other than the self, a social interaction? George H. Mead points out that the basic criterion of self-awareness—the ability to distinguish the "me" and the "not me"—depends on the presence of the "other"; and the self "would not be a self but for his relationship to others in the community of which he is a part."[4] This illustrates the connection between human rationality and relationality, and it allows us to say that our ability to exercise the rational faculty depends to a very large extent on our fundamentally social nature. After all, as I have discussed above, the unique human genome on the basis of which each human being is irreplaceable and intrinsically valuable is usually (and, until the recent advent of in vitro fertilization techniques, could only be) the product of a love relation between a man and a woman who decide not only to give love but to give life. Quite clearly, the conditions of being human are a complex interaction of biological, rational and relational factors.

In this regard, it is helpful to be reminded of John Macquarrie's four basic characteristics of human sociality in what would otherwise be a unique and irreplaceable individual.[5] The first characteristic is human sexuality: that human beings are either male or female points to our biological orientation toward a relation with another. While human sexual relations are often reduced to the purely biological dimension, they can only be fulfilled when they also involve the personal and social dimensions. Hence, the existence of each individual human being and the survival of the entire human species are dependent on social relations. The second pointer of human sociality is that before any human being becomes an independent and autonomous thinking self, she inevitably experiences a period of being surrounded and nurtured by others (usually a family) and exists in special relations to them. The reality most people come into contact with is a personal and social reality involving someone other than the self. A third indicator of human sociality is the unique human capacity for language, which facilitates communication with others. In this regard, Alistair McFadyen points out that the relational power of language is best demonstrated in how it shapes human identities through "patterns of communication and response in which we all are engaged."[6] Kevin Vanhoozer, writing from a strictly theological perspective, concurs that to be a person is first "to participate in the covenant of divine discourse as a faithful hearer and speaker"[7] and second to become a communication center in a web of commu-

---

[4]George Herbert Mead, *Mind, Self and Society*, ed. Charles W. Morris (Chicago: University of Chicago Press, 1974), p. 200.
[5]John Macquarrie, *In Search of Humanity: A Theological and Philosophical Approach* (New York: Crossroad, 1989).
[6]Alister I. McFadyen, *The Call to Personhood: A Christian Theory of the Individual in Social Relationships* (Cambridge: Cambridge University Press, 1990), p. 7.

nicative relationships with other fellow human persons. On this view, human beings are *called* into existence by God to be communicative and covenantal creatures, and human existence is a response to this divine call, both individually and corporately as the church, or *ekklesia* (the ones "called out of"). Finally, we possess an economic interdependence that betrays our sociality, especially in the inevitable economic phenomenon of the division of labor. In the economic sphere of modern society, no individual is truly self-sufficient: all our interests are inextricably intertwined, and we remain interdependent on each other for survival.

Personhood, Relation and Moral Rights

Ironically, the contemporary discussion of human personhood, which is often linked to the language of individual rights, speaks in favor of essential human sociality. Moral philosophers generally agree that personhood involves the entitlement to rights, privileges and duties; and as we have seen, Tooley normatively defines personhood itself as an entity with a right to life.[8] Since rights can only be claimed against the other, this presupposes a strong connection between personhood and sociality, at least as a consequence, if not a constitutive, factor. Yet some feminist writers believe that connecting personhood with moral rights introduces an undesirable individualizing element into the discussion. For example, Elizabeth Wolgast argues that such a connection has been fostered because we have adopted an atomistic model of the social world in which persons are self-centered individuals whose only mode of relating to other individuals is competitive and acquisitive and, thus, must be mediated and regulated by rights. She is of the opinion that an artificial connection between personhood and moral rights based on a distorted social model is particularly inappropriate for the discussion of issues relating to pregnancy, birth and parenthood.[9]

Mary Ann Warren also argues that the theoretical foundation of moral right is based on two assumptions, both of which are inclined to introduce an individualizing element. The first, called "the intrinsic properties assumption,"[10] limits the ascription of moral rights to individuals who have acquired certain intrinsic properties. While philosophers may disagree as to which intrinsic property or properties count as relevant to the ascription of rights, relational properties (e.g., being loved or being part of a community) are excluded

---

[7]Kevin Vanhoozer, "Human Being, Individual and Social," in *Cambridge Companion to Christian Doctrine,* ed. Colin E. Gunton (Cambridge: Cambridge University Press, 1997), p. 183.

[8]Michael Tooley, *Abortion and Infanticide* (New York: Oxford University Press, 1983), chap. 2.

[9]Elizabeth Wolgast, *The Grammar of Justice* (Ithaca: Cornell University Press, 1987), pp. 41-42.

[10]Mary Ann Warren, "The Moral Significance of Birth," *Hypatia* 4 (Fall 1989): 47.

because they are considered extrinsic to the individual. The second assumption, called "the single-criterion assumption," holds that as far as moral rights are concerned, a single property divides the world of the haves and the have-nots. Not only do these two assumptions preclude a relational basis of personhood and a social foundation of moral rights, but a closer look at the ascription of moral rights reveals that these assumptions are not consistently held, in that whatever intrinsic property is being used as the single criterion to define personhood is not always connected to the ascription of rights.

Walters provides an illustration of these difficulties. He takes self-consciousness as "the threshold of indisputably personal life," which admits of no degrees; once the threshold is passed, all persons have full moral status, and no moral lines can be drawn between persons.[11] Yet even though a newborn has not reached the threshold, it is granted moral standing because of its proximity to personal life. Walters justifies this on the basis that "the greater the *proximity* to personal life, the weightier is the animal's or human individual's moral status."[12] In other words, even though he generally subscribes to a single criterion of higher brain capacity, he is unable to hold to it consistently and is willing to agree that there are occasions in which the social relations of a marginal person may warrant ethical consideration.[13] He cites two observations to support this claim: the "quickening" experienced by the pregnant woman around sixteen to eighteen weeks of gestation, which results in a type of physiosocial bonding, and the pregnant woman's increasing identification with the growing child-to-be within her. He does not specify the extent to which social bonding counts in his proximate personhood; he simply states that after quickening is experienced, "the *meaning* that we attach to the developing fetus is all important for us."[14] Here the ascription of moral rights has been allowed to follow a sliding scale of some arbitrarily, although sensibly, chosen criteria: potentiality, development and social bonding. In this example, more than a single, extrinsic property is used to ascribe rights, and some kind of relational dimension is included for the moral, though not ontological, consideration of the fetus.

In a somewhat similar move, H. Tristram Engelhardt Jr. assigns the status of "social person" to patients suffering from severe Alzheimer's disease because these people were once "strictly defined persons," although their advanced dementia suggests that they no longer qualify. The same status may also be

---

[11]Walters, *What Is a Person?* p. 63.

[12]Ibid., p. 65.

[13]Ibid., p. 71.

[14]Ibid. Walters does not specify clearly the relationship between social bonding and personhood because his concern is primarily to show how social bonding may assist in treatment decisions rather than in defining personhood.

accorded to the whole class of persons-to-be, including viable fetuses (usually between twenty-four-weeks and twenty-six-weeks gestation), neonates, infants and even profoundly mentally retarded infants who, according to Engelhardt, will never become strictly defined persons. Their tentative status of personhood with some rights of protection is thus imputed on the basis of social considerations and not on the basis of the intrinsic property chosen as the defining criterion of personhood.[15]

These difficulties with the single-criterion assumption and the intrinsic property assumption make me inclined to agree with Warren that only when we set aside these two "individualizing" assumptions will it be possible to have a more socially sensitive account of moral rights. Some feminists have made such a shift in perspective. Writing in a context of the distribution of health care in the United States, Christine Gudorf states that "the only adequate bioethics is one that includes this simple principle: Promotion of the common good includes the good of *all* persons in the community."[16] By emphasizing *all* persons, this author wants to argue that people must be *treated* as persons and not simply as individuals filling some socially functional roles. This social sensitivity is also displayed in the writing of feminist theologians who, in seeing the Christian God as relational in essence, proceed to argue analogically for the relationality of the created world. Such a relational theology informs a feminist bioethical perspective that takes not only the human body seriously, but also the relational context of various bioethical issues. Specifically, this perspective is critical of bioethical principles that proceed from a model of personhood which emphasizes rationality and autonomy at the expense of the relational aspects of human personhood: caring, empathy, mutuality and community.[17]

Marjorie Maguire is a contemporary writer who attempts to articulate an explicitly relational account of personhood through the common feminist premises of relationality and embodiment.[18] She appeals to the Christian symbolism of the covenant, found in the Israelites' being called into a corporate personhood through a covenant of love freely willed by Yahweh. Based on this "Exodus peoplehood theology," she constructs an account of personhood

[15]H. Tristram Engelhardt Jr., *The Foundations of Bioethics* (New York: Oxford University Press, 1986), p. 117.

[16]Christine E. Gudorf, "A Feminist Critique of Biomedical Principlism," in *A Matter of Principles? Ferment in U.S. Bioethics,* ed. Edwin R. Dubose, Ron Hamel and Laurence J. O'Connell (Valley Forge, Penn.: Trinity Press International, 1994), p. 171.

[17]See for example Elisabeth Schüssler Fiorenza, *In Memory of Her: A Feminist Theological Reconstruction of Christian Origins* (New York: Crossroads, 1983).

[18]Marjorie Reiley Maguire, "Personhood, Covenant and Abortion," in *Abortion and Catholicism: The American Debate,* ed. Patricia Beattie Jung and Thomas Shannon (New York: Crossroad, 1988), pp. 100-120.

that reflects the "free and gracious act of love that establishes a covenant with the new reality that is being personed."[19] Specifically, Maguire proposes that the only agent who initiates the covenant love for prenatal life and allows it to become a human person is the mother, who thereby makes the fetus a person by accepting its relatedness to her. Applying the Buberian "I-Thou" insight,[20] Maguire says, "At the moment when the mother bonds with the fetus, the fetus becomes a Thou to her rather than an It."[21] In arguing for why the woman should be the human agency to mediate this covenant of love, she appeals to the biological facts that the ovum supplies the energy for the initial metabolic activities of the fertilized egg and that quickening, which signals the presence of an animated human life, is experienced only by the mother. In short, it is a form of natural law that links the beginning of personhood of the fetus to a covenant made by the pregnant woman.[22] From this, she moves on to demythologize her covenant theology by equating this "maternal covenant love" to a more secularized and more universally acceptable expression of maternal consent. To add a final twist to her account, Maguire suggests that a presumption of consent should be allowed when the fetus passes a certain point of development even if maternal consent is not available. She identifies this developmental point at a time when the brain and central nervous system of the fetus are sufficiently developed for viability, as the fetus is "no longer dependent on the mother to actuate its potentiality for relatedness and sociality."[23]

As appealing as Maguire's account may be, given its emphasis on relationality and embodiment, it suffers from several serious difficulties. To begin with, it is not at all clear how or why fetal viability is related to the presumption of maternal consent. If viability is chosen because the fetus's potentiality for relatedness can be actuated by someone other than the mother, it seems that viability is not a necessary condition. The father, whom Maguire considers merely a "biological donor," or any significant others may establish a covenant relationship with the previable fetus and thereby endow it with personhood, even as it resides within the womb of a woman who may not wish to establish such a covenant. An example can be found in the couple who donate both the egg and the sperm to produce an embryo to be gestated by a surrogate woman who agrees to the pregnancy solely on a contractual (monetary or altruistic) rather than a covenantal basis. Under such circumstances, it is difficult to see why the previable fetus is not a person on account of the genetic parents' continuing covenantal relationship of love; and if this

---

[19]Ibid., p. 108.
[20]I will examine Martin Buber's thought below.
[21]Maguire, "Personhood," p. 108.
[22]Ibid., p. 110.
[23]Ibid., p. 113.

is rejected, then there is no reason why the state of postviability would constitute such a strong presumption of consent. Maguire seems to assume that independent existence outside of the mother's body is crucial for "presumed consent" and a right to life.[24] However, it is uncertain whether she is willing to apply this criterion faithfully. For instance, would she grant the embryo created through in vitro fertilization the status of personhood since it exists outside the human body for the first several days of its life? The choice of viability is also a difficult one given the fact that advances in neonatology are incessantly pushing the point of viability—and with it the presumed consent and fetal personhood—earlier in the pregnancy.[25] Finally, relating viability to maternal covenant exposes Maguire's inconsistency in her understanding of the biblical notion of covenant. Her own choice of the calling of Israel as support for the covenant paradigm highlights the fact that the biblical notion of covenant often is a unilateral event sustained by God's unfailing love alone. Indeed, one of the main emphases of the biblical notion of covenant is the element of dependence in which one party (Israel) is to be totally dependent on the other (God). The choice to relate presumed maternal consent (covenant) with viability seems to go directly against the very spirit of the divine covenant on which her own account is based.

Perhaps it may be possible to see a relationship between viability and maternal consent (but not maternal covenant) in the sense that if the gestating mother does not consent and decides to expel the fetus out of her body, someone else may be permitted to consent to relate to the fetus and endow it with personhood. This then exposes the second weakness of Maguire's account— that she overlooks the enormous difference between the notion of covenant and the idea of consent. In the biblical tradition, a covenant can not be broken, even though it may be violated. Maguire's account of maternal consent can apparently be rescinded, since she allows for a second-trimester abortion for economic or social reasons even though the woman may have previously accepted the pregnancy.[26] Hence, ultimately Maguire's account commits the fundamental mistake of having too much faith in the human agency, namely, in the mother's mediating the covenant and conferring personhood. This is too much responsibility for humanity to bear. As we will soon see, human personhood is constituted by a covenant of love initiated by God and expressed in the creation of the human organism through the marriage covenant between the mother and the father. Once conceived, the divine-human covenant is established unilaterally by God—a covenant that no human being can put

---

[24]Ibid., p. 102.

[25]I will examine similar problems with the viability criterion in chapter sixteen.

[26]Ibid., pp. 115-16.

asunder. To have God's "personing creativity" decided in a personal moment of human covenantal love is to place far too much confidence in the human agency; and to look to the human agency to be "responsible for the creation of personhood or 'soul' "[27] is nothing less than a self-deificatory process in which the human agent usurps God's role.

In spite of these difficulties, as soon as we accept that human beings are inherently social, it will be difficult to regard all relationships (personal and otherwise) as irrelevant to the ascription of moral rights and the definition of personhood. After all, a definition of the person pertains to the personal life, which is actualized only in a social context. Arriving at a complete definition of personhood must, in addition to those individualizing physical and psychological dimensions that render the person a particular psychosomatic entity, go beyond these aspects to include the relational dimensions (social and religious) in which the personal life finds its ultimate meaning and fulfillment. As Albert Outler puts it:

> [The] primal origins, the continuing ground and final ends of human life are truly transcendental. . . . All our truly human experiences (identity, freedom, insight, hope, love) are also self-transcending—despite their being bracketed in space and time. . . . "Personhood" is not a part of the human organism, nor is it inserted into a process of organic development at some magic moment. It is the human organism oriented toward its transcendental matrix, in which it lives and moves and has its human being.[28]

It is for this reason that I am not satisfied with a definition of the person as an absolutely autonomous, self-sufficient and independent individual, for the relational or social humanness is of equal importance; indeed, my understanding of the "dyadic" structure of being and person mandates the relational dimension as constitutive of personhood. In what is to follow, I will review the historical development of the concept of the relational person in the (Western) philosophical, theological and biblical traditions to support this claim.

Relational Person in Modern Western Philosophical Thought

In spite of the individualistic bias in the West, since the latter part of the nineteenth century and especially the first half of the twentieth century we have witnessed a renewed attention in the relational dimension of a human person. Martin Buber (1878-1965), for example, has long been recognized as one of the most important "personalist" thinkers in the twentieth century primarily because of his emphasis on the importance of relation in defining person-

---

[27]Ibid., p. 109.

[28]Albert Outler, "Beginnings of Personhood: Theological Considerations," *Perkins Journal* 27 (Fall 1973): 28-34.

hood.[29] Despite the title he gives to his book *I and Thou,* the key to the concept is not the "I and Thou" but the hyphenated "I-Thou," which expresses Buber's fundamental principle of "the Between" or "Presence." In the ontology of the "hyphen," the Between or Presence, the individual is seen as a center of selfhood firmly located in the network of interpersonal relations. It is the foundation for individual and social existence, faith, morality and nature. Buber says:

> The fundamental fact of human existence is neither the individual as such nor the aggregate as such. . . . The fundamental fact of human existence is man with man. . . . I call this . . . the sphere of the "between." Though being realized in very different degrees, it is a primal category of human reality.[30]

To Buber, there is a polar nature of the self, which he represents in two word pairs: "I-Thou" and "I-It." "I-Thou" is the primary word of relation whereas "I-It" is the primary word of experiencing and using. The two are different in several respects. First, "the primary word *I-Thou* can only be spoken with the whole being. The word *I-It* can never be spoken with the whole being."[31] Second, the "I" of "I-Thou" is different from the "I" of "I-It" in that the latter "I" can be separated from the "It" whereas the former cannot be separated from the "Thou." Third, only to the "I" of the "I-Thou" is the reality disclosed as relation, as the Between.

> If I face a human being as my *Thou,* and say the primary word *I-Thou* to him he is not a thing among things, and does not consist of things. . . . Nor is he a nature able to be experienced and described. . . . But each time I do it he ceases to be *Thou.* . . . I do not experience the man to whom I say *Thou.* But I take my stand in relation to him, in the sanctity of the primary word.[32]

In other words, out of the primal unity of the "I-Thou," the "Thou" becomes an "It" through an objectification process. In the "I-It" encounter, the "It" can

---

[29]Martin Buber, *I and Thou,* 2nd ed. (New York: Charles Scribner's Sons, 1958). Even though it was Feuerbach who coined the term "I-Thou," his usage was limited primarily to interpersonal psychology; by contrast, it was Martin Buber who saw the ontological implications of the "I-Thou" relation. Incidentally, Walter Kaufmann, a recent translator of the work, argues that Buber's famous term "I and Thou" is best translated "I and You." As Kaufmann notes, the German "Du" is not a formal, archaic pronoun (as is thou), but rather "is spontaneous and unpretentious, remote from formality, pomp, and dignity." Kaufmann "I and You: A Prologue," in Buber, *I and Thou,* trans. Walter Kaufmann (New York: Simon and Schuster, 1970). While I will employ the accepted "I-Thou" terminology, we should nonetheless bear this qualification in mind.

[30]Martin Buber, *Between Man and Man,* trans. Ronald Gregor Smith (Glasgow: William Collins's Sons, 1979), p. 203.

[31]Buber, *I and Thou,* p. 3.

[32]Ibid., pp. 8-9.

be managed, manipulated, possessed and dispossessed, and the "I" emerges as the ego, the conscious subject, with the loss of the Between, or Presence. According to Buber, the finitude of humanity lies in the fact that every "I-Thou" can become an "I-It" through the objectification process, and he sees the growth of this increasingly oppressive objectification process in the West.

Buber believes that only in the "I-Thou" is personhood encountered. The "I" of the "I-Thou" is the "I" of a person, whereas the "I" of "I It" is merely an ego. A person is one who participates in the reality of the Between where the actualization of personhood takes place. "I become through my relation to the *Thou;* as I become *I,* I say *Thou.*"[33] It is important therefore to recognize that in Buber's "I-Thou" concept, the "I" and the "Thou" are not independent substances that are somehow enriched in the encounter. Rather, the "I" has actuality only as coactuality. There is no "I-as-such"; the only actual "I" is the "I" in relation. Yet at the same time there is no mutual absorption within the "I" and "Thou"; rather the "Distance," represented as a hyphen, is maintained, allowing for the space that respects the freedom and inwardness of the other.[34] The Between and the Distance, then, are the bases of a genuine community. Being a profoundly religious person with an intense sense of the immediacy and presence of the Divine, Buber viewed God as the eternal "Thou" who can never authentically become an object, "It." God therefore is the only reliable and complete ground by which to realize the possibility of every "I-Thou."

Gabriel Marcel (1889-1973), another contemporary "personalist" and "existentialist" philosopher, also rejects the Cartesian self based on the *cogito* because he believes that rationalism leads to an abstraction and depersonalization of the self and thus to the reification of the self.[35] Marcel argues that a manifestation of this strong rationalist tendency is the way we abstract ourselves from our experience in order to reflect on our own nature, and in so doing we separate ourselves from the modes of existence that are most basic to our being.[36] In his view, there is no such thing as an isolated experience of existence, and to believe that we have existence apart from ontological interaction with what is other than ourselves is an illusion.[37] For Marcel, to be is to participate as a "being-by-participation," and he specifically rejects René Descartes's emphasis on the *cogito* precisely because it negates the existential reality of participation in being and cuts the umbilical cord that binds the self to

---

[33]Ibid., p. 11.

[34]Martin Buber, *The Knowledge of Man* (New York: Harper & Row, 1966), pp. 59-61.

[35]Gabriel Marcel, *Creative Fidelity,* trans. Robert Rosthal (New York: Crossroad, 1982), p. 15.

[36]Kenneth Gallagher, *The Philosophy of Gabriel Marcel* (New York: Fordham University Press, 1975), p. 131.

[37]Ibid., p. xiii.

things. Marcel asks, "How can the existential world be resuscitated starting from a self that does not take part in it?"[38]

Thus, for Marcel, the proper foundation or beginning of metaphysics is not "I think" but "we are,"[39] so that to be living is to be open to a reality by which we enter into some sort of communion. A key concept in Marcel's thought is "availability," which has to do with one's openness and ability to be present to other realities and to allow what is other to be a presence in one's own experiences, as well as in one's own being.

> Availability is an opening upon the presence of another, not a way of access to certain goods he possesses. The available person is capable of being entirely with me; the unavailable person gives me only a provisionary loan on resources which lie at his disposal.[40]

In Marcel's thought, the French word *disponibilité* connotes openness, release, abandonment, welcoming, surrender and readiness to respond. The available person is able to receive from beyond the self and to give without limit of one's self. "The available person is hospitable to others; the doors of his soul are ajar."[41] The implication of this human openness to being, or availability, is that the human person is constituted by communion. Rather than conceiving the ego as a self-existing entity, it is *hypostasis* or "self" that emerges from a matrix of relations, which are characterized by the mutual penetration of the presence of self and other, ad infinitum. Marcel therefore can say that "I am constituted by my interaction with others." It is the "we" that creates the "I," and personhood is constituted in relation to an "other."[42]

John Macmurray (1891-1976), an important but much overlooked Scottish "personalist" philosopher, offers a similar critique of the Cartesian self. He argues that the *cogito* definition perpetuates an atomistic view of selfhood: "For thought is inherently private, and any philosophy which takes its stand on the primacy of thought, which defines the Self as a Thinker, is committed formally to an extreme logical individualism."[43] Withdrawn into itself, the Cartesian self is neither a true self nor a true person. To Macmurray, the self is first and fore-

---

[38]Ibid., p. 16.

[39]Gabriel Marcel, *Faith and Reality,* vol. 2 of *The Mystery of Being,* trans. Rene Hogue (London: Harvill, 1951), p. 9.

[40]Joe McCown, *Availability: Gabriel Marcel and the Phenomenology of Human Openness* (Missoula, Mont.: Scholars Press, 1978), p. 10.

[41]Gallagher, *Philosophy of Gabriel Marcel,* p. 26.

[42]I should add a note of caution here that while these "existentialist" philosophers have made some very important contributions toward understanding the relational dimension of human personhood, at times their exposition of the nature of the person is so one-sided in terms of relation and systems of relation that the person as a "substantial" entity with its "in-itself-ness" tends to disappear.

[43]John Macmurray, *The Self as Agent* (London: Humanities Press, 1991), p. 71.

most an agent, and hence the dictum "I think therefore I am" needs to be replaced by a dictum that gives primacy to action: "I do therefore I am."[44] Since thinking involves the mind only but doing engages both mind and body, by transferring the center of reference to action, the self recovers its body and becomes a "self-in-action." As an agent, the self exists only in dynamic relation with the other, ending the solitariness of the "Thinking Self" and restoring the self to its proper existence as a community of persons in relation.[45] In other words, a being's existence is constituted by active interrelations with a reality that is external to itself, the other: "Any agent is in necessity in relation to the Other. Apart from this relation, he does not exist."[46]

Furthermore, Macmurray believes not only that the self is constituted by its relation to the other, but that "the Other in this constitutive relation must itself be personal,"[47] that is, also acting as an agent. Hence, one's personal existence is constituted by the personal relation of persons as agents. While Macmurray joins Buber and Marcel in rejecting the Cartesian legacy, he does so via a different ontology of personhood, which he calls the "field of the personal." That is to say, the personal is derived from the reality of a community of "You and I," conceived as a plurality of agents in one field of action.[48] Macmurray finds a concrete example of persons as agents in the mother-child relationship. He notes that a young child is totally helpless and dependent on external assistance for survival. She does not even have animal instincts that would help her to respond to external stimuli, to avoid dangers and to adapt to her environment in order to survive. Her survival thus depends entirely on the intentional (rational) activity of the mother as an agent.[49] As Macmurray argues, "She can live only through other people and in dynamic relation with them. In virtue of this fact [she] is a person, for the personal is constituted by the relation of persons."[50]

The implications of this understanding of personhood are significant. If existence is conceived in terms of interrelated agents, then to exist entails having being within such a field: relatedness, rather than rationality, becomes the fundamental ground of the person. The capacity for rational reflection is a dimension of this field, not its defining characteristic. Macmurray identifies both logical and practical weaknesses in the Cartesian cognitive model, which is not adequate to serve as the criterion for defining persons. Like Buber and

---

[44]Ibid., p. 102.
[45]John Macmurray, *Persons in Relation* (Amherst, N.Y.: Humanities Press, 1991), p. 12.
[46]Ibid., p. 40.
[47]Ibid., p. 24.
[48]Macmurray, *Self as Agent*, p. 145; *Persons in Relation*, p. 27.
[49]Macmurray, *Persons in Relation*, pp. 44-63.
[50]Ibid., p. 51.

Marcel, he seeks to overcome the rationalism and egocentrism of modern philosophy by insisting that in conceiving of personhood, we must focus our attention not on the individual but on the matrix within which individuality takes shape and that such a matrix is found only in friendship and community. In an ideal community of persons,

> the self-realization of any individual person is only fully achieved if he is positively motivated towards every other person with whom he is in relation. We can therefore formulate the inherent ideal of the personal. It is a universal community of persons in which each cares for all the others and no one for himself.[51]

Though not a conventional Christian, Macmurray nevertheless grounds his vision of human nature and human community in the reality and intention of God.

This review shows that in contrast to those who advocate the more dominate Cartesian cognitive model, these personalist thinkers hold to an experience of the other in relations as more primal than the experience of the thinking self. Community is the context in which the person emerges. In their minds, apart from community, persons do not exist at all.

Trinitarian Understanding of Being as Relation

Historically the Christian theological interpretation of personhood has betrayed a strong psychological bias, primarily due to the influence of Augustine and his followers. But within the Latin tradition, we find an alternative way of thinking about persons in the writings of Tertullian, Hilary of Poitiers (c. A.D. 315-367) and Richard of St. Victor of the twelfth century. On the basis that God is not lonely or isolated, these theologians believe that God's creatures are not made to be isolated individuals. They also emphasize that humans as the image of God should reflect the distinctiveness and relatedness of the triune God, an approach that is more faithful to the biblical characterization of personhood (being), both divine and human. But the most fruitful attempt to develop a relational conception of the person has been undertaken by the Cappadocian fathers in the Greek church (Basil, Gregory of Nazianzus and Gregory of Nyssa). The basic term used by these Eastern church fathers is the New Testament word *hypostasis*. Initially it is used to express the objective self-revelation of the Son and Word of God incarnated in Jesus Christ;[52] however, upon deeper reflection on the threefold self-revelation of God, the term is found to be equally applicable to the Father and the Holy Spirit. In the course of devel-

---

[51]Macmurray, *Self as Agent*, p. 159.
[52]The New Testament usage of *hypostasis* in Heb 1:3 is in reference to Christ as "the exact representation of [God's] being" (NIV).

opment, *hypostasis* is converted from an abstract and impersonal term referring to "being" to a concrete one with a name *(onoma)* or face *(prosopon)*, or as T. F. Torrance puts it, a "self-subsistent self-identifying subject-being in objective relations with others." In other words, the term has become "suitable to express the identifiable self-manifestation of God in the incarnate economy of divine salvation as Father, Son and Holy Spirit—that is, as three distinctive hypostatic Realities or Persons."[53]

As the Cappadocian fathers reflect on the hypostatic interrelations of the three divine Persons *(hypostases)* within the one Being *(ousia)* of the Trinity, they come to the conclusion that "no divine Person is who he is without essential relation to the other two, and yet each divine Person is other than and distinct from the other two."[54] In other words, the Father is Father only because of his relation to the Son and the Spirit. The Son is Son only because of his relation to the Father and the Spirit. The Spirit is Spirit only because of his relation to the Father and the Son. The three divine Persons are what they are as a result of the ontic and holistic interrelations shared between them. In that sense, the relations are constitutive of the Persons; and as such they are "substantive relations" or "onto-relations." Specifically, these interrelations are not merely God's differing modes of existence; rather they are relations that belong intrinsically to what Father, Son and Holy Spirit are in themselves and in their mutual objective relations with one another. In sum, the original trinitarian conceptualization understands divine personhood as an onto-relational concept, which should have a significant bearing on the understanding of a relational personhood of the human being, insofar as we are creatures reflecting the Creator.

Since this doctrine of the Trinity affirms that God exists as a plurality of distinct Persons in communion, and if the relations between the divine Persons are onto-relations, the Cappadocian fathers draw the further implication that the very "essence" of God is relational. Person *(hypostasis)* is the way the divine Being *(ousia)* exists; personhood is then constitutive and expressive of "being," rather than simply an addition to "being."[55] This trinitarian ontology of personhood puts relation on equal footing to, if not ahead of, substance in the order of being. At the same time it establishes two new important ontological principles: first, persons are what they are by virtue of their relations to others,

---

[53]T. F. Torrance, *The Christian Doctrine of God: One Being Three Persons* (Edinburgh: T & T Clark, 1996), p. 156.

[54]Ibid., pp. 156-57.

[55]Such a doctrine replaces the Aristotelian ontology, which assumes substance is complete unto itself, irrespective of its relations (or lack thereof). Relations are what take place between the autonomous individual substances, and thus they are "accidental to," rather than constitutive of, being.

and second, there can be a sharing in being on account of persons.[56] These two principles allow the Cappadocian fathers to locate the real distinctiveness of Father, Son and Holy Spirit in the uniqueness of each Person, without having to postulate a difference in being/substance *(ousia)* between the divine Persons. This is succinctly delineated in the Nicean formulation *mia ousia, treis hypostases.* Simply put, this trinitarian theology asserts that the one God "exists" on account of the three Persons, Father, Son, Holy Spirit; boldly put, if God were not personal, he would not be God at all.

This theological interpretation of the relationality of divine personhood is entirely faithful to the biblical revelation of God as personally instantiated in the Father, Son and Holy Spirit, who are together involved in the divine activities of creation, redemption, sanctification and consummation. The Gospel of John particularly recognizes the need to account for the distinct personhood of Father, Son and Holy Spirit in such a way that the unity of God is not compromised. As a result, this Gospel provides the richest and subtlest account of divine distinction-within-unity: Father, Son and Holy Spirit are distinct divine Persons who play different roles within the one large life-giving enterprise. The Father consecrates and sends the Son for mission (Jn 10:36), the Son reveals and glorifies the Father, and the Holy Spirit makes the Son known; yet the relationship is not a one-way affair, because the Father also points to the Son, especially in the Son's baptism and transfiguration; and the Son points to the Spirit as the life-giving (Jn 6:63) and teaching (Jn 14:26) Spirit. In other words, the roles and even the ordering of the roles may be distinct, but there is a strong and unmistaken sense of mutuality between the distinct Persons.

On the basis of this distinctive mutuality of giving and receiving, the Gospel of John unequivocally presents a divine unity, oneness or "in-each-otherness" (Jn 10:30; 14:11). Within the three Persons, there is a reciprocity in knowledge, glorification and love, so that oneness and in-each-otherness become the overarching communal image of God. There is thus unity-in-triunity and triunity-in-unity in John's Gospel. By focusing their attention on the seriousness with which the Gospel expresses the unity and diversity of God's action, the Cappadocians have insisted on the notion of "being" as "being-in-communion": the being of God is unfolded in the relations of the three Persons. As one Eastern Orthodox commentator explains, the mystery of God exists as the mystery of Persons in communion; only in communion can God be who God is, and only as communion can God be at all.[57]

In the seventh and eighth centuries, the concept of *perichoresis* is formu-

---

[56]Colin E. Gunton, *The Promise of Trinitarian Theology* (Edinburgh: T & T Clark, 1991), p. 8.
[57]See John Zizioulas, *Being as Communion* (Crestwood, N.Y.: St. Vladimir's Seminary Press, 1993), pp. 45-48.

lated by Pseudo-Cyril and John of Damascus to further explain the dynamic relations between the Persons of the Trinity. *Perichoresis* derives either from the Greek root *chora* meaning "space" or "room," or from *chorein* meaning "to contain," "to make room" or "to go forward." This concept describes both a static and a dynamic component of the interactions between the divine Persons, and consequently its Latin equivalent requires two words: *circuminsessio* and *circumincessio,* respectively. In the more passive and static sense, *perichoresis* signifies that one person is in the others, occupying the same space as the others and filling the others with its presence. In a more active and dynamic sense, it signifies the interpenetration and permeation of one person with and in the others. This theological speculation is an attempt to express the eternal process of relating and communing, which early church fathers understood to be intrinsic to the three Persons.

Taking both the static and dynamic aspects of *perichoresis,* the three Persons of the Trinity are "being-in-one-another," with each divine Person irresistibly drawn to the other, taking his existence from the other, containing the other in himself (the static component), while at the same time actively enveloping and interpenetrating the other, co-inhering in the other, drawing life from the other and pouring himself out into the other (the dynamic component). While there is no coalescing, commingling or blurring of the individuality of each Person, neither is there separation from one another. There is only the communion of love in which each Person comes to express both what he is and, simultaneously, what the triune God is: vital, dynamic, ecstatic and relational.

Interpreted as union and communion, *perichoresis* gives expression to the fact that the distinctive Persons of Father, Son and Holy Spirit dwell *in* one another, not only with one another in the unity of one God. The Father *in* the Son and the Spirit, the Son *in* the Father and the Spirit, and the Spirit *in* the Father and the Son, dynamically coinhering or mutually containing essentially and enhypostatically within the Trinity. *Perichoresis* thus reinforces the wholeness of the Trinity since "no divine Person is he who he really and truly is . . . apart from relation to the other two in their mutual containing or interpenetrating of one another."[58] This model helps us to see how we may say that

> the whole God dwells in each Person and each Person is whole God. Since the fullness of the Godhead is complete in each of them as well as in all of them, it is as the one indivisible Holy Trinity that God is God and that God is one God, and therefore may be known . . . only as a Triune Whole.[59]

But the confirmation of the wholeness of the Trinity is not done at the

---

[58]Torrance, *Christian Doctrine,* p. 174.
[59]Ibid.

expense of the distinction of the three Persons because the concept of *perichoresis* strengthens our understanding of the interior hypostatic distinctions. In the first place, *perichoresis* affirms the full equality of the three divine Persons by declaring their identity in will, authority, judgment, energy, power or any other divine attribute. In the second place, *perichoresis* affirms the real distinctions between the divine Persons by showing that the oneness and communion found in the divine Persons' reciprocal relationships is in fact enabled rather than hampered by their differentiating qualities. Within the perichoretic movement of mutual indwelling, the three Persons are not just different from one another, but, in virtue of their incommunicable characteristics as Father, Son and Holy Spirit, they are also irreducible to one another. Each is unique, noninterchangeable and equal. Particularity, which serves to emphasize the distinctness of the Persons, is never sacrificed to the unity of the divine life. These three Persons, different and distinct, particular and irreducible, yet not separate, are bound up with each other so that one is not one without the other two, yet each exists in communion, which the one God eternally is.[60]

One may legitimately ask, what has a seventh-century concept of the Trinity to do with the twentieth-century conception of the modern person and the world we live in? Colin Gunton answers this question by arguing that if God exists perichoretically in his dynamic relatedness of Father, Son and Spirit, then the concept of *perichoresis* allows us to consider the world likewise as an order of things dynamically related to each other. The world is perichoretic in that everything in it contributes to the being of everything else, while at the same time the world is enabling everything to be what it distinctly is.[61] The basis of this dynamism of mutual constitutiveness is grounded in the belief that the world, as a dynamic order, is created just so by the free creativity of the Father, Son and Holy Spirit. Jürgen Moltmann shares a similar view, albeit with a slightly different justification. He sees that the perichoretic relations within the triune life are not confined to God only but also apply to God's relationship to the world, since the divine relationship to the external world is determined by the divine relationship within.[62] Furthermore, if there is a perichoretic interaction between God and the world, then the perichoretic model may be justly applied to the relationships between human persons, however imperfect they may be as finite and fallen creatures. The biblical doctrine of *imago Dei* (Gen 1:26-28) teaches that to be human is to be created in the image of God, and so the idea that human

---

[60]Ibid., p. 175.

[61]Colin E. Gunton, *The One, the Three and the Many* (Cambridge: Cambridge University Press, 1993).

[62]Jürgen Moltmann, *The Trinity and the Kingdom* (San Francisco: HarperSanFrancisco, 1991), p. 161.

beings should in some way be perichoretic is indeed plausible. As we shall see below in the discussion of the relational dimension of the image of God, Karl Barth seeks to justify the stance that human personhood (man-man) is derived from divine personhood (God-God). Catherine Mowry LaCugna also assumes an essential analogy between the relatedness of the divine Persons and human persons, since she holds that the relational ontology of personhood, relationship and communion is not exclusive to the divine life of God but is "the modality of *all* existence."[63]

In light of *perichoresis,* we see that both individualism, which says that we are what we are in separation from our neighbors, and collectivism, which makes us so involved with others in society that we lose particularity, are inadequate modern understandings of the human being and one-sided distortions of human personhood. *Perichoresis* provides a corrective for both in that while it promotes close relatedness by insisting that persons are defined in terms of their relations to other persons, it never does so at the expense of particularity. Rather it affirms that as creatures made in the image of God, we are closely bound up, for better or for worse, with other human beings in interpenetrating relationships that affirm both individuality and mutuality, equality and reciprocity. Specifically, it is not the modern view of self-fulfilling relations, but the inherently relational view that persons mutually constitute each other in giving and receiving, and thereby make each other what they are.

Hence, the trinitarian doctrine of divine personhood as reflected in God's own triune perichoretic life of agapeic love—unfolded in the divine activity of creation, redemption and renewal, and directed toward his creation—provides the Christian with a model of interpersonal relationship as well as with an ontological foundation for human personhood. In this regard, it is important to emphasize the proper conceptual order: it is not that the divine unity of personhood with its perfect diversity is based on human relations, nor that the human mind has access to the immanent, intradivine life of God. Rather, what is being claimed is that human personhood and community are based, pursued and achieved by understanding the economy of the triune God's interaction with human history.[64] The doctrine of Trinity and the concept of *perichoresis,*

---

[63]Catherine Mowry LaCugna, *God for Us: The Trinity and Christian Life* (San Francisco: HarperSanFrancisco, 1991), p. 250. Italics in original.

[64]In his book *Concepts of Person and Christian Ethics* (Cambridge: Cambridge University Press, 1997), Stanley Rudman is quite preoccupied with arguing that the link between divine and human personhood is indirect and precarious, being based on revelation and experiences in human life (pp. 175-88). My view here does not claim any direct knowledge of divine nature, but it is not clear why knowledge of divine personhood indirectly acquired through either revelation or human experience cannot be directly applied as a model for human personhood, as Rudman seems to suggest.

therefore, have far-reaching consequences for my understanding of a relational human personhood.

John Zizioulas, a contemporary Eastern Orthodox theologian, expounds this trinitarian insight and points out that

> the ontological question [of human personhood] is not answered by pointing to the "self-existent," to a being as it is determined by its own boundaries, but to a being which in its *ekstasis* breaks through these boundaries in a movement of communion. . . . It is not in its "self-existence," but in communion that this being is "itself" and thus is at all. This communion does not threaten personal particularity; it is constitutive of it.[65]

In Zizioulas's view, a person is thus not an autonomous individual but an open and ecstatic reality, one who refers to others for her existence. The actualization of personhood takes place in the self-transcending dynamic movement of freedom in love toward communion with other persons. This freedom to transcend the self and to be opened to the other is what Zizioulas calls "the *ekstasis* of being."[66] Every person, divine or human, is ecstatic; more precisely, every person comes into existence by her *ekstasis*. Specifically, human personhood can only be actualized in her self-transcendence and communion with God and her neighbors.

But in our fallen human nature, ecstatic self-expression is flawed and our capacity for *ekstasis* is compromised. As Zizioulas conceives it, our freedom for *ekstasis* is limited by our self-centeredness, individualism, sin and death. The atonement of human sin by the redemptive work of Christ and the subsequent participation in the life of God in Christ by the Holy Spirit entail a transformation into a new mode of existence that allows the person to transcend herself, to be free in love, to be a genuine event of communion. Salvation brings about an ontological change not in the sense that one kind of being becomes another kind of being, but in the sense that the new being is a new person *in* Christ through whom her personhood is actualized. This transformation then enables her to live with a new capacity for self-transcendence and relationship. Simply put, as we become persons in Christ, our personhood is being actualized in him; and as we live our lives in step with the Spirit, we become more like Christ and progressively actualize our potential as persons in him; and this "becoming-more-like-Christ" is an ongoing, continuous process that will not be completed until the end time, until the *eschaton*. Thus, as we shall see below, in a real sense, the Christian concept of person is both dynamic and eschatological, pointing toward a final *telos* of humanity in which human personhood will be perfected.

---

[65]John Zizioulas, "Human Capacity and Human Incapacity: A Theological Exploration of Personhood," *Scottish Journal of Theology* 28 (October 1975): 409.
[66]Ibid., p. 408.

Biblical Tradition of *Imago Dei* as Relational

Through the history of the Christian understanding of the *imago Dei*, one finds a view—in addition to the psychological (reason or rationality) and functional (e.g., the ability to rule, procreate) views—that understands the *imago* as fundamentally social and relational. For example, one of the Cappadocian fathers, Gregory of Nazianzus, believes that the individual alone cannot image God; indeed, not even the first couple Adam and Eve can fully do it. As he sees it, it takes the original "nuclear family" of Adam, Eve and Seth—three human persons sharing the same flesh and blood—to bring out in focus the image of the three divine *hypostases* existing as a divine unity.[67] As imperfect as the analogy may be, it does serve to emphasize the importance of human community in expressing the image of God. Indeed, every human person is either a man or a woman, and is the child of his or her parents; every human person's existence is determined by this "anthropological triangle," which consists of two sets of relationships: the relationship between husband and wife, which denotes the sociality of human persons in space, and the relationship between parents and children that signifies the community of the generations in time.[68] In this way, the image of God is expressed in true human community—the community of sexes and the community of the generations. Thus, in the various human communities, human beings are meant to express the image of the Trinity, the divine community of the Father, Son and the Holy Spirit.

Imago Dei *as man's triadic relation.* Barth presents a persuasive account in his *Church Dogmatics* that the relational nature of human beings is ultimately grounded on the basis that God is first and foremost a "relational" being himself, that is, in the "I-Thou" relationship within God himself, as manifested in the relationship between Father, Son and the Holy Spirit.[69] Specifically, Barth employs a christological model to develop his *analogia relationis:* as the incarnate Son (God-man), Jesus is reflecting the Father-Son relationship in the inner being of God (God-God). In the incarnation, "God repeats Himself in this relationship *ad extra* [God-man], a relationship proper to Himself in His inner divine essence [God-God]."[70] This eternal covenant (God-man) is then revealed and operative in time together with and through the humanity of Jesus (man-man). God-God, God-man and man-man then completes the threefold *analo-*

---

[67]Gregory of Nazianzus, *The Fifth Theological Oration: On the Holy Spirit,* in *The Nicene and Post-Nicene Fathers,* 2nd series, ed. Philip Schaff (Peabody, Mass.: Hendrickson, 1994), 7:318-28.

[68]Jürgen Moltmann, *God in Creation* (San Francisco: HarperCollins, 1991), p. 241.

[69]For a more thorough discussion on Barth's thought in this subject, see Stuart D. McLean, *Humanity in the Thought of Karl Barth* (Edinburgh: T & T Clark, 1981).

[70]Karl Barth *Church Dogmatics* 3/2, ed. G. W. Bromiley and T. F. Torrance (Edinburgh: T & T Clark, 1960), §45.1.

gia relationis.

According to Barth, since all human beings are created in the image of God through the Son, there exists in all human beings a basic creaturely form—the form of "I-Thou" relationships given by God.[71] Barth speaks of the image as the "plurality-in-man" or "being-in-togetherness," which he finds in the Genesis 1:27 (NRSV) text:

> So God created humankind in his image,
>   in the image of God he created them;
>   male and female he created them.

He sees in this text a clear indication that the image of the being created by God signifies existence in the "I-Thou" confrontation, that is, in the juxtaposition and conjunction of male and female.[72] Barth further claims that the confrontation of the "I-Thou" extends beyond the relation between husband and wife to the relation between human persons. On his view, any definition of the human person in which one is abstracted from the coexistence with other fellow humans is false: "It is not as he is for himself but with others, not in loneliness but in fellowship, that he is genuinely human, that he achieves true humanity, that he corresponds to his determination to be God's covenant-partner."[73] God exists as a "being-in-communion," and he creates humans for covenantal fellowship with himself and for fellowship with others. It is only in this sense that humankind is in his image. Barth summarizes it this way:

> That real man is determined by God for life with God has its inviolable correspondence in the fact that his creaturely being is a being in encounter—between I and Thou, man and woman. It is human in this encounter, and in this humanity it is a likeness of the being of its Creator.[74]

The "I-Thou" confrontation is constitutive for both God and humanity, and to remove it "is tantamount to removing the divine from God as well as the human from man."[75] Based on this ontology of relations, to be created in the image of God is to be in communion, to be self-transcendent, to be an ecstatic being, or, simply put, to be a person, oriented in proper relationship to God,

---

[71]"Man is created by God in correspondence with this relationship and differentiation [between the I and the Thou] in God Himself: created as a Thou that can be addressed by God but also an I responsible to God; in the relationship of man and woman in which man is a Thou to his fellow and therefore himself an I in responsibility to this claim" (ibid., 3/1, §41.2).

[72]Ibid.

[73]Ibid., 3/2, §45.2.

[74]Ibid., §45.1.

[75]Ibid., 3/1, §41.2.

fellow humanity and the rest of the creation. A human person cannot be complete in herself; she becomes complete only in relation to others.[76]

As relational beings reflecting the image of God, human beings are also meant to exist in harmony with the rest of creation, as evinced in the "cultural mandate" from God to exercise dominion over, serve, care for, preserve and cultivate creation for God's glory. As David J. A. Clines points out, in the ancient Near Eastern culture, possessing another's image means one performs material functions "as representative of one who is really or spiritually present, though physically absent."[77] According to Genesis 1:26 (NRSV), "God said, 'Let us make humankind in our image, according to our likeness; and let them have dominion over the fish of the sea and over the birds of the air and over every living thing that moves upon the earth.' " This clearly suggests that the human being is set on earth as a representative to exercise dominion over the rest of God's created world. The transcendent God wills his immanent presence on earth through the corporeal human who is created as his image. Further, Clines believes that "dominion" is a constitutive rather than a derivative part of the image, because he observes that in the ancient Near East, whenever the image of God is applied to a living person, it almost exclusively refers to the king; and Clines believes that in Genesis 1:26-28, the human being as the created image of God is described in royal terms and commanded to have dominion.[78] Hence, he concludes that "the command to have dominion (Gen. 1:26-28) does not advertise some function of man which may or may not devolve from his being the image; he has dominion only because he is the image."[79] On his view, the dominion of humanity over creation is an essential part of the image. I take exception to this opinion and believe that it confuses the function of the image with its content or structure. The biblical data evidently suggest that there are other functions besides dominion (e.g., "be fruitful and multiply") that accompany the image of God. I thus favor a broader relational understanding of the image in which dominion would be viewed as one of the concrete expressions of humanity's relational nature.

We can assume that before falling into sin, human beings are created to live in a perfect harmonious state of relation with the Creator, knowing his love and loving him in response, worshiping and enjoying him in total dependence.

---

[76]Also see similar views in Emil Brunner, *The Christian Doctrine of Creation and Redemption* (Philadelphia: Westminster Press, 1952), pp. 55-61, and John Macquarrie, "A Theology of Personal Being," in *Persons and Personality: A Contemporary Inquiry,* ed. Arthur Peacocke and Grant Gillett (Oxford: Basil Blackwell, 1987), p. 178.

[77]David J. A. Clines, "The Image of God in Man," *Tyndale Bulletin* 19 (1968): 87.

[78]Ibid., pp. 92-95.

[79]Ibid., pp. 97-98.

Today we vainly seek to live in a state of perfect harmony with our fellow humans, to recognize that as social beings, we all are in need of and should be open to each other, giving care to and receiving care from each other, loving and enriching each other and remaining totally interdependent. However, we have fallen far from Eden. Initially, as the unspoiled image of God, the first human beings were able to live fully as relational beings. After the Fall, the image of God in human beings has been severely disabled, a distortion that is reflected in all aspects of our relational life. Human beings no longer know the love of God; nor do we respond to him. Instead of worshiping God, we worship idols. Fallen human beings also tend to isolate themselves and withdraw from genuine relationships with fellow human beings. Instead of opening to another, they turn inward to themselves exclusively and become indifferent. Thus, as the corrupted image of God, human beings become alienated from each other, refusing to admit that they are mutually interdependent and instead proclaiming their independence and autonomy. As the deformed image of God, human beings are unable to relate to God's natural creation responsibly; they thus transform the Garden of Eden into a tower of Babel and in the process exploit and mutilate nature instead of caring for and preserving it.

Preservation of the *Imago Dei* as a Unilateral God-to-Man Relationship

Biblical tradition teaches that however poorly we may function in these three realms of relationships, human beings remain the image or representative of God (Gen 9:6; Jas 3:9). This is not because we may partially retain certain substantive capacities—such as rationality, morality or even relationality—but because God, in his faithfulness, continues to maintain his relation with us. To be the image of God is to refer first and foremost to the relationship God has toward us and to refer only secondarily to the relationship we possess by grace toward God and other fellow humans. The fact that God initiates the relationship and relates to us first is crucial. Since the Fall, we continue to be God's image because he continues to relate to us, albeit unilaterally; and as we have discussed, God's unilateral initiative in relating to us begins with a creational relation in which the substantial human person is created, and the umbilical cord of love through which God creates and sustains us has never been severed. It is perhaps for this reason that as the image of God, human beings are incurably religious.[80] Moltmann also implies that the image of God is to be found in God's particular relationship to human beings, and he maintains that "the relationship was resolved upon by God, and was created by him, and can

---

[80]Even staunch secularists often retain a dimension of religiosity. For instance, Carl Sagan maintained his faith in the SETI (Search for Intelligent Life) astronomy project with religious fervor throughout his life.

never be abrogated or withdrawn except by God himself."[81] Human beings may have sinned and thereby perverted our relationship with God, but human sin does not have the same effect on God's relationship to us, which remains unaltered. In this sense, the image of God is also a God-given status, gained through a unique relationship that God initiates, establishes and sustains.[82] So the image of God must be viewed first as a gift, and only secondarily as a response in our relationship of children to the Father, to other fellow human creatures and to the rest of creation.

Many passages in both the Old and New Testaments can be cited in support of God's unilateral covenantal relationship with human beings. In Psalm 139, King David is made aware not only that God wonderfully created his innermost being in his mother's womb (v. 13), but that in the secret place, in the depth of the earth, his unformed body is not hidden from the Creator-God (v. 15) and that all the days ordained for David have been written in God's book before one of them came to be (v. 16). The most remarkable thing about this psalm, in which David recounts his life, indeed his prenatal life, is his awareness of a very intimate and personal fellowship between God and himself; indeed, the "I-Thou" relationship between God and his creature is most pronounced in this psalm. It is God who has created, searched, known, surrounded, held and sustained David, who bears witness not so much to his relationship with God, but to God's relationship with him in a one-sided covenant of grace.[83] All of God's actions occur prior to our having any ability to consciously relate and respond to him, and we don't become God's image or persons by virtue of what we have, do or perform; it is God's loving and free initiative, intention and action to create us and to establish a relationship with us, and it is in this covenantal relationship that we are God's image on earth, which makes us persons. God is, and we are. Or as G. C. Berkouwer describes it:

> In all his relations and acts, [man] is never man-in-himself, but always man-in-relation, in relation to this history of God's deeds in creation, to this origin of an inalienable relation to his Creator. And this man is protected and maintained in his relation to God by him.[84]

We love because God first loved us (1 Jn 4:19).

If we are the image of God only on account of God's faithfulness in keeping

---

[81]Moltmann, *God in Creation,* p. 233.

[82]But it should also be stressed that the image of God is not merely a status, a position implied by Clifford E. Bajema in his *Abortion and the Meaning of Personhood* (Grand Rapids, Mich.: Baker, 1974), pp. 30-31; see also pp. 38-39.

[83]Other scriptural passages that support this line of argument include Job 31:15; Ps 22:9-10; 71:6; 119:73; Is 49:1, 5; Jer 1:5.

[84]G. C. Berkouwer, *Man: The Image of God* (Grand Rapids, Mich.: Eerdmans, 1962), p. 59.

his unilateral covenant of love and grace, then one remains wholly and entirely a person in God's image despite one's inability to respond to God's love in proper relationship to him, to fellow creatures and to the rest of creation because of one's developmental immaturity (e.g., being an embryo, a fetus or an infant), one's disability (e.g., being anencephalic, irreversibly comatose, in a persistent vegetative state, or severely mentally retarded or degenerated) or one's iniquity (being willfully sinful and godless). As Moltmann has written:

> The presence of God makes the human being undeprivably and inescapably God's image. . . . Even the human being who is totally *in*human remains a human being. . . . The dignity of human beings is unforfeitable, irrelinquishable and indestructible.[85]

In a similar manner, Barth believes that as human beings our very being is derived from God's freely given relationship to us. We are linked with a gracious God from the beginning whether we are conscious of it or not; we may ignore or forget the relationship, but we cannot destroy it. Barth summarizes this transcendental determination of the human existence as follows:

> That man is from God and is grounded, constituted and maintained by him, is an event which is willed, decided and effected by God. . . . In this event, he is created. In this event he is what he is by nature: soul and body in ordered unity. . . . He is, then, in virtue of the fact that God relates Himself to him in the event of this act. He lives, as the living God lives.[86]

It is on the basis of the *imago Dei* expressed in this divine-human covenantal relationship that all human beings possess equal dignity and worth regardless of the level of maturity they have achieved. The young and old, smart and stupid, infantile and senile, healthy and infirm are all equally in relation to God as his image. Thus, all humans—*not* just those who are rational or self-conscious—retain the right to life, for these rights are extended not on the basis of certain qualities achieved but because the human life has been freely created in love by God and lives in his creative purposes. Hence, the God-to-humankind covenantal relationship undergirds and conditions all our understanding of humanity, and it underwrites an ethic of personhood for our morality. Any description of human personhood and morality that omits this dimension would be found to be wanting. In forgetting or ignoring this reality, we can only contradict our own humanity in the image of God and become confused in our actions and decisions by the various complex issues at the beginning of life brought on by modern technology.

---

[85]Moltmann, *God in Creation,* p. 233, italics in original.
[86]Barth *Church Dogmatics* 3/2, §46.2.

6

The Temporal and Eschatological Dimensions of Human Personhood

*T*emporality and Potentiality

My analysis thus far suggests that the full actualization of human personhood is a function of the constant and dynamic interplay between the biological, psychological and relational (social/cultural) dimensions of the human being. That being the case, we can expect that these dimensions do not express themselves all at the same time nor express themselves with the same force at any given moment. Indeed, the very nature of their interactions can best be understood as processes by which each dimension influences, actualizes and ultimately fulfills the purpose of the other dimensions. These dynamic interactions between the various dimensions of a human being point to a temporal element in human personhood whereby it is possible to see human personhood as a series of unfolding events. As Clifford Geertz claims, "It is in man's career, in its characteristic course, that we can discern however dimly, his nature."[1] Geertz is saying that to define a person, we must account for her entire career, including what she has been, what she now is and what she may become. As a historical being, the

---

[1]Clifford Geertz, "The Impact of the Concept of Culture on the Concept of Man," in *New Views on the Nature of Man,* ed. John R. Platt (Chicago: University of Chicago Press, 1965), p. 116.

human person's biography begins when she is conceived and becomes a genetically unique individual. In Christian terms, the history of the human person begins when the personal God acts to initiate the relation with the person in the act of the person's creation—the person whom he calls forth to existence, with whom he will continue to relate and from whom he anticipates a response.

Successive stages in the unfolding of a human being imply that potentiality or capacity is an appropriate human characteristic. Sequential unfolding of various actualized and manifested achievements means that we cannot expect to see all dimensions of personhood displayed at one time, but we can anticipate within limits of certainty that the potentialities or capacities for various characteristics do exist and can be realized under certain favorable circumstances. Recognizing that human persons possess yet-to-be realized potentialities is to underline the fact that humans are both human *beings* as well as human *becomings*. Projections into the future are so important in human affairs that we may think of humans as eschatological beings, with their eyes always fixed just beyond the horizon. This means that instead of attributing personhood to an individual based exclusively on certain actualized characteristics, it is plausible, desirable and indeed necessary to consider human potentialities and capacities.

The three dimensions of human personhood I have discussed so far suggest that human personhood may be defined in terms of an interactive unfolding of biological, psychological and relational (social/cultural) potentialities. With the exception of the Christian conviction that God initiates the divine-human relation unilaterally in the act of creating the human person (itself a profoundly significant self-understanding not to be dismissed), in general, it is held that relations between human beings or social/cultural potentialities cannot be realized without the actualization of psychological potentialities, which in turn cannot be realized without the actualization of biological potentialities. This type of mutual dependency of the various dimensions of humanness does not entail that there are distinct boundaries or demarcations of development from one stage to another, like those found in the metamorphosis of a caterpillar to a butterfly. This is a mistake made by Lawrence C. Becker in his attempt to delimit the biological boundaries of human life and insist that the fetus, before the completion of a certain arbitrary metamorphic phase (which he chooses to be the formation of basic gross anatomical form and maturation of a set of histologically differentiated organs), is not yet a human "being" but only a human "becoming."[2] Baruch Brody also seems to have committed himself to this faulty line of reasoning in his proposal that brain activity, which no human being can lose without

---

[2]Lawrence C. Becker, "Human Being: The Boundaries of the Concept," *Philosophy and Public Affairs* 4 (Summer 1975).

ceasing to exist, is "the essence of humanity."[3] But the argument begs the question of why the completion of any arbitrarily determined metamorphic phase should carry any particular moral significance.

In an attempt to avoid the arbitrariness of having to precisely delineate the boundary of becoming/being, W. R. Carter creates the equally troubling problem of having to decide the degree of personhood an individual possesses and falls into another trap of creating the category of "marginal persons."[4] One may legitimately ask, does Karen Quinlin, in her state of irreversible coma, possess a sufficient degree of brain activity to be considered a person? Or is she only a marginal person, or worse, a nonperson? Again, what degree of personhood can the anencephalic baby be said to possess? These questions become very complex, and their answers arbitrary, if we seek to talk and measure in terms of degrees of personhood.[5]

Some of these conceptual difficulties arise from a common misunderstanding that the teleological organization of "potentialities" always exists as a form of hierarchy. It is certainly true that biological potentialities are teleologically oriented in that the unique pattern of human development is not random but ordered and purposeful. We observe for example, that the psychological capacity for rationality, which is crucial for social interaction and for making culture, is prepared very early in fetal brain development. I agree with Majorie Grene that "the whole structure of the [human] embryo, the whole rhythm of growth, is directed, from first to last, to the emergence of a culture-dwelling animal."[6] Human development has always demonstrated a unique pattern of direction toward the unfolding and fulfillment of certain characteristics and purposes, and this potentiality toward certain goals provides the most significant dimension in defining human personhood. But one cannot justify the conclusion that teleologically oriented potentialities are necessarily hierarchical, as Michael Polanyi implies when he visualizes human beings beginning as vegetative human life and growing into responsible persons.[7] Instead, the teleological organization of human development should be seen as a reminder that the different phases of development are actualizations of the various human potentialities (biological, psychological

---

[3]Baruch Brody, "On the Humanity of the Fetus," in *Abortion: Pro and Con,* ed. Robert L. Perkins (Cambridge, Mass.: Schenkman, 1974).

[4]W. R. Carter, "Once and Future Persons," *American Philosophical Quarterly* 17 (January 1980): 61-66.

[5]For a full discussion of the degrees of personhood and its implications for abortion, see chapter sixteen, "Moderation of the Extreme Positions via Re-evaluation of the Moral Status of the Fetus," below.

[6]Majorie Grene, *Approaches to a Philosophical Biology* (New York: Basic, 1968), p. 48.

[7]Michael Polanyi, *Personal Knowledge* (Chicago: Chicago University Press, 1974), p. 395.

and relational) and their interrelatedness and indebtedness to each other, rather than a gradation of priority.

Potentiality and Actuality

Another common difficulty in this understanding of potentialities results from an overstatement of the distinction between the capacity for and the potentiality of a certain function. In discussing higher mental functions, Michael Tooley distinguishes between potentiality and capacity, and he argues that fetuses only have potentiality for higher mental functions whereas comatose or sleeping persons have the actual capacity.[8] He claims that a comatose or sleeping person may be temporarily impeded from exercising that capacity due to certain factors (e.g., somnolence or reversible brain injury), but nonetheless that capacity is "immediately exercisable" once those factors are removed. In other words, to say that a comatose or sleeping person has the capacity for higher mental function is to say that he would behave and exhibit properties of higher mental function if the circumstances were more favorable. Fetuses on the other hand, Tooley argues, only have the potentiality for high mental functions and thus must undergo certain "constitutive transformations" that involve more than the mere elimination of negative factors before they will attain higher mental functions. Tooley concludes that one must have the capacity for higher mental functions in order to be a person; as fetuses only possess the potentiality for such properties, they are not persons and do not possess a right to life.[9]

Further reflection on Tooley's example suggests that the difference between the capacity and potentiality for higher mental function is more apparent than real and that it is more related to the complexity of the function being actualized or exercised. Tooley claims that exercising a certain "capacity" requires only the mere removal of certain obstacles whereas actualizing a certain "potentiality" necessitates further development or maturation, but this distinction can be understood as merely a difference in the immediacy of the function's exercisability. Nothing else in the capacity/potentiality distinction in his example suggests that a comatose or sleeping person is fundamentally different from an embryo/fetus; to the extent that capacity and potentiality both denote the availability of certain functions, so comatose or sleeping persons and embryos/fetuses both can be said to possess the inherent property of higher mental functions.

Patrick Lee further argues that the difference between the potentiality of an

---

[8]Michael Tooley, *Abortion and Infanticide* (New York: Oxford University Press, 1983). See also chapter sixteen, "Moderation of the Extreme Positions via Re-evaluation of the Moral Status of the Fetus," below.

[9]Ibid., pp. 146-57.

embryo (not immediately exercisable) and the capacity of a comatose or sleeping person (immediately exercisable) is not sufficient to be morally significant.[10] Adopting the Aristotelian classification, he considers such basic human potentialities to move, grow and reason to be "natural active potentialities" specific to and inherent in all human lives. In this significant sense, the embryo/fetus does have the active potential to perform higher mental acts because she already has that "positive factor" within herself—that is, the embryo/fetus is the self-same source of what she will become. In fact, once embryos/fetuses come to being, they actively develop themselves to the point where they can exercise these higher mental functions. Lee puts it this way: "being a thing which has the potentiality . . . is what confers *actual* personhood, and human embryos and fetuses have that characteristic actually, not just potentially."[11] To defend the conclusion that embryos and fetuses, who only potentially possess certain qualities, should carry the same moral weight as adults, who have already actualized these qualities, Lee points out that the action of terminating life bears primarily on potentialities rather than actualities, regardless whether the life is embryonic or adult. In killing, the one killed is deprived not of his past or present but of his future; what one actually is and has been cannot be removed, but what one may potentially become is lost. "Therefore, killing an unborn child is, in this respect, worse than killing an adult, because it deprives him or her of even more of life than the adult."[12] In other words, in certain instances, potentiality may be seen as more valuable than actuality, and not the other way around, as most modern people are inclined to think.

In connection with the discussion of potentiality and capacity, H. Tristram Engelhardt Jr. asks whether a person can maintain her personhood while asleep. He recognizes that as embodied self-conscious human beings, we are "spatiotemporally extended entities" and may become temporarily "un-self-conscious," due to the need for rest; as such, temporal discontinuities are to be expected. But he claims that as long as our embodiment is maintained through this span of "un-self-consciousness" so that the "physical substrate" of self-consciousness (and personhood) is not irreversibly damaged, the person's existence is likewise maintained. When that person resumes self-consciousness, we know who she is.[13] But Engelhardt does not think that the same can be said of the zygote or the fetus or even the young infant because

---

[10]Patrick Lee, *Abortion and Unborn Human Life* (Washington, D.C.: Catholic University of America Press, 1996), pp. 22-29.

[11]Ibid., p. 61.

[12]Ibid., pp. 61-62.

[13]H. Tristram Engelhardt Jr., *The Foundations of Bioethics* (Oxford: Oxford University Press, 1986), p. 122.

one does not yet know that person who will come to be "in" . . . that body. . . .
There is a difference in kind between a body that *is* someone's body, and a body
that *may become* someone's body. . . . One will need to distinguish between the
potentiality *to become* a person and the potentialities *of* a person. . . . There is a
difference in kind between knowing who is sleeping, in the case of an adult competent human, and knowing who a fetus will be.[14]

On this basis, Engelhardt attempts to justify the conclusion that a comatose
or sleeping person is still a person (and so cannot be violated) but a fetus is
only a possible person who could be prevented from being actualized
(through abortion): "Killing fetuses only prevents possible persons from
becoming persons."[15] It is apparent that Engelhardt has already made a decision as to who is and who is not a person before he says that as long as the
body's capacities are the capacities of a person, temporal discontinuities can be
bridged; but since the body of the fetus or infant presently belongs to no person, there is no identity to span or personhood to maintain. But it seems to me
that saying a body belongs to nobody is rather peculiar, to say the very least.

The Notion of a Potential Person

An important issue related to the discussion of human potentiality/actuality is
the popular notion of the "potential person," which says that embryos,
fetuses and infants are biological human lives that have inherent active
potentials to develop into a human person with all its characteristics but that
are not yet actual persons or "strict persons" (to use Engelhardt's terminology). On the same basis, the Warnock Committee recommends that "potential persons" such as embryos and fetuses should be afforded only some
protection[16] and that their full rights should be withheld until human potentiality is fully actualized with the attainment of self-consciousness and rationality. One may use the following analogy to dispute what is here claimed as
the difference between a potential person and an actual person. A forty-year-
old presidential aspirant may be said to be a potential president because
there is a possibility (potentiality) that he, as a candidate for that office, will
be elected. In this sense, a sperm or an ovum is a potential human being
because given certain circumstances (when they fuse), there is a possibility
for their becoming a human person. Gametes are, hence, only potential persons because they may not meet and unite to become a human being. On the
other hand, a president-elect is not merely a potential president, for unless

---

[14]Ibid.

[15]Ibid., p. 123.

[16]Warnock Committee, *Report of the Committee of Inquiry into Human Fertilisation and
Embryology* (London: Her Majesty's Stationery Office, 1984), p. 63. Cited in Norman M. Ford,
When Did I Begin? (Cambridge: Cambridge University Press, 1988), p. 98.

something drastic happens, he will be president. For all practical purposes, he is an actual president, preparing for his inaugural speech, getting ready to move in to the presidential office and so on. In time, he will perform more and more of the functions of a president. A zygote/embryo/fetus is in the same sense not a potential person, but a "person-elect"; and as a person-elect, she is already an actual person.

One of the fundamental problems with the notion of potential person arises from the failure to distinguish the potential *to cause* something to come into existence from the potential of something *to become* fully what it already is. A sperm and an ovum have the first type (the potential to cause), whereas an embryo has the second type (the potential to become); and the second type of potentiality already embodies actuality. Robert Joyce argues that a woman's potential to have babies is an actuality that a man does not have. Likewise, a human embryo's potential to reason, will and relate is an actuality that a sperm or an ovum does not have. The potential or capacity to engage in a certain action is an "actual potential" or "functional capacity," even though one is not engaging the action at the moment. Hence, a human embryo with the natural potential or capacity for reasoning, willing and relating to others is already a person, whether or not this natural potential or capacity is ever actualized.[17] The growth and development of the embryo, fetus or infant is the growth and development of a human person *to* maturity, rather than the growth and development of a nonhuman entity *into* a human person. As Paul Ramsey has written, "The human individual comes into existence as a minute information speck. . . . His subsequent prenatal and postnatal development may be described as a process of *becoming what he already is* from the moment he was conceived."[18]

Another fundamental problem with the notion of a potential person (especially notions of the "gradualist" variety) is the failure to distinguish between *being* a person and *functioning* as a person.[19] As I have discussed earlier, C. Stephen Evans sees in the doctrine of creation the basis for viewing human persons as "created substantial achievers"—persons created as beings, actualities or substances who are called to become, to achieve, to function and to relate to others. In short, human persons are beings created to become. But a "human being" is not thereby reduced to a "human becoming," because to

---

[17]Robert E. Joyce, "Personhood and the Conception Event," *The New Scholasticism* 52 (Winter 1978): 97-109; also see Lee, *Abortion,* pp. 22-29.

[18]Paul Ramsey, *Fabricated Man: The Ethics of Genetic Control* (New Haven, Conn.: Yale University Press, 1970), p. 11.

[19]For a more detail discussion of the gradualist principle and a potential person, see chapter sixteen, "Moderation of the Extreme Positions via Re-evaluation of the Moral Status of the Fetus," below.

become presupposes a being, however minimal that being may be.[20] The crucial significance of the Christian doctrine of creation is found in God's intention that human beings are so created: as substantial beings called with the capacities/potentials to become. As such, even those who must wait to actualize all the potentials to become, or who outright will never actualize to become at all, nevertheless continue to *be*.

Hence, personhood as such does not depend as much on the person's achievement of certain functions as on her being created to be in possession of such potentiality to perform those functions. The difference between "being a person" and "functioning as a person" must not be confused or conflated. If the capacity for higher mental functions is essential to human personhood, then an embryo or a fetus who possesses the potentiality for those capacities is a person. The fact that the fetus has not actualized that potentiality to any degree would not be a morally sufficient reason to call the fetus a nonperson. Lee makes a similar point when he suggests that the fetus is valuable not because of the functions (e.g., rational thought) she potentially may perform (a view that sees the fetus only as instrumentally valuable) but because the fetus with the active potentialities is identical with the adult who later possesses the actualized potential.[21]

Modern society's insistence on defining personhood in terms of function is largely due to a pervasive pragmatism undergirding the ethos of our time. Cardinal Joseph Bernardin reflects on being and functioning when he distinguishes between a "pragmatic humanism" and a "personalist humanism." He observes that the former is rooted in utilitarian philosophy, in which the value and dignity of certain "non-productive persons" (such as fetuses, infants, the comatose and the senile) may be diminished for the sake of the greatest good for society. Whatever value and dignity these individuals may be given or "extrinsically attributed" is based on a pragmatic budgeting and balancing of cost-analysis and benefit computation, with the "bottom line" always leaning in favor of the common good; the pursuit of this common good is sought even at the expense of the weak, voiceless, marginalized and disenfranchised. In pragmatic humanism, an individual's "right" depends on the "might" one can demonstrate. In short, it is a "might makes right" humanism.

In contrast, Bernardin wants to affirm a "personalist humanism" based on "a higher moral law" that affirms the "inherent value and dignity of every human person even if unwanted or undervalued by others." In other words, human dignity is rooted simply in "being human." This contrasts sharply with pragmatic humanism, which roots the human dignity in "doing human

---

[20]C. Stephen Evans, "Human Persons as Substantial Achievers," *Philosophia Reformata* 58, no. 1 (1993): 107-11.

[21]Lee, *Abortion*, p. 26.

things."[22] While he is right in his critique of the pragmatic approach of understanding the person, Bernardin is less than candid in his essay when it comes to stating clearly the basis of the inherent value and dignity of the human person. Without stating the basis of the human being made in God's image, it is not apparent why "being human" is more superior to "doing human things." After all, one is usually recognized and evaluated by what one does or what is done to one. What needs to be stated is the Christian perspective I have been advocating: *even if the fetus and the senile (i.e., nonproductive persons) cannot "do human things," they still command full dignity because God has not ceased to relate to them—they are still persons because they continue to be related to.* And this leads me to discuss the Christian tradition of seeing the *imago Dei* and human personhood from the eschatological perspectives.

The Eschatological Dimension of the *Imago Dei* in the Christian Tradition

As discussed earlier, on the basis of New Testament teachings (e.g., Jn 14:9; 2 Cor 4:4; Col 1:15; Heb 1:3), Karl Barth grounds his understanding of human nature in the God-man, Jesus Christ. For him, real human nature is revealed through the humanity of Jesus. As the Real Man, Jesus has the true creaturely form of humankind, that is, the form of "I-Thou" human relationship. He allows himself to be affected by the lives of his fellow companions and makes their cause his own. He sacrifices for and gives himself to them, and in so doing he is for humanity in a radical way. Hence, in Jesus we see the perfect correspondence and similarity between the human Jesus' being for God (his divinity; God-man) and his being for his fellows (his humanity; man-man). Barth says, "If the divinity of the man Jesus is to be described comprehensively in the statement that He is man for God, His humanity can and must be described no less succinctly in the proposition that He is man for man, for other men, His fellows."[23] To that extent, Jesus is the perfect *imago Dei.*

As the perfect image of God, Christ in his incarnation creates the necessary condition for humanity to be renewed in and conformed to his image (Rom 8:29). In the New Testament, to be in the image of God then is realized in the fellowship of believers with Christ—to become *imago Christi* through the agency of the Holy Spirit, expressed in a life of love for God, neighbors and the rest of creation. In 2 Corinthians 3:18 (NRSV), Paul speaks of how sinful

---

[22]Joseph Bernardin, "Medical Humanism: Pragmatic or Personalist?" *Health Progress* 66 (April 1985): 46-49.

[23]Karl Barth *Church Dogmatics* 3/2, ed. G. W. Bromiley and T. F. Torrance (Edinburgh: T & T Clark, 1960), §45.1.

humans "are being transformed into the same image from one degree of glory to another." It is no mere coincidence that in the image-renewing passages, Paul always uses the present tense: "are being transformed" (2 Cor 3:18), "is being renewed" (Col 3:10) and "to be renewed" (Eph 4:23). If the image of God is once-and-for-all realized in Christ, clearly Paul wants to emphasize that renewing the imperfect human image of God is a dynamic, ongoing and progressive process. In this process, *being* human is powerfully linked with *becoming* human, so that the endpoint of the image renewal is yet to be reached. In a sense, the New Testament describes the image of God in such a way that the doctrine of *imago Dei* has been transformed from a protological perspective to an eschatological perspective, with the implication that the final realization of the image of God in humankind will only be made manifest in the *eschaton*. As Jürgen Moltmann puts it, "In the messianic light of the gospel, the human being's likeness to God appears as a historical process with an eschatological termination; it is not a static condition."[24] In other words, the image of God is essentially dynamic and eschatological, and this means that the temporal dimension of human personhood includes an eschatological orientation.

The eschatological dimension of the human being as the *imago Dei* is quite explicitly stated by Paul in 1 Corinthians 15:49 (NRSV) when he says, "Just as we have borne the image of the man of dust, we will also bear the image of the man from heaven." The greater context of the passage is contrasting the first and the last Adam, implying that in this present life, we continue to bear the image of Adam and that only in the life to come shall we fully bear the image of Christ, the one from heaven. This eschatological dimension of the image of God is also found in John's teaching when he says, "Now we are children of God, and what we will be has not yet been made known. But we know that when he appears, we shall be like him, for we shall see him as he is. Everyone who has this hope in him purifies himself, just as he is pure." (1 Jn 3:2-3 NIV). John is emphasizing we are not expected to attain perfect likeness to Christ and God, the ultimate goal of our sanctification, until the end time. Although the image of God is now being progressively restored in those who are children of God, that restoration will only be completed in the life to come, when we shall perfectly glorify God as his image-bearers, at last fulfilling what we are intended to be, the perfected *imago Dei* and hence the *gloria Dei*.

This dynamic, progressive and eschatological understanding of the *imago Dei* is reflected in the teaching of some church fathers. Both Origen and Irenaeus teach that Adam and Eve were created like children, requiring that they

---

[24]Jürgen Moltmann, *God in Creation* (San Francisco: HarperSanFrancisco, 1991), p. 227.

grow before becoming perfect.[25] They interpret Genesis 1:26-28 as teaching that the "image" of God is a kind of potentiality for life in God that is given to the human being and that the "likeness" of God is the realization of that potentiality, a state when the human being comes closest to be like God.[26] The created human being possesses the image, which initiates the journey, but the likeness is achieved only at the end of one's journey. In Origen's words, "Man received the honor of the image at his first creation, but the full perfection of God's likeness will only be conferred upon him at the consummation of all things."[27] These church fathers describe this process of human development or actualization of human potentials as "deification." They recognize human nature as a dynamic, ongoing process; and they describe human life as a pilgrimage, with a history beginning in immaturity and imperfection, and progressing through various stages to greater and greater manifestations of the image, until it is ultimately consummated in total likeness with God. These two stages—from image to likeness of human maturation—as understood by these church fathers is important not only because it emphasizes the dynamic and teleological aspects of God's "image" and "likeness," but also because it means that human beings are not made and endowed with a fully realized perfection before they are called image-bearers of God. Rather, human beings are meant to respond to and to cooperate with God's grace through the use of their free will, slowly and gradually growing into perfection. The image of God and human personhood involves potentiality, development, progress and history.

This idea of humanity in a process of transition, moving toward a goal not clearly known, is majestically woven throughout the Bible, starting with the call of Abraham and culminating in the person of Jesus and his spiritual body, the church. It emphasizes that "a human person is a being-on-the-way," to use John Macquarrie's phrase, and on this side of glory, for us as human beings, the journey goes on until the end is reached. What may be the end of the human being-on-the-way? Or as the Westminster Shorter Catechism asks, what is the chief end of man? And the beatific response is, "To glorify God, and to enjoy him for ever." To glorify God and to enjoy him is to live in the reality of becoming what God wills us to become, living harmoniously in our relationships with God, the self, others and the world; as these relationships deepen

---

[25]Henri Crouzel, *Origen: The Life and Thought of the First Great Theologian,* trans. A. S. Worrall (San Francisco: Harper & Row, 1989), pp. 92-98; and Irenaeus of Lyon *Against Heresies* 4.38-39, in *Theological Anthropology,* ed. J. Patout Burns, S.J. (Philadelphia: Fortress, 1981), pp. 23-28.

[26]While I recognize their exegesis in this case as spurious, I may nonetheless glean the greater point.

[27]Origen *On First Principles* 3.6.1, quoted in Bishop Kallistos Ware, *The Orthodox Way,* rev. ed. (Crestwood, N.Y.: St. Vladimir's Orthodox Theological Seminary, 1979), p. 52.

and expand, we ourselves grow as persons in the image of God. Thus human persons are involved in a process of actualizing our potentiality/capacity to image God in love—to give oneself in love and to delight in receiving love. In giving us life, God creates us in love; in redeeming us, he opens up the potential for us to live in his love, which is in Christ Jesus; and in sanctifying us, he calls us to strive toward the human goal as "lovers-in-the-making"—limited, finite and defective, yet always on the way, by divine grace, toward a sharing in the life of God whose name is Love. Humans find joy in love—the love of God, self, fellow humans and the world.

Conclusion

I began this discussion of the human person as created relational "substance," and I have emphasized the unique dyadic structure of both substantiality and relationality. The created "substantial" person comes about because the triune God intends to relate to a particular person as expressed in and actualized through the act of creation, specifically in God's making it possible for a particular sperm to merge with a particular ovum, through the conjugal act of a male and a female joined in a marital covenant. *The formation of a zygote affirms God's intention to create a new human being as his image and to relate to this unique human being. This ongoing creational and relational act is established in a historical point of time and points to an eschatological future. Potentialities and capacities are given from the moment of God's creative act as part and parcel of the created "substance" and as tools needed by God's image-bearers to engage God and other creatures in relations. But God's relation with the created human person (substance, image) has already been established through the personal, unilateral and specific act of creation. What is essential to human personhood is this God-creature relationship, intentionally and unilaterally established by God.*

It is true that God intends, in the majority of cases, for his creatures to gradually actualize their capacities and potentialities to respond to the divine initiative by developing a relationship with him, other fellow creatures and the rest of creation. But that is not to say that these potentials and capacities have to be actualized before a human entity is a person. To make such an assertion amounts to claiming that the content of the created human "substance" is a set of unrealized capacities or potentialities and not an actualized God-creature relationship. What God intends and what he equips persons to achieve is "becoming"; but the person as a unique "being" is grounded in the establishment of a God-creature relationship in the unique creation of a particularized human "substance" initiated by God. In most cases, a "being" created in a divine-human personal relationship is meant to continue "becoming" more fully in all relationships. Nonetheless, a human being remains a person even without achieving a human becoming because she has *always been*—from the moment of her creation—a person involved in a personal, divine-human relation initiated by God.

In light of the above, it is important to realize that the starting point for the Christian interpretation of the human person as the *imago Dei* is not "the phenomenon human being" in the sense of what a human being is or can do.[28] This point of departure is based on a false inference, for the *imago Dei* is a theological term before it is an anthropological one. Hence, Christian anthropology is theocentric rather than anthropocentric: it tells us something about the God who creates an image for himself before it says anything about the human being who is created to be his image. It tells first and foremost of God's resolve to enter into a particular relationship with us through which we become persons in his image and by whom he is thereby glorified. Hence, the nature of human beings springs from God's relationship to them. If human nature is defined by God's relationship to human beings, then it is not to be determined by the possession of any particular characteristic, either potential or actualized. A human person can only be defined by what the triune God has done: whenever we speak of the human person we have to first speak of God.[29]

---

[28]Moltmann, *God in Creation*, p. 220.
[29]Barth *Church Dogmatics* 3/2, §46.2.

Part Two

Assisted
Reproductive
Technologies and
Personhood

7

Infertility and the Need for Assisted Reproductive Technologies

*T*he World Health Organization and the Canadian Royal Commission on Reproductive Technology consider a couple to be infertile if they have not conceived after two years of unprotected intercourse.[1] The 1982 United States National Survey of Family Growth reported that 8.5 percent of married couples were infertile,[2] and this agrees well with the Canadian Royal Commission's finding that 8.5 percent of all couples cohabiting for at least one year and 7 percent of couples cohabiting for two years failed to achieve pregnancy,[3] indicating that infertility is a widespread problem in North America.

Infertility in Women
Infertility in women can have a wide range of causes—including heredity, diet, climate, environmental factors (e.g., protozoa, bacteria, viruses)—and it may be

---

[1] *Proceed with Care: Final Report of the Royal Commission on New Reproductive Technologies,* 2 vols. (Ottawa: Canada Communications Group, 1993), 1:183.
[2] U.S. Congress, Office of Technology Assessment, *Fertility: Medical and Social Choices* (Washington, D.C.: U.S. Government Printing Office, 1988), p. 49.
[3] *Proceed with Care,* 1:180.

caused by anatomical, physiological or psychological abnormalities.[4] But the single most significant cause of infertility in women, accounting for about 25 to 35 percent of all incidences, is blocked or damaged fallopian tubes;[5] a large group of infectious diseases, collectively labeled "sexually transmitted diseases" (STDs), is by far the most significant source of damage to the fallopian tubes.[6] STDs include bacterial diseases such as gonorrhea, chlamydia and syphilis and viral diseases such as genital herpes, the human papilloma virus and the virus that causes AIDS. Both STDs, which cause extensive pelvic inflammation (especially in the fallopian tubes), and their treatments can inflict different kinds of physical damage to the reproductive organs, resulting in infertility.

Ovulatory dysfunction is the second leading cause of female infertility, accounting for between 15 and 20 percent of all cases. Ovulation commonly occurs about two weeks before the onset of a woman's menstrual period, at which point the egg is fertilizable for about 12 to 24 hours, and anything that causes an irregular menstrual cycle will significantly hamper a woman's ability to conceive. Endometriosis, a relatively rare disease, has been cited as another cause of infertility. Once dubbed "one-child sterility," it is estimated that 30 to 40 percent of patients with the disease become infertile.[7] The use of the intrauterine device (IUD) also leads to an increased incidence of female infertility, due to higher incidence of pelvic infections and fallopian-tube damages.[8] Various physical abnormalities—ranging from injuries due to surgical abortions or D & Cs (dilation and curettage procedures) or due to malformations of various parts of the female reproductive anatomy—have all been identified as causes of female infertility.[9] Smoking, including exposure to secondhand smoke, has been shown to decrease fertility. Women smokers have been found to develop

---

[4]C. R. Austin, *Human Embryos: The Debate on Assisted Reproduction* (Oxford: Oxford University Press, 1989), p. 86.

[5]Congress, *Fertility,* p. 49.

[6]This is hardly surprising since the fallopian tube plays an essential role early in pregnancy by attracting the eggs released from the ovary, transporting the sperm and the egg to the site of conception in the upper third portion of the tube, as well as creating an environment for fertilization and nurturing of the fertilized egg, and finally transporting the fertilized egg to the uterus. Damage to the fallopian tube as a result of infection can interfere with any of the above functions to cause infertility. See Stephen Genuis, *Reproduction Rollercoaster: Infertility and the Assisted Reproductive Technologies* (Edmonton: KEG Publishing, 1992), pp. 44-45.

[7]How endometriosis may cause infertility is unknown. Several reasons have been proposed, including sexual dysfunction, problems related to ovulation, malfunction of the fallopian tubes due to secretions produced by the endometrial implants, as well as a handicap in ovarian egg production and release; none of these reasons has been proven. For detail, see Genuis, *Reproduction Rollercoaster,* pp. 70-71.

[8]N. C. Lee, G. L. Rubin and R. Borucki, "The Intrauterine Device and Pelvic Inflammatory Disease Revisited: New Results from the Women's Health Study," *Obstetrics and Gynecology* 72, no. 1 (1988): 1-6.

[9]Genuis, *Reproduction Rollercoaster,* p. 46.

both abnormal growths that block their fallopian tubes as well as changes in the cervical mucus that prevent sperm from reaching the egg, and they are three to four times less likely to conceive than are nonsmokers. Women who drink more than one cup of coffee per day are half as likely to become pregnant per menstrual cycle as are women who do not drink coffee.[10] The Canadian Royal Commission reports that many agents found in the workplace and environment may adversely influence women's reproductive capacities in ways yet to be determined.[11]

Infertility in Men

Contrary to the conventional belief that infertility is entirely the problem of the "barren" woman, we now know that about 30 to 40 percent of infertility cases are related specifically to the male. For men, the most common reason for infertility is oligospermia (low sperm count), azoospermia (no sperm at all) or sperm that lack sufficient motility for effective fertilization. The specific causes of these conditions are largely unknown. Another cause of male infertility is varicocele, a condition where a collection of enlarged veins accumulates in the scrotum of the patient. It is speculated that the consequent rise in temperature of the scrotal sac and the testicles may exert a negative effect on the reproductive potential of the male.[12] As with women, men's fertility problems can be caused by smoking, alcohol and drug abuse. The studies done in this area are limited, but they do point to a relationship between substance abuse and both reduced sperm count and reduced motility in men. Sexually transmitted diseases may also produce a negative effect on male fertility, although the exact etiological mechanism has yet to be elucidated. More research is needed on infertility in men, including the role of STDs—especially given that the male-dominated medical profession tends to focus on female infertility.[13] About 10 to 20 percent of infertility cases, whether of the male or the female, have no apparent cause, and about another 15 to 20 percent are due to a combination of various factors. Infertility is thus a very complicated, multifaceted problem that demands an interdisciplinary response.

Emotional Impact of Infertility

Emotional responses to infertility are complex and will vary from couple to

---

[10]D. Evans, *Without Moral Limits* (Westchester, Ill.: Crossway, 1989), p. 96; also see *Proceed with Care,* 1:236.

[11]*Proceed with Care,* 1:270-72.

[12]Genuis, *Reproduction Rollercoaster,* pp. 48-49.

[13]Barbara Katz Rothman, "Infertility as Disability," in *Contemporary Issues in Bioethics,* 4th ed., ed. Tom L. Beauchamp and LeRoy Walters (Belmont, Calif.: Wadsworth, 1994), p. 215. This same disparity has been noted in the development of contraceptive technology.

couple depending on their psychological make-up, cultural background, religious beliefs and other personal convictions. In general, infertile couples experience deep emotional disturbances as well as psychosomatic problems.[14] Since infertile couples are not visibly ill, their problems are often overlooked, depriving them of the support, empathy and compassion that they need; because infertility commonly affects younger couples, often it is the first major crisis in their marriage, and they may not have developed the necessary skills to deal with the problem.[15] Grieving infertility is further complicated by the fact that couples remain unsure about exactly what to grieve, since there is no loss of a definite object to grieve about.[16] Isolated and withdrawn into their "secret" shame, the infertile couple may come to view everything in their environment differently: relationships, parental duties, spiritual well-being and self-esteem. Among these, the strain on the relationship of the infertile couple is the most profound. Common reasons for the alienation in infertile couples include unequal degrees of desire for a child, different abilities to cope with crisis, conflicting ideas on infertility alternatives, different attitudes toward investigation of and treatment for infertility.[17] Some marriages fail as a direct result of infertility. The couple may also develop physical signs and symptoms as part of the problem, including headaches, abdominal discomfort, general malaise and sleeping or eating disorders. Above all, infertile couples struggle with a sense of "incompleteness," since the ability to procreate is assumed to be an integral part of being human. This sense of a loss of human wholeness is often reinforced by the wider culture, which sees the couple's identity being critically tied to their ability to reproduce and which evaluates the integrity of their relationship on the basis of their ability to produce progeny. Only when we realize the full scope of the infertile couple's state of mental anguish can we begin to appreciate why a compassionate response is so necessary.

Is Infertility a Disease?

Many people refuse to consider infertility as a disease that warrants treatment because the condition does not threaten anyone's survival if left untreated. On this view, infertility is merely a couple's unfulfilled desire to have children of their own, and providing a child by artificial means should not be defined as

---

[14] D. Davis and C. Dearman, "Coping Strategies of Infertility," *JOGNN Clinical Studies,* May-June 1991, p. 221; F. Andrews, A. Abbey and L. Halman, "Stress from Infertility: Marriage Factors and Subjective Well-Being on Wives and Husbands," *Journal of Health and Social Behavior* 31 (September 1991): 240.

[15] Genius, *Reproduction Rollercoaster,* pp. 78-79.

[16] P. Mahlstedt, "The Psychological Component of Infertility," *Fertility and Sterility* 43, no. 3 (March 1985): 343.

[17] Genuis, *Reproduction Rollercoaster,* pp. 86-87.

medical treatment. Just as elective plastic surgery is considered to improve one's lifestyle but not one's health, so too procreation by artificial means is regarded as optional rather than essential. In an environment of scarce medical resources, treatment for infertility should not be a priority.[18] On the other hand, many disagree with this rather dogmatic approach of excluding infertility from the scope of medicine, since not all existing medical treatments are designed to exclusively treat life-threatening conditions.[19] Given that the desire to have children is so universal and that the ability to procreate assumes such paramount importance across all cultures, it seems reasonable to consider infertility as a dysfunctional state that falls within medicine's purview.[20] Barbara Rothman, writing from a feminist perspective, suggests that infertility should be regarded as a disability rather than as a disease because procreation, like walking and talking, is seen as a basic human function and those who lack it should be considered as "disabled." Disabilities are often caused by certain physiological or anatomical impairments, and appropriate medical treatment can sometimes eradicate the cause of the impairment. When infertility is viewed as a disability, treating a blocked fallopian tube is clearly a medical treatment; and if it is not possible to cure the cause of infertility, then treatment modalities that bypass the impairment can be used to offset the disability. In this context, assisted reproductive technologies such as donor insemination and in vitro fertilization are, in Rothman's view, justifiable means to overcome the handicap.[21]

In order to clarify this matter, I think it is important to define the meaning of "medical necessity" on the basis of the distinction between the "normal-functional model" and the "capability model."[22] The normal-functional model considers a condition to be a medical necessity only if the disadvantage is caused by a disease or a specifically diagnosed disability, and infertility secondary to fallopian tube blockage would be a medical necessity based on this model. The capability model considers treatment for anyone with a diminished capacity, whatever the cause, to be a medical necessity. On this model, all causes of infer-

---

[18]Evans, *Without Moral Limits*, p. 92; and Isobel K. Grigor, "Responses to Warnock: A Review," in *Embryos and Ethics: The Warnock Report in Debate*, ed. Nigel M. de S. Cameron (Edinburgh: Rutherford House, 1987), p. 86.

[19]Warnock Committee, "Report of the Committee of Inquiry into Human Fertilization and Embryology," in *Contemporary Issues in Bioethics*, 4th ed., ed. Tom L. Beauchamp and LeRoy Walters (Belmont, Calif.: Wadsworth, 1994), pp. 210-11; and Ian Donald, "Problems Raised by Artificial Human Reproduction," in *Embryos and Ethics: The Warnock Report in Debate*, ed. Nigel M. de S. Cameron (Edinburgh: Rutherford House, 1987), p. 74.

[20]Arthur L. Caplan, "The Ethics of In Vitro Fertilization," in *Contemporary Issues in Bioethics*, 4th ed., ed. Tom L. Beauchamp and LeRoy Walters (Belmont, Calif.: Wadsworth, 1994), p. 222.

[21]Rothman, "Infertility as Disability," pp. 211-26.

[22]James Sabin and Norman Daniels, "Determining 'Medical Necessity' in Mental Health Practice," *Hastings Center Report* 24, no. 6 (1994): 5-13.

tility, including the idiopathic ones, should be given treatment. Though the capability model may be a more ideal goal, in a context of limited medical resources, I believe the normal-functional model provides a better understanding of medical necessity when dealing with the infertility problem. This means treatment is warranted only when a treatable cause is identified. In this regard, the Canadian Royal Commission adopts the position that the most important criterion for employing assisted reproductive technologies is evidence for its effectiveness in relieving the infertile condition. The commission has researched the effectiveness of the in vitro fertilization with embryo transfer (IVF-ET) technique and concluded that it is only effective to treat fallopian tube blockage. The commission also regards it both unethical to employ IVF-ET for any other causes of infertility when the risks and effectiveness of its employment in those other infertile situations remain largely unproven, as well as irresponsible to use scarce public medical resources for such unproven procedures.[23]

Reproduction as a Right

The discussion of whether treating infertility is a medical necessity will eventually and inevitably lead to the question of whether a person has the right to procreate. In the late nineteenth century, the American eugenics movement led to a number of legal trials which established that forced sterilization was unconstitutional and that procreation was a fundamental right to be protected in the United States.[24] The right to procreate is further reinforced by the legalization of contraceptives and abortion, which has effectively established the corresponding right *not* to procreate. These legal precedents and ongoing debates can be expected to influence the individual's right to access the new reproductive technologies in the twenty-first century. But I believe that in a discussion of the right to procreate, it is important to differentiate two kinds of rights: positive and negative. By a negative right I simply mean that based on the principle of self-determination and respect for autonomy, one has the right to be left alone. But to claim that every infertile couple or single person should be provided access to reproductive assistance is to assert a positive right, which goes beyond the noninterference ethic of the negative right and claims that others have the *obligation* to facilitate one's right. It assumes that a particular social good should be distributed in an equitable way so that anyone who can demonstrate the need for that social good will be satisfied. The negative right is based on the principle of self-determination, and the positive right is based on the principle of justice; the two must not be confused. So while the

---

[23] *Proceed with Care,* 1:290-93. As for the use of fertility pills as a treatment, see Athena Liu, *Artificial Reproduction and Reproductive Rights* (Brockfield, Vt.: Dartmouth, 1991).

[24] Liu, *Artificial Reproduction and Reproductive Rights,* pp. 33-34.

right to procreate is a widely accepted negative right that should not be interfered with, the right to use assisted reproductive technologies to procreate as a positive right has yet to be established.

It has been suggested that in a just and caring society, patients' positive health care rights ought to be limited to a basic level, which means that a person is not entitled to every treatment she might desire and that not all potentially beneficial treatments should be made available to all.[25] Given this, one must ask whether assisted reproductive technologies (ARTs) can be considered part of a basic level of health care, comparable to vaccination against smallpox or polio. At the most basic level, ARTs simply do not rate as essential to human welfare in the same way that true necessities like vaccination, food and shelter do. It is difficult to make a convincing case that the right to procreate requires the society to provide every infertile couple access to IVF, unless an effectively treatable condition can be identified, as I have noted.[26]

The Right to Procreate and the Right to Create a Family

It is apparent that individuals, either single men or single women, cannot be said to have a right to reproduce, since naturally as individuals they cannot do so. The same can be said about same-sex couples or postmenopausal women. In claiming a procreative right, these people are really demanding the right to found a family (with the help of ARTs). This distinction is relevant even within the marital context. For instance, a couple's claim to the right to use donor sperm for artificial insemination, or the claim by a couple who are both sterile to the right to "reproduce" through ARTs, is based not so much on the right to reproduce, but on this right to found a family. The issue, therefore, is whether to grant certain individuals the right to found a family even if they cannot reproduce by themselves. Secular bioethics, based on a liberal humanism, has failed to produce a sound moral framework either to approve or to deny such requests. Consequently, some believe that a single woman should have the right to be artificially inseminated by donor sperm out of respect for her autonomy, while others, fearing that such a practice may undermine the integrity of the family and the society, argue that it should be denied on utilitarian grounds. In contrast, Christian orthodoxy is unequivocal in its insistence that a marital relationship be the criterion for one's right to reproduce and found a family. There is no Christian teaching that would permit a person who decides

---

[25]Leonard J. Weber, "In Vitro Fertilization and the Just Use of Health Care Resources," in *Reproduction: Technology and Rights,* ed. James M. Humber and Robert F. Almeder (Toronto: Humana, 1996), pp. 79-80.

[26]Weber, "In Vitro Fertilization," pp. 84-86; also see George Annas, "Regulatory Models for Human Embryo Cloning: The Free Market, Professional Guidelines and Government Restrictions," *Kennedy Institute Ethics Journal* 4 (1994): 235-49.

not to marry to bear and parent a child, simply because it is his or her wish.[27] The Roman Catholic teaching asserts that "the right to become a father and a mother [is] only through each other" and that "the parents find in their child a confirmation and completion of their reciprocal self-giving."[28] Thus, from a Christian point of view, the right to reproduce and have a family can only be discussed exclusively within the framework of marriage.

Reproduction as a Responsibility

While the society focuses on a right to reproduce, many Christians have adopted the view that there may in fact be a *responsibility* to reproduce, a view that sees perpetual voluntary infertility as a violation of God's direct decree.[29] In turn, medically treating those who are afflicted with infertility is considered as honoring this responsibility. The famous "cultural mandate" of Genesis 1:28, "be fruitful and multiply," is often taken as a proof text for this position.[30] However, any discussion of procreation as a responsibility must first be viewed in the context of the world's overpopulation. Non-Christian environmentalists have often blamed the world's overpopulation on those defending the Judeo-Christian heritage and while their criticisms may have been simplistic and biased, they serve to caution us against blindly defending the so-called responsibility to reproduce. Many biblical scholars feel strongly that the mandate to be fruitful and multiply must be interpreted within its cultural context: the ancient Israelite society needed to have as many children as possible for farming and warfare. This suggests that the imperatives of Genesis 1:26-28 are to be understood as context-dependent blessings designed to enhance and enrich human lives, rather than as burdensome commands. The world of Genesis 1:28 would thus have been one where abundant reproduction embodied such a blessing without qualification.[31] But in today's context, the world's current population problem may compel us to examine seriously

---

[27]John S. Feinberg and Paul D. Feinberg, *Ethics for a Brave New World* (Wheaton, Ill.: Crossway, 1993), p. 215.

[28]Cited in Bruce R. Reichenbach and V. Elving Anderson, *On Behalf of God: A Christian Ethic for Biology* (Grand Rapids, Mich.: Eerdmans, 1995), p. 148; also cited in Debra Evans, *Without Moral Limits* (Wheaton, Ill.: Crossway, 1989), p. 179.

[29]G. Farrell and W. Lazareth, *Population Perils* (Philadelphia: Fortress, 1979), p. 47.

[30]The Catholic Church would agree with this conclusion, given certain qualifications. See Congregation for the Doctrine of the Faith, "Instruction on Respect for Human Life in Its Origin and on the Dignity of Procreation: Replies to Certain Questions of the Day," in *Religious and Artificial Reproduction,* ed. Lisa Sowle Cahill and Thomas A. Shannon (New York: Crossroad, 1988).

[31]Raymond Van Leeuwen points out that Gen 24:60 shares the same grammatical structure as the procreation mandate and that the context dictates it to be clearly a blessing and not a command; see his "Breeding Stock or Lords of Creation?" *Christianity Today,* November 11, 1991, pp. 36-37.

whether producing more offspring can still be called a blessing.[32]

Furthermore, the responsibility to overcome infertility cannot be considered in isolation from the lifestyle we adopt both as individuals and as a society. I have alluded to the importance of STDs as a cause of infertility, for they damage the fallopian tubes and other parts of the female reproductive organs; here we need to emphasize the prevalence of STDs in the world due to our "sexually liberated" culture. Statistics indicate that in the United States alone 10 million people are assessed for STDs each year at public and private clinics.[33] It is quite obvious from these statistics that we must radically modify lifestyle and sexual behavior through education if STDs are to be checked and their contribution to infertility reduced. It would be hypocritical, to say the least, to advocate ARTs to relieve infertility and increase population growth when at the same time we live a lifestyle that is conducive to the development of infertility.

Arising from the Christian notion of responsibility to procreate is the problematic concept of "responsible parenthood." The assumption is that it is one's considered choice to assume the responsibility to become parents. But how responsible must we be before we can legitimately choose to become parents? For some, the dual charge of choice and responsibility has created an awesome burden of making perfect children (through reproduction) and making children perfect (through parenting), or of having no children at all. But this account of parenting turns our children into the products of human and technological achievements. It leads to the peculiar paradox of our times: that modern technology would use the most sophisticated skills available to assist those who are infertile to conceive, while at the same time

---

[32]Further evidence that procreation is a context-dependent blessing is found in the New Testament. For instance, there is a situation in which God would not deem it desirable (and therefore not a blessing) to have children: "Woe to those who are pregnant and to those who are nursing infants in those days!" (Mk 13:17 NRSV). Paul also indicated to the Corinthian church that there is a place and purpose for "eschatological celibacy" (1 Cor 7:1-7). If remaining single in certain situations for the furtherance of God's kingdom is an option, can we argue that in certain circumstances remaining childless can fall into that same category?

[33]Stephen Genuis, *Risky Sex,* 2nd ed. (Edmonton: KEG Publishing, 1992), p. 18. See also R. E. Johnson, et al., "A Seroepidemiologic Survey of the Prevalence of Herpes Simplex Virus Type 2 in the United States," *New England Journal of Medicine* 321, no. 1 (1989): 7-12, which reports that between 26 and 31 million people in the U.S. are presently infected with genital herpes. J. F. Jeffrey, "Human Papilloma Virus and Lower Genital Tract Dysplasia: Driver or Passenger?" *Society of Obstetricians and Gynecologists of Canada Bulletin* 10, no. 4 (1988): 5-15, reports that 20 percent of the female population between ages of 15 and 40 is harboring the human papilloma virus (HPV). Center for Disease Control, "Syphilis and Congenital Syphilis: United States 1985-88," *Morbidity and Mortality Weekly Report* 37 (August 1988): 486-89, reports that the rate of syphilis infection has been skyrocketing since 1987 and is at its highest level in forty years.

rejecting fetuses and unborns with the slightest flaws—ultimately reducing our options to either a perfect child or a dead child.[34]

Infertility and the Ethic of Personhood

I believe that the basic metaphor for having children is not choice and responsibility, but gift and stewardship. Christian tradition has always insisted that children are not ours but God's, and therefore ownership is not even determined on the basis of biology or consanguinity. In terms of the account of personhood I have established, we are provided with a moral framework that our children are created by God and entrusted to us as we act as procreators on behalf of God. Or, as Oliver O'Donovan puts it succinctly, children are "first and foremost begotten, not made."[35] They are gifts rather than parental achievements or properties to be designed and disposed of at will. And as gifts, they come to us as a given; they are not our choosing, nor are they under our control.[36] They bring joy and comfort when they arrive; but if they do not come, it may be the occasion to wait on and to relate to God and to relate to our spouse in the new context of infertility, rather than a necessary occasion for pain and despair. The ethic of personhood that emphasizes the vertical relationship with God and horizontal relationship with other God-loving persons as the most important constitutive elements of a person, would not see children as products of our autonomous will or the determinative will of our medical scientists, but rather as the result of the loving God willing them to come into this world as his image. For this reason, children always have a measure of independence from us and our rational choices. Contrary to the conventional belief that we (including Christians) should fight against infertility with any and all means available, the ethic of personhood relieves us of our burden to do all that is technologically possible to relieve infertility and cautions us to be patient and humble, guarding all our relations seriously, weighing all our options carefully and making all our decisions prayerfully.

---

[34]Stanley Hauerwas, *Truthfulness and Tragedy* (Notre Dame: University of Notre Dame Press, 1977), pp. 150-51.

[35]Oliver O'Donovan, *Begotten or Made?* (Oxford: Oxford University Press, 1984), p. 17.

[36]Hauerwas, *Truthfulness and Tragedy*, p. 153; also see Stanley Hauerwas, *A Community of Character* (Notre Dame: University of Notre Dame Press, 1981), p. 171.

8

Artificial
Insemination

*D*efinition, **Medical Procedure and Sperm Banks**

Artificial insemination (AI) continues to be the most basic and widely used ART procedure, and technically it is rather simple. A sperm sample is obtained from either the husband or a donor generally through masturbation, and the sample is then delivered by a syringe into the woman's vagina at the peak of her fertile cycle, about twelve hours immediately preceding ovulation. Achieving correct timing is essential for successful fertilization. The overall success rate for this procedure is between 60 and 80 percent.

In artificial insemination homologous (AIH) the sperm sample is obtained from the husband, and in artificial insemination donor (AID) the sperm sample is obtained from someone other than the husband.[1] Traditionally, artificial insemination has been used to overcome infertility in the husband who suffers from oligospermia, and a concentrated sperm sample is obtained from the husband for use in the procedure. Occasionally AIH is also used for the purpose of sex selection by the separation of sperms bearing X- and Y-chromosomes. If the husband cannot produce a viable sperm sample to successfully complete AIH, or if the husband carries a dominant gene for an inheritable disease such as hemophilia or Huntington's disease, or if the husband has a ejaculatory dysfunction, then a couple may find recourse in AID. Since the 1970s, AI has gained popularity because of two main factors: first, the sharp drop in the

---

[1]AID is also known as TDI (therapeutic donor insemination). The latter acronym is becoming the preferred option due to the resemblance of the former acronym to the acronym AIDS.

availability of babies for adoption due to effective birth-control methods and the legalization of abortion; and second, the desire to avoid genetic diseases. Recently, increased demands for AID has come from single women, homosexual couples and surrogate mothers. In Canada, it has been estimated that between 1,500 and 6,000 children are born each year through AID alone, representing between 0.4 and 1.5 percent of all children born in Canada.[2] A study conducted by the Office of Technology Assessment in the United States reports 30,000 births through AID and 35,000 through AIH in 1986-1987.

The rising popularity of AI has been accompanied by an increased use of sperm banks, an industry made possible by the technology of cryopreservation, which permits sperm samples to be frozen and stored for future use.[3] Initially developed for men who wanted to preserve their semen before undergoing vasectomy, sperm banks now serve other purposes, including sperm storage as insurance against health or occupational hazards and especially sperm storage for patients receiving radiation and chemotherapy for cancer. In recent years, with the increased prevalence of HIV infection, storing sperm in a sperm bank has become part of a routine practice for screening donated sperms: donor semen is taken, frozen and released for use only if two HIV blood tests done 6 months apart are sero-negative.

Ethical Concerns of AI and Sperm Banks

The use of AI and sperm banks has raised several ethical concerns.[4] Because the industry lacks standardized requirements, record keeping has long been a trouble spot, with some clinics or banks failing to keep detailed records of the clients and the sources of sperm. This results in situations in which sperm donors with particular diseases can infect many women before the diseases are detected.[5] Poor record keeping also makes it difficult to keep track of the number of times a particular donor's semen has been used with the result that in a small geographical area, or within a local minority group, consanguinity becomes a genuine possibility. Second, the lack of standardized screening procedures also allows the transmission of STDs, HIV-AIDS and other infectious diseases to the woman inseminated and subsequently to the child. Third, the use of sperm banks has eugenic implications since a couple may potentially

---

[2]*Proceed with Care: Final Report of the Royal Commission on New Reproductive Technologies,* 2 vols. (Ottawa: Canada Communications Group, 1993), 1:434.

[3]We will examine cryopreservation in more depth in chapter nine, "In Vitro Fertilization and Embryo Transfer," below.

[4]It should also be noted that the ovum can now be stored in much the same way as the sperm, so that even though the duration of storage is considerably shorter for the ovum, this discussion is not limited to the male part of the equation.

[5]*Canadian Royal Commission Newsletter,* December 1993, pp. 11-12.

choose what kind of child they would like, based on the general characteristics of the donor. The existence of "elite sperm banks"—which cater to those who want an "exceptional" child by storing only samples from Nobel Prize winners, super athletes, and so on—seems to legitimize the fear that the application of AI may degenerate into a tool of a new eugenics program.[6]

Confidentiality and Deception

Another major ethical issue in AID is the question of confidentiality. Donor identity is usually protected, and this raises a number of questions:

☐ Is confidentiality for the benefit of the donor or the couple?

☐ Is the donor, by remaining anonymous, thereby absolved of all responsibilities?

☐ Can the couple ever have access to the identity of the donor?

☐ Does the donor have the right to obtain information about the child?

☐ Does the resulting child have the right to know the identity of the biological father?

These questions entail much more than theoretical import, and the testimony of Margaret Brown, who discovered at age sixteen that she was a child of AID, captures their practical importance.

> I am a person created by donor insemination, someone who will never know half of her identity. I feel anger and confusion, and I am filled with questions. Whose eyes do I have? Why the big secret? Who gave my family the idea that my biological roots are not important? To deny someone the knowledge of his or her biological origins is dreadfully wrong. . . . In a world where history is a required academic subject and libraries have special sections for genealogy, I do not see how anyone can consciously rob someone of something as basic and essential as heritage. Parents must realize that all the love and attention in the world cannot mask that underlying, almost subconscious feeling that something is askew.[7]

There is no consensus on how to resolve this dilemma. Those who favor anonymity usually cite one or more of the following reasons:

☐ If donors' identities can be disclosed, the number of potential donors and potential parents may be reduced.

☐ With anonymity, we avoid the possibility of social stigmas being attached to the child.

☐ With anonymity, we protect the child from feeling estranged from the family she is raised in.

☐ Parents do have the prerogative to withhold certain information if neces-

---

[6]J. John, *Evangelical Ethics: Issues Facing the Church Today* (Phillipsburg, N.J.: Presbyterian & Reformed, 1993), p. 62.

[7]Margaret Brown, "Whose Eyes Are These, Whose Nose?" *Newsweek*, March 7, 1994, p. 12.

sary, so that while it *may* be prudent to inform the child in some cases, parents should not be obligated to do so.

☐ Parents have an obligation to maintain family stability by *not* disclosing this information, for disclosure may embarrass the parents and other family members when the problem of infertility is made public. This is particularly true for cultures that tend to see the connotation of immorality or adultery in AID.

On the other hand, many maintain that both anonymity and secrecy ultimately amount to deception, which undermines the parent-child relationship, and have undesirable consequences for the child if the truth is found out later in life. Based on experiences of adopted children and on our understanding of the significance of the biological/genetic dimension and embodiment of human personhood, we should acknowledge that the child's concern with her biological origin is more than mere curiosity. One's identity is so bound up with one's origin that the life of a child with an unknown biological parent is like a storybook with the first chapter missing. Hence the child's interest creates a strong presumption in favor of openness, as long as adequate protection is given to the various other parties involved.

To this end, Swedish law has tried to strike a compromise by giving the child, but not the social parents, the right to know the identity of the semen donor when the child reaches age eighteen. A compromise usually does not satisfy everybody, and even though social parents may still prefer that the donors remain anonymous so that the family will not be encumbered by any ambiguous donor half-relationships, the Swedish law feels that eighteen years is sufficient time for the development of family bonds such that the child's bonding with her social parents can be expected to far outweigh her attachment to her anonymous biological parent. Some donors also favor disclosure because they believe that a system of openness may offer them a socially recognized status as donors. In fact, disclosure of donor identity is not entirely unproblematic for the child, since she may become profoundly disturbed by the ambiguity between social and biological ties and thus confused over her true parentage. By delaying the disclosure of donor identity until the child is eighteen, the Swedish law is saying that the child may have a right to know *eventually* but that it is not in the child's best interest to be told before she attains a degree of maturity.

Morality of Germ-Cell Donation and the Human Biological Bond

Another key moral issue raised by AID pertains to the morality of germ-cell donation itself. Most nonreligious writers believe that as long as the donation is voluntary and preferably unremunerated, and as long as the donated gametes are known to be free from genetic defects, this practice presents no ethical problem. Some Christian scholars likewise believe that gamete donation can be theologically justified because while God can give his gifts of children directly to his stewards to care for, he can also use someone who lies outside the marriage to give an important gift to the childless couple through gamete donation. In short, they see AID as a gift from God to the infertile couple, delivered through the good stewardship of the donor. Further, they believe that the practice of AID affirms the human desire to procreate and to assume the parental vocation and helps people to realize that no one is completely self-sufficient— we are all dependent on others in the community to improve on one's quality and quantity of life.[8] These writers dismiss the significance of biology and the genetic link in human procreation as something which is psychological, and recommend careful psychological screening before using donor material in order to overcome any unnecessary emotional trauma.[9]

I cannot agree that there is no real moral difference between the donation of sperm and the donation of blood or organs, because I believe that the sperm cannot be seen merely as a body part. One obvious difference is that while an organ as a body part helps to restore function, the gamete is an "organ" that is involved in bringing forth a *new* life. In other words, the former is life-saving, whereas the latter is life-giving, and the two are hence not materially or morally equivalent. Besides, some have claimed that tissue organs do not convey "genetic individuality" but gametes do and thus may not be seen as freely exchangeable.[10] Whether gametes actually possess "genetic individuality" is open to question; but they do possess "genetic exclusivity," which not only is important for the maintenance of biological continuity with one's offspring, but also helps us to see the personal meaning and significance of the biological ties that exist between generations.[11]

Furthermore, to dismiss biological ties as inconsequential is highly counterintuitive. The very desire of many couples to have a child who is biologically "their own" suggests that parenting is not altogether "a-biological." Indeed, modern technologies such as IVF and AI were first developed to preserve the crucial connection between biology and parenting. This highlights the fact that ordinarily the parent-child relationship begins biologically in the physical relationship of parents to children. The parents assent to care for the child born to them because the relationship is already naturally and biologically established. To put it differently, the biological and genetic links between parents and chil-

---

[8]Bruce R. Reichenbach and V. Elving Anderson, *On Behalf of God: A Christian Ethic for Biology* (Grand Rapids, Mich.: Eerdmans, 1995), pp. 150-51.

[9]Ibid., p. 151.

[10]Oliver O'Donovan, *Begotten or Made?* (Oxford: Oxford University Press, 1984), p. 43.

[11]For an interesting discussion of the moral meaning of intergenerational continuity through genetic connection, see Gilbert C. Meilaender, *Bioethics: A Primer for Christians* (Grand Rapids, Mich.: Eerdmans, 1996), p. 13.

dren provide the "ordering of natural and social affinity," which gives full meaning to procreation and a stable structure for parenting. Loving and nurturing their children becomes an obligation that may be demanded and expected of them. These inalienable and nontransferable moral responsibilities are directly contingent on genetic connection, and to take genetic inheritance out of human procreation is to remove ourselves from the basis for accepting parenthood.[12] This implies that parenthood is rooted not entirely in the exercise of free choice, but also in the genetic continuity between parents and child.[13] From the perspective of the children's interest, if the parent's obligation to care for those whom one has created is contingent upon the genetic relation rather than an arbitrary volition, children will be provided with a set of preexisting social sanctions, which give them a more secure place in the world.[14] I see this also as important for human personhood to flourish and for the building of a better community for ourselves, because it seems good sense that we first learn to love those who are biologically tied to us before we come to love those who are not. To learn to love without a choice is a superior preparation for one's choosing to love and care for others.

I also do not think that the practice of adoption suggests one cannot draw moral proscriptions against AID on the basis of genetic continuity, because the practice of adoption should not be considered normative for parenting. Rather, it must be viewed only as an emergency stopgap measure, providing the necessary care for an otherwise unparented child abandoned by his natural parents due to natural or artificial causes. In other words, the primary purpose of adoption is to provide relief for the "neediest and the least among us" as an expression of neighborly love; the adoptive parents may benefit by having or adding a child to the family, but they are never intended to be the primary beneficiary of the child. As such, the primary purpose of adoption is not to fulfill an infertile couple's desire to have a family. Many couples have children of their own and go on to expand their families by adopting others. Hence, the mere existence of adoptive situations does not reduce the importance of the "biological" context of parenthood. However, emphasizing the biological con-

---

[12]For a similar view see Catholic writer Lisa Sowle Cahill's "The Ethics of Surrogate Motherhood: Biology, Freedom and Moral Obligations," *Law, Medicine and Health Care* 16 (Spring 1988): 65. For a Protestant perspective see O'Donovan, *Begotten or Made?* p. 48. For further discussion, please see chapter twelve, "Human Cloning and Stem Cells," below.

[13]Conversely, this implies that gamete donors may be held partially responsible for the children conceived. And as we will see in part three, "Abortion and Personhood," below, genetic connection is a valid reason for trying to persuade a rape/incest victim to keep her child.

[14]Elizabeth S. Anderson, "Is Women's Labor a Commodity?" in *Intervention and Reflection: Basic Issues in Medical Ethics,* 5th ed., ed. Ronald Munson (Belmont, Calif.: Wadsworth, 1996), pp. 540-41.

text of parenting is not to say that IVF or AID can be categorically prohibited on this basis, since genetic relation is being claimed as only a sufficient, but not a necessary, condition for parenting; but it provides a strong caution against and exercise some constraints upon a "free trade" of human gametes and gestational surrogacy as now practiced, as though the biological relationship with a child carries no moral responsibility or obligation at all.

The Unitive-Procreative Link of the Conjugal Act

Another moral objection to the use of AID or IVF with donor gametes is made on the basis that these procedures violate the marital bond of the couple. It is known that many couples report a feeling of guilt toward and alienation from each other after the procedure. Some couples even equate the procedure of AID to adultery. In the early twentieth century, trial courts in Canada and in the United States ruled that AID might constitute legal adultery, and this might have contributed to this unfortunate characterization of AID. I disagree with this legal position because all the crucial elements involved in adultery—including the intent and act of sexual relations with an extramarital third party as well as the deception, intimacy, lust and passion with someone outside the bond—are absent. Rather, the spouses are simply seeking to embody their love through assisted reproductive techniques.[15]

Even if AID is not an adulterous act per se, many believe that it violates the marriage bond and distorts the real meaning of the coital act. For this reason, many conservative religious communities, including the Roman Catholic Church, have consistently opposed AID and many other artificial reproductive procedures, considering them as "contrary to the unity of marriage, to the dignity of the spouses, to the vocation proper to parents, and to the child's right to be conceived and brought into the world in marriage and from marriage."[16] This injunction can be reduced to two issues: First, while the sperm donor is not physically invading the sexual relationship, he does become involved in and contributes materially to the procreative process, so that even though not definable as adultery, the act of sperm donation could amount to a violation of the intimacy of the marriage bond.[17] Second, AID

---

[15]Phyllis Creighton, *Artificial Insemination by Donor* (Toronto: Anglican Book Centre, 1977), pp. 11-16.

[16]Congregation for the Doctrine of the Faith, "Instruction on Respect for Human Life in Its Origin and on the Dignity of Procreation: Replies to Certain Questions of the Day," in *Religious and Artificial Reproduction,* ed. Lisa Sowle Cahill and Thomas A. Shannon (New York: Crossroad, 1988), pp. 158-59.

[17]Stanley Grenz, *Sexual Ethics* (Dallas: Word, 1990), p. 152. Grenz rejects the view that the invitation of a third party is intrinsically unethical, but he does note several potential psychological difficulties with such an arrangement.

undermines the nature and meaning of the coital act. Behind this moral suspicion of AID and other ARTs is a common Christian belief in the inseparable connection between the unitive and the procreative meanings of the conjugal act. On this basis, virtually all denominations within Christianity are united in their objection to the use of AID by unmarried heterosexual couples, lesbian couples or single women. We will consider these two connected issues together.

The Roman Catholic Church states its position in *Donum vitae* as follows: *"The fidelity of the spouses in the unity of marriage involves reciprocal respect of their right to become a father and a mother only through each other."*[18] The unity of marriage so defined implies that marital exclusivity includes the genetic, gestational and social dimensions of parenthood. Paul Ramsey makes the same point when he says that "to posit acts of sexual love beyond the sphere of responsible procreation (by definition, marriage) means a refusal of the image of God's creation in our own."[19] Both Protestants and Catholics base their objection on the belief that AID contradicts the nature and meaning of marriage as taught in the Scriptures and according to the tradition of the church. In other words, donation of gametes itself is a violation of the marriage covenant independent of any other potentially deleterious effects.

In order to justify these claims, Christians appeal to a biblical understanding of the divinely instituted marriage covenant on the basis of Genesis 2:18-25, where the impetus establishing the need of this relationship is the awareness that Adam's "aloneness" is not good—that is, it does not reflect the full plan and purpose of God's creation of humanity in his image. So God creates a partner for Adam, an equal counterpart corresponding to him. The passage then outlines at least three elements of this divinely given structure, which properly unites these two individuals in a covenant of marriage. First, a man is supposed "to leave" his father and mother, suggesting that marriage is to be accompanied by the initiation of a new family. Second, the man is then instructed "to cleave" to his wife, strongly suggesting the exclusive and permanent nature of the marriage bond, which is not to be broken. The result of this cleaving leads to the third and final element of becoming "one flesh." In the sexual sense, the man and woman become one body, but the extended meaning of this phrase includes the spiritual elements of commitment and purity.[20]

---

[18]Congregation for the Doctrine of the Faith, "Instruction," p. 518; emphasis in original.

[19]Paul Ramsey, *Fabricated Man: The Ethics of Genetic Control* (New Haven, Conn.: Yale University Press, 1970), p. 89. It should be noted that the Catholic Church and most Protestants, including Ramsey, would not agree exactly on the nature of the connection of these two meanings. However, they share enough common ground to consider their critiques of AID together.

[20]Janet Smith has suggested that "one flesh" might also refer to the incarnation of the couple's

In this context of biblical marriage, which emphasizes conjugal unity and fidelity, God then tells the first couple to be "fruitful and multiply" (Gen 1:28). The juxtaposition of the marriage covenant and the blessing to procreate establishes "the intimate connection between the love-giving and life-giving aspect of the one-flesh marital union,"[21] and it is precisely this union which AID and other ARTs threaten to destroy. Procreation is the fruit of the mutual love of the father and mother who are first united in marriage to become one flesh, and the child is thus a biological witness to the relation that exists between the husband and wife and "embodies the union of her father and mother."[22] Thus, procreation is more than merely the product of the fertilizing of the wife's egg, which AID inclines us to believe.

Procreation can never be reduced to such a simplistic biological level. As we have seen in the previous discussion of the theological meaning of personhood, the parents and child are said to form an "anthropological triangle" that reflects, however dimly, the relational life of the triune God.[23] In a marital union, the husband and wife not only express their own relational dimension as human persons, but in a real sense cause a new person to emerge out of it. It is only in this sense that, theologically, human begetting can be called procreation, for in the act of creation God creates humanity out of his love in the most personal manner and simultaneously establishes a personal relationship with us. For the human, to procreate is to create on behalf of God, and so it can only be accomplished through the love that unites the husband and wife. Giving life can only be accomplished in giving love, so that "the child is God's yes to such mutual self-giving"[24] between the husband and wife. As Ramsey puts it, "God created nothing apart from His love; . . . Neither should there be among men and women . . . any love set out of the context of responsibility for procreation, any begetting apart from the sphere of love."[25] Hence, to allow AID and other ARTs is to permit a radical despiritualization of the sexual union by separating its unitive and procreative dimensions.[26] It is for this reason that the Roman Catholic Church even finds the reliance on masturbation for collecting donor semen in ARTs objectionable: the procedure replaces rather than facilitates the con-

---

love in a new child in her *Humanae Vitae: A Generation Later* (Washington, D.C.: Catholic University of America Press, 1991), p. 131.

[21]Meilaender, *Bioethics,* p. 19.

[22]Ibid., p. 15.

[23]See the section "Biblical Tradition of *Imago Dei* as Relational" in chapter five, above.

[24]Meilaender, *Bioethics,* p. 14.

[25]Ramsey, *Fabricated Man,* p. 38.

[26]See also O'Donovan, *Begotten or Made?* p. 39; and M. R. Laffoon, *Artificial Insemination and In Vitro Fertilization: An Orthodox Perspective* (Portland, Ore.: Theological Research Exchange Network, 1986), p. 18.

jugal act and hence dissociates procreation from the sexual union.[27]

Maintaining the connection between the unitive and procreative meanings of the marital conjugal act is believed important for both promoting the vocation of parenthood and protecting the rights of the child. There is a continuity between the love that unites the parents in the conjugal act and the love with which they parent the child.[28] In other words, parenting is seen as both an act of begetting and a vocation to nurture. Any ART that employs gamete donation undermines the continuity of biological and social parenthood.[29] A second way AID may compromise parenting is through introducing life experiences in one partner that cannot be fully shared by the other. The use of donor gametes in AID implies that there is a genetic asymmetry in the relationship of the parents to the child; the wife is seen as the real mother of the child, and even though the husband is devoted and caring toward the child conceived through AID, the difference between his parental role and his wife's can hardly be missed. This leads to a loss of mutuality that interferes with the couple's ability to parent properly, having potentially damaging psychological effects on both the marital partners and the child.[30]

Maintaining the connection between the unitive and procreative aspects of the marital conjugal act is also important as a means of protecting the child's dignity by providing the foundation to see the child as equal to the parents. As I have discussed earlier, Christians believe in God as a Trinity of Persons whose own being is a community of love. In this eternal community, the Father begets the Son from his own being, and the Son is hence consubstantial with and equal in status and dignity to the Father. As the image-bearers of God, we are called to be fruitful and increase in the same manner.[31] That is to say, in human begetting, the parents also impart their nature to the offspring, who is therefore equal in dignity to the parents. With the participation of an anonymous third party in AID, or in the laboratory of science and medicine where embryos are being made and manipulated as products, it is very dubi-

---

[27] According to the Roman Catholic Church, masturbation is also objectionable because it is a solitary, sterile, disordered act.

[28] Laffoon, *Artificial Insemination,* p. 19.

[29] Hessel Bouma III et al., *Christian Faith, Health and Medical Practice* (Grand Rapids, Mich.: Eerdmans, 1989), p. 195.

[30] See similar views by Paul Lauritzen, "Pursuing Parenthood: Reflections on Donor Insemination," in *Second Opinion* 17, no. 1 (1991): 72; and Annette Baran and Rubin Pannor, *Lethal Secrets: The Shocking Consequences and Unresolved Problems of Artificial Insemination* (New York: Warner, 1989), p. 51.

[31] Grenz notes the fruitful increase of humans as analogical to divine generation: "Procreation constitutes an apt human analogy to the expansive love of God, which likewise creates the other as a product." *Sexual Ethics,* p. 74.

ous whether children so created can likewise claim the equality in dignity that parents are meant to endow on their children.[32]

Disconnecting the Unitive-Procreative Link

Most people appreciate the value of preserving the union-procreation link, but at the same time they recognize that an unqualified acceptance would entail a proscription of AID, other ARTs and even contraceptives. Some writers reason that while prima facie these two functions of human sexual intercourse should be preserved within the marriage, there may be situations in which it is still moral to separate the two functions. Specifically, it has been argued that even nature regulates the woman's ovulatory cycle in such a way that procreation is not always possible while the couple can engage in "love making." The use of the rhythm method for birth control takes advantage of nature's scheme, and it is not seen to have cheapened love, procreation or parenthood.[33] In response to this, I agree that the rhythm method or the Natural Family Planning method are superb examples of successful attempts to separate making love from making babies without intentionally severing the unitive and procreative link. But this is quite different from taking oral contraceptive for years to achieve the same purpose. The former takes advantage of what nature allows, whereas the latter "cheats" nature out of what she disallows.

Protestant ethicist Stanley Grenz takes a more philosophical approach and argues that there is no intrinsic connection between the unitive and procreative aspects of the sexual act. He sees in the sexual act several meanings beyond union and procreation, including a sacramental significance symbolizing God's mysterious love and a token of the couple's mutual submission and self-giving. He observes that all these meanings are not inseparably connected to the procreative meaning of the sexual act but maintain importance apart from it. On that basis, he concludes that the unitive-procreative connection is not inseparable and that technological assistance in procreation may be welcomed as God's gift, although he expresses reservation about any third-party involvement.[34] I agree with Grenz that all the nonprocreative meanings of the sexual act are not necessarily connected with the procreative meaning, and I also agree that even the unitive meaning may be dissociated with the sexual act and hence with procreation. This is so because all meanings, including the unitive but excepting the procreative, can be expressed in ways other than through the sexual act, although the sexual act most often brings with it the fullest unitive experience. By contrast, until the advent of modern ARTs, the procreative meaning

---

[32]Meilaender, *Bioethics,* p. 15.
[33]See for example, Reichenbach and Anderson, *On Behalf of God,* pp. 147-48.
[34]Grenz, *Sexual Ethics,* pp. 145-55.

could only be expressed through the sexual act. In other words, the relation between the sexual act and its procreative and nonprocreative meanings is not symmetrical: the procreative meaning is exclusively and inseparably tied to the sexual act, yet all the other nonprocreative meanings can be expressed in other ways.

This asymmetry implies that as long as people decide to express any of the nonprocreative meanings through nonsexual acts, these meanings will have nothing to do with procreation. But whenever the unitive and other nonprocreative meanings are expressed through the sexual act, the procreative meaning is necessarily involved. Indeed, if the sexual act is the most ultimate expression of the unitive meaning and if the couple decides to express it through the sexual act, then the unitive and procreative meanings are necessarily inseparably connected. This is not to say that all sexual acts will lead to procreation, for love-making acts do not always lead to baby-making—for instance, during certain periods in the menstrual cycle, in advanced age and in people inflicted with infertility. However, this does not change the conclusion reached above because in these instances, the procreative function is either temporarily or permanently disconnected from the sexual act. Hence, to focus on the inseparability of the unitive and procreative meanings of the sexual act, as some Catholics do, is certainly unwarranted; but to argue that these two aspects are separable and therefore AID and other ARTs are automatically justified is equally misconstrued. The real focus is on procreation itself. In the natural order of things, the sexual act is the only way to achieve procreation. Making babies can only come about through making love. If AID and other ARTs are to be justified, one would have to show why procreation can be ethically separable from the sexual act, and show this not merely by demonstrating that the unitive and procreative aspects of the sexual act are separable.

In this context, the contraceptive technology has artificially separated the normally connected unitive and the procreative aspects of the sexual act by removing the procreative aspect from the sexual act itself, so that it is now possible to have love making without baby making: that is, a couple can express unitive meaning through the sexual act without the procreative consequence. Some argue that if the use of contraceptives is morally justified (which has yet to be established here), then the use of ARTs should likewise be justifiable. The catchy phrase goes like this: If contraceptives can let us have love making without baby making, why can't we use ARTs to have baby making without love making? It is true that both contraceptives and ARTs are able to disconnect the sexual act from procreation and that both are artificial technologies. But are the similarities sufficient to justify ARTs? Even if contraception is justified or permitted, it does not automatically follow that ARTs would likewise be justified or permitted, for two things that share some common features are not necessarily equivalent, either materially or morally. Indeed, upon closer inspection, the differences become stark. In disconnecting the sexual act from procreation, contraception artificially induces a state of infertility; and in so doing it artificially prevents the procreation of a human life. ARTs on the other hand, by disconnecting the sexual act from procreation, take over the procreative function of the sexual act and artificially create life. It is evident that the two artificial technologies are radically dissimilar in nature and thus in their respective moral status as well. In the use of contraception, the sexual act is impoverished by the removal of its procreative significance if undertaken within the marital bond, is abused if the sexual act is undertaken outside of the marital bond and is degraded if the unitive aspect is absent. I conclude that the use of artificial contraceptives frustrates God's desire and will to hand out the gift of a life;[35] but in the use of ARTs, the sexual act is rendered superfluous for procreation, and thus human procreation is degraded to the product of scientific innovation rather than the fruit of human intimacy. In this instance, God is asked to accept the child when he has not given that gift of life.

Artificial Insemination and the Ethic of Personhood

From the perspective of the ethic of personhood that I have established in the first part of this work, one can expect that I will have considerable reservations about the employment of AID even with the proviso of allowing the revelation of the identity of the donor when the child attains adulthood. I do not believe that all the child's problems will be solved and all the wounds that she may have sustained, told or untold, will be healed simply by revealing the donor's identity. Before a child conceived of an AID parent attains minimal adulthood (and can be told of the donor's identity), there will have passed sixteen to eighteen years during which a form of collective deception has taken place within the entire relational matrix of the family as well as within the moral consciousness of each individual family member. The personhood I present in this work regards genuine relations with God and with God-loving persons as constitutive of our being and as the ongoing dynamic of our becoming more fulfilled persons. It should be quite obvious that the ethic derived from this account of personhood would not support a medical procedure of assisting reproduction if it might inflict a greater blow to the integrity of the persons in the family who are seeking to cure their lost wholeness due to infertility.

---

[35]This is a common argument used in Catholic circles. *Humanae Vitae* states that anyone using contraception "is defying the plan and holy will of God" (*Humanae Vitae: Encyclical Letter of Pope Paul VI on the Moral Principles Governing Human Procreation,* sec. 13). Smith suggests that insofar as married couples reject the call of transmitting life through contraception, they are "refusing to perform a service that God has asked of them." Smith, *Humanae Vitae: A Generation Later,* p. 104.

As far as using contraceptive devices and AI is concerned, the Roman Catholic Church automatically bans the use of any and all forms of contraceptive devices and all forms of AI by anyone—including the married couples—because of the church's unwarranted insistence on the inseparability of the unitive-procreative link. This has created much unnecessary harshness for many faithful followers. But as a result, the church does safeguard against the use of AID and all other ARTs with a framework of ethical reasoning. On the other hand, many Protestants accept the use of oral contraceptives and AIH on the misconstrued assumption that the unitive and procreative meanings of the conjugal act can be shown to be separable. But if this is the necessary justification, which I believe it is not, then the Protestants will find themselves much more vulnerable when arguing against the use of AID, IVF and other ARTs. In contrast, the ethic of personhood ultimately relies on an ethic of relation as its litmus test for the morality of any proposed human activity. When the family contexts warrant the employment of AIH or contraceptive devices to either increase or decrease the family size, respectively, I envision that human relationships *within* the family will be either enriched or preserved and not compromised in the process, and hence these methods are endorsable by the ethic of personhood. Yet this same ethic is under no obligation to support the use of AID, as I argue above, or the use of contraceptives by unmarried people, because it ultimately depersonalizes the two persons by undermining the relations between them. As we will see below, a personhood ethic also fails to find any good basis for endorsing other ARTs mainly because these technologies compromise the relational dimensions that constitute human personhood.

9

In Vitro Fertilization and Embryo Transfer

*D*efinition and Medical Procedure

In vitro fertilization and embryo transfer (IVF-ET) is a much more technically involved and dramatic procedure than artificial insemination is. Nonetheless, it has become an increasingly common procedure in infertility practice since it first received wide media coverage in 1978, when the first "test-tube baby," Louise Brown, was triumphantly ushered into the world by Steptoe and Edwards of Great Britain. At present, IVF-ET is widely accepted as a treatment for women with excessive, irreparable damage to their fallopian tubes. It is also used in the cases of an inability to ovulate, oligospermia, a failure to conceive due to abnormal genes or an unidentified inability to conceive.[1] It has been estimated that before 1989, the total number of babies born worldwide through IVF-ET was 40,578[2] and that in one five-year period between 1985 and 1990 there were over 12,000 IVF-ET deliveries just in the United

---

[1] It is important to note that the Canadian Royal Commission suggests that IVF has proven effective only when infertility is caused by blocked fallopian tubes. *Proceed with Care: Final Report of the Royal Commission on New Reproductive Technologies,* 2 vols. (Ottawa: Canada Communications Group, 1993), 1:498.

[2] J. Testart et al., "World Collaborative Report on IVF-ET and GIFT: 1989 Results," *Human Reproduction* 7, no. 3 (1992): 363.

States.[3] In 1993 alone, the number increased to 5,103 live IVF births in the United States.[4] There is no question that the number has been on the rise since then.

Technically, IVF-ET places considerable physical demands on women, because in order to harvest enough eggs, the woman is required to take drugs such as Pergonal, clomiphene citrate (Clomid) or pure follicular stimulating hormone (FSH-Metrodin) to achieve hyperovulation[5]—the so-called controlled ovarian hyperstimulation (COH). The side effects of these drugs include a higher incidence of premature birth with increased neonatal mortality and morbidity, increased incidence of ectopic pregnancy and ovarian hyperstimulation syndrome, which is characterized by severe pelvic pain and other symptoms.[6]

After drugs are given at the appropriate time of the woman's menstrual cycle, eggs may be harvested from the ovaries one of two ways: the eggs can be aspirated through a hollow suction needle inserted into the abdomen, which is guided by a fiber-optic laparoscope, while the woman is under general anesthesia; or the eggs can be extracted through a needle inserted through the vaginal wall, which is guided by close ultrasound surveillance. Sperm samples are usually obtained by masturbation, but they can also be obtained through epididymal sperm aspiration or microsurgical epididymal sperm aspiration (MESA). Eggs are generally fertilized soon after they are harvested, a process that takes twenty-four to thirty-six hours. After another forty-eight hours, when the embryos have grown to the eight- to sixteen-cell stage, embryo transfer is performed whereby two to four embryos[7] are transferred back into the woman's uterus for implantation. For successful implantation to take place, the timing of the transfer must coincide with the woman's natural hormonal cycle, and implantation usually occurs within days of transfer. It is

---

[3]Medical Research International and the Society for Assisted Reproductive Technology, The American Fertility Society, "In Vitro Fertilization-Embryo Transfer (IVF-ET) in the United States: 1990 Results from the IVF-ET Registry," *Fertility and Sterility* 57, no. 1 (1992): 15-24.

[4]Robert W. Shaw, W. Patrick Soutter and Stuart L. Stanton, eds., *Gynecology* (New York: Churchill Livingstone, 1997), p. 288.

[5]Hyperovulation usually results in four to seven eggs being released in one cycle, but as many as twenty have been reported. Donald E. Demarco, "Love Among the Test Tubes: Louise Brown Turns 10; *Humanae Vitae* Turns 20," in *Trust the Truth,* ed. Russell Smith (Braintree, Mass.: Pope John Center, 1991), p. 177.

[6]Other symptoms associated with ovarian hyperstimulation syndrome include ovarian enlargement, abnormal uterine bleeding, breast tenderness, development of ovarian cysts and their rupture with internal bleeding, bloating, stomach pain, jaundice, nausea and vomiting, headaches, dizziness, lightheadedness, blurred or double vision, nervousness and insomnia, thromboembolism and death.

[7]The Ethics Committee of the American Fertility Society adopts the term *pre-embryo* for the conceptus through the first two weeks of gestation and considers the moral status of a pre-embryo different from that of an post-14-day embryo; see chapter eleven, "Manipulation of Embryos," below, for a detailed discussion.

always possible that only one, more than one or none of the embryos will implant. A pregnancy is usually detectable two weeks after transfer.

The overall success rates of pregnancy and birth after IVF-ET range anywhere between 10 and 25 percent, and the success rate increases proportionally with the number of embryos transferred. The pregnancy has a 9 to 10 percent rate of success if one embryo is transferred, 12 to 15 percent rate for two embryos, 15 to 20 percent for three embryos, and 20 to 25 percent for four embryos.[8] The consequence of transferring a larger number of embryos is that the implantation of multiple embryos leads to multiple pregnancies. The multiple-pregnancy rates as related to the numbers of embryos transferred is as follows: one embryo, 2 percent; two embryos, 11.4 percent; three embryos, 26.2 percent; four embryos, 30.4 percent; five embryos 45.7 percent.[9] To balance the benefit of achieving pregnancy with the risk of unintended and dangerous multiple pregnancy, a medial number of three embryos is usually transferred. As expected, scientific efforts are ongoing around the world to reduce the numbers required for successful embryo transfer.

Medical Variations of IVF-ET

There are several procedures that are based on IVF-ET, but they differ in various ways. The first of these varieties, called zygote intra-fallopian transfer (ZIFT),[10] the embryo is placed in the fallopian tube instead of the uterus. Allowing the embryo to travel naturally down the path of the fallopian tube to the uterus has been shown to increase the chance for a successful pregnancy.[11] In gamete intra-fallopian transfer (GIFT)[12] two to four unfertilized eggs are mixed with the sperm sample and then the mixture is placed in the woman's fallopian tubes, ensuring that the gametes are placed in the most natural and optimal location for fertilization to take place in vivo. Since both ZIFT and GIFT require the woman to have at least one functioning fallopian tube, they are particularly useful for patients with pelvic adhesions or endometriosis. GIFT has been shown to have a 30 to 35 percent pregnancy rate, almost twice that of conventional IVF-ET. But since the procedure is also associated with increased tubal pregnancy and spontaneous miscarriage, the overall "take-

---

[8]M. Damewood, ed., *The Johns Hopkins Handbook of In Vitro Fertilization and Assisted Reproductive Technologies* (Boston: Little Brown, 1990), pp. 98-99.

[9]Stephen Genuis, *Reproduction Rollercoaster: Infertility and the Assisted Reproductive Technologies* (Edmonton: KEG Publishing, 1992), pp. 143-44. These numbers are based on statistics available in Australia and New Zealand between 1979 and 1984.

[10]This is also known as Tubal Embryo Transfer (TET) and Tubal Embryo Stage Transfer (TEST).

[11]Genuis, *Reproduction Rollercoaster,* pp. 149-51.

[12]This is also known as Tubal Ovum Transfer (TOT).

home baby" rate is perhaps only slightly better than the conventional IVF-ET.[13]

Pronuclear-stage transfer (PROST) refers to the transfer of a partially fertilized egg into the fallopian tube at the pronucleus stage, when the sperm has penetrated the egg but before the genetic material of the sperm and the egg have fused and combined. The advantage is that with PROST the fertilized egg can be transferred into the woman's body much sooner, so the patient can be discharged earlier to reduce the overall cost of the procedure.[14]

Several techniques have been developed to improve fertilization of the egg. With intra-vagina culture (IVC), a mixture of eggs and sperms are placed in an airtight container and left in the woman's vagina for fertilization to take place in vivo. At the end of forty-eight hours, embryo transfer is attempted following the regular IVF-ET protocol. The fertilization rate is comparable to that achieved in vitro with the advantage of considerable reduction in cost, since fertilization takes place inside the human body.[15] In subzonal implantation (SUZI), the sperm is directly injected through the outer shell of the egg to overcome any difficulties in egg penetration; and in intra-cytoplasmic sperm injection (ICSI) a single sperm is injected under micromanipulation into the cytoplasm of the egg. The fertilization rate by this procedure is as high as 25 percent even with immature sperms.[16] As a result, the combination of IVF and ICSI enables the clinician to overcome both female and male factors of infertility.

There is no question that ARTs offer hope to many infertile couples, but we must not overlook the moral challenges these technical innovations bring with them. As part of this moral evaluation, I will examine the harm to embryos and children so created, the harm to parents who use these technologies and the violation to the dignity of the human person through medicalization and commercialization of procreation by these technologies.

Potential Harm to Embryos Created Through ARTs

Some have estimated that the rate of chromosomal abnormality in embryos created by IVF is comparable to normal fertilization.[17] It is possible that the drugs used to stimulate hyperovulation may also damage the harvested eggs, which may account for the relatively high rate of implantation failure. However, IVF-ET adversely affects the survival of the embryo in ways other than by causing cellular or chromosomal abnormalities. Pregnancy rates increase when an increasing number of embryos are transferred, but what is often gone unno-

---

[13]Genuis, *Reproduction Rollercoaster,* p. 151.

[14]Ibid., pp. 148-49.

[15]Ibid., p. 142.

[16]*IVF Canada News* 5 (January 1994).

[17]Genuis, *Reproduction Rollercoaster,* p. 147.

ticed is the fact that the increase is not linear: increasing the number of embryos transferred from one to four (a fourfold increase) only increases the pregnancy rate from 10 percent to 25 percent (little better than a twofold increase). This suggests that the technique of multiple transfer itself decreases the chance of survival for each embryo transferred. Furthermore, when multiple embryos manage to implant and develop into fetuses, selective fetal reduction is often required in order to ensure the survival of just one or two fetuses to viability and beyond. Thus, for those who have a higher view of the dignity of the nascent life, the harm inflicted on embryos by IVF-ET is more actual than potential.

Potential Physical Harm to Children Conceived Through ARTs

In addition to finding a greater incidence of multiple births, studies have indicated that IVF and related technologies may inflict serious damage on a disproportionate number of children, rendering the ethics of ARTs questionable.[18] One small American study reports no significant difference in the incidences of physical or neurological abnormalities in IVF babies,[19] but others have suggested that overall there is a 2.2 percent chance of a birth defect in IVF-ET children, compared to a 1.5 percent chance in those conceived naturally.[20] Data from Australia indicate that IVF children are two or three times more likely to suffer spina bifida and transposition of the great vessels of the heart.[21] Data from France also indicate higher incidence of perinatal mortality among IVF babies than in the general population of babies conceived naturally.[22] Premature birth rates and neonatal death rates are eleven times higher in Australia and four times higher in France than the normal population.[23] Further, since the introduction and popularization of ICSI to overcome the male factor in infertility, a significant increase in sex-chromosome anomalies has been reported among children born after the employment of the ICSI technique.[24] Recently, the formation of chimera after the transfer of multiple embryos has been reported: The case involves an otherwise

---

[18]John A. Robertson, "Technology and Motherhood: Legal and Ethical Issues in Human Egg Donation," *Case Western Reserve Law Review* 39, no. 1 (1988): 1-38.

[19]Norma C. Morin et al., "Congenital Malformations and Psychosocial Development in Children Conceived by In Vitro Fertilization," *Journal of Pediatrics* 15, no. 2 (1989): 222-27.

[20]Genuis, *Reproduction Rollercoaster,* p. 148.

[21]National Perinatal Statistics Unit, Fertility Society of Australia, *In Vitro Fertilization Pregnancies: Australia and New Zealand 1979-1985* (Sydney: Pllancaster, 1987).

[22]French In Vitro National, "Pregnancies and Births Resulting from In Vitro Fertilization: French National Registry, Analysis of Data 1986 to 1990," *Fertility and Sterility* 64 (October 1995): 746-56.

[23]Phyllis Creighton, *Artificial Insemination by Donor* (Toronto: Anglican Book Centre, 1977), p. 28.

[24]Andre C. Van Steirteghem, "Outcomes of Assisted Reproductive Technology," *New England Journal of Medicine* 383 (1998): 194-95.

healthy male child with a partially empty sacrotal sac after birth, which was suspected to have an undescended testicle. In surgery, surgeons found an ovary and a fallopian tube instead. Presumably, two embryos, one male and one female, were fused in the very early stage of the child's embryogenesis.[25] One commentator laments that there has been a lack of risk analysis in the use of ARTs, and that when risks are discovered, there have been few attempts to rectify the situation. In particular there is an urgent need to implement systematic follow-up studies to determine the extent and severity of long-term physical, psychological and social harms to children conceived through IVF-ET techniques.[26] Even though these large, long-term controlled studies are still pending, there is evidence at this point to indicate that sufficient potential problems exist to justify cautioning against any carte blanche approval of the unconstrained production of IVF babies. Society's responsibility toward the welfare of the unborn far exceeds the unfulfilled desires of the infertile couple or the unquenchable curiosity of medical scientists.

Potential Psychological Harm to Children Conceived Through ARTs

The potential psychological harm to children conceived through IVF techniques is another ethical concern, especially when covert third-party donor or surrogacy arrangements are involved. These children often face a struggle of identity and social stigmatization.[27] As we have seen in cases involving AID where biological and social parents are different, children may be denied the stable sense of identity that comes from knowing one's biological heritage and family lineage. Likewise, IVF involving third parties either through gamete donation or surrogacy breaches the connection between nature (genetic or gestational linkage) and nurture (parental rearing) and obscures the child's identity within the family. Furthermore, as ARTs are increasingly accessed by people outside traditional marriage—including single persons, homosexual couples and unmarried heterosexual couples—psychologists are concerned that children reared in such nontraditional families may develop an impaired view of sexuality and procreation.[28] However, others see that there is no suffi-

---

[25]John C. S. Dean and Lisa Strain, "A True Hermaphrodite Chimera Resulting from Embryo Amalgamation After In Vitro Fertilization," *New England Journal of Medicine* 338, no. 3 (1998): 166-70.

[26]Lene Koch, "Physiological and Psychosocial Risks of the New Reproductive Technologies," in *Tough Choices: In Vitro Fertilization and the Reproductive Technologies,* ed. Patricia Stephenson and Marsden G. Wagner (Philadelphia: Temple University Press, 1993), pp. 122-34.

[27]Sidney Callahan, "The Ethical Challenge of the New Reproductive Technology," in *Medical Ethics: A Guide for Health Care Professionals,* ed. John F. Monagle and David C. Thomasma (Rockville, Md.: Aspen, 1988), pp. 26-37.

[28]Maureen McGuire and Nancy Alexander, "Artificial Insemination of Single Women," *Fertility and Sterility* 43, no. 2 (1985): 182-84.

cient evidence to show that single people and homosexual couples will necessarily provide an adverse family environment and subject their children to any
negative psychosexual developmental influences.[29] In support of the latter conclusion, both the Glover Report to the European Commission (1989) and the
Royal Commission on New Reproductive Technologies of Canada (1993) have
recommended that those outside traditional marriages be given access to these
technologies. So it seems that in a conflict of rights between a future child and
a nontraditional couple, those with the voices win.

I believe that there is sufficient circumstantial evidence indicating that IVF
together with the possibility of gamete donation and surrogate arrangements
will expose children to a variety of potential physical and psychosocial
harms. Even though unequivocal evidence is lacking, the burden of proof
must be borne by those who advocate the acceptability of these technologies, for harm to even a small proportion of those born is morally unjustifiable. I also believe that in bringing about a pregnancy where artificial
technologies are involved, those providing the technical expertise (i.e., the
physicians and scientists) share in the responsibility for the consequences.
Hence, the situation is complicated by professional and corporate interests.
Society's general reluctance to interfere with a single person's decision to
procreate through ARTs represents an irresponsible concession to parental,
professional and corporate interests and a gross injustice to the future child. I
thus tend to agree with the Warnock Report (published in Great Britain in
1985), which concludes that

> the interests of the child dictate that it should be born into a home where there is
> a loving, stable, heterosexual relationship and that, therefore, the deliberate cre-
> ation of a child for a woman who is not a partner in such a relationship is morally
> wrong.[30]

Utility and Justification of Harm

Some argue that even if the child will experience some physical and psychological harm, such harm may be excusable if the alternative to harm is nonexistence. In other words, better to have a defective offspring through ART than
no offspring at all; the harm of not having been born is greater than being
born with some psychological or physical handicaps.[31] This rationale can be
rejected for three reasons: First, in order for this argument to be successful, one

---

[29]Gillian Hanscombe, "The Right to Lesbian Parenthood," *Journal of Medical Ethics* 9 (September 1983): 133-35.

[30]Warnock Committee, *A Question of Life: The Report of the Committee of Inquiry into Human
Fertilization and Embryology* (Belfast: Her Majesty's Stationery Office, 1985), p. 11.

[31]John A. Robertson, "Procreative Liberty and the Control of Conception, Pregnancy and
Childbirth," *Virginia Law Review* 69, no. 3 (1983): 434.

would almost have to accept the presupposition that there are children preexisting in a state of limbo, who are anxiously waiting to be born, and that to prohibit IVF-ET would be to frustrate the child who otherwise would be born. Of course this whole pretense is absurd, since nobody accepts the existence of such an "existential orphanage." Second, one cannot compare harm incurred in the process of coming into existence through ARTs to the harm of nonexistence because in the state of nonexistence there is no child to be harmed and so there is no harm to speak of. Third, to admit such an argument would entail allowing any degree of harm to occur to children conceived through ARTs because it could always be said that they are better off alive. A new reproductive technology that consistently resulted in most children being born without legs could conceivably be justified.

Another argument used to justify the harm to children conceived through ARTs comes from the principle of utility, which is concerned with "producing the greatest possible balance of value over disvalue (or at least possible balance of disvalue, if only undesirable results can be achieved),"[32] and which undergirds many of the decisions and arguments surrounding the use of ARTs. That is to say, the harm to children born through ARTs is less than the good gained by the children, parents and other participants. Yet this argument is not entirely convincing for a number of reasons. First, while the principle of utility can often be applied to a larger social scale with more success, it is more difficult to use at a personal level where the subjective elements of individuals frequently reduce the utilitarian calculation to nothing more than the arbitrary personal preference of the individual. This is so because in applying the principle of utility to decisions of procreation, important personal, value-laden factors—such as one's convictions about children, the future, technology and parenting—are involved. Different people may share the same empirical information and use the same scientific methods and yet come to different conclusions about risks and benefits and morals. This lack of objectivity is particularly unhelpful in adjudicating conflicting interests between different individuals, and it prevents the proper assessment of the possible harms to the life that is created through ARTs.

Second, in balancing risks and benefits of ARTs, it is not sufficient for one to simply balance the columns of risks and benefits because, most importantly, one also needs to ask, "Who is taking the risks and who is getting the benefits?" Without asking these questions, utilitarian calculations may "balance the book" at the price of sacrificing justice. To allow one human being to assume risks for the sake of a good in which she does not participate is unjust, and this is applicable to ARTs in general and embryo experimentation

---

[32]Tom L. Beauchamp and James F. Childress, *Principles of Biomedical Ethics,* 4th ed. (Belmont, Calif.: Wadsworth, 1994), p. 26.

in particular. There is little doubt that embryo research will lead to some benefits, but it is not fair to impose the risk of research on those who neither voluntarily make the choice of risk nor benefit from such risk taking. A third difficulty with utilitarian calculations as applied to ARTs results from the complex task of identifying and assessing all the possible future harms and benefits of these technologies, which involve unknowns and probabilities. Taking embryo research again as an example, we see that while the risk to the embryos is a certainty, the benefit of finding a cure for a disease remains only a distant hope. Thus, embryo research becomes morally dubious if our only rationale for harming embryos is the vague "hope" of gaining some knowledge that may possibly contribute to the cure for a certain disease. I believe that the inherent arbitrariness of such calculations must be candidly acknowledged in order to make a more realistic moral assessment of the moral justification for the use of ARTs and embryo research.

When one considers these difficulties, the principle of utility is an insufficient principle to underwrite the procreative enterprise through ARTs. I maintain that the physical and psychosocial harms to the child produced via ARTs cannot be ignored and that the justifications to allow them will require something far more than the principle of utility. In the absence of better justifications, the burden of proof as to why such a compromise is morally justifiable remains on those who favor this technology.

Adverse Effects on Couples Using ARTs

ARTs have adverse effects not only on the child so created but also on the couple (or individual) seeking to have the child. Based on statistical data provided by the World Health Organization, the live-take-home baby rate per IVF cycle ranges from zero in the worst facilities to 8.5 percent in the best,[33] which is only slightly better than the rate for a comparable group of women waiting for IVF treatment. The pregnancy rate from IVF-ET for women with idiopathic infertility is so disappointing that some suggest that it would be preferable to do nothing for these patients. In view of the considerable financial investment IVF entails, it seems that the interest groups involved in the technology have not always been forthright in disclosing the odds of having a baby through this procedure. Further, since IVF is often the last resort for becoming pregnant, couples have rather unrealistic hopes and are often bitterly disappointed with the results of their investments—financially, physically and emotionally. This prompts some to state categorically that as a humanitarian response to infertility, IVF-ET is deceptive and thus anything but humane.[34]

---

[33]Varda Burstyn, "Making Babies," *Canadian Forum* 70 (March 1992): 12-13.
[34]Creighton, *Artificial Insemination*, p. 28.

The IVF-ET procedure itself is not free of risks, and it can be physically painful and emotionally disconcerting. Particular concerns have been raised with regard to the use of hormones to hyperstimulate the ovaries. The painful memory of those mothers using DES (diethylstilbestrol) who gave birth to female offspring susceptible to infertility and cancer should continue to serve as a warning against the frequent employment of hormones in high dosages. The long-term effects of the drugs used in the IVF-ET procedure are still unclear, and some researchers are concerned that women who have taken these drugs may become more susceptible to ovarian cancers and other neurological damages. It is thus not without reason that many feminists regard IVF-ET as a dangerous experiment on women. Furthermore, couples employing IVF-ET have also experienced unexpected emotional problems. Some husbands have reported emotional troubles after being forced to obtain the semen by masturbation, and some women have experienced adverse psychological reactions after impregnation. Finally, there is a concern that infertile women may be pressured into using ARTs against their will. An infertile woman's desire for children is itself partly shaped by the social pressures toward motherhood, which is intensified in a new way by ARTs. Women may experience a new obligation to employ these technologies even with all the known negative side effects on the future child and themselves.[35] Although ARTs ultimately aim to correct infertility and thus restore the affected couple to a state of wholeness, they may end up creating a scenario in which the cure is worse than the original disease. This must be part of the moral equation when we assess the ethics of ARTs.

Medicalization of Human Procreation and the Ethic of Personhood

The potentially negative effects of ARTs are not only felt by the immediate individuals involved; they can be shown to extend to the rest of the society as well. With the advent of ARTs, many are rightly concerned that some scientists and physicians—backed by profit-seeking corporations and operating under the guise of meeting the desires of desperate infertile couples out of a pure altruistic humanitarianism—are in fact engaged in the activity of changing and controlling human procreation and, with it, the very nature of human lives. The implications of control thus extend far beyond the infertile couple's own dilemma. Through the donation of gametes and the use of gestational surrogates, essentially anyone's egg can be combined with anyone's sperm and placed in an unrelated uterus to produce a child to be parented by yet some-

---

[35]Mary Ann Warren insists that the membership of ethics committees overseeing ARTs should be at least 50 percent women. See her essay "IVF and Women's Interests: An Analysis of Feminist Concerns," *Bioethics* 2 (January 1988): 44.

one else, fragmenting parenthood into genetic, gestational and social parts. What ART scientists seem to celebrate most is the fact that "the process is wholly independent of each of its contributors,"[36] the sobering result being that procreation is now in the hands of scientists, doctors and technicians rather than in the hands of the married couple. This directly challenges the ethic of personhood I propose here, which stresses that human personhood is not only characterized by relations, but ultimately constituted by relations. Specifically in terms of the procreation of life, God is the Creator and parents are the only legitimate "*pro*creators," through whom God gives the gift of life. Scientists, physicians, single people and same-sex couples who engage in IVF-ET are counterfeit "procreators." In the name of the progress of science and medicine on one hand, and in the name of the rights of freedom and autonomy on the other, medical and scientific professionals and their clients/consumers, respectively, are threatening to strip the onto-relational foundation from human personhood on the very first day of life's conception. I believe that by disrupting the foundation of the relational structure of human personhood, all the human persons involved in the process will be worse off as persons—will be depersonalized—in the process, some more directly and perhaps more visibly (e.g., the infant, the parent or the surrogate) and some indirectly and only opaquely (e.g., the physicians and the scientists). To the extent that modernity has allowed science to replace God and modern people are left all the more disoriented, modern anthropology has allowed scientific technological reproduction to replace divine-initiated human procreation. Modern persons are left all the more depersonalized.

The advent of embryo diagnosis (see chapter eleven, below) also means that IVF-ET will increasingly be used not only to treat infertility, but also to aid fertile couples with genetic problems. The prospect of diagnosing genetic disorders when the conceptus is only a three-day-old embryo means that more women will resort to using IVF-ET. In the long run, this technology will have the effect of increasing pressure to employ ARTs as a standard procedure for human procreation in the same way that cesarean section is viewed in the delivery of babies today. As embryo diagnosis becomes more popular, we can expect that it will be extended to the detection of nonfatal diseases as well as of predispositions to diseases. This in turn will recruit more couples who are deemed at-risk and will increase the perceived need for the technology to ensure a supposedly risk-free pregnancy and birth. As one writer summarizes the situation:

> Embryo diagnosis potentially creates a need for IVF among new groups of women, sets the stage for the spiraling development of new technologies (which

---

[36]Eugene C. Sandberg, "Only an Attitude Away: The Potential of Reproductive Surrogacy," *American Journal of Obstetrics and Gynecology* 160 (June 1989): 1442.

is an elevator up or slippery slope down depending on one's perspective), and creates new felt obligations for couples who might be happier conceiving through sexual intercourse and taking their chances on the usual outcome of having a healthy baby.[37]

Some even predict that in the near future women will not risk having a child by "in-body fertilization," which will be consider ed foolhardy, unhealthful and unsafe, and will instead choose IVF as the only satisfactory mode of procreation.[38] The once-unthinkable prospect has become a distinct possibility: in the very near future, sex will have nothing to do with procreation. In other words, medicalization will completely convert procreation to reproduction, and the power will be transferred from the "begetters" to the technical manipulators.

Commercialization, Fair Access of ARTs and the Ethic of Personhood

Closely associated with the medicalization of human procreation are the issues of commercialization of and access to ARTs. Particularly in the United States, ART is a very profitable industry ($2 billion annually) marked by intense competition, misleading advertising and fraud.[39] It has been shown that the ART industry is marred by unhealthy links between medical science and the pharmaceutical and biotechnological industries; it is marred as well by for-profit organizations' ethically questionable financial backing.[40] This close association between medical research and commerce raises questions about the motivation and objectivity in IVF research and about the need to continually watch the effect of economic forces on the spread of ARTs.[41]

There is reason to believe that both the bioethics community and the society at large have consistently underestimated the power of market forces and commercialism in shaping the demand for and uses of the various reproductive technologies. As a result, many ARTs are developed more for the market ideology and profit maximization than for the patient's best interest. Tragically, this subversive process unfolds under the guise of "reproductive liberty." If the medical profession is to retain its integrity as a moral profession, it must break with the current practice and set standards for ART that are based on medical

---

[37]Andrea Bonnicksen, "Genetic Diagnosis of Human Embryos," *Hastings Center Report Special Supplement* 22 (July-August 1992): S9.

[38]Ruth Hubbard, *The Politics of Women's Biology* (New Brunswick, N.J.: Rutgers University Press, 1990), pp. 167-68.

[39]Dr. Cecil Jacobson of Washington, D.C., was indicted on fifty-three counts of fraud and perjury related to his IVF practice and sentenced to five years in prison.

[40]For details see Burstyn, "Making Babies," p. 15.

[41]Phyllis Creighton, *Suspended in Time: The Frozen Human Embryo* (Toronto: Anglican Book Centre, 1994), p. 27.

but *not* market concerns.[42] Many believe that ARTs should be regulated under a broadly based national ethics panel that includes not only those directly involved with medicine, but nonresearchers and non-physicians as well, in order to reflect a broad range of societal values that transcend the market forces.[43]

My primary concern with the commercialization of ARTs is the assault on human dignity through the commodification of human beings, their bodies and their bodily products. Commercialization ensues as direct and indirect payments are made to hormone research and manufacture, gamete donors, surrogate mothers, laboratories, hospitals, physicians and scientists—resulting in the ART-produced children becoming commercial objects with a huge price tag in the marketplace. With the availability of embryo cloning (see chapter twelve below) companies could market cloned embryos (which have been frozen and stored in a warehouse, ready for shipment) by including in their advertisements the "finished" child (the "original") as a proof of the quality of the product for sale. This would not only commodify all embryos, but debase all children and destroy the dignity inherent in all human beings. The very thought of a commercial reproductive process that reduces a human creature— one God deemed so uniquely valuable as to relate to each one as his *imago*— to mere saleable merchandise would be totally incompatible with the account of personhood I present here and with the ethic derived from it, for a person is first constituted by the loving relation of God whose love is marked by its gratuitousness in creation, providence and in redemption, *all gratis*. This incompatibility is more than a matter of the sacred versus the secular, for as we will soon see, it is also a matter of the haves against the have-nots. It is important to stress that the inherent dignity is freely given by God and hence shared equally by *all* human beings regardless of their social status.

In response, some contend that as long as all parties are fully informed of the intentions of the procedures and as long as no one is coerced into participating in any of the reproductive arrangements, the dignity and value of human beings are not diminished even if the donors or surrogates are paid. But this overlooks the political and economic contexts in which some infertile women and surrogate mothers have to make their so-called informed decisions. Pressure and coercion in this area can be very subtle. For the infertile women whose lives are devalued because they cannot bear children, multiple

---

[42]George Annas is of the opinion that the cost of health care is out of control in the United States because medical goods are viewed as market goods, with the primary function being to earn money. See his "Regulatory Models for Human Embryo Cloning: The Free Market, Professional Guidelines and Government Restrictions," *Kennedy Institute Ethics Journal* 4 (1994): 240.

[43]Ibid., p. 245.

decisions are reduced to one choice: pay whatever the cost to have children.[44] On the other hand, those who sell gametes or act as surrogate mothers do it for financial rewards. The creation of a new economic underclass in which needy people earn a living by providing body parts and products to serve the reproductive purposes of the rich is more than a mere possibility. Exploitation is greatest in poorer countries, where a woman's reproductive capability becomes her only resource of livelihood and where she undertakes being pregnant solely for financial gain. Pricing the body inevitably leads to alienating the person from her own body and demolishing her self-esteem and dignity as a human person.

Others also contend that it would be unjustifiably paternalistic to decide on behalf of those who may earn money by participating in the commerce of the ARTs: people should have the right to do what they choose with their bodies, with or without remittance.[45] This argument can only be seen as another expression of the boundless individual autonomy rampant in the West. Surprisingly, some people are actually willing to purchase this autonomy, which is intended to protect a person's dignity, at the cost of the complete loss of personal dignity. Because of the real possibility of exploitation and the risk of inflicting irreversible damages on societal values, the Canadian Royal Commission has called for a complete ban on any possible commercial gain from surrogate arrangements and from the selling and buying of gametes, zygotes, embryos or fetuses because they "believe that certain aspects of the human experience must never be commercialized. . . . To allow commercial exchanges of this type would undermine respect for human life and dignity and lead to the commodification of women and children."[46] I find this position consistent with the ethic of personhood I have expressed above.

As alluded to earlier, the question of justice is closely related to the problem of commercialization of IVF-ET. The first area of concern is the cost that can amount to $6,000 to $8,000 per IVF-ET attempt. With a take-home baby rate of 10 to 25 percent, it is not uncommon for a couple to pay $20,000 to $30,000 for several attempts at IVF-ET.[47] When all the direct and indirect costs are factored in (e.g., research and development, training of specialists and technicians, treatment in the neonatal intensive care unit), some estimate the cost to be $50,000 to $100,000 per take-home baby. Hence, unless the procedures are publicly funded and not borne directly by the infertile couples, their availability will be severely restricted to those who can pay for them. In Canada, where

---

[44]Gregory E. Pence, *Classic Cases in Medical Ethics,* 2nd ed. (New York: McGraw-Hill, 1995), p. 109.

[45]Robertson, "Technology and Motherhood," pp. 1-38.

[46]*Proceed with Care,* 2:718.

[47]Genuis, *Reproduction Rollercoaster,* p. 180.

medicine is publicly funded, the questions are how to make these procedures equally accessible to all and which is the best way to use the limited resources available on these procedures. As I have discussed earlier, if we assume that IVF and other ARTs are legitimate medical treatments to relieve a disability affecting a basic and important human capacity, then access to such services must be fair, equitable and not contingent on the couple's ability to pay. In addition, access to IVF centers can be limited by other social factors, such as awareness of the available artificial reproductive services as well as geographical proximity to the centers. At the present time, no one disputes that the number of couples who are actually afflicted by infertility is greater than the number of couples receiving remedial reproductive services. Hence, any moral justification of ARTs cannot be acceptable unless this disparity is addressed.

Until these issues of access and justice are resolved, I believe that IVF-ET and other associative technologies should not be promoted; and, in the meantime, policy makers are well advised to allocate limited resources to the prevention rather than the "cure" of infertility. The cost to prevent infertility through more efficient diagnosis and treatment of pelvic inflammatory diseases (as well as through better sex education in schools to prevent the spread of STDs among teenagers) is estimated to be only a fraction of the cost to produce IVF babies. It has been estimated that for the cost of one IVF baby, thirty cases of infertility could be prevented. I agree with the conclusion "if equal and fair treatment for women at risk of suffering the anguish of infertility or sterility is the goal, the needs of far more women would be met by preventive reproductive health measures."[48] In sum, there is no question that medical scientists in ART have been making a lot of scientific achievements in the last century, but they have also created an equal amount of unsolved ethical problems about human nature and social justice. The ethic of personhood that I propose in this book cautions us that in regard to the technology of IVF-ET, the issues involved are of such a serious nature that there is no justifiable reason not to put a hold on the full-scale employment of the technology until a set of satisfactory and acceptable moral guideline is in place. It seems to me that any moral community would not desire—and for that matter, cannot afford—to do anything less than that.

---

[48]Creighton, *Suspended in Time,* p. 28.

10

Surrogate Gestational Motherhood

*D*efinition, Indications and Motivations

One of the most dramatic byproducts of IVF-ET is the unprecedented possibility of surrogate motherhood: now, for the first time, an embryo created in vitro can be transferred to a gestational woman other than the genetic mother who provides the egg or than the future social mother who will rear the child. Surrogacy is thus defined as an arrangement where one woman carries a pregnancy to term for another woman who is either unwilling or unable to do so. There are two types of surrogate mothers: In the first and medically simpler version, the surrogate is artificially inseminated with the sperm from the husband of the couple who has contracted her services. As the surrogate is also the genetic mother of the child, it is called "partial surrogacy." The surrogate mother may or may not charge a fee (commercial or noncommercial surrogacy), and after the birth, she agrees to relinquish the child to the contracting person or couple even though she is both the child's gestational and genetic mother. In partial surrogacy, there is a form of symbolic sexual replacement because the surrogate mother has to abstain from sexual intercourse with her own sexual partner while being inseminated with the contracting parent's sperm. So although partial surrogacy is medically simpler, it is morally and psychologically more complicated. The second version is "full surrogacy," in which both gametes containing all of the genetic material come from the contracting couple so that the surrogate mother only supplies the womb. For this reason the procedure is considered to have fewer moral and psychological complications, although it is medically more complex, since pregnancy is achieved via IVF-ET. Developed criteria for surrogate gestational mothers include the following:

☐ She should be between the ages of twenty-one and thirty-five.

☐ She should be a willing volunteer with children of her own.

☐ She should have no history of (past or present) STDs, infections, malignancy or substance abuse.

☐ She should not currently use medication or have used chemotherapy or radiation therapy in the past.

☐ She should possesses an intact reproductive system and a healthy lifestyle so as not to compromise the fetus.

☐ She should understand the contractual agreement.

When these criteria are met, prospective carriers will then be matched with contracting couples. After delivery, even though the contracting couple provides the gametes to produce the embryo, they have to adopt the newborn into their family.

The contracting couple may opt to make surrogacy arrangements for various medical and personal reasons. First, surrogacy is the option presented to a woman who has been born without a uterus, or who has undergone a previous hysterectomy but retains functioning ovaries, or who may have a nonfunctional uterus. Second, it is needed if pregnancy threatens the health of a woman who is otherwise fertile. Third, surrogacy is offered to a woman who cannot afford to have her career interrupted by a pregnancy or to a woman who simply wants a child without the experience of pregnancy. Fourth, single men or women may seek surrogate arrangements in order to have a child to whom they are genetically related. For most contracting couples, the procedure is chosen primarily for medical reasons. On the other hand, the surrogate mother's reasons and motivations for entering into this arrangement can be more complex, and the main ones identified are these:[1] First, 90 percent of surrogate mothers are motivated by remuneration. Second, about one-third do it as a cathartic means to deal with some past emotional trauma, and another one-third do it to work through guilt or other negative feelings, often associated with a past abortion or the giving up of a child for adoption. Third, some do it, at least in part, because they enjoy being pregnant. Fourth, many do it for an altruistic reason—giving an infertile couple "the gift of life." Fifth, some long for a close friendship with the future parents of the child. These findings, reported in United States, have been corroborated by similar studies in France

---

[1]H. T. Krimmel, *The Ethics of Reproductive Technology,* ed. K. Alpern (New York: Oxford University Press, 1992), pp. 58-59.

and Britain; and most surrogate mothers have been motivated by more than one reason. The Baby M case, the Calvert case and the Fereira-Jorge case summarized below, represent partial- and full-surrogate arrangements, and they illustrate many features, as well as some of the undesirable consequences, of both surrogacy arrangements.

The Baby M Case. In 1985, William and Elizabeth Stern decided to make a contract, through the Infertility Center of New York, with Mary Beth Whitehead for a partial-surrogacy arrangement, since pregnancy would cause Elizabeth Stern's multiple sclerosis to deteriorate. The couple agreed to pay Whitehead $10,000 to be inseminated with William Stern's sperm, to bear the child and to turn the baby over at birth to the Sterns for adoption. However, two days after the baby was born (on March 27, 1986), Whitehead pleaded to be allowed to keep the child; when the Sterns allowed her to take the baby home for a visit, she promptly departed for her mother's house in Florida and refused to give up the child as previously agreed. The Sterns obtained a court order, and the child was seized July 31, 1986. Subsequently, the Sterns and Whitehead both sought legal custody in court, and on March 31, 1987, the judge upheld the legality of the original contract and awarded the Sterns the legal adoption papers. However, on February 3, 1988, the New Jersey Supreme Court reversed this decision on the grounds that it violated state adoption laws because money had been exchanged for the child. In the end a intermediate position was reached: the Sterns were awarded the *custody* of Baby M because the court ultimately believed Baby M will fare better in their household.[2] The adoption agreement was set aside, and Whitehead remained Baby M's *legal* parent with visitation rights.

The Calvert Case. Crispina and Mark Calvert decided to seek a full-surrogacy arrangement since Crispina Calvert had her uterus surgically removed with ovaries left intact. Anna Johnson agreed to act as a gestational surrogate for a fee of $10,000. Ova were extracted from Crispina Calvert and mixed with Mark Calvert's sperm for IVF. A fertilized ovum was then implanted in Johnson and the pregnancy progressed without incident—until at the seventh month of gestation, when Johnson suddenly announced that she had changed her mind and filed suit to seek custody of the unborn child. After the baby was born (on September 19, 1990), the court initially granted both the Calverts and Johnson shared visitation rights, but when the California Superior Court reviewed the case the following month, Johnson's parental and visitation rights were terminated, and complete custody of the child was awarded to the Calverts.[3]

---

[2]Ronald Munson with Christopher A. Hoffman, *Intervention and Reflection: Basic Issues in Medical Ethics,* 5th ed. (Belmont, Calif.: Wadsworth, 1996), p. 494.
[3]Ibid., p. 497.

The Fereira-Jorge Case. Surrogacy arrangements involving a family member can be both simpler and more complicated. Karen and Alcino Fereira-Jorge wanted to have more children after Karen had her uterus removed due to complications from her first pregnancy. Karen's mother, Pat, volunteered to serve as a gestational surrogate, using Karen's ova fertilized in vitro by Alcino's sperm; and she successfully gave birth to triplets in September 1987. The arrangement did not involve payment to an outside stranger, but it threatened to cause the breakdown of family order by Pat giving birth to her own grand-children.[4]

Ethical Concerns Associated with Surrogate Motherhood

The Glover Report, published by the European Community in 1989, cites risks to the surrogate mother as one of the main ethical objections to surrogate arrangements. Since there is usually a fee involved, women in financial need are more likely to be surrogate mothers, which means their so-called free choice is merely that of a lesser evil than poverty. Surrogate mothers are thereby degraded to baby-making machines, and economic exploitation becomes inevitable (as I alluded to in the chapter nine). For example, in the Baby M case, the agency received $7,000 up front, simply for arranging the surrogacy with no other liability. Whitehead, on the other hand, was to receive $10,000 only after the surrogacy was completed. She had to agree to "assume all risks, including the risk of death," which for a "normal pregnancy" is nine maternal deaths for every 100,000 live births. If a miscarriage had occurred in the first five months, the contract would have been nullified and she would have received no compensation. If prenatal tests revealed fetal abnormalities, she would have been required to have an abortion at the Sterns's demand with all its physical and psychological risks to the pregnant mother. As one writer comments, the contract is "a calculation so cold as to embarrass a social order that licenses as a service works like this."[5]

Surrogate arrangement also exposes the woman to great emotional harm, most obviously from the forced severance of the mother-child relationship, as in both the Whitehead and Johnson cases. It is generally believed that a woman cannot carry a child for nine months without forming an emotional bond with the child.[6] The psychological literature describes specific maternal

---

[4]Joseph H. Howell and William F. Sale, eds., *Life Choices: A Hastings Center Introduction to Bioethics* (Washington, D.C.: Georgetown University Press, 1995), p. 284.

[5]Murray Kempton, "The Contract for 'Baby M,' " *New York Review of Books,* April 9, 1987, p. 44.

[6]"As David H. Smith has pointed out, when humans interact with animate beings over time, they tend to become personally involved, whether we are talking about 4-H kids and live-stock, or a researcher and a mouse tested over several months. Can we reasonably suppose

"attachment" patterns developed during pregnancy that create strong ties between mother and newborn.[7] As a result, most surrogate mothers experience grief upon giving up their children, and up to 10 percent require psychological intervention and support.[8] Also, commercial surrogacy requires that the surrogate mother deny her own feeling that she is a parent, rather than a contract laborer, as the pregnancy gradually progresses and that she repress whatever parental love she feels for the child.[9] In the whole process, the surrogate mother's emotions are manipulated, trivialized and rendered illegitimate by the market forces of a commercial transaction. A third source of emotional stress for a surrogate mother is related to the fact that upon the child's birth she may be summarily accused of being a "third party" who threatens the marital relationship of the contracting (social) couple, despite the fact that she "intrudes" into the couple only to the extent that she has been "invited" to do so. In other words, the contracting couple simultaneously seeks and resents the arrangement. The surrogate mother is hurt emotionally when she realizes that the contracting couple desires only the "product" of the surrogacy arrangement—that the couple resents the process itself and thus rejects her. Fourth, the contracting couple normally does not wish to maintain any continuing relationship with her after the baby has been handed over, which, as we have seen, conflicts with one of the key motives of surrogate mothers: to establish relationship. As one writer observes, "By taking advantage of the surrogate mothers' noncommercial motivations without offering anything but what the norms of commerce demand in return, these norms leave her open to exploitation."[10]

In response to these ethical concerns, some claim that womb lending or leasing is no more degrading than selling one's muscle power in hard labor, one's intellectual power in other more sedentary professions or one's physical appearance in the modeling profession; each trade carries its own professional hazards. Some feminist writers also argue that to prohibit a woman from hiring or being hired as a surrogate mother violates her reproductive freedom and is itself degrading. In spite of these contrary views, most people believe that the risk of economic exploitation is indeed inherent in any commercial surrogacy arrangement and thus commercial surrogacy should be outlawed. Indeed, this

---

that a woman could knowingly have the most intimate interaction with a fetus for nine months and not form a relationship with the fetus?" Thomas A. Shannon, *Surrogate Motherhood: The Ethics of Using Human Beings* (New York: Crossroad, 1988), p. 110.

[7]S. A. Garcia, "Reproductive Technology for Procreation, Experimentation and Profit," *Journal of Legal Medicine* 11, no. 1 (1990): 22-23.

[8]Elizabeth S. Anderson, "Is Women's Labor a Commodity?" in *Intervention and Reflection: Basic Issues in Medical Ethics,* 5th ed., ed. Ronald Munson (Belmont, Calif.: Wadsworth, 1996), p. 542.

[9]Ibid., pp. 541-43.

[10]Ibid., p. 541.

is the recommendation of the Canadian Royal Commission.

Not all exploitation needs to be of an economic nature. Women can be pressured to serve as surrogate mothers simply because they wish to be recognized as "good" women. In a male-dominated society, women are expected to be generous, loving, altruistic and sacrificial before they earn their praise. In this sense, surrogacy becomes an expression of gender exploitation. Furthermore, surrogate motherhood and IVF-ET degrade womanhood/motherhood by potentially dividing women into three classes: genetically superior women who become genetic mothers, physically strong women who become gestational mothers and wealthy, intelligent, gentle-tempered women who become social mothers.[11] This fragmentation of womanhood according to functional capacities violates the woman's holistic nature and thus undermines the woman's dignity. There are other ways the woman's personhood can be compromised in a surrogate arrangement. For example, the contract usually imposes conditions that curtail the activities and interests of the surrogate mother. She is prohibited from having intercourse with her usual partner, she cannot smoke or drink, and she must undergo invasive medical procedures such as amniocentesis. In short, the rights of the contracting couple and the interests of the future child override the surrogate mother's right of autonomy. Hence, in a surrogate arrangement, the surrogate mother lends not only her womb but her whole person, and many see this as comparable to prostitution or self-enslavement. Although these analogies are probably unnecessarily harsh, I agree that surrogacy violates the woman's personhood by requiring a commercial contract in which the woman's body is specifically and directly part of the trade. In sum, I strongly oppose surrogacy in general and commercial surrogacy in particular because they violate the dignity of the gestational mother, and this cannot be endorsed by the ethic of personhood that I espouse.

Problems Associated with Children Gestated by Surrogate Mothers

The Glover Report expresses concern that the child-to-be's welfare can be compromised by the surrogate arrangement in several ways.[12] First, the popular claim is that since social parenthood is much more important than either genetic or gestational parenthood, the child's only really significant relationship is with the contracting social parents in the surrogate arrangement. As long as the contracting couple has the child's best interests at heart, surrogate arrangements should be acceptable. But such a claim conflicts with the intuition of many people who, as we have seen, feel that genetic and gestational connections are crucial in engendering the spirit of self-sacrifice necessary in the nur-

---

[11]Gena Corea, *The Mother Machine* (New York: Harper & Row, 1985).
[12]Garcia, "Reproductive Technology," pp. 22-23.

turing and rearing of children. Under these circumstances, it is highly probable that the surrogate arrangement may deprive the child of the best care, love and nurturing available in conventional parenting. Further, by fragmenting the holistic connectedness of genetic, gestational and social parenthood, social parents are inclined to expect that the genetic and gestational parents are responsible for delivering a baby without disease or defect. If the child falls short of the contracting parents' expectations and is not fully accepted, the child may be a source of parental resentment and may grow up feeling and being treated like a piece of "factory seconds" merchandise.

This tendency to commodify the prospective child is reinforced by the motivations of the surrogate mother (to gain money, companionship and good feeling) and the motivations of the social parents (to fulfill needs, desires and curiosity).[13] Each of those motives essentially shows that the child is being conceived not as an end in herself, but as a means to satisfy the various needs of the parents, and this is ethically unacceptable. Some argue that many couples procreating naturally could be found guilty of the same motivations—they too use the child to gratify parental interests. This may well be true, but I believe that this fact in nowise justifies the *inherent tendency* within surrogacy for commodifying and hence dehumanizing and depersonalizing the child. Surrogacy can only be justified, or condemned, on the basis of what it actually does or does not do itself, not on what other naturally reproducing couples may also do otherwise. In commercial surrogacy, the child-to-be is specifically treated as though she is a piece of merchandise to be acquired, not as though she is a person. In so doing, great psychological damage is inflicted on the child.

The child may also incur psychological damage if the surrogate mother changes her mind and decides to keep the baby. As we have seen in the Baby M and Calvert cases, there is a distinct risk that the surrogate mother may be unwilling or unable to sever the bond formed with the child during gestation. In ruling on the Calvert case, the court suggested that a surrogate mother should not be a primigravida (first-time pregnancy), for only women who have given birth to children can know the bond that would have to be severed. However, even this restriction cannot guarantee that the surrogate mother will give up the child, for Whitehead had previously given birth to two children. This is why the law in Denmark forbids the surrogate mother from formally

---

[13]While many couples may seek surrogacy arrangements for perfectly good reasons, there is undoubtedly often a great sense of need or of curiosity, both of which can place great pressure on a child. William Stern (of the Baby M case) seems to illustrate the latter view when he described his reasons for seeking surrogacy: the idea of having children was "compelling." Ronald Munson with Christopher A. Hoffman, *Intervention and Reflection: Basic Issues in Medical Ethics,* 5th ed. (Belmont, Calif.: Wadsworth, 1996), p. 494.

giving up the child for adoption until three months after the birth. In the event that the surrogate mother decides to keep the baby, the contracting couple naturally feels that their child is unjustly being snatched away from them. Litigation for the custody of the child commonly ensues, especially in the United States, and the child may suffer from irreparable damage as a result of being passed around litigating parents while the legal case is being decided.

Many respond that not every child will necessarily develop emotional difficulties because of the commercial surrogate arrangement, and for those who do, their psychological problems can perhaps be dealt with by appropriate counseling when they become more mature. It is not rational to prohibit a practice based merely on some potential adverse feelings. Besides, it is most unlikely that the child is so harmed that she would have been better off if she had not been born. Admittedly, it is difficult to prove that the psychological damages inflicted on the child born of a surrogate mother would be so severe that the child would regret her existence. But as we have seen earlier, the point is not whether impaired existence is better than nonexistence, which itself is an untenable argument, but whether we have the right to deliberately set out to *create* a child with the probable problems associated with surrogacy. Even if we grant that a couple has the right to reproduce, it does not follow that they are justified to deliberately create a situation that inherently carries with it elements that are harmful to the child.

Lastly, conservatives from the Roman Catholic Church are critical of surrogacy, especially if it is a commercial surrogacy, saying that it is comparable to "baby-selling" and thus violates the dignity and the right of the child "who is to be conceived, carried in the womb, brought into the world and brought up by his own parents."[14] In response to this, some contend that any postulated "right" of the child to be created sexually within the marital bond requires that this right to be so strong that it trumps any interest of the childless couple. This also requires that being the child of a surrogate is such an indignity that, by comparison, honoring the rights of the childless couple to have a child basically counts for nothing.[15] It is argued, too, that this has not been demonstrated to be the case. But it seems that parental rights with respect to children are fiduciary in nature, which means that the proper exercise of parental rights is to maximize the best interest of the child, and this must surely include the preservation of the dignity of the child as a human being. What "commercial surrogacy has achieved

---

[14]Congregation for the Doctrine of the Faith, "Instruction on Respect for Human Life in Its Origin and on the Dignity of Procreation: Replies to Certain Questions of the Day," in *Religious and Artificial Reproduction,* ed. Lisa Sowle Cahill and Thomas A. Shannon (New York: Crossroad, 1988), p. 160.

[15]Bonnie Steinbock, "Surrogate Motherhood as Prenatal Adoption," *Law, Medicine and Health Care* 16 (Spring-Summer 1988): 48; Anderson, "Women's Labor," p. 539.

is to change the nature of parental rights from trusts to rights of use and disposal of properties owned."[16] If a child as a human person is of intrinsic value, no parental right can be so strong as to permit an arrangement that would rob the child of her right and dignity. I believe that a childless couple guided by an ethic of personhood would not choose to have children through means that degrade their personhood at the same time. In this context, surrogacy can only be regarded as a self-contradicting and self-defeating arrangement.

Surrogacy, ARTs and the Notion of Family

While our society often assumes that the family has inherent values—such as duty, responsibility, sacrifice and so on—modern people in the West are quite unsure of the real moral significance of a family and the sort of responsibility and duty entailed in having a family. Before the industrial revolution, the traditional family's strength as a social institution was to be found in the fact that the family functioned as an economic, political, educational and moral unit, with all the privileges and duties these activities involved. In this sense, the family was the basic building block of the society.[17] But in the modern Western society, the moral ideal of the culture has shifted from the family to the autonomous, self-determining, self-sufficient and free person. The family has thus been stripped of the various roles it used to play and the roles through which its existence used to be justified, and parents are no longer seen as having a direct function in regard to their children. In short, the family in the modern Western society has become morally irrational, and it appears to be nothing more than the part of life that the free person should learn to outgrow.[18] Some have hoped that after forfeiting its economic and political responsibilities, the family may perhaps concentrate on its primary role as a place of emotional support, intimacy, affection and care. After all, the industrialized society needs the family as a necessary refuge, "a haven in a heartless world" to protect people from the harsh reality of a competitive societal life.[19] But how well has the modern family flourished "as an event of affection and love"?[20] In a culture where individual autonomy and freedom are so emphasized that the courts deny both a husband's right to be informed of his wife's abortion decision and the parents' right to know of a minor's use of a contraceptive,[21] it is very diffi-

---

[16]Anderson, "Women's Labor," p. 539.

[17]Robert Nisbet, *Twilight of Authority* (New York: Oxford University Press, 1975), p. 257.

[18]Stanley Hauerwas, *A Community of Character* (Notre Dame: University of Notre Dame Press, 1981), p. 171.

[19]Christopher Lasch, *Haven in a Heartless World* (New York: Basic, 1977).

[20]Hauerwas, *Community of Character,* p. 169.

[21]In some parts of Canada, a minor may be allowed to make an autonomous decision to have an abortion without the parents' knowledge or approval.

cult to imagine what kind of family bonds, intimacy and care are actually possible. In reality, members in a modern family behave more or less in the same manner as they do in the society—that is, as friendly strangers at best and as individuals involved in "power struggles between independent principalities" at worst.[22] In other words, the individualistic ethos of the democratic society, which turns to the family for relief of some of the problems that it has created, duplicates the same problems for the family. We simply cannot cherish the family and at the same time adhere to ideologies and policies that work against it. We cannot expect that our social order rests on impersonal and rational principles and yet also hold our family together on the basis of personal intimacy. The family is likely in crisis because we are asking the family to do the impossible.

This uncertainty over the meaning and value of the family is both reflected in and compounded by the blurring of family boundaries introduced by ARTs and surrogacy. Consider the following example: a twenty-year-old woman from Rome gave birth in October 1988 to a boy conceived artificially using ova from her forty-eight-year-old mother and sperm from her thirty-five-year-old stepfather. The result is that the gestational/social mother is also the baby's genetic sister, the genetic mother is also the baby's grandmother, and the genetic father is also the baby's step-grandfather.[23] Thus, the development of ARTs has made it possible for many people other than the traditional two parents to be involved in the creation and identity of a child. AID results in a child with two "fathers"—one biological/genetic and one social/nurturing; IVF-ET with surrogate arrangements makes it possible for a child to have three "mothers"—one genetic, one gestational and one social. Such blurring of family boundaries has caused concern for family instability and an identity crisis in the child as well as practical concerns as to who will be responsible for the child in the case of the social parents' death or divorce.

In an attempt to minimize the gravity of these problems, some contend that many of the concerns raised by surrogacy are also raised by both the adoption process and blended families. In adoption there is a break between biological and social parenting, while blended families are created by remarriage subsequent to either divorce or death. If these situations are accepted by the society, then (these people claim) there is no reason why ARTs and surrogacy cannot likewise be accepted. In response, I must point out that although there are similarities between these situations, adoption and blended families are basically "rescue operations" to redeem certain unforeseen, unintended, ill-fated situations. ARTs and surrogacy fundamentally differ from these in that they cre-

---

[22]Hauerwas, *Community of Character,* p. 160.
[23]Garcia, "Reproductive Technology," p. 39.

ate the problems intentionally. They create a blended family with the *fore-knowledge* that it will blur the family lines.

Some also see that the advent of ARTs may be the occasion for society's adopting a more flexible and innovative view of the family in which the biological element plays only a relatively small role, allowing other elements such as legal definitions, social customs and "subjective intentions" to move to the fore. One such broadened definition of family proposes that

> family members are individuals who by birth, adoption, marriage, or declared commitment share deep personal connections and are mutually entitled to receive and obligated to provide support of various kinds to the extent possible, especially in times of need.[24]

Such a broad definition allows, of course, for the widespread utilization of reproductive technologies. The biological tie is no longer a defining factor in the family and thus family membership may change according to the circumstances. In AID, for example, the sperm donor is not considered the father, whereas in surrogacy he is. Carrying someone else's embryo does not make a mother in surrogacy, yet it does in IVF. An increased use of ARTs could therefore lead to defining family exclusively in nonbiological terms until the genetic link in families is all but eliminated. In fact, to base family membership with no reference to biology opens the door to our considering a baseball team or a group of dog lovers as a "family." That is, the family essentially becomes both everything and nothing. In light of the central role that embodiment and genetic ties have played in our understanding of personhood—together with the fact that families in our current society are historically the most unstable—such a broadened definition would undoubtedly lead to further deterioration of the status of the family. We caricature our culture's state of confusion when we promote a technology that is meant to assist people in creating a family yet simultaneously promotes an ethos to eliminate the very idea of family.

Assisted Reproduction, Freedom and the Ethic of Personhood

Assisted reproductive technologies and, in particular, surrogacy arrangements ultimately lead to the most fundamental issue of procreative freedom, understood as the ability for people other than heterosexual married couples to have reproductive choices without any constraint surrounding those choices. But such an account of freedom, as far as we can see, is nothing more than another expression of individual autonomy and self-determination. As in the case of abortion, freedom is being abused by women to fulfill their desire to

---

[24]Ruth Macklin, "Artificial Means of Reproduction and Our Understanding of the Family," *Hastings Center Report* 21 (January-February 1991): 10.

abort a child; in the use of ARTs, freedom is invoked to fulfill a couple's desire to create a child instead of aborting one. Single people and menopausal women in turn claim the same freedom to have children through ARTs, with homosexual couples quickly to follow. Although I do not deny that freedom is an important moral principle, neither do I believe that this modern expression of freedom serves us (as individuals or as a community) well as a moral guide to deal with issues raised by ARTs. To take parenting as an example, most people with experience as part of a family know that the family members do not exist merely as free, independent and autonomous individuals. Rather, as the ethic of personhood I espouse reminds us, family members are independent individuals in order that they can be freely and mutually dependent on each other, and in order that they can be connected in relationships in which self-giving sacrifice and interdependence, rather than self-determination and independence, are practiced for the purpose of building a family of authentic persons in relations. The modern interpretation of freedom, in my opinion, has not been sufficient to provide for an adequate account of personhood, and I have even less reason to believe that it provides sufficient moral guidance for underwriting a technology that creates new persons.[25] This is not to say that the ethic of personhood I espouse does not hold a high view of a person's individuality and independence, but I hold a similarly high view for the purpose of building a community.

Hence, my main critique of modernity's account of freedom, understood as autonomy, is its preoccupation with the individual, often at the expense of the collective whole. In this regard, one of the major ethical principles that the Canadian Royal Commission has adopted in its deliberation on ARTs is to emphasize a balance between the interests of the individual and those of society. The commission has expressed concern regarding a society that takes an exclusive interest in freedom, autonomy and individual rights while leaving little room for responsibility to the collective whole. Although Western society does not usually like to impose limits on freedoms or rights, the fact remains that sometimes individual rights must be sacrificed or curtailed for the good of the whole. This is not because of any inherent right of the majority in a democratic society, but rather because there are very few choices (if any) that the individual can make which do not somehow affect the larger society. When a society is exclusively preoccupied with the rights and autonomy of individuals, the effect of the decisions made by those individuals on the society as a whole is often overlooked. We lose sight of the fact that as a community of persons,

---

[25]For further discussion on reproductive liberty and family integrity, see the section "Destruction of the Traditional Family Structure by Cloning" in chapter twelve, "Human Cloning and Stem Cells."

we do live not solely as individuals but as an interconnected and interdependent whole. For this reason, the conviction of the Canadian Royal Commission is that when the interests of the society are being flattened, "individual rights can be limited."

The secular understanding of freedom as autonomy and self-determination presupposes the existence of a neutral self who has the capacity to will and to choose freely. But is a neutral self really possible? Augustine rejects such a possibility: in his view there is no neutral self that can be posited a priori. Rather, he understands freedom to be the capacity an agent has not to freely will or choose, but first to establish a self. To put it differently, freedom is the capacity to establish an identity, to secure the self upon some loyalty, and then to will and act in ways consistent with the established self. Whether an agent can freely will and choose depends on the ground upon which the self is established. In the account of personhood that I have described, the self (person) is established primarily by a relationship through the creational, redemptive and sanctifying work of the triune God, and established secondarily by relations with other God-relating persons in the self's surroundings. Only when a person is so established, is one then given the space to be truly free to will and to choose.[26]

When we understand freedom in light of the personhood ethic I advocate here, we see that how one exercises one's procreative choice reveals in some way one's identity as a person, establishes one's identity as a parent and determines to a large extent one's behavior as a parent in the future. In other words, the choice before us is more than the simple choice of which technology one will use to become a parent; the choice is informed by our established personal identity, which now creates a new parental identity with demands and expectations that on the surface are occasioned by the technologies, but that in fact are reinforced by the distortions of the manipulating parent who makes the choice. And on a larger scale, ARTs do deal not only with the beginnings of life, but also with the possibility of altering the fundamental essence of human nature and hence potentially affecting humanity's future. The employment of ARTs therefore ultimately determines the sort of persons, families and communities we are and want to become. Therefore, the ethic of personhood I

---

[26]In the Christian tradition, God, by his gracious invitation, calls people to reject the identity they have established upon some other "good" and to reestablish themselves upon him, from whom all goods are derived. In other words, God's grace in his invitation to human beings creates the condition and fulfillment of freedom, liberating the wrongly established selves into a new identity. God remains the condition and fulfillment of human freedom— the freedom to establish an identity upon him and to maintain integrity in the world through concrete choices that are consistent with a people set free by grace. For a well-summarized discussion of this Reformed tradition of freedom, see Hessel Bouma III et al., *Christian Faith, Health and Medical Practice* (Grand Rapids, Mich.: Eerdmans, 1989), pp. 13-15, 182-86.

espouse would be particularly sensitive to the vulnerability of a child whose identity can be manipulated by parents using technologies. Take for example a husband and wife who dream of seeing their child become a skilled surgeon and who employ all available technological means for the child to reach that end. Such a choice establishes a parental identity with certain expectations as well as an identity for the child that may not be freely owned by the child. Thus, if the child in his development displays an inclination to become a poet, the child's freedom will not be nurtured; instead he will be discouraged from developing into anything other than a skilled surgeon. The parental choice to exercise this sort of freedom sadly deprives a child of his true freedom; and the ethic of personhood that I have established would not find this morally acceptable, nor would it consider such a procreative choice a manifestation of true freedom, for the child's God-given freedom is sacrificed rather than nurtured.

11

Manipulation of Embryos

*T*he Moral Status of the Human Embryo and the Defeat of the Notion of a "Pre-embryo"

Pivotal to the acceptability of IVF and all related embryo technologies (including transfer, storage, research, diagnosis, treatment and cloning) is one's conviction regarding the nature, worth and moral status of the human embryo from its earliest beginnings. IVF technology has forced the determination of the beginning of a human being or human personhood to the forefront of the bioethics debate for one simple reason: for the first time in human history, a freshly fertilized zygote can be observed, handled, nurtured or discarded. Who or what is this zygote, which through cellular divisions develops first into an embryo and later into a fetus? Further, who determines what one can do to it, what use (if any) one can make of it, and what protection one should provide for it?

To specify the context, Edwards and Steptoe, the two scientists who pioneered IVF technology in the first half of the twentieth century, viewed the early embryos as so remotely related to adult human beings that they warranted no special protection,[1] and they discarded 99.5 percent of fertilized ova produced in their laboratory.[2] John Robertson, a contemporary legal expert, states that the "prevailing moral and legal consensus views early

[1]Marc Lappé, "Ethics at the Center of Life: Protecting Vulnerable Subjects," *Hastings Center Report* 8 (October 1978): 11-12.

[2]Donald E. O. Demarco, "Love Among the Test Tubes: Louise Brown Turns 10; *Humanae Vitae* Turns 20," in *Trust the Truth,* ed. Russell Smith (Braintree, Mass.: Pope John Center, 1991), p. 176.

embryos as too rudimentary in neurological development to have interests or rights."[3] On this view, endangering embryos would thus be justified within the same paradigm that justifies early abortion. On the other hand, the Ethics Advisory Board of the United States Department of Health, Education and Welfare asserted in their 1979 report that "the human embryo is entitled to profound respect," although it does not possess "the full legal and moral rights attributed to persons."[4] The board stated that IVF-ET is ethically acceptable for married couples but that research on human embryos can only be performed to establish the safety of IVF-ET and to yield important scientific information. Likewise, the U.K. Warnock Committee determined that the human embryo has a special status and "should be afforded some protection in law," although it does not have the status of "a living child or an adult."[5] Despite the opposition of conservative dissenting members, the committee endorsed both therapeutic and nontherapeutic experimentation on human embryos produced in vitro.[6]

Those who approach the issue from a Christian perspective, both Catholics and Protestants alike, adopt an extremely cautious attitude toward medical technologies when human embryos are involved. The Roman Catholic Congregation for the Doctrine of the Faith (CDF) pronounced in the *Donum Vitae* (1987) that "the human being must be respected—as a person—from the very first instant of his existence."[7] The CDF proceeds to argue the point not from explicitly philosophical or theological grounds, but mainly from scientific reasoning. It recognizes three debates in this matter: the beginning of human life, the individuality of the human being and the identity of the human person. To establish the embryo's full moral rights, the CDF relies on scientific evidence and falls back on "The Declaration on Procured Abortion" (1974),[8] which unequivocally states that

> from the time that the ovum is fertilized, a new life is begun which . . . modern genetic science brings valuable confirmation. It has demonstrated that, from the

[3]John A. Robertson, "Ethical and Legal Issues in Pre-implantation Genetic Screening," *Fertility and Sterility* 57, no. 1 (1992): 1.

[4]Department of Health, Education and Welfare, Ethics Advisory Board, "Report and Conclusions: HEW Support of Research Involving Human In Vitro Fertilization and Embryo Transfer" (Washington, D.C.: U.S. Government Printing Office, 1979), p. 107.

[5]Department of Health and Social Security, *Report of the Committee of Inquiry into Human Fertilization and Embryology* (London: Her Majesty's Stationery Office, 1984), p. 63.

[6]Ibid., pp. 90-91.

[7]Congregation for the Doctrine of the Faith, "Instruction on Respect for Human Life in Its Origin and on the Dignity of Procreation: Replies to Certain Questions of the Day," in *Intervention and Reflection: Basic Issues in Medical Ethics*, 5th ed., ed. Ronald Munson (Belmont, Calif.: Wadsworth, 1996), pp. 513-21.

[8]Ibid., p. 515.

first instant, the program is fixed as to what this living being will be: a man, this individual-man with his characteristic aspects already well determined.[9]

To this, the CDF adds in 1987 that human biological science confirms that "in the zygote resulting from fertilization the biological identity of a new human individual is already constituted."[10] The CDF thus argues that the beginning, individuality and identity of the human life all occur at conception on the basis that the scientific/genetic evidence is sufficiently strong to provide "a valuable indication for discerning by the use of reason a personal presence at the moment of this first appearance of a human life."[11] However, at this point the document departs from its overtly scientific argumentation and ventures into a philosophical proposition, equating *human being* with *human person* and asking, "How could a human individual not be a human person?"[12] Without providing an explicitly philosophical or theological argument, the CDF concludes that

> the human being is to be respected and treated as a person from the moment of conception; . . . his rights as a person must be recognized, [and] since the embryo must be treated as a person, it must also be defended in its integrity, tended and cared for, to the extent possible, in the same way as any other human being.[13]

This allows the CDF to draw a strong line on embryo manipulation, prohibiting all experimentation that is not directly therapeutic, and they condemn as immoral the production of human embryos for scientific use as disposable biological material.[14] I concur with the CDF's conclusion on the basis of my understanding that early embryos are human beings at the earliest stage of the developmental process and whose histories as human persons have been established by God's relationship with them in the very act of their creation.[15]

Some ethicists within the Roman Catholic Church have been critical of the CDF's position; Richard McCormick, S.J., for example, contends that there is a distinction between "genetic individuality," which he grants to a "pre-embryo,"[16] and "developmental individuality," which he believes a "pre-embryo" has not attained. McCormick draws from Clifford Grobstein's scientific opinion

---

[9]Ibid., p. 515.
[10]Ibid.
[11]Ibid.
[12]Ibid.
[13]Ibid.
[14]Ibid., pp. 513-21.
[15]See part one, "Foundations of Human Personhood," above, for details.
[16]McCormick prefers to use the term *pre-embryo* for the conceptus prior to the appearance of the primitive streak on the fourteenth or fifteenth day of gestation.

about the early development of the human embryo,[17] which holds to the following:

☐ Early blastomeres are totipotent.

☐ During the first two weeks of gestation, the conceptus is predominantly concerned with the formation of extra-embryonic rather than embryonic structures.

☐ Twinning and recombination are still possible before about fourteen days. McCormick then concludes that before the appearance of the primitive streak, the conceptus should be regarded as pre-embryonic rather than fully embryonic; and he maintains that the pre-embryo cannot be said to have attained developmental individuality, or "singleness," even though it may have acquired genetic individuality.[18] He maintains that a biologically stable subject should be present as "a minimal biological substrate for personhood"[19] and that such a stable subject is not present until implantation and the appearance of the primitive streak, when primary embryonic organization only begins, leading to the formation of a fetus eventually. The implication of this distinction is that "the embryo originates as a very small part of the pre-embryo, and coexists with the pre-embryo as the latter differentiates into the placenta, prior to the embryo becoming a fetus."[20]

It is true that many of the early conceptus's activities from the first to the fourteenth days are related to physiological interaction with the mother and are not directly involved in the formation of a fetus. But I believe that this fact itself does not support the conclusion that the embryo thereby only comes to exist after about fourteen days, when it is formed from a minuscule subset of cells generated by the fertilized egg.[21] Such an understanding fails to do justice to the biological and moral significance of that "tiny subset of the mass of cells," which from the morular stage onward (four to five days of gestation) is destined to form the fetus and later the adult. By focusing on the development of placental tissue, the term *pre-embryo* also creates the impression that the con-

---

[17]Clifford Grobstein, *Science and the Unborn: Choosing Human Futures* (New York: Basic, 1988). For a detailed discussion and critique of this and similar views, please refer to chapter two, "The Biological Dimension of Human Personhood," above.

[18]Richard McCormick, S.J., *Corrective Vision Explorations in Moral Theology* (Kansas City: Sheed & Ward, 1994), chap. 14.

[19]Ibid., p. 183.

[20]See D. Gareth Jones and Barbara Telfa, "Before I Was an Embryo, I Was a Pre-embryo—Or Was I?" *Bioethics* 9, no. 1 (1995): 37. It is important to note that despite the popularity the term *pre-embryo* has enjoyed, there is as yet no consensus regarding the exact moment when the pre-embryo becomes an embryo. Most place it at fourteen to sixteen days, but six to seven days, ten days and twenty-one days have also been used. See pp. 32-49 for a summary of these views.

[21]A. McLaren, "Embryo Research," *Nature* 320, no. 17 (1986): 570, cited in Jones and Telfa, "Before I Was," p. 39.

ceptus during those first fourteen days is far less important than the conceptus after that point. This notion overlooks the biological and moral significance of the placenta in maintaining the continuing existence of the embryo/fetus throughout the entire gestational period. The embryo/fetus simply cannot survive without the placenta. Recognizing the significance of the placental tissue, which arises from the early conceptus, D. Gareth Jones and Barbara Telfa suggest the designations *embryo-placenta* and *embryo-fetus* not so much to segregate the two, but precisely to emphasize that it is the whole of the embryo that gives rise to both the placenta and the fetus and that both therefore are biologically and morally significant. Even though many of the cells in the first fourteen days of embryonic development are destined to be extra-embryonic (embryo-placenta) and eventually discarded does not mean that the embryo under fourteen days old is of lesser value nor that it does not contain some very important part (embryo-fetus), because the whole embryo as an entity is essential for the well-being, growth and further development of that particular prenatal individual.[22] To compartmentalize and segregate the early conceptus into pre-embryo and embryo is to fail to appreciate the intricacies of the early development of the human embryo, which includes the establishment of the vital maternal-fetal relationship.

Finally, the pre-embryo designation has also attached far too much significance to the primitive streak, the embryologic developmental landmark, which is taken to mark the end of the pre-embryo and the beginning of an individual embryo. But as has already been discussed,[23] this view simply places more weight on the primitive streak than it can bear; it mistakenly takes the primitive streak as a permanent structure when in fact it is transitory, becoming progressively smaller and eventually disappearing once the mesoderm is formed around the third and fourth week of gestation. I believe that the primitive streak is a temporary signpost in the developmental continuum of the embryo, signaling that the embryo is becoming a more definitive entity by acquiring complex structures such as the notochord, neural tube, neural crest and so on. As a signpost, it has no distinctiveness of its own and does not perform any

---

[22]Jones and Telfa, "Before I Was," p. 43.

[23]See chapter two, "The Biological Dimension of Human Personhood," above. Norman Ford believes that the primitive streak marks the onset of the necessary condition for the *pro-embryo* (a term he prefers to *pre-embryo*) "to pass from the presence of a potential human individual to an actual human individual with potential." Norman M. Ford, *When Did I Begin?* (Cambridge: Cambridge University Press, 1988), p. 172. McLaren also believes that the primitive streak signals the point when the cells of the per-embryo's inner cell mass begin to display regional specifications, with cells for basic body tissues aligned in the corrective relative position; hence twinning is usually no longer possible afterwards, and thus this marks the onset of individuality. A. McLaren, "Where to Draw the Line?" quoted in Jones and Telfa, "Before I Was," p. 41.

exclusive organizational function to enable the emergence of an individual human being. The development of the embryo from fertilization onwards is a continuous process. Any arbitrary delineation of developmental stages or assignment of moral significance to a particular stage fails to do justice to the whole developmental continuum wherein the whole conceptus is maturing from the moment of fertilization as an individual human life. The notion of developmental individuality[24] on the designation of pre-embryo simply does not live up to the biological facts available.

While it is unlikely that any kind of consensus can be reached with regard to the nature, value and rights of embryos, most people would agree that even if the early embryo is not a person, it is nonetheless a human life with some moral standing.[25] This is a fundamentally significant matter not only for the embryo itself, but for humanity as a whole, because it reflects society's basic attitudes toward human life. As one writer puts it, "The way in which we define and treat the embryo . . . says something about how we see ourselves and who we want to be in the future."[26] Hence, blatant disrespect for the embryo erodes the value of human life in our society. Therefore, even though there is a lack of consensus on the status of the early embryo, I do not believe that the society has the right to do whatever it wishes to the embryo, even if the embryo is considered to be only a potential human person or a "possible future human life."[27] Any experimentation on the human embryo that is not done for the embryo's own benefit is done with great moral liability.

Cryopreservation of Surplus Embryos

As we have seen, IVF-ET and related procedures have very low successful-pregnancy rates. Multiple eggs are produced and fertilized in order to enhance the probability of a successful pregnancy, and often there will be extra embryos once the women successfully become pregnant. This raises the question of what should be done with these surplus embryos.

The first option is to simply discard all embryos that are not transferred. A second option is to immediately transfer all the embryos. Although this may increase the chances for conception, it also means that many embryos will not successfully implant and thus will be lost. It also increases the chance of a multiple pregnancy, which may entail selective fetal reduction, where one or more

---

[24]Grobstein, *Science and the Unborn,* p. 235.

[25]Richard McCormick, S.J., "Blastomere Separation: Some Concerns," *Hastings Center Report* 24 (March-April 1994): 15.

[26]Maureen Junker-Kenny, "The Moral Status of the Embryo," in *The Ethics of Genetic Engineering,* ed. Maureen Junker-Kenny and Lisa Sowle Cahill (London: SCM Press, 1998), p. 52.

[27]Paul Ramsey, "Shall We 'Reproduce'? The Medical Ethics of In Vitro Fertilization," *Journal of the American Medical Association* 220 (June 5, 1972): 1347.

of the fetuses are selectively aborted to allow the remaining fetuses a higher chance of survival. A third option would be to allow the extra embryos to develop outside the mother beyond the normal eight-cell stage to a point where early nerves or muscle tissues are formed, whereupon those tissues may be used for various scientific investigative purposes. A fourth option is to freeze the extra embryos for future use—either for repeated attempts of embryo transfer, if necessary, or for another child at some time in the future.[28] This reduces the pressure to transfer more than four embryos, lowers the incidence of multiple pregnancy and is considered by many to be the least morally problematic option. Cryopreservation of embryos is also advantageous for the following groups of people:

☐ people who need sterilization due to factors such as testicular or uterine cancer

☐ people who are terminally ill and wish to have their own offspring in the future

☐ women whose ovaries have been damaged or who find it too difficult to repeat the uncomfortable and costly laparoscopy to retrieve eggs

At present, cryopreservation of human embryos is not known to be associated with an increased incidence of adverse fetal effects, although the effect of long-term storage is not yet known. Donald Demarco notes that in the process of freezing, chemicals must be introduced to the embryo to prevent or moderate the formation of ice crystals at -8°C and that the effect of these "cryoprotectants" on the human embryo remains unknown.[29] Some people believe that since the embryo is the beginning of a human being, it should not be frozen and exposed to unknown risks. These people usually opt to fertilize no more than four ova and then transfer all the embryos obtained. However, for many medical personnel and infertile couples who hold a lower view of the embryo, cryopreservation is seen to offer many advantages, and it will continue to play a very important part in IVF-ET technology.

Preimplantation Embryo Diagnosis, Therapy and Experimentation

The IVF technologies also make it possible to diagnose genetic defects through pre-implantation biopsies of human embryos created in vitro, to determine the sex of the embryo, to detect sex-linked genetic diseases such as Duchenne's

---

[28]The first birth from the transfer of a thawed embryo was reported in Australia in 1985. By 1988, 824 frozen embryos were in storage in the U.S. The worldwide pregnancy rate in 1989 from previously frozen embryos was 13.5 percent (with 1,501 transfers) compared to a rate of 20.6 percent for fresh embryos (with 64,952 transfers). Phyllis Creigton, *Suspended in Time: The Frozen Human Embryo* (Toronto: Anglican Book Centre, 1994), p. 9.

[29]Demarco, "Love Among the Test Tubes," p. 181.

muscular dystrophy,[30] and to detect almost any genetic defect that has been characterized at the DNA level,[31] including cystic fibrosis, Tay-Sachs disease, hemophilia A and B and so on. Technically, on the third day after fertilization, when the embryo is at about the eight-cell stage, cells are removed from each embryo created in vitro for DNA analysis. Since the process can be completed within eight to twelve hours, unaffected embryos are transferred to the womb later on the same day. The subsequent development of the biopsied embryos is apparently unaffected by such procedures, at least when the biopsy is done at the eight-cell stage, presumably because at this early stage all the cells in the embryo remain totipotent.[32]

Embryo diagnosis would be particularly welcomed by couples who are known carriers or by couples who have already given birth to children with genetic disorders and who prefer not to go through prenatal screening with more traumatic techniques such as chorionic villus sampling or amniocentesis. The couple may be spared the weeks or months of anxiously waiting for the results. Embryo diagnosis therefore offers the following advantages:

☐ Parents can select the unaffected embryos for transfer to the womb, with a reasonable guarantee that if conception is successful the resulting fetus will be without the genetic defect known to exist in the family.

☐ It eliminates a deleterious recessive gene from a family's genetic line.

☐ It is attractive to couples who are known carriers of genetic disorders and who, for personal or religious reasons, resist abortion.

These couples may consider it morally preferable to discard "faulty" embryos than to abort a fetus after a prenatal test is positive. Hence, many see embryo diagnosis as a welcome addition to the medical repertoire for care of the prenatal life, and it may become a standard of care for women of advanced maternal age who have higher risks of genetic fetal anomalies. This positive affirmative attitude is apparently shared by ethicists of very diverse convictions, ranging from the conservative Roman Catholic Church's Congregation for the Doctrine of the Faith, to libertarian secularists such as Peter Singer.[33] As will be

---

[30]For a general overview, see Yury Verlinsky, Eugene Pergament and Charles H. Strom, "The Pre-implantation Genetic Diagnosis of Genetic Diseases," *Journal of In Vitro Fertilization and Embryo Transfer* 7, no. 1 (1990): 1-5. See also Robert G. Edwards, ed., *Preconception and Preimplantation Diagnosis of Human Genetic Disease* (Cambridge: Cambridge University Press, 1993).

[31]Kate Hardy and Alan H. Handyside, "Biopsy of Cleavage Stage Human Embryos and Diagnosis of Single Gene Defects by DNA Amplification" *Archives of Pathology and Laboratory Medicine* 116, no. 4 (1992): 388-92.

[32]Kate Hardy et al., "Human Preimplantation Development In Vitro Is Not Adversely Affected by Biopsy at the 8-Cell Stage," *Human Reproduction* 5, no. 6 (1990): 708-14.

[33]Congregation for the Doctrine of the Faith, "Instruction on Respect," cited in Munson with Hoffman, *Intervention and Reflection,* pp. 515-16, and Helga Kuhse and Peter Singer, eds.,

clear below, I take a more reserved position.

This new technology is also seen by many as the ultimate means to prevent disease because it allows us to correct genetic defects in embryos through site-specific gene therapy. Since the corrected gene will be incorporated in the reproductive (germ) cells of the future child, it will also be expressed in future generations.[34] Many have expressed grave concern about the morality of trans-mitting altered genes to future generations (see chapter eleven below), but others see in this new technology the ultimate form of preventive medicine. It should be particularly welcomed by those who hold the conviction that human life with the moral right to be protected begins at the moment of conception, since embryo diagnosis and therapy is theoretically aiming at and is potentially capable of preventing fetal loss via spontaneous abortion. In this connection, some scholars argue that strict anti-abortionists are morally obligated to pre-vent spontaneous abortion and that embryo therapy may be just one of these potential preventive measures.[35] The price to pay for this option is permitting diagnostic and therapeutic manipulations of the embryo at the very early stage of its development; but arguably, it may be seen as morally more acceptable than simply allowing the developing embryo to miscarry spontaneously at a later stage. For prospective at-risk parents for whom adoption is not available and who insist on having a child, I believe that gene therapy is only permissi-ble if the medical indications for it are incontrovertible and the risks of damage or destruction are excluded. Furthermore, I believe that decisions regarding genetic intervention should be made primarily by the parents, in order to pro-tect their interests in embryo diagnosis and therapy against the over-enthusi-asm of clinicians or scientists. This will also safeguard against any particular racial group's using the technology destructively against another group.[36]

Embryo Experimentation (New York: Cambridge University Press, 1990). Further, stiffer, more restrictive laws curtailing access to abortion may also unintentionally encourage the development of embryo diagnosis. See Andrea Bonnicksen, "Genetic Diagnosis of Human Embryos," *Hastings Center Report Special Supplement* 22 (July-August 1992): S6.

[34]This germ-line genetic modification has been successful in animals, in which foreign exoge-nous genes are introduced into the fertilized animal egg either by microinjection or through a viral vector. The resulting genetically modified embryos are then transferred to a female for gestation. At term, genetically modified offspring, or transgenic animals, as they are sometimes called, are produced. From these results one may infer that the technique to pro-duce transgenic human beings is theoretically available. However, since the success rate in producing transgenic animals is as low as 2 to 10 percent, the technique is not considered to be safe enough for human experimentation.

[35]Timothy F. Murphy, "The Moral Significance of Spontaneous Abortion," *Journal of Medical Ethics* 11 (June 1985): 79-83.

[36]James C. Peterson, "Ethical Standards for Genetic Intervention," in *Genetic Ethics: Do the Ends Justify the Genes?* ed. John F. Kilner, Rebecca D. Pentz and Frank E. Young (Grand Rapids, Mich.: Eerdmans, 1997), pp. 198-99.

Embryo Experimentation (Not Followed by Transfer)

Since IVF-ET is a relatively new medical innovation, it is crucial to continue refining IVF technology through research and development; some even think that using IVF-ET without continuing research is both medically unacceptable and morally wrong.[37] Many have also assumed that embryo research falls in the general area of medical and scientific inquiry relevant to human reproduction, since many areas of embryo research—including embryo implantation, differentiation and metabolism—are important not only for the improvement of IVF technology but also for the understanding and treatment of infertility in general. Since advocates of embryo research usually hold a low view of the embryo, which they consider to be lacking the individuality worthy of full personhood and protection, their main argument in favor of embryo experimentation is simply that essential knowledge about embryos will not be available unless research is performed on the embryos themselves. Since the research will benefit humanity in general, it is claimed to be justifiable even if the specific embryo research subject itself may not reap any benefit and will be allowed to die.[38] This was the position adopted by the United States Department of Health, Education and Welfare in 1989 and by the U.K. Warnock Committee in 1984, which approved experimentation on embryos up to fourteen days of age. Advocates of embryo research also believe that it is morally permissible to produce embryos solely and specifically for research,[39] partly because in their view the value of the embryo can never exceed the potential scientific/medical benefit that would be gained, and partly because relying on "surplus" embryos does not permit the large-scale embryo experimentation that needs to be performed.

Yet many do not share this eagerness to "volunteer" the embryo as a research subject. They contend that although the end of acquiring scientific knowledge is important, it will never justify the means of inflicting injury to a nascent life and then leaving it to die, for this not only violates the moral right of the embryo, but also undermines the value and dignity of human life and contradicts the primary meaning of embryo research—to create better and healthier lives. Depending on how one views the moral status of the embryo, any experimentation on embryos may be seen as a violation of the Helsinki Declaration, which not only requires the research subjects to be volunteers, but also holds the investigators responsible to protect and not harm the research

---

[37]Creighton, *Suspended in Time,* pp. 24-25.

[38]See, e.g., Michelle A. Muller, "The Use of Human Embryos and Fetal Tissue: A Research Architecture," in *Royal Commission on New Reproductive Technologies,* Ottawa, Ontario, January 1992.

[39]John A. Robertson, "Resolving Disputes over Frozen Embryos," *The Hastings Center Report* 19 (November-December 1989): 7-12.

subjects: "In research on man, the interest of science and society should never take precedence over considerations related to the well-being of the subject."[40] Therefore, even if embryo research means reaping many scientific benefits, it cannot be endorsed as moral. As far as creating embryos for the sole purpose of using them as research subjects, even if one does not accept the ethic of personhood I espouse, this position is still unjustified on a Kantian ethic. For to create human embryos merely as means to an end is incompatible with the notion of respecting human lives only as ends in themselves. Hence, many conservatives are willing to endorse experimentation on embryos only if they are surplus embryos left over from legitimate attempts at facilitating conception using IVF-ET.[41] They reason that since these surplus embryos will not be implanted, either due to having reached the maximal number of embryos transferred or due to having reached the maximum family size, they are doomed to die, and to perform experiments on them enables them to make a contribution to improve the quality of life of other human beings.[42] I feel that this argument is not completely satisfactory, for I see that these "surplus" embryos would never have been doomed had they not been created artificially in the first place. The ethic of personhood I espouse will not easily comprehend the idea of "surplus" or "redundant" human lives. A more convincing justification needs to be proffered as to why "surplus" embryos are made possible in the first place *before* we consider whether doing something harmful to them can be justified. To create and perform experiments on these "surplus" embryos places a heavy moral burden on the shoulder of the scientists as fellow human persons.

The Agnostic Nature of Embryo Research

A subject that has not received sufficient attention in the moral discussion of embryo therapy or research is the agnostic nature of the technologies involved. This agnostic nature is vividly illustrated by the fact that attempts failed forty times before the first human egg was successfully fertilized in vitro, which, after twenty-nine days of culture, had to be destroyed because it grew into a monstrosity.[43] In other words, every successful experiment carries a price tag of causing irreparable damages to or destruction of multiple nascent human lives.

[40]World Medical Association, "Declaration of Helsinki," in vol. 5 of *Encyclopedia of Bioethics,* ed. Warren Thomas Reich, rev. ed., Macmillan Library Reference U.S.A. (New York: Macmillan, 1995), p. 2767. The Helsinki Declaration, which was originally made in 1964, has been revised several times, most recently in 1989.

[41]Bruce R. Reichenbach and V. Elving Anderson, *On Behalf of God: A Christian Ethic for Biology* (Grand Rapids, Mich.: Eerdmans, 1995), p. 169. See also Bonnie Steinbock, *Life Before Birth: The Moral and Legal Status of Embryos and Fetuses* (New York: Oxford University Press, 1992).

[42]Reichenbach and Anderson, *On Behalf of God,* p. 169.

[43]Ramsey, "Shall We 'Reproduce'?" p. 1347.

For example, diagnostic manipulation of the blastomere may cause damage to the embryo, which, while escaping gross detection, may end up being spontaneously aborted; alternatively, the procedure may alter the embryo in such a way that it will not spontaneously abort even when it contains abnormalities that under more natural conditions would cause it to do so, resulting in the birth of a child with physical, personality or behavioral defects. Therapeutic corrections of genetic disorders in embryos cause concerns similar to those raised by other forms of manipulation. A primary fear lies with the safety of diagnostic biopsy of embryos. Even though preliminary studies suggest that there are no adverse effects on their subsequent development in vitro when one or two cells are removed from the embryos before implantation,[44] the long-term effect on the developing embryo in vivo is far from certain. The sobering fact is that scientists engaging in embryo diagnosis, therapy or research simply can never know what damages they may inflict upon these nascent human lives in the process of perfecting the technique; and since embryo manipulations involve the very biological substance that constitutes the human life, it is my opinion that until they can determine a way to exclude the possibility of embryonic damage or destruction in the process of developing the technology, scientists are not free morally to proceed in this area of research.

The second issue related to the agnostic nature of embryo intervention is the accuracy of embryo diagnosis. Technically, genetic diagnosis involves highly complex biochemical protocols with many possible experimental artifacts; coupled with the vast amount of human genetic information that has just become available in the last decade or two, premature and inaccurate conclusions are almost inevitable,[45] and exposure to false positive and false negative results is a grim reality.[46] False positive results may be taken as good news, though purchased with financial loss and emotional strain from the procedure; but false negative results may lead either to an unwanted abortion or to the birth of a child with an untreated defect. Often women with preimplantation embryo diagnosis have to resubmit themselves to subsequent prenatal tests with chorionic villus sampling (CVS) or amniocentesis as a form of backup measure, so we cannot expect that embryo diagnosis will render unnecessary the need of prenatal screening within the near future.

The last concern arises from the agnostic nature of germ-line therapy, which affects not only the treated embryo, but also all the future generations that may arise from it. First, I should note that current gene transfer and replacement

---

[44]Verlinsky, Pergament and Strom, "Preimplantation Genetic Diagnosis," pp. 1-5.

[45]Bonnicksen, "Genetic Diagnosis," S5-S6.

[46]A. L. Trounson, "Preimplantation Genetic Diagnosis: Counting Chickens Before They Hatch?" *Human Reproduction* 7, no. 5 (1992): 583-84.

technologies have very low success rates, so genes aimed at certain chromosomal loci may be inserted at the wrong place,[47] irreversibly altering the condition of the person and future generations for the worse. Second, even when a gene is successfully inserted at the right place, it may produce more than simply the intended effect because a single human gene may encode up to twenty different functions. This raises serious moral concerns for the subject of the genetic therapy as well as for the future persons who do not even yet exist and who cannot give their consent when this risk is entailed. Finally, even if a gene is inserted correctly and the positive effect can be demonstrated in the immediate beneficiary of the therapy, there is still no guarantee that the same genetic alteration may produce similar beneficial results for the generations to come. A genetic correction that is clinically valuable to one generation in one particular environment may not have equal value, or may not any value at all, or may even be harmful to future generations who might be living under an entirely different set of environmental conditions. And yet proponents of germ-line therapy naively assume that what is best for people living on earth in the present century will still be preferable for centuries in the future.[48] Moreover, the moral right of people of this generation does not include the right to deprive future generations of their right to inherit a "natural" genetic endowment uncontaminated by human manipulation. While a few see in germ-line therapy the fulfillment of the eugenic dream of a better humanity,[49] others are more reserved regarding its possibilities. The United Methodist Church in the United States rejects germ-line therapy because its long-term effects are uncertain; a similarly strong position has been adopted by the Council for Responsible Genetics of the United States, the German parliament and the government of Switzerland.[50] Jeremy Rifkin, a prominent critic of modern technology, also has called upon the United States Congress to outlaw any genetic engineering of human germ-line cells.[51]

My own position with respect to germ-line genetic intervention is constrained by an overall ethic of personhood that regards the embryo as person, even if she is only a very immature one. I believe that human embodiment and genetic makeup are important but that they are not the

---

[47]Thomas C. Caskey, "DNA-Based Medicine: Prevention and Therapy," in *The Code of Codes: Scientific and Social Issues in the Human Genome Project,* ed. Daniel J. Kevles and Leroy Hood (Cambridge: Harvard University Press, 1992), p. 129.

[48]Theodosius Dobzhansky, "Changing Man," *Science* 155 (January 27, 1967): 411.

[49]See, e.g., Pierre Teilhard de Chardin, *The Future of Man,* trans. Norman Denny (New York: Harper & Row, 1964); see also News Report, *Nature* 371 (September 29, 1994): 365-71.

[50]Roger Lincoln Shinn, *The New Genetics: Challenges for Science, Faith and Politics* (London: Moyer Bell, 1996), p. 125.

[51]Jeremy Rifkin, *Algeny: A New Word, A New World* (New York: Penguin, 1983).

exclusively deterministic parts of a person, for our relationships with others are just as important in making us persons. From a Christian perspective, one's relationship with God is not exhausted by the endowment of our unique genome, even though we gratefully acknowledge that God has given us the physical life we are living. Specifically, our relation with God is eschatologically oriented toward the final consummation—when humanity will be completely renewed and our personhood perfectly fulfilled. In other words, genetic therapy, either with somatic cells or germ-line cells, is only a means for relieving the suffering that comes with our fallenness, but it is not our ultimate hope.[52] Genetic therapy can lure us to believe in a false eschaton, a genetic utopia that our culture pursues idolatrously and in vain. In this context, I view genetic intervention or therapy (especially when it involves germ-line cells) as a morally risky undertaking that can only be endorsed as the means to prevent or remedy disorders that would otherwise result in great suffering and early death.[53] I also insist that genetic therapy should be used only as a tool to restore a person to wholeness rather than as a means to control human quality. Further, germ-line therapy, for all the uncertainties it involves for the future of humankind, should never be left in the hands of a few physicians and scientists working in the isolation of their laboratories; rather, the public should be fully educated to the complex issues involved, so that their diverse ethical views and social values can be freely and fully expressed in order to establish "a solid societal consensus." Indeed, germ-line gene therapy can so easily move toward eugenic enhancement intervention reminiscent of the Nazi effort that one nation or a small alliance of nations should not be allowed to monopolize and control this technology. Instead a dialogue about genetic intervention that involves future generations should include a global participation of all nations of the world because what is at stake is nothing less than the future of humanity as a whole.[54]

The Embryo as Patient

It is not an exaggeration to say that IVF-ET has made the human embryo a "newcomer" in this world. In its new status as a distinct human entity, the embryo confronts the world's values, judgment and vision of humanity's future; but as science keeps extending the frontiers of genetic diagnosis and

---

[52]See the next chapter for a more detailed discussion on hope.

[53]John C. Fletcher and W. French Anderson, "Germ-Line Therapy: A New Stage of Debate," *Law, Medicine and Health Care* 20 (1992): 31.

[54]Lisa Sowle Cahill, "Genetics, Ethics and Social Policy: The State of the Question," in *The Ethics of Genetic Engineering*, ed. Maureen Junker-Kenny and Lisa Sowle Cahill (London: SCM Press, 1998), p. xii.

therapy, embryo researchers are inclined to treat the embryos they have created as child-patients and to exercise proxy decision on behalf of the embryo.
But the embryos are not ordinary needy patients in any sense of the term,
because they would not have needed the "care" had they not been exposed to
risks or damages of their artificial conception in the first place. The scenario is
more accurately portrayed as follows: the scientists and clinicians decide for
the embryo what hazards it must bear in the various experimental interventions while choosing, at the same time, to give the embryo life in which to bear
these hazards. This seems to be morally dubious at best;[55] it is an inadequate
defense to say that one can monitor any mishaps during the embryo/fetus's
development, because it is morally indefensible to put a human life at risk and
then monitor its development in order to detect whether it has in fact material-
ized the risks. To complicate the morality of the undertaking further, one may
never know whether the damage detected is caused by the act of creation or
the act of monitoring since the latter, usually by CVS or amniocentesis, carries
risks of its own. Even if we set aside the morality of creating life to take risks
and consider the embryos as patients, these experimental procedures could
only be conducted with the explicit informed consent of the embryos either as
volunteers or as patients.[56] Since embryos cannot volunteer themselves nor
give consent as patients, scientists are not morally entitled to perform investigative experimentations on these embryonic "patients."

If anything can be seen with certainty as a positive development, the technology of embryo diagnosis and therapy has encouraged the notion of the
"embryo as patient" in the same way the technology of fetal diagnosis and
treatment has promoted the concept of the "fetus as patient." This is further
reinforced by the development of micromanipulation of the embryonic
genome, which enables clinicians to directly intervene to correct defects and
deficiencies in the embryo. In addition, the techniques of blastomere separation make it possible to clone embryos so that diagnostic procedures can first
be performed on the cloned embryo; transfer of the original embryo is suspended until after the cloned embryo is found to be genetically normal. In this
case, the cloned and "improved" embryo is seen by some as nothing more
than a biopsy from the original embryo that acts as an insurance for, and to
prevent harm to, the original embryo, thereby enhancing the original embryo's
status as patient. This is done, however, at the expense of sacrificing the life of
a cloned embryo, a sacrifice that, as we will see below, cannot be easily justi-

---

[55]Leon Eisenberg, "The Outcome as Cause: Predestination and Human Cloning," *Journal of
Medicine and Philosophy* 1, no. 4 (1976): 322.

[56]The voluntary role would be assumed if the investigation would not directly benefit the
embryo. Conversely, patient status would be assumed if such therapy could directly benefit
the embryo.

fied morally. Setting this moral ambiguity aside, we can see that the net effect of the advent of embryo diagnosis and therapy is a shift in the focus of attention from the couple who may carry the faulty gene to an "ailing embryo" who needs to be rescued from a genetic disorder. To view the embryo as a patient, in turn, encourages the development of more diagnostic techniques specifically designed for this new population of patients, fosters a therapeutic relationship between the clinician and the embryo, and provides a broader base for regarding the embryo both as a patient and as a person. For one who views embryos as merely disposable biological materials, this new scenario becomes a threat because "the embryo as patient runs the danger of personalizing the embryo and further confusing the question of the beginnings of life . . . [and] sets the stage for elevating the embryo to the status of an entity with rights."[57] But for those who accord embryos high moral value, the fact that embryos can be diagnosed and treated separately lends further support to the conviction that a human person begins at conception, requiring that the embryos be treated with the respect granted to persons. Despite this perceived benefit of embryo technology, the price at which it comes seems deplorably enormous to me.

Embryo Manipulation and Eugenics

Another main concern with the development of genetic manipulation of the embryo is the eugenic motive behind it. Robert G. Edwards, one of the pioneers of IVF, openly admitted that for him the primary purpose of this technology is to improve the genome of the offspring rather than to relieve the infertile couple. Under the guise of producing healthier babies—though actually exploiting parents' fears of bearing children with anomalies and of being responsible for their wrongful births—unscrupulous IVF promoters can now seize yet more control of the very substance of life in order to further their eugenic agenda. In turn, the decision as to who would require genetic analysis and the standard on which the decision is based are removed from the prospective parents and put in the hands of the IVF scientists. Many see that neither IVF-ET nor prenatal diagnosis have had any "liberating consequences" for women[58] and regard IVF-ET as a violation of the couple's moral right of self-determination. On the other hand, the couple seeking IVF must realize that the fear which renders them vulnerable to exploitation is in fact the fear of facing human suffering and the fear of not being in control, as well as the fear of randomness and chance in life. Mistakenly, embryo diagnosis is perceived as the new hope for avoiding suffering and for regaining control of life.

The eugenic motive in embryo diagnosis is also revealed in the use of the

---

[57]Bonnicksen, "Genetic Diagnosis," p. S58.
[58]See Creighton, *Suspended in Time*, p. 30.

technology to screen for nonfatal conditions, such as hereditary blindness or deafness, or simply for preferred physical characteristics in order to yield "designer babies." Even though many have argued that altering multigenic traits such as intelligence, ability and beauty is highly unlikely because such complex characteristics come about not by design but by the parents' having passed on the right combination of genes,[59] others insist that in principle the technique of embryo selection is applicable to any identifiable gene even though it may take several generations to determine the result.[60] Hence the use of the technology will inevitably expand beyond eliminating diseases to designing desirable traits. But the most serious moral problem associated with the ability to screen out fetuses with nonlethal disorders is that the people who are born with such disorders will be devalued.[61] It seems likely that unless the public is made aware of these moral issues, the new eugenic movement of the twenty-first century will be driven not by legal or political coercion, as was the case in previous centuries, but by consumer choices, made under the pressure of an economy-driven IVF industry.

Embryo Manipulation and the Ethic of Personhood

While I do not want to be unsympathetic to couples who potentially may conceive embryos with certain defects, I should nonetheless evaluate the potential uses of genetic diagnosis and therapy in light of certain principles derived from the ethic of personhood I espouse. Christians always remember that we are persons because God first relates to us by giving us the gifts of life. Since our children are persons in the same way we are, it follows that we as parents and as stewards can only receive children in trust from God as gifts and nurture them as those who are entrusted to us, even when they are not perfect or when they bring pain and suffering. In a sense, as persons we do not simply choose to have children; we have children because we feel called to do so. Having children is the human persons' way to tell the world that, struggling though we may be, we yet trust the divine Person as our Creator and Redeemer and that, in spite of the suffering in the world, we affirm that he is still very much in control.[62] For this reason, in the Christian tradition children are not treated as their parents' possessions, nor will they be raised for the gratification or glorification

---

[59]See, e.g., Marilyn Monk, "Embryo Research and Genetic Disease," *New Scientist* 6 (January 1990): 56-59.

[60]Tabitha M. Powledge, "Springtime for Fetal Tissue Research?" *Hastings Center Report* 21 (March-April 1991): 5-6.

[61]For a more detailed discussion, the reader may refer to the section "Prenatal Screening and Nonfatal Genetic Defects" in chapter eighteen, below.

[62]Stanley Hauerwas, *Truthfulness and Tragedy* (Notre Dame: University of Notre Dame Press, 1977), p. 151.

of the family. Rather, as John Chrysostom of the fourth century insists, Christian couples are called to raise children in order that they may be a people *unto* God.[63] This means that the primary purpose of parenting is not to design "perfect" children through the best technologies available or to nurture children to their full potential through education; rather, the primary calling of parenting is to teach children the love of God and the Christian belief that there is no meaningful human existence apart from a redeemed relationship with God.[64] In other words, it is the divine-human relation that has to be given priority and emphasized, for this is how a human person is initiated and how she flourishes and matures. This does not mean that all Christians must have children, but this is what it means for Christians to have children. Knowing that this is the primary purpose of Christian parenting relieves us of the unnecessary burden of making perfect children and making children perfect, for children are not the ultimate hope of our future. The Child on whom the world's only hope depends has been born "unto you" (Lk 2:11), whether or not we have children of our own. Hence, as Karl Barth has written:

> The burden of the postulate that we should and must bear children, heirs of our blood and name and honor and wealth, . . . is removed from us all by the fact that the Son on whose birth alone everything seriously and ultimately depended has now been born.[65]

Another important way the ethic of personhood provides a moral guide by which we can evaluate IVF and embryo manipulation is by giving us an understanding of the Christian community and its relation to children. Considering IVF and related technologies prompts us to ask, what sort of community are we and what sort do we hope to be, what kind of attitudes toward parenting should we encourage, and which values about human existence do we want our children to have?[66] In other words, it is not only a moral question of whether IVF and related technologies are right or wrong, but also a moral discernment and judgment of whether this kind of technology is consistent with the character of the community and the persons who are members of it. In this regard, one of the most intriguing phenomenon in our society is that although infertile people are frantically seeking ways to realize their reproductive freedom by procreating through technologies, fertile people are simultaneously

---

[63]Ibid., p. 142.

[64]Vigen Guroian, *Ethics After Christendom: Toward an Ecclesial Christian Ethic* (Grand Rapids, Mich.: Eerdmans, 1994), p. 142.

[65]Karl Barth, *Church Dogmatics* 3/4, trans. A.T. Mackay et al. (Edinburgh: T & T Clark, 1961), §54.2.

[66]Also see the insightful remarks by Stanley Hauerwas, *Suffering Presence: Theological Reflections on Medicine, the Mentally Handicapped and the Church* (Notre Dame: University of Notre Dame Press, 1986), p. 143.

fighting to extend their reproductive freedom by stopping procreation through contraception, abortion and sterilization. Is it possible that the enthusiasm for assisted reproductive technologies may represent an effort to neutralize a concealed societal guilt regarding the widespread use of abortion and a poor social policy that discriminates against women and children? The issue of technological reproduction therefore acutely raises the question of the kind of community genuine persons ought to have: is it a community that cares for and nurtures children, including the so called "defective children" naturally born to us, or is it a community that technologically "produces" perfect children and refuses to tolerate the "defective"? I believe that it is inconsistent with the ethic of personhood for a community to have a scandalous infant mortality rate, or to have handicapped children who are not cared for, or to have a liberal abortion policy that categorically deprives every fetal life diagnosed with genetic defects, lethal or nonlethal, while endorsing the use of enormous resources on developing esoteric reproductive technologies for the privileged few. The same ethic challenges commercial contracts for gamete donation or surrogacy because such contracts tempt the poor to treat their body's reproductive capacities as marketable commodities to be purchased by the rich. If we believe that all these arrangements violate the ethic of personhood and compromise the integrity of all persons who make up the community, then we are justified in protesting against IVF, embryo manipulation and other forms of ARTs and surrogacy.

12

Human Cloning
and Stem Cells

*D*efinition, Technical Procedures and Applications of Cloning
In our society today, few other words evoke as strong a reaction as the word *cloning* because it raises questions of self-identity, personhood, determinism and the ethical boundaries of technology. The word *clone* comes from the Greek *klon,* which means a twig or branchlet, and cloning describes the botanical process of budding.[1] In contemporary usage, however, the word has moved from this unassuming etymology into the realms of science fiction and bioethical debate. With its increased usage has come a growing ambiguity of meaning, as illustrated in the turmoil created by the Stillman-Hall experiment in 1993.[2] It is prudent, therefore, to begin by defining the varying terminological uses of the word *cloning.*

The most widespread use of the term *cloning* has been shaped by a host of science fiction such as Aldous Huxley's *Brave New World* (1932),[3] which revolves around the idea of creating a genetically identical human being by copying a single mature cell. The scientific literature, on the other hand, has

---

[1]Jacques Cohen and Giles Tomkin, "The Science, Fiction and Reality of Embryo Cloning," *Kennedy Institute of Ethics Journal* 4, no. 3 (1994): 194.

[2]Phillip Elmer-Dewitt, "Cloning: Where Do We Draw the Line?" *Time,* November 8, 1993, pp. 37-42.

[3]Others include David M. Rorvik's *In His Image: The Cloning of a Man* (1978), I. Levin's *The Boys of Brazil* (1977) and the movies *Sleeper* (dir. Woody Allen), *Jurassic Park* (dir. Steven Spielberg) and *Multiplicity* (dir. Harold Ramis).

used the term *cloning* to denote a much less sensational procedure, which can be subdivided into three general categories:

☐ gene cloning, in which individual genes are multiplied to generate extra genetic material for research

☐ cell cloning, in which specific differentiated cells or undifferentiated stem cells from embryos are multiplied to study their specific biology

☐ embryo cloning, in which the nucleus is removed from an ovum and replaced with the nucleus of a totipotent stem cell from an early embryo (nuclear transplantation)

Since early embryonic cells are totipotent up to the four-cell or even the eight-cell stage, a maximum of eight embryos may be cloned from one embryo by this technique.[4] Terminological confusion began in 1993 when Jerry Hall and Robert Stillman reported that they had succeeded in creating an artificial zona pellucida (a natural surface "coat" that covers the embryo) for human embryos, thus allowing the embryo to be split at the four- or eight-cell stage and for each of the subsequent new cell clusters to be surrounded with an artificial zona pellucida.[5] The procedure, better known as *blastomere separation,*[6] has been referred to as *cloning* in the scientific literature by Hall and Stillman, but this terminology is disputed by others.[7]

In contrast to the skepticism that surrounds Hall and Stillman's work, there is little doubt over Ian Wilmut's successful cloning of the sheep Dolly, which was cloned from a differentiated cell of an adult sheep's mammary gland. The main scientific innovation in this case is the reversal of a fully differentiated somatic cell nucleus to its original totipotential state, leading to the production of a "cloned" embryo with a genome identical to the animal that donated the nucleus (a procedure more formally known as somatic cell nuclear transfer, or SCNT). The embryo was subsequently implanted into the uterus of another ewe, which eventually gave birth to Dolly.[8]

---

[4]Cohen and Tomkin, "Science, Fiction and Reality," p. 195.
[5]Their paper is titled "Experimental Cloning of Polyploid Embryos Using an Artificial Zona Pellucida."
[6]It is also referred to as *totipotency evaluation* or *artificial twinning.*
[7]Cohen and Tomkin, "Science, Fiction and Reality," p. 196.
[8]Technically, mammary cells were first removed from a pregnant ewe and starved in a nutrient-free culture for one week in order to stop their normal cycle of cell division. The "quiescent" cell was then put alongside an unfertilized egg that had its nucleus removed, leaving behind an intact cytoplasm. Electric current was used to fuse the cells, with the cytoplasm of the unfertilized egg accepting the quiescent nucleus, which reverted to a totipotential state. Under the stimulation of a second round of electrical current, normal cellular division resumed to form an implantable embryo. Ian Wilmut et al., "Viable Offspring Derived from Fetal and Adult Mammalian Cells," *Nature* 385 (February 27, 1997): 810-13.

Apart from scientific curiosity, the possible application of cloning[9] was never seriously debated until the 1960s, and even then, the interest was largely theoretical, for no one had yet been able to provide a good reason for *why* it should be done.[10] However, the situation has changed radically since the successful cloning of Dolly; most scientists agree that the basic technique for human cloning from somatic cells is already in place, and once the technique is perfected, the possibility of useful applications will become an actual reality. For example, since the success rates for IVF lie between 10 and 25 percent and because some mothers are simply incapable of producing multiple eggs suitable for fertilization despite hyperovarian stimulation and multiple egg retrieval, embryo cloning is thus a very promising procedure that can raise the odds of achieving a successful pregnancy through IVF even if only a limited number of embryos are available.[11] Even for those couples who are capable of producing multiple embryos, embryo cloning stands as an attractive cost-efficient alternative to expensive, physically uncomfortable egg retrieval. Embryo cloning also makes preimplantation diagnosis much easier by creating a twin embryo for the sole reason of genetic diagnosis and thus eliminating the risk to the embryo that would be implanted, although it is done at the cost of sacrificing the artificially cloned embryo.[12]

Other applications of cloning, whether through blastomere separation or SCNT, include creating identical twins separated by a time interval, providing an adult with her own twin to raise, providing a replacement for a child who dies and donating or selling embryos to others.[13] A demand for cloning could also arise from the desire to acquire a form of "life" or "health" insurance by guaranteeing that a suitable donor exists, although recent success in the technique whereby a culture of human embryonic stem cells is coaxed to differentiate into organ cells for "transplant" may render the cloning of a whole human being for the purpose of transplant unnecessary (see the discussion below).

---

[9]For the remainder of this chapter, the term *cloning* will include the procedure introduced by the Stillman-Hall experiment in 1993—blastomere separation.

[10]In the late 1960s Nobel laureate Joshua Lederberg sparked the first serious bioethical discussions on cloning. Key figures in these early debates included Paul Ramsey and Joseph Fletcher.

[11]Robert Stillman ("Experimental Cloning of Polyploid Embryos Using an Artificial Zona Pellucida," 1993), cited in National Advisory Board on Ethics in Reproduction, "Report on Human Cloning Through Embryo Splitting: An Amber Light," *Kennedy Institute of Ethics Journal* 4, no. 3 (1994): 254. Blastomere separation has also been shown to increase the implantation success of cattle embryo from 60 to 100 percent, while still maintaining some control over the breeding process. See Cohen and Tomkin, "Science, Fiction and Reality," p. 197.

[12]Elmer-Dewitt, "Cloning," p. 39.

[13]National Advisory Board on Ethics in Reproduction, "Report on Human Cloning Through Embryo Splitting: An Amber Light," *Kennedy Institute of Ethics Journal* 4, no. 3 (1994): 254.

Further research into this area could expand scientists' understanding of genetic diseases and their activation, of the transition from totipotency to differentiation and of how this process can be reversed. It could also conceivably be used to further eugenic motives of gene selection.[14] As the potential applications of cloning technology increase, their ethical problems also multiply, and to these latter issues I will now turn.

Potential Harms to Cloned Persons

Potential harms to a clone may be psychological or physical. To begin with, psychological harm can be done to a child if his parents deliberately decide to clone twins. Cloned twins can either be implanted simultaneously so they are born and grow up like natural twins,[15] or the cloned embryo could be frozen and implanted at a later time, thus producing "split" twins of significantly different ages and providing the condition for an adult to raise his baby twin. Since split twins are without parallel in nature, their potential to cause psychological harm is clearly much more serious, leading some to contend that the birth of the younger of the split twins amounts to nothing less than a wrongful birth. Others reject this as an overly pessimistic conclusion and caution against indulging too much on such a speculative situation where parents would decide to bring the cloned embryo to term decades after the first child is born.[16] They believe it is more likely that parents would choose to implant the cloned embryo at most only a few years after the first, thus allowing various factors, including finances and other parental resources, to be distributed more ideally than if the children had been born together. We believe the assumption that every parent will embrace these noble intentions is based on a naive view of human nature. Many parents have children for selfish reasons and care more for the fulfillment of their own needs and desires than for those of their children. Thus, it behooves us to consider every possible scenario, including that of a twin being born decades later, no matter how improbable it may sound. History and our experience of human nature demand nothing less.

The situation is different if the cloning is undertaken for the purpose of providing a "replacement child" for a lost one. If the parents accept the fact that

---

[14]John A. Robertson, "The Question of Human Cloning," *Hastings Center Report* 24, no. 2 (1994): 9.

[15]Some have shown that natural identical twins appear to have fewer psychological problems than children born as singlets, and argued that twins born simultaneously thus justify the creation of twins through cloning to achieve the psychological benefits. For a more detailed discussion, see Ruth Macklin, "Splitting Embryos on the Slippery Slope," *Kennedy Institute of Ethics Journal* 4, no. 3 (1994): 218; and Robertson, "Question of Human Cloning," p. 10.

[16]Macklin, "Splitting Embryos," pp. 218-19.

genotype does not fully determine phenotype, they may be able to view their cloned child as a unique individual to be loved for its own sake, rather than as a mere replica of the first.[17] But if the parents are firm believers in genetic determinism (see chapter twelve below) and expect a cloned replica of the original—a child with the same traits and characteristics found in the first child—then the divergent phenotypic development of different traits in the cloned twin will be met with profound disillusionment and disappointment. In this case, the child will suffer great emotional distress both from the unjust expectation placed on her and from the parents' ultimate disappointment when she fails to meet that expectation.

Human cloning may conceivably also inflict physical harm to the offspring so created, even though the extent of potential physical harm is not yet known, since the first human clone has yet to appear. But this does not stop some eager scientists from garnering support for the safety of human cloning by citing that the cattle industry has seen years of experience of embryo cloning with no demonstrable defects occurring in the offspring produced through this technique.[18] Furthermore, it has been claimed that the number of clones via blastomere separation is limited since embryonic cells retain their totipotency only for a maximum of three cell divisions, allowing a maximum number of eight cloned embryos. Assuming that 20 percent of these cloned embryos implant successfully, the idea of high multiple copies is simply a technological impossibility,[19] thus falsifying the claim that high multiple pregnancy will end prematurely with increased perinatal morbidity and mortality. Based on these speculative evidences, enthusiastic and overly optimistic scientists have drawn the unwarranted conclusion that human embryo cloning should pose no greater biological risks to children than normal conception and birth already do.

However, no reliable data are available to support such optimism; in fact the experiences of SCNT in the cloning of Dolly have confirmed the concern that a great potential for physical injuries occurred in clones. For example, before the successful cloning of Dolly, 277 attempts in cloning were made, only twenty-nine of which resulted in embryos that survived for longer than six days. A total of thirteen pregnancies were achieved, and all but Dolly miscarried, many of the miscarried embryos having had malformations. Given the differences between humans and sheep, no one can guarantee that all human clones with congenital malformations will necessarily miscarry. Further, it has

[17]Robertson, "Question Human of Cloning," p. 11.
[18]Cohen and Tomkin, "Science, Fiction and Reality," p. 197.
[19]Ibid., pp. 199-200; and Robertson, "Question of Human Cloning," p. 11.

recently been confirmed that Dolly has a significant chromosomal anomaly (telomere erosion), with its long-term physical effects including life span still to be determined. Concern for the effects of cloning is shared by the United States National Bioethics Advisory Commission (USNBAC), which submitted its report to President Clinton in June 1997 and recommended that "current scientific information indicates that this technique is not safe to use in humans at this time . . . [due to] unacceptable risks to the fetus and/or potential child."[20] However, I believe it is a mistake for USNBAC to assume that once the technique is deemed physically safe it also becomes ethically permissible, for human cloning involves far more than the contingent issue of harm/safety and the utilitarian balance of risk/benefit. Potential physical and psychological harms are certainly real enough, but they are short-term problems that are likely to be overcome technically. What is truly at stake are the potential long-term effects on structures of society and family, on individual identity and dignity, and indeed on our very nature as humans. Sadly, while those holding the modern secular worldview respond to human cloning with a vague uneasiness, they are unable to counter with anything better than an ad hoc morality, as with the USNBAC recommendation. Thus it is important for us to examine some of the deeper issues involved in order to respond to them with a moral conviction that is grounded on a firmer normative basis.

The Loss of Uniqueness of the Cloned Person

Another moral concern about human cloning is the violation of the cloned person's right to his individual genetic identity and uniqueness. One of the most awe-inspiring aspects of human existence is the fact that unless one has an identical twin, no two individuals have ever been genetically identical; there was never anyone like me in the history of humankind, and there never will be anyone like me in the future—each one of us can take pride in our genetic uniqueness. However, despite the undeniable importance of the genetic code to each individual, many question the legitimacy of claiming genetic uniqueness as a right.[21] Specifically, two arguments have been advanced to refute the idea that cloning compromises one's uniqueness and worth. The first argument suggests that such an idea amounts to a quantification of the worth of human uniqueness in the same way a print's monetary worth decreases according to the number of copies made. But it is an indignity to assume that human worth

---

[20]Cited in Ronald Cole-Turner, "At the Beginning," in *Human Cloning: Religious Responses,* ed. Ronald Cole-Turner (Louisville, Ky.: Westminster John Knox, 1997), p. 133. While the recommendation shows sensitivity to the safety of the potential child, the ban is made entirely on a risk/benefit calculation rather than on a normative basis.

[21]See, e.g., Macklin, "Splitting Embryos," p. 218.

is derived and assessed in the same way as the worth of a print.[22] The second argument says that if human worth is determined on the basis of genetic uniqueness, then natural twins would somehow be less worthy than non-twins. And if genetic uniqueness is a right, then natural twins would either be cheated of that right or be exempted from it. As no one has ever made these suggestions, it is not easy to establish the claim that genetic uniqueness is a right and that clones are of a lesser worth.

The claim that cloning endangers human uniqueness has also been challenged by those who insist on the distinction between genetic and individual uniqueness, which in turn is based on two different theories of human development: preformationism and epigenesis. Preformationism posits that all growth in living beings constitutes merely an unfolding of what was already there from the beginning. On this view, one can equate genetic uniqueness with individual uniqueness, since one's human uniqueness is predetermined by one's genetic endowment. In essence, preformationism is basically a principle of genetic determinism. On the other hand, the theory of epigenesis disputes this position and posits that successive developments lead to the emergence of new properties and new structures.[23] In this model, the genome merely determines a range of possibilities and initiates a specific sequence of events, but the final outcome of these events depends on the genes' interaction with the external environment. Consequently, identical genotypes do not end up in identical phenotypes. There is no simple genetic determinism of who one will become.[24]

Furthermore, many supporters of cloning also argue that in the cloning procedure, whether done by using embryos or somatic cell nuclear transfer, the cytoplasm of the "original" and the "clone" are actually different.[25] Cell nuclear transfer technique involves placing the nucleus of the donor cell into the cytoplasm of the enucleated ovum, which contains different mitochondria than that found in the donor cell. Since mitochondrial DNA are known to interact with

---

[22]Ibid., p. 216.

[23]Leon Eisenberg, "The Outcome as Cause: Predestination and Human Cloning," *Journal of Medicine and Philosophy* 1, no. 4 (1976): 321.

[24]Richard Lewontin militates against a preformationist view. He notes that humans (and all other organisms) are a unique product of three factors: genetics interacting with the environment, further randomized by a "fluctuating asymmetry" or "developmental noise," which occurs in unpredictable patterns as an organism develops. Thus determinism remains impossible, even in theory. Lewontin, *Biology as Ideology* (Concord, Ontario: Anansi, 1991), pp. 26-27.

[25]Martin LaBar, "The Pros and Cons of Human Cloning," *Thought* 59 (1984): 319-33, cited in Ruth Macklin, "Splitting Embryos on the Slippery Slope," *Kennedy Institute of Ethics Journal* 4, no. 3 (1994): 217.

the nuclear genetic material, and because the cytoplasm of the ovum itself is also known to play a role in programming the nuclear DNA, the original and the clone are said to have significantly different genetic material to start with. Furthermore, the postnatal development of the human brain is known to be influenced by the interaction between the social environment and the individual,[26] giving rise to unique personalities even among identical twins. In sum, this view argues that human cloning does not undermine human uniqueness, and to claim that it does confuses genetic uniqueness with individual uniqueness, which is far more significant in one's becoming unique.

I believe that the differences between the original and the clones derived from it have been exaggerated, and I also think that the epigenetic process has limited application to cloning. We can imagine that if a person, for instance, Michael Jackson, is cloned one hundred times, the clones together as a group will differ far more from other people than from each other, even though one may detect some differences among the one hundred Michael Jacksons. In short, they would appear as a herd, each nothing more than a variation on the same theme, with each individual's uniqueness eliminated.[27] Hence, even if we set aside the issue of an individual's right to uniqueness, cloning nonetheless threatens our idea of individuality in a very profound way because part of the richness—and indeed mystery—of being human is provided by the marvelous diversity within humankind that results from our unique genomes. While I believe that it takes far more than the genome to make a person unique, the technology of cloning threatens to reduce a human person to merely duplicable genetic material. This genetic reductionism undermines our basic understanding and appreciation of human personhood, even if it cannot be shown to specifically impact the uniqueness of the cloned person or the original from whom she is derived.

Cloning Violates Human Dignity

Cloning has also been charged with violating the basic human dignity. But what *is* human dignity? Is it something inborn? Is it endowed by others in a social setting? Or is it bestowed through divine fiat by God? I believe that human dignity is not a static property inherent in our human nature; rather, it arises primarily from the relational pole of our personhood, expressed in giving and receiving within our human existential network. For a Christian, human dignity is ultimately derived from and given through God relating to us

---

[26]Eisenberg, "Outcome as Cause," p. 325.
[27]David M. Byers, "An Absence of Love," in *Human Cloning: Religious Responses,* ed. Ronald Cole-Turner (Louisville, Ky.: Westminster John Knox, 1997), p. 75.

first in our creation, then in our redemption and eventually in consummation.[28] So defined, human dignity can be expressed by the Kantian maxim that a person is to be treated never as a means, but always as an end. Given this delineation, cloning can be shown to violate human dignity in several ways. Whatever the motivation for cloning, the original has certain expectations of the roles the clone would play or the qualities it should display. All the clone's initiative may be stifled under the original's expectations, so that the clone's life is reduced to being a means to satisfy the desires of the original. Also, the original values whatever qualities he is looking for in the clone rather than valuing the cloned person himself. The clone's value as a person will be diminished if those expected qualities are missing or if he is simply incapable of fulfilling the role demanded. This jeopardizes the status of the clone as an end in itself and thus violates his dignity as a human person.

Further, cloning technologies can be shown to be driven by economic and market forces, potentially turning cloned children into commodities. Attempts to patent particular genotypes are already underway in the United States, and most patents are intended to turn human genes into commercial products. Conceivably a person may be cloned as a replacement or substitute for a lost child. The assurance that the clone will be loved as much as the lost child does not alter the indignity of being a secondary replacement for the lost child. A person who is cloned to provide perfectly compatible organs for transplant is produced to be a "spare part" supplier—her sole purpose of existence is to provide organs exclusively for the original. Cloning also makes possible the production of different kinds of specialized human beings to meet different societal needs, such as an unskilled labor force, military personnel, scientists and so on.

It is evident that cloning is, essentially, an assertion of the power of one human being over another, and this violates the clone's dignity and rights as a person not only because the clone has not consented to play the expected role, but also because the cloned person's freedom is removed even in the technological process of his coming into life. The ethic of personhood I advocate maintains that each human being has an inherent dignity as a creature of God, who has dignified each human being with an unprecedented and unpredetermined genome through his providential combination of one's parents' genetic material, and secondly in one's freedom to respond and relate to God and ultimately to participate in the life of God through the Son, Jesus Christ. In virtue of one's unpredictable genetic composition, the human person is freed

---

[28]Compare Ted Peters, "Cloning Shock: A Theological Reaction," in *Human Cloning: Religious Responses,* ed. Ronald Cole-Turner (Louisville, Ky.: Westminster John Knox, 1997), p. 22.

to flourish and develop toward the future and destiny that is uniquely hers. At this most fundamental level, cloning is incompatible with the notion of human dignity and freedom because the human clone is literally created in the image of another human being's genome and is destined to fulfill the will of another human being.

Destruction of the Traditional Family Structure by Cloning

The prospect of large-scale human cloning intensifies the erosion of the family structure spurred on by other ARTs. For instance, who are the clone's parents? The notion of procreative liberty that underwrites modern ARTs presumes that a child is an outcome of parental reproductive choices. But such a procedural principle is meant to serve a negative function: preventing people in a pluralistic society from imposing unwarranted restrictions on each other in their reproductive decisions. But this principle of parental choice based on individual decisions is not meant to provide the positive meaning of procreation that grows out of the parents' love relationship. Hence, ARTs, including human cloning, should be evaluated only from the normative frameworks of parental relationship and familial integrity, rather than from the procedural framework of reproductive liberty; the true moral task, then, is to evaluate the extent to which the various ARTs, including cloning, either conform to or deviate from such a normative ordering of procreation and family. I discussed the unitive aspect of the conjugal act as a normative basis of human procreation earlier;[29] here I will argue for another normative basis of procreation on the grounds of the natural ordering of the family. According to Brent Waters, a family formed by a genetically unrelated couple with offspring related to each other and to both parents provides "the ordering of natural and social affinity."[30] The spouses initiate the one-flesh *unfolding* love that opens to the begetting of children, who in turn establish the *enfolding* relationship of a family. The family is thus seen as the embodiment of "an unfolding and enfolding of familial love,"[31] without which the family only exists as a collection of cohabiting individuals grouped together due to necessity rather than affinity.

Because the family is the result of an unfolding and enfolding love, it is also a "place of unconditional belonging . . . bounded by the proper ordering of choice and chance."[32] Parents may choose when to have children and how

---

[29]See chapter eight, "Artificial Insemination," above.

[30]Brent Waters, "One Flesh? Cloning, Procreation and the Family," in *Human Cloning: Religious Responses,* ed. Ronald Cole-Turner (Louisville, Ky.: Westminster John Knox, 1997), pp. 78-90.

[31]Ibid., p. 83.

[32]Ibid., p. 85.

many children to have, but they have to leave to chance the precise "quality" of their children. Cloning allows a prediction of qualities, so belonging becomes conditional on the expected character of offspring, and parenthood is reduced to a form of self-fulfillment through managed breeding rather than through the unfolding and enfolding familial love. Furthermore, since no parent or male participation is necessary in cloning, the assault on the family will be complete, with the institution being rendered socially and biological unnecessary, if not irrelevant. In sum, cloning negates the biological roles of parents and distorts the ordering of a family's natural and social affinity by depriving the cloned child of a defined role in the family as well as a full sense of familial relatedness and belonging. However, American ethicist Ronald Cole-Turner rejects this "natural order of the family" as narrow and as discriminatory against unconventional families, and he believes it is susceptible to misuse.[33] Ultimately, he is suspicious of the notion of "natural order," for he remains skeptical of fallen humanity's ability to properly discern this aspect of human reality. I believe that this suspicion and skepticism are both unnecessary and ungrounded and that they do not justify the conclusion that "cloning is a matter of indifference."[34] Rather, I believe that there is a natural order of procreation and family that we disregard at our own peril.

Cloning and Eugenics

Cloning always raises the specter of eugenics because it allows for the direct genetic customization of the embryo. John Robertson openly hails the increase in eugenic control made possible by embryo cloning and regards it as "the right of adoptive parents."[35] Ruth Macklin also supports the use of cloned embryos for genetic improvement. She bases her argument on two claims: First, sacrificing one conjoined twin to save the other is profoundly different from submitting a cloned embryo to genetic manipulation to benefit the original. While the former may be ethically objectionable, the latter is not. Second, to clone an embryo for diagnostic purposes is ethically equivalent to obtaining a biopsy from an organism to determine its health status.[36] However, these arguments fail to account for one crucial fact: the cell biopsy from an organism does not develop into a whole organism, whereas the cloned cell will develop into an embryo and a fetus if its life is not sacrificed. Hence its life cannot be disregarded in the same way that one of the conjoined twins cannot be sacrificed without moral risk.

---

[33]Cole-Turner, "At the Beginning," p. 128.
[34]Ibid.
[35]Robertson, "Question of Human Cloning," p. 12.
[36]Macklin, "Splitting Embryos," p. 222.

On the other hand, many scholars hold a more pessimistic view of the eugenic implications of cloning. After the announcement of the Stillman-Hall experiment, Jeremy Rifkin proclaims in true prophetic style that this is "the dawn of the eugenics era."[37] Many fear that the search for the perfect genetic quality of life will eventually degenerate into the redesigning of human nature. The German program of eugenics in the twentieth century confirms that positive eugenics is conducive to abuses of power, used against the marginalized and disenfranchised minorities. The French National Ethical Committee warns that "the research is paving the way for a choice of a future child according to a quality that will have been defined by the manipulator."[38] George Annas makes a further observation that American society is now largely driven by its own market forces, and one does not need to wait for a regime like Nazi Germany to make the eugenics nightmare come true; the capitalist impulse will do fine on its own. I share the conviction that the association between cloning and eugenics is sufficient enough to render cloning morally suspect.

Cloning and the Threat to Biodiversity

When embryo diagnosis becomes common enough to include the diagnosis of nonfatal diseases, many embryos that would otherwise have grown to adulthood will be eliminated. While many see removing undesirable traits as beneficial to humanity, we must not overlook the price that has to be paid as certain genes are selectively and increasingly eliminated with these embryos, reducing the genetic diversity of future generations of the human race. This problem will be further exacerbated when SCNT becomes available for human cloning. As I noted before, sexual reproduction ensures the reshuffling of genes in every new human being born, which guarantees genetic diversity by adding new genomes to the human gene pool and which helps to overcome some of the inherent genetic weaknesses passed on by the parents. Widespread employment of cloning as a mode of human reproduction, especially cloning by SCNT, will lead to a gradual deterioration of genetic quality and a diminution of genetic variability. Leon Eisenberg warns that a wide-scale employment of cloning will lead to a biological disaster because it will restrict the diversity of the human gene pool. In particular, the reduction would slowly erode our adaptability to the wide range of ecosystems we now inhabit and confine us to a very narrow ecological niche. Karen Lebacqz contends that this will become a real issue only if cloning is used on a large scale, a highly

---

[37]Jeremy Rifkin, cited in Elmer-Dewitt, "Cloning: Where Do We Draw the Line?" p. 41.
[38]French National Ethical Committee, "Discussion on Ethical and Judicial Aspects of Embryo Research," *Human Reproduction* 4, no. 2 (1989): 206-17.

unlikely proposition in her view, and so she dismisses the concern as premature.[39] But Robertson, otherwise an outspoken advocate of "procreative liberty," concedes that "cloning might fall outside the bounds of reproduction,"[40]
and thus outside the realm of procreative liberty, precisely because it involves
gene replication rather than gene formation by the union of the DNA from
human gametes.

From the perspective of human evolution, we see asexual cloning as a
closed process, producing a new human being with an unchanged genetic
identity, whereas sexual reproduction is an open process, providing for continuous genetic innovation and increasing the efficiency of human survival. If we
assume that in human evolution we have moved from asexual to sexual reproduction for good reasons, it would seem highly illogical (and much less exciting) to revert back to asexual reproduction simply because we have the
technological means to do so. Such a restriction on human genetic diversity
violates the biological principles basic to the evolution of the human race.[41]
From a Christian viewpoint, sexual reproduction is an order ordained by God
in creation; by returning to asexual reproduction, cloning represents not only a
retreat from the advancement of human evolution, but a violation of divine
order that is crucial for the survival of the human race.

Cloning, with its eugenic vision, ultimately represents humanity's attempt to
define itself and to determine its destiny. Through this technology, modern
humanity seeks to become either the creator or a "co-creator"; however, I
believe that even the latter concept is not biblically sustainable. Christians
should remember the story of the Tower of the Babel, which shows how the
human ambition to be like God through technological power brought cata-
strophic chaos. The New Testament affirms that human renewal and perfection
will only come in the new heaven and new earth brought about by the Creator, rather than through technology. Given the finiteness and fallibility of
humanity—which should always be the context for the critical evaluation of
any human technological progress—we are not likely to achieve human perfection through reproductive innovations; the impediment to perfection is
within us. Another factor that should provide the context for evaluating technological progress is the relational dimension of human personhood. One
needs to ask whether a particular innovation would promote or retard human
relationships with God, with fellow human beings and with the rest of the cre-

---

[39]Karen Lebacqz, "Genes, Justice and Clones," in *Human Cloning: Religious Responses,* ed.
Ronald Cole-Turner (Louisville, Ky.: Westminster John Knox, 1997), p. 51.
[40]John A. Robertson, "Genetic Selection of Offspring Characteristics," *Boston University Law
Review* 76 (June 1996): 438.
[41]Eisenberg, "Outcome as Cause," p. 322.

ated order. Every instance of human scientific progress, particularly those that have the potential to tamper with the nature of human life, as is the case with human cloning, must first be submitted to the basic litmus test of the fundamental meaning of human personhood. In this way we may move beyond the extremes of either a Luddite rejection or a naive affirmation of all technologies, seeking only those technologies that truly further us as persons and as communities. For if this basic goal is lost, what then is the purpose of improving the human lot when the process does not lead to the fulfillment of the persons it seeks to improve?

Stem Cells: Types, Sources and Uses

Stem cells are cells with the inherent potential to further specialize and give rise to other cell types; and in an optimal artificial culture medium, they may grow and divide for an inordinate or indefinite period of time. Stem cells are known to originate from as many as four or five different sources, and with the speed at which new scientific discoveries are made no doubt more will be found with time. For the purpose of facilitating ethical discussion, I will classify cells into two main categories, depending on whether they derive from the embryo (Type 1) or bypass the embryo (Type 2). Type 1 stem cells may come from surplus embryos donated by couples who have been successfully treated in an IVF clinic and have extra embryos that are no longer needed. James Thomson and his associates received such donated embryos from IVF clinics after he obtained informed consent from these donor couples, and subsequently they isolated pluripotent cells from the inner cell mass of the embryos at their blastocyst stage and successfully cultured the cells to produce a pluripotent stem cell line.[42] Pluripotent stem cells, either existing naturally in the inner cell mass of the blastocyst or existing in isolation as a cultured stem cell line, have the potential to further specialize and commit themselves to a even more restricted area of functions (e.g., they become blood stem cells and give rise to various blood cells such as red blood cells, white blood cells, platelets and so on). Functionally committed stem cells are called "multipotent" stem cells, and their ability to further specialize is, as far as we know, limited to cells within the general scope of the same function. In the course of the normal development of a human embryo, the pluripotent stem cells in the inner cell mass give rise to various multipotent stem cells, which go on to become all of the more than two hundred tissues and organs of the whole human body. A few multipotent stem cells are found to survive in children and adults, and one

---

[42]James A. Thomson et al., "Embryonic Stem Cell Lines Derived from Human Blastocysts," *Science* 282 (November 6, 1998): 1145-47.

of them, namely, the blood stem cells, is needed for our survival. Another source of Type 1 stem cells is the cloning technique, particularly using SCNT (discussed earlier in this chapter), whereby the nucleus of a mature and functionally fully committed somatic cell is reversed to its original totipotent state. In a sense, the body cell, with the help of technology, can find its way back to where it originally has begun! Once the body cell reverts back to the totipotent zygotic state, it is only a matter of several cycles of cell division before the blastocyst will appear and the inner cell mass, with the pluripotent cells, can be harvested again. On November 26, 2001, Advanced Cellular Technology, a private biotechnology company, reported its success in cloning a human embryo from an unfertilized human egg. The company announced that its intention is not to implant the embryo and produce a fetus; rather it plans always to harvest and produce therapeutically useful stem cells.

Type 2 stem cells, according to my classification, originate from sources that bypass the human embryo and hence avoid the moral difficulties associated with it. Michael Shamblott and his associates isolated germ cells from the fetus in regions that are known to develop into gonadal tissues.[43] They discovered that the cells are similar to the pluripotent cells isolated by Thomson and his associates from the embryonic inner cell mass. As I have mentioned above, blood stem cells are found in the bone marrow of children and adults. Stem cells have also been found in the placenta and umbilical cord blood from live births. Recent research findings also suggest that neuronal stem cells can be isolated from adult (live or cadaver) nerve tissues. But the number of stem cells are still very limited, compared to the more than 220 tissue and organ cellular types that make up the human body. A small spark of hope may be generated by the recent findings in animal studies that some multipotent stem cells may be switched to produce several different cell types (e.g., neuronal stem cells switched to produce blood cells). While this is theoretically possible, since SCNT has essentially shown that cellular "de-differentiation" or "de-specialization" is possible, the data available so far are too preliminary to make any conclusions. In addition, this line of research is also limited by

☐ the limited number of stem cells identified in human adults and children

☐ the limited number of different types of stem cells these adult stem cells can become through "de-differentiating"

☐ the reduced likelihood that adult stem cells can be cultured to become cell lines when compared to pluripotent cells of the embryo

---

[43]Michael J. Shamblott et al., "Derivation of Pluripotent Stem Cells from Cultured Human Primordial Germ Cells," *Proceedings of the National Academy of Sciences of the United States of America* 95 (November 10, 1998): 13726-31.

Much more research needs to be done to overcome these limitations before this promising source of stem cells is to become a reality.

There is no question as to the scientific and medical values of stem cell research. The study of the progressive specialization of the stem cell—from the original totipotent state (restricted to the first two to three cycles of cell divisions of the zygote) to the pluripotent state and then to the multipotent state (before they finally cease to be stem cells and end their journey as somatic cells)—throws light on many previously unknown key steps in the control of cellular growth, differentiation and specialization; and this will be crucial in the understanding of many disease states such as birth defects and cancers. Stem cell research will also make available a large number of human tissue and organ cell types such as heart cells, kidney cells and liver cells for testing the efficacy and toxicity of new drugs. But most exciting of all, with the availability of pluripotent stem cells, they can be coaxed into any number of different tissue stem cells. Theoretically, a form of therapy other than the conventional medical or surgical form is now possible through cellular replacement. When this new therapy is fully available, it is entirely conceivable that a patient with heart dysfunction due to destruction of heart muscle mass from a heart attack may receive and be benefited from an infusion of heart stem cells! This cell therapy will be applicable to a number of conditions that affect many people in the world today: for example, diabetes, Parkinson's disease, muscle diseases, cancers and bone diseases such as osteoporosis, just to name a few. However, several obstacles have to be removed before this therapy comes into practice. For one thing, scientists have yet to identify the exact mechanism that directs a pluripotent stem cell to switch to a tissue-specific stem cell. Secondly, unless every recipient of cell therapy uses his or her own pluripotent cells produced through the SCNT technique (which is too time-consuming to be used in an emergency), the tissue rejection arising from histo-incompatibility akin to that encountered in organ transplants will also have to be overcome before this new therapy can be put to use.

The Promise of Stem Cells and the Ethic of Personhood

Prior to 1999, the United States federal government explicitly outlawed the use of federal funds for human embryo research, including stem cell research. But on January 15, 1999, the Department of Health and Human Services made the arbitrary and controversial decision to divorce the act of doing research on the pluripotent stem cells from the act of isolating the stem cells from the embryo and thereby destroying the embryo. It is believed that this dissociation legitimizes federal funding of embryo-derived (Type 1) stem cell research. One may suppose that this line of reasoning is also supported by legislation that provides for federal funding to use fetal tissue obtained from elective abortions. But in this case, it is clearly stipulated that fetal tissues must be obtained from abortions performed for reasons entirely unrelated to research reasons. To harvest stem cells from embryos leading to their very own destruction would not easily be said to have fulfilled a similar requirement; and this also applies to embryos created by cloning through SCNT technique. So it would seem that the ethic of personhood that I espouse is consistent with the well established international ethical norms against the use of any human subject for research purposes—including embryos and fetuses within and without the womb—as explicitly stated in official statements such as the Nuremberg Code, the Declaration of Helsinki and the United Nations Declaration of Human Rights.

Our only options, then, are Type 2 stem cells. I believe that, among the choices available, fetal stem cells from aborted fetuses are the least acceptable from the perspective of a personhood ethic. I agree that if a woman's abortion is not motivated by any research objective, then the research specimen obtained, stem cells in this case, is not directly linked to the death of the fetus in a causal sense; but this in no way implies that one can do anything with the fetus so aborted. In my opinion, any and all activities connected to the fetus are related to the abortion and the death of the fetus—the only difference being that some are more proximately related and some are more distantly related. The pregnant woman who decides to terminate her pregnancy irresponsibly, for trivial reasons, may find that by donating the fetal corpse for stem cell research, she can ease her conscience and avoid facing the disintegration that has come upon her. I therefore reject this source of stem cells as morally unacceptable, but I want to encourage the scientific community to continue in the following alternative directions:

☐ Obtain naturally miscarried fetuses and fetuses from certified medically required abortions.

☐ Search for more different stem cells in adults and children.

☐ Search for cellular mechanisms that help multipotent stem cells to switch to pluripotent stem cells. If successful, this will be most promising, because these cells originate from one's own body and do not involve the creation of embryos, which makes the process compatible with philosophical and theological positions.

☐ Continue research on the potential of umbilical cord blood and placental blood.

☐ Search for mechanisms that stop the SCNT cloning process at the pluripotent stem cell level. I am aware that this proposal is theoretical and speculative, but if it is successful, it has all the advantages of the second and third recommendations above. In fact, in terms of the cellular de-differentiation processes involved, all these options rely on making the same cellular reversal from somatic cells or multipotent stem cells to pluripotent stem cells but not any further "backward."

To conclude, let me reiterate that I believe that stem cell research holds great promise for medicine and offers hope for sick people who otherwise have little option but to suffer and die. I see this new technology as the most exciting and most fruitful, positive development to come out of a century of advances in reproductive science and technology, and I think it may potentially make a great contribution toward relieving much unnecessary and sometimes meaningless suffering. But I only endorse stem cells within the ethic of personhood that I have established and defended. I want to say again that this ethic has no room for Type 1 stem cells, for using them reflects a total disregard for the value of embryonic lives and treats them as objects and means and not as ends. On the other hand, I do not share the sort of religious sentiment that categorically condemns stem cell research. I believe that the ethic of personhood easily accommodates all Type 2 stem cell research except stem cells derived from most elective abortions currently being done in North America for reasons already stated—therapeutic abortions and miscarriages excepted. I am even prepared to endorse SCNT-originated stem cells, in either the multipotent or the pluripotent forms, if and when SCNT technology can be refined to the point that the "nuclear potential reversal process" can somehow be arrested at the stage of either the multipotent or the pluripotent stage and not continue all the way to the totipotent stage. My endorsement is predicated on my belief that the pluripotent stem cells obtained through SCNT techniques or through cellular reversal (de-differentiation), as in the few reported cases of animal multipotent stem cells switching to pluripotent stem cells, are not *fully* embryonic in nature. That is to say, the pluripotent stem cells so derived will not give rise to a complete fetus with the placenta and other supportive structures, for only a totipotent stem cell from an early embryo with no more than three cycles of cell divisions is capable of giving rise to a complete embryo that goes on to develop to a fetus and become deliverable as an infant. Since the harvest of pluripotent stem cells from cell reversal techniques bypasses stem cells with full embryonic nature, and as long as one can be sure that no actual or potential embryonic life is being destroyed, then such an endorsement is not in conflict with the ethic of personhood I espouse.[44]

---

[44]In the event that subsequent studies show that pluripotent stem cells can revert back to the totipotent state either spontaneously or under stimulation, then this endorsement will have to be revised.

13

The Human
Genome Project

*H*istory, Development and Application

The Human Genome Project (HGP) stands at the forefront of embryonic and genetic research as an international endeavor to determine the precise specifications, chromosomal locations and molecular composition of the 50,000 to 100,000 genes and multiple regulatory elements constituting the human genome.[1] To this end, the project has three specific goals:

☐ developing genetic and physical maps

☐ determining the genome sequence of human beings and other model organisms[2]

☐ producing a set of "reference data" accessible through a computer database.[3]

In short, the HGP is an initiative to create an encyclopedia of the human genome.[4] The project is divided into three five-year phases, with the first phase focusing on the construction of a low-resolution genetic map with fifteen hundred specific markers and physical linkage sites identifying the ordered, over-

---

[1]Charles DeLisi, "The Human Genome Project," *American Scientist* 76 (September-October 1988): 488.

[2]Francis Collins and David Galas, "A New Five-Year Plan for the U.S. Human Genome Project," *Science* 262 (October 1993): 43.

[3]T. D. Yager, D. A. Nickerson and L. E. Hood, "The Human Genome Project: Creating an Infrastructure for Biology and Medicine," *Trends in Biochemical Sciences* 16 (December 1991): 454.

[4]Victor McKusick, "Mapping and Sequencing the Human Genome," *New England Journal of Medicine* 320 (April 6, 1989): 913.

lapping and purified fragments of DNA that cover particular regions of the human genome. The second phase will further refine the human genetic and physical maps and complete some pilot sequencing projects on a scale larger than in phase one. Finally, the third phase will concentrate on sequencing the entire three billion base pairs of the human genome.[5] Given adequate funding to cover the estimated $200 million annual budget (given in 1988 U.S. dollars) for the worldwide effort, the project—which was scheduled to be completed by 2005—was in fact nearly completed by the end of 2000.[6]

The HGP obviously has enormous implications for understanding human biology and pathology. James Watson (co-discoverer of DNA's structure) is not exaggerating when he proclaims that the completed project will provide all the answers to "the chemical underpinnings of human existence"[7] and the understanding of many genetically linked inheritable diseases, such as cystic fibrosis, Huntington's chorea and other diseases caused by a defect in a single gene. Locating defective genes by mapping and unraveling their code through sequencing would reveal how they differ from their normal counterparts and thus provide an essential key to developing methods for early diagnosis and treatment. In the past, genetic scientists have encountered much difficulty in mapping the positions of genes involved in multigene diseases such as diabetes and schizophrenia, but the HGP has led to the development of new technologies that allow quicker scanning of the genome as a whole rather than analyzing one marker at a time.[8] However, the enthusiasm about the HGP is not shared by some more cautious scientists who insist that the project is methodologically flawed on at least two counts: first, it is reductionistic to assume that the relationship between a defective gene and disease is a directly causal one; second, there is as yet no support for the assumption that the existence of a statistically averaged and hence unified human genome can be called "normal" because the existence of such a fundamental human genome has yet to be proven. I believe that these criticisms provide a much needed qualification to many of the grandiose claims made of the project, and the applicability of the information obtained from the HGP to specific individuals may be more limited than is often assumed.[9]

---

[5]Yager, Nickerson and Hood, "Human Genome Project: Creating an Infrastructure," p. 458.

[6]Victor McKusick, "The Human Genome Project: Plans, Status and Applications in Biology in Medicine," in *Gene Mapping: Using Law and Ethics as Guides,* ed. George Annas and Sherman Elias (New York: Oxford University Press, 1992), p. 18.

[7]James D. Watson, "The Human Genome Project: Past, Present and Future," *Science* 248 (April 1990): 44.

[8]Technically this involves moving away from the traditional linkage analysis to genomic mismatch scanning (GMS) and representational difference analysis (RDA). Peter Aldhous, "Fast Tracks to Disease Genes," *Science* 265 (September 1994): 2008-10.

[9]Richard Lewontin, *Biology as Ideology* (Concord, Ontario: Anansi, 1991), p. 50.

Ethics of the Human Genome Project

Most researchers agree that while the HGP may not have caused an "ethical earthquake" itself, ethical issues arise from two situations the project introduces: First, because the project's scope is so large, it increases the range of health problems with ethical concerns. Second, because we will be able to identify disease genes that potentially everyone may carry, the project poses an enormous challenge to the health care system, to families and to individuals.[10] Therefore, the HGP has given enormous emphasis to the ethical reflection and deliberation on the project. In Canada and in the United States, a full 7.5 percent and 3 percent, respectively, of the program budget has been reserved to fund research into "medical, ethical, legal and social issues" (MELSI) stemming from genome research.[11] Specifically this ethical research will address questions about the responsible use of genetic research, about the ways to maximize the benefits to human welfare and about the means to guard against abuses.[12] MELSI is also mandatory for all other countries that participate in the HGP.

Use and Usefulness of Genetic Information

The first moral issue of the HGP is how to protect a person's privacy by preventing the enormous amount of personal genetic information from becoming unnecessarily accessible by the public, including employers and insurance companies. Since this new and sensitive genetic information will be largely in the hands of physicians, discreet disclosure of information will become even more critical than before. But the proper use of such information raises many equally serious questions of profound ethical concerns. For example, will employers use the newly acquired genetic information to deny prospective candidates employment because they may possibly develop genetic traits or diseases in the future, say, in ten to fifteen years? Will insurance companies be able to raise premiums or deny insurance to those with genetic susceptibility to disease?[13] How can we ensure tighter record keeping and standardize disclosure policies in doctors' offices?[14] Are doctors prepared to counsel patients

---

[10]See also Francis Collins, "Medical and Ethical Consequences of the Human Genome Project," *Journal of Clinical Ethics* 2 (Winter 1991): 264; and Eric Juengst, "Human Genome Research and the Public Interest: Progress Notes from an American Science Policy Experiment," *American Journal of Human Genetics* 54 (January 1994): 122.

[11]"Canadian Bioethics Report," *Humane Medicine* 10 (October 1994): 295-300.

[12]Eric Juengst, "The Human Genome Project and Bioethics," *Kennedy Institute of Ethics Journal* 1 (March 1991): 71-72.

[13]A chilling Orwellian future, where individuals are admitted to or excluded from positions of power and prestige simply based on their genome, is depicted in the science fiction film *Gattica* (dir. Andrew Niccol).

[14]S. McCrary and William Allen, "The Human Genome Initiative and Primary Care," in *Health*

about the various practical implications of testing—such as insurance coverage, and employment—and other psychological, economic and social implications the genetic information may have for the patient? What if the patient does not wish to know her own genetic information but some other third party is affected by the same information? Finally, are physicians sufficiently aware of their own attitude and personal values toward the genetic information that will influence patients' decisions?[15] It seems to me that the HGP yields far more genetic information than it provides answers for how to use that information.

An equally pressing issue is the usefulness of the genetic information itself. Most researchers agree that as the HGP progresses and significant genes and gene markers continue to be discovered, the ability to identify defective genes through DNA testing will exceed the development and availability of appropriate therapy to treat these defects, resulting in the so-called diagnostic-therapeutic gap.[16] Since we have this gap, we must ask serious moral questions, particularly because in our society, information is power. For instance, we must ask, what is the usefulness of genetic information—and what are the consequences of having such information—in the absence of a cure or helpful treatment other than "therapeutic" abortions?[17] Another most significant factor that compromises the usefulness of this new genetic information is the "physician's knowledge gap," that is, the physician's lack of knowledge to interpret probabilistic genetic information and the physician's lack of confidence to offer appropriate therapeutic option or advice. Furthermore, physicians' low tolerance for uncertainty, their negative attitudes toward being responsible for genetic counseling and testing, and a general unfamiliarity with the ethical issues raised by testing are significant barriers between physicians and genetic medicine. It seems to me that unless these problems are resolved as quickly as the advances in genetic knowledge through the HGP are made, the usefulness of genetic technology is limited as far as meeting the needs of patients is concerned.[18]

In sum, the HGP brings with it a host of new information and diagnostic

---

Care Ethics: Critical Issues, ed. John F. Monagle and David C. Thomasma (Gaithersburg, Md.: Aspen, 1994), pp. 9-10.

[15]Gail Geller and Neil Holtzman, "Implications of the Human Genome Initiative for the Primary Care Physician," *Bioethics* 5 (October 1991): 323.

[16]Juengst, "Human Genome Research," p. 123.

[17]Theodore Friedmann, "Opinion: The Human Genome Project: Some Implications of Extensive 'Reverse Genetic' Medicine," *American Journal of Human Genetics* 46 (March 1990): 407-14.

[18]For a general discussion with special focus on primary care physicians, see Geller and Holtzman, "Implications of the Human Genome Initiative," pp. 319-24; and Lori Whittaker, "The Implications of the Human Genome Project for Family Practice," *Journal of Family Practice* 35 (September 1992): 198-99.

capabilities that will affect tremendously not only patients, but also physicians, who may not yet fully understand how genetics will penetrate their professional practice and place new responsibilities on them. The "new" genetics will shift the focus of medicine from crisis management care to more preventative/predictive medicine;[19] but even more significantly, physicians are required not only to respond to patients' complaints of illness, but to provide insights into their destinies.[20] This is due to the fact that the HGP has engendered a new perspective in human nature, and to this topic of great moral concern I will now turn.

Changes in the Understanding of Human Nature, Health and Disease

From a philosophical point of view, many are justifiably concerned that the HGP may subtly but profoundly impact how we define the human being, health and disease. A particular fear is that a type of reductionism similar to modernity's comparison of the human body to a machine will be extended—that the HGP will further reduce the machine to its molecular components consisting of a set of genetic blueprints that the body's biochemical reactions will follow precisely. Using such a metaphor of blueprints or charts to describe the genome diminishes the differences between individuals to their DNA codes. This "geneticization" of human nature negatively affects the way we think about ourselves as unique individuals, diminishes our valuation of human life and undermines our personhood.[21]

With this increased focus on genes and genetic makeup, many also fear that the HGP specifically promotes a deterministic view of the human being, health and disease. How the individual will be, how he can be or how he ought to be will be viewed largely, if not exclusively, as genetically determined; this genetic determinism will also manifest itself in a simple genetic explanation of health and disease. This reinforces the modern scientific (mis)understanding of human reality by taking real life out of the context of its situation in order to control the object being investigated. In the case of human diseases, genes only provide a partial picture of a bigger story that involves complex interactions and combinations. As I have already discussed, genes influence but do not determine human traits.[22] No human characteristic is absolutely genetically determined, because genes generally act indirectly

---

[19]M. Therese Lysaught, "From Clinic to Congregation: Religious Communities and Genetic Medicine," *Christian Scholars Review* 23 (March 1994): 329.

[20]Dorothy Wertz and John Fletcher, "Privacy and Disclosure in Medical Genetics Examined in an Ethics of Care," *Bioethics* 5 (July 1991): 227.

[21]Abby Lippman, "Led (Astray) By Genetic Maps: The Cartography of the Human Genome and Health Care," *Social Science and Medicine* 35 (December 1992): 1470.

[22]See chapter eleven, "Manipulation of Embryos," above.

and they interact with the environment. At various stages of human development, genes are being turned on or off and are acting entirely differently from how they act in other stages. In fact, even diseases themselves, such as repeated seizures, can activate specific genes. Hence, the context is just as essential to the genes' function as is their code.[23] The HGP may map out the genes, but it will never determine the manner and the environment in which the mapped genes will be phenotypically expressed, and therein lies the limitation of deterministic and reductionistic arguments applied to human beings. The HGP will be very useful for analyzing the parts, but when we look at the whole, we see a mystery that transcends the individual genetic parts of the human being. Genes should be understood in the context of the whole human being and her environment, and not the other way around; but the HGP and other genetic technologies tempt us to see human beings in the contexts of the human genome and to thereby ignore other dimensions of our personhood including relationality, spirituality and responsibility.[24] By forgetting the multidimensional nature of human personhood and the interactions between the biological/molecular and the environmental/societal levels, which are just as important as genetics to the health and disease of the person, genetic technology shifts from external to internal causes of disease, with the result that normal genetic variations are described as "defects," "flaws," "disorders" and "deleterious genes."[25] Such language not only falsifies the actual explanatory power of genetics, but also distorts our true understanding of the nature of health, disease and personhood.

Further, genetic reductionism and determinism change how society views, treats and acts toward those we define as "abnormal." With the "geneticization" of human health and disease, we are inclined to identify the person with the disorder that afflicts the person—a person is disabled, rather than having a disability; she is diabetic, instead of suffering from diabetes—when in reality a person is more than her disease. By identifying the disease with the individual's destiny, we move into a dangerous territory, especially in fetal diagnosis, where we begin to support a belief that it is not the genetic disease that needs to be corrected, but the defective child that needs to be eliminated. As Leon Kass warns, the notion that "defectives" should not be

---

[23]For a similar viewpoint, see V. Elving Anderson, "Resisting Reductionism by Restoring the Context," in *Genetic Ethics: Do the Ends Justify the Genes?* ed. John F. Kilner, Rebecca D. Pentz and Frank E. Young (Grand Rapids, Mich.: Eerdmans, 1997), pp. 85-87.

[24]Henk Jochemsen, "Reducing People to Genetics," in *Genetic Ethics: Do the Ends Justify the Genes?* ed. John F. Kilner, Rebecca D. Pentz and Frank E. Young (Grand Rapids, Mich.: Eerdmans, 1997), pp. 75-83.

[25]See also Philip Boyle, "Genetic Grammar: 'Health,' 'Illness' and the Human Genome Project," *Hastings Center Report Special Supplement* 22 (July-August 1992): S1.

born is "a principle without limits."[26] If the "defective" person escapes prenatal diagnosis and abortion, our society's more heinous response, given the principle of identifying human disease with destiny, is to activate the social mechanisms of separation, discrimination and stigmatization, thus further accentuating the artificial segregation of the "normal" and the "abnormal." The HGP and other genetic programs may even lead us to differing views of human nature, which in turn lead to differing social choices in favor of those we classify as normal.[27] In sum, genetic advances have a great potential to benefit the human race, but they also have the potential to segregate the human community into various kinds of persons with different and conflicting natures: some to be accepted, some to be genetically manipulated, some to be eliminated. Wisely and cautiously employed, the HGP may contribute toward the relief of some human suffering, but to ignore the potential risks associated with the project will lead to human conditions far worse than what they intend to cure.

Modern Medical Technology as Humanity's Hope

It is fair to say that in the West, the general public attitude toward genetic technologies in general, and the HGP in particular, is one of excitement rather than caution. One of the main reasons for such an attitude, in my assessment, is that the public has adopted a utopian view of medical technology as humanity's ultimate hope. As I have previously suggested, the biomedical approach to modern medicine has reduced the human body to essentially biochemical and biophysical processes, with "machine" as its most fitting metaphor. This understanding of the human being has undoubtedly provided an impetus for the great technical progress in medicine, but it has done so at the price of allowing medicine to be entirely under the grips of medical technology.[28] Concomitant with this mechanization of the human body and technologization of medicine is "a dilution of the religious valency of the reality of this world"[29] and the loss of both the transcendent dimension

---

[26]Leon Kass, "Implications of Prenatal Diagnosis for the Human Right to Life," in *Ethical Issues in Human Genetics: Genetic Counseling and the Use of Genetic Knowledge,* ed. Bruce Hilton et al. (New York: Plenum, 1973), p. 190. Also see my chapter eighteen.

[27]Bartha Maria Knoppers, "Genetic 'Ab-normality,' " in *Human Dignity and Genetic Heritage,* Protection of Life Series (Ottawa: Law Reform Commission of Canada, 1991), p. 43.

[28]For a succinct and useful discussion of this historical development, see Henk Jochemsen, S. Strijbos and J. Hoogland, "The Medical Profession in Modern Society: The Importance of Defining Limits," in *Bioethics and the Future of Medicine: A Christian Appraisal,* ed. John F. Kilner, Nigel M. de S. Cameron and David L. Schiedermayer (Grand Rapids, Mich.: Eerdmans, 1995), p. 25.

[29]Romano Guardini, *Religie en openbaring* (Hilversum, Holland: P. Brand, 1963), p. 32, cited in ibid., p. 25.

of reality and the eschatological hope beyond earthly existence. In our modern culture, the "here and now" is the only real nature of reality, and health and medicine are the sole content of humanity's hope. The most popular religion of the present age is a perfect society made possible by science and technology, and individual eternal life is realized by complete health made possible by medicine. In this regard, in the Christian church, especially in North America where most medical technologies have originated, the emphasis of the gospel has been shifted to health and wealth rather than love of God and our neighbors. Equipped with this counterfeit religion or gospel, modern people, including Christians, develop mythological expectations for medical technology, assuming that it will help humanity exercise full control over life and health—even defeating death. Thus this mythologization of technology not only accounts for the modern obsession with health and medical technology, but also explains modern people's rejection of their own finitude, with the result that we no longer can accept the reality that as embodied human beings, we are finite, limited, fragile and vulnerable to aging, disease and death.[30] Modern technology, understood as part and parcel of modern secularization, should alert us to the need to critically evaluate the technological bias of our time. As a conclusion to this section on technology and the procreation of human lives, I now discuss the Christian understanding of technology, value and hope.

Technology and Value

Many philosophers and scientists believe that technology in itself is value-neutral and that morality comes into play only when technology is employed, and this optimism is also shared by Christian scholars.[31] The assumption here is that technologies are neither moral nor immoral but amoral, and as neutral their usage is entirely decided by human values in particular contexts. But such a view appears to be naive, and it directly contradicts human experience. One only needs to recall how the stethoscope, laparoscope, CT scans, MRIs, prenatal screening and genetic counseling were all introduced initially as options, but subsequently they have become socially enforced procedures. In other words, technology has a life of its own and generates its own demand. Ultimately technologies are able to move from being optional to mandatory because they covertly determine our options by shaping our values. As Neil Postman points out, technologies subtly change the society's definition of

---

[30]Also see Jochemsen, Strijbos and Hoogland, "Medical Profession," p. 16.

[31]For example John S. Feinberg and Paul D. Feinberg assert that "misusing technology for evil is not logically inevitable." *Ethics for a Brave New World* (Wheaton, Ill.: Crossway, 1993), p. 290.

"knowing" and "truth"; they inform us as to what is real, natural, reasonable, necessary and inevitable; and they "alter those deeply embedded habits of thought which give to a culture its sense of what the world is like."[32] This is so because intrinsic in every technology is an ideological bias that subtly predisposes one to see the world in one way and not the other, and to value one thing over another. In this sense, medical technologies do not merely service medicine, but also shape our medical ideologies, values and practices.

In light of this, one has good reason to be concerned with how genetic technology may ultimately redefine human nature. I have already discussed how modern genetic ideology has effectively reduced human beings to DNA, and how it has allowed genetic technologists to exercise control over humanity's destiny. However, this is not a conspiracy planned by the technocrats, with the patients as totally unwilling victims; rather, modern people have willingly assumed the role of medical consumers and have contributed much in reinforcing this form of technological imperative by supporting and demanding that technology. As modern consumers, they have accepted the Enlightenment premise that science and technology are powers over nature and necessary sources of human progress and welfare. As a result, most modern people choose to ignore the controlling power such technology may exercise over their lives, which C. S. Lewis sadly sees too clearly when he says that "what we call man's power over Nature [technology] turns out to be a power exercised by some men over other men with Nature as its instrument."[33]

Technology, then, is value-laden and not value-neutral, and it possesses a power that shapes human values and controls medical practices. It both legitimates and authorizes people to perform certain actions and achieve certain ends to the detriment of those who are helpless, disfranchised or marginalized. This was not so in the premodern days, when people in the West still believed in God and the society lived by the principle that all the goodness arising from knowledge and technology ultimately comes from God and so must reflect God's goodness. Such a theology provides order and meaning to human existence, stipulates the limits and purpose for technology and progress, and protects society from the tyranny and subordinating power of technology. Much of modern society's abuse of and confusion about medicine stems from the fact that it has allowed theology to be replaced by technology as its controlling ideology. This idolatrous situation can only be rectified by bringing medical technology once again under the guidance of a biblical theology of creation, providence, stewardship and eschatology, wherein our Christian hope lies.

---

[32]Neil Postman, *Technopoly: The Surrender of Culture to Technology* (New York: Vintage, 1993), p. 12.

[33]C. S. Lewis, *The Abolition of Man* (London: Harper Collins, 1978), p. 35.

Creation and Providence

In approaching creation and providence we note that there is a particular nuance between *creation* and *creating;* while *creation* is primarily a theological term, the verb form *creating* is consistently used in the Bible.[34] This open nature of creating implies God's continuing activity in sustaining the world that he has brought into being (Gen 8:22; Ps 104:27). Were God to withdraw his sustaining providence, the world would perish or, more specifically, simply cease to exist. While this view of divine providence underlines how the world is radically contingent upon God, it does not mean that the world is thereby closed to all new possibilities and the future is wholly determined by the present. Rather, it emphasizes that any new possibilities we anticipate are entirely dependent on the mercy of God, so that creation's openness is ultimately an openness to the goodness and sovereignty of God.

Regrettably, some theologians have insisted on understanding creation's openness in such a manner as to imply that the cosmos has an unfinished character that human beings are charged by God to finish. Ronald Cole-Turner, for example, sees the HGP as an opportunity to participate in God's work of continuing creation.[35] The Bible speaks of the stability and actuality of the original creation, as evidenced by the institution of the sabbath (Gen 1—2; Ps 93:1; 102:25; Is 45:11-12), but it says nothing about God's creation as unfinished. Correspondingly, it is incorrect to think of God's providence as a kind of continuous creation *(creatio continua)* and of humans' participation in it as cocreators. Rather, a biblical understanding of the openness of creation fundamentally denies the self-containing and self-sufficient nature of the created world and affirms the continuing providential care of the Holy Spirit, who has been present from the beginning (Gen 1:2).[36] Creation's openness therefore emphasizes its total dependence on God and his goodness, and creation can be called "good" only to the extent that through it the goodness of the Creator is manifested and experienced; it is not "good" because it is intrinsically good, actually or potentially. This implies that in order for creation to be "good," it should exist and function in a way that fulfills the Creator's intention and purpose—communion, relationship and love—and this reflects the goodness of the triune God-Creator because in eternity he is communion, relationship and love. Technology as part of creation can only be guided by this litmus test: one must determine whether it conforms to the good character of God and whether it allows all his creation to experience the goodness of its Creator.

---

[34]Larry Rasmussen, "Creation, Church and Christian Responsibility," in *Tending the Garden,* ed. Wesley Granberg-Michaelson (Grand Rapids, Mich.: Eerdmans, 1987), p. 116.

[35]Ronald Cole-Turner, *The New Genesis: Theology and the Genetic Revolution* (Louisville, Ky.: Westminster John Knox, 1993).

[36]James M. Houston, *I Believe in the Creator* (Grand Rapids, Mich.: Eerdmans, 1980), p. 105.

Humanity, Nature and Stewardship

A distorted perception of humanity and creation as inherently adversarial is a fundamental underpinning of the modern development of technology, which in turn breeds an uneasy relationship between technology and creation. To most modern people, creation (or nature) is an enemy that threatens human welfare, and science and technology offer the sure hope of victory in this ongoing battle. But such an adversarial and triumphal posture ignores the fact that as embodied beings we are children of Spirit as much as children of nature. We may transcend nature in certain important ways, but our embodied state is connected to and dependent on nature; and for us to live "over against" nature is both dualistic and unrealistic. The Bible puts the human being neither over, nor under, but within nature. As the Creator's stewards, we have been given the mandate to exercise dominion in creation: to fill, to rule and to care for the earth. While this does not imply that we have an anti-technological spirit, it does imply that we must bring the development and employment of technology under the guidance of biblical stewardship. Bruce Reichenbach and V. Elving Anderson interpret stewardship as a warrant, in the name of human betterment, to engage in genetic engineering (including germ-line cell manipulation) in order to redesign human beings to be genetically and intellectually more superior.[37] But are stewards really called to improve upon creation? And if so, do we have license to redesign human genetic structures? Some also believe that the mandate to rule, a word in Hebrew that connotes subjugation, empowers human stewards to do whatever they can through technology. But even Reichenbach and Anderson agree that the human power to rule is not self-derived but delegated by God, and therefore its exercise should be consistent with the intention and purpose of the Creator for the creation.[38] This, together with the explicit mandate to take care of the land (Gen 2:15)—which means to serve, preserve, guard, protect, cultivate and benefit—leads to the conclusion that we are called to be stewards accountable to God. But modern people behave more like autonomous agents or despots, exploiting and destroying nature and redesigning human beings in our own image rather than living as God's. In this context, technology has the potential to elevate human beings from stewards to gods, empowering them to perform tasks that properly only belong to God and to change what only God has the right to change. But as the Tower of Babel reminds us, this is a dangerous development, for God's stewards should not play God but should remain accountable to him.

---

[37]Bruce R. Reichenbach and V. Elving Anderson, *On Behalf of God: A Christian Ethic for Biology* (Grand Rapids, Mich.: Eerdmans, 1995), pp. 50-51.
[38]Ibid., p. 52.

To help us be accountable stewards, Reichenbach and Anderson suggest five questions that we may consider before we employ any technology:[39]

☐ What are we obligated to change?

☐ Are changes merely permissible or obligatory?

☐ For what purpose are we to change creation?

☐ What are the limits of the change?

☐ What are the limits of the risks of any proposed change?

To this list I suggest we may add five more:

☐ What are we prohibited to change?

☐ Is the proposed change consistent with an accountable steward?

☐ Does the change make us more dependent on or more independent of God?

☐ Does the proposed change alienate us from our neighbors and nature or draw us closer to them?

☐ Is God's goodness more manifested and experienced through the proposed change or less?

Even if we accept the premise that in a fallen world, being God's steward involves a moral injunction to change certain parts of the creation, it is still very dubious that we have the right to directly alter the human genome, especially in germ-line cell therapy and human cloning. For none of the questions in the list can be positively and certainly affirmed as far as genetic engineering is concerned. I believe that stewardship of technological innovations should be guided by a purpose that is clearly in line with the purpose and intention of the Creator. In other words, our criterion for the legitimacy of any proposed change should be that it facilitates the fulfillment of God's purpose for creation.

Hope, Sins Against Hope and the Ethic of Personhood

I believe that, fundamentally, God creates out of love in order that creation may enjoy fellowship with him. If relationship and communion express the essential nature of God and, consequently, the created nature of humanity as the image of God, then the function of the image or steward must be exercised for the improvement of relationships. It follows that the ethic of personhood derived from this theology is obligated to endorse changes and improvements only on a part of the creation that clearly frustrates the Creator's intention for relationship, but that this ethic is prohibited from endorsing changes that actually or potentially undermine our dependence on God or our interdependence on fellow human beings and the rest of the creation. This means that as God's stewards and God-loving persons, we should not do everything that can be done. God has always imposed limits on his own creatures and the risks they

---

[39]Ibid., pp. 56-66.

may undertake, including their aspirations and achievements (Gen 11); and this means there are certain things only God can do and achieve—such things that humans, in their hubris, should not even attempt.

In this regard, we are reminded of Thomas Aquinas's teaching of the two sins against hope: despair and presumption. According to Aquinas, there are two kinds of despair: The first comes from "a distaste for spiritual things, and not to hope for them as arduous goods,"[40] and modern society has clearly committed this sin in expurgating all theological underpinnings from its previously Christian anthropology. The second kind of despair arises from a lack of confidence in the infinite goodness of God. Modern culture also commits this sin by choosing to place its confidence in science and technology rather than in God and by allowing the goodness of God's intention for communion, fellowship, relationship and love to be replaced by autonomy, control, manipulation and exploitation. When genuine hope in God, guaranteed by the resurrection of the Son, Jesus Christ, is overshadowed by modernity's Tower of Babel, people lose what the author of Hebrews called the "anchor for the soul," resulting in a directionless fall to despair unprecedented in human history. How else can one explain society's maddening quest for technological advances to improve, create and extend life and, at the same time, to seek to terminate lives with abortion, euthanasia and assisted suicide?

According to Aquinas, the second sin people commit against hope is presumption. We modern people clearly commit this sin by assuming that we are able to create a "new heaven and new earth" and are able to fulfill God's promises of eternal blessing by the human power of science and technology. As Aquinas comments, "Such like presumption seems to arise directly from pride, for it is owing to a great desire for glory, that a man attempts things beyond his power."[41] Modern society needs to repent of the sins of despair and presumption in its exclusive reliance on technological achievements, and it must relocate itself in the Christian resurrection hope that is anchored in God. When modern human beings decide to set their vision on a counterfeit model of perfection—which comes through the knowledge of their own genome instead of through the perfect image of the invisible God, the *imago Christi*—they have overlooked the eschatological dimension of human personhood. For in the process of our human becoming, the Holy Spirit gives us the gifts of maturity, integrity and "wholesomeness" as we live a life conforming to the perfection of the Son, who always wills to please the Father. And as we pursue this life, our relationships with God and with God-loving persons are enriched

---

[40]Thomas Aquinas, *Summa Theologiae* Q20A4, trans. Fathers of the English Dominican Province (Westminster, Md.: Christian Classics, 1981), p. 1256.
[41]Ibid., p. 1258.

and our personhood is made more wholesome, enabling us to exercise the ethic that is congruous of our personhood—that each of us is a being who enables a doing that will enrich and not undermine other beings.

Part Three

Abortion and Personhood

14

The Two Extreme Positions

*T*he established views on abortion are roughly divided into two diametrically opposed camps commonly labeled as pro-choice and pro-life, respectively supported by liberal and conservative ideologies. These positions are considered to be extreme in that they both hold absolutist positions on the moral status of the fetus. For the extreme liberal, the fetus has no moral right to life at all throughout most of the nine months of its gestation, and abortion is therefore a trivial surgical procedure to be chosen by the woman privately or, at most, in consultation with her physician. In contrast, the extreme conservative accords the fetus full moral standing at the time of conception and believes abortion is almost always morally akin to homicide. Even though these two positions may lead to radically different fates for the fetal life, they actually share a similar absolutist method for assessing the fetus's moral standing, a method that results in their respective extreme views of the fetus and their relatively simplistic treatments of the morality of abortion.[1]

The Extreme Liberal Position

Of the two features characterizing the abortion issue—the unique nature of the fetus and the unique mother-fetus relationship within the maternal-fetal dyad—the extreme liberal position is seriously concerned only with the latter; and

---

[1]To reduce the pro- and anti-abortion positions to two is obviously simplistic. In reality they represent two ends of a spectrum of opinions. The limited scope of this volume entails such a simplification.

even within their consideration of the maternal-fetal dyad, only the interest of the mother needs to be taken into account, since the fetus is not regarded as a person possessing sufficient rights or interests to balance those of the mother, who alone is considered a full moral being. While the fetus may end up dead as a result of the abortion, it cannot be said to have been harmed or injured, and abortion does not pose a genuine moral dilemma. Bereft of any moral standing, the fetus is reduced to the status of a mere thing that can be disposed of at the discretion of its mother. Naturally, such an extreme position, which reduces a fetus to a mere thing, requires careful defense, and Michael Tooley has attempted to provide just that.[2]

The Moral Status of the Fetus

Tooley defines a moral being as one with "a moral right to life."[3] He first argues that there are two radically different ways an entity may lack certain rights, illustrated as follows:

☐ A child does not have a right to smoke.

☐ A newspaper does not have a right not to be torn up.[4]

Both the child and the newspaper lack a certain right here, but the crucial difference is that the newspaper can never possess *any* rights, whereas the child may have other rights, although not the one described in this instance. This raises the question of whether a fetus is more akin to a newspaper or a child. Tooley contends that the concept of rights is based on the concept of interest, and it is absurd to award rights where no interests are present. This is why the newspaper's right can be easily dismissed whereas the child's right raises a substantive moral issue. Tooley calls this the "particular-interests principle": that is, "an entity cannot have a particular right, R, unless it is at least capable of having some interest, I, which is furthered by having right, R."[5] Individuals, therefore, cannot have a right to life unless they can be shown to have an interest in sustained life. Furthermore, in order to have such an interest, the same entity must possess "the concept of a continuing self, or subject of experiences, and other mental states."[6] Since a fetus is clearly not yet capable of possessing the concept of a continuing self as established by memory, it can have neither interest nor right and is not a being with moral status. Tooley concludes that abortion neither violates the fetus's right to life, since it has none, nor creates a serious moral issue.

---

[2]Michael Tooley, "In Defense of Abortion and Infanticide," in *The Problem of Abortion,* ed. Joel Feinberg (Belmont, Calif.: Wadsworth, 1973), pp. 122-24.

[3]Ibid., p. 120.

[4]Ibid., p. 123.

[5]Ibid., p. 125.

[6]Ibid., p. 132.

Mary Ann Warren also defends the extreme liberal position on abortion by denying the fetus the right of life,[7] although her approach differs from Tooley's. To defend a woman's right to obtain an abortion, she contends that a fetus is not a human being in the morally relevant sense of the term and is thus without a full-fledged right to life, because even in the final stages of its development the fetus fails to show any of the attributes which she asserts a human being must possess in order to qualify as "humanity in the moral sense," namely, a person.[8] In fact, Warren believes that a fetus is less personlike than the average mature mammal or than even the average fish.[9] For her, the distinction between genetic humanity (fetus) and human personhood (pregnant woman) supplies the crucial reason why abortion is not a weighty moral decision: A fetus "cannot be said to have any more moral right to life than, let us say, a newborn guppy, . . . and a right of that magnitude could never override a woman's right to obtain an abortion, at any stage of her pregnancy."[10] Almost all writers who define personhood in terms of "psychological" achievements are committed to a similar extreme liberal position on abortion whereby a fetus is not considered a person or member of a moral community because it has not achieved certain arbitrarily chosen psychological capabilities (rationality, cognition, self-consciousness and so on). Hence, abortion is not considered a moral issue.

The "Actuality Principle"

In denying the fetus moral standing or membership in a moral community, what Tooley, Warren and others have done is to adopt the so-called actuality principle of human personhood, which stipulates that "only beings with a developed capacity for conscious self-reflective intelligence have a right to life."[11] This principle implies that not only is personhood to be primarily defined in some arbitrarily chosen and usually rationalistic and moral terms, but that even possessing the potential for these capacities is insufficient to qualify a being as a person. Only what is actualized is relevant for the designation of personhood and the assignment of the right to life. This is consistent with Tooley's definition of a "person as an entity that possesses at least one of those enduring, non-potential properties."[12] Or, as Robert Wennberg puts it,

---

[7]Mary Ann Warren, "On the Moral and Legal Status of Abortion," in *The Problem of Abortion*, ed. Joel Feinberg (Belmont, Calif.: Wadsworth, 1973), pp. 102-19.

[8]Ibid., p. 112.

[9]Ibid., p. 114.

[10]Ibid.

[11]Robert N. Wennberg, "The Right to Life: Three Theories," in vol. 2 of *Readings in Christian Ethics,* ed. David K. Clark and Robert V. Rakestraw (Grand Rapids, Mich.: Baker, 1996), p. 36.

[12]Michael Tooley, *Abortion and Infanticide* (New York: Oxford University Press, 1983), p. 87.

"according to the actuality principle, . . . no person has a right *to come into* existence; they only have a right to *remain* in existence."[13] This means that the severely retarded, the irreversibly comatose, fetuses and infants are not persons with rights to life. They may be human beings in the sense that they belong to the human species, but they are not human persons. Human personhood according to the actuality principle requires the satisfaction of a set of arbitrary criteria as suggested by Tooley and others.

Failure of the Extreme Liberal Position

As appealing as these suggestions may be to their liberal proponents, I believe that none of them succeeds on the strength of argument. To begin with, each criterion or set of criteria chosen for qualification of personhood tend to prove either too much or too little. For instance, Tooley's criterion of the person as "a continuing, self-same, experiencing entity" excludes not only fetuses and infants but also many Buddhists, who do not believe in a concept of the self, and those who subscribe to the Humean "bundle concept" of the self—even though these human beings are highly sophisticated cognitively. Likewise, Warren's proposal to link the reasoning capacity to the ability to solve complex problems also excludes many persons whom Warren otherwise wants to include.[14] Thus, the liberal definition of personhood "is simply too narrow, and guilty of implicit, unintentional conceptual provincialism."[15] In the second place, the connection between personhood and right to life fails to capture some of the more nuanced refinements of the notion of rights. As L. W. Sumner suggests, rights can be differentiated further into "welfare-rights" and "property-rights"; and using the example of an autistic person who presumably cannot desire to continue to live, Sumner argues that if people around the autistic person make it possible for him to live a happy life, such a person has been benefited by the provision without having a corresponding desire. Given the concept of welfare-rights, such a person can then be considered to have a right to life without a corresponding interest.[16] Hence, the only necessary condition for one's having the welfare-right to something is that this something serves the welfare of the one who receives it. It is not necessary for the receiver to have desired it. If continued

---

[13]Wennberg, "Right to Life," p. 37.

[14]Warren, "Moral and Legal Status," p. 112; see the list of Warren's criteria in the section entitled "Contemporary Bioethical Viewpoints," found in chapter three, "The Psychological Dimension of Human Personhood," above.

[15]Michael Wreen, "Abortion: The Extreme Liberal Position," *Journal of Medicine and Philosophy* 12 (August 1987): 245.

[16]L. W. Sumner, ed., *Values and Moral Standing,* vol. 8 of *Bowling Green Studies in Applied Philosophy* (Bowling Green, Ohio: Bowling Green State University Press, 1986), p. 62.

existence serves the welfare of the fetus or infant, then she acquires the right to life in virtue of this and not from a conscious desire for life.

Finally, the actuality principle itself is also freighted with fundamental short-comings: First, no convincing and comprehensive argument has been presented to demonstrate that personhood can only be "conferred" on entities who *actually* manifest certain traits; in other words, the differences between actuality, capacity and potentiality have not been sufficiently ascertained for them to be employed in the definition of personhood. Second, with so many proposed personhood-defining criteria, it is still not clear on what basis one chooses one characteristic over another. Merely asserting that certain traits belong to the concept of personhood is not enough. One must show why those traits or characteristics are either morally significant or morally necessary conditions for personhood with a right to life. Even if one accepts that descriptively a being has to possess certain psychological capabilities before it can be called a person, it does not automatically follow that all and only descriptive persons are normatively entitled to the right to life. It seems to me that the actuality principle fails to clarify the ambiguity and confusion of the descriptive and normative senses of the word *person.*

I thus conclude that the actuality principle and the various criteria it underwrites do not provide a self-evident answer to the question of the moral status of the fetus. The extreme liberal position has failed to provide adequate reasons for why the fetus is not a person while simultaneously showing that certain adults are persons. However, not only has this position failed to provide an adequate rationale, there is a significant further reason *not* to accept this position, as we shall now see.

Abortion and Infanticide

I mentioned earlier that Tooley's criteria exclude both fetuses *and* infants from personhood. Since Tooley and many others like him discern no morally relevant difference between early and late fetuses, they likewise do not find a morally relevant difference between the fetus one day before birth and the infant one day post-birth. Fetuses and infants alike do not possess the actual characteristics that would qualify them as persons. Therefore, on their view, early infanticide, like abortion, is a justifiable act.

Warren admits that the objection to infanticide carries with it significant emotional force, but she feels that "its logical force is far less than it may seem at first glance."[17] She suggests that one of the reasons why people require a stronger moral justification for infanticide than for abortion is that neonates are very close to being persons. She compares killing neonates to killing dolphins,

---

[17]Warren, "Moral and Legal Status," p. 116.

whales, chimpanzees and other very "personlike creatures." Another reason she thinks the society may find it harder to justify infanticide is that infants can be adopted by others and they provide much pleasure to others. Regarding infants born with physical or mental handicaps, the society may prefer the expenses of institutional care to the burden of guilt that comes with killing handicapped infants. But Warren insists that from a theoretical point of view, infants have no right to life; and however unpalatable it may seem, infanticide is not a violation of the infant's rights. She further argues that it is not "morally backward" to practice infanticide if a society is so poor that it simply cannot care for the neonate without also endangering the survival of existing persons. Likewise, when an infant is born with a severe physical handicap such that her life is guaranteed to be very short or very miserable, "it is not morally wrong to terminate treatment so that the infant may die painlessly."[18] But Warren's account of the morality of infanticide is entirely based on consequentialist grounds and, as one critic remarks, it "leaves out entirely the idea that infanticide, like other homicides, is a wrong to the child who is killed, because it deprives the child of his life."[19]

Tooley also recognizes the implications of his view of personhood for infanticide. He suggests that the opposition to infanticide is a matter of social taboo and is not based on sound rational or moral principles. It is wrong only because most people are offended by it, and its moral wrongness cannot be rationally demonstrated. To justify his own position on infanticide, he uses the analogy of a car theft, arguing on the basis of "a basic intuition" that one's obligation not to remove the car from its owner is conditional upon the owner's desire not to have it taken away. By that he implies that if the owner does not care whether his car is taken away, then one generally does not violate the owner's right in taking the car.[20] In response, Sumner rightly argues that there is no good reason to accept such a basic intuition. He points out that on most theories of property-rights, it is not necessary for the owner to continue to have a desire for the object owned in order to maintain continued ownership. For example, one can completely lose interest in and desire for a car one owns, but one does not thereby forfeit one's ownership of the car. Likewise, a two-year-old infant may acquire ownership of property through inheritance without being able to have an interest in or a desire for it. That being the case, it is not clear why infants cannot have the right to life even if they are incapable of desiring to live.[21] Hence, Tooley's argument is inadequate because he

---

[18]Ibid., p. 118.

[19]Bonnie Steinbock, *Life Before Birth: The Moral and Legal Status of Embryos and Fetuses* (New York: Oxford University Press, 1992), p. 53.

[20]Tooley, *Abortion and Infanticide*, p. 60.

[21]Sumner, ed., *Values and Moral Standing*, p. 63.

fails to ground fetuses' and infants' right to life on a theory of rights that will support the crucial link between rights and desires. I thus agree with the conclusion that "until such a theory is provided we have no reason to accept Tooley's view of the moral status of the fetus, especially when it violates some of our basic moral intuitions."[22]

Furthermore, Tooley never seems to determine exactly when an infant acquires the necessary right to life in order not to be killed; instead, he claims that infanticide cannot be said to be morally wrong because the vast majority of cases for which infanticide is desirable—such as anencephaly, Tay-Sachs disease and trisomy 18—manifest themselves within a week after birth when infants are not yet capable of having a concept of a continuing self with an interest in their own continued existence. Hence he pragmatically and arbitrarily chooses "a week after birth, as the interval during which infanticide will be permitted."[23] But this is hardly convincing, for if one adheres to his criterion of personhood as a continuing self with an interest in one's own continued existence, it is conceivable that, given the slow pace of postnatal development, a child may not acquire moral standing and the right to life until she is at least two, three or even four years old. So it is in fact a matter of *years* during which infanticide may still be morally justified, if we adhere to Tooley's definition of personhood—an unsettling and highly counterintuitive proposition to say the least!

To summarize, the extreme liberal position commits the error of oversimplification in its moral treatment of abortion. By adopting a rationalistic and "actualist" definition of personhood, which strips the fetus of any moral rights, the extreme liberal takes the position that the fetus has no stake in the abortion decision. No consideration is given to the special relationship that exists between the pregnant woman as a person and the fetus as a person or at least as a developing person. Since the fetus is not a person and hence has no right to life, the pregnant woman has no obligation or responsibility to it. Hence abortion presents no moral dilemma, and abortion requires no moral justification. None of these conclusions can be endorsed by the ethic of personhood that I have advocated. But such an extreme view of the fetus's moral status is in fact shared by only a few, and even many in the pro-choice camp feel that the fetus must count, however minimally, as some kind of moral being in the abortion conflict. For many of these moderate liberals, allowing the fetus a full right or partial right to life does not necessarily mean that abortion can never be justified. It only means that the justification for abortion and even the advocacy of a liberal permissive abortion policy do not have to be dependent on an

---

[22]Ibid., p. 64.
[23]Tooley, "Defense," p. 133.

outright denial of the fetus's personhood and moral standing. I will have more to say about this in the following sections after I review the basic tenets of the extreme conservative position.

The Extreme Conservative Position

While the extreme liberal pro-choice position views an abortion as no more serious than an appendectomy, the extreme conservative pro-life position sees abortion as nothing less than a form of homicide. This position rests its case on ascribing full moral standing to the fetus, hence endowing the fetus with the same right to life as is granted to a normal human adult. This position does not discount the mother's right to decide what may happen in and to her body; rather, it simply argues that the fetus's full right to life is almost always weightier than the mother's right of autonomy. For many Christians, including the official Roman Catholic Church and the more conservative brands of Protestantism, who usually espouse this conservative position, the beliefs that God alone is the Lord of life and that it is morally wrong to take the lives of other innocent human beings provide additional support for their position.

Moral Standing and the Moment of Conception

Since the extreme conservatives ascribe full moral status to the fetus with a right to life at par with an adult's, the definition of human personhood has naturally become the most decisive factor in their argument.[24] The conservative Catholic Hospital Association of the United States and Canada affirms that "every unborn child must be regarded as a human person, with all the rights of a human person, from the moment of conception."[25] Protestant ethicist Francis Beckwith makes a similar declaration when he asserts that "the unborn are biologically members of the species Homo Sapiens. . . . It follows that the unborn entity, from the moment of conception, is fully human."[26] This ascription of full moral humanity to fetuses has its foundation in the natural-law tradition: human fetuses share the nature of all humanity.[27] As noted earlier, John Noonan states that "the criterion for humanity, thus, was simple and all-

---

[24]See, e.g., John T. Noonan Jr., "An Almost Absolute Value in History," in *The Problem of Abortion*, ed. Joel Feinberg (Belmont, Calif.: Wadsworth, 1973), p. 9; Robert F. Drinan, "The Inviolability of the Right to Be Born," in *Abortion and the Law*, ed. David T. Smith (Cleveland, Ohio: Western Reserve University Press, 1967), p. 107; Francis J. Beckwith, *Politically Correct Death* (Grand Rapids. Mich.: Baker, 1993), p. 91.

[25]*Ethical and Religious Directives for Catholic Hospitals* (St. Louis: Catholic Hospital Association of the United States and Canada, 1965), p. 4.

[26]Beckwith, *Politically Correct Death,* p. 153.

[27]This sets aside theological answers such as the possession of a soul or the image of God (which is really the religious equivalent of the humanistic term *human* and which cannot be said to be a natural property verifiable by empirical tests).

embracing: if you are conceived by human parents, you are human."[28] Any fetus conceived by human parents is in possession of a human genetic code, and as far as Noonan is concerned, "a being with a human genetic code is man."[29] In short, extreme conservatives adopt the genetic basis I have discussed in the first section of this book as the positive argument for conception's being the decisive moment of humanization.

Christian conservatives in turn buttress this conclusion, derived from genetics, with further theological convictions. Paul Ramsey is most critical of the secular view of the sanctity of life as "something inherent in man" because he believes that whatever sanctity or dignity a human person ever possesses "is a dignity that is alien to him."[30] In other words, personhood or the dignity of a human being directly results from God's creation of and relation to the individual, and thus it is not at all dependent on anything inherent in a particular human being, whether she be a student, a scientist, a mother or a fetus. Everyone has the same title to life immediately from God. So, for Ramsey, the primary value of a human life is ultimately grounded in the value God puts on it, and what human beings acquire later in life are only relative values. To define the personhood and sacredness of a human life by relative values is to confuse the primary with the relative. In terms of the primary value God places on all human beings, "no one is ever much more than a fellow fetus."[31] Ramsey concludes that the dignity, sanctity, awe, meaning and worth of a human life are derived from "the fact that from all eternity God resolved not even to be God without this particular life."[32] This is entirely consistent with my theological understanding of human personhood, articulated in part one; and that being the case, the fetus is a full person commanding our support, respect and protection for the same reason that any human being is a person: because of God's relationship with him.

If all Christians agree that personhood comes by way of a certain relationship with God, then there is less agreement as to the minimal basis for this relationship. Wennberg has argued that the possession of "an actualized capacity for personal agency and rationality"[33] is the minimal condition for God having a relationship with a human being. This implies that God can have a unique relationship with human beings only *after* they have become persons

---

[28]Noonan, "Almost Absolute Value," p. 9.

[29]Ibid., p. 13.

[30]Paul Ramsey, "The Morality of Abortion," in *Life or Death: Ethics and Options,* ed. D. H. Labby (Seattle: University of Washington Press, 1968), p. 71.

[31]Ibid., p. 72.

[32]Ibid., p. 75.

[33]Robert N. Wennberg, *Life in the Balance: Exploring the Abortion Controversy* (Grand Rapids, Mich.: Eerdmans, 1985), p. 51.

and thus have become distinct from animals. But in so implying, Wennberg seems to have confused primary and relative values as suggested by Ramsey. This account of personhood would suggest that the reverse is the case: personhood is attained not *before* God's relationship with us but *because* of it. The minimal basis for and proof of God's unique relation to human beings is found not in human rationality, morality or spirituality, but in the very emergence (creation) of a human life, embodied in and witnessed by the physicality of the fetus. On this view, the physicality of the fetus is in itself sufficient as the basis for God's covenantal relationship with the human being. Human personhood does not rise above our physicality; rather, our personhood is only possible as we are embodied through our physicality.[34] As a result, those who advocate criteria for personhood above and beyond the physical can be seen as modern-day gnostics. Stanley Hauerwas states, "Those who assume that abortion is a relatively insignificant moral matter because the fetus is only 'physical' are but Manichees in a new form."[35] Therefore, if physicality is the minimally sufficient quality necessary for full personhood, then there is no reason to suppose that the conceptus is not a full human person.

In defending the importance of the physicality of the human life, I am affirming the value of human life in general, rather than simply providing a defense of the fetus. I am not saying that the physical nature of the fetus is so important that it wholly determines the meaning of life, "but rather [that] the idea of life determines why it is significant to regard the *conceptus* as an important aspect of life."[36] Hence, I don't see that anything can be called too extreme if conservatives hold the assumption that the physical property of being human also serves as the criterion of moral standing to provide the basis for granting the fetus the right to life. There is thus both a biological (descriptive) and a moral (normative) meaning to the term *being human,* and the two are considered inseparable and are possessed by all human beings no matter how immature or abnormal they may be. In adopting this position, the extreme conservatives should not be accused of confusing the distinction between "descriptive" and "normative" personhood, as the extreme liberals may have done in their espousal of the actuality principle. Rather, the extreme conservatives have simply demonstrated more ably that their description of humanity as "genetic humanity" is inextricably tied to and sufficient for normative personhood. Thus Noonan may declare, "To say a being was human was to say it had a destiny to decide for itself which could not be taken from it by another man's

---

[34]Stanley Hauerwas makes a similar point in *Vision and Virtue* (Notre Dame: University of Notre Dame Press, 1981), pp. 150-51.

[35]Ibid., pp. 151-52.

[36]Ibid., p. 152.

decision."[37] This means that extending an entity of membership to the species *Homo sapiens* automatically entails the assignment of the moral right to life. This is sometimes called the "species principle," which many conservatives believe to be defensible.

The Species Principle, Fetal Right to Life and the Ethic of Personhood

According to the species principle, human life earns the moral right to life not because of any characteristics or traits it possesses or will possess in due course, but because of species membership, which is extended to any being conceived of human parents—including infants, adults, the retarded, the anencephalic and the irreversibly comatose. It gives to all members the same strong right to life, so every human life is inviolate because of its membership in the species *Homo sapiens*. This view has the advantage of being decisive and clear in specifying precisely who is entitled to being treated with value, dignity and the right to life. But to avoid being accused of speciesism (a label some would equate to racism or sexism), proponents of the species principle must be able to provide an answer for this question: Why is membership in the human species so significant morally that all such members are entitled to have a right to life?

Christians who espouse the species principle have formulated two versions of the principle on the basis that human beings are created in the image of God. The first version states that the divine image is found in certain members of the human species who reflect the divine nature by either actually or potentially exercising rational, moral and spiritual agency. The presence of these divine image-bearers in turn "sanctifies" the whole species *Homo sapiens,* so that even those who are not image-bearers are endowed with a right to life. The second version holds the view that all members of the human species are in the image of God and thus possess a right to life.[38]

Some consider the second version—which views *Homo sapiens* as a whole to be the recipient of divine valuation as the image of God—to be problematic[39] because it can seem as if there is nothing particularly special about the species *Homo sapiens:*

> God is free to determine who shall bear his image, and he has directly conferred this status on those who happen to be members of the human species; therefore God could have just as easily decided to confer the special status of image-bearer on apes or ants.[40]

Wennberg contends that this separation of the special status of divine

---

[37]Noonan, "Almost Absolute Value," p. 13.
[38]Wennberg, *Life in the Balance,* pp. 127-28.
[39]Ibid., p. 134.
[40]Ibid.

image-bearer from one's nature as a rational agent is highly arbitrary and that it runs against most people's expectation that the valuation with a divine image should be linked to some noticeable characteristics. For how else would it be apparent that a divine image exists at all? Hence he believes that one's special status as an image of God should be "inextricably tied to one's nature as a person who can respond to God, enter into relationship with him, and be morally and spiritually accountable to him."[41] But this would mean that God does not confer the status of divine image on those who cannot participate in his purposes, including the severely retarded and the irreversibly comatose, because they have neither the capacity nor the potential for personal life. In an insightful essay, Michael Wreen defends the species principle on philosophical grounds without using religious symbols such as the image of God. He first argues that even though human persons and human bodies are not the same entities, personal identity is at least closely tied to bodily identity. He considers this relationship a "quasi-metaphysical linkage" between the concepts of the human person and the bodily human being.[42] This explains why it is easier for us to identify with human "nonpersons" than with intelligent nonhuman persons. Wreen is not arguing that such a conceptual connection between human persons and human beings constitutes a metaphysical basis to support the claim that basic rights should be accorded to biological human beings per se. Rather, he merely wants to point out that "the metaphysical gridwork which supports the flow [of basic rights] to persons has a structure which, in some sense, includes human beings."[43] It is as if the concept of a person is caught up with that of a human being.

In the second place, Wreen points out that a human being functions as a human person only if certain conditions are available: food, water, air, time, ability, opportunity and so on. He calls these the "empirical preconditions for human personhood,"[44] which are pervasive and important features of human existence because they set limitations on human personal existence. If they are not available, human persons as we know them would not exist. Furthermore, whether these empirical preconditions for human personhood are satisfied in the development of a particular person is largely a matter of chance, contingency, luck and the laws of nature. This implies that in the world we live in, human personhood is not easily separable from being human, in all its biological, social, physical and psychological dimensions. The claim that only human persons are entitled to certain rights is an abstraction that over-

---

[41]Ibid.
[42]Michael Wreen, "In Defense of Speciesism," *Ethics and Animals* 5 (1984): 50.
[43]Ibid.
[44]Ibid.

looks these empirical factors, which are woven into our lives. Hence, Wreen concludes that "it is not personhood *simpliciter* which ensures the possession of basic rights, but personhood *cum* its linkage to humanity and its world-bound constraints and contingencies."[45] Finally, Wreen argues that if human beings can be prevented from becoming persons due to chance occurrences that we cannot foresee, prevent or avoid, then the principle of equality or simply fairness should nonetheless require us to ascribe basic rights to them,[46] because in regard to basic rights, human nonpersons and human persons are in the same existential boat. On this view, all members of *Homo sapiens* normally go on to become persons, and a few are not persons just because they were denied the opportunity to become or to remain persons. A basic morality should redress this moral imbalance and make up for "nature's inhumanity to humanity" by extending basic rights to all members of the species *Homo sapiens*.[47]

Even if the species principle is accepted so that the fetus is granted full moral status, the conservatives have yet to reckon with the fact that it is possible for human beings with equal rights to come into conflict with each other in a way that may require adjudication. But in the context of the abortion debate, the conservatives always insist on the natural-law tradition that it is wrong to kill if someone possesses moral standing and is innocent, and the act of killing is direct.[48] Hence, once the moral standing of the fetus is affirmed, it is relatively easy for the extreme conservatives to argue that abortion is the direct taking of an innocent life, an act to be condemned and proscribed. This prohibition is an absolute demand even in difficult concrete situations,[49] and as Beckwith puts it, "Almost every act of abortion is intended to kill the unborn, an entity that is fully human. Therefore, almost every act of abortion is prima facie wrong."[50] If the extreme conservative position is redeemable at all, it will hinge on how meaningful the word *almost* can be. Sometimes the conservatives give the impression that not only is the prohibition of taking innocent life absolute, but so is life in general and fetal life in particular. The biblical tradition indeed affirms that life is precious, but there is an understanding that life may be licitly surrendered, especially in the relationships of persons. As Jesus says, "No one has greater love than this, to lay down one's life for one's friends" (Jn 15:13 NRSV). Conservatives who insist on absolutizing the life of the

---

[45]Ibid., p. 57.
[46]Included among such unfortunate human nonpersons would be the fetus, the infant, the senile and the retarded.
[47]Ibid., p. 53.
[48]L. W. Sumner, ed., *Values and Moral Standing*, p. 87.
[49]Josef Fuchs, *Natural Law* (New York: Sheed & Ward, 1965), p. 123.
[50]Beckwith, *Politically Correct Death*, p. 153.

fetus do so at the expense of overlooking the significance of relationships as personhood flourishes. As a result they fail to locate the abortion issue in the essential network of personal and social relations, which includes but is not exhausted by the maternal-fetal dyad.

In sum, given my account of personhood with its emphasis on the importance of embodiment, I would not expect to disagree with the species principle in a major way. It is fair to say that the ethic of personhood that I espouse shares with the speciest position a firm commitment to honor the fetal right to life on the basis that the early conceptus has the physical substance that enables the eventual emergence of a full person. However, my account of personhood is not limited to one's embodiment because of its dyadic structure, which emphasizes the equal importance of a being's relationality. In contrast, the species principle itself does not explicitly require the involvement of relations. Consequently, the species principle and the extreme conservative position it supports often find themselves rigidly constrained in an anti-abortion stand that betrays an indifference to the interests of the pregnant woman in the maternal-fetal dyad as well as to other relations in her surroundings, which in fact deserve careful consideration and attention. In this regard, the ethic of personhood I embrace offers a greater sensitivity to and support for the importance of the network of relations surrounding the pregnant woman, for as I have shown, in my account of human personhood, relationality has an ontological status equal to that of the human substance in the constitution of the person.

15

Moderation of the Extreme Positions via Consideration of the Pregnant Woman's Rights

W e have seen the limitations inherent in both the actuality principle, by which the liberals deny moral standing and right to life to the fetus and infant, and the species principle, by which the conservatives defend the moral standing of the fetus at the expense of ignoring the interests of the mother. By either totally denying or totally affirming of the moral status of the fetus, these extreme positions have made fetal personhood the singular decisive factor in the abortion issue, and as a consequence they have allowed the value and the rights (or absence thereof) of the fetus to preempt the consideration of all other values—maternal, familial and social. This "one-dimensionality" of the extreme positions narrows the number of issues in the abortion debate to only a few that bear exclusively on the moral status of the conceptus. Since the 1970s both liberals and conservatives have attempted several different approaches to overcome these limitations, including a more genuine consideration of maternal rights and other social factors, such as the role of the physician, the husband or male partner as well as the family, the society and the values they embody. I will first examine the different interpretations of the maternal rights of the pregnant woman and the way these rights may moderate the extreme positions, and then I will evaluate their conclusions.

Maternal Rights of the Pregnant Woman

According to Joel Feinberg, a woman's right to an abortion is a discretionary right, that is, it is a right to choose; correlated with this right is a duty of others not to interfere with or withhold the necessary means for its exercise.[1] But discretionary rights are subject to limits, which can be discovered by examining the basis on which a discretionary right is grounded. According to Feinberg, the right to an abortion is thought to be associated with at least three fundamental rights:

☐ property rights

☐ right to self-defense

☐ right to bodily autonomy

   To this list I add

☐ abortion right gained through the use of the principle of double effect

☐ right of privacy

I will try to analyze how these rights may help to modify the extreme positions on abortion.

Property Rights and Abortion

It is a prevailing trend within the pro-choice culture to argue that because fetal ontology does not entitle the fetus to any rights and because the ontological status of the mother is not disputed, a discussion of a woman's right to an abortion can thereby be reduced to a defense of one's property right over one's body.[2] This view considers a fetus as literally a "part" of a woman's body, like an organ or a tumor. As such, a woman may choose to have any part of her body, including an organ or tumor, removed at will, for property right includes the right of disposal.[3] However, if a fetus is viewed as one's property in the same way as we would view one's car, for example, it may be argued that the right to do whatever one wants to with the fetus should be shared by both the mother and the father, who contributes an equal amount of genetic heritage to the fetus and may therefore claim just as much right to ownership as the mother claims. Such an idea of sharing/equality of paternal and maternal rights over the embryo/fetus is even more obvious in cases where conception is achieved through in vitro fertilization. Furthermore, if fetuses are merely

---

[1]Joel Feinberg, "Abortion" in *Matters of Life and Death,* ed. Tom Regan (New York: Random House, 1980), p. 203.

[2]Ruth Macklin, "Liberty, Utility, Land Justice: An Ethical Approach to Unwanted Pregnancy," *International Journal of Gynecology and Obstetrics Supplement* 3 (1989): 40-41.

[3]Feinberg, "Abortion," pp. 183-217.

property, then there is no reason why they cannot be commercially bought or sold. But if the fetus is granted any measure of moral standing, which entitles it to even a minimal degree of right to life (a consideration only a few would unhesitatingly dismiss), then it is against all moral logic to consider the fetus as property at somebody else's disposal.

Some may argue that a woman does not need to consider her ownership of the fetus as akin to her ownership of a car; rather she needs to view the fetus as an organ of her body like her kidney, over which she exercises full control and which she can have removed from her body and donated to others at will. But conceptually it is problematic to view the fetus as the pregnant woman's organ. What function would this "organ" serve? Further, the analogy of organ donation implies the preservation of integrity and intactness of the organ; hence the analogy is more applicable to adoption than to abortion. At any rate, regardless of the fetus's personhood status, most people view the fetus not simply as an organ of the mother's body, but as an independent entity temporarily growing inside her. As will be considered in some detail later, recent developments in neonatal medicine—with the fetus emerging as an independent patient—reinforces this view.

The pro-choice liberals may make a further retreat in their argument to retain the property right rationale by arguing that a pregnant woman does not own the fetus but she owns her body, particularly the womb in which the fetus takes residence. In this case, the pregnant woman is conceived of as a landowner and the fetus is viewed as an occupant, a relationship in which the woman is entitled to expel the occupant when certain conditions are not met. All these actions can be done in the name of merely exercising one's property rights. But this argument fails for several reasons. First, most people will find it morally offensive to think of one's body, in this case the womb, in terms of property and ownership, thereby rendering it vulnerable to commercialization and commodification. Second, most people will also wonder whether the legal concept of property right entitles a property owner to evict a tenant who fails to meet whatever terms of the rental agreement on a cold winter night, say at -40°C, when it is certain the tenant will die from exposure within a few minutes. If no real-estate property rights can be exercised at the expense of homicide, then no vindication of a woman's property right of her body can justify abortion. Further, in a real-estate property rental agreement, the tenant has rights, and she may appeal to an independent third party such as a rental board if she feels her rights have been violated. A rental agreement is thus always a two-way street, and the woman's right to abortion is not supported by this notion of property right. Finally, viewed from the broader perspective of the understanding of personhood discussed in the first part of this book, it is difficult to see how persons will flourish and be fulfilled if the basis of their relationality is grounded on a transactional basis of property. I therefore agree with the conclusion that property rights simply cannot support the moral weight of an abortion.[4]

Direct Abortion and the Maternal Right of Self-Defense

Even the extreme conservatives, who presume that the fetal right to life overrides any and all other maternal interests, are compelled to consider maternal rights when the mother's life is being threatened by the pregnancy. Can abortion be justified when the mother's life is being threatened by the pregnancy? If the answer is affirmative, how can it be justified? If the conservatives in fact hold the natural-law rule that it is always wrong to directly kill an innocent human being with moral standing, then abortion can never be justified unless either the fetus is not innocent or the killing is not direct. If the fetus is not innocent, then the mother's act of abortion could be considered justifiable on her right of self-defense; and if the killing is indirect, then the abortion is rendered permissible on the basis of the principle of double effect.

I shall first present the argument of direct abortion and the maternal right of self-defense. Three cases of direct abortion will suffice to illustrate the situation: the first case involves a pregnant mother with chronic hypertensive heart disease, who may die if her pregnancy goes beyond the second trimester. A second example is the need to crush the skull of a hydrocephalic fetus (craniotomy) to effect a vaginal stillbirth when either routine vaginal or cesarean delivery threatens to kill both mother and child. Finally, we consider a third, less straightforward case, where a fetus poses an indirect threat: a woman who is four-months pregnant is found to have cancer of the uterus. An early operation gives her a good chance of being cured, but waiting any longer will greatly reduce her chance for survival.[5] All three cases involve conflict situations in which continuation of the pregnancy will lead to the death of both the mother and the fetus (although in the third case, the fetus might possibly survive) and in which the only way to save the mother is to take medical action that will kill the fetus. Is abortion justified in these cases? How?

Common opinion would hold that there should be no moral ambiguity in these cases, that the mother should be saved without question and that the abortion justified on utilitarian grounds.[6] However, some believe that this argu-

---

[4]Ibid., pp. 205-6.

[5]This case is adapted from Ronald Munson with Christopher A. Hoffman, *Intervention and Reflection: Basic Issues in Medical Ethics,* 5th ed. (Belmont, Calif.: Wadsworth, 1996), pp. 105-6.

[6]Hauerwas would argue that the situation in the third example is not that clear. "It may well

ment focuses too much on the good outcome, namely, the survival of the mother, when the real question does not pertain to the justification for saving the mother. Rather, the task is to provide a moral justification for the direct killing of the fetus without disregarding outright the sanctity of the fetal life.[7] Hence, the maternal right to self-defense has been proposed as the basis for the moral justification for killing the fetus. Feinberg points out that the right to self-defense should be qualified by the principle of "proportionality," according to which the act of self-defense by force should be proportional to, though not identical to, the severity of the harm that is inflicted by the assailant.[8] While this principle is sometimes used to justify the use of lethal force to prevent harms that are less serious than death, it also implies that one may not be entitled to inflict in self-defense an injury excessively greater than the injury to be avoided. Applied to the abortion situation, this qualification would disallow most abortions because the harms to be avoided by the mother are usually relatively trivial compared to the death of the fetus. The right to self-defense only justifies the few rare cases, including those cited above, in which the pregnant woman's life is genuinely being threatened and in which she will certainly die without an abortion.

The self-defense argument as a justification of abortion is also challenged by the fact that this right is usually applicable only if the aggressor is morally at fault. In other words, the right to self-defense presupposes the presence of a guilty aggressor.[9] But what if the aggressor is innocent? Feinberg considers the case in which the aggressor is not morally at fault, as in the case of an attacker who is temporarily insane. In such a case, the aggressive act is recognized as wrong and therefore unjustified, but because the aggressor either does not mean it or cannot help it, the aggression is excusable. Applying this to the case of abortion, one can certainly establish that the fetus is innocent since it is too immature to be a moral agent; and if its presence constitutes an unjustified aggression, it surely could not help it since it has not put itself in that aggressive position. But some may argue that it is morally justifiable to kill even an innocent aggressor if such action is necessary to save one's life.[10] But is the fetus in fact an aggressor? Feinberg believes that the fetus is not only innocent, it is not even an

---

be that a woman is so committed to a particular understanding of the nature of human life that she willingly suffers the possibility of her own death in order to be faithful to that commitment which her whole life as wife and mother as expressed to that time." Stanley Hauerwas, *Vision and Virtue* (Notre Dame: University of Notre Dame Press, 1981), p. 152.

[7]Paul Ramsey, "The Morality of Abortion," in *Life or Death: Ethics and Options,* ed. D. H. Labby (Seattle: University of Washington Press, 1968), p. 81.

[8]Feinberg, "Abortion," p. 206.

[9]Ibid., p. 207.

[10]Ibid., pp. 207-8.

aggressor.[11] On this basis, he seems to question the validity of using the self-defense argument to justify abortion at all. On the other hand, L. W. Sumner argues that the fetus need not be considered totally innocent. According to this author, innocence can be understood as either absence of guilt or absence of threat. In the sense of moral guilt, a fetus must be morally innocent. But a morally innocent person may still pose a threat, and in this sense a fetus may not be innocent, and hence the mother is permitted to kill in self-defense.[12]

Paul Ramsey accepts the general validity of the right to self-defense in justifying direct abortion when the pregnant woman's life is threatened, and he provides yet another argument for its moral justification. To begin with, he insists that even in "direct abortion" both the motivation of the moral agent and the intention of the action must not be the death of the fetus. Motivationally, the agent wants to save the mother, but "the death of the fetus can and should be radically *unwanted*,"[13] so that at least "in the motivational realm, a person does not altogether deny the equality of these two lives to God, or direct his own human love upon the one and not the other."[14] The intention of the act also must not be the death of the fetus, but only its incapacitation.[15] However, in employing the notion of incapacitation, Ramsey is portraying the fetus as an aggressor, even though admittedly it is "only doing what comes naturally, i.e., growing and attempting to be born. But this, objectively and materially, is aggressing upon the life of the mother."[16] In an attempt to absolve the fetus of culpability, Ramsey introduces the distinction between a materially and a formally guilty aggressor. A material aggressor is that agency which threatens someone's safety without any intention to do so. Ramsey uses an analogy of war to explain this. In war, two opposing soldiers do not have a direct or personal intention to kill each other. Rather, they are the material bearers of the forces in conflict, which need to be stopped and can be incapacitated in two ways: by death or by surrender. Because the soldier is merely the bearer of a material force and not a formally guilty aggressor, it is the tragedy of war that sometimes the death of the soldier is necessary in order to stop the material aggression he carries, but it is profoundly unethical to take the life of a surrendered soldier. Applying this to a life-threatening pregnancy, we see that the fetus is not innocent as a material aggressor, but it is not "formally" (that is, deliberately and culpably) an aggressor either, and the need to incapacitate the

---

[11]Ibid., p. 208.
[12]L. W. Sumner, *Abortion and Moral Theory* (Princeton: Princeton University Press, 1981), p. 108; for a detailed discussion of self-defense, see pp. 106-14.
[13]Ramsey, "Morality of Abortion," p. 82.
[14]Ibid.
[15]Ibid., p. 84.
[16]Ibid.

fetus from materially bearing its force against the mother is the tragedy of abortion. Ramsey argues that in war as in terminating a life-threatening pregnancy, no wickedness is done because in both cases the motive of the agent and the intention of the action—what is wanted and intended—is not the death of another human being but "the incapacitation of a life that is exerting materially aggressive fatal force upon the life of another."[17]

While I recognize Ramsey's ingenuity in lessening the fetus's burden of guilt as a mere bearer of material aggressive force, his claim that no wickedness is done in war or even in an abortion to save the life of the pregnant woman seems to run against common sense. I think it is more reasonable to hold that a lesser wickedness is done in these cases and to admit that the deaths of soldiers and fetuses are still evil. Another weakness of the self-defense approach is the creation of an adversarial stance between the mother and the fetus, and to some writers such a disharmonious characterization of the maternal-fetal dyad is found to be unacceptable. For example, Baruch Brody argues that the fetus is innocent not only because "the condition of guilt is not satisfied," but because "the condition of condition" is not satisfied, since the fetus has not taken any action that threatens the life of the mother, either formally or materially. Brody concludes that the mother cannot justify aborting the fetus via a self-defense right, even when its continued existence threatens her life.[18] I acknowledge the reality of a situation in which the mother's life may genuinely be endangered by the fetus, but I do not believe that the maternal-fetal relationship would thereby need to be characterized in terms of aggressor-defender relation, because such a characterization distorts the being of the persons involved as well as the relation that exists between them. A pregnancy in which the mother's life is genuinely threatened is a tragic situation, and the abortion has to take place for pragmatic and usually utilitarian reasons rather than on the grounds of fetal aggression and maternal rights of defense. The loss of the fetal life is unquestionably a (lesser) evil, and the action taken, though necessary, needs to be repented of. In this fallen world we live in, a tragedy that takes place in any relation between two persons should be acknowledged, admitted and accepted without compounding the situation by resorting to unnecessary and unhelpful distortions.

Indirect Abortion and the Principle of Double Effect

Another tactic conservatives often use to justify abortion while preserving the

---

[17]Ibid., p. 86; cf. Naomi Wolf, "Our Bodies, Our Souls," *The New Republic,* October 16, 1995, pp. 26-35.

[18]Baruch Brody, *Abortion and the Sanctity of Human Life: A Philosophical View* (Cambridge: MIT Press, 1975), pp. 6-12.

absolute prohibition on the direct killing of the innocent is the principle of double effect, which seeks to show that even if the fetus is innocent, abortion can sometimes be justified if the killing can be shown to be indirect. Briefly, the principle states that when an action can produce both a good and a bad effect, the action is permissible if all of the following four conditions are met:

☐ The act itself, independently of its effects, must be good, indifferent or at least not forbidden.

☐ The bad effect must not be the means to the good effect.

☐ The good effect of the act is intended, and the bad effect is foreseen but not intended.

☐ The reason for exercising the cause to produce the good effect must be proportionate to the seriousness of the bad effect.

The case of an ectopic pregnancy illustrates a legitimate operation of the principle. In an ectopic pregnancy the fetus is developing in the fallopian tube instead of the uterus. Unless salpingectomy (excision of the tube) is performed, which also entails the death of the fetus, the mother is in danger of dying from tubal rupture, in which case the fetus will also die. All four conditions required by the principle of double effect are fulfilled in this example: the act of salpingectomy is a neutral surgical procedure generally not forbidden; the bad effect of fetal death is only the indirect result but not the means to the good effect of saving the mother's life; the saving of the mother's life is intended, but the foreseen death of the fetus is never intended; and both the good and bad effects are more or less equally balanced in importance. Conservatives argue that excision of a tubal pregnancy is therefore an indirect act of killing an innocent moral being and is permissible. This is in contrast to performing a fetal craniotomy to save the mother's life in the case of a hydrocephalic fetus, in which both the mother and the child will perish if either vaginal or cesarean delivery is attempted. In this case, the death of the fetus is intended and employed as the direct means to save the mother, and the second and third conditions of the principle of double effect are thus not satisfied. In the traditional teaching of Roman Catholicism, this act of killing cannot be said to be indirect and fetal craniotomy is hence forbidden, unless one justifies the procedure by resorting to the self-defense argument, which we have found to be not always sustainable.

In theory, the double-effect principle justifies fewer abortions than does the self-defense argument because it treats the maternal-fetal situation as symmetrical: neither the mother nor the fetus has a privileged moral claim to survival over the other. But in practice, the principle of double effect has been criticized for the tendency to artificially inflate the number of indirect abortions because the description of any medical procedure is flexible enough so that the death of the fetus can often be shown not to be the means of saving the mother. The principle is thus not immune to abuse. But on the whole, I feel that it is a commendable principle because it has the merit of refusing to abandon the important rule against directly killing innocent people while allowing certain action to achieve some good in a tragic situation, even if this results in an unintended evil like the indirect death of the fetus. Likewise, some moderate conservatives see the principle as a positive attempt by theologians to enable action in difficult situations.[19] Above all, the principle encourages people to weigh values in our moral decision-making and to recognize that certain difficult ethical dilemmas cannot always be resolved by an absolutist approach. As one writer concludes, "The natural end of appeal to the double effect is thus a case-by-case analysis of abortion and a moderate abortion policy."[20]

Maternal Right to Bodily Autonomy

The most important attempt to moderate the absolute all-or-none positions on the abortion issue has been provided by Judith Thomson. Even though Thomson does not embrace the conservative view that all fetuses have the right to life, she is willing to grant such a right to the fetus for the sake of argument. Instead of focusing exclusively on the moral status of the fetus or on the property and defense rights of the mother, she wants to take seriously the unique and complex relation between the fetus and the mother and to show that abortion in certain instances can be morally justified based on the maternal right of bodily autonomy. In her essay "A Defense of Abortion"—which was by 1986 "the most widely reprinted essay in all of contemporary philosophy"[21]—Thomson basically raises this question: Even if the fetus is granted personhood, we are still confronted with two conflicting rights: the fetal right to life and the maternal right of bodily autonomy. How can one discern which of these rights is weightier? Thomson's now famous analogy of "the plugged-in violinist" provides the starting point for the discussion:

> You wake up in the morning and find yourself back to back in bed with an unconscious violinist. A famous unconscious violinist. He has been found to have a fatal kidney ailment, and the Society of Music Lovers has canvassed all the available medical records and found that you alone have the right blood type to help. They have, therefore, kidnapped you, and last night the violinist's circulatory system was plugged into yours, so that your kidneys can be used to extract poisons from his blood as well as your own. The director of the hospital now tells you,

---

[19]David Granfield, *The Abortion Decision* (Garden City, N.Y.: Doubleday/Image, 1971), p. 139.
[20]L. W. Sumner, ed., *Values and Moral Standing,* vol. 8 of *Bowling Green Studies in Applied Philosophy* (Bowling Green, Ohio: Bowling Green State University Press, 1986), p. 121.
[21]W. Parent, introduction to *Rights, Restitution and Risk,* by Judith J. Thomson (Cambridge: Harvard University Press, 1986), p. vii.

"Look, we're sorry the Society of Music Lovers did this to you—we would never have permitted it if we had known. But still, they did it, and the violinist now is plugged into you. To unplug you would be to kill him. But never mind, it's only for nine months. By then he will have recovered from his ailment, and can safely be unplugged from you."[22]

This analogy parallels an unwanted pregnancy in several ways. Both contain the elements of exclusively necessary dependence, temporary attachment and the existence of a connection without consent. Thomson contends that just as it would be morally permissible to detach oneself from the violinist who will be left to die, it is also morally permissible for a pregnant woman to remove the fetus from her body, even if it has a right to life.

Thomson's analogy raises the important question as to the nature of the fetus's right to life: does the fetus's right to life demand that others sustain that life at all costs (a positive claim right), or does it merely demand that it not be cavalierly terminated (a negative claim right)? Thomson argues that right to life can only be understood as a negative claim right. In the case at hand, even if the kidnapped victim is not justified in taking the life of the violinist, he is not morally obligated to sustain the violinist's life at any cost to himself. Likewise, a fetus's right to life does not mean that it has the right to everything it needs to sustain its life, particularly with regard to the use of the mother's body. The fetus's right to life is not absolute but is limited by the mother's right of bodily autonomy. As Thomson states, "Having a right to life does not guarantee having either a right to be given the use of or a right to be allowed continued use of another person's body."[23] Just as the violinist's right to life does not include the right not to be disconnected, so too the fetus's right to life does not include the right not to be aborted.

However, Thomson makes it clear that the mother's right to her bodily autonomy does not include the right to ensure the death of the fetus. In her example of the violinist, if the kidnapped person were to unhook himself from the violinist and by some miracle the violinist survived, that person would have no right to turn around and slit the violinist's throat. Likewise, the pregnant woman only has a right to relieve herself of the burden of pregnancy but not to directly kill the fetus.[24] Thus, Thomson's analogy of the plugged-in violinist is an attempt to show that an abortion is not the killing of a fetus but the act of withdrawing life support from it. The fetal death that ensues, like the certain death of the violinist, is not a violation of the fetal right to life but an unin-

---

[22]Judith J. Thomson, "A Defense of Abortion," in *The Problem of Abortion,* ed. Joel Feinberg (Belmont, Calif.: Wadsworth, 1973), p. 122.
[23]Ibid., p. 130.
[24]Ibid., p. 139.

tended side effect that results from the fetus's inability to survive without maternal support, which the woman is not obligated to provide.

Despite its being popularly accepted in some circles, Thomson's argument is problematic for several reasons. Although it is probably true that some cases of abortion are not instances of intentional killing, the vast majority are. Abortions are usually motivated either to avoid the condition of pregnancy or to avoid the responsibility of having a child. Only the first motive provides the condition for nonintentional killing; as for the second motive, the death of the future child is the only way (except for adoption) to remove the responsibility. Since the majority of abortions are motivated by the second reason, most cases of abortion are intentional killing.[25] Hence, Thomson's argument only covers those minority cases where it can be shown that the motive is to avoid pregnancy and that death is really only an unintended side effect, as in the case of terminating a life-threatening pregnancy. Further, it does not appear that Thomson's argument can justify all cases of nonintentional killing in abortion either, because of the various limitations on such a justification. The first limitation is that the side effect (fetal death) must be an inevitable and necessary consequence of the main intention (maternal bodily autonomy). If there exists a possible alternate implementation of the main intention that does not include the side effect, then the side effect cannot be justified on the basis of the main intention. In the example of terminating a life-threatening pregnancy, an abortion with fetal death may be justified only with the previable fetus, since postviable pregnancies could be "terminated" without necessarily causing the death of the fetus. Another limitation on nonintentional killing is the need to show that the moral necessity of the main intention must be sufficiently serious to warrant the undesirable and harmful side effect. In most abortions, however, the harm sustained by the fetus is invariably fatal, whereas the harm that the pregnant woman seeks to avoid by having the abortion is usually nonfatal and mostly minor, if not trivial. These cases of nonintentional killing can hardly be justified. Hence I conclude that although Thomson's distinction between intentional killing and nonintentional killing with death as a side effect is valid, it does not even apply to those few cases where the death of the fetus truly is only a side effect because of the disproportionate severity of the unintended side effect, namely, the end of the fetal life.

By raising the issue of the mother's bodily autonomy, Thomson's analysis has succeeded in showing that a variety of factors bear on the unique and complex maternal-fetal relation, which in turn affects the fetus's right to life as well as the duties and obligations of the mother. Through the analysis of sev-

---

[25]Compare Patrick Lee, *Abortion and Unborn Human Life* (Washington D.C.: Catholic University of America Press, 1996), p. 115.

eral examples, Thomson has identified four such factors:[26]

☐ the voluntary or involuntary nature of the pregnancy

☐ the burden of the pregnancy to the mother

☐ benefit to the fetus if pregnancy is continued

☐ the elapsed duration of pregnancy as an indicator of acceptance of parental responsibility

Given these factors, Thomson's example of the plugged-in violinist roughly corresponds to the case of a sick and desperately frightened fourteen-year-old schoolgirl having become pregnant due to rape. In such a situation, the pregnancy comes about involuntarily and the continuation of pregnancy will probably result in both emotional and physical harm to the young mother. These two factors may significantly modify the fetus's right to life. Furthermore, the future prospect of such a child is rather dubious; and if the mother requests an abortion as soon as she discovers her pregnancy, thus indicating her reluctance to assume parental responsibility, it would seem that Thomson's violinist analogy may apply.

But in real life, these factors are rarely all present in one case, or they may appear in different degrees and in various combinations. Consider a case in which the pregnancy is carefully planned and is proceeding normally when the woman suddenly decides, in the sixth month of pregnancy, that she wants an abortion because of an unexpected promotion at work. Thomson recognizes that in such a case, the mother's right of autonomy is a manifestation of her self-centeredness, callousness and outright indecency. And yet, she maintains that the right remains inviolable. Thomson herself raises the question as to what one should do if asked to be hooked up to the violinist for one hour in order to save his life. Thomson acknowledges that to refuse assistance in such cases would be highly indecent, but she insists that an "ought" does not translate into a right to demand access to or use of someone's body. Refusal to help the violinist for the hour would be "greedy, stingy, callous—but not unjust."[27] The distinction between decency and justice is stressed. In a case in which the burden of the pregnancy is not a large sacrifice, then it would be indecent, albeit not immoral, to refuse to assume parental responsibility. To carry such a pregnancy to term is to practice a "Minimally Decent Samaritanism" as an act of supererogation,[28] but no one is obligated to be a minimally decent Samaritan. In sum, Thomson's nuanced arguments suggest that the fetus's right to life does not render abortion always impermissible; by granting that the fetus has the right to life and then

---

[26]Compare Sumner, *Abortion and Moral Theory,* p. 69.

[27]Thomson, "Defense of Abortion," p. 133.

[28]Ibid.

arguing how that right can be modified, restricted or neutralized by the mother's right of bodily autonomy, she justifies abortion in the case of a pregnancy that results from rape, a pregnancy that threatens the mother's life and a pregnancy that is otherwise burdensome. Yet her arguments also effectively moderate the extreme liberal position because a woman's right of bodily autonomy does not render abortion with the certain death of the viable fetus always permissible either.

In my assessment, Thomson's contribution to the abortion debate is to be found in her emphasis that the morality of abortion is influenced by a multitude of interconnected factors involved in each case. Thomson asserts that "there are cases and cases, and the details make a difference,"[29] and she considers her account meritorious precisely because "it does *not* give a general yes or a general no."[30] Thomson's argument means that the morality of abortion can only be decided on a case-by-case basis; that there could always be exceptions; and that one can only be sure of the morality of each case after one carefully weighs the various factors present in it, including maternal voluntariness to pregnancy, risk to maternal life or health, presence of fetal deformity and the subsequent environment into which the child-to-be will be born. Contextual factors and particularities of circumstances are the foci of many who advocate for what may be called a "pragmatic" approach to abortion, which I will address in chapter sixteen. But a pragmatic approach is entirely consistent with an ethic of personhood which insists that the appropriateness of both fetal and maternal rights must be evaluated in the context of a relational understanding of personhood and, for the case at hand, the maternal-fetal relationship.

Maternal Right of Privacy: *Roe* v. *Wade*

Two years after Thomson first published her landmark essay advocating the pregnant woman's right of bodily autonomy, the United States Supreme Court confirmed such a right in its 1973 *Roe* v. *Wade* decision, which declared unconstitutional a Texas statute outlawing all abortions except when the life of the mother was genuinely threatened. In her search for a safe, elective, nontherapeutic legal abortion, "Jane Roe," a woman from Dallas, Texas (whose true name is Norma McCorvey), decided to challenge the constitutionality of the state law. The defendant, Henry Wade, was the district attorney of Dallas County. The Supreme Court argued that a woman has a right to act for her own well-being as a part of a more general right of privacy. Eight years prior to this decision, the Supreme Court had already decided in *Griswold* v. *Connecti-*

---

[29]Ibid.
[30]Ibid., p. 139.

cut that a state might not prohibit the use of contraceptive pills by a married couple because such a prohibition violates the couple's personal right of self-determination as guaranteed by the "constitutional right to privacy." In *Roe* v. *Wade,* the Court extended this right to include the right of abortion.

Even though the United States Constitution does not explicitly mention any right of privacy, some legal scholars consider that such a right is implied either in the Fourteenth Amendment's concepts of personal liberty and restriction on state action, or in the Ninth Amendment's reservation of rights to the people. Further, they believe that such a privacy right can only be extended to those fundamentally personal activities related to marriage, procreation, contraception, family relationships, child rearing and education of children.[31] The Supreme Court judged that such a right is broad enough to include a woman's right to decide whether or not to continue her pregnancy. Other scholars accept a constitutional right of privacy but disagree that such a right includes the right to the abortion. The Supreme Court in the *Roe* v. *Wade* decision took a middle-of-the-road approach by declaring that while the right of privacy is broad enough to include abortion decisions, it is not an absolute right and must be subject to limitations imposed by the state's interests to protect maternal health, uphold medical standards and protect prenatal life at some crucial point of fetal development. With that in mind, the court ruled that the abortion decision must be left to the woman and the physician in the first trimester, but after that period the state may regulate the abortion procedure in ways reasonably related to maternal health; after the fetus is viable (usually between twenty-three to twenty-six weeks of gestation), the state may regulate or even prohibit abortion in order to protect the fetus.

Since the *Roe* v. *Wade* decision in 1973, the number of legal abortions performed annually in the United States has grown to about 1.5 to 2.0 million. Despite the undesirable—indeed tragic—social outcomes, my assessment of the *Roe* v. *Wade* decision is not entirely negative. In light of my understanding of human personhood, I agree with the court's insistence that the right of privacy is a fundamental right which is crucial for the protection of an individual from any unwarranted governmental intrusion into matters of personal import, including procreation. While I appreciate the Court's decision to consider the viable fetus's right to protection by the state, I believe that the assignment of fetal right to the developmental stage of viability is arbitrary and unsatisfactory (see chapter sixteen below). From the perspective of the personhood ethic I embrace, I am uncomfortable with this arrangement because it has the net effect of pitting fetal right against maternal right in a situation where intimate personal relationship is involved. I see personal privacy as a relational notion;

---

[31]Munson with Hoffman, *Intervention and Reflection,* pp. 97-102.

it functions generally to protect against unnecessary intrusions by "impersonal" parties. But in the case of abortion, the personal decision is immersed in a complex relational context that involves the mother, the spouse, the physician, the family and the "person" of the fetus. It is only within the pregnant woman's entire relational network that I believe the woman can properly exercise her right of privacy in the abortion decision.

Abortion and Female Sexuality

Including female sexuality as an important factor in the abortion issue stems from the popular feminist position of addressing female sexuality as an instrument to accomplish social and psychological equality with men. It is often argued that women, to maintain their psychological parity with men, must have free exercise of heterosexual intercourse. However, in order to achieve this free exercise of female sexuality, access to abortion must be assured so that the psychological equality is not burdened by the constant threat of pregnancy. In other words, pro-choice feminists seek to gain their "right" to express their sexuality without the encumbrance of biological bondages such as pregnancy, childbirth and nursing in the same way that men do. Given this position, opponents of abortion are often characterized as acting from a discomfort with female sexual autonomy and equivalency.

But this pro-choice feminist view of female sexuality is completely errant because it fails to recognize that female and male sexuality are fundamentally different. The full scope of female sexual pleasure includes orgasm, conception, gestation, birth and nursing. It is thus utterly erroneous to elevate orgasm as the reigning characteristic in opposition to and at the expense of the other female sexual functions. As Sidney Callahan states, "Women as compared to men possess a sexuality that is more complex, more intense, and more extended in time, involving higher investment, risks, and psycho-social involvement."[32] Because of this difference, female sexuality does not flourish within the same circumstances as does male sexuality. A more male-oriented model of erotic sexuality is inclined toward sexual permissiveness without long-term commitment or reproductive focus. Women, however, thrive when sex acts are embedded within deep emotional bonds and secure long-term commitments. Women thus require a model that recognizes every stage of their sexual cycle. The limited scope of the male model, however, is quite destructive for the average woman. So while abortion may alleviate the short-term burden of a pregnancy, it will only do so at the price of allowing the woman's body to become more like a man's.[33] Callahan and others insist that justice can-

---

[32]Sidney Callahan, "Abortion and the Sexual Agenda," *Commonweal* 25 (April 1986): 237.
[33]Ibid., p. 239.

not be done to true female sexuality simply by creating circumstances, such as abortion, that enable women to participate in a male sexual model on equal footing with men. Instead, true feminism should work toward a world that endorses and supports women within their own unique sexual model. From the perspective of a multidimensional personhood, the complexity of female embodiment may be acknowledged and respected; it is part of the dignity of female personhood that abortion threatens to remove.

Naomi Wolf depicts what a female-oriented model of the social situation may look like:

> There would be no coerced sex without serious jail time; safe contraceptives would be affordable and available for the taking in every public health building; there would be economic parity for every woman, and basic economic subsistence for every baby born.[34]

Such a society would also work toward stable human relationships and long-term sexual commitments.

> In such a world . . . we would probably use a very different language about . . . the rare and doubtless traumatic event of abortion. That language would probably call upon respect and responsibility, grief and mourning, [sin and repenting]. In that world, . . . passionate feminists might well hold candlelight vigils at abortion clinics, standing shoulder to shoulder with the doctors who work there, commemorating and saying goodbye to the dead.[35]

Feminist Critique of Rights

Many have assumed that the discussion on the merits of various rights is unanimously endorsed by pro-choice advocates, especially when such a discussion takes place within a feminist context. This is not entirely true, for many feminists believe that a language of maternal rights—be it property, self-defense, bodily autonomy or personal privacy—is fundamentally inappropriate in the context of pregnancy and abortion because such language misconstrues the relationships that constitute authentic personhood. Specifically, such language promotes a property model of relationships rooted in an extractive view of power, which is absolutely at odds with the feminine principles of nurture, care, relationships and day-to-day responsibility. Maura Ryan is of the opinion that by resorting to a language of rights, women have merely adopted the patriarchal model for themselves, instead of truly promoting a feminist alternative.[36] Many feminists also are not persuaded by the argument that the right to

---

[34]Wolf, "Our Bodies," p. 35.

[35]Ibid. "Sin and repenting" is my addition.

[36]Maura Ryan, "The Argument for Unlimited Procreative Liberty: A Feminist Critique," *Hastings Center Report* 20 (July-August 1990): 6-12.

abortion is essential to the woman's social equality, because such argument presupposes that a woman's biological capacity to bear children is a natural handicap which prevents her from attaining full social equality. Besides, these feminists do not agree that social equality should be accomplished by pitting women against their own offspring. Some believe this approach is psychologically and politically destructive, and other even see that abortion is being used by men as yet another manipulative tool for controlling women. As one provocatively comments, "Women will never climb to equality and social empowerment over mounds of dead fetuses."[37] Far from "liberating" women, permissive abortion—justified with the language of the woman's right—makes abortion a purely private matter, deprives the pregnant woman of a support network and allows those involved to abdicate their responsibility.[38] As a result, free access to abortion in fact undermines women's claim to and quest for social equality.

At a more fundamental level, many feminists recognize that debates about fetal personhood bear an eerie resemblance to the not-so-ancient debates over the personhood of women and blacks. Such debates are the result of a patriarchal system where lesser orders of life are granted rights only when the powerful choose to do so, not when society sees that all human beings have equal worth due to their intrinsic value as persons. As Callahan astutely observes, "Women are the most recent immigrants from non-personhood. It is, therefore, chilling to see pro-choice feminists demanding continued access to assembly line, technological methods of fetal killing."[39] In denying the personhood of the fetus, the woman seeking abortion risks invalidating her own personhood. There is also a fear that the denial of the fetal right to life may go beyond the maternal-fetal dyad to involve the dehumanizing of all children. Ryan warns that making the personhood of the fetus subject to the mother's choice is but one step toward a choice for a particular kind of child as a product or commodity. To claim that parental choice alone determines the personhood of the fetus thus promotes a dehumanization and marginalization of life in general.[40]

Some recent studies focusing on the phenomenological experience of the pregnant woman also seriously question the appropriateness of using maternal rights to justify abortion. In pregnancy, the woman only gradually becomes aware that her fetus is an entity separate from herself. This awareness leads to a gradual psychic differentiation between mother and fetus and

---

[37]S. Callahan, "Abortion and the Sexual Agenda," p. 236.

[38]Ibid. Reports show that approximately 30 percent of women have an abortion because someone else wants it. Compare Daniel Callahan, "The Abortion Debate: Can This Chronic Illness Be Cured?" *Clinical Obstetrics and Gynecology* 35, no. 4 (1992): 787.

[39]S. Callahan, "Abortion and the Sexual Agenda," p. 234.

[40]Ryan, "Argument for Unlimited Procreative Liberty," p. 8.

is usually accompanied by the mother's increasing emotional attachment to her fetus. The status of the fetus is thus strongly influenced by the mother's phenomenological experience of it. It is for this reason that "quickening" is such an important benchmark in pregnancy for so many cultures. The implication is that the fetus acquires increasing importance as the phenomenological experience of the pregnancy deepens and the assessment of the pregnancy increases in value. This understanding can have consequences in both directions. On the one hand, it can be used to argue for early abortions, which would be experienced as a matter of not wanting a future child, rather than of killing a person.[41] On the other hand, such a phenomenological understanding of pregnancy can also point to the opposite direction by bringing about a heightened awareness among women that abortion is killing a life, which will result in a strong sense of guilt and self-reproach.[42] Thus some feminists advocate switching from an emphasis on maternal rights in pregnancy to a focus on the importance of the actual experiences of the pregnant woman. Such experiences clarify the fact that because pregnancy takes place within the woman's body, any decision to continue or terminate a pregnancy will have profound effects on the woman as a whole person, not just on her rights.[43]

Abortion and Maternal Responsibility

Recognizing the limitation and inappropriateness of the rights language in the ethical discourse of abortion, some feminists have initiated a radically different approach to the abortion issue by emphasizing responsibility instead of rights. Thomson is the first to hint that, among other things, responsibility for a pregnancy is a moral factor in the abortion debate (albeit, for her, a small factor). Her analogy of the plugged-in violinist implies that only in a rape-induced pregnancy is a woman totally without responsibility. But if the woman engages in sexual intercourse voluntarily, then, Thomson hints, a mother "has a special kind of responsibility for it [the

---

[41]Ibid., p. 152; see also Catriona Mackenzie, "Abortion and Embodiment," *Australian Journal of Philosophy* 70, no. 2 (1992): 151. The phenomenological assessment extends to physical evidence as well as societal conventions and personal feelings. Gordon thus states that "the physical evidence of the bloody fetal stuff shows that abortion is a dramatic event, but not the death of a child" (Gordon, "Moral Choice," p. 81).

[42]Compare K. Kallenberg et al., "The Disposal of the Aborted Fetus—New Guidelines: Ethical Considerations in the Debate in Sweden," *Journal of Medical Ethics* 19 (March 1993): 32-36. In Sweden, the law governing the disposal of aborted fetuses was changed in 1982 largely due to the increasing unwillingness of hospital employees to simply "throw away" fetuses aborted after the twenty-eighth week.

[43]Susan Sherwin, *No Longer Patient: Feminist Ethics and Health Care* (Philadelphia: Temple University Press, 1992).

fetus], not possessed by any independent person."[44] Hence, even though Thomson denies that a biological relationship between the pregnant woman and the fetus automatically imposes any special responsibility per se on the mother,[45] she nevertheless holds that in some pregnancies the woman may be held at least partially responsible, and so not all cases of abortion are morally permissible.

Mary Ann Warren is very critical of this "extremely unsatisfactory outcome" of Thomson's argument. As an extreme liberal pro-abortionist, Warren is concerned that if responsibility is not dismissed altogether, then it will not be possible to defend the right to abortion for the woman who gets pregnant due to contraceptive failure or carelessness or for the woman who gets pregnant intentionally and then changes her mind.[46] Hence she asserts that "the moral right to obtain an abortion is not in the least dependent upon the extent to which the woman is responsible for her pregnancy."[47] But it is clear to most that if abortion involves rights, then responsibility must be a relevant issue in the abortion debate.

If responsibility is in fact a relevant moral factor, then one may ask, when is a woman responsible for her pregnancy? Despite the apparent simplicity of parental responsibilities, their origin is a controversial topic. Three models have been proposed: the biological model, the consent model and the causal responsibility model.[48] The biological model suggests that responsibility arises from the biological relationship between progenitor and fetus. This model generally affirms the extreme pro-life position by maintaining that parental responsibility begins as soon as a child is conceived. It also clearly states that one can become a parent unwillingly, without consenting to be one. One main shortcoming of this model is its failure to account for the existence and validity of instances of step-parenthood.

The consent model is, in a sense, the opposite of the biological model. It suggests that parenthood is an act of kindness or supererogation rather than a strict obligation;[49] and in general terms, it would cohere with the extreme liberal position, allowing abortion even when it is assessed from the perspective of parental duty. The model is attractive for its simplicity and comprehensiveness, and it practically covers all cases of parenthood. The model, however, is

---

[44]Thomson, "Defense of Abortion," p. 131.

[45]Ibid., p. 138.

[46]Mary Ann Warren, "On the Moral and Legal Status of Abortion," in *The Problem of Abortion*, ed. Joel Feinberg (Belmont, Calif.: Wadsworth, 1973), p. 108.

[47]Ibid., p. 107.

[48]These three models are taken from M. E. Winston, "Abortion and Parental Responsibility," *Journal of Medical Humanities and Bioethics* 7, no. 1 (1986): 33-56.

[49]Ibid., p. 41.

not without its own problems. For instance, one must ask, to whom is consent given? For parenthood within marriages, spouses can give consent to each other. But what about for parenthood of single mothers? To whom do they consent—themselves, society, God? Further, some believe that consent is neither a sufficient nor a necessary condition of parenthood. For example, consent is not a sufficient reason to determine parental responsibility for having the custody of children in divorce or child-abuse cases. The case of fathers who avoid child-support payments also illustrates that consent is not considered necessary in all cases of parental responsibility either.

The causal responsibility model is considered by some as the one that most appropriately describes the origin of parental responsibility. M. E. Winston defines this model as follows: "If x is through his or her own free action directly and forseeably causally responsible for the creation of a human offspring y, then x has a parental responsibility towards y."[50] Although this model reflects the biological model in ascribing responsibility to the consequence of action rather than choice, it excuses individuals from parental responsibility in cases where they cannot be held responsible for their actions. Such cases would include pregnancy resulting from rape and the pregnancy of an incompetent woman or a minor. In the cases of rape and incompetence, it may be argued that the mother cannot be held fully responsible for the action leading to pregnancy and, therefore, for the child. Similarly, if our society generally does not hold minors fully responsible for their actions, they too may arguably be excused from full parental responsibility. The following case illustrates some of the benefits this model provides:[51] M. C. was a twenty-two-year-old retarded woman possessing the intellect of a child. Much to the dismay of her parents, she became pregnant as a result of sexual relations with her uncle. While recognizing the importance of biological ties, the causal responsibility model would excuse the woman from her parental role by recognizing her incompetence to assume responsibility for her actions. Hence the causal responsibility model balances parental responsibility with a certain degree of flexibility not present in the biological model.

In the context of maternal responsibility, Patricia McEvoy describes two types of situations in which it is particularly difficult to determine whether a woman is responsible for her pregnancy:[52]

Case 1: Sarah, a corporate lawyer in her early 30s, has had the same mate for 5 years but never intended to have children. She has used oral contraceptives for 7

---

[50]Ibid., p. 39.
[51]Munson with Hoffman, *Intervention and Reflection,* pp. 104-5.
[52]Patricia McEvoy, "Is a Woman Responsible for Being Pregnant?" *Journal of the Canadian Medical Association* 146, no. 4 (1992): 604.

years but has avoided sterilization because she wants to reserve the right to change her mind. She becomes pregnant.

Case 2: Diane, in her mid-20s, has been slightly depressed since the termination of her relationship with her boy friend. She had unintentionally become intoxicated at a party, and the alcohol caused her to behave out of character and she ended up having sex with a man she met at the party. The severe intoxication also caused her to forget her diaphragm and she became pregnant.

Both cases can be characterized as contraceptive failures: the first case is unforeseen and unexpected, whereas the second case is due to forgetfulness induced by intoxication. How should parental responsibility be determined in these two cases? Can it be assumed that Sarah is responsible for the failure of her contraceptive? Should Diane be held responsible for her intoxication? McEvoy believes that we need to have guidelines for determining and assessing responsibility in these more complex cases. Some would argue that a person who uses contraceptives has by that action expressed the intention not to produce offspring, so that any pregnancy due to contraceptive failure must be both unintended and unforeseen.[53] Likewise, Thomson would argue that since Sarah has taken the necessary and reasonable precautions to avoid pregnancy, she should not be held responsible for the failure of the contraception. Thomson uses the analogy of a burglar gaining entrance into a house after the homeowner opens a window for ventilation. She argues that the homeowner is not responsible for the burglar's entrance and that the burglar has no right to stay.[54] But it may be argued that the analogy is limited by the fact that the burglar actively takes advantage of the opened window to gain entrance into the house, whereas in a pregnancy due to contraception failure, the fetus does not take any active part to become a resident of the woman's womb.

Others contend that no contraceptive precaution is absolutely safe, and therefore users take for granted a certain degree of contraceptive failure. Hence, if the failure rates of contraceptives are made known and taken seriously, as they should be, then contraceptive failure cannot be considered as unforeseen and the consequence as without responsibility. Having made an effort to avoid a known consequence of one's action—with the full knowledge that the effort is not 100 percent foolproof—does not absolve one from responsibility for any unlikely consequence of the action. It is also important to emphasize the passive and dependent nature of the child in the mother's womb in order to see why the parents should assume responsibility for the act that leads to pregnancy due to contraceptive failure. Unlike the burglar who

---

[53]Winston, "Abortion and Parental Responsibility," p. 45.
[54]Thomson, "Defense of Abortion," p. 132.

actively enters the unguarded house, the fetus is made dependent on the woman through the sexual act she voluntarily performs. Sarah and her partner, therefore, have a specific duty to, and can be held responsible for, the pregnancy.

As for Diane's case, it would appear that one should be more sympathetic to her predicament since she becomes inebriated because she is depressed, which in turn contributes both to her having sexual intercourse with a stranger and to her forgetting to take the necessary precautions to avoid the consequence of such an action. Despite the sympathy one may feel for Diane, I am of the opinion that she remains responsible for her actions. Consider an analogous situation in which a business executive becomes drunk to relieve the pressures at work then proceeds to drive home in an inebriated state and causes an accident, damaging another car. Just as the executive is responsible for the damages incurred, so also is Diane responsible for the pregnancy. Simply because one can understand and sympathize with another's regrettable action does not mean that it is excusable and that its consequence and responsibility are absolvable. This is particularly true when removing the consequences entails taking a human life.

An even more pressing issue in parental responsibility is the male partner's role. As we have seen, issues such as women's equality and bodily autonomy have made the abortion decision into a woman's sole prerogative, leaving the male partner without any role or right in the decision-making. Some argue that if the male partner has neither rights nor responsibilities concerning the abortion decision, logically he has no responsibilities for the pregnancy. But does one necessarily follow from the other? Becoming pregnant and seeking abortion involve two separate acts. The action leading to pregnancy requires the participation of both the man and the woman. The fact that the woman alone is the "carrier" of the pregnancy and the one to decide whether to abort can provide no reason for reducing the man's responsibility, for he is an equal participant in the original action that lead to pregnancy. The fact that the man is physically more "detached" from the pregnancy may give him the illusion that he can avoid facing the consequences of his action, but he is nonetheless responsible. Child-support laws in most Western countries support this viewpoint by making the father financially responsible for his child.

An entirely new type of shared responsibility, which involves the scientific/medical community and the society, has been proposed by Christine Overall. Addressing the specific case of multiple pregnancies resulting from induced hyperovulation, she charges that the need for selective abortion has been created by the use of fertility drugs, often coupled with the technology of in vitro fertilization and embryo transfer, and yet the responsibility of choosing whether to abort some or carry all the fetuses is thrust upon the woman alone.

Overall instead blames the society and the scientific/medical community for construing infertility as a "problem" in the first place and for then pressuring women to undergo treatments to enhance fertility. For her, the debate over the responsibility for and the morality of selective abortion "exemplifies a classic no-win situation for women, in which medical technology generates a solution to a problem itself generated by medical technology."[55] Overall's argument implies that medical, technological and societal factors are themselves "responsible" to a large degree for these pregnancies, and the woman should not be asked to shoulder the responsibility alone.

Responsibility, Decision, Conscience and the Ethic of Personhood

I have already shown how the issue of maternal responsibility has been countered in two ways: either by claiming that the fetus is not a moral being (Tooley and Warren) and hence the mother is not responsible or by claiming that, regardless of fetal moral standing, the woman's right of bodily autonomy excuses her from any moral responsibility to continue the pregnancy (Thomson). Catriona Mackenzie rejects both Warren's and Thomson's arguments because, in her opinion, they concede too much at the outset to the conservative notion of responsibility. She distinguishes between moral and causal responsibility and then charges that the "conservative" notion of responsibility has conflated this distinction by assuming that because the woman is causally responsible for bringing a fetus into being, she is necessarily morally responsible to maintain the existence of the fetus.[56] In so doing, conservatives create a paradigm that is fundamentally oppressive to women. Instead, she contends that a true concept of responsibility starts with "decision responsibility," which takes into account the matrix of circumstances in which a woman finds herself when making a decision between abortion and maternity. Moral responsibility, asserts Mackenzie, cannot be construed simply and exclusively in terms of responsibility toward the fetus, no matter what its moral status is. Rather, moral responsibility has a wider focus—on the self, on relations with significant others, on a person's other commitments or projects. Given the matrix created by all these factors, the balance of individual responsibilities may well render a decision to abort as moral. In the framework of this matrix, according to this author, causal responsibility thus only has a potential to become moral responsibility.[57]

On this view, parental responsibility is a decision responsibility, and it arises

---

[55]Christine Overall, "Selective Termination of Pregnancy and Women's Reproductive Autonomy," *Hastings Center Report* 20 (May-June 1990): 8.
[56]Mackenzie, "Abortion and Embodiment," p. 139.
[57]Ibid., pp. 140-41.

only after the woman has chosen, within her own matrix, to assume that responsibility and to make a commitment to bring a future child into existence. When a woman decides to have an abortion, she has decided against such a commitment and responsibility.[58] In other words, parental responsibility is an assumed responsibility that is undertaken after the parents have balanced various factors and arrived at a reasoned decision. In Mackenzie's opinion, deciding against assuming parental responsibility does not necessarily mean that the mother has relinquished moral responsibility, for the decision against assuming parental responsibility may, under certain circumstances, be the most morally responsive and responsible course of action, depending on all the other factors the woman needs to consider. However, Mackenzie's argument raises an important question concerning the relation between the pregnant woman's decision matrix and her rights, which are grounded in an understanding of the woman as an autonomous, independent bearer of specific rights. I feel that it is incoherent to claim that the woman is dependent on a matrix of commitments when establishing her moral responsibility while simultaneously asserting that she is completely independent when it comes to assessing her rights. It would seem that the rights and responsibilities of a woman would have to cohere to a greater degree than this before this account of responsibility is acceptable.

I like to suggest that reproductive responsibility cannot be easily or adequately defined by an abstract ethical framework provided by the notions of causal, moral or decision responsibility without taking into consideration the reality of reproduction itself as a paradigm to serve as an ethical framework. Reproduction and pregnancy teach us that "we are born into some obligations and some are born to us"[59] and that our moral responsibility includes the necessary and enriching acceptance of these obligations, which are not entirely a matter of autonomous choice. By placing a premium on individual autonomy and active choice, liberals distort morality into becoming exclusively a matter of human agency and decisive action. As a result, "willing, planning, choosing one's moral commitments through the contracting of one's individual resources becomes the premier model of moral responsibility,"[60] and in so doing, procreation is turned into a contractual arrangement from which any woman may withdraw at will. But morality is never restricted to the contractual agreements of isolated individuals, and matters of procreation and parenting often entail involuntary relationships just by our being part of the interdependent human community. Indeed, true parenthood neither comes from free choice alone, nor is it something that is entirely determined by our responsibility. When par-

---

[58]Ibid., pp. 141-42.
[59]Ryan, "Argument for Unlimited Procreative Liberty," p. 10.
[60]S. Callahan, "Abortion and the Sexual Agenda," p. 235.

enthood is understood in light of true personhood, which is both autonomous and relational, we will find the proper synthesis of the two in which the woman freely chooses as a self-determinative agent to exercise responsibility in self-giving to relate to and to care for a new life, even when its presence may have been uninvited and unexpected. In so doing, the woman displays the highest human moral capacity and an expanded sense of responsibility. From this perspective, the question of assessing a woman's responsibility for her pregnancy is at most only partially relevant since moral acceptance includes acceptance both of those situations for which we are responsible and of those for which we are not.

Lastly, the reality of reproduction also teaches us that moral responsibility pertaining to matters of abortion or maternity is related more to conscience than to decisions. Wolf points out that abortion decisions are never pure, morally responsible decisions, as is often claimed by pro-choice advocates. Freedom to choose our responsibilities often means that we are free to choose them irresponsibly. Therefore true moral responsibility cannot occur without a significant role for personal conscience, something pro-choice advocates have failed to acknowledge. The reality of procreation belies the description of abortion as merely a personal decision, for it is really a matter of intense moral struggle with one's personal conscience: selflessness against selfishness and responsibility against irresponsibility.[61] Wolf rightly suggests that the only way to deal with the issue of conscience is within a framework of sin and redemption, which are ultimately understood as a broken relationship with God in the context of atonement, reconciliation and God's redemptive grace. To enter into the framework of sin and redemption, we must also recognize the evil of an abortion as it is: the death of an innocent human being. In terms of the ethic of personhood that I espouse, any claim of the pregnant woman's various rights, any assessment of the moral status of the fetus, any movement of the conscience to accept or to reject the expected or the unexpected pregnancy, and any exercise of the freedom to be responsible for the care of the fetus only make sense within the framework of a restored relationship with God and others. In other words, the woman's right to abort a fetus only acquires a true moral foundation of responsibility and conscience when one's own ethic of personhood regains a sense of integrity and wholeness.

---

[61]Wolf, "Our Bodies," pp. 32-34.

16

Moderation of the Extreme Positions via Re-evaluation of the Moral Status of the Fetus

*A*lternative **Biological Decisive Moments in Fetal Development**
Many writers are concerned that species membership as a criterion of moral standing for the fetus may be less than convincing because it is not easy to demonstrate a deep connection between the natural property of species membership and the possession of moral rights. For example, L. W. Sumner argues that at best, species membership can function only as an indicator of moral standing, but not as a criterion, because it has not exhibited any intrinsic relevancy to moral standing.[1] Robert Wennberg is essentially arguing for the same point, although his is cloaked in a religious garb. To these writers, other human characteristics—such as sentience, rationality, moral agency and so on—share a deeper connection with moral standing and hence are better criteria. In response to these criticisms, many conservatives begin to retreat from the extreme position that the acquisition of the human genome is the begin-

---

[1]L. W. Sumner, ed., *Values and Moral Standing,* vol. 8 of *Bowling Green Studies in Applied Philosophy* (Bowling Green, Ohio: Bowling Green State University Press, 1986), p. 92.

ning of a person with a right to life; they opt instead for other significant but less extreme "decisive moments" of personhood. The advantage of this move is that presumably the further one can push the moral threshold of the fetal life away from the time of fertilization, the greater the "window" one gains for the use of abortifacient contraceptives, embryo manipulation and abortion. The net result is a moderation of the conservative stance on the issues of abortion and artificial reproductive technologies. To this end, several biologically significant "decisive moments" in fetal development have been identified:

☐ the formation of the "primitive streak"
☐ the emergence of brain function
☐ the attainment of sentience
☐ the point of viability
☐ the actual birth

I have already discussed in some detail the debate on the significance of the "primitive streak" and conclude that although it is an important biologic landmark, it cannot be considered the decisive moment.[2] I will now review the other four "decisive moments" discussing the emergence of brain function and the attainment of sentience together, and the point of viability and the actual birth together, since these two pairs of concepts are quite closely related.

Emergence of Brain Function and Sentience as Decisive Moments

Emergence of the brain as the defining criterion for personhood has been most noticeably advocated by Baruch Brody in his important book *Abortion and the Sanctity of Human Life*.[3] Brody contends that the fetus acquires a moral right to life only when a functioning brain appears at about six weeks of gestation. As a typical "essentialist," he holds that any particular class of living being must possess certain essential characteristics to qualify for its membership, and the absence or loss of these traits will conversely disqualify membership. For human beings, he contends that brain function is that essential property.[4] He grounds his premise on the rationale that since total and irreparable cessation of brain function (brain death) is how the end of a human life is defined, then likewise the possession of a functioning brain should be the mark of a living human life. Since the brain of a six-week-old fetus is really only a potentially functioning brain, he compares it with an individual with reversible brain damage and argues that both have a right to life because both have brains with potential for normal functioning.

---

[2]See chapter two, "The Biological Dimension of Human Personhood," above.
[3]Baruch Brody, *Abortion and the Sanctity of Human Life: A Philosophical View* (Cambridge: MIT Press, 1975).
[4]Ibid., p. 108.

But it is difficult to see the relevancy of comparing a comatose person with reversible brain damage and a six-week-old fetus whose brain does not even have all the neuronal synaptic connections in place to perform any critical function at that stage of development. The brain emerges in preparation for the future maturation of the fetus into adulthood, when the human life reaches a level of complexity that requires the integrative function of the brain. In fact, it seems more convincing if the comparison is used to argue *against* the use of brain function as the definition of human life. As H. Tristram Engelhardt Jr. sees it, the brain function of a six-week-old fetus is a potentiality of an *abstract* nature whereas the brain function of a reversibly comatose person is concrete and belongs to a human life that has "already in the past developed into a full-blown human person."[5] When the reversibly comatose patient recovers, she will resume all the higher brain functions necessary for her personal existence, whereas the six-week-old fetus's brain merely indicates the potentiality to develop such integrative and personal functions and for some does not sufficiently meet the criterion for personhood. In short, in the case of a reversibly comatose person, the prospect of resuming the integrative and personal functions confers the right to life, rather than the potentiality for such functions conferring this right in a six-week-old fetus. Thus, the analogy between the reversibly comatose person and the six-week-old fetus breaks down.

Despite these weaknesses in the argument, Brody is not alone in employing a brain-function criterion for personhood. Hans-Martin Sass also sees great conceptual advantage in the "symmetry" between "brain life" and "brain death." He proposes a "Uniform Determination of Life Protection Act" to guarantee "the protection of human life from the presence of neuro-neuronal connections in the cortical plate zone, when personal life becomes imminent, to the absence of integrated brain functions, when somatic death becomes imminent."[6] He suggests that the beginning of brain life is present around the tenth week after conception; and he believes that with such a brain-life criterion, all other "moral criteria of differentiating between abortive, contraceptive, and contraimplantive techniques become irrelevant."[7] That is to say, before the tenth week of gestation, there is no moral difference between using the birth-control pill, using an IUD or having an abortion.

I believe that the fundamental weakness with the brain-life criterion is the

---

[5]H. Tristram Engelhardt Jr., "Viability, Abortion and the Difference Between a Fetus and an Infant," *American Journal of Obstetrics and Gynecology* 116 (June 1, 1973): 431.

[6]Hans-Martin Sass, "The Moral Significance of Brain-Life Criteria," in *The Beginning of Human Life,* ed. F. K. Beller and R. F. Weir (Boston: Kluwer Academic, 1994), p. 66; cf. Hans-Martin Sass, "Brain Life and Brain Death," *Journal of Medicine and Philosophy* 14 (February 1989): 45-49.

[7]Sass. "Moral Significance," p. 66.

incorrect assumption that brain function is the essential characteristic of a human being. A mature human being cannot lose brain function without ceasing to exist because the brain organizes all the other bodily organs and thus provides the crucial condition for the human organism to exist as an integrated whole. Hence the brain is required only after the human organism has reached a certain level of complexity. Up to the sixth or even the tenth week of gestation, the human organism is too immature to require brain functions for its maintenance. Thus, in the entire continuum of a human life, brain function is an essential function only for a mature human life but not a developing human life, and so it cannot be used to define the initiation of life. Furthermore, the so-called symmetry between "brain life" and "brain death" is more apparent than real, and it creates conceptual confusion rather than providing conceptual advantage. The function of the brain is asymmetrical for the beginning of life (as opposed to the end of life) of a human organism, and it does not cover the whole continuum of human life. Hence, brain function cannot be considered the essential characteristic for membership of the class of human being.

Another decisive moment for fetal personhood is the attainment of the brain-related capacity for sentience. The chief proponents of this view include L. W. Sumner, Samuel Gorovitz and Bonnie Steinbock.[8] Sumner calls sentience "a third way" of according moral right to life, in contradistinction to either species membership or rationality. He argues that if morality is a matter having to do with the promotion and protection of interests or welfare, then it deals exclusively with beings who are conscious or sentient, since only these beings can have desires that can be satisfied or frustrated and have the capacity to be benefited or harmed. This means that we owe moral duties only to sentient creatures. Since the animal kingdom is characterized by "a hierarchy of sentience," this position commits Sumner to a gradation of moral standing, from no moral standing granted to nonsentient beings, to maximum moral standing granted to a normal adult human being.[9]

Basing his conclusions on biological evidence for the neuromaturation of the human brain, Sumner judges that first-trimester fetuses are certainly not yet sentient, while third-trimester fetuses most probably possess some degree of sentience, with the threshold of sentience falling somewhat in the second semester. Even though Sumner admits that there may be a class of fetus around the threshold stage whose sentience and moral standing are difficult to determine, he is satisfied that a fetus is probably sentient by the end of the second

---

[8]See L. W. Sumner, *Abortion and Moral Theory* (Princeton: Princeton University Press, 1981); Samuel Gorovitz, *Doctors' Dilemmas: Moral Conflict and Medical Care* (New York: Oxford University Press, 1982); Bonnie Steinbock, *Life Before Birth: The Moral and Legal Status of Embryos and Fetuses* (New York: Oxford University Press, 1992).
[9]Sumner, *Abortion and Moral Theory*, p. 144.

trimester so that sentience and viability coincide roughly at the same time around the twenty-sixth week of gestation.[10] On this basis, Sumner ascribes moral standing to a third-trimester sentient fetus equal to that of a newborn infant; he equates all early abortions, done in the first trimester and early in the second trimester, with the use of contraception.[11] Similarly, Steinbock argues in favor of using sentience as a criterion for granting moral status to fetal life, arguing that before the fetus becomes conscious and sentient, it is incapable of experiencing pleasure and pain and has no interest in its continued existence, so therefore the presentient fetus is not being harmed by being killed.[12] Applying the same criterion, she contends that if it can be factually ascertained that anencephalic babies are totally lacking in conscious awareness and sentience, they are unable to be harmed and there is no good moral reason to prohibit harvesting their organs.[13] For Steinbock, the criterion of moral personhood is ultimately founded on *interest* as something worthy of protection and promotion: "The possession of interests is therefore a minimal condition for both rights and moral status."[14] Since interest is the object of a desire, which only a sentient being can have, it follows that only sentient beings can have interests.

One of the difficulties of using sentience/interest as a criterion of personhood and moral standing is the assumption that consciousness or some similar psychological faculty is a prerequisite for human personhood; I have already shown that this is mistaken.[15] Another faulty assumption inherent in assigning moral value to sentience is the implication that a particular thing is rendered "good" by the fact that it is desired.[16] But, in fact, whether the object of our desire—our interest—is intrinsically valuable or not is independent of our desire or preference. We may be desirous of something that is harmful to us, and we may reject something that is intrinsically good. The fetus cannot become "good" just because it is sentient or capable of desire or preference; and the sentience criterion cannot be used to exclude early fetuses from moral standing just because they have no desire.

Another weakness of the sentience criterion is the difficulty in its application. If one grants full and equal moral standing to all sentient beings, then there will be no moral difference between killing a mouse and killing a human being. But if we distinguish between the moral standing of mice and human

---

[10]Ibid., p. 150.

[11]Ibid., pp. 151-53.

[12]Steinbock, *Life Before Birth,* p. 24.

[13]Ibid., p. 35.

[14]Ibid., p. 10.

[15]See chapter three, "The Psychological Dimension of Human Personhood," above.

[16]Patrick Lee, *Abortion and Unborn Human Life* (Washington, D.C.: Catholic University of America Press, 1996), p. 53.

beings, then on what basis do we grant equal moral standing to viable fetuses in late pregnancy and mature human beings, since late-term fetuses are almost certainly less highly sentient than older human beings? This exposes yet another fundamental problem with the criterion of sentience: its failure to distinguish between a desirable quality possessed by a being and the intrinsic value of the being itself. A human being is an intrinsically valuable person who acquires varying degrees of sentience over the course of her development and cannot be equated to a sentient mouse, which is intrinsically less valuable. A late-term fetus who is less sentient than a fully developed adult possesses a moral standing equal to the adult's because they are both of equal intrinsic value. As I have discussed in the first section of this book, a substantial achiever has to be a substance before it achieves anything; the value of the substance is due to its intrinsic dignity and not the degree of its achievement. And as I shall discuss in connection with the "gradualist theory" later in this chapter, moral standing is not graduated proportionately to certain characteristics or qualities acquired, but instead is linked to the intrinsic value of the being itself. Sentience therefore cannot be the criterion of personhood or of the fetus's moral status.

Fetal Viability and Birth as Decisive Moments

Fetal viability is defined as the point at which the fetus can survive *ex utero* if necessary. At the popular level, it has enjoyed wide acceptance as the "decisive moment" at which the fetus acquires personhood and the right to life. The justices of the United States Supreme Court adopted this viewpoint in *Roe* v. *Wade* (1973) when they used fetal viability as the developmental watershed dividing fetuses that merit legal protection from those that do not. The Court justified its decision on the belief that at viability, the fetus presumably has the capability of meaningful life outside the mother's womb.[17] Many intuitively hold that if the fetus is not independently viable, then it has not acquired the intrinsic value to have the right to life.

Despite its wide popular appeal, this argument is beset by several problems. To begin with, it is not at all clear what sort of intrinsic value viability imparts to the fetus that it does not already possess. The ability to exist independently outside the womb seems to describe viability rather than explain its significance. As John Noonan puts it, "The unsubstantial lessening in dependence at viability does not seem to signify any special acquisition of humanity."[18] Besides, early fetuses are not the only category of human beings who are not

---

[17]*Roe v Wade*, 410 US 113 (1973), p. 163.
[18]John T. Noonan Jr., "An Almost Absolute Value in History," in *The Problem of Abortion*, ed. Joel Feinberg (Belmont, Calif.: Wadsworth, 1973), p. 10.

viable independently. Many acutely ill adult patients are dependent on both machines and other people to stay alive. In many ways they are hardly independent human beings; yet no one seems to want to claim that their intrinsic value as persons is compromised and that their right to life is diminished as a result. One may argue that fetal nonviability represents a dependence on someone's body, whereas an adult sick person is ultimately dependent on a machine. In this regard it is useful to recall that in some cases of conjoined twins, one twin is so dependent on the other twin's body for existence that once the twins are separated, the dependent twin will die. Yet no one would call one twin a person and the other a nonperson.[19] And if we adapt Judith Thomson's famous "plugged-in violinist" for use in the present context, we may consider a technically plausible scenario in which the violinist can only be kept alive by being plugged into someone else's body for a short time.[20] At that point, the violinist is also dependent on someone's body, but he is nonetheless a person with the right to life, even if his right to be plugged into someone's body may be denied.[21]

I believe that the link between fetal viability, fetal personhood and the right to life is a tenuous one. The fetus's physical dependency on the mother's body (which is normally granted) is not unique and has nothing to do with its personhood and right to life. To use fetal viability as a criterion for personhood is to confuse independence with distinctness[22] or to unjustifiably make the former a necessary condition for the latter. The fetus is no less distinct as an individual person and member of the human species just because he or she is not able to exist independently of another human being. Furthermore, fetal viability as a criterion is unreliable in defining fetal personhood, for medical technology is constantly pushing fetal viability to earlier and earlier stages of pregnancy, thus entailing a constant revision of the time when a fetus acquires personhood. Not many people would find it reasonable to link the attainment of human personhood to the advancement and availability of medical technology.

To get around these criticisms, Engelhardt proposes a social interpretation of what otherwise would be considered a purely biological concept of viability. He argues that by attaining viability and the ability to exist *ex utero,* the fetus changes its status to that of a "child," its "biological structure" is changed to a "social structure," and the maternal-fetal relationship is converted to a

[19]Richard Werner, "Abortion: The Ontological and Moral Status of the Unborn," *Social Theory and Practice* 3, no. 1 (1974): 201-22.

[20]Judith J. Thomson, "A Defense of Abortion," in *The Problem of Abortion,* ed. Joel Feinberg (Belmont, Calif.: Wadsworth, 1973).

[21]Jonathan Glover makes the same point using another analogy in his *Causing Death and Saving Lives* (New York: Penguin, 1977), pp. 124-25.

[22]Lee, *Abortion,* p. 73.

mother-child relationship. On this basis, he contends that "as soon as the fetus actualizes its potential viability, it can play a full social role and can be understood as a person."[23] In this new role, a personality can be "imputed," and there is a new moral obligation to the viable "child." Such a social understanding of viability, in Engelhardt's opinion,

> legitimizes both the permission of [aborting] the pre-viable fetus and the proscription of [aborting] the post-viable fetus, and preserves many of the social values which enhance the dignity of the human person . . . without recourse to metaphysical doctrines concerning human nature.[24]

While it is meritorious to conceive personhood in terms of sociality and relationality, Engelhardt's argument can be faulted for several reasons. In the first place, he does not say that the fetus becomes a person when it attains viability; in fact he repeatedly uses words and phrases such as *imputed to, construed as, understood as* and *acted upon as if it were* to convey the notions that the viable fetus is *not* a person in its own right and that its personal status is merely bestowed by the significant others around it. Personhood as a status bestowed goes against my understanding that human relations presuppose personhood rather than conferring it, and personhood entails an agreement between the fetus's parents, which is not always achieved.[25] In the second place, Engelhardt himself recognizes that as medical technology advances, viability becomes a moving target, with the result that the time at which the fetus is socialized to become a child is likewise a changing one. The only reason why this is not problematic for Engelhardt is that ultimately for him "the fetus has not yet actually achieved essentially human characteristics. . . . In any absolute sense, there is not yet a *rational* animal on hand."[26]

In many ways, Engelhardt's arguments are more applicable to the moral significance of birth than to the concept of viability. Birth is an important milestone in the development of a human being, and even though it does not represent a critical leap in the physiological maturation of the fetus such that it carries the fetus beyond a certain significant moral threshold, its moral significance is not to be underestimated for several reasons. First, in countries that follow the English common law, birth endows the human individual with the standing of a legal person. Second, it represents a significant stage of fetal growth, marking the fetus's readiness to move from an in utero habitat to the outside of the womb. It marks the end of the fetus's unique dependence on

---

[23]Engelhardt., "Viability," p. 432.
[24]Ibid., p. 433.
[25]Germain Grisez, "When Do People Begin?" *Proceedings of the American Catholic Philosophical Association* 63 (1989): 28.
[26]Engelhard, "Viability," p. 433.

the mother as a biologically inseparable organic unity and the beginning of
other forms of social dependency. Third, birth marks the beginning of the
infant's existence as a socially recognizable and responsive member of a
human community. From that moment on, he can be heard, seen, touched,
dressed, cared for and truly be known. Birth constitutes a quantum leap in
social bonding and enables the human being to engage in an exclusive human
network that reaches beyond his mother.[27] Through birth, the infant becomes a
biologically and socially separate human being, even though many philosophers are still not prepared to grant him the full moral standing of a person.

Like Engelhardt, Mary Ann Warren may be credited for being sensitive to
the social nature of persons and for recognizing the moral significance of the
birth event. But her most pressing underlying motive to upgrade the moral
status of the "birthed" infant—even at the price of increasing the moral culpability of infanticide—is to safeguard the woman's autonomous right to abortion, even late abortions. As she admits, "The presumption that being born
makes no difference to one's moral rights creates problems for the liberal
view of abortion."[28] Hence, assigning moral significance to the event of birth
avoids the undesirable move to retreat to a moderate position on abortion.
But Warren does not believe that the event of birth changes any of the
infant's intrinsic property so as to give him a stronger right to life; and as we
have seen, Warren considers infanticide as humanitarian when committed
under harsh economic conditions.[29] In sum, despite the feeble attempts she
makes to assign some moral significance to the event of birth, her conclusion
is not too different from Sumner's verdict that "birth is a shallow and arbitrary
criterion of moral standing."[30] In my assessment, birth is a milestone in a person's development of his relational network, which represents a significant
actualization of the human being's personhood, although it is not itself a criterion of personhood.

The Modified Use of Rationality as a Criterion of Human Personhood

As we have seen, the conservatives have been challenged to grant moral standing to fetuses only in virtue of their possession of certain characteristics instead
of by arbitrarily connecting species membership to their moral right to life.
One of the more unexpected moves conservatives make is to resort to the use
of a modified form of rationality as the criterion of personhood, a criterion that

---

[27]Loren E. Lomansky, "Being a Person—Does It Matter?" in *The Problem of Abortion,* ed. Joel
Feinberg (Belmont, Calif.: Wadsworth, 1973), quoted in Mary Ann Warren, "The Moral Significance of Birth," *Hypatia* 4 (Fall 1989): 56.

[28]Warren, "Moral Significance," pp. 48-49.

[29]Ibid., p. 54.

[30]Sumner, *Abortion and Moral Theory,* p. 53.

is also used by most extreme liberals to exclude fetuses and infants as persons with a right to life. To avoid reaching a conclusion similar to the liberals', conservatives appeal to two arguments that they hope will circumvent some of these conceptual difficulties: a natural-kind argument and the closely related argument involving the notion of potentiality.

The Natural-Kind Argument

Briefly stated, the principle underlying this argument is this: "If respect is owed to beings because they are in a certain state, it is owed to whatever, by its very nature, develops into that state."[31] In other words, because normal mature human adults are rational beings that merit moral standing, similar moral standing should be extended to other members of the same "natural kind" regardless of whether these other members are themselves rational, partially rational or not rational at all. Fetuses, infants, the profoundly retarded and the irreversibly comatose are thus permitted to "ride the moral coattails of the paradigm rational being."[32] It matters not that a fetus is considerably less rational than a mature dog, for the fetus acquires moral standing by being a creature of a rational nature. While the natural-kind argument cleverly avoids using membership of the human species as a criterion of moral standing, the end result is that being human is nevertheless sufficient for such moral standing. The main problem with this argument is that, in the final analysis, nonrational human beings are given moral standing essentially because they have a resemblance to rational human beings. But it remains unclear why that resemblance should count for more than the difference that exists between rational and nonrational human beings. Further, one may argue that rational human beings and nonhuman rational beings also exhibit a significant resemblance, and it is not easy to see why their resemblance does not count morally.

The Potentiality Argument

The potentiality argument[33] says that if the possession of a certain characteristic or property (e.g., self-consciousness) endows any "organism" with a serious right to life, then any organism potentially possessing this characteristic or property has a serious right to life even now.[34] In other words, a right to life is possessed not only by persons but by all who in the course of the normal

---

[31]Alan Donagan, *The Theory of Morality* (Chicago: University of Chicago Press, 1977), p. 171.
[32]Sumner, ed., *Values and Moral Standing*, p. 97.
[33]Please refer to chapter six, "The Temporal and Eschatological Dimensions of Human Personhood," where I have addressed the concept of potentiality in some detail. Here I shall develop this theme in the context of abortion.
[34]Philip E. Devine, *The Ethics of Homicide* (Ithaca: Cornell University Press, 1978), p. 94.

unfolding of their intrinsic potential will become persons. Unlike the natural-kind argument, the potentiality argument does not extend moral standing to the boundaries of the human species. Being human is not sufficient for having moral standing; one has to have a potential for the morally relevant property of being human in order to merit the right to life. And according to the potentiality argument (in contrast to the natural-kind argument), if one takes rationality as a criterion of personhood, the irreversibly comatose and the severely retarded will not be granted a right to life. For this reason, conservatives rely increasingly on fetal potentiality in their treatment of abortion because it allows them to take a more moderate position—allowing for the abortion of the severely retarded and the anencephalic—while prohibiting abortion of the fetus with normal potentials.

Two criticisms have been raised against such use of the potentiality principle. First, if we suppose that rationality is the criterion of moral standing, and thus it is an intrinsic good that should be promoted and protected, the principle of potentiality does not distinguish whether it seeks to preserve the quality of rationality or it wants to protect the potential individual rational life. If it is the former, it would follow that even actually or potentially rational beings may be sacrificed as long as such a course of action can be shown to maximize rationality. In other words, conservatives who espouse the potentiality principle would have to prove that they in fact value the potential person more than the potential quality the potential person bears—a proof that is not provided by the principle itself. Thus the potentiality principle will only serve to moderate the conservative view of abortion with considerable moral risk.[35] The second criticism, which may be considered a *reductio ad absurdum,* claims that when the potentiality principle is carried to its logical extreme, human sperms and ova effectively become potential persons, rendering contraception just as morally wrong as abortion is. Hence, contraception becomes a form of homicide, and in this case the potentiality argument fails to make a moral distinction between contraception and abortion.[36] However, it is possible to dismiss this second criticism by showing that it confuses the notion of "potential person" with "person with potential," which I have discussed earlier. If the fetus as a "potential person" is understood as a "person with potential," then there is no way to see the sperm and ovum as "potential persons." A fetus is a person with potential that will be actualized in its normal course of development; but the sperm and ovum are not "potential persons" in this sense because sperms and

---

[35]Compare Michael Wreen, "The Possibility of Potentiality," in vol. 8 of *Bowling Green Studies in Applied Philosophy,* ed. L. W. Sumner (Bowling Green, Ohio: Bowling Green State University Press, 1986), pp. 140-41.

[36]Sumner, *Abortion and Moral Theory,* pp. 104-5.

ova will never develop into persons on their own. The sperm and the ovum, however, do have the potentiality to be fused together in the process of fertilization to become a "person with potential" in the form of a zygote.

Some Christian writers who generally take a conservative stand on the issue of abortion appear to espouse the potentiality argument with enthusiasm. In broad terms, they find the principle supported by the biblical tradition as well as a number of Judeo-Christian theological themes. Specifically it is believed that the argument captures the moral perspectives embedded in such concepts as life as a gift and a trust from the creator God who has a divine intention to see the biological human that he has created become a full personal human being with rational, moral and spiritual capacities. Yet the way the potentiality argument has been used by these Christian writers is too uncritical and often mistaken. For example, Christian ethicist Lewis Smedes apparently embraces the principle because of its ability to portray the dynamic aspect of fetal development: "Growth into personhood is dynamic, gradual, complex; its beginning is obscure."[37] He feels that the early fetus up to less than six weeks is sufficiently removed from later stages of development that it cannot be considered a person,[38] although he concedes that even as a potential person in the process of becoming a person, it is "a genuine being in its own right, not just a piece of its hostess' tissue," and should not be aborted without a good reason.[39] Here Smedes has apparently contradicted the argument of the potentiality principle enunciated by Alan Donagan, whom he quotes: "If respect is owed to beings because they are in a certain stage, it is owed to whatever by its nature develops into that state."[40] Donagan's axiom is usually understood to mean that if personhood is owed to a mature human being, it is also owed to a fetus whose nature it is to develop into the same. Given this definition, it is difficult to see how a normal fetus less than six weeks old can be excluded. Due to this misinterpretation of the principle of potentiality, Smedes defines the fetus as a mere potential person rather than an actual person and suggests that the pregnant woman's welfare might be weightier than the welfare of the early fetus.[41] While I do not discount the possibility that the pregnant woman's welfare may in rare circumstances justify an abortion, I do not believe that this justification should come by denying personhood to the early fetus, and it is mistaken to do so on the basis of the principle of potentiality.

D. Gareth Jones is another Christian writer who also believes the potentiality principle is an option for Christians because it treats the developmental

---

[37]Lewis Smedes, *Mere Morality* (Grand Rapids, Mich.: Eerdmans, 1983), p. 137.
[38]Ibid., p. 134.
[39]Ibid., p. 132.
[40]Ibid., p. 133.
[41]Ibid., p. 134.

continuum of the fetus with utter seriousness and, on that basis, he claims for the fetus a right to life and respect.[42] But Jones goes on to say that the fetus's right is only proportional to its stage of fetal development because "the probability of an older fetus becoming an actual person is much greater than that of a very early embryo becoming a person."[43] Here, Jones (like Smedes) is treating the fetus as an entity that has yet to become a person. His misinterpretation of the potentiality principle is responsible for yet another misunderstanding: that the principle "is prepared to assess fetal capabilities in terms of the extent of its biological development,"[44] which I do not believe the principle intends to do. I believe that the application of the principle must avoid the potential/actual dichotomy that the principle seeks to refute. In terms of personhood and the moral right to life, the potential is the actual.

The Gradualist Theory

It seems likely that one source of this misunderstanding is the writers confusing the potentiality principle with the so-called gradualist theory, which in turn makes use of a proportionality principle. The gradualist theory holds that the personhood or the moral worth of the fetus is proportional to the gradual actualization of certain potentialities relevant to the determination of moral worth or personhood. For example, Sumner argues that since the fetus only gradually actualizes its potentiality of sentience, it only gradually attains full personhood and full moral standing. He then concludes that the fetus has no moral standing at all before the first trimester since it is pre-sentient, and from the end of the first trimester to term, as the fetus gradually acquires increasing degrees of sentience, it acquires a proportional increment of moral right to life.[45] The gradualist theory is essentially a pragmatic position based on the intuition that (1) a late abortion is more serious morally and requires a stronger justification than an earlier one and (2) killing infants is seriously objectionable. A fetus's right to life would thus be a matter of degree of fetal development, and the fetus's claim to life must be increasingly respected as its unique biological potential unfolds.

Support for this gradualist theory is strong partly because it seems to fit our common moral intuition and partly because rights are usually conceptualized as a matter of degree. Individuals acquire a particular right when they satisfy

---

[42]D. Gareth Jones, *Brave New People: Ethical Issues at the Commencement of Life* (Downers Grove, Ill.: InterVarsity Press, 1984), p. 164.

[43]Ibid., p. 163.

[44]Ibid.

[45]L. W. Sumner, "A Third Way," in *The Problem of Abortion,* ed. Joel Feinberg (Belmont, Calif.: Wadsworth, 1973), pp. 71-93.

the relevant criterion; some individuals may have more right than others, and those who no longer satisfy the criterion may lose the right. Applying this theory to human development, an embryo that has not developed the physiological basis for personal life has minimal or no right to life; a near-term fetus would have more right to life than a second-trimester fetus, an infant more than a prenatal fetus, and an older child more than an infant. It is important to note that this increasing right to life is linked to the increasing physical or psychological maturation of the fetus in the course of its prenatal development.

At this point we begin to see how the potentiality principle may be confused with the gradualist theory's claim that as the fetus's biological and psychological potential unfolds and matures, its claim to life should be increasingly respected. Even if we regard the fetus as a potential person rather than as a person with potential, the potentiality of the fetus still only refers to its inherent capacity to develop into a person, and as such, it does not admit of degrees. The actualization of the capacity may come in increments, but the capacity itself is a matter of either all or none. If potential personhood refers to this capacity, then the principle of potentiality does not lead to the conclusion that personhood comes in degrees. As I have alluded to earlier, it is not the characteristic itself that is intrinsically valuable; rather, what is intrinsically valuable is the organism itself. So even if we accept rationality or sentience as the criterion of personhood, it is the person who is intrinsically valuable and not sentience or rationality per se. To allow degrees of moral standing and the fractionalization of personhood is to fail to see that what is intrinsically valuable and what has moral worth is the human being who possesses the potentiality for a certain characteristic (sentience, rationality and so on). In other words, the embryo/fetus is not merely instrumentally valuable as a vehicle or recipient of what is of value; rather, the embryo/fetus is intrinsically valuable as the bearer of the potentiality of some worthy characteristics. An embryo, a second-trimester fetus and a neonate all possess the same potentiality for personhood and, on that criterion, the same right to life.

Robert Wennberg also discusses this gradualist theory in his book *Life in the Balance* and appears to see considerable merit in it. In the first place, he is impressed by the theory because it is in agreement with most people's intuitive beliefs that an older child or adult would have a stronger right to life than a fetus or an infant because people detect personal life in the former but not in the latter.[46] He apparently agrees with this popular but mistaken feeling. Writing in a Christian context, he recognizes that in order to adopt this gradualist position, he needs to get around the principle of potentiality and the "individ-

---

[46]Robert Wennberg, *Life in the Balance: Exploring the Abortion Controversy* (Grand Rapids, Mich.: Eerdmans, 1985), pp. 115-16.

ual-specific" divine intention in the creation of human life, both of which are at odds with any notion of degree of moral standing or right to life. To get around the divine intention of creating life, he uses an analogy of someone who first intends to plant a tree and then "kills" the tree at different stages of its subsequent development: as a seed, a seedling and a sapling. He argues that having an original intention does not necessarily commit one never to thwart the execution of the intention even if it has already been initiated.[47] What is important to realize is that one needs increasingly stronger reasons to justify abandoning the original intention. He specifically believes that "the category of intention" is compatible with the notion of degrees of right and wrong,[48] and he sees nothing wrong with invoking the divine intention of creating life as a moral category while simultaneously adopting a gradualist position to justify some first-trimester abortions. What Wennberg fails to see is the obvious limitation of his analogy: the person who intends to plant the tree and subsequently "kills" it is the same person, whereas in abortion, it is God who intends to create life and the human being who determines the degrees of personhood and terminates the nascent life. The analogy has thus not provided the argument needed to harmonize the divine intention of creating and the human action of aborting lives.

With regard to the principle of potentiality, Wennberg apparently recognizes that potentiality is something inherent in human nature and does not admit of degrees. In this regard, he cannot be said to have confused the principle of potentiality with the gradualist principle. He acknowledges that "a full-term infant, a six-month-old fetus, and a newly fertilized ovum all possess the same potentiality for personhood; none possesses it less and none possesses it more."[49] To get around the incompatibility between the notion of potentiality and degrees of moral standing, Wennberg needs to find what he considers to be a "nonmoral" variable that admits degrees, in order to gauge "the *increasing* strength of a fetus's claim to life." He finds that "nonmoral property" in the physiological development and maturation of the fetal brain and central nervous system, which he believes can be quantifiably assessed in degrees and correlated to the fetus's moral standing and right to life. Furthermore, he reassures us that one need not fear that "emphasizing the biological maturation of the fetus as the crucial nonmoral property would in any way entail abandoning the concept of potentiality, for where no natural potential for personhood exists, no special status can exist either."[50] Here by "natural potential" Wenn-

---

[47]Ibid., p. 115.
[48]Ibid., p. 114.
[49]Ibid., pp. 116-17.
[50]Ibid., p. 117.

berg is referring to "the biological basis for a personal being," and he sees the gradualist theory as serving the function of linking the incremental maturation of "the unique *biological* potential" to an increasing degree of right to life. In other words, without denying that human potentiality confers the fetus with personhood and a right to life, the gradualist theory "simply adds the further claim that as the unique *biological* potential unfolds and takes shape, this claim to life must be increasingly respected."[51]

I find the last claim rather problematic. In the first place, Wennberg believes that this theory enables him to morally justify some abortions.[52] So the theory does not take on the positive connotation that "life must be increasingly respected"[53] as Wennberg has wished; on the contrary, since what can be increased can also be decreased, the theory in fact supports the position that the right to life can be so diminished at some stages of fetal development that abortion is justifiable. At a more fundamental level, Wennberg's approval of the gradualist theory is based on several flawed assumptions. First, he assumes that fetuses are potential persons rather than persons with potentials. I have already discussed the difficulties with such a notion of potential person. Second, he assumes that the biological maturation of the fetus is in the realm of "nonmoral property," a concept he never elaborates or justifies. If by "nonmoral property" he simply means a biological variable that is accessible to quantitative assessment, I may find it acceptable. But he goes on to state that "the nonmoral property . . . cannot be a potentiality for personhood,"[54] implying that biological maturation is unrelated to human potentiality and personhood. This is perhaps the fundamental flaw in Wennberg's account of personhood. Taking rationality as the ultimate criterion of attaining personhood, what Wennberg values is the property of rationality itself rather than the human being with the potentiality for rationality. For him, the various stages of the fetus's biological development are only the means for the development of that which is truly valuable: that is, the rationality of the person. Meanwhile, the embryo, fetus or infant is at best a vehicle or recipient of this intrinsically valuable property. I have argued that if the physical organism itself is intrinsically valuable as the substantial pole of the human being, then it is so from the time it begins to be, not just from when it acquires a property such as rationality. It is quite obvious that the reason Wennberg chooses brain development as the unique biological nonmoral property to apply the gradualist theory is that it is the biological substrate for rationality and other related mental activities, which are his key defin-

---

[51]Ibid.
[52]Ibid., p. 115.
[53]Ibid., p. 117.
[54]Ibid.

ing characteristics of human personhood. But by calling his account "the gradualist variant of the potentiality principle,"[55] he artificially conflates the two principles to serve his purpose and, in the process, confuses them.

Further, Wennberg's account of the gradualist theory cannot be consistently employed to gauge the fetus's and the infant's right to life. Since neonates and infants do not acquire the capacities for personal agency for up to at least two years, the consideration of degree in the claim to the right to life ought to continue in the postnatal period if the gradualist theory is to be held consistently. This point has been emphasized by Philip Devine, who asserts that "if personhood or humanity admits of degrees before birth, then it would seem it must admit of degrees after birth as well. . . . But few would hold and fewer still teach that a ten-year-old child can be killed on lighter grounds than an adult."[56] In a somewhat surprising move, for the period of infancy in which the infant is still "subpersonal" (to use Wennberg's term), he abandons the development of the brain and the central nervous system as a gauging device and switches to "personal characteristics."[57] He does not tell his readers exactly what these "personal characteristics" are and how they are to be measured, nor does he explain why the development of the brain and the central nervous system can no longer be the standard in the postnatal period. Here Wennberg falls back on the common moral intuition that "indeed, by the time of birth, the infant's claim to a right to life is so strong and the occasions for a serious conflict of rights so rare . . . that talk of degrees of a right to life has no real practical import."[58] But this does not really avoid the inescapable conclusion of the gradualist theory that a one-year-old infant who does not have the capacity for personal life has a lesser claim to life than a four-year-old child. Wennberg in fact believes that this is consistent with our moral instinct that a ten-year-old child has a greater claim to life than an infant with emerging personhood, and the infant has more than a neonate totally devoid of personal characteristics. In Wennberg's view, these counterexamples do not weaken the gradualist theory but provide support for it.[59]

Potentialist, Gradualist and Rationalist Accounts and the Ethic of Personhood

It is apparent that the main problem with many conservatives' attempt to moderate their account of fetal status is their insistence on retaining the choice of rationality as a natural human property that confers moral standing and, in the case

---

[55]Ibid., p. 112.

[56]Devine, *Ethics of Homicide*, pp. 79-80.

[57]Wennberg, *Life in the Balance*, p. 116.

[58]Ibid., p. 119.

[59]Ibid., pp. 118-19.

of conservative Christians' attempts, the choice of a rationalistic account of the image of God as the basis of human personhood. In contrast to the account of personhood I propose here, the conservatives' argument maintains that a human being is not a person until it displays rational capacity, which then confers a right to life. I have shown that no matter how one understands rationality, it is a set of abilities: consciousness, self-consciousness, language use, beliefs and so on. Obviously not all members of the human species have achieved rationality. Fetuses and infants have not yet achieved it; the severely retarded will never achieve it; and the irreversibly comatose have both achieved and lost it. By choosing rationality as a criterion of moral standing, many human beings—including fetuses and infants—are excluded from having a right to life. I have shown in earlier chapters that liberals such as Michael Tooley, Mary Ann Warren and Peter Singer use traits and activities related to rationality as a standard of personhood to exclude fetuses from claiming a right to life; it is therefore quite surprising to see so many conservatives embrace the same Enlightenment sentiment by adopting the same criterion. Perhaps their intention is to preserve a special status for human beings—an intention that betrays a trace of speciesism, screening out other animal species. But even this purpose is not well served because as I have noted above, other beings such as apes, dolphins and whales certainly possess a level of rationality not readily distinguishable from human beings'. At any rate, as far as humans are concerned, this choice will make it difficult for proponents to extend moral standing to a large number of human beings because rational abilities are typically achieved only at a relatively advanced stage of human development. As I have shown, the potentiality-cum-gradualist principle is a rather ill-fated attempt to rescue developing fetuses and infants. Further, the so-called overflow principle, which states that "respect for persons also extends . . . to things closely associated with persons,"[60] is sometimes invoked to provide some right to life to those who are severely retarded or irreversibly comatose. But just as the gradualist theory enables its proponents to allow a gradation of rights to life from an early conceptus to an adult person, so too the "overflow" principle accomplishes nothing more than a token service in granting a minimal amount of respect to the severely retarded, which will be "less than what we would give a person (or potential person) and more than we would give a mere animal."[61] One can see that the embarrassing positions are unavoidable if one decides to constrain oneself by employing rationality as a standard for moral standing and by needing to establish degrees of right to life as a pragmatic approach to solve moral dilemmas.

Smedes also argues that the fetus only acquires an increasing right to life

---

[60]Devine, *Ethics of Homicide,* p. 101.
[61]Wennberg, *Life in the Balance,* p. 105.

as it matures, although he does not mean that anyone can freely kill a fetus that is several weeks old. Rather, he is using the notion of the fetus's potential personhood, however incorrectly constructed, to enable a moderate position on abortion. This means that in the event that the mother's needs conflict with the fetus's, the maternal needs cannot be dismissed. Smedes specifically considers that such a modified understanding of the fetus's moral status will enable society to deal with exceptional circumstances, such as pregnancies that result from rape or incest, as well as several extreme but not uncommon social hardships. He cites the example of a pregnant woman who has severe chronic debilitating asthma, who is raising four children, who is married to an unsympathetic and unemployed alcoholic and who requests to have an abortion. He makes a plea that the mother's circumstances should be seriously considered.[62]

I believe that human life is not absolute and inviolable and that not even the fetus has an unqualified right to protection. If one gives consideration to the mother because one is genuinely interested in her very desperate situation, then I agree with Smedes that it would be morally irresponsible to refuse any consideration of her needs and rights. But I do not agree that the considerations given to the mother should be either correlated to an agnosticism toward the fetal personhood or accomplished through an unjustified modification (reduction) of fetal personhood. These are obviously major influences in Smedes's mind when he says that

> growth into personhood is dynamic, gradual, complex; its beginning is *obscure.* Over against uncertainty about the fetus, we weigh the certainty of misery and pain for the living persons who would be driven to desperate disadvantage by the birth of the child. . . . May it ever be God's will that a mother abort a fetus?[63]

While Smedes can be applauded for his tender sensitivity and his desire to consider pragmatic factors beyond the fetus itself, there is room for improvement in this anthropology of agnosticism and uncertainty. As we will see in the next chapter, the ethic of personhood I espouse allows for a flexibility that in extremely difficult situations, such as the example raised by Smedes, the pregnant woman's circumstances need to be considered even while we grant the fetus the right to life. For the ethic of personhood recognizes that the pregnant woman's responsibilities to herself and her family are generally less weighty when compared to the moral value of her unborn child, yet it also realizes that these responsibilities need not be trivialized, just as the value of the fetal life need not be absolutized.

---

[62]Smedes, *Mere Morality,* p. 135.
[63]Ibid., p. 137.

17

Consideration of
Pragmatic Factors

*A*bortion as a Multifaceted Decision-Making Process

Daniel Callahan has criticized the narrow focus of the ongoing abortion debate for having exclusively focused on the fetal right to life against the maternal right to self-determination, and he has argued that the morality of abortion must include a consideration of the social factors surrounding the pregnancy. Tracing the history of the movement to legalize abortion from the 1950s to the late 1960s, he observes that the "pro-choice" movement was based on several contentions apart from the woman's right to choose an abortion. For example, people were concerned with the adverse effects of illegal abortions on women's health, the unavailability or ineffectiveness of contraceptives, the economic and domestic circumstances that may force women into unwanted pregnancies as well as the effect of unwanted children on the welfare of both women and children alike.[1]

In contrast, since the early 1970s (especially after the *Roe* v. *Wade* decision), the pro-choice movement was forced into a defensive position involving an ideological shift from the original arguments for social reform to an exclusive emphasis and focus on the woman's right to choose.[2] This shift was primarily due to the emergence of a politically strong, well-organized and well-financed

---

[1] Daniel Callahan, "An Ethical Challenge to Prochoice Advocates: Abortion and the Pluralistic Proposition," *Commonweal* 117 (November 1990): 682.

[2] Daniel Callahan, "The Abortion Debate: Can This Chronic Illness Be Cured?" *Clinical Obstetrics and Gynecology* 35, no. 4 (1992): 785-86.

"pro-life" movement, which has successfully focused on the moral status of the fetus.[3] For example, in the contemporary pro-choice argument, little or nothing is said anymore about the social harms of unwanted pregnancies, about the terrible or tragic choice posed by an abortion or about the moral nature of that choice. Further, practically nothing is said about the need to reduce the number of abortions. As a pro-choice advocate, Callahan finds this ideological shift alarming because it has the net effect of reducing the moral issue of abortion to the pregnant woman's right to choice and her process of choosing, at the expense of the moral content of the choice. Callahan asks, "Is every abortion choice equally justifiable? Are there no moral standards for the making of such choices?"[4] On the other hand, the Christian conservatives' exclusive focus on the fetal right to life also allows the Christian community to overlook the oppressive social factors affecting pregnant women and the Christian community's responsibility to directly participate in their relief. I believe that one abortion choice is not as equally unjustifiable as another, given the unique circumstances of each pregnancy; and the Christian community had best ask itself what responsibility it is prepared to bear—other than pointing out the absolute wrongness of any abortion.

It is true that the public generally supports legal abortion; but when confronted with a specific abortion decision, people are still concerned with the precise particular circumstances involved. For example, a general consensus may be easily reached in favor of an abortion when the mother's life is endangered by the pregnancy; a more reserved acceptance is likely when the pregnancy is the result of rape or incest or due to extremely harsh economic or social reasons. But when an abortion is being considered as an alternative to contraception or simply for convenience, the acceptability is drastically reduced. For this reason, the public has never been unambiguously pro-choice or pro-life, because in the public mind the distinction between a general support of legal abortion and the morally justifiable reasons for a particular case of abortion must be maintained and not be casually dismissed.[5]

This qualified acceptance of abortion has been shared by many writers in the abortion debate. L. W. Sumner is rightly critical of both the extreme conservative and the extreme liberal views precisely because of the inherent reductionism with which they treat a complex issue. The "simplicity" of these views may have made them more readily comprehensible and marketable in the public forum, but this simplicity "deprives us of our familiar reference points in the

---

[3]See, e.g., G. R. Dunstan and M. J. Seller, *The Status of Human Embryos: Perspectives from Moral Tradition* (London: Oxford University Press, 1988).
[4]Callahan, "Abortion Debate," p. 786.
[5]Ibid.

abortion landscape."[6] Consequently, in my opinion, it is wrong to assume a simple solution for a problem as complex as abortion. We need a view of abortion that is responsive to all of the elements involved in the situation: the moral status of the fetus, the rights of the pregnant woman and any morally relevant pragmatic social factors. In any serious case of abortion, these elements will converge to render the problem perplexing and divisive. We need to be reminded that "only complex views do justice to abortion."[7] In turn, acknowledging that abortion is a multifaceted decision-making process means deciding the morality of abortion only on a case-by-case basis, even if all cases are to be mourned and repented. If we want to preserve the status of abortion as a serious moral issue and reach a just decision for each individual abortion choice, we must weigh the various factors present in each case, adopt a nuanced position that is willing to make some distinctions among and between reasons for abortion, and resist the temptation to find a simple formula that will outweigh the various factors involved. Among the various types of requests for abortion, perhaps the most traumatic cases are those involving rape and incest. Here is a good example in which the pragmatic factors are so strong that any simplified generalization to deny abortion is itself morally in question.

Pregnancy Due to Rape

Abortion in the case of pregnancy due to rape is unique not only because the pregnancy is one the woman has not voluntarily participated in, but also because rape is such a violent act that it often causes emotional harms which can take a lifetime to heal. The full horror is exemplified in the following case.

A twelve-year-old girl moved with her family from India to Sterling Heights, Michigan.[8] After she visited a doctor in the spring of 1998 for what had earlier been diagnosed as digestive problems, it was discovered she was twenty-seven weeks pregnant. The girl later confessed in court papers that her seventeen-year-old brother had raped her the previous winter. Her family prepared to take her to Kansas for an abortion, as Michigan prohibits abortions after the twenty-fourth week. However, the family-court authorities in Michigan intervened and removed her from her parents' custody, on the basis that the girl sharing a room and a bed with her elder brother constituted abuse. The girl's doctor argued in court that she could face physical and mental complications were the pregnancy allowed to proceed and that there was a high probability the baby would be born with genetic abnormalities. As a result, the prosecu-

---

[6]L. W. Sumner, *Abortion and Moral Theory* (Princeton: Princeton University Press, 1981), p. 124.

[7]Ibid, p. 73.

[8]Suzanne Siegel and Bill Roy, "Youth, Incest and Abortion," *Newsweek*, August 10, 1998, p. 52.

tors withdrew the charge and the girl underwent a partial-birth abortion in Wichita, Kansas, on July 1, 1998.

Four reasons have been advanced by liberals to justify abortion in these difficult cases:

☐ to redress an act of grave injustice by removing the "product" of the unjust act

☐ to repel the fetus as an aggressor against the woman's integrity

☐ to uphold a woman's right to abort a fetus she has not voluntarily conceived

☐ to safeguard the mental health of the pregnant woman

I will consider each of these arguments in turn.

With respect to the first argument favoring the removal of the product of the unjust act, there is no question that a woman who is raped and becomes pregnant is a victim of a horribly unjust crime of violence, so that the situation often evokes emotions of revenge and hatred. For this reason alone, rapists are punishable by death in some jurisdictions.[9] Hence, it would be insensitive, to say the least, to charge the woman and her family of harboring unjustified emotions. Although these feelings of revenge are entirely understandable, a distinction should still be made between the fetus and the act through which the fetus is conceived. The fetus is certainly the product of a violent and unjust act of crime, but it is as innocent as the pregnant mother. There is nothing violent, unjust or criminal about the fetus's existence. Consequently, it is not easy to see how the injustice of the original rape crime can be removed or redressed by killing an innocent human being with a right to life. An act of rape simply cannot be erased by committing a second unjust act—abortion. And just because the rape victim has been unjustly violated, she is not morally justified in then unjustly violating an innocent third party, even when the third party happens to be the product of the first violent act. It simply is not just.

The second argument in favor of repelling the fetus-aggressor operates on a self-defense rationale against the fetus. However, as with the previous argument, the innocence of the fetus refutes the suggestion that it is an aggressor that deserves to be expelled from the mother's womb. The fetus may have come about through the act of an aggressor, but is not itself an aggressor, and an abortion on this basis is an unjust and immoral act against an innocent human being. Moreover, since abortion is often perceived as an attack on the woman's body, it is very dubious whether a second bodily attack—an abortion—would restore the woman's acute sense of loss of integrity from the first attack, the rape.

The third argument claims that the involuntary nature of the pregnancy

---

[9]John Noonan, "How to Argue About Abortion," in *Morality in Practice,* 2nd ed., ed. James Sterba (Belmont, Calif.: Wadsworth, 1994), p. 151.

should absolve the woman of any responsibility to the future child. As we have seen, this is really what Judith Thomson's analogy of the "plugged-in violinist" is trying to show.[10] While this argument is morally relevant, it provides a good reason only for giving the future child up for adoption after delivery but not for killing the fetus by abortion. Furthermore, it has been suggested that even though the rape/incest victim did not choose to conceive, the fetus is nonetheless from her; and given the importance of physical embodiment in any comprehensive account of personhood, it is not unreasonable to see that such a unique genetic and biological relation is morally significant enough to assess the mother some duty to the fetus.[11] Unlike Thomson's analogy of the "plugged-in violinist," in which the victim is involuntarily hooked up to a perfect stranger with whom he has no genetic and biological ties whatsoever, a rape victim is in fact hooked up to someone who is in essence a bit of herself, and the needy life in question is entirely dependent on her as a mother. Emphasizing the moral significance of this biological relation, reinforced by the gestational bond of pregnancy, not only strengthens the "connectedness" of the rape victim to the life conceived, but may also allow her to meet the challenge of assuming responsibility for the life as the means to regain her integrity and dignity.

In many ways the fourth reason presents the most serious justification for abortion in the case of rape. The emotional stress and psychological damage that a continued pregnancy would bring as a reminder of the rape cannot be lightly dismissed. Indeed, the damages are so deep and extensive that many such victims never fully recover. Further, the damage also goes beyond the victim—affecting her relations with others, especially her husband (if she is married) and other family members, who may or may not be sympathetic. Another important source of psychological trauma for the pregnant rape victim comes from the relationship between the woman and her children. A woman relates to the children she bears in such a way that her whole personal identity as a unique individual—her sense of personal worth in life, and her very motherly nature to share a bit of what she uniquely is to others—is entirely tied to her status as mother.[12] If this is how a mother identifies herself with her child (or children), then asking a woman to bear a child whom she can only identify as

---

[10]See, e.g., Susan Teft Nicholson, *Abortion and the Roman Catholic Church* (Notre Dame: University of Notre Dame Press, 1978), pp. 54-55. Judith Thomson makes this analogy in "A Defense of Abortion," in *The Problem of Abortion,* ed. Joel Feinberg (Belmont, Calif.: Wadsworth, 1973).

[11]Compare Patrick Lee, *Abortion and Unborn Human Life* (Washington D.C.: Catholic University of America Press, 1996), p. 122.

[12]Also see Michael Wreen, "Abortion and Pregnancy Due to Rape," *Philosophica* 21 (1992): 213.

"a living emblem of the rape" may indeed be equivalent to torture. To have the child is to identify with the rape and the rapist through motherhood. I agree that "this is the sort of massive assault on a person's very being that men never face, and no man can ever really know . . . what it would be like to be pregnant due to rape."[13] An abortion request may not be denied for this reason alone, especially by a group of male ethicists or church elders!

As reasonable as this argument may be, such is not the whole experience of many women. In David Reardon's survey of 225 pregnant victims of rape or incest, the vast majority of women actually wished to carry their children to term. The evidence shows that the pressures to abort come primarily from friends, family and society in general as a result of prejudicial, discriminatory and even superstitious views against such "tainted women" and their children, who have been "conceived in sin." Reardon concludes that "it is the social pressure to hide (abort) these pregnancies which needs to be eliminated, not the innocent children."[14] He confirms that in difficult circumstances such as rape or incest, those women who carried on with the pregnancy were better able to reestablish their self-images and regain a sense of control over their lives than women who did not carry to term. This emphasizes that the rape victim should always be provided with counseling through a strongly sympathetic support group, but her decision, regardless of which direction it takes, must be fully respected. Should she decide to abort, I can only say that within the limitations of our human wisdom to discern what is the best for the victim, and within the limitations of our human capacity to counter the overwhelming evil forces that have impacted the pregnant woman, she has chosen abortion as the lesser of the two evils. Christians must take this position also, for the victims' choice must be respected and they must be left alone to face their own God even though their fallenness still needs to be acknowledged, the act of abortion still needs to be repented of, and the life of the aborted still needs to be mourned.

Psychological Effects of Abortion

While the psychological trauma to pregnant rape victims who choose abortion can be easily characterized, the emotional responses of pregnant women to abortion in general are difficult to assess, and are often ignored as an important pragmatic factor in the decision-making process of abortion. Before the mid 1970s, the medical profession and the public were aware of abortion's possible negative emotional consequences, but actual reports were scanty and too vague to make any definite conclusions.[15] However, in the early 1980s, after the so-

---

[13]Ibid., p. 217.
[14]David C. Reardon, *Aborted Women: Silent No More* (Westchester, Ill.: Crossway, 1987), p. 205.

called posttraumatic stress disorder (PTSD) was applied to Vietnam veterans with direct war trauma experience, a similar label, postabortion syndrome (PAS), was applied to women suffering the psychological effects of abortion. Despite the sensation PAS has created, as well as the attention it has received, there is no consensus as to the actual existence of such a syndrome. Those who advocate the existence of this condition understand PAS to be similar to PTSD and define it as a "disorder that seems to be brought about by stress involved with the abortion itself and that, for one reason or another, the aborted woman is unable to process."[16] Others assume a more skeptical position, questioning whether the syndrome even meets the American Psychiatric Association's definition of "trauma."[17] The controversial nature of the matter can be seen in the report prepared by former United States Surgeon General C. Everett Koop, who conducted an extensive survey of the literature and interviewed twenty-seven groups of experts and lay people on the subject, and then came to the conclusion that "the data were insufficient . . . to support the premise that abortion does or does not produce a postabortion syndrome and that emotional problems resulting from abortion are minuscule from a public health perspective."[18] Koop summed up his findings by stating that "the available scientific evidence about the psychological sequelae of abortion simply cannot support either the preconceived belief of those pro-life or of those pro-choice."[19] Given Koop's personal pro-life stand, his conclusion is particularly significant.

One of the main reasons why it has been so difficult to evaluate the psychological effects of abortion on a woman has to do with the methodological problems that complicate interpretation of the findings. These methodological problems include the lack of standardized methods for several factors: data collection, group sizes, study design, patient characteristics, abortion proce-

---

[15]See A. J. Margolis et al., "Therapeutic Abortion Follow-up Study," *American Journal of Obstetrics and Gynecology* 110, no. 2 (1971): 243-49; and Ian Kent et al., "Emotional Sequelae of Elective Abortion," *British Columbia Medical Journal* 20, no. 4 (1978): 118-19.

[16]Terry L. Selby and Marc Bockmon, *The Mourning After: Help for Post-Abortion Syndrome* (Grand Rapids, Mich.: Baker, 1990), p. 15. The term "aborted women" is a standard term in the psychological literature that is used in place of the more awkward "women who have had an abortion."

[17]Rachel Benson Gold, *Abortion and Women's Health: A Turning Point for America?* (New York: Alan Guttmacher Institute, 1990).

[18]C. Everett Koop, hearing before the Human Resources and Intergovernmental Relations Subcommittee of the Committee on Governmental Operations, 101st Cong., 1st sess., 1989, quoted in Allan Rosenfeld and Sara Iden, "Abortion: Medical Perspective," in *Encyclopedia of Bioethics*, rev. ed., 5 vols., ed. Warren T. Reich, Macmillan Library Reference U.S.A. (New York: Simon & Schuster, 1995), 1:4.

[19]C. Everett Koop, "The U.S. Surgeon General on the Health Effects of Abortion," in *Population and Development Review* 15, no. 1 (1989): 174. His finding came as a severe shock to members of the pro-life movement who were hoping to gain yet one more weapon in their arsenal against abortion rights.

dures, the length of time between abortion and assessment, and the way of recording symptoms. As a result of these many methodological problems, which are augmented by investigators' biases, the literature on the psychological impact of induced abortion is often contradictory.[20] In spite of these shortcomings, several groups of investigators conclude that for most women, abortion is accompanied by emotional relief experienced as a deliverance from the crisis of an unwanted pregnancy. While short-term grief, guilt and depressive reactions may occur, long-term psychiatric sequelae are rare, with only 5 to 10 percent of women experiencing serious psychological after-effects. On the whole, negative emotions, reflecting concerns such as personal loss or social disapproval, typically are not experienced as strongly as are positive emotions, and there is very little evidence that women show any sign of permanent psychopathology after abortion. Any occurrence of clinically significant psychological postabortion sequelae is most likely associated with risk factors that are tangential to the abortion itself but are commonly found in other stressful life situations. While these findings do not deny that abortion is a weighty moral choice for women, they do challenge the idea that every abortion is followed by a postabortion syndrome. Consequently, the author considers it morally irresponsible to exaggerate the psychological danger of abortion, which is negligible at best.[21]

Other investigators dispute this conclusion. For example, David Rasmussen and N. Holst compared 27,234 women who had abortions with 71,378 women who carried a pregnancy to term and found that the risk of psychiatric admission was substantially higher for the former group of women (18.4 per 10,000 versus 12 per 10,000).[22] A review conducted in Saskatchewan, Canada, also found that postabortion women had mental disorders 40.8 percent more often than postpartum women. This finding has been corroborated by a five-year study in Alberta, Canada, which showed that of the women who had abortions, 25 percent made visits to psychiatrists, compared to 3 percent in the general population.[23] These studies do not provide firm numbers of women who experience psychological distress after abortion, partly because women are generally reluctant to be forthcoming in the interviews about their abortion and

---

[20]Susan J. Blumenthal, "Psychiatric Consequences of Abortions: Overview of Research Findings," in *Psychiatric Aspects of Abortion,* ed. N. Stotland (Washington, D.C.: American Psychiatric Press, 1991), pp. 19-20.

[21]Ibid., p. 32. See also Nancy Adler, Henry P. David, Brenda N. Major, Susan H. Roth, Nancy F. Russo, and Gail E. Wyatt, "Psychological Response After Abortion," *Science* 248 (April 1990): 41-44; and J. A. Rosenfeld, "Emotional Responses to Therapeutic Abortion," *American Family Physician* 45, no. 1 (1992): 137-40.

[22]Summarized in report by L. L. DeVeber et al., "Postabortion Grief: Psychological Sequelae of Induced Abortion," *Humane Medicine* 7 (August 1991): 203-9.

[23]Ibid., p. 204.

partly because their negative reactions may surface years after the actual abortion experience.[24] However, these studies do suggest that women who have an abortion are more likely to suffer adverse reactions than are women who carry a child to term. In a survey reported by Douglas Brown and his colleagues that was conducted with forty-five women who had abortions, 64 percent spoke of having more than incidental and transient grief. A number of women spoke of other negative after-effects:[25]

☐ suicidal ideation (15.5 percent)
☐ phobic responses to infants (13.3 percent)
☐ recurrent nightmares (13.3 percent)
☐ marital discord (15.5 percent)
☐ fear of men (8.9 percent)
☐ disinterest in sex (6.7 percent)

More than a third of the women related these symptoms directly to the abortion. Even if significant negative effects occur in only a small percentage of women, these effects is still a significant health care problem, particularly in light of the 2.0 million abortions a year that occur in the United States alone.

An investigation conducted by a private U.K. commission of inquiry, which studied the operation and consequences of the U.K. abortion law, yielded similar results: both short-term and long-term psychological effects do occur,[26] with the total number of affected women estimated to be 10 percent. The commission further noted that the estimate is conservative due to a high attrition rate in follow-up studies. Both physicians and women involved seem to be equally unenthusiastic about follow-up visits after an abortion. There is also a general reluctance for the woman who has experienced adverse postabortion effects to return to the clinic or to the physician who originally performed the abortion. This attrition rate is even more pronounced in medium- or long-term follow up studies because many psychological symptoms have a delayed onset, sometimes only triggered by the birth of a subsequent child years later. Much of the controversy about postabortion psychological effects is linked to this factor. The commission also conducted follow-up interviews with postabortion women, and most of them showed a high degree of ambivalence; many wished they had not had the abortion, and some even felt that they had killed their babies.[27] These studies suggest that even if the rate of incidence of

---

[24]Ibid.
[25]Douglas Brown, Thomas E. Eklins and David B. Larson, "Prolonged Grieving After Abortion: A Descriptive Study," *Journal of Clinical Ethics* 4, no. 2 (1993): 120.
[26]Stephanie J. Smith, "Post-Abortion Syndrome: Fact or Fiction?" in *Bioethics and The Future of Medicine: A Christian Appraisal,* ed. John F. Kilner, Nigel M. de S. Cameron and David L. Schiedermayer (Grand Rapids, Mich.: Eerdmans, 1995), pp. 171-75.
[27]Ibid., pp. 175-76.

psychological effects is difficult to ascertain, their occurrence can hardly be denied. When anecdotal evidence of women who experience postabortion psychological effects is taken into consideration, the incidence of psychological distress experienced by these women is not low enough that it can be dismissed or ignored.

From a decision-making point of view, what matters most is the ability to identify special groups of women who may be more susceptible to developing negative postabortion sequelae.[28] It is generally agreed that the following categories of women are particularly more vulnerable: young teenage women with fragile self-esteem who elect not to tell their parents about the abortion or whose parents oppose the abortions; women who do not receive social support for their decision to abort; women who have negative feelings toward their partners; women who have second-trimester or late-pregnancy abortions; women who have greater difficulty in deciding whether to have an abortion; women who hold strong religious beliefs; women with previous psychiatric histories; and women who have multiple abortions. Another group of women who are exposed to high risk of psychological injury from an abortion are those forced to abort because of genetic anomalies or severe fetal defects. In these cases, the pregnancy is fundamentally wanted, planned and personally meaningful, and the abortion will prove psychologically much more traumatic than in any other circumstance. One report indicates that these women are at high risk of prolonged psychiatric difficulties requiring treatment or hospitalization in the twelve months after the abortion.[29] Another report shows that 99 percent of women experienced depression as an immediate response to the abortion, with many expressing the belief that only the subsequent birth of a normal child would be able to heal their pain.[30] It is therefore undisputed that postabortion sequelae have a much higher incidence among these women, and this factor must be considered in an abortion decision. Lastly, it has been noted that, in general, the severity of the abortion-induced emotional problems is directly proportional to the gravity of the reason for having the abortion. Women with the most serious reasons to have an abortion—such as pregnancy due to rape—are likely to have the most severe postabortion emotional problems.[31] Such a possibility constitutes a strong pragmatic reason not to recommend abortion hastily, and it suggests that the emotional distress from the violence of rape is better dealt with through long-term counseling rather than

---

[28]DeVeber et al., "Postabortion Grief," pp. 203-9; Adler et al., "Psychological Response," pp. 41-44; Rosenfeld, "Emotional Response," p. 138.

[29]Rosenfeld, "Emotional Response," p. 138.

[30]B. Blumberg, "The Psychological Sequelae of Abortion Performed for a Genetic Indication," *American Journal of Obstetrics and Gynecology* 122, no. 7 (1975): 805.

[31]Reardon, *Aborted Women,* chaps. 4-6.

through terminating the pregnancy.

To summarize, even if conclusive evidence is lacking for or against a full-blown postabortion syndrome, there can be no doubt that the psychological effects of an abortion must be considered by the woman as an important pragmatic factor in the decision of whether to have an abortion. The psychological complexity of abortion itself is evidence that abortion is more than a conflict of rights between the mother and fetus. Naomi Wolf, a well-known feminist writer and supporter of woman's right to abortion, describes her own experience as follows:

> I had an abortion when I was a single mother and my daughter was two years old. I would do it again. But you know how in the Greek myths when you kill a relative, you are pursued by Furies? For months it was as if baby's Furies were pursuing me.[32]

Social factors may render her abortion inculpable, but it inflicts psychological damage nonetheless. A similar experience is recalled by Linda Bird Francke in a letter originally published in *The New York Times*. While not regretting her abortion, she still grieved:

> I have this ghost now. A very little ghost that only appears when I'm seeing something beautiful, like the full moon or the ocean last weekend. And the baby waves at me. And I wave at the baby. "Of course we have room," I cry to the ghost. "Of course we do."[33]

A few weeks after her letter was published, she wrote a reply to the firestorm of response that emphasized the ambivalence many women experience: "It is not black-and-white as the laws governing abortion are forced to be. Rather it is the gray area whose core touches our definition of ourselves that produces 'little ghosts' in some, and a sense of relief in others."[34] The complex psychological sequelae of abortion are indeed intriguing, for they transcend the neatly defined pro-choice and pro-life boundaries. Recognition of this aspect of abortion would go a long way to help those who are contemplating an abortion and those who are living with one.

The Pregnant Woman's Socioeconomic Environment

Among the pragmatic factors that render abortion a highly complex issue are economic hardship and social environment, and the latter includes significant human relationships such as the one between the woman and her partner and

---

[32]Naomi Wolf, "Our Bodies, Our Souls," *The New Republic,* October 16, 1995, p. 26.
[33]Linda Bird Francke, "Abortion: A Personal Dilemma," in *Morality in Practice,* 2nd ed., ed. James Sterba (Belmont, Calif.: Wadsworth, 1994), p. 197.
[34]Ibid., p. 198.

between the woman and her physician. Pro-choice advocates often make two rather questionable assumptions regarding abortion: first, once the woman is given the freedom to make a choice, she will necessarily make free choices; and second, the choice freely made is always automatically right. However, both these assumptions contradict the evidence. For instance, the decision to have an abortion is often critically influenced, if not outright determined, by economic realities. Many women seek abortions simply because they cannot afford the expenses required to raise a child. This economic pressure is particularly acute in minority groups and among teenagers. It is not a coincidence that in the United States, economically underprivileged young black women are proportionately the largest group to choose abortion. While it may not be possible to prove that there is a direct correlation between a decrease in financial resources and an increased rate of abortion, empirical facts suggest that such a correlation likely exists. To support the thesis that poverty and abortion are linked, it has been pointed out that the United States has the world's most liberal abortion laws as well as the poorest social support system for women, mothers and children.[35]

However, the pressures influencing the abortion decision are not felt only by the economically marginalized. Even among more privileged middle-class professional women, the intense competition they face in society, the instability of the job market and the enormous physical and emotional stress involved in trying to maintain both a career and a parental role all converge to make having children a virtually next to impossible task. As a result, abortion becomes for many an inevitable solution to an unwanted pregnancy. In addition, pressure for an abortion may come from the woman's partner, who himself desires career advancement and a certain lifestyle more than he desires to raise a family at a certain time. Thus, virtually any woman in society may be forced to consider abortion as a result of social and economic pressures. These pressures suggest that even though women may have won the freedom to make abortion decisions, their decisions are not necessarily free. A large number of reports suggest that many women have been coerced by others or by their social circumstances into having an abortion that they would not have voluntarily chosen.[36] Many of the so-called free choices are in fact made under the constraint of socioeconomic circumstances.

This analysis suggests that, tragically, abortion is often used as an alternative to an adequate social policy for women, children and families—a cheap solution proffered under the rubric of free reproductive choice. But there is in fact much more to choosing freely than simply having access to a particular alter-

---

[35]M. A. Glendon, *Abortion and Divorce in American Law: American Failures, European Challenges* (Cambridge: Harvard University Press, 1987).

[36]Callahan, "Abortion Debate," p. 788.

native. For women to make moral decisions regarding abortion, they must be provided with wider options to choose from. And for this to occur, there need to be improvements in the various social services available to women. Society and religious communities, such as the church, must provide for the protection and benefit of pregnant women and their "unwanted" children. It is only through the possibility of other options (e.g., adoption, social and financial support) that abortion can be considered a real option. Only then will pregnant women begin to have choices that are truly free.

Counseling and the Role of the Physician

If the pregnant woman seeking an abortion is to be truly able to make a decision that is both free and moral—with due consideration for the medical, psychological and social aspects of abortion—then she must be provided with the proper venues for uncovering and communicating her needs and concerns as she receives advice and assistance. When considering an abortion, the pregnant woman often turns first to her physician; yet, strangely enough, physicians' rights and responsibilities are seldom discussed in the abortion literature.[37] The United States Supreme Court decision in *Roe* v. *Wade* is often understood as vindicating the rights of women to procure an abortion. What is less often appreciated is that it equally vindicates the physician, whose legal right to provide abortion according to his professional judgment is ensured.[38] The ethical basis for the physician's right to perform abortions rests on the principle of the physician's autonomy to practice his profession and his duty to protect the privacy and confidentiality of the patient from intrusion and serious physical harm. But the physician's right is not unlimited; it is restricted largely by patient autonomy and state interest. While the state's interest to protect the fetus may at times limit a physician's right to perform an abortion,[39] the potential conflict between patient autonomy and physician autonomy may lead to a far more complex and sensitive situation. Although the woman's desire for and consent to an abortion is prima facie the ethical necessity for an abortion, such a desire and consent in itself does not logically or ethically oblige a physician to provide such service.[40] In the complex relational matrix formed by the physician-patient relationship, there would not be such a thing as an "abortion on demand." A position demanding the physi-

---

[37]For a brief general discussion on physician attitudes, see John M. Westfall, Ken J. Kallail and Anne D. Walling, "Abortion Attitudes and Practices of Family and General Practice Physicians," *Journal of Family Practice* 33, no. 1 (1991): 47-51.

[38]W. G. Bartholome, "Ethics and the Termination of Pregnancy: The Physician's Perspective," in *Ethical Issues at the Outset of Life,* ed. William B. Weil Jr. and Martin Benjamin (Boston: Blackwell Scientific Publications, 1987), p. 116.

[39]Ibid., p. 117.

[40]Ibid., p. 114.

cian to acquiesce destroys the physician-patient relationship so crucial to patient welfare and reduces the physician to an amoral technician or a mere provider of technical services. I believe that in addition to discerning the woman's desire and willingness, the physician as a moral agent must also be able to verify his decision to perform a particular abortion as ethically justifiable. Such an exchange of values and desires can only be accomplished in an open dialogue between the physician and the patient, which would include preabortion counseling and postabortion support as well as informing the patient of possible alternatives to abortion. Because of the importance of this dialogue, abortion clinics must provide the physician who works in such settings the opportunity to fulfill this particular ethical obligation.

Both the rising number of annual abortions (close to 2 million in the United States) and the fact that 40 percent of all women who undergo abortions have had at least one previous abortion suggest that there is a growing tendency for women to depend on abortion as the first line of defense against unwanted pregnancy.[41] Consequently, many physicians begin to realize that their professional responsibility is also an important component in a woman's abortion decision, particularly those pregnancies due either to contraceptive failure or to a failure to use contraception. Preventing a situation such as contraceptive failure may result in abortion being seen as the responsibility of both the physician and the woman rather than the woman's sole responsibility. For this reason, some view contraceptive failure as one occasion in which "the physician can be said to have at least a prima facie obligation to perform an abortion."[42] Even though I do not endorse this view, it does serve to emphasize the physician's duty.

Another of the physician's important responsibilities is providing serious and responsible counseling for the woman seeking abortion. This is particularly a challenge to physicians who work in a clinic situation, which involves a large number of abortions on a daily basis. Under these conditions, it may take a special effort or even sacrifice on the physician's part to explore the pregnant woman's own thinking about why she feels that an abortion is the best option. This reflection includes her own thinking about what abortion is, the implications for her life after she has made that particular choice, the possibility that she may have been unknowingly influenced or knowingly coerced into considering the abortion, and some psychological or even physical sequalae she may need to anticipate. In this regard the physician should encourage the pregnant woman to wait a few days before she finalizes her decision to have an abortion, so she may have sufficient time to consider the full range of options before she freely makes her choice and gives truly informed consent.

---

[41]Callahan, "The Abortion Debate," p. 684.
[42]Bartholome, "Ethics and the Termination of Pregnancy," p. 118.

Many see this exercise of caution as an important way to respect a woman's autonomy. Given the importance of counseling as part of the abortion procedure, an open and constructive dialogue between physician and patient—including all the necessary elements of trust, honesty, compassion and authenticity—is crucial for the ethical, well-managed care of a pregnant woman seeking an abortion.

One way in which this needed physician-patient openness can be compromised is through the state's attempt to influence abortion decisions by regulating the type of information physicians may or may not provide their patients when obtaining informed consent. For example, in 1986 the United States Supreme Court struck down a statute of the city of Akron requiring physicians to personally communicate some specific information to a pregnant woman when counseling her for abortion: this information included the statement that "the unborn child is a human life from the moment of conception," a description of the anatomical and physiological characteristics of the unborn child and a warning that abortion is a major surgical procedure that can result in serious physical and psychological complications.[43] The Supreme Court reasoned that the information provided in this ordinance is not the sort of professional guidance that the pregnant woman seeks, and so the physician should not be compelled to provide it. Ironically, the Court felt that such a statute is the antithesis of informed consent because it interferes with the doctor's ability to communicate freely with the patient. What the Supreme Court failed to see is that by striking down the ordinance, it committed the very mistake it sought to correct. The Akron law was an attempt to ensure that a physician must provide certain vital information when counseling a pregnant woman for family planning so that the woman can make an informed decision. Thus, by regulating what a physician *may not say,* the Court worked *against* a free dialogue between physician and patient, compromised the relationship between the two parties and ultimately violated the woman's autonomy as well the physician's.

The Pregnant Woman and Her Family

When a pregnant woman is deciding whether to have an abortion, her relationships with her family members must be seen to be as crucial a factor in her decision-making process as is her relationship with her physician. Preoccupied with a biomedical model of disease in which illness and treatment are seen as conditions that only occur *within* the body of the patient and thus do not affect anyone else, the medical profession has mistakenly construed pregnancy as a

---

[43]G. J. Annas, "The Right of Privacy Protects the Doctor-Patient Relationship," *Journal of the American Medical Association* 163, no. 6 (1990): 860.

medical condition concerning only the pregnant woman, rather than as the social and relational event it truly is.[44] In such a model, the pregnant woman is regarded as a weak and vulnerable patient to be protected from not only the condition of pregnancy but also the family. But those in the medical profession are becoming more aware that the prevalent ethic, which appeals exclusively to patient autonomy, compromises family interest. John Hardwig argues that the concept of patient autonomy is meaningless unless it is combined with consideration of family well-being and respect for the autonomy of other significant members (e.g., the pregnant woman's spouse and children).[45] This is particularly true in abortion cases, since the decision to terminate the pregnancy affects the pregnant woman as well as all those who have an interest in the fetus—particularly the fetus's father. The autonomy of other family members is systematically undercut if they are excluded from the decision-making process. On this view, family conferences would be mandatory, especially when the lives of family members could be demonstrated to be significantly affected by the abortion decision; such a scenario applies to many if not most cases of abortion. Often the physician and the family of the pregnant woman are put in an adversarial position, an unfortunate development due largely to the values of privacy and confidentiality that have been placed on the physician-patient relationship. The physician is charged with the responsibility to protect the patient from those who seek access to the patient's confidential medical information, including not only the state but also her spouse and her family.[46]

In the West, the moral significance of the father's role within the decision-making process to have an abortion has been entirely ignored. If both parents agree that the pregnancy should be terminated, then the role and responsibility of the father can be said to be subsumed under that of the mother. But if the parents disagree, then the decision to abort is regarded as the woman's sole prerogative, ethically justified by her autonomous rights. However, it has been argued that in certain cases the woman's choice to terminate a pregnancy may well cause wrongful harm to the father, specifically as a morally unacceptable offense against the father's reproductive autonomy.[47] According to G. W. Harris, the father's reproductive autonomy is limited by maternal consent, since a man can neither reproduce on his own nor force a woman to reproduce with him. In cases of rape, maternal consent is never given, and thus the father has no claim to reproductive autonomy regarding the conceived fetus. Harris

---

[44]Barbara Katz Rothman, "The Tentative Pregnancy: Then and Now," *Fetal Diagnosis and Therapy* 8, no. 1 (1993): 60-63.

[45]John Hardwig, "What About the Family?" *Hastings Center Report* 20 (March-April 1990): 5-10.

[46]Bartholome, "Ethics and the Termination of Pregnancy," p. 112.

[47]G. W. Harris, "Fathers and Fetuses," *Ethics* 96 (April 1986): 594-603.

believes that the same logic is applied to a relationship pursued for sexual pleasure only: if the woman becomes pregnant, she does so without giving her consent to reproduce. In both situations, the man has no claim to reproductive autonomy, for he cannot force parenthood on a woman who never agreed to conceive a child.[48]

In cases where consent for potential reproduction has been given, the father does have a claim to reproductive autonomy. For example, in a marriage where both partners are open to the idea of having children, consent can be assumed even when it is not explicitly stated. The societal understanding of marriage allows for and reinforces the expectation that children form a normal part of a healthy marriage. Once a man can reasonably assume that his partner consents to producing offspring, his reproductive autonomy is established, and he may claim to have a "morally legitimate interest" in the fetus. It would seem that with certain abortions, the reproductive autonomy of the man and his morally legitimate interest in the fetus may be said to have been violated. This would make those abortions morally suspect for this reason alone. But in the three decades since *Roe* v. *Wade,* the courts in the United States have not resolved the issue of men's rights regarding abortion, especially with respect to spousal consent and notification for an abortion. In *Planned Parenthood of Central Missouri* v. *Danforth,* the United States Supreme Court decided that "the State may not constitutionally require the consent of the spouse as a condition for abortion during the first 12 weeks of pregnancy, which is considered to be a decision entirely up to the pregnant woman alone."[49] The Court then reasoned that because the state itself could not prohibit abortion before twelve weeks, neither could it delegate authority to prohibit abortion. However, one may question whether women should at least be required to notify their spouses of their decision to abort for the sake of state interest in family protection. But in the case of *Planned Parenthood of Southeastern Pennsylvania* v. *Casey,* the Court decided that partner notification would potentially interfere with the woman's right to choose, would present an undue burden on the woman's abortion decision and does not serve the states' interest in family protection. Thus, at least in the United States and for the foreseeable future, the autonomy of the pregnant woman far outweighs any interest of the family or the reproductive autonomy of the spouse.

Another potential spousal right is the man's interest in his potential offspring. As we have already seen, it can be argued that a father has a morally legitimate interest in the fetus once his reproductive autonomy has been estab-

---

[48]Ibid., p. 597.
[49]S. M. Davies, "Partners and the Abortion Decision," in *Abortion, Medicine and the Law,* ed. J. D. Butler and D. F. Walbert (New York: Facts on File, 1992), p. 224.

lished and that this interest is violated if a woman unilaterally chooses an abortion. S. M. Davies acknowledges that "if the man and the woman are married or in an ongoing relationship, both partners have an interest in the procreative potential of that relationship."[50] However, Davies goes on to state that the man's interest in his offspring is precisely that—merely an interest, and not a right. He concludes that a man's interest alone can never outweigh a woman's right to choose. Enforcing a man's interest could only be constitutional if a man and a woman were in agreement so that the woman would not be deprived of her constitutional right to make the decision herself. In sum, the current ethos of the society is such that while the man's interest in his potential offspring and the state's interest in the stability of the family are important, they cannot justify a legally compelled restriction of a woman's private right to choose an abortion. This trend favoring maternal autonomy and privacy will probably continue until such a time when our society realized that this does more harm than good to the pregnant woman. Until our society realizes the significance of relations in the flourishing of persons and in building the moral fiber of our society, individual autonomy will always have an upper hand over the interest of the community, even the most intimate community of the family. Until then the power of the pregnant woman to unilaterally abort her previable fetus will, sadly, remain unchallenged.

Lonely Abortion and the Ethic of Personhood

In this chapter, I have reviewed a variety of scenarios that have a bearing on the abortion decision-making process. These cases express pragmatic issues more than philosophical principles or theological dogmas. Through this analysis, I observe that our society's prevailing values of individualism and autonomy have underwritten a moral framework of abortion that isolates the pregnant woman from her usual social network of relations—her spouse, children, siblings, parents, colleagues and close friends—and essentially reduces her decision-making partners to her physician alone, whose participation is often uncertain. We can see how this has deprived the significant persons of making a contribution at this important juncture of the woman's life, no matter whether they are for, against or neutrally supportive of her decision. Instead, most women are left to make a decision alone and to bear the consequences alone. The ethic of personhood I adopt would want to cherish all the relationships involved, including the relationship the pregnant woman has with herself. I leave open the possibility of honoring a rape victim's request for an abortion for this reason: if we are convinced that she is not to be persuaded against an abortion within the time available to live at peace with herself, then

---

[50]Ibid., p. 227.

her personhood must be protected and preserved as a priority. But more positively, the personhood ethic mandates that the physician provide extensive counseling to all pregnant women seeking abortions before and during the abortion decision-making process. I also believe that excluding the woman's spouse and immediate family from the decision-making process is at odds with the ethic of personhood I espouse, because in the long run such a unilateral decision undermines the personhood of the parents, the covenant partnership that binds them together and the integrity of the family they bring forth, which (I believe, in the original scheme of things) has the best chance to exemplify the various dimensions of human personhood God has ordained.

18

Prenatal Screening and Fetal Genetic Defects

*S*ince the 1980s advances in the medical technology of prenatal screening have allowed early detection of fetal defects and their genetic causes. For instance, while in the past ultrasonic visualization was the only way to determine defects and disorders before birth, it has recently become possible to diagnose genetic abnormalities in the first trimester through chorionic villus sampling (CVS) and in the early second trimester through amniocentesis, thus allowing for the possibility of aborting a defective fetus as early as possible.

However, screening procedures carry considerable risks. It is a standard assumption in genetic counseling that in one out of two-hundred cases screening will result in spontaneous abortion.[1] In a large series of amniocentesis, the rate of miscarriage is reported to be 1.6 percent, and fetal damage without miscarriage is also reported in 0.3 percent of all cases.[2] Screening by CVS is accompanied by a 3.2 percent rate of miscarriage as well as the development of malformations

---

[1]S. Clark and G. DeVore, "Prenatal Diagnosis for Couples Who Would Not Consider Abortion," *Obstetrics and Gynecology* 73, no. 6 (1989): 1035-37.

[2]Neil M. Macintyre, Llew Keltner and Dorothy A. Kovacevich, "The Impact of an Abnormal Fetus or Child on the Choice for Prenatal Diagnosis and Selective Abortion," in *Abortion, Medicine and the Law,* edited by J. D. Butler and D. F. Walbert (New York: Facts on File, 1992), p. 532.

ranging from strawberry hemangiomas to limb reduction.[3] CVS is also notorious for its inability to detect neural tube defects. Some believe that even ultrasound is not entirely harmless, perhaps exposing the fetus to the carcinogenic effects of ionizing radiation.[4] Despite these known risks, advocates of prenatal screening claim that the benefits produced by screening fetuses outweigh any potential harms. For example, one of the greatest benefits of prenatal screening is the "peace of mind" given to the parents when they know they have a normal pregnancy.[5] Furthermore, if testing reveals a fetal anomaly, such "early warning" allows the parents to prepare themselves emotionally, physically and financially; if fetal abnormalities such as diaphragmatic hernia, abdominal wall defects, congenital heart defects or myelomeningocele are discovered, the parents may consider experimental fetal surgery (see chapter nineteen below) or choose cesarean section to enhance fetal outcome.[6] The good of trying to prevent or ameliorate genetically based medical or disabling conditions is also considered as a worthy goal. These benefits have led many physicians and geneticists to support prenatal screening, although the definite presence of risks has prompted some in the medical profession to suggest that screening should not be a mandatory procedure. Rather, they believe screening should be made available only with parental consent[7] and should only take place where high-quality laboratory work is available.

Genetic Screening, Fatal Defects and "Wrongful Life"

Screening results in adult patients involving the BRCA1 and BRCA2 genes in connection with inherited breast and ovarian cancer and the APC gene for colon cancer[8] have encouraged the medical profession to provide early prenatal genetic screening through CVS and amniocentesis, in the hope that fetal genetic therapy—including the use of the experimental but highly promising fetal stem cell transplantation technique—may be provided.[9] However, since at the present time prenatal diagnosis only rarely leads to fetal therapy, that is,

---

[3]J. Boss, "First-Trimester Prenatal Diagnosis: Earlier Is Not Necessarily Better," *Journal of Medical Ethics* 20 (September 1994): 146-51.

[4]Macintyre, Keltner and Kovacevich, "Impact of an Abnormal Fetus," p. 531.

[5]Clark and DeVore, "Prenatal Diagnosis," p. 1035.

[6]Ibid., p. 1036.

[7]J. Fletcher, "Ethical Issues in Genetic Screening, Prenatal Diagnosis and Counseling," in *Ethical Issues at the Outset of Life,* ed. William B. Weil Jr. and Martin Benjamin (Boston: Blackwell Scientific Publications, 1987), p. 68; and J. Fletcher and D. Wertz, "Ethics and Decision Making About Diagnosed Fetal Anomalies," in *Reproductive Risks and Prenatal Diagnosis,* ed. M. Evans (Norwalk, Conn.: Appleton & Lange, 1992).

[8]David Allan, "Ethical Boundaries in Genetic Testing," *Canadian Medical Association Journal* 154, no. 2 (1996): 241.

[9]Boss, "First-Trimester Prenatal Diagnosis," pp. 146-51.

since the diagnostic-therapeutic gap remains wide, one would think that conditions without treatment prospects are not candidates for this procedure. But in reality it has become standard practice to screen and abort fetuses who are suspected to be carrying certain abnormal genes. It has been reported that pregnancies affected with diseases, especially those fetuses likely to develop intellectual impairment or likely to have short life expectancy after birth, are currently aborted almost uniformly.[10] Scientists and ethicists look toward a future when screening techniques are able to separate the more severe cases, where abortion may possibly be morally justified, and the minimally affected cases, for which therapy may be an option, thus eliminating abortion as the only inevitable alternative. But until this level of diagnostic sophistication is reached, the chief goal of prenatal diagnosis will be detecting and aborting abnormal fetuses.[11] Hence the whole technology of prenatal screening is a morally uncertain undertaking.

Aborting a fetus with severe or fatal genetic defects is often thought to be defensible as a protection of the woman's right of autonomy, because such a pregnancy generates anxiety and the prospect of a burdensome parenthood. Besides, this abortion has very reasonable medical ends in view: prevention of genetic disease, elimination of suffering, preservation of medical and financial resources, and protection of the human gene pool.[12] Many physicians and geneticists also believe that eliminating pregnancies with lethal genetic defects through elective abortion is only doing what nature often does through spontaneous abortion.[13] But clearly all the reasons provided serve primarily the interests of the pregnant woman and the benefit of the society at large, but do not necessarily benefit or serve the interests of the fetus.

Recently, a new argument has been advanced to justify the abortion of fetuses with genetic defects for the sake of protecting the fetus itself. Mary Ann Warren argues that not to have a child is neither right nor wrong, but to have a very unhappy child is morally objectionable because "it results in the frustration of the interests of an actual person in the future."[14] This line of reasoning has led to the new tort of "wrongful life"—the moral wrongness of bringing children with serious diseases and disabilities into the world—based

---

[10]Peter G. Pryde et al., "Prenatal Diagnosis: Choices Women Make About Pursuing, Testing and Acting on Abnormal Results," *Clinical Obstetrics and Gynecology* 36 (September 1993): 506.

[11]Compare Fletcher, "Ethical Issues," p. 77; Allan, "Ethical Boundaries," p. 243.

[12]Leon Kass, "Implications of Prenatal Diagnosis for the Human Right to Life," in *Ethical Issues in Human Genetics: Genetic Counseling and the Use of Genetic Knowledge,* ed. Bruce Hilton et al. (New York: Plenum, 1973), p. 193.

[13]Ibid., p. 197.

[14]Mary Ann Warren, "Do Potential People Have Moral Rights?" in *Obligations to Future Generations,* ed. R. I. Sikora and Brian Barry (Philadelphia: Temple University Press, 1978), p. 25.

on the notion that existence itself can be an injury.[15] In a wrongful-life suit, the physician is held responsible not for causing the child's impairment, but for allowing the birth of an impaired child who otherwise would not have been born.[16] In other words, it is based on the premises that the child would be better off never having been born, that the child has an interest or right *not* to be born and that any child born under such conditions has been unjustly harmed. Joel Feinberg suggests that this "right not to be born" is a way of referring to the plausible moral requirement that no child be brought into the world unless certain very minimal conditions of well-being are assured. If a child is brought into existence among conditions so dismal that all of the child's most basic interests, those essential to existence, are completely doomed, it can be said that the child has been wronged.[17] Feinberg concludes that harm can thus be caused to a person before birth. The kind of cases that may conceivably be called wrongful life should be very rare conditions such as Tay-Sachs disease, trisomy 13 and trisomy 18, in which the infant is severely physically and mentally handicapped and suffers from intense chronic pain, rendering his life subjectively akin to torture. In these conditions, someone who acts as the infant's advocate may choose by proxy for the infant and declare that his life is sufficiently awful that nonexistence is rationally preferable,[18] in the sense that "the choice is one that a rational person would *have to* make."[19]

But how does one decide on someone else's behalf that nonexistence is preferable? Since no living human being has claimed to have experienced the state of nonexistence, it is not plausible to say that nonexistence is preferable to the existence of an impaired existence. A "proxy chooser" is therefore taking on a difficult and morally ambiguous task. Hence, it is difficult if not impossible to have the necessary level of confidence and certainty that bringing such a child into existence would be wrong. "Handicaps, even severe ones, do not necessarily make a child better off dead, or better off unborn."[20] I conclude that only when a child's existence is of such a doomed-to-defeat quality can the child be said to have been wronged or harmed by being brought to exist-

---

[15]Bonnie Steinbock, "The Logical Case for 'Wrongful Life,' " *Hastings Center Report* 16, no. 2 (1986): 15-20.

[16]This is in contrast to a "wrongful birth" suit in which the plaintiffs are the parents who claim that they have been deprived of the option to abort by negligent physicians. For detail, see Bonnie Steinbock, *Life Before Birth: The Moral and Legal Status of Embryos and Fetuses* (New York: Oxford University Press, 1992), pp. 114-18.

[17]Joel Feinberg, *Harm to Others* (New York: Oxford University Press, 1984), p. 101, quoted in Steinbock, *Life Before Birth*, p. 119.

[18]Steinbock, *Life Before Birth*, p. 120.

[19]Ibid., p. 123.

[20]Ibid., p. 121.

ence. To assess the infant's life as wrongful life whenever it does not meet a
so-called minimally decent existence is hence unwarranted. If the notion of
wrongful life can be applied at all, it must be limited to a small number of
extreme cases.

It is of interest to note that the idea of wrongful life is endorsed widely even
among conservative Christians who agree that fetuses inflicted with conditions
like Tay-Sachs disease, trisomy 13 and trisomy 18 warrant the designation of a
wrongful life, justified as a form of "loyalty to the child."[21] On the other hand,
some conservative Christians still wonder how one could take a nascent life
without violating the sanctity of life or usurping the sovereign rule of God, justifying their position with the argument that if God wants to take the child's
life, he will do it himself. I take the position that these cases are extreme examples of creation's tragic fallenness, and as such, they represent the sort of
human suffering that cannot be explained or rationalized—suffering that goes
beyond the categories of rightness or wrongness. By grace, some may be able
to accept such experience of suffering, with the eyes of faith, as a mystery; others however, may not be able to do so, especially when the suffering of the
child is kept in mind. The response to this tragic situation should be decided
by the parents before their own God, whether they accept or reject the tragic
life they have conceived, the life presumably allowed by God.

Prenatal Screening and Nonfatal Genetic Defects

Clearly cases where the fetus's life is so doomed that nonexistence is preferable are rare. A more common scenario in prenatal screening involves cases in
which the infant's condition puts her in such a disadvantageous position that
she is unable to develop or do any of the things human beings normally can
do: these conditions may include cases such as congenital blindness and deafness, spina bifida, thalassemia, hemophilia, cystic fibrosis, trisomy 21 and so
on. These patients may experience disabilities and pain, but their disabilities
lead to diminished capacities rather than total incapacitation; and their pain,
though at times considerable, would often be controllable. Thus it is very
doubtful whether these children would prefer nonexistence or would assess
their life as "wrongful." In *Berman* v. *Allan* (1979) the New Jersey Supreme
Court held that Sharon Berman, who was born with Down syndrome, would
be able to love and be loved and to experience happiness and pleasure, and
therefore it could not be concluded that she would be better off unborn.[22] Yet

---

[21]Hessel Bouma III et al., *Christian Faith, Health and Medical Practice* (Grand Rapids, Mich.:
Eerdmans 1989), pp. 227, 250.
[22]Steinbock, *Life Before Birth,* p. 116; also see Bouma et al., *Christian Faith,* p. 228, and John
A. Robertson, "Involuntary Euthanasia of Defective Newborns: A Legal Analysis," *Stanford
Law Review* 27, no. 2 (1975): 254.

society continues to endorse the abortion of fetuses with nonfatal genetic defects, generally on the bases of societal good, parental or familial good and fetal good (i.e., the good of the child-to-be). I shall examine each of these arguments in turn.

Genetic Abortion for the Good of the Society

David Allan argues that the selective abortion of defective fetuses may be morally justifiable because of the financial, medical and emotional burden of caring for such children.[23] The society would presumably be best served by the elimination of these genetically defective fetuses. This societal-good argument is vulnerable for several reasons. First, it is undisputed that currently the affluent have disproportionate access to technologies such as CVS and amniocentesis, so that prenatal screening is primarily available to middle- and upper-class women. However, if this inconsistency is not corrected by making prenatal screening programs available to all groups of pregnant women known to be at risk, genetic detection and selective abortion will be restricted to a certain social class. In time, disorders that are now unrelated to socioeconomic factors, such as the Down syndrome, could become a defining mark of the lower stratum of the society. The societal good that is originally invoked to justify these prenatal screenings and abortions would not have been achieved, but would in fact have been adversely affected by them.[24] Second, many matters of social importance are not reducible to financial costs and may not be quantifiable at all. For instance, how do we measure the negative effect of genetic abortion on societal values such as care or trust? And how do we objectively measure the amount of burden these children will place on society? To assert that these children have little or nothing to give society in return for the expenses their caretakers incur is a gross misreading of the human spirit. People are often inspired and led to be better individuals as a direct result of contact with "flawed" individuals. One only needs to read the experiences of Henri Nouwen to appreciate this.[25] For many, the benefits these people can bring to the moral fiber of society and the very qualities of theirs that we recognize as distinctly human would far exceed any financial expenditure. Finally, it is as-

---

[23]Allan, "Ethical Boundaries," p. 242.

[24]Abby Lippman, "Prenatal Genetic Testing and Screening: Constructing Needs and Reinforcing Inequities," parts 1 and 2, *American Journal of Law and Medicine* 17, nos. 1 and 2 (1991): 36. It is interesting to note that for many authors the concept of social stratification through prenatal screening is a greater horror than the killing of fetuses. This may be a peculiar consequence of the North American obsession with social equality.

[25]E.g., *The Road to Daybreak* (Doubleday, 1988) and *The Return of the Prodigal Son* (Doubleday, 1992), and *The Inner Voice of Love* (First Image, 1988) and *Creative Ministry* (First Image, 1978).

sumed that by eliminating genetic defects through abortion, the human gene pool will be improved. But our present knowledge of the complexity of human genetic diversity does not warrant this claim. Through the elimination of genetically defective fetuses, which may otherwise have a chance to reproduce, genetic diversity may be affected in ways we cannot yet foresee.[26] It seems that if we were truly worried about "genetic pollution," then we would be more concerned with controlling mutagenesis from environmental pollution[27] than with aborting fetuses with nonfatal genetic defects. The argument in favor of nonfatal genetic abortion for the good of the society cannot be sustained.

Genetic Abortion for the Good of the Family

A second argument that has been commonly used to justify selective abortion of fetuses with nonfatal genetic conditions is based on the assumption that a defective child impedes both the qualitative and quantitative good of a family. But the issue of familial good is ambiguous and is largely dependent on whether the pregnancy is wanted to begin with. If the pregnancy is unwanted, the parents may justify aborting the fetus even if the certainty of the diagnosis is very low;[28] but if the pregnancy is wanted, a high degree of accuracy and certainty for the diagnostic results becomes important because parents tend to cling on to the smallest chance that the fetus may be unaffected and thus decide for birth over abortion. Positive test results have a detrimental impact on the family, especially when the pregnancy is wanted. Most often the parents' first reaction is denial, which is followed by anger, usually directed at the physicians and spouses. Legal suits may be launched,[29] and marriages may break down. Although these consequences may be the same for defects discovered after birth, the crisis is often exaggerated by prenatal screening because of the added stress of having to decide for or against an abortion. The family is thus confronted with the "awesome responsibility" either "to spare [the] child from its own life"[30] or to allow the child to be born into certain suffering. Often parents decide to forfeit a wanted pregnancy in order to avoid bringing a suffering child into the world.[31] But for some, it may just be possible

---

[26]Andrea Bonnicksen, "Genetic Diagnosis of Human Embryos," *Hastings Center Report Special Supplement* 22 (July-August 1992): S6.

[27]Kass, "Implications of Prenatal Diagnosis," p. 195.

[28]Ruth R. Faden et al., "Prenatal Screening and Pregnant Women's Attitudes Toward the Abortion of Defective Fetuses," *American Journal of Public Health* 77, no. 3 (1987): 290.

[29]Macintyre, Keltner and Kovacevich, "Impact of an Abnormal Fetus," p. 536.

[30]Barbara Katz Rothman, *The Tentative Pregnancy* (New York: Viking, 1986), p. 61.

[31]Compare Stephen Post, "Huntington's Disease: Prenatal Screening for Late Onset Disease," *Journal of Medical Ethics* 18, no. 2 (1992): 76.

to see that the suffering associated with having a defective child is not entirely without value for the family. The family good may in fact be enhanced if the burden of the defective child is seen instead as an opportunity for the family members to mature and grow as they learns to live with suffering.[32]

Prenatal Screening and Sex Selection

As part of the larger question of familial good, prenatal screening has been linked to a parental right to fetal sex selection. The strongest and presumably most legitimate argument for such a parental right is to screen for gender-related conditions such as red-green color blindness or the deficiency of enzyme glucose-6-phosphate dehydrogenase (G-6-PD), a condition that affects many black Americans and that is usually asymptomatic, unless the person is exposed to fava beans in her diet or the antimalarial drug primaquinone. Exposure to these food or drug products may lead to the serious but not life-threatening condition of hemolytic anemia. Other sex-linked diseases include Duchenne's muscular dystrophy, a serious progressive, degenerative muscular disease that leads to early death in the male victim's teens; hemophilia A and B, involving the impairment of the clotting factor VIII and IX, respectively; and the Lesch-Nyhan syndrome, which is characterized by progressive neurological problems in the affected patients, who usually do not survive beyond their late twenties. These conditions are caused by defective genes located in the X-chromosome, and since the male has only one X-chromosome, he is much more susceptible to them,[33] providing the reason for prenatal sex selection. However, I believe that none of these conditions justifies prenatal sex selection at all. Serious diseases such as hemophilia, Duchenne's muscular dystrophy and Lesch-Nyhan syndrome can best be prevented by screening the prospective mother as a carrier of the defective gene and then advising her against becoming pregnant. For conditions that are not lethal, such as color blindness or G-6-PD deficiency, the affected person can live a basically normal life with only minimal restrictions. Since a woman who is a carrier only exposes her male offspring to a 50 percent risk of acquiring the defective gene, prenatal sex selection to "screen out" (abort) male fetuses entails a grave moral wrong— eliminating all male fetuses, half of whom do not even have the defective gene, and half of whom are only affected by genetic conditions that can be controlled.

---

[32]Kass, "Implications of Prenatal Diagnosis," p. 196.

[33]Since females have two X-chromosomes, the expression of these conditions in the female would require either a dominant defective gene or a pair of recessive genes, both of which are uncommon. Females are thus usually spared of these diseases but a male will be affected if such a defective gene is present, regardless whether it is dominant or recessive. Sex-linked disorders are therefore usually found in males.

Another argument often used to defend sex selection is limiting population growth. For families intent on having a child of a particular gender, screening for sex selection would ensure that the child will only be of the desired gender and would prevent the birth of children of the undesired gender. The problem is that there is absolutely no evidence that population trends are in any way related to parental preferences to have children of either gender.[34] Moreover, in cultures that manifest a strong preference for male progeny (e.g., China and India), the number of females being aborted could become inordinately high, with the result that the usual balance between male and female is upset, posing greater dangers to population stability. Some studies also suggest that sex selection can be the result of the mother's desire for companionship, manifested in a desire to have a daughter.[35] The argument in the mother's favor implies that the sex choice enhances the quality of life of the child and of the parents by satisfying this desire. The concept of "companionship" is not justifiable, since it entails the practice of sex discrimination, not to mention the gross injustice of exterminating the fetal life simply because it is not the preferred gender.[36]

I believe that the strongest argument *against* accepting screening for sex selection is that it undermines the only significant moral reason for justifying prenatal diagnosis: to prevent the rare but serious untreatable and fatal diseases. By allowing the procedure to serve the function of something as comparatively frivolous as sex selection to satisfy personal desires or cultural needs, prenatal screening will be turned from a diagnostic tool into a tool for eugenic motivations of "customizing" one's baby. Eventually gender would be only one of the attributes parents can choose—along with body height; straight teeth; eye, hair and skin color; and so on.[37] Not only would such a development direct important attention away from the more serious use of prenatal screening, it would also commodify and commercialize human life in the most unacceptable way. If we judge that is not justifiable, what then is the best way to prevent this practice? Laws against prenatal screening for sex selection would probably not be feasible at this time in most Western countries because abortion is allowed for almost any reason. Another option would be withholding information about fetal sex when prenatal testing is done for medical reasons unrelated to detection of sex-linked disorders. This option is consistent with the accepted medical practice of nondisclosure of incidental information and need not be seen as a form of medical paternalism.[38] The problem of vio-

---

[34]Dorothy Wertz and John Fletcher, "Fatal Knowledge? Prenatal Diagnosis and Sex Selection," *Hastings Center Report* 19, no. 3 (1989): 22.
[35]Ibid.
[36]Ibid., p. 23.
[37]Ibid.
[38]Ibid., p. 27.

lating patient autonomy can also be avoided if from the outset the physician provides the parents with a list of information that will and will not be disclosed. In this case, the patient's autonomy would be justly balanced with a recognition of the physician's values.[39]

Prenatal Screening for the Good of the Fetus

Another argument (in addition to the "good of society" and "good of the family" arguments) for justifying prenatal screening for nonfatal genetic defects in the fetus has been advanced by geneticists and physicians in the name of serving the good of the fetus. It is an argument based on the "quality-of-life standard"—also called the "natural standard" because of the assumption that nature itself judges many of these fetuses unfit to live and initiates spontaneous abortion.[40] But how does one determine something as ambiguous as the "natural standard" or whether someone is fit or unfit to live? As Paul Ramsey points out, such a position implies that a society would not be able to accept into the human community any infant until a full-fledged postbirth examination ensures that the infant meets the natural standard.[41] Moreover, this approach of denying the fetus its right to life based on arguments of a quality-of-life standard is highly problematic. Unless the future child's life is short, doomed and amounts to nothing less than torture, I believe the quality-of-life standard should not be applied to deny her right to life. This standard also runs into problems with the more recent concept of the fetus as a patient, which has an important influence on the goals of prenatal screening. Because prenatal testing is currently beneficial mainly to the woman and because it most likely has a negative effect on the fetus, the fetal-patient's autonomy and her best interests are violated. The only way to circumvent this problem is to argue that abortion in this case is indeed a benefit for the fetus, for the fetus's impaired quality of life makes death more preferable—but I have already demonstrated the problems with such an assessment.

In order to overcome this difficulty, some liberal writers would like to extend the application of a "natural standard" to a broader class of fetuses who are inflicted with handicaps and disabilities but not with the more severe cases of genetic defects.[42] These authors suggest that when parents decide to have children, a certain decent minimum quality of life should be provided in

---

[39]Jeffrey Botkin, "Prenatal Screening: Professional Standards and the Limits of Parental Choice," *Obstetrics and Gynecology* 75 (May 1990): 880.

[40]Kass, "Implications of Prenatal Diagnosis," p. 197.

[41]Paul Ramsey, "Screening: An Ethicists View," in *Ethical Issues in Human Genetics: Genetic Counseling and the Use of Genetic Knowledge,* ed. Bruce Hilton et al. (New York: Plenum, 1973), p. 157.

[42]Bonnie Steinbock and Ron McClamrock, "When Is Birth Unfair to the Child?" *Hastings Center Report* 24, no. 6 (1994): 16-22.

order to qualify as good parents. It is morally wrong, they say, for prospective parents to justify bringing into existence a handicapped and impaired child by saying that the child's life, though miserable, is not so awful that he would prefer nonexistence. They conclude that when a decent minimum of quality of life is not reached and the children are still brought to existence, they are being victimized by the parents' decision.[43] As a form of quality control and assurance, prospective parents are thus under a moral obligation to have children only after reflecting on the quality of life the children are likely to experience, and prenatal screening is said to provide that opportunity for quality control. Using the "decent minimum" rationale to justify prenatal screening and abortion of genetically defective fetuses is based on the assumption that the suffering of a miserable life is thereby prevented. But how can we be sure that people who are "retarded" are in fact suffering on account of their "retardation"? For instance, a person with Down syndrome may have a diminished capacity for cognitive functions, but this limitation also protects him from fully realizing that he is retarded in the way others perceive him. We simply do not know how much the retarded suffer from their disability because we will never be able to be truly *in* their position unless we are similarly disabled. The decent-minimum standard involves judgments of another's quality of life that are highly subjective and too unreliable to establish a standard of "awfulness of life." Too often the good of the fetus is defined by the values of the parents, which is an unfair guideline for determining when genetic abortion may be permissible. Besides, much of what we consider as handicaps or disabilities are in fact social constructions created by the society's prejudiced values and needs. As Stanley Hauerwas suggests, in a society that values cooperation more than competition and ambition,[44] the suffering of retardation—which for many would justify abortion—might not even exist. What we should fear most is that, in our relentless pursuit of normal or minimally decent children, we will make the concept of "normality" the defining criterion of a life worth living. "Defectives should not be born" becomes an Orwellian principle without limits.[45]

This emphasis on the parents' responsibility to ensure a decent minimum quality of life for their offspring has also become part of the common defense that prenatal screening is necessary for certain women who are "at risk" and thus "need" to be tested in this manner. I like to point out the concept of "need" is a highly flexible and value-laden one, much influenced by the domi-

---

[43]Ibid., p. 19.
[44]Stanley Hauerwas, *Suffering Presence: Theological Reflections on Medicine, the Mentally Handicapped and the Church* (Notre Dame: University of Notre Dame Press, 1986), p. 161.
[45]Kass, "Implications of Prenatal Diagnosis," p. 192.

nant societal ethos on matters of health and disease, normality and abnormality. A society that automatically labels any woman over thirty-five years old as "high risk" can easily create specific needs for that high-risk group. Today, our culture is dominated by the language and tools of genetics, so our concepts of health and disease have been reduced to a form of genetic determinism. Yet the actual life process and disease states are much more complicated than simple genetic determination, being influenced by a unique interaction between genes and the environment.[46] Prenatal diagnosis, treated almost as a "ritual" of pregnancy—at least for white middle-class women in North America—is a striking example of genetically deterministic thinking and a culturally constructed need.[47] It is doubtful whether prenatal genetic screening can ever live up to the expectation of being an insurance policy for parents, guaranteeing that their fetuses have attained a decent minimum in quality, for the simple reason that certain conditions, particularly those related to mental retardation, may not be exclusively or even primarily genetic in nature. Many cases of mental retardation are related to postnatal developmental factors such as environmental deprivations, nutritional deficiencies and other medical mishaps, including untreated febrile conditions. No matter how sophisticated prenatal genetic screening might become in the future, it is unrealistic to expect that it will ever be able to identify these disorders and eliminate them through a permissive abortion policy. Even if prenatal screening is required of all pregnant women, the "retarded" will continue to live among us.[48] I must conclude that prenatal screening is a rather poor means for reassuring women about the quality of their pregnancy. Alleviating the general social and economic inequalities among women, guaranteeing provision of good basic health care, reducing harmful environmental influences, educating mothers about the harmful effects of substance abuse (including cigarette smoking, alcohol and cocaine) and creating a society supportive of pregnancy in general are much more important ways to reassure women that their pregnancy will have a good outcome.

The idea that pregnant women need prenatal screening is also driven by the assumption that it is specifically a woman's duty to seek out such preventative measures. This peculiar duty seems to have arisen from the fact that in North American at least, the health of the family, especially of the children, is usually seen as the mother's sole responsibility. Prenatal screening is thus seen as an extension of the mother's duties as a caregiver. At the same time, a pregnant woman is so bombarded by behavioral directives with respect to her preg-

---

[46]Richard Lewontin, *Biology as Ideology* (Concord, Ontario: Anansi, 1991), p. 27.

[47]Lippman, "Prenatal Genetic Testing," p. 16.

[48]Compare Hauerwas, *Suffering Presence*, pp. 162-63.

nancy and the care for her future child that she often feels incompetent. This sense of incompetence renders a pregnant woman particularly vulnerable to prenatal diagnosis, since it is presented as aiding her in her overwhelming task. External verification thus becomes more important to her than her own sense of self and her own intuition.[49] Furthermore, as in all other areas of biotechnology, prenatal screening is being driven to a certain extent by commercial logic. The commercialization of these procedures creates the need for laboratories which in turn must increase consumer demand to keep each laboratory working at capacity. In this manner, prenatal diagnosis may easily become a necessary routine procedure in obstetric care, not so much freely chosen by the prospective mother as an exercise of her maternal duty of care-giving, but mandated by the general attitudes of the society, the medical profession and the biotechnology industry.

In this context, it is ironic to see the argument put forward by some that prenatal screening increases women's reproductive choices and thus their reproductive control. It is true that testing increases control, but it would seem that such control resides more in the hands of persons other than the pregnant woman herself. Geneticists and obstetricians decide what is healthy or normal and what is not. They are thus the group that gains power over decisions to continue or to terminate pregnancy. Other potential participants who may stand to gain control include the government and insurance companies. Newborn screening for phenylketonuria (PKU) is carried out in the United States with universal approval; yet, in only four states are health insurers required to cover the costs of the special foods children with PKU need. The prenatal testing cannot be said to have increased the woman's choice in this context.[50] If we view the needs and demands of prenatal screening in a larger social context, it is much harder to speak about free choice, reproductive autonomy and parental responsibility.[51]

As women rely increasingly on prenatal test results to validate their pregnancy, prenatal screening subtly compromises motherhood by putting the pregnancy in a provisional status, so that until the lab confirms negative test results, the status of pregnancy need not, indeed *cannot,* be acknowledged or accepted. Prenatal diagnosis becomes a slowly pulsing amber light, warning prospective mothers that they must not rush to experience the intimate union with the fetus until after the completion of a quality control procedure. The test thus renders a confirmed pregnancy tentative and conditional, creating essen-

---

[49]Lippman, "Prenatal Genetic Testing," p. 30.

[50]Ibid., p. 35.

[51]E. A. Gates, "Ethical Considerations in Prenatal Diagnosis," *Western Journal of Medicine* 159, no. 3 (1993): 393; also see Lippman, "Prenatal Genetic Testing," p. 32.

tially "a pregnancy without a baby."[52] This has a profoundly negative effect on the pregnant woman's experience, for she has a unique opportunity and privilege to relate to a new human being at the most vulnerable and dependent period of that being's existence. This relationship requires an unconditional commitment to the child by the pregnant woman. Prenatal screening renders such a commitment tentative and delays the bonding between mother and fetus, which severely compromises the woman's experience and the fetus's ability to flourish. Pregnancy—the most personal and intimate event a human being can ever experience—has taken on a contractual nature, with the prenatal diagnosis acting as the arbitrator who controls the contract and determines the conditions that must be fulfilled. This radical deconstruction of women's understanding and experience of pregnancy is perhaps the most damaging of all the implications of prenatal screening. As one writer laments, "Disabilities will always be with us. That will never change. But mothers will suffer and motherhood will have changed. That has consequences. That is of consequence."[53]

Prenatal Screening and the Suffering of the Disabled Community

The wide support that prenatal screening enjoys is partly due to the ethos of our society, which is obsessed with physical perfection and which has driven us to require such "health care" services as elitist sperm banks, genetic manipulations, plastic surgery and so on in order to restore people's health to normal or to a decent minimum. Does our vast new genetic knowledge enrich our reproductive lives, enhance our tolerance of differences, increase our acceptance of human finitude and strengthen our communities? Or does it enslave us to live under the "tyranny of the normal" or the "decent minimum" without enhancing "quality standards" in our life as a whole? Stephen Post rightly points out that this "tyranny of the normal" is by no means a fixed standard,[54] and if we ask the disabled community about their self-perceptions of their quality of life, we will realize that their perception of their disability is strikingly different from that held by the rest of the society. Most disabled people will affirm that a large part of their suffering results not from their physical impairments, but from the many obstacles they face in society—from technology, law, architecture and both individual and corporate attitudes. They do not suffer as much from their impairments as from a society that despises the impaired. The argument that a reduced quality of life justifies selective abortion

---

[52]Barbara Katz Rothman, "The Tentative Pregnancy: Then and Now," *Fetal Diagnosis and Therapy* 8, no. 1 (1993): 60-63.

[53]Ibid., p. 63.

[54]Post, "Huntington's Disease," p. 76.

thus clashes with the professed experience of people who actually live with a disability. Critically, most do not believe that the suffering produced either directly or indirectly by their disability is a sufficient reason to avoid life.[55]

Many fear that a widespread application of prenatal screening will have an enormous negative effect on the public perception of disability. Prenatal screening is already being explicitly promoted as beneficial because it will reduce the number of disabled people in society. This development will inevitably increase societal pressure to reduce funding of programs that benefit persons with disabilities, and there is evidence that social support for parents with disabled children is waning. It is entirely possible that our aversion toward "abnormal" children will grow in the foreseeable future to such an extent that mothers will be *required* to abort their genetically disabled fetuses despite the variability and unpredictability of the severity of the prenatally diagnosed condition. If we regard persons with disabilities as a definable social group that has faced great oppression and stigmatization, then we must regard prenatal screening and its influence on societal values as nothing less than a form of social abuse.[56] For this reason, the disabled community in Canada uniformly condemns prenatal diagnosis and genetic screening and demands that such programs be banned and not supported by government funding.[57]

Prenatal screening and genetic abortion have revealed how our society has forgotten the basic reality of human suffering. Given that we now have so many tools to control our lives, we forget that suffering is very much a part of the human reality, whether or not one has a disability. As we have seen, the painful life from which we are trying to spare our children simply does not match the quality of life that disabled persons perceive themselves as having. Yet our society is insistent that they are suffering and that if we do not prevent them from coming into this world, we are guilty of bringing about a "wrongful life." Certainly these people need special care, and their handicapped condition should never be regarded as insignificant or trivial; but their suffering must not be exaggerated or used as an excuse to eliminate them when they are quite willing and able to live up to the challenges of their suffering. Perhaps their presence in our midst is a crucial reminder that as a community we need to show greater sensitivity and sympathy to those who are in need, rather than seeking to eliminate them in the name of mercifully preventing suffering. The ethic of personhood I espouse demands at least that much from us.

---

[55]D. Kaplan, "Prenatal Screening and Its Impact on Persons with Disabilities," *Fetal Diagnosis and Therapy* 8, no. 1 (1993): 65.

[56]Ibid., p. 69.

[57]Varda Burstyn, "Making Perfect Babies," part 2, *Canadian Forum* 70 (April 1992): 18.

Our society's readiness to embrace prenatal screening and genetic abortion ultimately reflects its inability to face the suffering of which the genetically handicapped remind us. Our technological culture has given us a triumphalistic mindset, manifested in the illusion that we can overcome any difficulty. We are thus so accustomed to being in control that these genetically handicapped people become an unfriendly reminder of our finitude, limitations, neediness and dependency—all part of our real nature, which we are unable to face. Hence these defective fetuses must be eliminated as wrongful lives. I believe that our community, Christian or otherwise, is better off eschewing prenatal screening and genetic abortion. Rather, we should embrace the disabled people in our midst both because in their neediness and dependency, they help us face our own finitude, and because as human beings they deserve no less. In providing and receiving care, both the able and the disabled become better persons.

The Anencephalic Fetus and Neonate

A rare and especially tragic example of a prenatally diagnosed defective fetus is the anencephalic. Lacking the neocortex, the anencephalic is without sentience as a fetus and consciousness as a neonate. Since she is incapable of feeling pain and her postnatal life is measured in hours or days, it is doubtful whether the concept of "wrongful life" can be applied to her. Before I discuss the moral status of an anencephalic fetus/neonate, I will briefly describe her pathophysiology.

To begin with, though *anencephaly* literally means "without brain," it refers not to the complete absence of the head or brain, but rather to the congenital absence of a developed forebrain, skull and scalp due to the failure of the exposed anterior portion of the neural tube to form a forebrain during the first month of gestation.[58] Depending on the level of the brain stem's development, an anencephalic neonate may be capable of supporting basic vital functions such as a heartbeat and breathing for a short time. While the cause of anencephaly is not known, all the current data suggest a polygenic or multifactorial etiology: chromosomal abnormalities, mechanical factors and poorly understood geographic factors have been listed as possible reasons for the disorder.[59]

Pregnancy with an anencephalic fetus carries an increased risk to both the mother and the fetus. Approximately 65 percent of these fetuses die in utero.

---

[58]D. A. Shewmon, "Anencephaly: Selected Medical Aspects," *Hastings Center Report* 18 (October 1988): 11.

[59]Medical Task Force on Anencephaly, "The Infant with Anencephaly," *New England Journal of Medicine* 322, no. 1 (1990): 669-70.

Of those that survive until birth, 55 to 75 percent are stillborn. The vast majority of live-born neonates with the disorder die within the first twenty-four to forty-eight hours after birth because the brain stem may also be too underdeveloped or too defective to perform the basic integrative function required for a vegetative state outside the womb. Only rarely would the anencephalic fetus survive for longer than a week or more. Due to the complete absence of a cerebral cortex, anencephalics permanently lack consciousness.[60] Blindness as well as anomalies of the middle and inner ears are not uncommon, and hormone levels are reduced markedly because the hypothalamus is missing.[61] Between 13 and 33 percent of live-born anencephalics also show defects of nonneural organs such as the heart, liver and kidneys. The direct cause of death for live-born anencephalics has been poorly understood and remains essentially unknown. Endocrine abnormalities may be the most likely factor, leading to fatal electrolyte imbalances, which result in cardiac arrhythmia—the most likely immediate cause of death.

Frank Chervenak, best known for his work in the area of the maternal-fetal dyad, is a strong advocate for the patient status of the postviable fetus, toward whom he believes the physician should have beneficence-based obligations. As a result, he is strongly opposed to abortion of the postviable fetus and sees it as a violation of the physician-patient relationship. However, he makes the anencephalic fetuses the one exception to this position.[62] In his view, in the total absence of sentience and consciousness, it is difficult to construe one's actions as either harming or benefiting the fetus, and the balance between beneficence-based obligations tips favorably toward the mother. Thus abortion in this case is morally justifiable, albeit never mandatory.[63] The third-trimester abortion of anencephalic fetuses would thus be allowed, according to this position, only because of the unique characteristics of these fetuses and the resulting lack of a possible beneficence-based obligation toward it.

A more conservative approach in handling the anencephalics has been proposed by the Catholic hospitals in North America. The proposal is an attempt to justify an early induction of labor of the anencephalic fetus in

---

[60]Even though the brain stem is known to be able to take over cortical functions, it is felt that evidence of consciousness and experience of pain are distinctly lacking in these anencephalic neonates.

[61]W. Holzgreve and F. K. Beller, "Anencephalic Infants as Organ Donors," *Clinical Obstetrics and Gynecology* 35, no. 4 (1992): 823.

[62]F. A. Chervenak and L. B. McCullough, "When Is Termination of Pregnancy During the Third Trimester Morally Justifiable?" *New England Journal of Medicine* 310, no. 8 (1984): 501-4.

[63]Chervenak and McCullough feel that for other fetuses with severe defects, either the defects are not diagnosed with absolute certainty or their condition may allow for a longer span of postnatal life and a "greater opportunity for a meaningful existence than is generally appreciated." Ibid., pp. 502-3.

order to preserve the hospital's integrity as a Catholic institution.[64] In this proposal, the mother is regarded as the primary decision-maker, and the hospital is ethically warranted to respect the decision of the mother either to "interrupt the pregnancy" or to carry to term. The proposal permits "interrupting the pregnancy" by early induction because it is felt that there is a significant difference between "abortion" and induction. Although both may be referred to as abortion, the proposal argues that inducing an anencephalic pregnancy prematurely is a different act than abortion because the motivation is different. Since the anencephalic has neither the capacity nor the potential for human experience of benefit or harm, the pregnancy is a futile one; the anencephalic fetus is best regarded as irreversibly dying, so that an early induction of such pregnancies means only relief from a fatally flawed and futile process. From the mother's point of view, it is the condition of anencephaly and not the induction of labor that kills the fetus, just as it is not the death of the fetus but the discontinuation of the pregnancy that brings relief. These distinctions are important for one's understanding of the intentions that lead to the early induction of delivery. The proposal further stipulates that if an anencephalic infant is delivered alive, no medical treatment other than humane supportive care will be provided, and organ removal should be avoided.

While the proposal is laudable for its careful attempt to differentiate the issues involved, it is not without problems. First, the proposal is very ambivalent about the anencephalic's status as a person. It attempts to sidestep the whole issue of personhood by calling the fetus a human life and justifies this approach by arguing that the focus should be on the fetal physical flaws and the dying process instead of on abstract theoretical categories. But this move is unacceptable because both radical physical flaws and dying processes presuppose certain living entities, so their significance depends on whether it is somebody dying or merely some *thing* dying. A second problem is the use of maternal risk to justify removing the flawed and dying human life, comparing the induction to the removal of an ectopic pregnancy and other such medical situations that pose life-threatening risk to the mother. Yet a comparable magnitude of risk posed by the anencephalic fetus to the maternal health or life has never been demonstrated.

Conservative Protestant writer Francis J. Beckwith seems to have misjudged more severely when he puts the anencephalic fetus in the same category as a teratoma, which seems to imply that he may not even be certain that he is dealing with a human being. Hence, he remains uncommitted as to whether an

---

[64]James F. Drane, "Anencephaly and the Interruption of Pregnancy: Policy Proposals for HECs," *HEC Forum* 4, no. 2 (1992): 103-19.

abortion can be justified.[65] Hessel Bouma III and his associates consider the anencephalic fetus "not a potential person because deformities prevent it from coming even close to having God-imaging capacities," and thus they recommend the abortion of what they consider to be a "meaningless life."[66] Similarly, Robert Wennberg believes that since personhood would never emerge in these anencephalic infants, they have no prospect for personal existence and their death is therefore not tragic.[67] However, one would have to ask exactly what kind of "human life" these authors consider the anencephalic fetus to be? Would they have reservations if an anencephalic fetus were to be buried immediately after it is delivered "alive"? Would they object if organs were removed for transplantation from such a living being while it is breathing spontaneously? And if they would not, what kind of rationale, I wonder, can they offer? The question as to what sort of human entity exists during the several hours, days and sometimes weeks of life that these anencephalic infants have remains unanswered. If they are neither persons nor potential persons, *what* then are they?

It seems that the attitude toward the anencephalic infant inadvertently exposes some of the hidden weaknesses and ambiguities of many current concepts of personhood. To the extent that I believe human personhood is grounded not on any capacities the human being can achieve, but on the relation God establishes with the creature he creates, I find it difficult to consider the anencephalic fetus as anything other than a person—albeit a terribly and irremediably defective one. Since the anencephalic infant, if born, will not be suffering as will neonates with other severe conditions such as Tay-Sachs, trisomy 13 and trisomy 18, there is no justification for abortion on the basis of "wrongful life." In the event that such an unfortunate one is born alive, she is born a human person, and her short life as a person must be respected and treated with dignity as we would treat any irreversibly dying person. No heroic or futile treatments need to be provided, but neither should her organs be harvested for transplant. She dies and rests in peace as a person.

Prenatal Screening and the Ethic of Personhood

To summarize, Christians view parenthood as a vocation and children as gifts from God to be embraced whether they are normal and bright or handicapped and retarded.[68] Furthermore, Christians in general consider the sanctity of life as weightier than the quality of life, and as such the supreme value of human

---

[65]Francis J. Beckwith, *Politically Correct Death* (Grand Rapids, Mich.: Baker, 1993), p. 68.

[66]Bouma III et al., *Christian Faith*, p. 227.

[67]Robert N. Wennberg, *Life in the Balance: Exploring the Abortion Controversy* (Grand Rapids, Mich.: Eerdmans, 1985), p. 34.

[68]For a more detailed discussion on Christian parenting, see chapter seven, "Infertility and the Need for Assisted Reproductive Technologies," above.

life is nonnegotiable, even when the life involves much suffering, when it serves no apparent useful purpose, or even when it appears to stand in the way of the good of humankind. This is because Christians believe that those afflicted and handicapped with genetic disorders can still enjoy meaningful lives as persons in all their relations with God, the people around them and the rest of the creation. God's special concern for the weak, fragile, powerless and marginalized—as demonstrated throughout Scripture— requires not only that we respect equally those afflicted with disease and those who are healthy, but also that persons who are blessed with good health should step forward as advocates specifically for these people. The long Christian tradition of good Samaritanism also motivates Christians, both individually and in their institutions, to care for the weak, the needy and the downtrodden. We live in a fallen world, and genetic defects are but one manifestation of this fallenness. Society as a whole may reject those who fail to meet the so-called decent minimum, but this is a position that Christians can never share, for the Christian tradition holds that all human beings are created equal as the image of God and that we all strive toward the perfect image.

In addition to a high valuation of life and an advocacy for the weak, Christians also have a unique perspective on suffering that is shared by only a few others in our society. In the current debate on prenatal screening and abortion, it is difficult to find any positive appreciation for the role of suffering, either on the part of those afflicted with diseases or on the part of those caring for them. To most Christians, the community's uncritical and permissive attitude toward the screening and abortion of fetuses not only questions our relationship with and trust in God, but also reminds us of the Christian understanding of the nature and meaning of suffering and of our willingness to endure it. Hauerwas equates caring for the retarded to loving God: "God's face is the face of the retarded; God's body is the body of the retarded; God's being is that of the retarded. . . . In the face of the retarded we are offered an opportunity to see God."[69] The point Hauerwas really tries to make is that we need to receive the genetically handicapped into our community because they serve as a reminder of our true nature as creatures in total dependence on God and thus on one another. In other words, as human persons living in a community—Christians and non-Christians together—we ought to see those in the community afflicted with genetic disorders as providing us with an opportunity for our "relational personhood" to flourish, for us to give and to receive those who suffer, whereby we become better persons. Prenatal screening, if it is done, should only be undertaken in order that the community is better prepared to welcome the afflicted.

---

[69]Hauerwas, *Suffering Presence,* pp. 178-79.

Medical Technological Innovations and the Status of the Unborn

*S*ince the 1980s two new developments in medicine have contributed to a change in public awareness of the nature and status of the early conceptus and the fetus, which in turn has altered the public viewpoint on abortion. On one hand, the development of abortifacients has fostered an insensitivity to the presence of the early conceptus and a concomitant moral indifference regarding the destruction of this nascent human life by these agents. On the other hand, the development of various surgical interventions aimed directly at the fetus has promoted the concept of the fetus as a patient, which recognizes the fetus as an individual human being whose well-being can be protected and promoted quite independently of her mother's. In this chapter I will first focus on the abortifacients and then follow with a brief discussion of the fetus as a patient.

Oral Contraceptives and Abortifacients

In the greater controversy over abortion, the relationship between contraception and abortion is rarely explored, and yet in a very practical sense, this gray area is where the abortion controversy begins. Both pro-life and pro-choice advocates agree that preventing conception is qualitatively different from terminating an early pregnancy. But when it comes to judging when a type of birth control acts as a contraceptive and when it acts as an abortifacient, the discussion rapidly becomes more complex. This is because contraceptives, broadly defined, operate by one or more of three physiological mechanisms:

☐ preventing the fertilization of the ovum by the sperm via a barrier or anovulant

☐ preventing the implantation of a fertilized egg

☐ destroying the developing embryo

In this discussion, I will assume a narrow definition of "contraceptive" to refer to those that inhibit pregnancy only via the first category—that is, by clearly *preventing* conception.[1] Conversely, all methods that work exclusively post-conception (the second or third category) will be referred to as "abortifacients," and methods that have the potential to operate in any one or a combination of these three mechanisms will be qualified as "abortive contraceptives." My concern is with the latter two types of birth control, which contain at least a *potential* to be abortifacient.

Traditionally, oral contraceptives (OCs) are understood to prevent pregnancy by preventing conception through suppressing ovulation. In other words, they are truly contraceptives. But this is true only if the estrogen content in a "birth-control pill" is sufficiently high. If the estrogen level is low, OCs will prevent pregnancy by thickening the cervical mucus to prevent sperm penetration or will alter the endometrium to discourage the implantation of an fertilized egg. To minimize undesirable side effects associated with high levels of estrogen, there is a tendency among women to prefer formulations with a low estrogen content, so that these low-estrogen OCs operate more as abortifacients than as contraceptives. In OCs that include progestin, how pregnancy is suppressed depends on the dosage and response of the woman's own hormone levels through her cycle, and it is even more difficult to assess whether these OCs act as contraceptives or abortifacients.[2] Progestin-only pills (also called "mini-pills") do not contain estrogen, which results in fewer side effects but higher pregnancy rates. The scientific data suggest that this formulation fails to prevent ovulation in over 50 percent of cases, implying that it primarily acts by preventing sperm penetration or embryo implantation; that is, it acts as an abortifacient. These uncertainties are also found in triphasic pills, biphasic pills and tricyclic pills.[3] In general, the trend

---

[1] I will also refer to these as "fertility control" methods. By contrast, *birth control* will be used as an umbrella term to refer to all methods that prevent birth (both contraceptive and abortifacient).

[2] Nicholas Tonti-Filippini, "The Pill: Abortifacient or Contraceptive? A Literature Review," *Linacre Quarterly* 62, no. 1 (1995): 5-8.

[3] Ibid., pp. 9-10.

in OCs is for patients as well as providers to prefer formulations that operate more as abortifacients (or as "abortive contraceptives") than as strict contraceptives, in order to reduce side effects without sacrificing efficacy. In the last decade, injectables and subcutaneous implants containing progestins have been developed. Their mechanism of action is similar to progestin-only OCs.[4] The emergency contraception pill (also called the "morning-after pill"), is a regimen of four estrogen-progestin OCs taken over a twelve-hour period in pairs within seventy-two hours of intercourse. A high estrogen and progestin peak ensues, with heavy bleeding occurring soon after, and the chance of pregnancy is reduced by about 75 percent.[5] Its mode of action is probably abortifacient, though it may act through ovulation suppression if it is taken in the woman's cycle.[6]

Intrauterine Devices and Abortifacients

The intrauterine device (IUD) is one of the most widely used abortive contraceptive methods in the world, even though its usage is less popular in North America. The two most common intrauterine devices are the copper-bearing IUDs, the Copper-T-380-A (marketed as ParaGard) and the Multiload IUD. In one study, the efficacy of Cu-T-380-A has been found to be comparable to oral contraception and even sterilization.[7] There are also progestin-releasing IUDs, which emit steady, low doses of Levo-norgestrel and which are effective for over five years.[8] IUDs most likely operate by their spermicidal effect through the copper ions, preventing the ovum from becoming fertilized,[9] although most people believe that all IUDs operate *at least in part* as an abortifacient by interfering with the implantation of the fertilized egg. The progestin-releasing IUD operates by preventing the embryo's implantation, hence its primary mode of operation is abortifacient rather than contraceptive.

RU 486, lauded by some as "perhaps the greatest breakthrough in fertility control technology since the discovery of oral contraceptives,"[10] is a synthetic steroid that acts as a progesterone antagonist, leading to a reduced progesterone level in the uterus. As progesterone is necessary for maintaining the uter-

---

[4]George F. Brown, "Long-Acting Contraceptives: Rationale, Current Development and Ethical Implications," *Hastings Center Report Special Supplement* 25, no. 1 (1995): S13.

[5]C. E. Ellerston and C. C. Harper, "The Emergency Contraception Pill: A Survey of Knowledge and Attitudes Among Students at Princeton University," *American Journal of Obstetrics and Gynecology* 173 (November 1995): 1438-40.

[6]Tonti-Filippini, "The Pill," p. 11.

[7]I. Chi, "What We Learned from Recent IUD Studies: A Researcher's Perspective," *Contraception* 48 (August 1993): 83.

[8]Brown, "Long-Acting Contraceptives," p. S13.

[9]Chi, "What We Learned," p. 83.

[10]Brown, "Long-Acting Contraceptives," p. S13.

ine lining, the reduced progesterone level causes the uterine lining to be sloughed off and the embryo expulsed along with it.[11] When used alone, RU 486 has a 60 to 85 percent rate of success for a complete abortion, and the rate rises to 95 percent when prostaglandin is added. A delay of thirty-six to forty-eight hours is required between taking RU 486 and the prostaglandin, rendering the abortion a gradual process that may stretch over two or three days.[12] Within thirty-six to forty-eight hours, bleeding equivalent to a heavy menstrual period ensues, lasting eight to fifteen days. Side effects include abdominal cramping, nausea and occasionally bleeding heavy enough to require a blood transfusion. Due to the uncertain effect RU 486 may have on the fetus, when the drug does not clearly induce a medical abortion, a follow-up surgical abortion may be required.

Recent research aims to develop abortifacient vaccines for long-term effects on fertility. One of the most promising abortifacient vaccines is the human chorionic gonadotropin (HCG) vaccine, which attacks HCG, a hormone produced by the human embryo that is necessary for the maintenance of the uterine endometrium in the first few months of pregnancy. Any drop in the levels of this hormone in the first six to ten weeks will terminate the pregnancy by causing the certain death of the embryo/fetus.[13]

The above survey of birth-control methods reveals a historical progression from oral contraceptives with comparatively low abortifacient potentials to RU 486, which operates solely as an abortifacient. Such a shift is not accidental—it is underpinned by important ideological and practical social ties between contraception and abortion. Ideologically, both contraception and abortion are expressions of the individual's right to reproductive choice. Once the right to control fertility (through contraception) is granted, there is no reason why the right cannot be extended to control birth (through abortion), since contraception and abortion are both grounded in the same right.[14] Another attitude supported by both contraception and abortion is the desire to avoid children, which is also closely tied to the reproductive right[15]

---

[11]D. DiPerri, "RU 486, Mifepristone: A Review of a Controversial Drug," *Nurse Practitioner* 19 (June 1994): 59.

[12]M. Berer, "Inducing a Miscarriage: Women-Centered Perspective on RU 486/Prostaglandin as an Early Abortion Method," *Law, Medicine and Health Care* 20 (Fall 1992): 207.

[13]L. Roberge, "Abortifacient Vaccines: Technological Update and Christian Appraisal," in *Bioethics and the Future of Medicine: A Christian Appraisal,* ed. John F. Kilner, Nigel M. de S. Cameron and David L. Schiedermayer (Grand Rapids, Mich.: Eerdmans, 1995), p. 179.

[14]Betsy Hartman, *Reproductive Rights and Wrongs* (New York: Harper & Row, 1987), p. 242. Hartman goes on to say that "properly performed, abortion is a woman's safety net and one of the most important reproductive rights of all" (p. 249).

[15]The fact that contraception is "against conception" (and thus "anti-child") is often used as

and which can be seen to consist of two aspects: first, the adult's economic and practical desire to be able to have sex without making a baby, and second, the desire to have a child born wanted.[16] However, since contraception can fail even under the best of conditions, abortion has to complement birth-control methods to ensure that no unwanted babies will be born.

The relationship between contraception and abortion has also been supported socially through the rulings of American courts. In the United States Supreme Court's decision in *Griswold* v. *Connecticut* (1965), married couples were guaranteed the right to use contraception. The contraceptive right was later extended to include abortion in the *Roe* v. *Wade* decision (1973), which cited *Griswold* as providing partial precedent. Thus, the social acceptance of abortion can be seen as building on the recognition of a reproductive right to contraception.[17] The connection between contraception and abortion is made even closer because they are also seen as necessary in the attempt to check the rapidly expanding world population. In the war against overpopulation, contraception and abortion serve as coservants together harnessing the incessant multiplication of the teeming masses.[18]

A Moral Evaluation of Abortifacients

Thus, for both ideological and practical reasons, the acceptance of contraception has contributed to the acceptance of abortifacients and abortion. In the context of this complex relationship between contraception and abortion, I will evaluate the social and ethical implications of RU 486, since it is the first major abortifacient available. The most startling implication of RU 486 is the privatization of the abortion procedure it introduces. RU 486 allows a new dimension of privacy in birth control, which becomes more like going to a family-planning clinic for contraception.[19] This will result in a lessened accountability of the public, and the individual physician, the woman and

---

a Catholic argument to proscribe all contraception. A common argument is that conception is a human good and that it is always evil to directly thwart the actualization of human goods, as contraception does. Compare Joseph Boyle, "Contraception and Natural Family Planning," in *Why Humanae Vitae Was Right,* ed. Janet Smith (San Francisco: Ignatius, 1993).

[16]American Academy of Pediatrics, *Statement of Goals,* 1978, quoted in Eugene F. Diamond, "'Every Child Should Be Born Wanted'—A Dubious Goal," *Linacre Quarterly* 52, no. 2 (1985): 105.

[17]Incidentally, this relationship—whereby contraception contributes to an acceptance of abortion—is one of the arguments the Roman Catholic Church uses to proscribe all types of contraception. See *Humanae Vitae,* sec. 17.

[18]Andrezej Kulczycki, Malcom Potts and Allan Rosenfeld note that no society has ever achieved low fertility rates without finding recourse to abortion. See "Abortion and Fertility Regulation," *Lancet* 347 (June 15, 1996): 1663.

[19]Berer, "Inducing a Miscarriage," p. 199.

her partner to an extent that they can evade moral scrutiny almost entirely.[20] Furthermore, as women are provided the opportunity to take an abortifacient in the privacy of their homes, the transparency of the issues within the abortion debate will be greatly reduced, and the pro-life movement will be weakened as it loses its opponent in the public debate. The identity of pro-choice abortionists will also change from individual doctors or clinics to pharmaceutical companies, opponents that are obviously too powerful and that are more difficult to directly protest against, with the expected result that the balance between the pro-choice and pro-life views will be upset and tipped in favor of the former.

Second, RU 486 will have serious implications for the woman's experience, for with it abortion shifts from a surgical to a medical procedure. The appropriate level of counseling, more readily provided in the structured clinical setting, will not be available; and many see this as a significant psychological threat to the woman. One study reports that only 24 percent of women have preferred the home environment to the hospital because "the miscarriage of a fetus at home is a lonely, physically trying, frightening, and demoralizing experience—one that culminates in the woman viewing her own dead child in a terrifying mass of blood, clot, and tissue."[21] On the other hand, some argue that experiencing the abortion at home allows a greater chance for loved ones and other social networks to support the woman at a difficult time. They also see that with RU 486, the physical trauma associated with surgical abortion is replaced by the more "natural" process of a medical abortion. Some women have referred to abortions with RU 486 as "a premeditated miscarriage," with a "natural" feel that greatly reduces the emotional pain involved. In addition, the two to three days over which a RU 486-induced abortion occurs allows women more time to disengage emotionally from their pregnancy—a fitting period in which they may emotionally come to terms with the abortion.[22] In this connection, some women believe that RU 486 increases their personal control over the procedure and that it allows them to avoid the helpless feelings and humiliation commonly associated with surgical abortion. But this overlooks the fact that this new power to decide and to act comes with a new responsibility and ownership that is often too traumatic and burdensome for the woman. As one puts it, "I took the decisive action, I killed the child, there were no intermediaries."[23] Further, their sense of increased autonomy and control may be more apparent than real, and it is by no means clear that RU 486 will in fact mean-

---

[20]Lisa Sowle Cahill, " 'Abortion Pill RU486': Ethics, Rhetoric and Social Practice," *Hastings Center Report* 17 (October-November 1987): 5.

[21]Bernard Nathanson, "The Abortion Cocktail," *First Things* 59 (January 1996): 25.

[22]Berer, "Inducing a Miscarriage," pp. 200-204.

[23]Ibid., p. 201.

ingfully accord women more autonomy. It has been contended that the clinical involvement in a medical abortion may be even greater than was the case with the surgical abortion, involving multiple office visits, blood tests, ultrasonic investigations and strict medical supervision.[24] While this is not necessarily a bad thing, it certainly is a far cry from the experience touted by defenders of the so-called "private" abortion pill. Many also see the use of RU 486 as a direct threat to the autonomy of the women who use these methods by the physicians who prescribe it and by the pharmaceutical companies which manufacture it. As I have noted, there is a persistent ignorance in the public over the crucial distinctions of the mechanism of action between contraceptives and abortifacients, and the medical establishment remains surprisingly ambivalent on the issue. The terminological confusion is further compounded by the term *contragestive,* which is now frequently used in place of *abortifacient* in references to RU 486.[25] If by changing the terminology the medical professionals intend to conceal the drug's abortive action, then this intention must be considered as deceptive, thus violating the woman's autonomy and her right of informed consent for her choice of the contraceptive method.

Lastly, the use of abortifacients such as RU 486 poses a direct threat to the nascent human life and confronts the society with the grave matter of justice to the conceptus. The moral concerns are intensified as medical researchers relentlessly pursue the development of abortifacient vaccines. It has been estimated that with an abortifacient vaccine (e.g., HCG vaccine, Trophoectoderm antigen vaccine), a sexually active woman might be terminating up to twelve embryos a year,[26] so that while the number of conventional abortions may statistically decrease, the actual number of abortions taking place would actually increase exponentially. As abortion becomes more readily and less visibly available through abortifacients, there is a concurrent decrease in the perceived need to be both morally accountable and responsible for the destruction of the conceptus. "In a sense, if there is no body, then there exists no crime. . . . Self-deception will grow as this technology becomes more commonplace."[27] That abortifacients encourage insensitivity toward the nascent human life is the most serious threat posed by this medical innovation.

In summary, clearly abortifacients like RU 486 make abortion safer, easier and cheaper; and many who would object morally to the use of abortion as a means of birth control may even find abortifacients acceptable, either due to their ignorance of the abortifacients' mechanism of action or due to a false belief that abortifacients

---

[24]Nathanson, "Abortion Cocktail," p. 25.
[25]Tonti-Filippini, "The Pill," p. 11.
[26]Roberge, "Abortifacient Vaccines," p. 182.
[27]Ibid., p. 184.

terminate a life of less moral import than a more fully developed fetus. In many ways, RU 486 will serve as a template for the trend of future birth-control methods and will allow a previously unavailable level of choice and privatization of the abortion procedure. For the pro-choice advocates in the abortion debate, guaranteed access to RU 486 would be little short of a coup; meanwhile, pro-life advocates fear that the demedicalization of the procedure and the concomitant loss of accountability for women undergoing the abortion could have devastating effects both on the pregnant woman and on the nascent human life inside her womb.

The Maternal-Fetal Dyad: The Fetus as a Patient

While the presence and value of the early conceptus have been increasingly ignored by physicians and the public due to the development and use of abortive contraceptives, there has emerged within rank-and-file medical practitioners the new concept of the fetus as a patient, which has exerted an enormous force on the abortion debate in a positive direction—diametrically opposite to the effect of abortifacients. This comes about largely as a result of advancements in medical technology that have made possible not only sophisticated diagnosis of fetal defects, but also the surgical correction of some of these conditions.[28] Insofar as the fetus is now seen as having disorders that can be diagnosed and treated quite independently of the mother, it has become a patient. In addition to the practical effect it has made on clinical prenatal care,[29] the concept also carries with it tremendous ethical significance, for if the fetus is accepted as an independent patient, the physician will be morally obligated to protect and promote fetal interests in addition to the interests of the pregnant woman. This concept profoundly changes our understanding of the "maternal-fetal dyad" and has contributed much to upgrade the

---

[28]M. R. Harrison, M. S. Golbus and R. A. Filly, eds., *The Unborn Patient: Prenatal Diagnosis and Treatment*, 2nd ed. (Philadelphia: W. B. Saunders, 1990), p. 6.

[29]Compare these works by L. B. McCullough and Frank Chervenak: *Ethics in Obstetrics and Gynecology* (New York: Oxford University Press, 1994); "The Fetus as Patient: Implications for Directive Versus Nondirective Counseling for Fetal Benefit," *Fetal Diagnostic Therapy* 6 (1991): 93-100; "An Ethically Justified Clinically Comprehensive Management Strategy for Third-Trimester Pregnancies Complicated by Fetal Anomalies," *Obstetrics and Gynecology* 75 (March 1990): 311-16; "Does Obstetric Ethics Have Any Role in the Obstetrician's Response to the Abortion Controversy?" *American Journal of Obstetrics and Gynecology* 163 (November 1990): 1425-29; "Nonagressive Obstetric Management: An Option for Some Fetal Anomalies During the Third Trimester," *Journal of the American Medical Association* 261 (June 1989): 3439-40; "When Is Termination of Pregnancy During the Third Trimester Morally Justifiable?" *New England Journal of Medicine* 310, no. 8 (1984): 501-4; "Clinical Guides to Preventing Ethical Conflicts Between Pregnant Women and Their Physicians," *American Journal of Obstetrics and Gynecology* 162 (February 1990): 303-7. See also Monica J. Casper, *The Making of the Unborn Patient: A Social Anatomy of Fetal Surgery* (New Brunswick, N.J.: Rutgers University Press, 1998).

moral status of the fetus, while at the same time it raises new ethical dilemmas when patients' rights and physicians' obligations conflict *within* the dyad.

Fetal Diagnosis and Therapy and the Maternal-Fetal Dyad

The evolution of the concept of the fetus as a patient has been in tandem with the gradual development of fetal diagnosis, beginning with manual palpation of fetal activity, through the auscultative detection of fetal heartbeat, to the more sophisticated electronic fetal monitoring and monitoring of gestational hormonal levels. Also, amniotic fluid analysis through amniocentesis and chorionic villus biopsy make possible both the prenatal diagnosis of a number of inheritable metabolic and chromosomal disorders and the clinical assessments of other disorders. But the development of sonography as a direct means of visualizing the living fetus via a safe, noninvasive imaging technology has been by far the most significant breakthrough in the understanding and perception of the fetus. This method provides accurate delineation and measurement of normal and abnormal fetal anatomy and activity, including the rhythmic motions of the heart and its valves. Further, at the emotional level it has allowed the fetus to be seen "kicking and rolling, breathing [and] . . . swallowing . . . and emptying its bladder"[30]—almost as a human person. All of a sudden, seen through the eye of the sonographer, the fetus appears no longer as a passive seed buried in the darkness of the uterine organ, but as a lively human being flourishing actively in a human womb. With the development of high-resolution, real-time scanners, it is now possible to visualize any part of the fetal anatomy in exquisite detail.[31] As one author comments, "The possibility of visualizing their fetus in real time has had a powerful effect on many expectant parents. . . . It gives their fetus a reality and individuality not otherwise captured by verbal or other descriptions."[32] Sonography has also had a profound effect on many doctors, including an influential pro-choice physician who admits that this technology has convinced him to reject abortion as immoral.[33]

While ultrasonographic methods are useful for diagnosing fetal anatomic

---

[30]Harrison, Golbus and Filly, eds., *Unborn Patient*, p. 6.

[31]Compare A. C. Fleischer et al., eds., *The Principles and Practice of Ultrasonography in Obstetrics and Gynecology,* 4th ed. (Norwalk, Conn.: Appleton & Lange, 1991).

[32]Daniel Callahan, "How Technology Is Reframing the Abortion Debate," *Hastings Center Report* 26 (February 1986): 35.

[33]Bernard Nathanson, *The Hand of God* (Washington, D.C.: Regenery, 1996). Nathanson notes, "When ultrasound in the early 1970s confronted me with the sight of the embryo in the womb, I simply lost my faith in abortion on demand. This change was, in its way, a clean and surgical conversion" (p. 140).

defects, other genetic and biochemical abnormalities are better detected through direct analysis of fetal tissues obtained through amniocentesis and chorionic villus sampling. Cordocentesis (fetal blood sampling) and other fetal-tissue biopsies (including skin, liver and muscle) can now be performed under the guidance of real-time sonography. Finally, the newest noninvasive imaging technique, which employs nuclear magnetic resonance technology, holds out promise not only that we will be able to define fetal anatomy, but that we will be able to ascertain the actual chemical definition of fetal tissue. Because these procedures involve direct fetal visualization or tissue sampling, they contribute significantly to the conceptualization of the fetus as an independent patient.

Most early twentieth-century techniques of fetal diagnosis were developed to detect serious inheritable diseases or congenital malformations that are largely incompatible with postnatal life, so most prenatal fetal diagnoses lead to elective abortions. But recent developments have encouraged direct interventive therapy to correct some of these fetal anomalies. Since A. W. Liley first reported his successes in intrauterine blood transfusion to fetuses,[34] the medical community has continued to refine its fetal therapeutic repertoire for direct fetal therapy—particularly surgical corrective procedures for a wide range of conditions. Hydrocephaly, a condition in which fluid and increasing pressure build up inside the fetal skull, leading to brain damage and severe mental retardation, is one of the first targets for fetal surgery: doctors can implant a shunt in utero to drain the fluid from the fetus's skull.[35] Other fetal conditions treated by prenatal surgery include congenital diaphragmatic hernia, which causes the abdominal contents of the fetus to fill the chest cavity and compress the fetal lungs, and severe bilateral hydronephrosis, which causes urine blockage.[36] Together with developments in fetal diagnosis, these fetal surgical/therapeutic refinements have the net effect of gradually advancing the concept of the fetus as an independent patient.

---

[34] A. William Liley, "Intrauterine Transfusion of Fetus in Hemolytic Disease," *British Medical Journal* 2 (November 1963): 1107-9.

[35] Mark I. Evans et al., "Fetal Surgery in the 1990s," *American Journal of Diseases of Children* 143 (December 1989): 1432. These authors reported that as of July 1, 1989, thirty-eight out of forty-five fetuses survived the prenatal shunt surgery. Of these, twenty-four infants with multiple congenital problems did not fare very well, suffering from varying degrees of mental handicaps. The remaining fourteen who were without multiple congenital problems were normal up to one year after birth.

[36] R. H. Murray, "Ethical Issues in Fetal Surgery," *American College of Surgeons Bulletin* 70 (June 1985): 6-10; and John A. Robertson, "The Right to Procreate and in Utero Therapy," *Journal of Legal Medicine* 3 (September 1982): 333-66. Many fetuses with diaphragmatic hernia died after birth despite prenatal surgical repair of the hernia.

The Maternal-Fetal Dyad as a Duality

In the past, the fetus has always been viewed as an "integral part" of the mother; and in that sense, the maternal-fetal dyad is treated as one complex patient. One of the most important implications of seeing the fetus as an independent patient is a radical modification of the nature of the relationship between mother and fetus from unity to duality: that is, now we see the fetus as a distinct patient in its own right. There is, however, little agreement on a number of questions that come with this new development:

☐ Does the duality begin to exist at the moment of conception or only at some later point in the pregnancy?

☐ Which agency has the right to determine when the maternal-fetal dyad becomes a dual patient?

☐ What does this shift mean in practical terms for the physician?

☐ What different moral implications may this concept entail, especially in terms of the fetus's right not to be aborted vis-à-vis the pregnant woman's right to bodily autonomy?

The most extreme view rejects the possibility that the maternal-fetal dyad can ever be a duality. For example, Barbara Katz Rothman insists that "a pregnant woman is one person, not two. Third parties, therefore, may legitimately protect and care for the fetus only by protecting and caring for her."[37] Mary Ann Warren, noted earlier for her extremely liberal position on abortion, represents the view that the duality of the maternal-fetal dyad is a possibility, but that this reality emerges only *after* the woman has made the choice not to abort the fetus. Thus, if abortion is chosen, the duality never comes to exist, whereas if the decision is made *not* to abort, then the maternal-fetal duality is called into existence.[38] It should be clarified, however, that it is not the particular decision to carry the pregnancy to term that establishes the duality, but the very act of making the decision not to abort; and the physician's obligation to the dyad as a duality only begins after the woman has made such a decision. Warren's model is clearly influenced by her pro-abortion stance, but it raises important questions: Is the obligation of the physician to the fetus really only initiated through the mother's consent in such a way that any enhancement of the fetal benefit is primarily due to the physician's obligation to the mother? Or can the physician's duties be understood as existing independently of the mother's desire or choice, in direct obligation to the fetus?

A third view, represented by L. B. McCullough and Frank Chervenak, argues

---

[37]Barbara Katz Rothman, cited in Mary Ann Warren, "Women's Rights Versus the Protection of Fetuses," in *The Beginning of Human Life,* ed. F. K. Beller and R. K. Weir (Boston: Kluwer Academic, 1994), p. 288; also see Janet Gallagher, "Fetus as Patient," in *Reproductive Laws for the 1990s,* ed. S. Cohen and N. Taub (Clifton, N.J.: Humana, 1989).

[38]Warren, "Women's Rights," p. 289.

that the duality of the maternal-fetal dyad should not entirely be a function of maternal desire. These authors are particularly interested to know *when* the fetus becomes a patient such that the physician has direct obligation to the fetus. They come to the conclusion that once the fetus reaches viability, there is an expectation that it will achieve independent moral status later, which establishes the necessary and sufficient ground for the fetus to become a patient accessible to the physician.[39]

Their view is also supported by John A. Robertson, who states that "the fetus going to term is a 'patient' by virtue of the expectation that it will be born alive,"[40] an expectation that is not reliable until the fetus is viable. While these authors never explicitly state why a reliable expectation only arises after the fetus has reached viability, they have clearly been influenced by the United States Supreme Court's decision in *Roe* v. *Wade,* where the postviable fetus is considered to possess the "potentiality for life." Their own position on the immorality of third-trimester abortions for fetal defects also suggests why viability is so important in their framework.[41] If abortion after viability is ruled out, the physician must always deal with the postviable fetus as a patient and with the maternal-fetal dyad as a duality. This position is also consistent with the society's expectation that the mother has a moral obliga-tion to refrain from nonlethal harm to the fetus and to enhance fetal benefit.[42] This is best seen in most countries of the world by widespread efforts aimed at promoting and preserving fetal health through antenatal medical care and public health education of pregnant women. In that context, viability is important for the initial decision of whether or not to abort:

> After viability, the fetus's increasing nearness to actual rather than merely potential life strengthens its moral claim against being killed to the point where it overrides the mother's right to choose not to bear a child, though not so far as to force her to risk her life in doing so.[43]

On this basis, Chervenak and McCullough conclude that the maternal-fetal dyad exists as a duality in all cases after the fetus has reached viability, when the fetus becomes an independent patient, and they expect that all the moral obligations owed to it be honored. Since the viable fetus cannot be said to

---

[39]McCullough and Chervenak, "The Fetus as a Patient: An Essential Ethical Concept for Mater-nal-Fetal Medicine," *Journal of Maternal-Fetal Medicine* 5 (1996): 117.

[40]John A. Robertson, "Legal Considerations in Fetal Treatment," in *The Unborn Patient: Prena-tal Diagnosis and Treatment Patient,* 2nd ed., ed. M. R. Harrison, M. S. Golbus and R. A. Filly (Philadelphia: W. B. Saunders, 1990), p. 20.

[41]Chervenak and McCullough, "When Is Termination," p. 502.

[42]T. H. Murray, "Moral Obligations to the Not-Yet Born: The Fetus as Patient," *Clinics in Perin-atology* 14 (June 1987): 331.

[43]Ibid., p. 332.

have an autonomy that needs to be respected, the physician is obliged to treat the fetus as a patient on the basis of beneficence-based principles, with its own beneficence-based rights independent of the mother. Under certain circumstances the maternal autonomy-based freedom to make decisions regarding the fetus can be justifiably limited.[44]

A Relational Model of the Maternal-Fetal Dyad

Regardless of whether the duality of the dyad is established on the basis of maternal decision or fetal viability, both views agree that mother and fetus should be seen as individual, independent patients who may have conflicting rights that have to be balanced against each other. Susan Mattingly has expressed reservation about this duality model because it fails to come to terms with the fact that the two patients exist in a basic biological unity. She argues that even if medicine, philosophy and ethics are beginning to see the fetus as an independent entity, the fact that the fetus exists *inside* the mother and forms a biological unity with the mother simply cannot be dismissed or ignored.[45] Even if conflicts were to occur in the two-patient model, "conflict between maternal and fetal needs occur within, not between, patients."[46] Mattingly suggests that the problem arises from a basic deficiency in traditional Western medicine, which treats patients as autonomous individuals without any regard to their dependency on personal and social relationships.[47] Mattingly appeals to the model of family medicine, which espouses a biopsychosocial model of health and disease that moves beyond the organic circumstances of the patient to consider the greater context of familial relationships. If one views the maternal-fetal dyad in this greater context, the relationship of dependence in the maternal-fetal dyad would be seen as medically relevant; the medical profession may be more able to see that since the fetus's dependency is not transferable from the mother to anyone else, it has a special claim upon her.[48] If an occasion arises in which the mother requires treatment that may be harmful to the fetus or vice or versa, a physician may be better able to guide her in making these decisions in a context of her relationship both with the fetus and with other persons in her life.[49]

---

[44]McCullough and Chervenak, "Does Obstetric Ethics Have Any Role," p. 1426.

[45]Susan S. Mattingly, "The Maternal-Fetal Dyad: Exploring the Two-Patient Obstetric Model," *Hastings Center Report* 22 (January 1992): 16.

[46]Ibid., p. 15.

[47]Ibid., p. 17.

[48]Ibid., pp. 16-18.

[49]Respect for the professional-patient relationship in a relational model of the maternal-fetal dyad also prevents physicians from being carried away in their enthusiasm for the fetus due to the excitement of the new medical innovations in fetal diagnosis and therapy. This is sig-

A unique example illustrating the duality, unity and relationship of dependence that exist within the maternal-fetal dyad can be found in a case where the fetus was allowed to mature to viability inside the womb of the mother after she was pronounced brain dead.

> A previously healthy twenty-seven-year-old primigravida (woman experiencing her first pregnancy) at twenty-two-weeks gestation presented herself to the hospital with a five-day history of severe headaches, vomiting and disorientation. Four hours after presentation, the patient experienced a generalized seizure and respiratory arrest, which led the patient to lapse into coma. When she was pronounced brain dead two days later, the decision was made to maintain the mother's bodily functions to save the fetus. The hospital was successful in maintaining cardiorespiratory support to the mother for sixty-three days, at which point the fetus was delivered by cesarean section. The male infant was initially cared for in the neonatal intensive care unit and then was taken home. On follow-up examination at eighteen months of age, he appeared to be healthy and developing normally.[50]

This case demonstrates that even as the fetus has become a patient quite independent of his mother, he is still fully linked to and dependent on the mother in a biological unity. As a result, the physician's dilemma cannot simply be misconstrued as a conflict between the duty to benefit the fetus and the duty to respect the woman's autonomy. Rather, this case enables the physicians to see how, by retaining the dimension of unity in the duality, they can retain the professional goal of helping the pregnant woman to fulfill her role of trust to the fetus.[51] It not only presents an instance of the medical rescue of the fetus from death, but magisterially illustrates the interdependent nature of the maternal-fetal dyad in which there are two persons, yet one patient.

Such an interdependent relationship within the maternal-fetal dyad resonates well with the understanding that relationality is a constitutive dimension of the human person,[52] and I believe that a relational model of the maternal-fetal dyad as the basis of ethical discourse is superior to the other rights-based models in which maternal and fetal rights are always presented as being in opposition to each other. A relational model avoids these inherent adversarial consequences even in situations of conflict; for if one

---

nificant because the technology now at their disposal has a potential to render the fetus a far more "interesting" patient than the pregnant woman. Gallagher, "Fetus as Patient," p. 192.

[50]For a full account of this case, see D. R. Field et al., "Maternal Brain Death During Pregnancy: Medical and Ethical Issues," *Journal of the American Medical Association* 260, no. 6 (1988): 816-17.

[51]Mattingly, "Maternal-Fetal Dyad," p. 17.

[52]See chapter five, "The Relational Dimension of Human Personhood," above.

accepts the premise that the "self" only emerges within relationships, then all autonomous decisions are necessarily relational decisions.[53] The relational model stresses relationships, rather than individual rights, as the primary moral concern. Thus while the rights-based model cannot require persons to be self-sacrificial, the relations-based model may encourage people to be so. Christians may draw from their tradition the additional resources of viewing the maternal-fetal dyad as a perichoretic relation of mutual interaction, interpenetration and interdependency that is modeled after the relational life of the triune God, who exists not only in eternity as a "unity-in-trinity" but also as the incarnate Son, embracing a life of self-sacrifice for the lives of others.[54]

Conflicts Within the Maternal-Fetal Dyad

Regardless of whether the maternal-fetal dyad is understood as a duality, a unity or both, one still needs to deal with potential conflicts within the dyad in the event that the mother rejects medical intervention necessary for the fetus. Treatments with regard to the maternal-fetal dyad can be classified into three categories:

☐ direct treatment for the mother to indirectly benefit the fetus, in which case the mother herself directly benefits from the treatment

☐ direct medical or surgical intervention for fetal benefit, in which case the mother is at best neutral in regards to the intervention, and at worst is directly harmed by it

☐ cesarean delivery to enhance fetal outcome, in which case the mother is always directly harmed by the treatment of the fetal patient[55]

The second and third categories of treatment contain potential conflicts: the mother might refuse a treatment that is harmful to her, even if it is beneficial to the fetus. In that situation the mother may elect to leave the fetus untreated or to have an abortion. Some believe that if a successful treatment for a certain fetal defect is available, abortion cannot be easily justified, and that the need to improve fetal quality of life would preclude her carrying a defective fetus to term without allowing it to benefit from available treatment. On this view, maternal autonomy is less weighty than either the fetus's quality of life or its right of life, so that abortion is proscribed and treatment is mandatory, regard-

---

[53]See also Jane Trau, "Treating Fetuses: The Patient as Person," *Journal of Medical Humanities* 12, no. 4 (1991): 173-75.

[54]Again see chapter five, "The Relational Dimension of Human Personhood," above, for more detail.

[55]Alan R. Fleishman and Ruth Macklin, "Fetal Therapy: Ethical Considerations, Potential Conflicts," in *Ethical Issues at the Outset of Life,* ed. William B. Weil Jr. and Martin Benjamin (Boston: Blackwell Scientific Publications, 1987), p. 123.

less of whether maternal consent is volunteered or not.[56] We can see that the availability of fetal treatment makes it more difficult to justify aborting on grounds of fetal defect. But the argument that the availability of treatment makes that treatment mandatory is more disputable. The fetus's right not to be aborted does not automatically commit the pregnant woman to surgery. Besides, it may very well be morally acceptable, under certain circumstances, to carry a defective fetus to term without treatment. Therefore, it can be predicted that physicians will be increasingly confronted with a new dilemma: whether to respect the woman's decision to leave the fetus with his defect untreated or to respond to the need of the fetus, who may benefit from fetal therapy.[57]

A Rights-Based Approach to Conflict Resolution

In a rights-based approach, both the mother and the fetus are assumed to be bearers of rights who stand in opposition to each other and compete for dominance.[58] In this situation, as long as one insists on resolving conflicts through the rights approach, the adjudication of conflicts between fetal and maternal rights will likely be sought in the legal realm, with the only possible (and undesirable) resolution often coming under the strong arm of legal coercion. As a result, despite the fact that neither the Canadian nor the American legal system has statutes that criminalize "fetal abuse,"[59] the law nonetheless has an increasing tendency to regulate the behavior of pregnant women in order to prevent such abuse. Typically, legal intervention in pregnancy takes the form of either prebirth seizures (compelling a woman to act or to refrain from acting a certain way during pregnancy) or postbirth sanctions (punishing a woman after birth for specific behavior that has caused fetal harm during pregnancy). The criminal behavior ranges from refusal of treatment, to "lifestyle choices"

---

[56]W. Ruddick and W. Wilcox, "Operating on the Fetus," *Hastings Center Report* 22 (October 1992): 11.

[57]John C. Fletcher, "The Fetus as Patient: Ethical Issue," *Journal of the American Medical Association* 246 (August 4, 1981): 772-73.

[58]Janet Gallagher argues that the fetus's status as a patient is different from the status of a full person in the United States. She is particularly concerned that if the fetus is given the status of a person, it will lead to a "nightmarish scenario" in which court enforcement of fetal patienthood may mandate physicians "to a willingness to treat pregnant women as vessels to be used, risked and discarded." Gallagher, "Fetus as Patient," pp. 198-200.

[59]The Law Reform Commission of Canada still defines *person* as "a human being which has proceeded completely and permanently from its mother's body in a living state and capable of independent survival." In the United States, the *Harvard Law Review* states, "No state has yet passed a statute that explicitly criminalizes 'fetal abuse.' " Law Reform Commission of Canada, *Working Paper 58: Crimes Against the Foetus* (1989), p. 63; and "Maternal Rights and Fetal Wrongs: The Case Against the Criminalization of 'Fetal Abuse,' " *Harvard Law Review* 101, no. 5 (1988): 995.

(particularly drug abuse) during pregnancy, to deliberate prenatal harm inflicted on the fetus.

In Canada, two recent sensational court cases have launched the issue of fetal rights to the forefront of public debate. The first case involved a twenty-two-year-old woman, "Ms. G.," a mother of three children, who had been sniffing glue and paint thinner for eight years.[60] As a result of her addiction, two of her children had already suffered neurological damage, and when a Manitoba court discovered that Ms. G. was pregnant again and was continuing in her habit, it ruled that she should be restricted to a residential drug-treatment facility until the birth of her child. After her baby was born healthy and she overcame her addiction, the sanctions against Ms. G. were dropped.[61]

The second case is illustrative of postbirth sanctions and involved Brenda Drummond, a woman from the small town of Carleton Place, Ontario. She was charged with attempted murder in June 1996, when a lead pellet was discovered in the brain of her newborn son.[62] Apparently she had shot an air gun into her vagina, presumably with the intention to kill the fetus. The baby boy was born on May 28, 1996, at her own condominium and was taken to the hospital where his condition deteriorated quickly. On the third day at the hospital the doctors performed a brain scan and discovered the pellet. Soon after, charges were filed, but Drummond's lawyer argued that the case should not go to trial because under Canadian law the unborn fetus has no rights,[63] and even if it did, those rights should not supersede the mother's. The attempted murder charges against Drummond were later dropped.

In New York, the Nassau County Department of Social Services has a long-standing policy to remove a newborn infant from the custody of its mother if it is discovered that she used illegal drugs during her pregnancy. In a comment on his 1988 ruling that a pregnant woman's use of cocaine was an act of neglect, Judge Joseph De Maro of the Nassau County family court said, "There is no reason to treat a child in utero any differently from a child ex utero where the mother has decided not to destroy the fetus or where the time allowed for such destruction is past."[64] In other words, once the woman foregoes her right to abortion, she is not free to act in any way she pleases during the course of her pregnancy but instead

[60]Chris Wood, "Beyond Abortion," *Maclean's,* August 19, 1996, pp. 14-15.

[61]Janice Tibbetts, "Rights of Fetus Spotlighted in Manitoba, U.S.," *Vancouver Sun,* October 30, 1997.

[62]Patricia Chrisholm, "Does a Fetus Have Rights?" *Maclean's,* August 19, 1996, pp. 16-19.

[63]A 1991 Supreme Court decision in Canada declared that fetuses have no rights.

[64]Tamar Lewin, "When Courts Take Charge of the Unborn," *The New York Times,* January 9, 1989, p. A11, cited in Bonnie Steinbock, *Life Before Birth: The Moral and Legal Status of Embryos and Fetuses* (New York: Oxford University Press, 1992), p. 134.

is obligated to care for the health of the fetus.[65] In addition, the strength of the state's interest in the future child is sufficiently strong to justify legal coercion of the mother.[66] While some applaud the state's tendency to represent the interest of the child-to-be—thus pushing for clearer legal guidelines and stricter legal control—many others are less than enthusiastic toward any legal involvement or coercion within the maternal-fetal dyad. Warren acknowledges that the child-to-be has the right not to be inflicted with harm that frustrates optimal fetal outcome, but she argues that legal involvement is completely inappropriate for the maternal-fetal dyad, insisting that such "obligations are better left to the conscience of the individual and to moral persuasion than to the coercive force of the law."[67] Others also see the difficulty in drawing appropriate lines and thus the possibility of misuse and abuse. Bonnie Steinbock contends that while removing newborns from crack-addicted mothers is reasonable, removing a child from a mother because she uses marijuana for recreation and relaxation inflicts harm on the child by depriving her of her mother.[68] Removing children from their homes is always a traumatic event and may have disastrous consequences for the children; this action is often taken in the name of protecting the children, when in reality the removal of the children is being used as a way to punish their parents. Others also see that fetal abuse cannot be the same as child abuse for the simple reason that the fetus, by definition, resides inside the body of the pregnant woman. Thus one cannot assess the fetus's interests and rights independently of the mother's.[69] I believe that persuasion, education, counseling and arbitration are better means of resolving maternal-fetal conflicts, leaving legal coercion only as the very last resort.

---

[65]L. J. Nelson, "Legal Dimensions of the Maternal-Fetal Conflict," *Clinical Obstetrics and Gynecology* 35 (December 1992): 739.

[66]Ibid., p. 740. However, even if legal statues were to be implemented, there are several concerns that would need to be dealt with. The first concern is due process. In the cases that have been reported to have occurred so far, the mother did not have a fair hearing at court, was not assisted by a lawyer and in some cases did not even know that a judge's decision had been sought and obtained in her case. (See ibid., p. 742.) This clearly violates the constitutional right to due process guaranteed in Canada and the United States in all cases, and would have to be guaranteed should fetal health and outcome be legislated. A second matter concerns the fetus itself. As several authors have correctly pointed out, it is impossible to create a legal statute for "fetal abuse" without clarifying the legal status of the fetus in general. (See ibid., pp. 742-43; cf. "Maternal Rights," pp. 1003-5.) Although these objections do not rule out the possibility of legal statutes for fetal rights, they indicate that the process would be more complex and large-scale than first evident.

[67]Warren, "Women's Rights," p. 289; cf. Nelson, "Legal Dimensions," pp. 743-44; and L. J. Nelson and N. M. Miliken, "Compelled Medical Treatment of Pregnant Women: Life, Liberty and Law in Conflict," *Journal of the American Medical Association* 259, no. 7 (1988): 1060-66.

[68]Bonnie Steinbock, *Life Before Birth: The Moral and Legal Status of Embryos and Fetuses* (New York: Oxford University Press, 1992), p. 135.

[69]"Maternal Rights," p. 1000.

Court-Ordered Cesarean Deliveries

The most prevalent example of legal intervention in the maternal-fetal dyad is found in the cases where a mother is ordered by the court to submit to a delivery by cesarean section to enhance fetal outcome. Since 1980, when the first of these situations occurred, a number of cases have been discussed widely in the literature. In 1981, a Georgia court ordered a cesarean on a nonconsenting woman after the physician testified that the baby had a 99 percent chance of not surviving normal birth. The court's decision was based on the state's interest in protecting potential life as provided by the *Roe* v. *Wade* decision.[70] In 1987, a Washington hospital obtained a court-ordered cesarean for Angela Carder—a twenty-seven-year-old semicomatose woman with terminal cancer who was in her twenty-sixth week of pregnancy—against the expressed wishes of the woman's husband and physician. The fetus died two days after the surgery, and the woman died two weeks later, with the surgery cited as a factor contributing to her death.[71] In a Michigan case, the court ordered a woman with complete placenta previa to "present herself" to the hospital for cesarean delivery. The woman refused, went into hiding, and subsequently gave birth vaginally to a healthy baby.[72] These cases illustrate the immense complexity involved in the area of court-ordered cesarean sections. While these better-known cases have revealed the fallibility of medical and legal judgments, in other less publicized cases, the court order most likely saved the life of the fetus or the lives of both the fetus and the mother.

Many reasons have been provided in the argument that court-ordered cesareans are not recommendable. The most credible reason is that the woman is exposed to greater risk for the benefit of the fetus. Yet many see in the *Roe* v. *Wade* decision the necessary support for justifying such an increase in maternal risk when it is necessary to protect the fetus. While it is clearly not the spirit of the *Roe* v. *Wade* decision to support legislation that may expose the pregnant woman to an unreasonable amount of risk, I believe that these scholars are right to conclude that court-ordered cesarean may be justifiable so long as the risk faced by the fetus if it is not treated is greater than the risk faced by the woman undergoing the intervention.[73] Another reason often cited to oppose court-ordered cesareans is the "slippery slope" effect that follows these legal interventions. It is feared that these precedents may eventually lead to a totalitarian surveillance and control of pregnant women.[74] Even though this fear is

---

[70]Warren, "Women's Rights," p. 292.

[71]Nelson, "Legal Dimensions," p. 744.

[72]Gallagher, "Fetus as Patient," p. 186.

[73]John E. B. Myers, "Abuse and Neglect of the Unborn: Can the State Intervene?" *Duquesne Law Review* 23 (November 1984): 18; Nelson, "Legal Dimensions," p. 741.

[74]M. Evans et al., "Coercion for Fetal Therapy?" in *The Beginning of Human Life*, ed. F. K. Beller

not entirely ungrounded, one must not be led to think that pregnant women are likely to be forced to undergo surgical delivery for reasons other than the prevention of fetal death. A realistic and serious concern, especially in the dramatic case of court-ordered cesareans, is the potential antagonism that can be set up between the mother and fetus. This creation of such an adversarial relationship may have grievous consequences for mother-and-child bonding and may cause her to form a negative attitude toward future pregnancies.[75] Some have attempted to minimize the antagonism within the maternal-fetal dyad, most notably by requiring that any surgical intervention involving the maternal-fetal dyad must have prior review by and approval of a "fetal review committee" consisting of multidisciplinary specialists and ethicists who will discuss each case and its unique set of surrounding circumstances.[76] The goal is to anticipate and prevent antagonistic feelings through "counseling and educating women so that they can make their own informed decisions."[77] While the long-term success of these efforts remain to be seen, it is clear that a rights-based approach—which finds recourse to legal coercion to achieve conflict resolution—engenders a sentiment of distrust, fear and resentment that is most inappropriate and unfortunate in the intimate context of the maternal-fetal dyad.

The Fetus as a Patient and the Ethic of Personhood

As an alternative to the rights-based approach, many prefer a consequentialist view, which focuses on the desired goal or outcome of a situation as the determinative factor for choosing appropriate actions toward the maternal-fetal dyad.[78] Such an approach is ultimately concerned with balancing the risks and benefits of all parties equitably. There are several serious problems with this approach when it is applied to intervention in pregnancy. First, it would be a mistake to assume physicians can make infallible prenatal diagnoses, and in many cases the medical situation that leads to the need for cesarean delivery is in fact a misdiagnosis, as seen in some of the cases of forced cesarean delivery discussed above. Coupled with the problem of misdiagnosis is the formidable task of predicting outcomes. This is especially true in the new and largely experimental area of fetal surgery, and accurately predicting the eventual outcome of treatment for particular fetal problems remains difficult. Also, it is extremely difficult for the pregnant woman to objectively balance the risks and

---

and R. F. Weir (Netherlands: Kluwer Academic Publishers, 1994), p. 323; also see L. J. Nelson, "The Mother and Fetus Union: What God Has Put Together, Let No Law Put Asunder?" also in *The Beginning of Human Life*, p. 312.

[75]Compare "Maternal Rights," p. 1011.

[76]Ruddick and Wilcox, "Operating on the Fetus," p. 10.

[77]Evans et al., "Coercion for Fetal Therapy?" pp. 321-22.

[78]Fleischman and Macklin, "Fetal Therapy," p. 137.

benefits of all parties, analyze alternatives and come to a reasoned decision in a crisis situation where she is already suffering from considerable mental and physical stress.[79] Despite these obvious shortcomings, the consequentialist approach retains a distinct advantage over the rights-based model in that it is not necessarily adversarial. If a common goal for all parties can be agreed upon, there is a much better chance of promoting harmony for all involved than would be the case with a rights-based approach.

However, in my opinion, the ethic of personhood that I espouse—which takes the maintenance, enrichment and harmony of relations as the primary criteria of ethics—offers the best chance of providing ethical parameters in response to conflicts within the maternal-fetal dyad. This ethic, as discussed earlier, is based on the premise that human personhood is experienced and nurtured only in relationships. The pregnant woman is involved with the obstetrician in a patient-physician relationship, and the fetus inside her is involved with another surgeon in a separate patient-physician relationship. The fetus also has a relationship with his biological father, who has made contributions other than just the gametes. However, the fetus also has a special relationship with the pregnant woman because of his unique, exclusive and nontransferable dependence on her. And ultimately the fetus has a unique relationship with God, who has created him in his image. It is only within this matrix of relationships that a way for conflict mediation can be expected to emerge. While an ethical framework that honors these relationships would tend to promote a mother's willingness to enhance fetal well-being, an ethic of personhood does not automatically require the pregnant woman to embrace a life of self-sacrifice. Therefore treating the fetus at great risk to the mother is usually not contemplated. Any invasion of the mother's body in the face of maternal refusal is only considered with utter seriousness and demands the strongest justification. No such justification would be granted if the therapy would "merely" enhance fetal quality of life; however, such a justification may be deemed acceptable in those rare cases where the life of the fetus is at serious risk and the risk to the pregnant woman is not life-threatening.[80]

Further, this ethic of personhood does not mandate forceful intervention, nor does it encourage the employment of legal means as a way to enforce fetal protection, because both forceful intervention and legal coercion in this context are hardly conducive to the nurturing of relationships that make us persons. Persuasion and education should be the means of achieving the desired goal. In exercising the ethic of personhood to resolve conflicts, participation of

---

[79]Alan R. Fleischman, "The Fetus Is a Patient," in *Reproductive Laws for the 1990s,* ed. S. Cohen and N. Taub (Clifton, N.J.: Humana, 1989), p. 252.

[80]For a similar view also see Trau, "Treating Fetuses," pp. 175-79.

and support from other members in the pregnant woman's immediate network of relations—especially the spouse and the physicians—are crucial. Viewed from this perspective, the protection of fetal life can actually be accomplished with an enhancement to, rather than a diminution of, the woman's dignity and autonomy.

In sum, the medical advances in fetal diagnosis, therapy and surgery have allowed medical professionals to treat the maternal-fetal dyad as a duality and have provided the opportunity to see the fetus as an independent patient. For those who refuse to see the fetus as a person, the status of the fetus as a patient still may not be sufficient to change their mind. But it cannot be denied that this developing human life is in fact establishing an expanding network of relations. Previously regarded as a rather passive resident of the dark womb—considered no more than a part of the woman's body, such as her appendix or as a parasite—the fetus is put in the limelight before "onlookers," including the mother, the father, the physician, the surgeon, the radiologist, the nurses and other personnel, who have an intense interest in her well-being and who are prepared to invest an enormous energy and effort to protect her interest as a patient, if not a person. The emerging concept of the fetus as a patient inevitably increases the fetus's status as a moral being and reminds the world that she is being related to by an increasing number of persons outside of the mother's body. I am particularly encouraged by this development, for the fetal person is enhanced through the enrichment of the relational dimension of her life, and her interests are acknowledged and, when necessary, protected by moral persons. As William Liley, the "father of fetal surgery," wrote:

> We may not all live to grow old but we were each once a foetus ourselves. . . . Is it too much to ask therefore that perhaps we should accord . . . to fetal personalities and behavior, rudimentary as they may appear by adult standards, the same consideration and respect?[81]

And for those of us who live in the Christian tradition, we should likewise be reminded that it is God who has formed each one of us from the dust of the ground and breathed into us the breath of life whereby we are related to him. And in respecting each embryo and fetal life, we are honoring the life-creating God.

---

[81]A. William Liley, "The Foetus as a Personality," *Australia and New Zealand Journal of Psychiatry* 6, no. 2 (1972): 105.

Selected Bibliography

Ackerknecht, Erwin H. "The History of Psychosomatic Medicine." *Psychological Medicine* 12 (February 1982): 17-24.

Adler, Nancy, Henry P. David, Brenda N. Major, Susan H. Roth, Nancy F. Russo and Gail E. Wyatt. "Psychological Response After Abortion." *Science* 248 (April 1990): 41-44.

Allan, David. "Ethical Boundaries in Genetic Testing." *Canadian Medical Association Journal* 154, no. 2 (1996): 241-44.

Anderson, Elizabeth S. "Is Women's Labor a Commodity?" In *Intervention and Reflection: Basic Issues in Medical Ethics.* 5th ed. Edited by Ronald Munson. Belmont, Calif.: Wadsworth, 1996.

Andrews, F., A. Abbey and L. Halman. "Stress from Infertility, Marriage Factors, and Subjective Well-Being of Wives and Husbands." *Journal of Health and Social Behavior* 32, no. 3 (1991): 238-54.

Annas, George. "Regulatory Models for Human Embryo Cloning: The Free Market, Professional Guidelines and Government Restrictions." *Kennedy Institute of Ethics Journal* 4 (September 1994): 235-49.

———. "The Right of Privacy Protects the Doctor-Patient Relationship." *Journal of the American Medical Association* 263, no. 6 (1990): 858-61.

Aquinas, Thomas. *Summa Theologiae.* Translated by Fathers of the English Dominican Province. Westminster, Md.: Christian Classics, 1981.

Ashley, B. M., O.P. "Pro-Life Evangelization." In *New Technologies of Birth and Death.* St. Louis: Pope John XXIII Medical-Moral Research and Education Center, 1980.

Ashley, Benedict, and Albert Moraczewski. "Is the Biological Subject of Human Rights Present from Conception?" In *The Fetal Tissue Issue: Medical and Ethical Aspects.* Edited by Peter Cataldo and Albert Moraczewski. Braintree, Mass.: Pope John Center, 1994, p. 49. Quoted in Patrick Lee, *Abortion and Unborn Human Life* (Washington, D.C.: Catholic University of America Press, 1996) p. 98.

Athanasius. *Epistula ad Adelphium* 3. In *A Select Library of Nicene and Post-Nicene Fathers of the Christian Church.* Edited by P. Schaff and H. Ware. Reprint ed., Grand Rapids, Mich.: Eerdmans, 1952.

———. *On the Incarnation of the Word.* In vol. 4 of *The Nicene and Post-Nicene Fathers.* 2d series. Edited by Philip Schaff. Peabody, Mass.: Hendrickson, 1994.

Augustine. *City of God.* Translated by Henry Bettenson. Harmondsworth, U.K.: Penguin, 1984.

———. *The City of God.* In vol. 2 of *The Nicene and Post-Nicene Fathers.* 2d series. Edited by Philip Schaff. Peabody, Mass.: Hendrickson, 1994.

———. *The Greatness of the Soul, The Teacher.* In vol. 9 of *Ancient Christian Writers.* Edited by Johannes Quasten and Joseph C. Plumpe. New York: Newman, 1978.

———. *The Trinity.* Translated by Edmund Hill, O.P. New York: New York City Press, 1991.

Austin, C. R. *Human Embryos: The Debate on Assisted Reproduction.* Oxford: Oxford University Press, 1989.

Bajema, Clifford E. *Abortion and the Meaning of Personhood.* Grand Rapids, Mich.: Baker, 1974.

Baran, Annette, and Rubin Pannor. *Lethal Secrets: The Shocking Consequences and Unresolved Problems of Artificial Insemination.* New York: Warner, 1989.

Barth, Karl. *Church Dogmatics.* Edited by G. W. Bromiley and T. F. Torrance. Edinburgh: T & T Clark, 1961.

Bartholome, W. G. "Ethics and the Termination of Pregnancy: The Physician's Perspective." In *Ethical Issues at the Outset of Life.* Edited by William B. Weil Jr. and Martin Benjamin. Boston: Blackwell Scientific Publications, 1987.

Beauchamp, Tom L., and James F. Childress. *Principles of Biomedical Ethics.* 4th ed. Belmont, Calif.: Wadsworth, 1994.

Becker, Lawrence C. "Human Being: The Boundaries of the Concept." *Philosophy and Public Affairs* 4 (Summer 1975): 334-59.

Beckwith, Francis J. *Politically Correct Death.* Grand Rapids, Mich.: Baker, 1993.

Bedate, C. A., and R. C. Cefalo. "The Zygote: To Be or Not to Be a Person." *Journal of Medicine and Philosophy* 14, no. 6 (1989): 641-45.

Behm, Johannes. "Kardia." In vol. 3 of *Theological Dictionary of the New Testament.* Edited by Gerhard Kittel and Gerhard Friedrich and translated by G. W. Bromiley. Grand Rapids, Mich.: Eerdmans, 1965.

Beller, F. K., and R. F. Weir, eds. *The Beginning of Human Life.* Netherlands: Kluwer Academic Publishers, 1994.

Berer, M. "Inducing a Miscarriage: Women-Centered Perspective on RU 486/Prostaglandin as an Early Abortion Method," *Law, Medicine and Health Care* 20 (Fall 1992): 199-208.

Berkouwer, G. C. *Man: The Image of God.* Grand Rapids, Mich.: Eerdmans, 1962.

Bernardin, Joseph. "Medical Humanism: Pragmatic or Personalist?" *Health Progress* 66, no. 3 (1985): 46-49.

Blumberg, Bruce D. "The Psychological Sequelae of Abortion Performed for a Genetic Indication." *American Journal of Obstetrics and Gynecology* 122, no. 7 (1975): 799-808.

Blumenthal, Susan J. "Psychiatric Consequences of Abortions: Overview of Research Findings." In *Psychiatric Aspects of Abortion.* Edited by N. Stotland. Washington, D.C.: American Psychiatric Press, 1991.

Bolton, V. N., P. J. Oades and M. H. Johnson. "The Relationship Between Cleavage, DNA Replication and Gene Expression in the Mouse 2-Cell Embryo." *Embryology and Experimental Morphology* 79 (1984): 139-63.

Bonnicksen, Andrea. "Genetic Diagnosis of Human Embryos," *Hastings Center Report Special Supplement* 22 (July-August 1992): S5-S11.

Boss, J. "First Trimester Prenatal Diagnosis: Earlier Is Not Necessarily Better." *Journal of*

Medical Ethics 20, no. 3 (1994): 146-51.

Botkin, Jeffrey. "Prenatal Screening: Professional Standards and the Limits of Parental Choice." *Obstetrics and Gynecology* 75 (May 1990): 875-80.

Bouma, Hessel, III, Douglas Diekema, Edward Langerak, Theodore Rottman and Allen Verhey. *Christian Faith, Health and Medical Practice.* Grand Rapids, Mich.: Eerdmans, 1989.

Boyle, Joseph. "Contraception and Natural Family Planning." In *Why Humanae Vitae Was Right.* Edited by Janet Smith. San Francisco: Ignatius, 1993.

Braude, Peter, V. Bolton and S. Moore. "Human Gene Expression First Occurs Between the Four- and Eight-Cell Stages of Preimplantation Development." *Nature* 332 (March 31, 1988): 459-61.

Brody, Baruch. *Abortion and the Sanctity of Human Life: A Philosophical View.* Cambridge: MIT Press, 1975.

———. "On the Humanity of the Fetus." In *Abortion: Pro and Con.* Edited by Robert L. Perkins. Cambridge, Mass.: Schenkman, 1974.

Brown, Douglas, Thomas E. Eklins and David B. Larson. "Prolonged Grieving After Abortion: A Descriptive Study." *Journal of Clinical Ethics* 4, no. 2 (1993): 118-23.

Brown, George F. "Long-Acting Contraceptives: Rationale, Current Development and Ethical Implications." *Hastings Center Report Special Supplement* 25 (January-February 1995): S1-S8.

Brown, Margaret. "Whose Eyes Are These, Whose Nose?" *Newsweek,* March 7, 1994, p. 12.

Brunner, Emil. *The Christian Doctrine of Creation and Redemption.* Philadelphia: Westminster Press, 1952.

———. *Man in Revolt.* Translated by Olive Wyon. Philadelphia: Westminster Press, 1939.

Buber, Martin. *Between Man and Man.* Translated by Ronald Gregor Smith. Glasgow: William Collins' Sons, 1979.

———. *I and Thou.* 2d ed. New York: Charles Scribner's Sons, 1958.

———. *The Knowledge of Man.* New York: Harper & Row, 1966.

Burstyn, Varda. "Making Babies." *Canadian Forum* 70 (March 1992): 12-17.

———. "Making Perfect Babies." Part 2. *Canadian Forum* 70 (April 1992): 13-17.

Byers, David M. "An Absence of Love." In *Human Cloning: Religious Responses.* Edited by Ronald Cole-Turner. Louisville, Ky.: Westminster John Knox, 1997.

Cahill, Lisa Sowle. " 'Abortion Pill RU486': Ethics, Rhetoric and Social Practice." *Hastings Center Report* 17, no. 5 (1987): 5-8.

———. "The Ethics of Surrogate Motherhood: Biology, Freedom and Moral Obligations." *Law, Medicine and Health Care* 16 (Spring 1988): 65-71.

———. "Genetics, Ethics and Social Policy: The State of the Question." In *The Ethics of Genetic Engineering.* Edited by Maureen Junker-Kenny and Lisa Sowle Cahill. London: SCM Press, 1998.

Callahan, Daniel. "The Abortion Debate: Can This Chronic Illness Be Cured?" *Clinical Obstetrics and Gynecology* 35, no. 4 (1992): 783-91.

———. "An Ethical Challenge to Prochoice Advocates: Abortion and the Pluralistic Proposition." *Commonweal* 117 (November 1990): 681-87.

———. "How Technology Is Reframing the Abortion Debate." *Hastings Center Report* 16, no. 1 (1986): 33-42.

Callahan, Sidney. "Abortion and the Sexual Agenda." *Commonweal* 25 (April 1986): 232-38.

————. "The Ethical Challenge of the New Reproductive Technology." In *Medical Ethics: A Guide for Health Care Professionals.* Edited by John F. Monagle and David C. Thomasma. Rockville, Md.: Aspen, 1988.

Caplan, Arthur L. "The Ethics of In Vitro Fertilization." In *Contemporary Issues in Bioethics.* 4th ed. Edited by Tom L. Beauchamp and LeRoy Walters. Belmont, Calif.: Wadsworth, 1994.

Carter, W. R. "Once and Future Persons." *American Philosophical Quarterly* 17 (January 1980): 61-66.

Casell, Eric J. *The Nature of Suffering and the Goals of Medicine.* Oxford: Oxford University Press, 1991.

Caskey, Thomas C. "DNA-Based Medicine: Prevention and Therapy." In *The Code of Codes: Scientific and Social Issues in the Human Genome Project.* Edited by Daniel J. Kevles and Leroy Hood. Cambridge: Harvard University Press, 1992.

Casper, Monica J. *The Making of the Unborn Patient: A Social Anatomy of Fetal Surgery.* New Brunswick, N.J.: Rutgers University Press, 1998.

Center for Disease Control. "Syphilis and Congenital Syphilis: United States 1985-88." *Morbidity and Mortality Weekly Report* 37 (August 1988): 486-89.

Chamblin, J. Knox. *Paul and the Self: Apostolic Teaching for Personal Wholeness.* Grand Rapids, Mich.: Baker, 1993.

Chervenak, F. A.. and L. B. McCullough. "When Is Termination of Pregnancy During the Third Trimester Morally Justifiable?" *New England Journal of Medicine* 310, no. 8 (1984): 501-4.

Chi, I-Cheng. "What We Have Learned from Recent IUD Studies: A Researcher's Perspective." *Contraception* 48 (August 1993): 81-108.

Chrisholm, Patricia. "Does a Fetus Have Rights?" *MacLean's,* August 19, 1996, pp. 16-18.

Clark, Mary T. "Christ and Trinity." In *Augustine.* Washington, D.C.: Georgetown University Press, 1994.

Clark, S., and G. DeVore. "Prenatal Diagnosis for Couples Who Would Not Consider Abortion." *Obstetrics and Gynecology* 73, no. 6 (1989): 1035-37.

Clarke, W. Norris, S.J. *Explorations in Metaphysics: Being-God-Person.* Notre Dame: University of Notre Dame Press, 1994.

————. *Person and Being.* Milwaukee: Marquette University Press, 1993.

————. "To Be Is to Be Substance-in-Relation." In *Metaphysics as Foundation.* Edited by Paul A. Boggaard and Gordon Treash. New York: State University of New York Press, 1993.

Clines, David J. A. "The Image of God in Man." *Tyndale Bulletin* 19 (1968): 53-103.

Cohen, Jacques, and Giles Tomkin. "The Science, Fiction and Reality of Embryo Cloning." *Kennedy Institute of Ethics Journal* 4, no. 3 (1994): 193-203.

Cole-Turner, Ronald. "At the Beginning." In *Human Cloning: Religious Responses.* Edited by Ronald Cole-Turner. Louisville, Ky.: Westminster John Knox, 1997.

Congregation for the Doctrine of the Faith. "Instruction on Respect for Human Life in Its Origin and on the Dignity of Procreation: Replies to Certain Questions of the Day." In *Intervention and Reflection: Basic Issues in Medical Ethics.* 5th ed. Edited by Ronald Munson. Belmont, Calif.: Wadsworth, 1996.

Cooper, John W. *Body, Soul and Life Everlasting.* Grand Rapids, Mich.: Eerdmans, 1989.

Corea, Gena. *The Mother Machine.* New York: Harper & Row, 1985.

Creighton, Phyllis. *Artificial Insemination by Donor.* Toronto: Anglican Book Center, 1977.

————. *Suspended in Time: The Frozen Human Embryo.* Toronto: Anglican Book Centre, 1994.

Crosby, I. M., F. Gandolfi and R. M. Moor. "Control of Protein Synthesis During Early Cleavage of Sheep Embryos" *Journal of Reproduction and Fertility* 82, no. 2 (1988): 769-75.

Crouzel, Henri. *Origen: The Life and Thought of the First Great Theologian.* San Francisco: Harper & Row, 1989.

Damewood, M., ed. *The Johns Hopkins Handbook of In Vitro Fertilization and Assisted Reproductive Technologies.* Boston: Little Brown, 1990.

Davidson, Eric H. *Gene Activity in Early Development.* London: Harcourt Brace Jovanovich, 1986.

Davies, S. M. "Partners and the Abortion Decision." In *Abortion, Medicine and the Law.* Edited by J. D. Butler and D. F. Walbert. New York: Facts on File, 1992.

Davis, D., and C. Dearman. "Coping Strategies of Infertility" *JOGNN Clinical Studies* 20, no. 3 (1991): B12-B18.

Davis, John J. *Evangelical Ethics: Issues Facing the Church Today.* Phillipsburg, N.J.: Presbyterian & Reformed, 1993.

Dean, John C. S., and Lisa Strain. "A True Hermaphrodite Chimera Resulting from Embryo Amalgamation After In Vitro Fertilization." *New England Journal of Medicine* 338, no. 3 (1998): 166-69.

Demarco, Donald E. O. "Love Among the Test Tubes: Louise Brown Turns 10; *Humanae Vitae* Turns 20." In *Trust the Truth.* Edited by Russell Smith. Braintree, Mass.: Pope John Center, 1991.

Department of Health and Social Security. *Report of the Committee of Inquiry into Human Fertilization and Embryology.* London: Her Majesty's Stationery Office, 1984.

Descartes, René. "Meditations on First Philosophy." In *The European Philosophers from Descartes to Nietzsche.* Edited by Monroe Beardsley. New York: Modern Library, 1960.

DeVeber, L. L., Janet Ajzenstat and Dorothy Chisholm. "Postabortion Grief: Psychological Sequelae of Induced Abortion," *Humane Medicine* 7 (August 1991): 203-9.

Devine, Philip E. *The Ethics of Homicide.* Ithaca, N.Y.: Cornell University Press, 1978.

Devorkin, Mark B., and Eva Devorkin-Rastl. "Functions of Maternal mRNA in Early Development." *Molecular Reproduction and Development* 26, no. 3 (1990): 261-97.

Diamond, Eugene F. " 'Every Child Should Be Born Wanted'—A Dubious Goal," *Linacre Quarterly* 52, no. 2 (1985).

DiPerri, D. "RU 486, Mifepristone: A Review of a Controversial Drug." *Nurse Practitioner* 19, no. 6 (1994): 59-61.

Dobzhansky, Theodosius. "Changing Man." *Science* 155 (January 1967): 409-15.

Donagan, Alan. *The Theory of Morality.* Chicago: University of Chicago Press, 1977.

Donald, Ian. "Problems Raised by Artificial Human Reproduction." In *Embryos and Ethics: The Warnock Report in Debate.* Edited by Nigel M. de S. Cameron. Edinburgh: Rutherford House, 1987.

Donceel, Joseph. "Immediate Animation and Delayed Hominization." *Theological Studies* 31, no. 1 (1970): 76-105.

Doran, Kevin. *What Is a Person: The Concept and the Implications for Ethics.* Lewiston, N.Y.: Edwin Mellen Press, 1989.

Drane, James F. "Anencephaly and the Interruption of Pregnancy: Policy Proposals for HECs." *HEC Forum* 4, no. 2 (1992): 103-19.

Drinan, Robert F. "The Inviolability of the Right to Be Born." In *Abortion and the Law.*

Edited by David T. Smith. Cleveland, Ohio: Western Reserve University Press, 1967.

Dunstan, G. R., and M. J. Seller. *The Status of Human Embryos: Perspectives from Moral Tradition.* London: Oxford University Press and King Edward's Hospital Fund for London, 1988.

Edwards, Robert G., ed. *Preconception and Preimplantation Diagnosis of Human Genetic Disease.* Cambridge: Cambridge University Press, 1993.

Eichrodt, W. *Theology of the Old Testament II.* London: SCM Press, 1967.

Eisenberg, Leon. "The Outcome as Cause: Predestination and Human Cloning." *Journal of Medicine and Philosophy* 1, no. 4 (1976): 318-31.

Ellerston, C. E., and C. C. Harper. "The Emergency Contraception Pill: A Survey of Knowledge and Attitudes Among Students at Princeton University." *American Journal of Obstetrics and Gynecology* 173, no. 5 (1995): 1438-45.

Elmer-Dewitt, Phillip. "Cloning: Where Do We Draw the Line?" *Time,* November 8, 1993, pp. 18-21.

Engelhardt, H. Tristram, Jr. *The Foundations of Bioethics.* New York: Oxford University Press, 1986.

―――. "Viability, Abortion and the Difference Between a Fetus and an Infant." *American Journal of Obstetrics and Gynecology* 116 (June 1, 1973): 429-34.

Ethical and Religious Directives for Catholic Hospitals. St. Louis: The Catholic Hospital Association of the United States and Canada, 1965.

Evans, C. Stephen. "Healing Old Wounds and Recovering Old Insights: Toward a Christian View of the Person for Today." In *Christian Faith in the Modern World.* Edited by Mark Noll and David Wells. Grand Rapids, Mich.: Eerdmans, 1988.

Evans, D. *Without Moral Limits.* Westchester, Ill.: Crossway, 1989.

Evans, M., M. Johnson, B. Nelson and W. Holzgrieve. "Coercion for Fetal Therapy?" In *The Beginning of Human Life.* Edited by F. K. Beller and R. F. Weir. Boston: Kluwer Academic, 1994.

Evans, Mark I., Arie Drugan, F. A. Manning and M. R. Harrison. "Fetal Surgery in the 1990s." *American Journal of Diseases of Children* 143, no. 12 (1989): 1431-36.

Faden, Ruth R., A. Judith Chwalow, Kimberly Quaid, Gary A. Chase, Cheryl Lopes, Claire O. Leonard and Neil A. Holtzman. "Prenatal Screening and Pregnant Women's Attitudes Toward the Abortion of Defective Fetuses." *American Journal of Public Health* 77, no. 3 (1987): 288-90.

Farrell, G., and W. Lazareth. *Population Perils.* Philadelphia: Fortress, 1979.

Feinberg, Joel. "Abortion." In *Matters of Life and Death.* Edited by Tom Regan. New York: Random House, 1980.

―――. *Harm to Others.* New York: Oxford University Press, 1984.

Feinberg, John S., and Paul D. Feinberg. *Ethics for a Brave New World.* Wheaton, Ill.: Crossway, 1993.

Fenton, John Y., ed. *Theology and Body.* Philadelphia: Westminster Press, 1974.

Field, D. R., Elena A. Gates, Robert K. Creasy, Albert R. Jonsen and Russell K. Laros. "Maternal Brain Death During Pregnancy: Medical and Ethical Issues," *Journal of the American Medical Association* 260, no. 6 (1988): 816-22.

Fisher, Anthony. " 'When Did I Begin?' Revisited." *Linacre Quarterly* 58, no. 3 (1991): 59-68.

Fleischman, Alan R. "The Fetus Is a Patient." In *Reproductive Laws for the 1990s.* Edited by S. Cohen and N. Taub. Clifton, N.J.: Humana, 1989.

Fleischman, Alan R., and Ruth Macklin. "Fetal Therapy: Ethical Considerations, Potential

Conflicts." In *Ethical Issues at the Outset of Life*. Edited by William B. Weil Jr. and Martin Benjamin. Boston: Blackwell Scientific Publications, 1987.

Fletcher, J. "Ethical Issues in Genetic Screening, Prenatal Diagnosis and Counseling." In *Ethical Issues at the Outset of Life*. Edited by William B. Weil Jr. and Martin Benjamin. Boston: Blackwell Scientific Publications, 1987.

Fletcher, J., and D. Wertz. "Ethics and Decision Making About Diagnosed Fetal Anomalies." In *Reproductive Risks and Prenatal Diagnosis*. Edited by M. Evans. Norwalk, Conn.: Appleton & Lange, 1992.

Fletcher, John C. "The Fetus as Patient: Ethical Issue." *Journal of the American Medical Association* 246 (August 4, 1981): 772-73.

Fletcher, John C., and W. French Anderson. "Germ-Line Therapy: A New Stage of Debate." *Law, Medicine and Health Care* 20, nos. 1 and 2 (1992): 26-39.

Fletcher, Joseph. "Four Indicators of Humanhood: The Enquiry Matures." *Hastings Center Report* 4, no. 6 (1974): 4-7.

———. "Indicators of Humanhood: A Tentative Profile of Man." *Hastings Center Report* 2, no. 5 (1972): 1-4.

Ford, Norman M. *When Did I Begin?* New York: Cambridge University Press, 1988.

Francke, Linda Bird. "Abortion: A Personal Dilemma." In *Morality in Practice*. 2d ed. Edited by James Sterba. Belmont, Calif.: Wadsworth, 1994.

Frankfurt, Harry G. "Freedom of the Will and the Concept of a Person." *Journal of Philosophy* 68, no. 1 (1971): 5-20.

French In Vitro National. "Pregnancies and Births Resulting from In Vitro Fertilization: French National Registry, Analysis of Data 1986 to 1990." *Fertility and Sterility* 64 (October 1995): 746-56.

French National Ethical Committee. "Discussion on Ethical and Judicial Aspects of Embryo Research." *Human Reproduction* 4, no. 2 (1989): 206-17.

Fuchs, Josef. *Natural Law*. New York: Sheed & Ward, 1965.

Gallagher, Janet. "Fetus as Patient." In *Reproductive Laws for the 1990s*. Edited by S. Cohen and N. Taub. Clifton, N.J.: Humana, 1989.

Gallagher, Kenneth. *The Philosophy of Gabriel Marcel*. New York: Fordham University Press, 1975.

Garcia, S. A. "Reproductive Technology for Procreation, Experimentation and Profit." *Journal of Legal Medicine* 11, no. 1 (1990): 1-57.

Gates, E. A. "Ethical Considerations in Prenatal Diagnosis." *Western Journal of Medicine* 159, no. 3 (1993): 391-95.

Geertz, Clifford. "The Impact of the Concept of Culture on the Concept of Man." In *New Views on the Nature of Man*. Edited by John R. Platt. Chicago: University of Chicago Press, 1965.

Genuis, Stephen. *Reproduction Rollercoaster: Infertility and the Assisted Reproductive Technologies*. Edmonton: KEG Publishing, 1992.

———. *Risky Sex*. 2d ed. Edmonton: KEG Publishing, 1992.

Gilligan, Carol. *In a Different Voice*. Cambridge, Mass.: Harvard University Press, 1982.

Glendon, M. A. *Abortion and Divorce in American Law: American Failures, European Challenges*. Cambridge: Harvard University Press, 1987.

Glover, Jonathan. *Causing Death and Saving Lives*. (New York: Penguin, 1977).

Gold, Rachel Benson. *Abortion and Women's Health: A Turning Point for America?* New York: Alan Guttmacher Institute, 1990.

Gorovitz, Samuel. *Doctors' Dilemmas: Moral Conflict and Medical Care*. New York:

Oxford University Press, 1982.

Granfield, David. *The Abortion Decision*. Garden City, N.Y.: Doubleday/Image, 1971.

Gregory Nazianzen. *The Fifth Theological Oration: On the Holy Spirit*. In vol. 7 of *The Nicene and Post-Nicene Fathers*. 2d series. Edited by Philip Schaff. Peabody, Mass.: Hendrickson, 1994.

Gregory of Nyssa. *De hom. opif.* C.16, MG 44, 180A.

———. *On the Making of Man*. In vol. 5 of *The Nicene and Post-Nicene Fathers*. 2d series. Edited by Philip Schaff. Peabody, Mass.: Hendrickson, 1994.

Grene, Marjorie. *Approaches to a Philosophical Biology*. New York: BasicBooks, 1968.

Grenz, Stanley. *Sexual Ethics*. Dallas: Word, 1990.

Grigor, Isobel K. "Responses to Warnock: A Review." In *Embryos and Ethics: The Warnock Report in Debate*. Edited by Nigel M. de S. Cameron. Edinburgh: Rutherford House, 1987.

Grisez, Germain. *Abortion: The Myths, the Realities and the Arguments*. New York: Corpus, 1970.

———. "When Do People Begin? The Ethics of Having Children." *Proceedings of the American Catholic Philosophical Association* 63 (1989): 27-47.

Grobstein, Clifford. *Science and the Unborn: Choosing Human Futures*. New York: BasicBooks, 1988.

Gudorf, Christine E. "A Feminist Critique of Biomedical Principlism." In *A Matter of Principles? Ferment in U.S. Bioethics*. Edited by Edwin R. Dubose, Ron Hamel and Laurence J. O'Connell. Valley Forge, Penn.: Trinity Press International, 1994.

Gunton, Colin E. *The One, the Three and the Many*. Cambridge: Cambridge University Press, 1993.

———. *The Promise of Trinitarian Theology*. Edinburgh: T & T Clark, 1991.

Guroian, Vigen. *Ethics After Christendom: Toward an Ecclesial Christian Ethic*. Grand Rapids, Mich.: Eerdmans, 1994.

Hanscombe, Gillian. "The Right to Lesbian Parenthood." *Journal of Medical Ethics* 9, no. 3 (1983): 133-35.

Hardwig, John. "What About the Family?" *Hastings Center Report* 20, no. 2 (1990): 5-10.

Hardy, Kate, and Alan H. Handyside. "Biopsy of Cleavage Stage Human Embryos and Diagnosis of Single Gene Defects by DNA Amplification." *Archives of Pathology and Laboratory Medicine* 116, no. 4 (1992): 388-92.

Hardy, Kate, Karen L. Martin, Henry J. Leese, Robert M. Winston and Alan H. Handyside. "Human Preimplantation Development In Vitro Is Not Adversely Affected by Biopsy at the 8-Cell Stage." *Human Reproduction* 5, no. 6 (1990): 708-14.

Harris, G. W. "Fathers and Fetuses." *Ethics* 96, no. 3 (1986): 594-603.

Harris, John. "In Vitro Fertilization: The Ethical Issues." *Philosophical Quarterly* 33, no. 132 (1983): 217-37.

Harrison, M. R., M. S. Golbus and R. A. Filly., eds. *The Unborn Patient: Prenatal Diagnosis and Treatment*. 2d ed. Philadelphia: W. B. Saunders, 1990.

Hartman, Betsy. *Reproductive Rights and Wrongs*. New York: Harper & Row, 1987.

Hartshorne, Charles. "Concerning Abortion: An Attempt at a Rational View." *The Christian Century* 98 (January 21, 1981): 42-45.

Hauerwas, Stanley. *A Community of Character*. Notre Dame: University of Notre Dame Press, 1981.

———. *Suffering Presence: Theological Reflections on Medicine, the Mentally Handicapped and the Church*. Notre Dame: University of Notre Dame Press, 1986.

————. *Truthfulness and Tragedy.* Notre Dame: University of Notre Dame Press, 1977.

————. *Vision and Virtue.* Notre Dame: University of Notre Dame Press, 1981.

Hellegers, André E. "Fetal Development." *Theological Studies* 31 (March 1970): 3-9.

Holzgreve, W., and F. K. Beller. "Anencephalic Infants as Organ Donors." *Clinical Obstetrics and Gynecology* 35, no. 4 (1992): 821-36.

Howell, Joseph H., and William F. Sale, eds. *Life Choices: A Hastings Center Introduction to Bioethics.* Washington, D.C.: Georgetown University Press, 1995.

Hubbard, Ruth. *The Politics of Women's Biology.* New Brunswick, N.J.: Rutgers University Press, 1990.

Hume, David. *A Treatise of Human Nature.* Oxford: Clarendon, 1964.

Iglesias, Teresa. "What Kind of Being Is the Human Embryo?" In *Embryos and Ethics: The Warnock Report in Debate.* Edited by Nigel M. de S. Cameron. Edinburgh: Rutherford House, 1987.

Irenaeus of Lyon. *Against Heresies.* In *Theological Anthropology.* Edited by J. Patout Burns, S.J. Philadelphia: Fortress, 1981.

IVF Canada News 5 (January 1994).

Jeffrey, J. F. "Human Papilloma Virus and Lower Genital Tract Dysplasia: Driver or Passenger?" *Society of Obstetricians and Gynecologists of Canada Bulletin* 10, no. 4 (1988).

Jones, D. Gareth. *Brave New People: Ethical Issues at the Commencement of Life.* Downers Grove, Ill.: InterVarsity Press, 1984.

Jones, D. Gareth, and Barbara Telfa. "Before I Was an Embryo, I Was a Pre-embryo—Or Was I?" *Bioethics* 9, no. 1 (1995): 32-49.

Joyce, Robert E. "Personhood and the Conception Event." *The New Scholasticism* 52 (Winter 1978): 97-109.

Junker-Kenny, Maureen. "The Moral Status of the Embryo." In *The Ethics of Genetic Engineering.* Edited by Maureen Junker-Kenny and Lisa Sowle Cahill. London: SCM Press, 1998.

Kaiser, Christopher B. *The Doctrine of God: A Historical Survey.* Westchester, Ill.: Crossway, 1982.

Kallenberg, Kjell, Lars Forslin and Olle Westerborn. "The Disposal of the Aborted Fetus—New Guidelines: Ethical Considerations in the Debate in Sweden," *Journal of Medical Ethics* 19, no. 1 (1993): 32-36.

Kant, Immanuel. *Fundamental Principles of the Metaphysic of Morals.* Indianapolis: Bobbs-Merrill, 1949.

Kaplan, D. "Prenatal Screening and Its Impact on Persons with Disabilities." *Fetal Diagnosis and Therapy* 8, no. 1 (1993): 64-69.

Kass, Leon. "Implications of Prenatal Diagnosis for the Human Right to Life." In *Ethical Issues in Human Genetics: Genetic Counseling and the Use of Genetic Knowledge.* Edited by Bruce Hilton, Daniel Callahan, Maureen Harris, Peter Condliffe and Burton Berkely. New York: Plenum, 1973.

Kempton, Murray. "The Contract for 'Baby M.' " *New York Review of Books,* April 9, 1987, p. 44.

Kent, Ian, R. C. Greenwood, Janice Loeken and W. Nicholls. "Emotional Sequelae of Elective Abortion." *British Columbia Medical Journal* 20, no. 4 (1978): 118-19.

Kierkegaard, Søren. *Concluding Unscientific Postscript.* Translated by David F. Swenson and Wlater Lowrie. Princeton, N.J.: Princeton University Press, 1941.

————. *Philosophical Fragments.* Translated by David Swenson. Princeton, N.J.: Princeton University Press, 1962.

Kilner, John F. "Post-Abortion Syndrome: Fact or Fiction?" In *Bioethics and the Future of Medicine: A Christian Appraisal.* Edited by John F. Kilner, Nigel M. de S. Cameron and David L. Schiedermayer. Grand Rapids, Mich.: Eerdmans, 1995.

Kleinig, John. *Valuing Life.* Princeton: Princeton University Press, 1991.

Koch, Lene. "Physiological and Psychosocial Risks of the New Reproductive Technologies." In *Tough Choices: In Vitro Fertilization and the Reproductive Technologies.* Edited by Patricia Stephenson and Marsden G. Wagner. Philadelphia: Temple University Press, 1993.

Kollar, Edward J., and Michael Alcalay. "The Physiological Basis for Psychosomatic Medicine: A Historical View." *Annals of Internal Medicine* 67, no. 4 (1967): 883-95.

Koop, C. Everett. "The U.S. Surgeon General on the Health Effects of Abortion." *Population and Development Review* 15, no. 1 (1989): 172-82.

Krimmel, H. T. *The Ethics of Reproductive Technology.* Edited by K. Alpern. New York: Oxford University Press, 1992.

Kuhse, Helga, and Peter Singer. *Should the Baby Live?* Oxford: Oxford University Press, 1985.

Kulczycki, Andrezej, Malcom Potts and Allan Rosenfeld. "Abortion and Fertility Regulation." *Lancet* 347 (June 15, 1996): 1663-69.

LaCugna, Catherine Mowry. *God for Us: The Trinity and Christian Life.* San Francisco: HarperSanFrancisco, 1991.

Laffoon, M. R. *Artificial Insemination and In Vitro Fertilization, An Orthodox Perspective.* Portland, Ore.: Theological Research Exchange Network, 1986.

Lappé, Marc. "Ethics at the Center of Life: Protecting Vulnerable Subjects." *Hastings Center Report* 8, no. 5 (1978): 11-13.

Larsen, William J. *Human Embryology.* New York: Churchill Livingstone, 1993.

Lasch, Christopher. *Haven in a Heartless World.* New York: BasicBooks, 1977.

Lauritzen, Paul. "Pursuing Parenthood: Reflections on Donor Insemination." *Second Opinion* 17, no. 1 (1991): 57-76.

Law Reform Commission of Canada. *Working Paper 58: Crimes Against the Foetus* (1989).

Lebacqz, Karen. "Genes, Justice and Clones." In *Human Cloning: Religious Responses.* Edited by Ronald Cole-Turner. Louisville, Ky.: Westminster John Knox, 1997.

Lee, N. C., G. L. Rubin and R. Borucki. "The Intrauterine Device and Pelvic Inflammatory Disease Revisited: New Results from the Women's Health Study." *Obstetrics and Gynecology* 72, no. 1 (1988): 1-6.

Lee, Patrick. *Abortion and Unborn Human Life.* Washington, D.C.: Catholic University of America Press, 1996.

Lewin, Tamar. "When Courts Take Charge of the Unborn." *The New York Times,* January 9, 1989, p. A11.

Lewontin, Richard. *Biology as Ideology.* Concord, Ontario: Anansi, 1991.

Liley, A. William. "The Foetus as a Personality." *Australia and New Zealand Journal of Psychiatry* 6, no. 2 (1972): 99-105.

———. "Intrauterine Transfusion of Fetus in Hemolytic Disease." *British Medical Journal* 2 (November 1963): 1107-9.

Lipowski, Z. J. "Psychosomatic Medicine: Past and Present" (3 Parts). *Canadian Journal of Psychiatry* 31, no. 1 (1986): 2-21.

Lippman, Abby. "Prenatal Genetic Testing and Screening: Constructing Needs and Reinforcing Inequities." Parts 1 and 2. *American Journal of Law and Medicine* 17, nos. 1 and 2 (1991): 15-50.

Liu, Athena. *Artificial Reproduction and Reproductive Rights.* Brockfield, Vt.: Ashgate, 1991.

Locke, John. *An Essay Concerning Human Understanding.* 4 vols. London: Tho. Basset, 1690. Abr. ed. edited by A. D. Woozley. New York: Meridian, 1974.

Lomansky, Loren E. *Persons, Rights and the Moral Community.* Oxford: Oxford University Press, 1987.

MacIntyre, Neil M., Llew Keltner and Dorothy A. Kovacevich. "The Impact of an Abnormal Fetus or Child on the Choice for Prenatal Diagnosis and Selective Abortion." In *Abortion, Medicine and the Law.* Edited by J. D. Butler and D. F. Walbert. New York: Facts on File, 1992.

Mackenzie, Catriona. "Abortion and Embodiment." *Australian Journal of Philosophy* 70, no. 2 (1992).

Macklin, Ruth. "Artificial Means of Reproduction and Our Understanding of the Family." *Hastings Center Report* 21, no. 1 (1991): 5-11.

———. "Liberty, Utility, Land Justice: An Ethical Approach to Unwanted Pregnancy." *International Journal of Gynecology and Obstetrics Supplement* 3 (1989): 37-49.

———. "Splitting Embryos on the Slippery Slope." *Kennedy Institute of Ethics Journal* 4, no. 3 (1994): 209-25.

Macmurray, John. *Persons in Relation.* Amherst, N.Y.: Humanities Press, 1991.

———. *The Self as Agent.* London: Humanities Press, 1991.

Macquarrie, John. *In Search of Humanity: A Theological and Philosophical Approach.* New York, Crossroad, 1982.

Maguire, Marjorie Reiley. "Personhood, Covenant and Abortion." In *Abortion and Catholicism: The American Debate.* Edited by Patricia Beattie Jung and Thomas A. Shannon. New York: Crossroad, 1988.

Mahlstedt, P. "The Psychological Component of Infertility." *Fertility and Sterility* 43, no. 3 (1985): 335-46.

Marcel, Gabriel. *Creative Fidelity.* Translated by Robert Rosthal. New York: Crossroad, 1982.

———. *Faith and Reality.* Vol. 2 of *The Mystery of Being.* Translated by Rene Hogue. London: Harvill Press, 1951.

Margolis, A. J., L. A. Daviso, K. H. Hanson, S. A. Loos and C. M. Mikkelsen. "Therapeutic Abortion Follow-up Study." *American Journal of Obstetrics and Gynecology* 110, no. 2 (1971): 243-49.

"Maternal Rights and Fetal Wrongs: The Case Against the Criminalization of 'Fetal Abuse.'" *Harvard Law Review* 101, no. 94 (1988): 994-1013.

Mattingly, Susan S. "The Maternal-Fetal Dyad: Exploring the Two-Patient Obstetric Model." *Hastings Center Report* 22, no. 1 (1992): 13-18.

McCormick, Richard, S.J. "Blastomere Separation: Some Concerns." *Hastings Center Report* 24, no. 2 (1994): 14-16.

———. *Corrective Vision Explorations in Moral Theology.* Kansas City: Sheed & Ward, 1994.

McCown, Joe. *Availability: Gabriel Marcel and the Phenomenology of Human Openness.* Missoula, Mont.: Scholars Press, 1978.

McCullough, L. B., and Frank Chervenak. "Clinical Guides to Preventing Ethical Conflicts Between Pregnant Women and Their Physicians," *American Journal of Obstetrics and*

Gynecology 162, no. 2 (1990): 303-7.

———. "Does Obstetric Ethics Have Any Role in the Obstetrician's Response to the Abortion Controversy?" *American Journal of Obstetrics and Gynecology* 163 (November 1990) : 1425-29.

———. "An Ethically Justified Clinically Comprehensive Management Strategy for Third-Trimester Pregnancies Complicated by Fetal Anomalies." *Obstetrics and Gynecology* 75 (March 1990): 311-16.

———. *Ethics in Obstetrics and Gynecology.* New York: Oxford University Press, 1994.

———. "The Fetus as Patient: Implications for Directive Versus Nondirective Counseling for Fetal Benefit." *Fetal Diagnostic Therapy* 6 (1991): 93-100.

———. "Nonagressive Obstetric Management: An Option for Some Fetal Anomalies During the Third Trimester," *Journal of the American Medical Association* 261, no. 23 (1989): 3439-40.

———. "When Is Termination of Pregnancy During the Third Trimester Morally Justifiable?" *New England Journal of Medicine* 310, no. 8 (1984) : 501-4.

McEvoy, Patricia. "Is a Woman Responsible for Being Pregnant?" *Journal of the Canadian Medical Association* 146, no. 4 (1992).

McFadyen, Alistair. *The Call to Personhood: A Christian Theory of the Individual in Social Relationships.* Cambridge: Cambridge University Press, 1990.

McGuire, Maureen, and Nancy Alexander. "Artificial Insemination of Single Women." *Fertility and Sterility* 43, no. 2 (1985): 182-84.

McLaren, Anne. "Embryo Research." *Nature* 320 (April 1986): 570.

McLean, Stuart D. *Humanity in the Thought of Karl Barth.* Edinburgh: T & T Clark, 1981.

Mead, George Herbert. *Mind, Self and Society.* Edited by Charles W. Morris. Chicago: University of Chicago Press, 1974.

Medical Research International, Society for Assisted Reproductive Technology and the American Fertility Society. "In Vitro Fertilization-Embryo Transfer (IVF-ET) in the United States: 1990 Results from the IVF-ET Registry." *Fertility and Sterility* 57, no. 1 (1992): 15-24.

Medical Task Force on Anencephaly. "The Infant with Anencephaly." *New England Journal of Medicine* 322, no. 10 (1990): 669-74.

Meilaender, Gilbert C. *Bioethics: A Primer for Christians.* Grand Rapids, Mich.: Eerdmans, 1996.

———. *Body, Soul and Bioethics.* Notre Dame: University of Notre Dame Press, 1995.

Moltmann, Jürgen. *God in Creation.* San Francisco: HarperSanFrancisco, 1991.

———. *The Trinity and the Kingdom.* San Francisco: HarperSanFrancisco, 1991.

Morin, Norma C., et al. "Congenital Malformations and Psychosocial Development in Children Conceived by In Vitro Fertilization." *Journal of Pediatrics* 15, no. 2 (1989): 222-27.

Mork, Marilyn. "Embryo Research and Genetic Disease," *New Scientist* 125 (January 6, 1990): 56-59.

Muller, Michelle A. "The Use of Human Embryos and Fetal Tissue: A Research Architecture." In *Royal Commission on New Reproductive Technologies.* Ottawa, Ontario: 1992.

Munson, Ronald, ed. *Intervention and Reflection: Basic Issues in Medical Ethics.* 5th ed. Belmont, Calif.: Wadsworth, 1996.

Murphy, Timothy F. "The Moral Significance of Spontaneous Abortion." *Journal of Medical Ethics* 11, no. 2 (1985): 79-83.

Murray, T. H. "Ethical Issues in Fetal Surgery." *American College of Surgeons Bulletin* 70 (June 1985).

———. "Moral Obligations to the Not-Yet Born: The Fetus as Patient." *Clinics in Perinatology* 14 (June 1987): 329-43.

Myers, John E. B. "Abuse and Neglect of the Unborn: Can the State Intervene?" *Duquesne Law Review* 23, no. 1 (1984): 1-76.

Nathanson, Bernard. "The Abortion Cocktail." *First Things* 59 (January 1996): 23-26.

———. *The Hand of God.* Washington, D.C.: Regenery, 1996.

National Advisory Board on Ethics in Reproduction. "Report on Human Cloning Through Embryo Splitting: An Amber Light." *Kennedy Institute of Ethics Journal* 4, no. 3 (1994): 251-82.

National Perinatal Statistics Unit, Fertility Society of Australia. *In Vitro Fertilization Pregnancies: Australia and New Zealand 1979-1985.* Sydney: Pllancaster, 1987.

Nelson, James B. *Body Theology.* Louisville, Ky.: John Knox Press, 1992.

Nelson, L. J. "Legal Dimensions of the Maternal-Fetal Conflict." *Clinical Obstetrics and Gynecology* 35, no. 4 (1992): 738-57.

———. "The Mother and Fetus Union: What God Has Put Together, Let No Law Put Asunder?" In *The Beginning of Human Life.* Edited by F. K. Beller and R. F. Weir. Boston: Kluwer Academic, 1994.

Nelson, L. J., and N. M. Miliken. "Compelled Medical Treatment of Pregnant Women: Life, Liberty and Law in Conflict." *Journal of the American Medical Association* 259, no. 7 (1988): 1060-66.

Nicholson, Susan Teft. *Abortion and the Roman Catholic Church.* Notre Dame: University of Notre Dame Press, 1978.

Nisbet, Robert. *Twilight of Authority.* New York: Oxford University Press, 1975.

Noonan, John T., Jr. "An Almost Absolute Value in History." In *The Morality of Abortion: Legal and Historical Perspective.* Edited by John T. Noonan Jr. Cambridge, Mass.: Harvard University Press, 1970.

———. "How to Argue About Abortion." In *Morality in Practice.* 2d ed. Edited by James Sterba. Belmont, Calif.: Wadsworth, 1994.

Northoff, G., M. A. Schwartz and O. P. Wiggins. "Psychosomatics, the Lived Body and Anthropological Medicine: Concerning a Case of Atopic Dermatitis." In *The Body in Medical Thought and Practice.* Edited by Drew Leder. Boston: Kluwer Academic, 1992.

Nutwell-Irving, Diane. "Scientific and Philosophical Expertise: An Evaluation of the Arguments on Personhood." *Linacre Quarterly* 60 (February 1993): 18-46.

O'Connor, D. J. "Substance and Attributes." In *The Encyclopedia of Philosophy.* Edited by Paul Edwards. New York: Macmillan, 1967.

O'Donovan, Oliver. *Begotten or Made?* Oxford: Oxford University Press, 1984.

Outler, Albert. "Beginnings of Personhood: Theological Considerations." *Perkins Journal* 27 (Fall 1973): 11-34.

Overall, Christine. "Selective Termination of Pregnancy and Women's Reproductive Autonomy." *Hastings Center Report* 20, no. 3 (1990): 6-11.

Pastrana, Gabriel. "Personhood and the Beginning of Human Life." *The Thomist* 41, no. 1 (1977): 247-94.

Pence, Gregory E. *Classic Cases in Medical Ethics.* 2d ed. New York: McGraw-Hill, 1995.

Peters, Ted. "Cloning Shock: A Theological Reaction." In *Human Cloning: Religious Responses.* Edited by Ronald Cole-Turner. Louisville, Ky.: Westminster John Knox,

1997.

Peterson, James C. "Ethical Standards for Genetic Intervention." In *Genetic Ethics: Do the Ends Justify the Genes?* Edited by John F. Kilner, Rebecca D. Pentz and Frank E. Young. Grand Rapids, Mich.: Eerdmans, 1997.

Pettersen, Alvyn. *Athanasius.* Ridgefield, Conn.: Morehouse, 1995.

Polanyi, Michael. *Personal Knowledge.* Chicago: Chicago University Press, 1974.

Post, Stephen. "Huntington's Disease: Prenatal Screening for Late Onset Disease." *Journal of Medical Ethics* 18, no. 2 (1992): 75-78.

Powledge, Tabitha M. "Capital Report: Springtime for Fetal Tissue Research?" *Hastings Center Report* 21, no. 2 (1991): 5-6.

Proceed with Care: Final Report of the Royal Commission on New Reproductive Technologies. 2 vols. Ottawa: Canada Communications Group, 1993.

Prokes, Mary Timothy, F.S.E. *Toward a Theology of the Body.* Grand Rapids, Mich.: Eerdmans, 1996.

Pryde, Peter G., Arie Drugan, Mark P. Johnson, Nelson B. Isada and Mark I. Evans. "Prenatal Diagnosis: Choices Women Make About Pursuing, Testing and Acting on Abnormal Results." *Clinical Obstetrics and Gynecology* 36 (September 1993): 496-509.

Quasten, Johannes. *Patrology.* 4 vols. Westminster, Md., and Allen, Tex.: Christian Classics, 1994-1995.

Ramsey, Paul. *Fabricated Man: The Ethics of Genetic Control,* New Haven, Conn.: Yale University Press, 1970.

———. "The Morality of Abortion." In *Life or Death: Ethics and Options.* Edited by D. H. Labby. Seattle: University of Washington Press, 1968.

———. *The Patient as Person.* New Haven, Conn.: Yale University Press, 1970.

———. "Screening: An Ethicists View." In *Ethical Issues in Human Genetics: Genetic Counseling and the Use of Genetic Knowledge.* Edited by Bruce Hilton, Daniel Callahan, Maureen Harris, Peter Condliffe and Burton Berkely. New York: Plenum, 1973.

———. "Shall We 'Reproduce'? The Medical Ethics of In Vitro Fertilization." *Journal of the American Medical Association* 220 (June 5, 1972): 1346-50.

Reardon, David C. *Aborted Women: Silent No More.* Westchester: Crossway, 1987.

Reich, Warren T., ed. *Encyclopedia of Bioethics.* Rev. ed. New York: Free Press, 1995.

Reichenbach, Bruce R., and V. Elving Anderson. *On Behalf of God: A Christian Ethic for Biology.* Grand Rapids, Mich.: Eerdmans, 1995.

Rifkin, Jeremy. *Algeny: A New Word, A New World.* New York: Penguin, 1983.

Roberge, L. "Abortifacient Vaccines: Technological Update and Christian Appraisal." In *Bioethics and the Future of Medicine: A Christian Appraisal.* Edited by John F. Kilner, Nigel M. de S. Cameron and David L. Schiedermayer. Grand Rapids, Mich.: Eerdmans, 1995.

Robertson, John A. "Ethical and Legal Issues in Pre-implantation Genetic Screening." *Fertility and Sterility* 57, no. 1 (1992): 1-11.

———. "Genetic Selection of Offspring Characteristics." *Boston University Law Review* 76 (1996): 421-82.

———. "Involuntary Euthanasia of Defective Newborns: A Legal Analysis." *Stanford Law Review* 27, no. 2 (1975): 213-69.

———. "Procreative Liberty and the Control of Conception, Pregnancy and Childbirth." *Virginia Law Review* 69, no. 3 (1983): 405-64.

———. "The Question of Human Cloning." *Hastings Center Report* 24, no. 2 (1994): 6-14.

————. "Resolving Disputes over Frozen Embryos." *The Hastings Center Report* 19, no. 6 (1989): 7-12.

————. "The Right to Procreate and In Utero Therapy." *Journal of Legal Medicine* 3, no. 3 (1982): 333-66.

————. "Technology and Motherhood: Legal and Ethical Issues in Human Egg Donation." *Case Western Reserve Law Review* 39, no. 1 (1988): 1-38.

Rosenfeld, J. A. "Emotional Responses to Therapeutic Abortion." *American Family Physician* 45, no. 1 (1992): 137-40.

Rothman, Barbara Katz. "Infertility as Disability." In *Contemporary Issues in Bioethics*. 4th ed. Edited by Tom L. Beauchamp and LeRoy Walters. Belmont, Calif.: Wadsworth, 1994.

————. *The Tentative Pregnancy*. New York: Viking, 1986.

————. "The Tentative Pregnancy: Then and Now." *Fetal Diagnosis and Therapy* 8, no. 1 (1993): 60-63.

Ruddick, W., and W. Wilcox. "Operating on the Fetus." *Hastings Center Report* 12 (October 1982): 10-14.

Rudman, Stanley. *Concepts of Person and Christian Ethics*. Cambridge: Cambridge University Press, 1997.

Ryan, Maura. "The Argument for Unlimited Procreative Liberty: A Feminist Critique." *Hastings Center Report* 20, no. 4 (1990): 6-12.

Sabin, James, and Norman Daniels. "Determining 'Medical Necessity' in Mental Health Practice." *Hastings Center Report* 24, no. 6 (1994): 5-13.

Sandberg, Eugene C. "Only an Attitude Away: The Potential of Reproductive Surrogacy." *American Journal of Obstetrics and Gynecology* 160, no. 6 (1989): 1441-46.

Sass, Hans-Martin. "Brain Life and Brain Death: A Proposal for a Normative Agreement." *Journal of Medicine and Philosophy* 14, no. 1 (1989): 45-59.

————. "The Moral Significance of Brain-Life Criteria." In *The Beginning of Human Life*. Edited by F. K. Beller and R. F. Weir. Boston: Kluwer Academic, 1994.

Schneiderman, L. J., N. S. Jecker and A. R. Jonsen. "Medical Futility: Its Meaning and Ethical Implications." *Annals of Internal Medicine* 112, no. 12 (1990): 949-54.

Schüssler Fiorenza, Elisabeth. *In Memory of Her: A Feminist Theological Reconstruction of Christian Origins*. New York: Crossroad, 1983.

Selby, Terry L., and Marc Bockmon. *The Mourning After: Help for the Post-Abortion Woman*. Grand Rapids, Mich.: Baker, 1990.

Shannon, Thomas A. *Surrogate Motherhood: The Ethics of Using Human Beings*. New York: Crossroad, 1988.

Shannon, Thomas A., and Allan B. Wolter. "Reflections on the Moral Status of the Pre-Embryo." *Theological Studies* 51 (December 1990): 603-26.

Shaw, Robert W., W. Patrick Soutter and Stuart L. Stanton, eds. *Gynecology*. New York: Churchill Livingstone, 1997.

Sherwin, Susan. *No Longer Patient: Feminist Ethics and Health Care*. Philadelphia: Temple University Press, 1992.

Shewmon, D. A. "Anencephaly: Selected Medical Aspects." *Hastings Center Report* 18 (October 1988): 11-19.

Shinn, Roger Lincoln. *The New Genetics: Challenges for Science, Faith and Politics*. London: Moyer Bell, 1996.

Siegel, Suzanne, and Bill Roy. "Youth, Incest and Abortion." *Newsweek,* August 10, 1998, p. 52.

Singer, Peter. *Rethinking Life and Death: The Collapse of Our Traditional Ethics.* New York: St. Martin's Press, 1994.

Singer, Peter, Helga Kuhse, Stephen Buckle, Karen Dawson and Pascal Kasimba, eds. *Embryo Experimentation.* New York: Cambridge University Press, 1990.

Smith, Janet. *Humanae Vitae: A Generation Later.* Washington, D.C.: Catholic University of America Press, 1991.

Smith, Stephanie J. "Post-Abortion Syndrome: Fact or Fiction?" In *Bioethics and the Future of Medicine: A Christian Appraisal.* Edited by John F. Kilner, Nigel M. de S. Cameron and David L. Schiedermayer. Grand Rapids, Mich.: Eerdmans, 1995.

Sommerville, James. "Maurice Blondel and the Philosophy of Action." *Spiritual Life* 7, no. 2 (1961): 114.

Spinoza, Benedict de. *Ethics.* In *Chief Works,* vol. 2. New York: Dover, 1951.

Steinbock, Bonnie. *Life Before Birth: The Moral and Legal Status of Embryos and Fetuses.* New York: Oxford University Press, 1992.

———. "The Logical Case for 'Wrongful Life.' " *Hastings Center Report* 16, no. 2 (1986): 15-20.

———. "Surrogate Motherhood as Prenatal Adoption." *Law, Medicine and Health Care* 16 (Spring-Summer 1988).

Steinbock, Bonnie, and Ron McClamrock. "When Is Birth Unfair to the Child?" *Hastings Center Report,* 24, no. 6 (1994): 15-21.

Strawson, P. F. *Individuals.* London: University Paperbacks, 1964.

Suarez, Antoine. "Hydatidiform Moles and Teratomas Confirm the Human Identity of the Preimplantation Embryo." *Journal of Medicine and Philosophy* 15, no. 6 (1990): 627-35.

Sumner. L. W. *Abortion and Moral Theory.* Princeton: Princeton University Press, 1981.

Sumner, L. W., et al., eds. *Values and Moral Standing.* Vol. 8 of *Bowling Green Studies in Applied Philosophy.* Bowling Green, Ohio: Bowling Green State University Press, 1986.

Teichman, J. "The Definition of Person." *Philosophy* 60, no. 232 (1985): 175-85.

Teilhard de Chardin, Pierre. *The Future of Man.* Translated by Norman Denny. New York: Harper & Row, 1964.

Tertullian. *Against Marcion.* In vol. 3 of *The Ante-Nicene Fathers: The Writings of the Fathers down to A.D. 325.* Edited by Alexander Roberts and James Donaldson. 1885-1887. Reprint, Peabody, Mass.: Hendrickson, 1994.

———. *On the Resurrection of the Flesh.* In vol. 3 of *The Ante-Nicene Fathers: The Writings of the Fathers down to A.D. 325.* Edited by Alexander Roberts and James Donaldson. 1885-1887. Reprint, Peabody, Mass.: Hendrickson, 1994.

Testart, J., M. Plachot, J. Mandelbaum, J. Salat-Baroux, R. Frydman and J. Cohen. "World Collaborative Report on IVF-ET and GIFT: 1989 Results." *Human Reproduction* 7, no. 3 (1992): 362-69.

Thomson, Judith J. "A Defense of Abortion." In *The Problem of Abortion.* Edited by Joel Feinberg. Belmont, Calif.: Wadsworth, 1973.

———. *Rights, Restitution and Risk.* Cambridge: Harvard University Press, 1986.

Tibbetts, Janice. "Rights of Fetus Spotlighted in Manitoba, U.S." *Vancouver Sun,* October 30, 1997.

Tillich, Paul. "Meaning of Health." In *On Moral Medicine: Theological Perspectives in Medical Ethics.* Edited by Stephen E. Lammers and Allen Verhey. Grand Rapids, Mich.: Eerdmans, 1987. Originally published in *Perspectives in Biology and Medicine*

5 (Fall 1961): 92-100.

Tocqueville, Alexis de. *Democracy in America*. Edited by J. P. Mayer. Translated by George Lawrence. New York: Doubleday/Anchor, 1969.

Tonti-Filippini, Nicholas. "The Pill: Abortifacient or Contraceptive? A Literature Review." *Linacre Quarterly* 62, no. 1 (1995).

Tooley, Michael. *Abortion and Infanticide*. New York: Oxford University Press, 1983.

———. "In Defense of Abortion and Infanticide." In *The Problem of Abortion*. Edited by Joel Feinberg. Belmont, Calif.: Wadsworth, 1973.

Torrance, T. F. *The Christian Doctrine of God, One Being Three Persons*. Edinburgh: T & T Clark, 1996.

Trau, Jane. "Treating Fetuses: The Patient as Person." *Journal of Medical Humanities* 12, no. 4 (1991): 173-81.

Trounson, A. L. "Preimplantation Genetic Diagnosis: Counting Chickens Before They Hatch?" *Human Reproduction* 7, no. 5 (1992): 583-84.

U.S. Congress, Office of Technology Assessment. *Fertility: Medical and Social Choices*. Washington, D.C.: U.S. Government Printing Office, 1988.

U.S. Department of Health, Education and Welfare, Ethics Advisory Board. *Report and Conclusions: HEW Support of Research Involving Human In Vitro Fertilization and Embryo Transfer*. Washington, D.C.: U.S. Government Printing Office, 1979.

Van Leeuwen, Raymond. "Breeding Stock or Lords of Creation?" *Christianity Today*, November 11, 1991, pp. 36-37.

Vanhoozer, Kevin. "Human Being, Individual and Social." In *Cambridge Companion to Christian Doctrine*. Edited by Colin E. Gunton. Cambridge: Cambridge University Press, 1997.

Verlinsky, Yury, Eugene Pergament and Charles H. Strom. "The Pre-implantation Genetic Diagnosis of Genetic Diseases." *Journal of In Vitro Fertilization and Embryo Transfer* 7, no. 1 (1990): 1-5.

Vogel, Arthur A. *God's Presence in Man's World*. London: Geoffrey Chapman, 1973.

Walters, James W. *What Is a Person? An Ethical Exploration*. Urbana: University of Illinois Press, 1997.

Waltke, Bruce. "Reflections from the Old Testament on Abortion." *Journal of the Christian Medical Society* 19, no. 1 (1988).

Ware, Bishop Kallistos, *The Orthodox Way*. Rev. ed. Crestwood N.Y.: St. Vladimir's Orthodox Theological Seminary, 1979.

Warnock Committee. *A Question of Life: The Report of the Committee of Inquiry into Human Fertilization and Embryology*. Belfast: Her Majesty's Stationery Office, 1985.

———. "A Question of Life: The Report of the Committee of Inquiry into Human Fertilization and Embryology." In *Contemporary Issues in Bioethics*. 4th ed. Edited by Tom Beauchamp and LeRoy Walters. Belmont, Calif.: Wadsworth, 1994.

Warren, Mary Ann. "Do Potential People Have Moral Rights?" In *Obligations to Future Generations*. Edited by R. I. Sikora and Brian Barry. Philadelphia: Temple University Press, 1978.

Warnock, Mary. "In Vitro Fertilization: The Ethical Issues." *Philosophical Quarterly* 33 (July 1983): 238-49.

———. "IVF and Women's Interests: An Analysis of Feminist Concerns." *Bioethics* 2 (January 1988).

———. "The Moral Significance of Birth." *Hypatia: Special Issue—Ethics and Reproduction* 4, no. 3 (1989): 46-65.

————. "On the Moral and Legal Status of Abortion." In *The Problem of Abortion.* Edited by Joel Feinberg. Belmont, Calif.: Wadsworth, 1973.

————. "Women's Rights Versus the Protection of Fetuses." In *The Beginning of Human Life.* Edited by F. K. Beller and R. K. Weir. Boston: Kluwer Academic, 1994.

Waters, Brent. "One Flesh? Cloning, Procreation and the Family." In *Human Cloning: Religious Responses.* Edited by Ronald Cole-Turner. Louisville, Ky.: Westminster John Knox, 1997.

Weber, Leonard J. "In Vitro Fertilization and the Just Use of Health Care Resources." In *Reproduction: Technology and Rights.* Edited by James M. Humber and Robert F. Almeder. Toronto: Humana, 1996.

Weiner, H. "The Prospects for Psychosomatic Medicine: Selected Topics." *Psychosomatic Medicine* 44 (December 1982): 491-517.

Wennberg, Robert N. *Life in the Balance: Exploring the Abortion Controversy.* Grand Rapids, Mich.: Eerdmans, 1985.

————. "The Right to Life: Three Theories." In vol. 2 of *Readings in Christian Ethics.* Edited by David K. Clark and Robert V. Rakestraw. Grand Rapids, Mich.: Baker, 1996.

Werner, Richard. "Abortion: The Ontological and Moral Status of the Unborn" *Social Theory and Practice* 3, no. 1 (1974): 201-22.

Wertz, Dorothy, and John Fletcher. "Fatal Knowledge? Prenatal Diagnosis and Sex Selection." *Hastings Center Report* 19, no. 3 (1989): 21-27.

Westfall, John M., Ken J. Kallail and Anne D. Walling. "Abortion Attitudes and Practices of Family and General Practice Physicians." *Journal of Family Practice* 33, no. 1 (1991): 47-51.

Wilkes, Kathleen V. *Real People.* Oxford: Clarendon, 1987.

Wilmut, Ian, A. E. Schnieke, J. McWhir, A. J. Kind and K. H. S. Campbell. "Viable Offspring Derived from Fetal and Adult Mammalian Cells." *Nature* 385 (February 27, 1997): 810-13.

Winston, M. E. "Abortion and Parental Responsibility." *Journal of Medical Humanities and Bioethics* 7, no. 1 (1986): 33-56.

Wolf, Hans Walter. *Anthropology of the Old Testament.* Translated by Margaret Kohl. Philadelphia: Fortress, 1974.

Wolf, Naomi. "Our Bodies, Our Souls." *The New Republic,* October 16, 1995, pp. 26-35.

Wolgast, Elizabeth. *The Grammar of Justice.* Ithaca: Cornell University Press, 1987.

Wood, Chris. "Beyond Abortion." *Maclean's,* August 19, 1996, pp. 14-15.

Wreen, Michael. "Abortion and Pregnancy Due to Rape." *Philosophica* 21 (1992): 201-20.

————. "Abortion: The Extreme Liberal Position." *Journal of Medicine and Philosophy* 12, no. 3 (1987): 241-65.

————. "In Defense of Speciesism." *Ethics and Animals* 5 (1984): 47-60.

————. "The Possibility of Potentiality." In vol. 8 of *Bowling Green Studies in Applied Philosophy.* Edited by L. W. Sumner. Bowling Green, Ohio: The Applied Philosophy Program at Bowling Green State University, 1986.

Yu, Carver T. *Being and Relation: A Theological Critique of Western Dualism and Individualism.* Edinburgh: Scottish Academic Press, 1987.

Zaner, Richard. "Body—I. Embodiment: The Phenomenological Tradition." In *Encyclopedia of Bioethics.* Edited by Warren T. Reich. New York: Simon & Schuster, 1995.

————. *The Context of Self: A Phenomenological Inquiry Using Medicine as a Clue.* Athens: Ohio University Press, 1980.

————. *Ethics and the Clinical Encounter.* Englewood Cliffs, N.J.: Prentice-Hall, 1988.

Zizioulas, John. *Being as Communion*. Crestwood, N.Y.: St. Vladimir's Seminary Press, 1993.

———. "Human Capacity and Human Incapacity: A Theological Exploration of Person-hood." *Scottish Journal of Theology* 28, no. 5 (1975): 401-47.

Index of Subjects